Introduction to
The Netherlands

Although almost half of it was once under water, the Netherlands is one of the most urbanized – and densely populated – nations on earth, with a huge amount of interest packed into a relatively small area. A remarkable country – no more than the size of the US state of Maryland – it's a largely man-made affair, around half of which lies at or below sea level. Its fertile, pancake-flat landscape is gridded with drainage ditches and canals, beneath huge open skies, while the country's towns and villages are often pristine and unchanged places of gabled townhouses, pretty canals and church spires. Despite the country's diminutive dimensions, each town is often a profoundly separate place with its own distinct identity – indeed there's perhaps nowhere else in the world where you can hear so many different accents, even dialects, in such a small area. In spring and summer the bulbfields provide bold splashes of colour, and in the west and north the long coastline is marked by mile upon mile of protective dune, backing onto wide stretches of perfect sandy beach.

A major colonial power, the Dutch mercantile fleet once challenged the English for world naval supremacy, and throughout its seventeenth-century Golden Age, the standard of living was second to none. There have been a few economic ups and downs since then, but today the Netherlands is one of the most developed countries in the world, with the highest population density in Europe. It's an international, well-integrated place too: most people speak English, at least in the heavily populated west of the country; and most of the country is easy to reach on a public transport system of trains and buses, whose efficiency may make British and American visitors weep with envy.

Successive Dutch governments have steered towards political consensus – indeed, this has been the drift since the Reformation, when the competing pillars of Dutch society learnt to live with – or ignore – each other, aided by the fact that trading wealth was making most people richer. Almost by accident, Dutch society became tolerant, and, in

ABOVE CUBE HOUSES, ROTTERDAM **RIGHT** BROUWERSGRACHT AND HERENGRACHT CANALS, AMSTERDAM its enthusiasm to blunt conflict, progressive. These days, many insiders opine that the motive behind liberal Dutch attitudes towards drug use and prostitution isn't freewheeling permissiveness so much as apathy –and even that is under threat, with an official clampdown on Amsterdam's coffeeshop culture. In addition, the country's avowed multiculturalism has been severely tested in recent years, with the shootings of Theo van Gogh and the politician Pim Fortuyn persuading many to reassess the success of the Netherlands' consensual politics.

Where to go

Mention you're going to the Netherlands and most people assume you're going to **Amsterdam**. Indeed for such a small and accessible country, the Netherlands is relatively unknown territory. Some people may confess to a brief visit to Rotterdam or Den Haag (The Hague), but for most visitors Amsterdam *is* the Netherlands, the assumption being that there's nothing remotely worth seeing elsewhere. To accept this is to miss much, but there's no doubt that the capital has more cosmopolitan dash than any other Dutch city, both in its restaurant and bar scene and in the pre-eminence of its three great attractions. These are the Anne Frank Huis, where the young Jewish diarist hid away during the World War II Nazi occupation; the Rijksmuseum, with its wonderful collection of Dutch paintings, including several of Rembrandt's finest works; and the peerless Van Gogh Museum, with the world's largest collection of the artist's work.

In the west of the country, beyond Amsterdam, the provinces of **Noord-** and **Zuid-Holland** are for the most part unrelentingly flat, reflecting centuries of careful reclamation work as the Dutch have slowly pushed back the sea. These provinces are

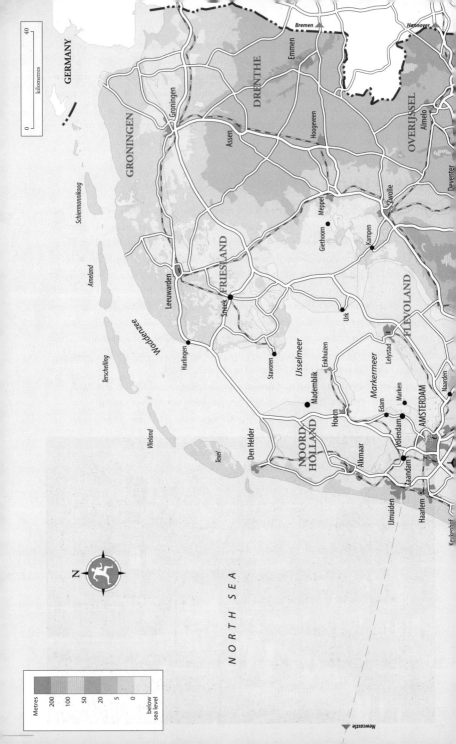

FACT FILE

The Netherlands has a **population** of just over 16.6 million people. Of these, some 790,000 live in the capital, Amsterdam, 620,000 in Rotterdam and 500,000 in Den Haag (The Hague). "**Holland**" comprises just two of the twelve Dutch provinces: Noord-Holland around Amsterdam, and Zuid-Holland around Rotterdam and Den Haag.

One-fifth of the Netherlands is made up of water. Without protection, two-thirds of the country would be regularly flooded. The lowest point in the Netherlands – at seven metres below sea level – is also Europe's lowest point.

With 20 million bikes in the country – 1.25 for every inhabitant – the Netherlands has the highest level of bicycle usage in the world. However, one bike is stolen every minute of every day around the country.

The Netherlands is a constitutional **monarchy** presided over by Queen Beatrix, who was crowned in 1980. The country's bicameral **parliament** sits in Den Haag and comprises an Upper House or First Chamber of 150 directly elected deputies and a Lower House or Senate of 75 senators.

Every year each Dutch person eats four kilos of Dutch liquorice or *drop*, which comes in a never-ending supply of sweet, salty and flavoured varieties. Often sold in pharmacies, it was once believed to have medicinal properties, and is as Dutch as tulips and clogs.

The Dutch concept of *gezelligheid* has no direct translation, but loosely speaking it means cosy, convivial or fun – and it's the mission of Dutch folk to create a *gezellig* atmosphere or enjoy a *gezellig* time on most occasions.

predominantly urban, especially Zuid-Holland, which is home to a grouping of towns known collectively as the Randstad (literally "rim town"), an urban sprawl that holds all the country's largest cities and the majority of its population. Travelling in this part of the country is easy, with trains and buses that are fast, inexpensive and efficient; highlights include easy-going **Haarlem**; the old university town of **Leiden**; **Delft**, with its attractive medieval buildings and diminutive, canal-girded centre; and the gritty port city of **Rotterdam**, festooned with prestigious modern architecture. **Den Haag (The Hague)**, is well worth a visit, too, a laidback and relaxing city, seat of the Dutch government and home to several excellent museums. Neither should you miss the **Keukenhof gardens**, with the finest and most extensive bulbfields in the country. To the north of Amsterdam, the old Zuider Zee ports of **Enkhuizen** and **Hoorn** are very enticing, as is the small town of **Alkmaar**, with its unashamedly touristy cheese market, and the small villages and unspoilt dunescapes of the **coast**.

Beyond lies a quieter, more rural country, especially in the far north where a chain of low-lying islands – the **Frisian Islands** – separates the open North Sea from the coast-hugging Waddenzee. Prime resort territory, the islands possess a blustery, bucolic charm, and thousands of Dutch families come here every summer for their holidays. Apart from **Texel**, the islands lie offshore from the coast of the province of **Friesland**. Friesland's capital, **Leeuwarden**, is a likeable, eminently visitable city, while neighbouring **Groningen** is one of the country's busiest cultural centres.

To the south, the provinces of Overijssel and Gelderland are dotted with charming old towns, notably **Deventer** and **Zutphen**, while their eastern portions herald the Netherlands' first few geophysical bumps as the landscape rolls up towards the German frontier. Here also are two

CLOCKWISE FROM TOP BRIDGE OVER THE HERENGRACHT, AMSTERDAM; CYCLISTS NEAR UTRECHT; ROTTERDAM CARNIVAL

diverting towns: **Arnhem**, much rebuilt after its notorious World War II battle, but a hop and a skip from the open heaths of the **Hoge Veluwe National Park**, and the lively college town of **Nijmegen**.

Further south still are the predominantly Catholic provinces of Limburg, Noord-Brabant and Zeeland. The last of these is well named (literally "Sealand"), made up of a series of low-lying islands and protected from the encroaching waters of the North Sea by one of the country's most ambitious engineering plans, the **Delta Project**. Heading east from here, you reach Noord-Brabant, gently rolling scrub-and farmland which centres on the historic cities of **Breda** and **'s Hertogenbosch**, and the more modern manufacturing hub of **Eindhoven**, home to electronics giant Philips. The hilly province of Limburg occupies the slim scythe of land that reaches down between the Belgian and German borders, with its cosmopolitan capital, **Maastricht**, being one of the Netherlands' most convivial cities.

When to go

The Netherlands enjoys a temperate **climate**, with relatively mild summers and moderately cold winters. Generally speaking, temperatures rise the further south you go. This is offset by the prevailing westerlies that sweep in from the North Sea, making the wetter coastal provinces both warmer in winter and colder in summer than the eastern provinces, where the more severe climate of continental Europe has an influence. As far as rain is concerned, be prepared for it at any time of year.

QUEEN'S DAY

The Queen in question isn't one of the flamboyant transvestites hanging around Rembrandtplein but Holland's reigning monarch, **Queen Beatrix**, whose official birthday is celebrated throughout the country on April 30. The ensuing fiesta is Amsterdam's Mardi Gras, Beerfest and street carnival all rolled into one – which, in a city famed for its easy-going, fun-loving population, manages to crank the party volume a few notches higher still. The street party blasts away for a full 24 hours uninterrupted, from the evening of April 29 – Queen's Night – to the evening of April 30, when the citizens of Amsterdam reclaim the streets, parks, squares and canals of the town from tourists, motorists and officialdom for one glorious party.

Author picks

We've spent loads of time in the Netherlands over the years, but there are some things we like to do, or places we have to visit, every time we return. Here's a selection of our favourites.

Blissful beaches There are great sandy beaches all over the Netherlands, but some of the best are on the islands in the north, where vast areas of virgin golden sand soak up the summer crowds with ease. Try the southwest of Texel (see pp.134–138), or the western end of Schiermonnikoog (see p.220) for the biggest and emptiest stretches. For more life, and wonderful dunes to hike through, head to Bloemendaal-aan-Zee (see p.110).

Classic bike ride Our favourite cycle track is the North Sea Route from Zeeland to Den Helder – you can cycle the whole route if you're lucky enough to have the time, or just pick an individual stretch, from the watery expanses of Zeeland to the duneside paths further north.

Carnival chaos Few people realize the Low Countries' capacity for celebrating Carnival – if you don't fancy braving the enormity of Queen's Day in Amsterdam (see p.35), try the Bergen-op-Zoom Carnival (see p.305), our favourite, where they party better than most.

Modernist architecture There's so much to choose from in the Netherlands, from the Rietveld Schröderhuis in Utrecht (see p.189) to Dudok's Hilversum Town Hall (see p.140) to Berlage's Beurs (see p.52) right in the heart of Amsterdam.

Faces from the past The Dutch Golden Age was an era of great portraiture, when artists such as Rembrandt, Frans Hals and Vermeer left a magnificent record of the time and its people – many of them, grim-faced, black-hatted Dutch burghers staring out of the gloom. Perhaps the most powerful pair of paintings you'll ever see is Hals' penetrating portraits of the elders of the Haarlem almshouse in which he died, on display *in situ* (p.107).

> Our author recommendations don't end here. We've flagged up our favourite places – a perfectly sited hotel, an atmospheric café, a special restaurant – throughout the Guide, highlighted with the ★ symbol.

FROM TOP QUEEN'S DAY, AMSTERDAM; DUNES, DE COCKSDORP, TEXEL; HILVERSUM TOWN HALL

21

things not to miss

It's not possible to see everything that the Netherlands has to offer in one trip – and we don't suggest you try. What follows is a selective and subjective taste of the country's highlights, in no particular order: cosmopolitan cities, peaceful villages, memorable landscapes and outstanding museums. All entries have a page reference to take you straight into the Guide, where you can find out more.

1 EASTERN DOCKLANDS, AMSTERDAM
Page 73
There's plenty to see in the Netherlands apart from Amsterdam, but it would be a strange trip that missed out the picturesque capital altogether. It's not all clogs 'n' canals, though – head off the tourist track to the city's Eastern Docklands, newly developed and home to some cutting-edge architecture.

2 DEN HAAG (THE HAGUE)
Page 152
Den Haag's reputation for dourness is completely undeserved: it boasts a first-rate restaurant scene, smart hotels and enough prime museums to exhaust even the most energetic sightseer – the Binnenhof and Mauritshuis alone are reason enough to visit

3 HOGE VELUWE NATIONAL PARK
Page 257
A richly forested swathe of dunes and woodland in the middle of the country. Cycle your way around thanks to a fleet of free-to-use white bicycles.

4 THE ELFSTEDENTOCHT
Page 205
If you're very lucky you may be able to watch the speed-skaters of Friesland as they tear round the province's canals in this infrequently staged open-air race.

5 DELTA PROJECT AND EXPO
The series of huge dykes and flood-barriers in the far-flung western province of Zeeland, which bear witness to the country's long battle to hold the sea at bay, is celebrated in an adjacent exhibition hall.

6 ANNE FRANK HUIS, AMSTERDAM
A poignant and personal evocation of the Nazi persecution of the Jews. The photo shows the bookcase behind which the Frank family hid for two years.

7 FRISIAN ISLANDS
Of the string of wild and windswept holiday islands off the northern Dutch coast, Terschelling is the most popular, a fine spot for walks and bike rides amid the dunes.

8 CYCLING
No country in Europe is so kindly disposed towards the bicycle than the pancake-flat Netherlands: you'll find bike paths in and around all towns, plus long-distance touring routes taking you deep into the countryside.

9 KEUKENHOF GARDENS
Some seven million flowers are on show in these extensive gardens, which specialize in daffodils, narcissi, hyacinths and – of course – tulips.

6

7

8

9

14

10 TEXEL
Page 134

With its distinct identity and feel, Texel is the most accessible of the Dutch islands, just a couple of hours north of Amsterdam by train and ferry.

11 'S HERTOGENBOSCH
Page 294

This lively market town features an intricate old quarter of canals and picturesque bridges, plus a stunning cathedral.

12 VAN GOGH MUSEUM, AMSTERDAM
Page 76

Quite simply the best and most comprehensive collection of van Gogh's work anywhere.

13 FRANS HALS MUSEUM, HAARLEM
Page 107

Often neglected, Hals was one of the finest of the Golden Age painters, his later canvases acutely dark and broody.

14 SOUTHWEST FRIESLAND
Page 197

Touring the small towns and villages of this region shows a whole different side to the country than the more urbanized southwest.

15 KRÖLLER-MÜLLER MUSEUM
Page 257

This superb art museum and sculpture garden is set in the heart of the Hoge Veluwe National Park.

15

16 THE BIESBOSCH
Page 185

As an escape from Dutch urban life, the reedy marshes and lagoons of the Biesbosch are hard to beat.

17 INDONESIAN FOOD
Page 32

Thanks to the Netherlands' colonial adventures in Southeast Asia, restaurants around the country prepare some of the finest Indonesian cuisine outside Indonesia.

18 WADLOPEN
Page 221

One novel way of getting to the Frisian Islands is to try guided *wadlopen* or "mud-walking" from the mainland at low tide.

19 DELFT
Page 163

Eulogized by Vermeer, Delft's centre is particularly handsome, and its market square is one of the country's best.

20 MAASTRICHT
Page 274

This atmospheric, laidback city in the far south, squeezed between the porous Belgian and German borders, offers a worldly outlook and a superb old quarter.

21 IJSSELMEER
Page 112

This beautiful inland lake, formerly the Zuider Zee, lies at the heart of the Netherlands and represents the country at its watery best, with charming old ports like Hoorn and Enkhuizen and former islands like Urk to explore.

Itineraries

The Netherlands beyond Amsterdam is a bit of a mystery to most people, even to those who live there – which, of course, is part of its charm. However, to save you having to read through the entire Guide before deciding where to go we've put together a few itineraries to help you out.

A GRAND TOUR

The Netherlands is a small country, so you can see the best of it within a week – that is if you don't linger too long in Amsterdam.

❶ Amsterdam A good place to start, and small enough that you can see its highlights in a day or two. **See pp.46–100**

❷ Haarlem Only fifteen minutes from the capital, but a place apart, with a nice old centre and plenty to see, including the fantastic Frans Hals Museum. **See pp.105–111**

❸ Utrecht Lively student town just half an hour from Amsterdam that retains its cobbled old centre. **See pp.186–191**

❹ Delft The Netherlands' most handsome provincial town with plenty of historical attractions and the most classically beautiful canal-riven Dutch town centre. **See pp.163–168**

❺ Biesbosch The country's most significant and accessible wetland, easily explorable by boat or bike. **See p.185**

❻ Texel The most accessible of the Dutch islands, and a wonderfully relaxing place of dunes, birds, beaches and gentle cycling, and with some great places to stay. **See pp.134–138**

❼ Enkhuizen Perhaps the most enchanting of the old Zuider Zee ports, its face firmly turned towards the water around its busy inner harbours, and with the excellent Zuider Zee Museum as a bonus. **See pp.121–125**

❽ Groningen The northern part of the country's major urban centre, with a huge university population and a buzzy centre full of bars and restaurants. **See pp.221–227**

THE GREAT OUTDOORS

You don't normally think of the Netherlands as a place to experience the Great Outdoors, but it is a fantastic destination for many outdoor activities, from horseriding to sailing to some other, more specifically Dutch pursuits.

❶ Wadlopen in Friesland There's nothing more Dutch – or more enjoyable – than the guided walks you can do between the north coast and the islands of the Wadden Sea. **See p.221**

❷ Sailing The Netherlands is a boaty kind of place all round, but the lakes and waterways of Friesland are the best place to take to the water, or there are plenty of opportunities on the IJsselmeer. **See p.112**

❸ Skating You can, of course, do this anywhere if the weather is cold enough, but there's nothing better than following at least part of the course of the famous Elfstedentocht race through Friesland. **See p.205**

❹ Horseriding The countryside is well suited to all kinds of equestrian activities, especially the Hoge Veluwe National Park. **See pp.257–260**

❺ Windsurfing and surfing There's no better place for both activities than Renesse in

ABOVE SAILING, FRIESLAND; DELFT POTTERY; VAN GOGH'S BEDROOM

Zeeland's Schouwen-Duiveland, where you can rent boards and wet suits and seek out the plentiful waves and wind. **See p.318**

ART AND CULTURE

The Netherlands is known for its art and boasts some top-class collections. Several smaller towns hold a fantastic selection of Dutch painting and sculpture, and visiting some of these lesser-known museums and galleries makes for a great trip.

❶ **Amsterdam** When it reopens, the Rijksmuseum will reclaim its rightful place in the top ten of European galleries; until then you still have the Van Gogh Museum, the newly reopened Stedelijk and the excellent Amsterdam Historisch Museum, to name just three.

❷ **The Frans Hals Musuem** It's worth visiting Haarlem for this museum alone – to see paintings by Frans Hals and others in the almshouse where he lived his final days. **See p.107**

❸ **The Mauritshuis** This elegant seventeenth-century mansion in The Hague is home to one of the finest concentrations of Dutch and Flemish paintings in the world. **See p.153**

❹ **Boijmans van Beuningen Museum** A vast collection of Flemish, Dutch and modern art awaits in this amazing museum in Rotterdam. **See p.173**

❺ **Centraal Museum, Utrecht** Utrecht is home to an extensive fine art collection with a local focus, including great works by Jan van Scorel, the Utrecht School, as well as Gerrit van Rietveld and Miffy's Dick Bruna. **See p.188**

❻ **Kröller-Muller Museum** Perhaps the country's finest collection of late nineteenth-century and modern paintings and sculptures, housed in a wonderful location in the Hoge Veluwe park. **See p.257**

❼ **Rijksmuseum Twente** It may be a bit of a trek, but Enschede's Rijksmuseum Twente is as good a small collection of Dutch art as you'll find outside the major museums. **See p.270**

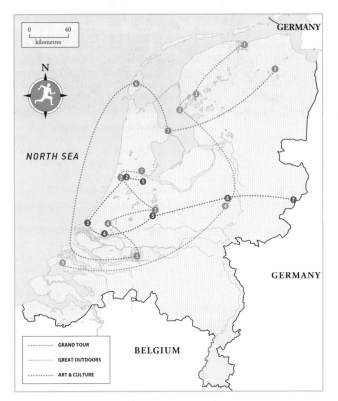

COFFEESHOP AND BIKE, AMSTERDAM

Basics

Getting there

There are plenty of flights from a bevy of UK airports to Amsterdam's Schiphol (pronounced **skip-oll**) airport as well as a sprinkling of flights to several second-string Dutch airports, primarily **Eindhoven** and **Rotterdam**. Alternatively, travelling from the UK to the Netherlands by train via the Channel Tunnel is just as easy and about the same price as a flight, and neither, if you live in the southeast of the UK, does it take much longer. You can also get there by long-distance bus, which is usually the most affordable option, though more time-consuming. By car and ferry, deals for drivers on ferry routes into Dutch and Belgian ports are particularly competitive.

From North America and Canada the main decision is whether to fly direct – easy enough as Amsterdam's Schiphol is a major international air travel hub – or to route via London, picking up a budget flight onwards from there. From Australia and New Zealand, all flights to Amsterdam require one or two stops on the way; from South Africa, there are direct flights.

Flights from the UK

Amsterdam is one of the UK's most popular short-haul destinations and its international airport, **Amsterdam Schiphol**, is extremely easy to reach. Among many operators, easyJet, Jet2, Air France and British Airways all have flights to Amsterdam, but the airline with the widest range of flights is KLM, who fly there direct and nonstop from Aberdeen, Birmingham, Bristol, Cardiff, Durham Teeside, Edinburgh, Glasgow, Humberside, Leeds, Liverpool, London Heathrow, Manchester, Newcastle, Norwich and Southampton. Alternatively, Ryanair flies from London Stansted to

Eindhoven and CityJet flies from London City Airport to **Rotterdam**.

Prices for flights to Amsterdam vary enormously, but begin at about £170 return from a regional airport, slightly less from London. **Flying times** are insignificant: Aberdeen and London to Amsterdam takes one and a half hours, one hour from Norwich.

Flights from Ireland

Flying from Ireland, Aer Lingus has daily flights to Amsterdam from Dublin and Cork, easyJet flies to Amsterdam from Belfast, and Ryanair has flights from Dublin to Eindhoven.

Prices for flights vary considerably, but begin at about €140 return from Dublin to Amsterdam. **Flying times** are modest: Dublin to Amsterdam takes one hour and forty minutes.

Flights from the US and Canada

Amsterdam's Schiphol airport is among the most popular and least expensive gateways to Europe from North America, and finding a convenient and good-value flight is rarely a problem. **Direct, nonstop flights from the USA** are operated by KLM and Delta Airlines, but many more airlines fly **via London** and other European centres – and are often cheaper because of it. **KLM** offers the widest range of flights, with direct or one-stop flights to Amsterdam from several US cities, and connections from dozens more. Return **fares** from major cities in the US to Amsterdam start at around US$900, but average around US$1500. **Flying times** to Amsterdam on direct flights are as follows: New York (7hr 10min), Chicago (8hr 30min), Atlanta (10hr), and Los Angeles (11hr).

From Canada, KLM flies direct to Amsterdam from Vancouver (9hr 30min) and from Toronto (7hr 10min). **Fares** from Toronto go for around Can$1200, while from Vancouver you can expect to pay around Can$1500.

A BETTER KIND OF TRAVEL

At Rough Guides we are passionately committed to travel. We believe it helps us understand the world we live in and the people we share it with – and of course tourism is vital to many developing economies. But the scale of modern tourism has also damaged some places irreparably, and climate change is accelerated by most forms of transport, especially flying. All Rough Guides' flights are carbon-offset, and every year we donate money to a variety of environmental charities.

Flights from Australia and New Zealand

There are no direct/nonstop flights **from Australia** or **New Zealand** to the Netherlands and most itineraries will involve at least one stop in the Far East – Singapore, Bangkok or Kuala Lumpur – before proceeding onto Amsterdam (or the gateway city of the airline you're flying with). You can get tickets to Amsterdam from Sydney, Melbourne or Perth for AUS$1500–2500, NZ$2000–3000 from Auckland.

Flights from South Africa

From South Africa, KLM offers **direct/nonstop flights** to Amsterdam from Cape Town and Johannesburg. With other airlines, you will have to change at a gateway city – for example Lufthansa via Frankfurt – but this can often be more economical. As for sample **fares**, direct/nonstop return flights with KLM from South Africa begin at about ZAR7000. The **flying time**, direct, is about 11 hours.

AIRLINES

Aer Lingus Ⓦ aerlingus.com
Air France Ⓦ airfrance.co.uk
British Airways Ⓦ britishairways.com
CityJet Ⓦ cityjet.com
Delta Airlines Ⓦ delta.com
easyJet Ⓦ easyjet.com
Jet2 Ⓦ Jet2.com
KLM Ⓦ klm.com
Ryanair Ⓦ ryanair.com

By train from the UK

Eurostar trains (Ⓦ eurostar.com) departing from London St Pancras (plus Ebbsfleet and Ashstead in Kent) reach Brussels via the Channel Tunnel in a couple of hours. In Brussels, trains arrive at Bruxelles-Midi station (Brussel-Zuid in Dutch), from where there are onward services to Rotterdam (1hr 10min) and Amsterdam Centraal station (2hr) with two high-speed train companies, **Fyra** (Ⓦ fyra.com)

and **Thalys** (Ⓦ thalys.com). Eurostar can arrange **through ticketing** from any point in the UK to any point in the Netherlands, as can Rail Europe (Ⓦ raileurope.co.uk). A standard return **fare** from London to Amsterdam, with some flexibility, costs around £150, but special deals and bargains are commonplace. Obviously enough, **travelling time** from London to Amsterdam depends on how long you have to wait for the connection in Brussels – but 5 hours in total is about average.

For other Dutch destinations accessible from Brussels, consult the encyclopedic website of Dutch Railways, **NS** (Ⓦ ns.nl).

By train and ferry from the UK

Stena Line (Ⓦ stenaline.co.uk), in conjunction with Greater Anglia trains (Ⓦ greateranglia.co.uk), operates the **Dutchflyer**, an inexpensive if somewhat time-consuming rail-and-ferry route from the UK to the Netherlands. **Trains** depart London's Liverpool Street station bound for Harwich, where they connect with the **ferry** over to the Hook of Holland – the Hoek van Holland (though you can also join the Dutchflyer at stations in between Liverpool Street and Harwich). The whole journey takes between eight and nine hours, including the six-hour ferry crossing. From the Hook, there are frequent trains onto Rotterdam (every 30min to 1hr; 30min), from where you can reach a host of other Dutch towns. One-way **fares** start at £39, or £90 on an overnight sailing, cabin included – cabins are compulsory on overnight sailings. **Tickets** are available from Greater Anglia trains.

By ferry from the UK

Three companies operate **car ferries** from the UK to the Netherlands. They are Stena Line (Ⓦ stenaline.co.uk) with services from Harwich to the Hook of Holland (6hr); **DFDS Seaways** (Ⓦ dfdsseaways.co.uk) from Newcastle (North Shields) to IJmuiden near Amsterdam (16hr); and **P&O Ferries** (Ⓦ poferries.com) from Hull to Europoort, 40km west of Rotterdam (11hr).

RAIL PASSES

Pan-European **Inter-Rail** and **Eurail passes** can include the Dutch railway network and there's also a **Holland Rail Pass**, which entitles the holder to between three to five days unlimited rail travel within one month. The rules and regulations regarding all these passes are complicated – consult the website of the umbrella company, **Rail Europe** (Ⓦ raileurope.com). Note that some passes have to be bought before leaving home. Note also that Dutch railways sells a competitively priced, one-day unlimited railcard for €47.

Tariffs vary enormously, depending on when you leave, how long you stay, if you're taking a car, what size it is and how many passengers are in it. As a sample fare, a weekend excursion from Hull to the Europoort for two adults, a car and a cabin might cost as little as £120 each way.

Driving from the UK

To reach the Netherlands **by car or motorbike from the UK**, you can either take a ferry (see opposite) or use **Eurotunnel**'s shuttle train through the Channel Tunnel (W eurotunnel.com) from Folkestone to Calais. Eurotunnel **fares**, which are charged per vehicle including passengers, depend on the time of year, time of day and length of stay and the journey takes about 35min. As an example, a five-day return fare in the summer costs in the region of £100. Advance booking is advised. Amsterdam is roughly 370km from the Eurotunnel exit in Calais, Rotterdam 200km, Arnhem 260km.

By bus from the UK

Travelling by **long-distance bus** is generally the cheapest way of reaching the Netherlands from the UK, but it is very time-consuming: the main route, from London to Amsterdam, takes around twelve hours. There are three or four services daily and all of them use the Eurotunnel. For timetable details, consult the operator, **Eurolines** (W eurolines.co.uk). One-way **fares** start from as little as £30, £60 return. There are discounts for seniors (60+) and the under-26s.

Getting around

Getting around the Netherlands is rarely a problem: it's a small country, and the longest journey you're ever likely to make – say from Amsterdam to Maastricht – takes under three hours by train or car. Furthermore, the public transport system is exemplary, a fully integrated network of trains and buses that brings even the smallest of villages within easy reach, and at very reasonable prices too. Train and bus stations are almost always next door to each other, and several of the larger cities also have a tram network.

By train

The best way of travelling around the Netherlands is by **train**. The system – one of the best in Europe – is largely, though not exclusively, operated by **Nederlandse Spoorwegen** (NS; Dutch Railways; W ns.nl). NS trains are fast, mostly modern, frequent and very punctual; fares are relatively low; and the network of lines comprehensive. NS domestic services come in two types: the speedy **Intercity** for city-to-city connections; and the **Stoptrein**, (or Sprinter), which operates on local routes and stops pretty much everywhere.

Several **other train companies** operate long-distance/international, high-speed services across the Netherlands, principally **Fyra** (W fyra .com) and **Thalys** (W thalys.com), whose services connect Amsterdam and Rotterdam, and **ICE** trains linking Amsterdam with Utrecht and Arnhem. At larger train stations in the Netherlands, there are separate hi-speed train ticket desks (W nshispeed.nl).

Fares and tickets

Ordinary **fares** are calculated by the kilometre, diminishing proportionately the further you travel: for example, a standard one-way fares from Amsterdam to Maastricht costs €23.20, Rotterdam €13.60 and Leeuwarden €23. For a one-way ticket, ask for an *enkele reis*; a return trip is a *retour*. Same-day return tickets (*dagretour*) can knock between ten and forty percent off the price of two one-way tickets for the same journey, but returns are normally double the price of one-way tickets. First-class fares cost about eighty percent on top of the regular fare.

BUYING A TRAIN TICKET

Buying an NS train ticket is not as straightforward as you might expect. With the exception of the machines at Amsterdam Centraal Station and Schiphol airport, the automatic, mutilingual **ticket machines** in every station concourse do not accept foreign credit cards or debit cards – and only a few (around a quarter) accept cash (coins not notes). The same applies – and with the same exceptions – to NS ticket offices; note also that if you buy a ticket at a ticket office, they apply a small surcharge per transaction of €0.50. Neither can you purchase an NS ticket online with either a foreign debit card or a credit card.

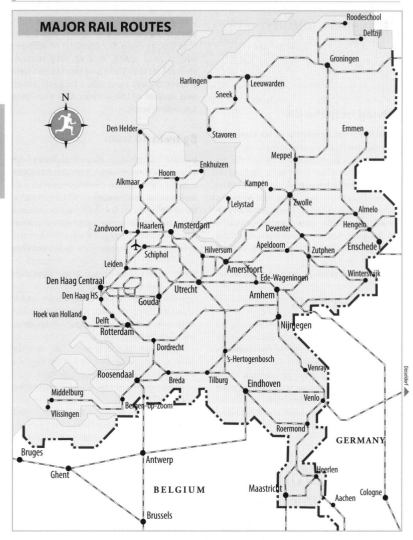

MAJOR RAIL ROUTES

N

With any ticket, you're free to stop off anywhere en route and continue your journey later that day, but you're not allowed to backtrack. **Timetables** are online and mounds of information on special deals and discounts are available at all major train stations. Note that you are not allowed to buy a ticket on the train – travel without a ticket and you will be fined on the spot (€35).

NS discount tickets and deals

NS offers a variety of **discount tickets and deals**, perhaps the most useful of which is the **Dagkaart**

(Day Travel Card) for unlimited travel on any train in the system and costing just €47 in second-class; first-class is €80. There's also the **Weekendretour** (Weekend Return), which costs the same as a day return (see p.25), but you can spread your outward and return journeys over a weekend from Friday (7pm+) to Monday (4am) with an added day thrown in when there is a public holiday. A third possibility is the family-orientated **Railrunner**, which charges just €2.50 per journey for up to three children aged 4–11 travelling with an adult. Note also that the OV-Chipkaart (see box opposite) can

PLANNING A JOURNEY

For pre-departure information on your **train journey**, the "Journey Planner" feature on the NS website (🅦ns.nl) is hard to beat. Type in your departure and arrival points (train station or street address), and it will not only tell you how long it takes to get to the nearest station, but also what platform your train leaves from, how many changes to make (and where, with platform numbers), and how much your ticket will cost. A comparable service, but this time including all public transport, is provided on 🅦9292.nl.

be used on the NS network. For further information on deals and discounts, consult 🅦ns.nl.

Treintaxi

With NS's **treintaxi scheme**, rail passengers can be assured of a taxi to and/or from around thirty train stations in the NS network. The largest stations – Amsterdam Centraal and Den Haag CS, for example – are not part of the scheme and it only applies within the city limits of each participating station. To get to the station at the start of your journey, call the national *treintaxi* number ☎0900 873 4682 (premium line, only within the Netherlands) at least half an hour in advance. On arrival at your local station, you can either book a *treintaxi* for your destination when you buy your ticket, or wait till you get there – and pay the taxi driver direct (for a small extra fee). The **fixed-rate price** per person per *treintaxi* ride is €4.80. Note that *treintaxis* are not the same as regular taxis – you may well, for instance, have to share with other people taking a similar route. The cabs are identifiable by a "*treintaxi*" sign on the roof and they have a separate rank – usually with summoning buttons – outside train stations.

By bus and tram

Supplementing the train network are **buses** – run by a patchwork of local companies but again amazingly efficient and reaching into every rural nook and cranny. **Ticketing** is straightforward as the whole country is divided into public transport zones and you can either use your **OV-chipkaart** (see box below) or pay the driver instead. Bear in mind also that in more remote rural areas some bus services only operate when passengers have made advance bookings: local **timetables** indicate where this applies. Regional bus timetable books, costing around €3, are sold at some train station bookshops and most VVVs (see p.43), or you can plan your journey **online** at 🅦9292.nl.

Within **major towns**, urban public transport systems are extensive, inexpensive and frequent, which makes getting around straightforward and hassle-free; most bus and tram services run from 6am until about midnight and your OV-Chipkaart is valid on all services. Urban "**Park and Ride**" (or **Transferium**) schemes are commonplace.

THE OV-CHIPKAART

The whole of the Netherlands is divided up into public transport zones with a **nationwide ticketing system** valid on all the country's buses, trams and metros. The ticketing system works via the **OV-Chipkaart** (🅦ov-chipkaart.nl), which comes in several types and two formats – paper and plastic. Paper OV-chipkaarts begin with the 1hr ticket (€2.70) and then the 24hr ticket (€7.50), 48hr (€12) and 72hr (€16). All these paper tickets can be purchased from most tram and bus drivers, many VVVs and some hotels. They need to be checked against an electronic reader when you enter and leave the public transport system – if you forget, the card soon stops working.

For extended stays, you might consider purchasing a rechargeable, plastic OV-Chipkaart, which come in two main types, personalized and anonymous; both cost €7.50. These are valid for five years and are sold at train and bus stations, including automatic ticketing machines (though see box, p.25). Before your journey, you load up the card with the required/desired credit and check it against the reader when you enter and again when you leave the public transport network. There is an initial boarding fee of €4 – so your OV-Chipkaart must have a minimum credit of €4 – but when you leave the system this is automatically reimbursed. Finally, note that plastic (but not paper) OV-Chipkaart can also be used on the NS train network.

By car

For the most part, **driving** round the Netherlands is pretty much what you would expect: smooth, easy and quick. The country has a uniformly good road network, with most of the major towns linked by some kind of motorway or dual carriageway, though snarl-ups and jams are far from rare. Rules of the road are straightforward: you drive on the right, and **speed limits** are 50kph in built-up areas, 80kph outside, 120kph on motorways – though some motorways have a speed limit of 100kph, indicated by small yellow signs on the side of the road. Drivers and front-seat passengers are required by law to wear seat belts, and penalties for drunk driving are severe. There are no toll roads, and although **fuel** is expensive, at around €1.85 per litre (diesel €1.50), the short distances mean this isn't too much of an issue.

Most foreign **driving licences** are honoured in the Netherlands, including all EU, US, Canadian, Australian and New Zealand ones. If you're **bringing your own car**, you must have adequate insurance, preferably including coverage for legal costs, and it's advisable to have an appropriate breakdown policy from your home motoring organization too.

Renting a car

All the major **international car rental agencies** are represented in the Netherlands. To rent a car, you'll have to be 21 or over (and have been driving for at least a year), and you'll need a credit card – though some local agencies will accept a hefty cash deposit instead. **Rental charges** are fairly high, beginning around €250 per week for unlimited mileage in the smallest vehicle, but include collision damage waiver and vehicle (but not personal) **insurance**. To cut costs, watch for special deals offered by the bigger companies. If you go to a smaller, local company (of which there are many), you should proceed with care: in particular, check the policy for the excess applied to claims and ensure that it includes a collision damage waiver (applicable if an accident is your fault) as well as adequate levels of financial cover. If you **break down** in a rented car, you'll get roadside assistance from the particular repair company the rental firm has contracted. The same principle works with your own vehicle's breakdown policy providing you have coverage abroad.

Cycling

One great way to see the Netherlands, whether you're a keen cyclist or an idle pedaller, is to travel by **bike** (*fiets*). Cycle-touring can be a short cut into Dutch culture and you can reach parts of the country – its beaches, forests and moorland – that might otherwise be (relatively) inaccessible. The mostly flat landscape makes travelling by bike an almost effortless pursuit, although you can find yourself battling against a headwind or swallowed up in a shoal of cyclists commuting to work.

The short distances involved make it possible to see most of the country with relative ease, using the nationwide system of well-marked **cycle paths**: a circular blue sign with a white bicycle on it indicates an obligatory cycle lane, separate from car traffic. Red lettering on signposts gives distances for fairly direct routes; lettering in green denotes a more scenic (and lengthy) mosey. Long-distance (LF) routes weave through the cities and countryside, often linking up to local historic loops and scenic trails.

The Dutch as a nation are celebrated touring cyclists, and bookshops are packed with **cycling books and maps**; however, for all but the longest trips the maps and route advice provided by most tourist offices are fine. If you're looking for a **place to stay** after a day in the saddle, the best advice is to visit a member of the **Vrienden op de Fiets** (see p.29).

Bike rental

You can **rent a bike** from most NS train stations for €7.50 a day, plus a deposit of anywhere between €50 and €150 depending on the model. Most bikes are single-speed, though there are some 3-speeds to be had, and even mountain bikes in the hillier south. You'll also need some form of **ID**. The snag is that cycles must be returned to the station from which they were rented, making onward hops by rented bike impossible. Most **bike shops** – of which there are many – rent bicycles out for around the same amount, and they may be more flexible on deposits: some may accept a passport in lieu of cash. In all cases, advance reservations are advised.

Taking your bike on an NS **train** is allowed – and the bike carriages have a clear cycle symbol on the outside. You'll need to buy a flat-rate ticket (*dagkaart fiets*; €6) for your bike, which is valid for the whole day. Space can be limited, despite the variety of ingeniously folding bikes favoured by locals, and because of this you won't be allowed on with your bike during the morning and evening rush hours (6.30–9am & 5.30–6pm), except in July and August.

Note that in the larger cities in particular, but really anywhere, you should never, ever, leave your bike **unlocked**, even for a few minutes – bike stealing is a big deal in the Netherlands. Almost all train stations have somewhere you can store your bike safely for less than a euro.

Accommodation

Inevitably accommodation is one of the major expenses of a trip to the Netherlands – indeed, if you're after a degree of comfort and style, it's going to be the costliest item by far. There are, however, budget alternatives, principally private rooms (broadly bed and breakfast arranged via the local tourist office), campsites and a scattering of HI-registered hostels. During the summer and over holiday periods vacant rooms can be scarce, so it's wise to book ahead. In Amsterdam, room shortages are commonplace throughout the year, so advance booking is always required; hotel prices are about thirty percent higher here than in the rest of the country.

Hotels

All **hotels** in the Netherlands are graded on a star system. One-star and no-star hotels are rare, and prices for two-star establishments start at around €70 for a double room without private bath or shower, €80 with en-suite facilities. Three-star hotels cost upwards of about €85; for four- and five-star places you'll pay €125-plus. Generally, the stated price includes **breakfast**, except in the most expensive and the very cheapest of hotels.

You can book ahead easily by calling the hotel direct – English is almost always spoken. Within the Netherlands, you can also make same-night bookings in person through any tourist office for a nominal fee. Alternatively, three useful **booking websites** are ⓦweekendcompany.nl (in Dutch & German only); ⓦweekendjeweg.nl (Dutch only); and the **Netherlands' Board of Tourism's** ⓦholland.com.

Private rooms

One way of cutting costs is to use **private accommodation** – rooms in private homes that are let out to visitors on a bed-and-breakfast basis, sometimes known as **pensions**. Prices are quoted per person and are normally around €20–30 with breakfast usually included. You mostly have to go through the local tourist office to find a private room: they will either give you a list to follow up independently or will book the accommodation themselves and levy a minimal booking fee. Note, however, that not all tourist offices are able to offer private rooms; generally you'll find them only in the larger towns and tourist centres and characteristically a good way from the centre. In some of the more popular tourist destinations the details of these "B&Bs" are listed in tourist brochures.

Vrienden op de Fiets

If you're cycling or walking round the Netherlands, you will find the organization **Vrienden op de Fiets** (Friends of the Bicycle; ☎079 323 8556, ⓦvriendenopdefiets.nl) an absolute bargain. For an annual joining fee ("donation") of €8, you'll be sent a book with several hundred Dutch addresses where you can stay the night in somebody's home for a fixed tariff of €19 per person; all you have to do is phone/email 24 hours in advance. Accommodation can range from stylish townhouses to suburban semis to centuries-old farmhouses – and staying in somebody's home can give a great insight into Dutch life. Hosts are usually very friendly, offer local information and will provide a breakfast of often mammoth proportions to send you on your way.

ACCOMMODATION PRICES

Throughout this Guide we give a headline price for every accommodation reviewed. This indicates the lowest price you're likely to pay for a double or twin room with breakfast, in high season (usually June to mid-Aug), barring regularly offered **weekend discounts and special deals**; the price includes breakfast, unless otherwise stated. Single rooms, where available, usually cost between 60 and 80 percent of a double or twin. At **hostels**, we sometimes give two prices – the price of a double room, if available, and of a dormitory bed – and at **campsites**, the cost of two people plus car and tent pitch.

TOP 5 HOTELS WITH CHARACTER

The Netherlands has a fantastic range of hotels from grand Art Nouveau buildings to renovated thatched cottages. Here are five of the country's most individual places to stay.

Stempels, Haarlem. See p.111
Hotel Molendal, Arnhem. See p.264
Hotel de Harmonie, Giethoorn. See p.251

De Posthoorn, Monnickendam. See p.113
Hotel de Mug, Middelburg. See p.311

Hostels

If you're travelling on a tight budget, an **HI hostel** may well be your accommodation of choice. **Stayokay** (Ⓦstayokay.com) is the HI-affiliated Dutch hostelling association and they operate twenty-seven hostels across the Netherlands. **Dorm beds** are the norm, in four- to ten-bunk rooms, though the smaller dorms can also be rented as family rooms and some hostels have double and single rooms. For the most part, they represent extremely good value, offering clean and comfortable accommodation at rock-bottom prices.

Dorm beds **cost** €25–40 per person per night including breakfast, €50 for a bed in a double room, depending on the season and the hostel's facilities; there are no age restrictions. Both city and country locations can get very full between June and September, when you should **book in advance**. Most Stayokay hostels accept online bookings. Meals are often available – about €13 for a filling dinner – but there are no self-catering facilities. If you're planning on spending several nights in hostels, it makes sense to join your home HI organization before you leave in order to avoid paying surcharges, though you can join at the first Dutch hostel you stay at instead.

In addition to Stayokay hostels, the larger cities – particularly Amsterdam – have a number of **private hostels** offering dormitory accommodation and almost invariably double- and triple-bedded rooms too. Prices are broadly similar, but standards vary enormously; we've given detailed reviews, where appropriate, in the Guide.

Camping and trekkers' huts

There are plenty of **campsites** in the Netherlands and most of them are very well equipped. Prices vary greatly, depending on the facilities available, but in the more deluxe you can expect to pay around €25 for a pitch including electrical hook-up and car parking, plus €3–5 per person. All tourist offices have details of their nearest sites, and we've mentioned a few campsites in the Guide. A list of selected sites is available on the **Eurocampings** website (Ⓦeurocampings.co.uk).

If you don't mind having basic facilities, look out also for **minicampings**, which are generally signed off the main roads. These are often family-run – you may end up pitched next to a family's house – and are informal, inexpensive and friendly. Details of registered minicampings can be found in the accommodation section of the provincial guides sold at every tourist office. Some campsites also offer **trekkers' huts** (*trekkershutten*) – frugally furnished wooden affairs that can house a maximum of four people for about €30 a night. You can get details of the national network, with good information in English and a list of sites in each province, from the **Stichting Trekkershutten Nederland** (Ⓦtrekkershutten.nl).

Food and drink

The Netherlands may not be Europe's gastronomic epicentre, but the food in the average Dutch restaurant has improved by leaps and bounds in recent years, and there are any number of places serving a good, inventive take on home-grown cuisine. All the larger cities also have a decent assortment of ethnic restaurants, especially Indonesian, Chinese and Thai, plus lots of cafés and bars – often known as eetcafés – that serve adventurous, reasonably priced food in a relaxed and unpretentious setting. The Netherlands is also a great country to go drinking, with a wide selection of bars, ranging from the chic and urbane to the rough and ready. Considering the country's singular approach to the sale and consumption of cannabis, you might choose to enjoy a joint after your meal rather than a beer – for which you will have to go to a "coffeeshop" (see p.37 & p.92).

Food

Dutch **food** tends to be higher in protein content than variety: steak, chicken and fish, along with filling soups and stews, are staples, usually served up in substantial quantities. It can, however, at its best, be excellent, with lots of restaurants – and even bars and eetcafés – offering increasingly adventurous crossovers with French cuisine, all at good-value prices.

Breakfast

In all but the cheapest and most expensive of hotels, **breakfast** (ontbijt) will be included in the price of the room. Though usually nothing fancy, it's always substantial: rolls, cheese, ham, hard-boiled eggs, jam and honey or peanut butter are the principal ingredients. Many bars and cafés serve rolls and sandwiches in similar mode, although few open much before 8am or 8.30am.

A standard cup of **coffee** is bitter and strong and served black with koffiemelk (evaporated milk) on the side, but lots of places – especially city coffee shops (of the non-dope variety) – have moved up a notch, serving mochas, cappuccinos and so forth. **Tea** generally comes with lemon – if anything; if you want milk you have to ask for it. **Chocolate** (chocomel) is also popular, hot or cold; for a real treat, drink it hot with a layer of fresh whipped cream (slagroom) on top. Some cafés also sell aniseed-flavoured warm milk (anijsmelk).

Snacks

Dutch **fast food** has its own peculiarities. Chips/fries (friet or patat) are the most common standby; vlaamse or "Flemish" style sprinkled with salt and smothered with huge gobs of mayonnaise (frietesaus) are the best, or with curry, sateh, goulash or tomato sauce. If you just want salt, ask for patat zonder; fries with salt and mayonnaise are patat met. You'll also come across kroketten – spiced minced meat (usually either veal or beef), covered with breadcrumbs and deep-fried – and fricandel, a frankfurter-like sausage. All these are available over the counter at evil-smelling fast-food places, or, for a euro or so, from coin-op heated glass compartments on the street and in train stations.

Much tastier are the **fish specialities** sold by street vendors, which are good as a snack or a light lunch: salted raw herring, rollmops, smoked eel (gerookte paling), mackerel in a roll (broodje makreel), mussels and various kinds of deep-fried fish are all delicious. Look out, too, for "green" or maatje herring, eaten raw with onions in early summer: hold the fish by the tail, tip your head back and dangle it into your mouth, Dutch-style. Another snack you'll see everywhere is shoarma or **shwarma** – also known as doner kebab, shavings of lamb pressed into a flat pitta bread – sold in numerous Middle Eastern restaurants and takeaways for about €3. Other, less common, street foods include **pancakes** (pannenkoeken), sweet or spicy, also widely available at sit-down restaurants; **waffles** (stroopwafels), doused with syrup; and, in November and December, oliebollen, greasy **doughnuts** sometimes filled with fruit (often apple) or custard (as a Berliner) and traditionally eaten on New Year's Eve.

Sandwiches

Bars often serve sandwiches and rolls (boterham and broodjes) – mostly open, and varying from a slice of tired cheese on old bread to something so embellished it's almost a complete meal – as well as more substantial dishes. A **sandwich** made with French bread is known as a stokbrood. In the winter, erwtensoep (or snert) – thick **pea soup** with smoked sausage, served with smoked bacon on pumpernickel – is available in many bars, and makes a great buy for lunch, at about €5 a bowl. Alternatively, you can sample the **uitsmijter** (a "kicker-out", derived from the practice of serving it at dawn after an all-night party to prompt guests to depart). Now widely available at all times of day, it comprises one,

---

TOP 5 CAKES AND COOKIES

Dutch cakes and cookies are always good, best eaten in a banketbakkerij (patisserie) with a small serving area; or bought in a bag and munched on the hoof. Here are some of our favourites.

Amandelkoekjes Cakes with a crisp cookie outside and melt-in-the-mouth almond paste inside.

Appelgebak Chunky, memorably fragrant apple-and-cinnamon pie, served hot in huge wedges, often with whipped cream (met slagroom).

Mergpijpjes Soft cakes with a layer of almond on the outside and dipped in chocolate at both ends.

Speculaas Crunchy cinnamon cookie with the texture of gingerbread.

Stroopwafels Butter wafers sandwiched together with runny syrup.

DUTCH CHEESE

Dutch cheeses may not be as rich and varied as, say, those of France or Switzerland, but they can certainly be delicious. Most Dutch cheeses are pale yellow, like the most famous of them, **Gouda**, in which differences in taste come with the varying stages of maturity: *jong* (young) cheese has a mild flavour, *belegen* (16–18 weeks old) is much tastier, while *oud* (mature) can be pungent and strong, with a grainy, flaky texture. The best way to eat it is as the Dutch do, in thin slices (cut with a cheese slice, or *kaasschaaf*) rather than large chunks. Among other names to look out for, the best known is **Edam**, semi-soft in texture but slightly creamier than Gouda; it's usually shaped into balls and coated in red wax ready for export, but is not eaten much in the Netherlands. **Leidse** is simply a bland Gouda laced with cumin or caraway seeds; most of its flavour comes from the seeds. **Maasdam** is a Dutch version of Emmental or Jarlsberg, strong, creamy and full of holes, sold under brand names such as Leerdammer and Maasdammer. You'll also find Dutch-made Emmental and Gruyère.

two or three fried eggs on buttered bread, topped with a choice of ham, cheese or roast beef; at about €5, it's another good budget lunch.

Full meals

Most cafés, **bars and café-bars** serve food, everything from sandwiches to a full menu – in which case they may be known as an **eetcafé**. This type of place is usually open all day, serving both lunch and an evening meal. Full-blown **restaurants**, on the other hand, tend to open in the evening only, usually from around 5.30 or 6pm until around 10pm. Especially in the smaller towns, the Dutch eat early, around 7.30 or 8pm; after about 10pm you'll find many restaurant kitchens closed.

If you're on a budget, stick to the **dagschotel** (dish of the day) wherever possible, for which you'll pay around €10. It's usually a meat or fish dish, heavily garnished with potatoes and other vegetables and salad; note, though, that it's often only served at lunchtime or between 6 and 8pm. Otherwise, you can pay up to €25 for a meat or seafood main course in an average restaurant. **Vegetarian** dining isn't a problem. Many eetcafés and restaurants have at least one meat-free menu item, and you'll find a few veggie restaurants in

most of the larger towns, offering full-course set meals for €10–15 – although bear in mind that they often close early (7/8pm).

Ethnic cuisine

As for **foreign cuisines**, the Dutch are particularly partial to **Indonesian** food and Indonesian restaurants are commonplace: *nasi goreng* and *bami goreng* (rice or noodles with meat) are good basic dishes, though there are normally more exciting items on the menu, some very spicy; chicken or beef in peanut sauce (*sateh*) is always available. Or you could try a **rijsttafel** – a sampler meal, comprising rice and/or noodles served with perhaps ten or twelve small, often spicy dishes and hot sambal sauce on the side. Usually ordered for two or more people, you can reckon on paying around €25 per person. **Surinamese** restaurants are much rarer, being largely confined to the big cities, but they offer a distinctive, essentially Creole cuisine – try *roti*, flat pancake-like bread served with a spicy curry, hard-boiled egg and vegetables.

Italian food is ubiquitous, with pizzas and pasta dishes starting at a fairly uniform €8 or so in most places.

FIVE FAVOURITE RESTAURANTS

The Netherlands has a great variety of places to eat serving every imaginable cuisine. Here are five of our favourites.

Belhamel, Amsterdam. A winning combination of Art Nouveau decor, excellent food and great views. See p.89

Lucius, Amsterdam. No mistake, this brasserie-style restaurant serves the city's best seafood. See p.88

Soestdijk, Groningen. Smashing restaurant with a highly creative menu, ranging from

Italian to Indonesian dishes. See p.226

Stempels, Haarlem. Smooth and polished, sleek and slick, this is the most stylish of restaurants. See p.111

Ut Lieuwke, Maastricht. Lovely premises and delicious Franco-Dutch cuisine – no wonder the place is so popular. See p.283

FIVE FAVOURITE BARS

Visiting a Dutch bar is an integral part of the Netherlands experience – check out our top five joints to take a tipple.

't Arendsnest, Amsterdam. Great place to sample Dutch beer from all the country's many breweries. See p.91
De Oude Mol, Den Haag. If you thought Den Haag lacked character, think again: this lovely old bar has oodles of atmosphere. See p.162
Het Papeneiland, Amsterdam. Must be one of the cosiest neighbourhood bars in the country. See p.91
In de Wildeman, Amsterdam. No music, no distractions, it's the beer that counts – and this bar has more than two hundred different brews on offer. See p.91
Der Witz, Groningen. Genial customers, friendly bar staff and a great atmosphere in the heart of Groningen. See p.126

Drinking

Most **drinking** is done in the laidback surroundings of a brown bar (*bruin kroeg*) – so called because of the colour of the décor – or in more modern-looking places, everything from slick designer bars, minimally furnished and usually catering for a younger crowd, to cosy neighbourhood bars. Most bars **stay open** until around 1am during the week and 2am at weekends, though some don't bother to open until lunchtime, a few not until 4 or 5pm.

Though they're no longer common, you may also come across **proeflokaalen** or tasting houses. Originally the sampling premises of small distillers, these are now small, old-fashioned bars that only serve spirits (and maybe a few beers) and sometimes close early (around 8pm).

Beer

The Netherlanders' favourite tipple is **beer**, mostly Pilsener-style lager usually served in a relatively small measure (just under a half-pint, with a foaming head on top) – ask for *een pils*. Away from Amsterdam expect to pay around €2–3, or €3–4 in Amsterdam. Predictably, beer is much cheaper from a supermarket, most brands retailing at just under €2 for a half-litre bottle. The most common Dutch brands are Heineken, Amstel and Grolsch, all of which you can find more or less nationwide. Expect them to be stronger and more distinctive than the watery approximations brewed abroad under licence.

For something a little less strong, look out for *donkenbier*, which is about half the strength of an ordinary Pilsener beer. There are also a number of **seasonal beers**: rich, fruity *bokbier* is fairly widespread in autumn, while year-round you'll see *witbier* (a wheaty, white beer) such as Hoegaarden, Dentergems or Raaf – refreshing and potent in equal measure, and often served with a slice of a lemon or lime.

Around the country, you'll also spot plenty of the better-known **Belgian brands** available on tap, like Stella Artois and the darker De Koninck, as well as bottled beers like Duvel, Chimay and various brands of the fruit-flavoured Kriek. There are also an increasing number of local, independent breweries: see box below for five of the best.

Wine and spirits

Wine is reasonably priced – expect to pay around €5 for an average bottle of French white or red in a supermarket, €15 in a restaurant. As for spirits, the

FIVE OF THE BEST: ARTISAN BREWERIES

Brouwerij Brand Limburg Ⓦ brand.nl. The country's oldest brewery turns out a limited range of dark and blond beers plus a particularly tasty, cherry-coloured *Dubbelbock*.
Brouwerij Emelisse Kamperland Ⓦ emelisse.nl. Distinctive stuff – try their Imperial Russian Stout.
Brouwerij de Koningshoeven Tilburg. The Netherlands only Trappist brewery produces several strong dark ales, notably *La Trappe*
Quadrupel. Distributed by the country's second largest brewer, Bavaria (Ⓦ bavaria.com).
Brouwerij de Molen Amsterdam Ⓦ brouwerijdemolen.nl. Several good brews from this discrete little brewery – look out for their *Hemel & Aarde* (Heaven & Earth).
Gulpener Limburg Ⓦ gulpener.nl. Burgeoning brewery noted for its tasty lagers made from prime ingredients; their *Gulpener Oud Bruin* is an especially tangy dark ale.

indigenous drink is **jenever**, or Dutch gin – not unlike British gin, but a bit weaker and oilier, made from molasses and flavoured with juniper berries. It's served in a small glass (for around €2) and is traditionally drunk straight, often knocked back in one gulp with much hearty back-slapping. There are a number of varieties, principally *Oud* (old), which is smooth and mellow, an d *Jong* (young), which packs more of a punch – though neither is extremely alcoholic. The older *jenevers* (including *zeer oude*, very old) are a little more expensive but stronger and less oily. In a bar, ask for a *borreltje* (straight *jenever*) or a *bittertje* (with angostura); if you've a sweet tooth, try a *bessenjenever* (flavoured with blackcurrant). A glass of beer with a *jenever* chaser is a *kopstoot*. Imported spirits are considerably more expensive.

Other drinks include numerous **Dutch liqueurs**, notably *advocaat* or eggnog; sweet, blue *curaçao*; and luminous green *pisang ambon*. There is also an assortment of luridly coloured fruit brandies best left for experimentation at the end of an evening – or perhaps not at all – plus a Dutch-produced brandy, *vieux*, which tastes as if it's made from prunes but is in fact grape-based. Various regional **firewaters** include *elske* from Maastricht – made from the leaves, berries and bark of alder bushes.

The media

English-speakers will find themselves quite at home in the Netherlands as Dutch TV broadcasts a wide range of British programmes, and English-language newspapers are readily available too.

Newspapers and magazines

British newspapers are on sale in every major city on the day of publication. Newsagents located at train stations will almost always have copies if no one else does. Current issues of UK and US magazines are widely available as well, as is the *International Herald Tribune*.

Of the **Dutch newspapers**, *NRC Handels-blad* (Ⓦnrc.nl) is a right-of-centre paper that has perhaps the best international news coverage and a liberal stance on the arts; *De Volkskrant* (Ⓦvolkskrant.nl) is a progressive, leftish daily; the popular right-wing *De Telegraaf* (Ⓦtelegraaf.nl) boasts the highest circulation figures in the country and has a well-regarded financial section; while *Algemeen Dagblad*

(Ⓦad.nl) is a right-wing broadsheet. The left-of-centre *Het Parool* ("The Password"; Ⓦparool.nl) and the news magazine *Vrij Nederland* ("Free Netherlands"; Ⓦvn.nl) are the successors of underground Resistance newspapers printed during wartime occupation. The Protestant *Trouw* ("Trust"; Ⓦtrouw .nl), another former underground paper, is centre-left in orientation with a focus on religion.

Television and radio

Dutch TV isn't the best, but English-language programmes and films fill up a fair amount of the schedule – and they are always subtitled, never dubbed. The big global cable and satellite channels are routinely accessible in hotel rooms and most give access to a veritable raft of foreign television channels, including Britain's BBC1 and BBC2.

SMT **Dutch radio** has numerous stations catering for every niche. Of the **public service stations**, Radio 1 is a news and sports channel, Radio 2 plays AOR music, Radio 3 plays chart music and Radio 4 classical, jazz and world music. Of the **commercial stations**, some of the main nationwide players are Radio 538, Veronica and Noordzee FM; most of them play chart music. The Dutch Classic FM, at 101.2FM, plays mainstream classical music, with jazz after 10pm. There's next to no **English-language programming**, apart from the overseas-targeted **Radio Netherlands** (Ⓦrnw.nl), which broadcasts Dutch news in English, with features on current affairs, lifestyle issues, science, health and so on. Frequencies and schedules for the BBC World Service (Ⓦbbc.co.uk /worldservice), Radio Canada (Ⓦrcinet.ca) and Voice of America (Ⓦvoanews.com) are listed on their respective websites.

Festivals and events

Across the Netherlands, most annual festivals are arts- or music-based affairs, confined to a particular town or city, though there is also a liberal sprinkling of folkloric events celebrating one local event or another – the Alkmaar cheese market (see p.129) being a case in point. Most festivals take place during the summer and the local tourist office can be guaranteed to have all the latest details.

JANUARY

Elfstedentocht (Eleven Cities' Journey) Friesland
Ⓦ elfstedentocht.nl. Annual ice-skating marathon along the frozen rivers
of Friesland, starting and finishing in Leeuwarden. Weather permitting.

FEBRUARY

Holland Flowers Festival Enkhuizen Ⓦ hollandflowersfestival.nl.
The world's largest covered flower show held over five days in late
February.

Lent carnivals All sorts of shenanigans at the beginning of Lent in
Breda, 's Hertogenbosch, Maastricht and other southern towns. Late Feb
to early March.

MARCH

Keukenhof Gardens Lisse Ⓦ keukenhof.nl. World-renowned floral
displays in the bulbfields and hothouses of this large, sprawling park. Late
March to late May. See p.150.

APRIL

Alkmaar Cheese Market Alkmaar Ⓦ www.kaasmarkt.nl. Held
every Friday (10am–12.30pm), from the first Friday in April to the first
Friday in September. See p.129.

ABN AMRO Marathon Rotterdam Ⓦ rotterdammarathon.nl. Popular
long-distance run beginning in the city centre. Held on a Sunday in April.

Queen's Day (Koninginnedag) April 30. This is one of the most popular
dates in the Dutch diary, a street event *par excellence*. Celebrations in honour
of Queen Beatrix take place throughout the Netherlands, but festivities in
Amsterdam tend to be the wildest of the lot, with the city's streets and canals
lined with people dressed in ridiculous costumes. Anything goes, especially if
it's orange – the Dutch national colour. This is also the one day of the year
when goods can be bought and sold tax-free to anyone on the streets, and
numerous stalls are set up in front of people's houses.

MAY

Scheveningen Sand Sculpture Festival Scheveningen
Ⓦ sandsculptures.nl. Hard-working teams descend on the resort from
all over Europe to create amazing sand sculptures, which are left for three
weeks for visitors to admire. May to mid-June.

Herdenkingsdag (Remembrance Day) There's wreath-laying all
over the country and a two-minute silence is widely observed in honour
of the Dutch dead of World War II. May 4.

Bevrijdingsdag (Liberation Day) The country celebrates the 1945
liberation from German occupation with music, outdoor festivals and
processions. May 5.

Breda Jazz Festival Breda Ⓦ bredajazzfestival.nl. Has open-air
concerts and street parades over four days in late May.

Pinkpop festival Landgraaf, near Maastricht Ⓦ pinkpop.nl. A
top-ranking, three-day open-air rock festival held at the end of May.

JUNE

Holland Festival Amsterdam Ⓦ hollandfestival.nl. This
month-long performing arts festival covers all aspects of both national
and international music, theatre, dance and the contemporary arts.
Throughout June.

Oerol Festival Terschelling Ⓦ oerol.nl. A ten-day event featuring
theatre and stand-up comedy; mid- to late June.

JULY

North Sea Jazz Festival Rotterdam Ⓦ northseajazz.com.
Outstanding three-day jazz festival showcasing international names as
well as local talent. Multiple stages and a thousand musicians. Mid-July.
See also p.175.

Woodstock69 Bloemendaal aan Zee Ⓦ woodstock69.nl. Festival
held on Bloemendaal beach and featuring live percussion, dance acts and
plenty of revelry. Begins in April and runs through to September, but July
and August are the busiest – and best – months. There are daily shows in
high season, weekend shows in the shoulder season.

Internationale Vierdaagse Afstandmarsen Nijmegen
Ⓦ 4daagse.nl. One of the world's largest walking events, with over
30,000 participants walking 30–50km per day over four days. Late July.

AUGUST

Sneek Week Sneek Ⓦ sneekweek.nl. International sailing event in
Sneek, with around 1000 boats competing in over thirty classes. Early Aug.

Amsterdam Gay Pride Amsterdam Ⓦ amsterdamgaypride.nl. The
city's gay community celebrates with street parties and performances, as
well as a "Canal Pride" flotilla of boats parading along the Prinsengracht.
First or second weekend.

Grachtenfestival Amsterdam Ⓦ grachtenfestival.nl. For nine days,
international musicians perform classical music at historic locations in the
city centre. Includes the Prinsengrachtconcert, one of the world's most
prestigious open-air concerts, featuring a stage over the canal and a
promenading audience. Mid-August.

SEPTEMBER

Open Monumentendag (Open Monument Day)
Ⓦ openmonumentendag.nl. For two days in September, monuments
and historical attractions that are normally closed or have restricted
opening times throw open their doors to the public for free. Second
weekend.

OCTOBER

Amsterdam Marathon Amsterdam Ⓦ amsterdammarathon.nl.
Popular city marathon starting and finishing inside the Olympic Stadium
and passing through the city centre along the way. Held in early/mid-Oct.

NOVEMBER

Crossing Border The Hague Ⓦ crossingborder.nl. Four-day festival
that aims to cross artistic boundaries with performances by over a
hundred international acts presenting the spoken word in various forms,
from rap to poetry. Second or third week.

Parade of Sint Nicolaas Amsterdam. The traditional parade of
Sinterklaas (Santa Claus) through the city on his white horse, starting
from behind Centraal Station where he arrives by steamboat, before
proceeding down the Damrak towards Rembrandtplein accompanied by
his helpers, the Zwarte Pieten ("Black Peters") – so called because of their
blackened faces – who hand out sweets and little presents. It all finishes
on the Leidseplein. Second or third Sunday.

International Documentary Film Festival Amsterdam
Ⓦ idfa.nl. Arguably the world's largest documentary film festival, held over ten days in Amsterdam and showing around 250 domestic and international documentaries. Mid- to late November.

DECEMBER

Pakjesavond (Present Evening) Nationwide. Pakjesavond, rather than Christmas Day, is when Dutch kids receive their Christmas presents. If you're in the Netherlands on that day and have Dutch friends, it's worth knowing that it's traditional to give a present together with an amusing poem you have written caricaturing the recipient. For the children, legend asserts that presents are dropped down the chimney by Zwarte Piet (Black Peter) as Sinterklaas rides across the rooftops on his white horse. Traditionally, kids sing songs to make Sinterklaas happy in the weeks before Pakjesavond as there is always the chance of being caught by Zwarte Piet (if you haven't been good) and sent to Spain – where Sinterklaas lives – in a brown bag. December 5.

Sports and outdoor activities

Most visitors to the Netherlands confine their exercise to cycling (see p.28) and walking, both of which are ideally suited to the flatness of the terrain and, for that matter, the excellence of the public transport system. The Netherlands also offers all the sporting facilities you would expect of a prosperous, European country, from golf to gymnasia, swimming pools to horseriding, plus one or two more distinctive activities: these include Korfball, canal ice skating, though this is of course dependent on the weather being cold enough, and the idiosyncratic pole sitting, wherby participants literally sit on top of a pole for as long as possible.

Beaches and watersports

The Netherlands possesses some great **sandy beaches** on both its western and northern coasts, although it has to be admitted that the weather is notoriously unreliable – some say bracing – and the North Sea is really rather murky. There are a number of fully-fledged seaside resorts – such as Zandvoort (see p.109) and Scheveningen (see p.159) – but there are nicer, quieter stretches of coast, most notably amid the wild dunes and beaches that make up the **Nationaal Park Zuid-Kennemerland** near Haarlem (see p.110). There are also long sandy strands right

across the islands of the Waddenzee from Texel to Schiermonnikoog and these beaches are popular for **windsurfing** and **kitesurfing**. The lakes of Friesland and the IJsselmeer are good for **sailing**, particularly the yachting centre of Sneek (see p.205).

Spectator sports

The chief spectator sport is **football** (soccer) and the teams that make up the country's two professional leagues attract a fiercely loyal following. Big-deal clubs include PSV Eindhoven (Ⓦ psv.nl); Feyenoord from Rotterdam (Ⓦ feyenoord.nl); and Amsterdam's Ajax (Ⓦ ajax.nl). The football season runs from September to May, and matches are traditionally held on Sunday at 2.30pm, with occasional games at 8pm on Wednesday. Tickets for key matches are notoriously hard to come by.

Played from one end of the Netherlands to the other, **Korfball** (Ⓦ korfball.com) is a home-grown sport cobbled together from netball, basketball and volleyball, and played with mixed teams and a high basket. To watch a game, ask for fixture details at the local tourist office.

Culture and etiquette

The traditional view of the Netherlands is of a liberal country, where drugs and prostitution are both legal and homosexuality is widely accepted. However, this reputation disguises the fact that the population of the Netherlands is very diverse and a large number of its inhabitants fret about the decriminalization of drugs and the legalization of prostitution, while the gay and lesbian scene flourishes in Amsterdam above everywhere else in the country.

Drugs

Thousands of visitors come to the Netherlands in general, and Amsterdam in particular, just to get **stoned**. In the Netherlands the purchase of **cannabis** is decriminalized and this has proved to be a real crowd puller, though it's not without its problems: many Amsterdammers, for instance, get mightily hacked off with "**drug tourism**", as do folk in border towns, who have to deal with tides of people popping over the international frontier to the first **coffeeshop** they see. The irritation is such that there have been recent moves to both reduce the number of coffeeshops and restrict access to

Dutch citizens only, who will have to show a valid "weed card" to get served – at time of writing it's not clear what the future will hold for the coffeeshop.

Fundamentally, however, the Dutch government's attitude to soft drugs remains unchanged: the use of cannabis is tolerated but not condoned, resulting in a rather complicated set of rules and regulations. These permit users to buy very small amounts for **personal use only** – which means possession of up to 5g and sales of up to 5g per purchase in coffeeshops are OK. Needless to say, never, ever buy dope on the street and don't try to take any form of cannabis out of the country. A surprising number of people think (or claim to think) that if it's bought in Amsterdam it can be taken back home legally; this story won't wash with customs officials and drug enforcement officers, who will happily add your stash to the statistics of national drug seizures, and arrest you into the bargain.

As far as **other drugs** go, a series of serious incidents prompted the Dutch government to ban the sale of **magic mushrooms**, making them just as illegal as hard drugs. That said, you can still purchase the "grow-your-own" kits or buy truffles, which are claimed to have a similar effect. Despite the existence of a lively and growing trade in cocaine and heroin, possession of either could mean a stay in one of the Netherlands' lively and ever-growing jails. Ecstasy, acid and speed are as illegal in the Netherlands as they are anywhere else.

Coffeeshops

When you first walk into a **coffeeshop**, how you buy the stuff isn't immediately apparent – it's illegal to advertise cannabis in any way, which includes calling attention to the fact that it's available at all. What you have to do is ask to see the **menu**, which is normally kept behind the counter. This will list all the different hashes and grasses on offer, along with (if it's a reputable place) exactly how many grams you get for your money. The in-house dealer will be able to help you out with queries. Current **prices** per gram of hash and marijuana range from €7 for low-grade stuff up to €20 for top-quality hash and a bit more for really strong grass.

The **hash** you come across originates in various countries and is much like you'd find anywhere, apart from **Pollem**, which is compressed resin and stronger than normal. **Marijuana** is a different story, and the old days of imported Colombian, Thai and sensimelia are fading away. Taking their place are limitless varieties of "**Nederwiet**", Dutch-grown under UV lights and more potent than anything you're likely to have come across. Skunk, Haze and Northern Lights are all popular types of Dutch weed, and should be treated with caution – a smoker of low-grade British draw will be laid low (or high) for hours by a single spliff of skunk. You would be equally well advised to take care with **space-cakes** (cakes or biscuits baked with hash), which are widely available: you can never be sure exactly what's in them; they tend to have a delayed reaction (up to two hours before you notice anything strange – don't get impatient and gobble down another one); and once they kick in, they can bring on an extremely intense, bewildering high (10–12hr is common). You may also come across **cannabis seeds** for growing your own: while locals are permitted to grow a small amount of marijuana for personal use, the import of cannabis seeds is illegal in any country, so don't even think about trying to take some home.

Finally, one oddity is that in July 2008, **smoking tobacco** was banned in coffeeshops (as well as bars and restaurants), though smoking hash remained perfectly permissible: there has been some back-tracking on this, however, and some places now have separate smokers' dens, though the majority do not – hence the pile up on the pavement outside.

Gay and lesbian travellers

The Netherlands ranks as one of the top **gay-friendly** countries in Europe, with the superstar of the country's gay and lesbian scene being, of course, Amsterdam – here attitudes are tolerant, bars are excellent and plentiful, and support groups and facilities unequalled. In the other major cities of the Netherlands, while the scene isn't anywhere near as extensive, it's well organized: Rotterdam, The Hague, Nijmegen and Groningen, for example, each has a visible and enjoyable gay nightlife. The native **lesbian** scene is smaller and more subdued: many politically active lesbians move in close-knit communities, and it takes time for foreign visitors to find out what's happening.

The **COC** (Ⓦcoc.nl), the national organization for gay men and women, dates from the 1940s and is actively involved in gaining equal rights for gays and lesbians, as well as informing society's perceptions of gayness. Every city of any size has a branch office and they offer help, information on events and promotions – and many have a sociable coffee bar too. **Gay legislation** is particularly progressive – for example same-sex marriage and adoption by same-sex partners were legalized in 2001. The age of consent is 16.

Consider timing your visit to coincide with **Amsterdam's Gay Pride** (ⓦ amsterdampride.nl) on the first weekend in August. Celebrations are unabashed, with music, theatre, street parties and floats parading through the streets. The other major deal is **Queen's Day** – not that sort of queen, but with lots of gay parties anyway, and held on April 30.

Children

In general terms at least, Dutch society is sympathetic to its **children** and the tourist industry follows suit. Extra beds in hotel rooms are usually easy to arrange; many restaurants (though not the very smartest) have children's menus; concessions for children are the rule, from public transport through to museums; and baby-changing stations are commonplace. Pharmacists (*apotheek*) carry all the kiddy stuff you would expect – nappies, baby food and so forth.

Travel essentials

Addresses

These are written, for example, as Haarlemmerstraat 15 III, meaning the third-floor (US fourth-floor) apartment at no. 15 Haarlemmerstraat. The ground floor is indicated by **hs** (*huis*, "house") after the number; the basement is **sous** (*sousterrain*). The figures **1e**, **2e**, **3e** and **4e** before a street name are abbreviations for Eerste, Tweede, Derde and Vierde, respectively – the first, second, third and fourth streets of the same name. Some **side streets**, rather than have their own name, take the name of the street that they run off, with the addition of the word *dwars*, meaning crossing – so Palmdwarsstraat

is a side street off Palmstraat. **T/O** (*tegenover*, "opposite") in an address shows that the address is a boat: hence "Prinsengracht T/O 26" would indicate a boat to be found opposite building no. 26 on Prinsengracht. Dutch postcodes are made up of four figures and two letters.

Climate

The Netherlands enjoys a temperate **climate**, with relatively mild summers and moderately cold winters. Generally speaking, **temperatures** rise the further south you go, with the south of the country perhaps a couple of degrees warmer than the north and east for much of the year. This is offset by the prevailing **westerlies** that sweep in from the North Sea, making the wetter coastal provinces both warmer in winter and colder in summer than the eastern provinces, where the more severe climate of continental Europe has an influence. As far as **rain** is concerned, be prepared for it at any time of year.

Concessions

Concessionary rates apply at almost every sight and attraction as well as on public transport. Rates vary, but usually children under 5 go free and kids over 5 and under 15/16 get a substantial discount. There are senior discounts too, but the age of eligibility is rising in increments from 65+ to 67+ by 2023. Family ticket deals are commonplace. See also "Museum cards", p.41.

Crime and personal safety

By comparison with many other parts of Europe, the Netherlands is relatively free of **crime**, so there's little reason why you should ever come into contact with

AVERAGE MONTHLY TEMPERATURES AND RAINFALL

	Jan	Feb	Mar	Apr	May	Jun	Jul	Aug	Sep	Oct	Nov	Dec
AMSTERDAM												
Max/min °C	5/1	6/0	9/2	12/4	17/8	19/10	21/13	22/12	18/10	14/7	9/4	7/2
Max/min °F	41/34	43/32	48/36	54/39	63/46	66/50	70/55	72/54	64/50	57/45	48/39	45/36
Rainfall (mm)	62	43	59	41	48	68	66	61	82	85	89	75
Sun hr/day	2	3	4	6	7	7	7	7	4	3	2	1
MAASTRICHT												
Max/min °C	5/0	6/0	10/2	13/4	18/8	20/11	23/13	23/13	19/10	14/7	9/3	6/1
Max/min °F	41/32	43/32	50/36	55/39	64/46	68/52	73/55	73/55	66/50	57/45	48/37	43/34
Rainfall (mm)	61	51	61	46	64	74	67	58	60	63	66	70
Sun hr/day	2	3	4	5	6	6	6	6	4	4	2	1

the Dutch police. However, there is more **street crime** than there used to be and wherever you go at night it's always better to err on the side of caution. Using public transport any time of the day or night isn't usually a problem, but if in doubt take a taxi, and if you're on a bike, make sure it is well locked up – bike theft and resale is a major industry here. Be especially vigilant in the big cities, especially in Rotterdam and Amsterdam, where the Red Light District can have an unpleasant, threatening undertow (although the crowds of people act as a deterrent). In Amsterdam, there has also been a spate of street crimes in which thieves impersonate plain-clothes police, flashing false IDs: only very rarely will genuine non-uniform officers stop you in the street, so be sceptical if you are stopped in this manner.

If you do have to approach the Dutch police, you'll mostly find them courteous, concerned and usually able to speak English. If you have something stolen, make sure you get a copy of the **police report** or its number – essential if you are to make a claim against your insurance.

As for **offences you might commit**, drinking and driving is treated harshly and although you're allowed to be in possession of cannabis for personal use (up to 5g), anything more can result in confiscation by the police. It's not illegal to smoke cannabis in public, but it is frowned upon and you can be fined – stick to the coffeeshops (for more on drugs, see p.36). If you're **detained by the police**, you don't automatically have the right to a phone call, although in practice they'll probably phone your consulate for you – not that consular officials have a reputation for excessive helpfulness. If your alleged offence is a minor matter, you can be held for up to six hours with or without questioning (though note that midnight to 9am is not counted – tough luck if you are arrested at 11.59pm).

Electricity

The current is 220 volts AC, with standard European-style two-pin plugs. British equipment needs only a plug adaptor; American apparatus requires a transformer and an adaptor.

Entry requirements

Citizens of the EU/EEA, including the UK and Ireland, plus citizens of Australia, New Zealand, Canada and the US do not need a **visa** to enter the Netherlands if staying for ninety days or less, but they do need a current **passport**. Travellers from South Africa, on the other hand, need a passport

and a tourist visa for visits of less than ninety days; visas must be obtained before departure for the Netherlands and are available from the Dutch embassy (see below).

For stays in the Netherlands of **longer than ninety days**, EU/EEA residents (with the exception of Bulgarian and Romanian nationals) will have few problems, but everyone else needs a mix of **visas and permits. In all cases,** consult your Dutch embassy at home before departure.

DUTCH EMBASSIES ABROAD

Australia Ⓦ netherlands.org.au.
Canada Ⓦ netherlandsembassy.ca.
Ireland Ⓦ ireland.nlembassy.org.
New Zealand Ⓦ newzealand.nlembassy.org.
South Africa Ⓦ southafrica.nlembassy.org.
UK Ⓦ dutchembassyuk.org.
US Ⓦ dc.the-netherlands.org.

Health

Under **reciprocal health arrangements**, all citizens of the EU and EEA (European Economic Area) are entitled to free or discounted medical treatment within the Dutch public health-care system. Non-EU/EEA nationals are not entitled to free or discounted treatment and should, therefore, take out their own medical insurance – though some countries, for example Australia, do have limited mutual agreements. EU/EEA citizens may want to consider private health insurance too, in order to cover the cost of the discounted treatment as well as items not within the EU/EEA's scheme, such as dental treatment and repatriation on medical grounds. Note also that the more worth-while policies promise to sort matters out before you pay (rather than after) in the case of major expense; if you do have to pay upfront, get and keep the receipts. For more on insurance policies and what they cover, see p.40.

Health care in the Netherlands is of a high standard and rarely will **English speakers** encounter language problems – if the doctor or nurse can't speak English themselves (which is unlikely) there will almost certainly be someone at hand who can. Your local pharmacy, tourist office or hotel should be able to provide the address of an English-speaking doctor (or dentist).

If you're **seeking treatment under EU/EEA reciprocal public health agreements**, double-check that the medic is working within (and seeing you as) a patient of the public health-care system. This being the case, you'll receive reduced-cost/

government-subsidized treatment just as the locals do; any fees must be paid upfront, or at least at the end of your treatment, and are non-refundable. Sometimes you will be asked to produce documentation to prove you are eligible for EU/EEA health care, sometimes no one bothers, but technically at least you should have your passport and your **European Health Insurance Card** (**EHIC**) to hand. If, on the other hand, you have a **travel insurance policy covering medical expenses**, you can seek treatment in either the public or private health sectors, the main issue being whether – at least in major cases – you have to pay the costs upfront and then wait for reimbursement or not.

Anyone planning to stay in the Netherlands for **more than ninety days** (even when coming from another EU/EEA member state) is required by Dutch law to take out private **health insurance**.

Pharmacies

Minor ailments can be remedied at a **drugstore** (*drogist*). These sell non-prescription drugs as well as toiletries, tampons, condoms and the like. A **pharmacy** (*apotheek*) – generally open Monday to Friday 9.30am to 6pm, but often closed Monday mornings – is where you go to get a prescription filled. There aren't many 24-hour pharmacies, but the local tourist office, as well as most of the better hotels, will supply addresses of ones that stay open late.

Insurance

Prior to travelling, it's a good idea to take out **travel insurance** to cover against theft, loss and illness or injury. Before paying for a new policy, however, it's worth checking whether you already have some degree of cover: for instance, EU/EEA health-care privileges apply in the Netherlands (see p.39), some all-risks home insurance policies may cover your possessions when overseas, and many private medical schemes include cover when abroad.

A typical **insurance policy** usually provides cover for loss of baggage, tickets and – up to a certain limit – cash or cheques, as well as cancellation or curtailment of your journey and medical costs. Most of them exclude so-called **dangerous sports** – horseriding, windsurfing and so forth – unless an extra premium is paid. Many policies can be chopped and changed to exclude coverage you don't need – for example, sickness and accident benefits can often be excluded or included at will. If you do take **medical coverage**, ascertain whether benefits will be paid as treatment proceeds or only after your return home, and whether the policy has a 24-hour medical emergency number. When securing **baggage cover**, make sure that the per-article limit will cover your most valuable possessions. If you need to **make a claim**, keep receipts for medicines and medical treatment. In the event you have anything stolen, you should obtain a crime report statement or number.

Internet

Almost all the country's hotels, B&Bs and hostels provide **internet access** for their guests either free or at minimal charge. Many cafés offer internet access too, as does every library, where services are free but usually time-limited. If you are bringing your own laptop, the useful website Ⓦ kropla.com gives information about **electrical systems** in different countries as well as international codes.

Mail

The Dutch postal system has been privatized and is now run by **TNT** (Ⓦ postnl.nl). TNT has closed many of the old post offices, replacing them with counters within large stores and supermarkets, though these can be difficult to track down. Fortunately, **stamps** are sold at a wide range of outlets, including shops and hotels, and TNT has not reduced the number of **postboxes**, which are legion.

Maps

There are lots of Netherlands **road maps** on the market and for the most part they are widely available both at home and in the Netherlands. The **Hallwag** (Ⓦhallwag.com) map is particularly good and is also one of the more detailed (at 1:200,000), a feat it accomplishes by being double-sided; it also includes an index. The problem – and this even applies to the Hallwag – is that the Netherlands is such a crowded country that following any fold-out road map can be very difficult: if you're doing any serious driving, you're best off investing in a Road Atlas. The best is the **Nederland Road Atlas** (1:100,000) produced by **ANWB** (Ⓦanwb.nl), the main Dutch touring organization; it includes an index and has detailed insets of major Dutch towns and cities. ANWB also publishes a whole raft of **specialist/regional maps**, including waterproof maps specifically designed for cyclists.

As for **city maps**, your first port of call should be the local tourist office, which will almost invariably supply free, reasonably good-quality maps. Otherwise, **Falk** city maps are usually the cream of the cartographic crop with the exception of Amsterdam, where the best map is our own **Rough Guide Map to Amsterdam**, (1:16,000 & 1:10,000), which has the added advantage of being waterproof and rip-proof. This map also marks all the key sights plus the location of many restaurants, bars and hotels.

Money

The **currency** of the Netherlands is the **euro** (€), divided into 100 cents. The **exchange rate** for one euro at time of writing was €0.84 to the British pound; 1.34 to the US dollar; 1.33 to the Canadian dollar; 1.24 to the Australian dollar; 1.59 to the New Zealand dollar; and 10.02 to the South African Rand. There are euro **notes** of €500, €200, €100, €50, €20, €10 and €5, and **coins** of €2, €1, 50c, 20c, 10c, 5c, 2c and 1c, but note that many retailers will not touch the €500 and €200 notes with a bargepole – you have to break them down into smaller denominations at the bank.

For the most up-to-date rates, check the currency converter website Ⓦoanda.com.

ATMs are liberally distributed around every city, town and large village in the Netherlands – and they accept a host of debit cards without charging a transaction fee. Credit cards can be used in ATMs too, but in this case transactions are treated as loans, with interest accruing daily from the date of withdrawal. All major **credit/debit cards**, including American Express, Visa and MasterCard, are widely accepted in most shops, restaurants and cafés, as well as in ATMs. Typically, Dutch ATMs give instructions in a variety of languages.

You can change **foreign currency** into euros at most banks, which are ubiquitous; banking hours are Monday to Friday 9am to 4pm, with a few big-city banks also open Thursday until 9pm or on Saturday morning. All are closed on public holidays (see box below).

Mosquitoes

These pesky blighters thrive in the country's canals and can be a real handful (or mouthful) if you are camping. An antihistamine cream such as Phenergan is the best antidote, although this can be difficult to find – in which case preventative sticks like Autan or Citronella are the best bet.

Museum cards

If you're planning to visit more than just a couple of Dutch museums, you'll save money with a **Museum-kaart** (Museum Card; Ⓦmuseumkaart.nl), which gives free entry to over 400 museums and galleries nationwide. It costs €40 for a year (less if you're 18 or under) and you can purchase one at any participating museum – most major museums are in the scheme.

Opening hours

The Dutch weekend fades painlessly into the working week with many smaller shops and

---

PUBLIC HOLIDAYS

Public holidays (*Nationale feestdagen*) provide the perfect excuse to take to the streets. The most celebrated of them all is **Queen's Day** – Koninginnedag – on April 30, which is celebrated everywhere but with particular abandon in Amsterdam.

January 1 New Year's Day	**May 5** Liberation Day
Good Friday (although many shops are open)	**Ascension Day** (40 days after Easter)
Easter Sunday	**Whit Sunday & Monday**
Easter Monday	**December 25 & 26** Christmas
April 30 Queen's Day	**December 31** New Year's Eve

INTERNATIONAL CALLS

PHONING HOME FROM THE NETHERLANDS

To make an **international phone call from the Netherlands**, dial the appropriate international access code as below, then the number you require, omitting the initial zero where there is one.

Australia ☎0061

Canada ☎001

New Zealand ☎0064

Republic of Ireland ☎00353

South Africa ☎0027

UK ☎0044

US ☎001

PHONING THE NETHERLANDS FROM ABROAD

To call a number in the Netherlands **from abroad**, dial the local international access code, then ☎31, followed by the number you require, omitting the initial zero where there is one. Note that numbers prefixed ☎0800 are toll-free and those prefixed ☎0900 are premium-rated – a (Dutch) message before you're connected tells you how much you will be paying for the call. Frustratingly, a number of tourist offices have telephone numbers with special prefixes – including ☎0800 and ☎0900 – which prevent them from being called from outside the Netherlands.

---

businesses, even in Amsterdam, staying closed on Monday mornings until noon. **Normal opening hours** are, however, Monday to Friday 8.30/9am to 5.30/6pm and Saturday 8.30/9am to 4/5pm, and many places open late on Thursday or Friday evenings. **Sunday** opening is becoming increasingly common, with many stores and shops in every city open between noon and 5pm.

Most **restaurants** open for dinner from about 6 or 7pm, and though many close as early as 9.30pm, a few stay open past 11pm. **Bars**, **cafés and coffeeshops** are either open all day from around 10am or don't open until about 5pm; all close at 1am during the week and 2am at weekends. **Nightclubs** generally function from 11pm to 4am during the week, though a few open every night, and some stay open until 5am at the weekend.

Phones

Almost all of the Netherlands has **mobile phone** (**cell phone**) coverage at GSM900/1800, the band common to the rest of Europe, Australia and New Zealand. Mobile/cell phones bought in North America will need to be able to adjust to this GSM band. If you intend to use your mobile/cell phone in the Netherlands, note that call charges can be excruciating – particularly irritating is the supplementary charge you often have to pay on incoming

---

EMERGENCY NUMBERS

Ambulance ☎113

Fire ☎110

Police ☎112

---

calls – so check with your supplier before you depart. You may find it cheaper to buy a **Dutch SIM card**, though this can get complicated: many mobiles/cells will not permit you to swap SIM cards and the connection instructions for the replacement SIM card can be in Dutch only. If you overcome these problems, you can buy SIM cards at high-street phone companies, which offer myriad deals beginning at about €5 per SIM card. **Text messages**, on the other hand, are normally charged at ordinary or at least bearable rates – and with your existing SIM card in place. The Dutch **phone directory** is available (in Dutch) at ⓦdetelefoongids.nl.

Shopping

The Netherlands has a flourishing **retail sector** and each of its large towns and cities is jammed with department stores and international chains. More distinctively, the big cities play host to scores of **specialist shops** selling everything from condoms to beads. There are certain obvious Dutch goods – tulips, clogs and porcelain windmills to name the big three – but it's the Dutch flair for **design** that is the most striking feature, whether it's reflected in furniture or clothes.

Normal **opening hours** are Monday to Friday 8.30/9am to 5.30/6pm and Saturday 8.30/9am to 4/5pm, though many smaller outlets take Monday morning off and larger stores and shops often open late on Thursday or Friday evenings. In the cities, Sunday opening is increasingly common (noon–5pm) and many supermarkets stay open until about 8pm every night. Also in the cities, a handful of **night shops** – *avondwinkels* – stay open into the small hours or round the clock. Out in the sticks, on the other hand, Saturday afternoon can be a retail desert with just about everywhere closed. Most towns have a **market day**, usually midweek (and sometimes Sat morning), and this is often the liveliest time to visit, particularly when the stalls fill the central square, the *markt*.

Clogs

You'll see **clogs** – or *klompen* – on sale in all the main tourist centres, usually brightly painted and ready for the nearest mantelpiece or even wall. They are not typical: about three million wooden clogs are made in the Netherlands every year and the unpainted variety are the chosen footwear of thousands of Dutch workmen, who swear they are safe and sound – apparently they pass all European safety standards with flying colours.

Smoking

In 2008, **smoking tobacco** was prohibited inside all public buildings, including train and bus stations, as well as in restaurants, clubs, bars and cafés. It was also banned in (dope-smoking) coffeeshops – which created some rather odd situations. Four years on, however, there has been some relaxation of the ban: for instance, small bars, where only the owner works, can permit their customers to smoke tobacco if they wish. There are also outside smoking areas on train station platforms. One in four Netherlanders still puffs away.

Time zones

The Netherlands is on **Central European Time** (**CET**) – one hour ahead of Greenwich Mean Time, six hours ahead of US Eastern Standard Time, nine hours ahead of US Pacific Standard Time, nine hours behind Australian Eastern Standard Time and eleven hours behind New Zealand. There are, however, minor variations during the changeover periods involved in **daylight saving**. The Netherlands operates daylight saving time, moving clocks forward one hour in the spring and one hour back in the autumn.

Tipping

Tipping isn't quite as routine a matter as it is in the US or even in the UK. However, you are expected to leave something if you have enjoyed good service – up to around ten percent of the bill should suffice

in most restaurants, while taxi drivers may expect a euro or two on top of the fare.

Tourist information

The **Netherlands' Board of Tourism and Conventions** (NBTC) operates an all-encompassing website (Ⓦ holland.com), which highlights upcoming events and is particularly strong on practical information. It also publishes a wide range of brochures and guides. Once in the Netherlands, almost every place you visit will have a **tourist office**, most of which are known as a **VVV** (pronounced *fay-fay-fay*), with a distinctive triangular logo. Staff are nearly always enthusiastic and helpful, and speak excellent English. In addition to handing out basic maps (often for free) and English-language information on the main sights, many tourist offices keep lists of local accommodation, which they can book for a small fee.

Most tourist offices sell **province guides** which list every type of accommodation, from plush hotels to campsites, albeit almost always in Dutch. However, establishments must pay for inclusion, so the listings are not comprehensive.

Travellers with disabilities

Despite its general social progressiveness, the Netherlands is only just getting to grips with the requirements of people with **mobility problems**. In Amsterdam and most of the other major cities, the most obvious difficulty you'll face is in negotiating the cobbled streets and narrow, often broken pavements of the older districts, where the key sights are often located. Similarly, provision for people with disabilities on the country's urban **public transport** is only average, although improving – many new buses, for instance, are wheelchair-accessible.

Practically all **public buildings**, including museums, theatres, cinemas, concert halls and hotels, are obliged to provide access, and do. Places that have been certified wheelchair-accessible now bear the **International Accessibility Symbol** (IAS). If you're planning to use the Dutch train network and would like assistance on the platform, phone the Bureau Assistentieverlening Gehandicapten (Disabled Assistance Office; daily 7am–11pm) on ☎ 030 235 7822 at least 24 hours before your train departs, and there will be someone to help you at the station. NS, the main train company, publishes information about train travel for people with disabilities at Ⓦ ns.nl and in various leaflets, stocked at main stations.

Amsterdam

THE SINGEL CANAL

1

Amsterdam

With every justification, AMSTERDAM is one of Europe's top short-break destinations. It's a compact, instantly likeable city, that's appealing to look at and pleasant to walk around. An intriguing mix of the parochial and the international, it has a welcoming attitude towards visitors and a uniquely youthful orientation, shaped by the liberal counter-culture that took hold in the 1960s. Also engaging are the buzz of its open-air summer events and the intimacy of its clubs and bars, not to mention the Dutch facility with languages: just about everyone you meet in Amsterdam will be able to speak near-perfect English, on top of their own native Dutch and often French and German too.

Amsterdam has three world-famous sights, the **Anne Frank Huis**, the **Van Gogh Museum** and the **Rijksmuseum**, with its wonderful collection of Rembrandt paintings. In addition, there is a slew of lesser known attractions, from the Resistance Museum through to the Royal Palace on the Dam, though for many visitors the city's **canals** are its main draw – take a cruise or a stroll around the **Grachtengordel** and you'll see why. Beyond the sights, Amsterdam also boasts an unparalleled selection of drinking places, be it a traditional, bare-floored **brown café** or one of the city's many designer bars and grand cafés. The city's **nightlife** and **cultural events** have a similarly innovative edge, with offerings that are at the forefront of contemporary European film, dance, drama and music. In addition, Amsterdam boasts one of the world's leading classical **orchestras**, a platoon of great **clubs**, and one of Europe's liveliest and largest **gay scenes**.

The Old Centre

The **Old Centre** was where Amsterdam began, starting out as a fishing village at the mouth of the River Amstel and then, when the river was dammed in 1270, flourishing as a trading centre and receiving its municipal charter from a new feudal overlord, the Count of Holland, in about 1300. Thereafter, the city developed in stages, each of which was marked by the digging of new canals and, after a particularly severe fire in 1452, by the abandonment of timber for stone and brick as the main building materials. Today, it's the handsome stone and brick buildings of subsequent centuries, especially the seventeenth, which provide the Old Centre with most of its architectural highlights.

THE CITIZEN'S HALL AT THE KONINKLIJK PALEIS

Highlights

❶ The Koninklijk Paleis Witness Amsterdam in its full Golden Age glory at the Royal Palace, which began life as Amsterdam's Stadhuis (Town Hall). **See p.53**

❷ Grachtengordel Amsterdam's "girdle" of canals are the city at its most beautiful, especially along and around the Brouwersgracht. **See pp.59–66**

❸ Anne Frank Huis A poignant memorial to the Holocaust, this is Amsterdam's most visited sight by a mile. **See p.60**

❹ Museum Willet-Holthuysen Amsterdam's merchant class lived in style and comfort – as the interior of this opulent canal house reveals. **See p.65**

❺ Hortus Botanicus See Amsterdam in bloom – at the city's excellent botanical gardens. **See p.72**

❻ De Hollandsche Schouwburg Of the several memorials to the Jews of Amsterdam, this is perhaps the most moving. **See p.72**

❼ Rijksmuseum World-beating collection of Dutch paintings from the Golden Age including Rembrandt's wonderful *Night Watch*. **See pp.75**

❽ Van Gogh Museum The world's largest collection of van Gogh's paintings, shown to advantage in this modern, purpose-built gallery. **See pp.76**

HIGHLIGHTS ARE MARKED ON THE MAP ON PP.48–49

1

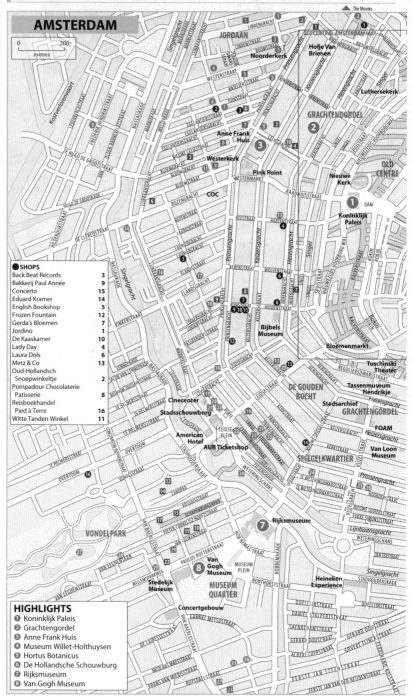

▲ The Movies

AMSTERDAM

0 ⎯⎯ 200
metres

JORDAAN

LINDENGRACHT

SEE CENTRAL AMSTERDAM MAP

Noorderkerk

Hofje Van
Brienen

WESTERSTRAAT

Luthersekerk

TUINSTRAAT

GRACHTENGORDEL ❷

Anne Frank
Huis ❸

Westerkerk

Nieuwe
Kerk

OLD
CENTRE

Pink Point
WESTERMARKT

COC

RAADHUISSTRAAT

DAM ❶

Koninklijk
Paleis

CINEMA

Bijbels
Museum

Bloemenmarkt

Tuschinski
Theater

DE GOUDEN
BOCHT

Tassenmuseum
Hendrikje

Stadsarchief
GRACHTENGORDEL

Cinecenter

Stadsschouwburg

American
Hotel

AUB Ticketshop

Leidseplein

FOAM

Van Loon
Museum

SPIEGELKWARTIER

OVERTOOM

Rijksmuseum ❼

VONDELPARK

PAULUS POTTERSTRAAT

Van
Gogh
Museum ❽

MUSEUM
PLEIN

Heineken
Experience

Stedelijk
Museum

MUSEUM
QUARTER

Concertgebouw

SHOPS

Back Beat Records	3
Bakkerij Paul Année	9
Concerto	15
Eduard Kramer	14
English Bookshop	5
Frozen Fountain	12
Gerda's Bloemen	7
Jordino	1
De Kaaskamer	10
Lady Day	4
Laura Dols	6
Metz & Co	13
Oud-Hollandsch	
Snoepwinkeltje	2
Pompadour Chocolaterie	
Patisserie	8
Reisboekhandel	
Pied à Terre	16
Witte Tanden Winkel	11

HIGHLIGHTS

❶ Koninklijk Paleis
❷ Grachtengordel
❸ Anne Frank Huis
❹ Museum Willet-Holthuysen
❺ Hortus Botanicus
❻ De Hollandsche Schouwburg
❼ Rijksmuseum
❽ Van Gogh Museum

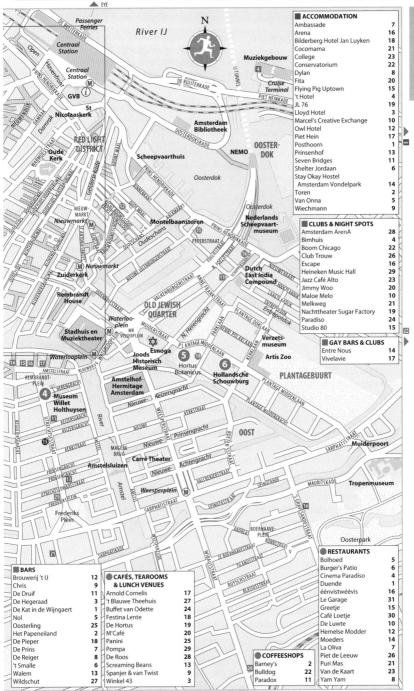

EYE

Passenger Ferries

River IJ

N

Muziekgebouw

DE RUIJTERKADE

Open

Centraal Station

Centraal Station

GVB

St Nicolaaskerk

Damrak

Cruise Terminal

PIET HEINKADE

OOSTERDOK

Amsterdam Bibliotheek

NEMO

OOSTER-DOK

RED LIGHT DISTRICT

Oude Kerk

Scheepvaarthuis

Oosterdok

Oosterdok

NIEUW-MARKT

Nieuwmarkt

Montelbaanstoren

Nederlands Scheepvaart-museum

Nieuwmarkt

Oudeschans

PEPERSTRAAT

PRINS HENDRIKKADE

Dutch East India Compound

Zuiderkerk

Rembrandt House

OLD JEWISH QUARTER

Waterloo-plein

Stadhuis en Muziektheater

MR VISSERPLEIN

Esnoga

Verzets-museum

Waterlooplein

AMSTELSTRAAT

BLAUWBRUG

Joods Historisch Museum

Hortus Botanicus

Hollandsche Schouwburg

Artis Zoo

PLANTAGEBUURT

PLANTAGE MIDDENLAAN

REMBRANDT-PLEIN

Amstelhof-Hermitage Amsterdam

Museum Willet Holthuysen

Keizersgracht

Nieuwe-

KEIZERSGRACHT

KERKSTRAAT

OOST

Nieuwe- Prinsengracht

SARPHATISTRAAT

Muiderpoort

River Amstel

MAGERE BRUG

Carré Theater

Nieuwe- Achtergracht

Amstelsluizen

PRINSENGRACHT

UTRECHTSEDWARSSTRAAT

Weesperplein

VALCKENIERSTRAAT

MAURITSKADE

Tropenmuseum

Frederiks Plein

SARPHATIKADE

WEESPERZIJDE

SARPHATISTRAAT

BOERHAAVE-PLEIN

Oosterpark

2E BOERHAAVESTRAAT

RUYSCHSTRAAT

BLASIUSSTRAAT

ACCOMMODATION
Ambassade	7
Arena	16
Bilderberg Hotel Jan Luyken	18
Cocomama	21
College	23
Conservatorium	22
Dylan	8
Fita	20
Flying Pig Uptown	15
't Hotel	4
JL 76	19
Lloyd Hotel	3
Marcel's Creative Exchange	10
Owl Hotel	12
Piet Hein	17
Posthoorn	1
Prinsenhof	13
Seven Bridges	11
Shelter Jordaan	6
Stay Okay Hostel Amsterdam Vondelpark	14
Toren	2
Van Onna	5
Wiechmann	9

CLUBS & NIGHT SPOTS
Amsterdam ArenA	28
Bimhuis	4
Boom Chicago	22
Club Trouw	26
Escape	16
Heineken Music Hall	29
Jazz Café Alto	23
Jimmy Woo	20
Maloe Melo	10
Melkweg	21
Nachttheater Sugar Factory	19
Paradiso	24
Studio 80	15

GAY BARS & CLUBS
Entre Nous	14
Vivelavie	17

RESTAURANTS
Bolhoed	5
Burger's Patio	6
Cinema Paradiso	4
Duende	1
éénvistwéévis	16
Le Garage	31
Greetje	15
Café Loetje	30
De Luwte	10
Hemelse Modder	12
Moeders	14
La Oliva	7
Piet de Leeuw	26
Puri Mas	21
Van de Kaart	23
Yam Yam	8

BARS
Brouwerij 't IJ	12
Chris	9
De Druif	11
De Hegeraad	3
De Kat in de Wijngaert	1
Nol	5
Oosterling	25
Het Papeneiland	2
De Pieper	18
De Prins	7
De Reiger	8
't Smalle	6
Walem	13
Wildschut	27

CAFÉS, TEAROOMS & LUNCH VENUES
Arnold Cornelis	17
't Blauwe Theehuis	27
Buffet van Odette	24
Festina Lente	18
De Hortus	19
M'Café	20
Panini	25
Pompa	29
De Roos	28
Screaming Beans	13
Spanjer & van Twist	9
Winkel 43	3

COFFEESHOPS
Barney's	2
Bulldog	22
Paradox	11

28 & 29

1

ORIENTATION

Amsterdam's layout is determined by its **canals**. The oldest part of the city is the **Old Centre**, an oval-shaped area dating from the thirteenth century and featuring a jumble of antique streets and narrow little canals. It's here that you'll find two of the city's most historically important buildings – the Koninklijk Paleis (Royal Palace) and the Nieuwe Kerk – as well as the industrialized eroticism of the **Red Light District**. Encircling the Old Centre are the canals of the **Grachtengordel** – or "Girdle of Canals" – the Singel, followed by Herengracht, Keizersgracht and Prinsengracht, all dug in the seventeenth century as part of a planned expansion to create a uniquely elegant urban environment. This is Amsterdam at its prettiest and it is here that the city's merchant class built their grand mansions, typified by tall, graceful, decorated gables, whose fine proportions are reflected in the still, olive-green waters below. The Grachtengordel is also home to the city's most famous sight, the **Anne Frank Huis**.

Beyond the Grachtengordel, the **Jordaan** to the west remains the traditional heart of working-class Amsterdam, although it has experienced a degree of gentrification: its maze of streets and narrow canals make it a pleasant area to wander. On the east side of the centre is the **Old Jewish Quarter**; since the German occupation of World War II, this area has changed more than any other – its population gone and landscape altered – but there are several poignant reminders of earlier times, most notably the first-rate **Jewish Historical Museum** and the Hollandsche Schouwburg. Beyond the southern boundary of the Grachtengordel lies the **Museum Quarter**, which holds a trio of top-ranking museums, the **Rijksmuseum**, internationally famous for its Rembrandts, the **Van Gogh Museum**, with its peerless collection of van Goghs, and the **Stedelijk Museum** of modern and contemporary art. Together, these form a cultural prelude to the sprawling greenery of the nearby **Vondelpark**, Amsterdam's loveliest park.

Strolling across the bridge from **Centraal Station** brings you onto the **Damrak**, the spine of the Old Centre and the thoroughfare that once divided the **Oude Zijde** (Old Side) of the medieval city to the east from the smaller **Nieuwe Zijde** (New Side) to the west. The Damrak culminates in **Dam Square**, flanked by two of Amsterdam's most impressive buildings, the Koninklijk Paleis (Royal Palace) and the Nieuwe Kerk. From here, it's a brief ramble south to both the **Spui**, one of the city's most engaging open spaces, and the first-rate **Amsterdam Museum**, which tracks through the city's eventful history.

To the east of Damrak is the **Red Light District**, which stretches up to Nieuwmarkt. It's here that you'll find many of the district's finest buildings, though the seediness of the tentacular red-light zone tends to dull their charms. That said, be sure to spare time for two delightful churches – the Amstelkring and the Oude Kerk. Just beyond the reach of the Red Light District is **Nieuwmarkt**, a fairly mundane start to the **Kloveniersburgwal**, which forms one of the most beguiling parts of the Old Centre, with a medley of handsome old houses lining the prettiest of canals. From here, it's a short walk west to **Muntplein**, a busy junction where you'll find the floating flower market.

Centraal Station

Stationsplein

With its high gables and cheerful brickwork, the neo-Renaissance **Centraal Station** is an imposing prelude to the city. At the time of its construction in the 1880s, it aroused much controversy because it effectively separated the centre from the River IJ, source of the city's wealth, for the first time in Amsterdam's long history. Nowadays both the station and **Stationsplein** outside are mired in fresh controversy on account of ambitious plans to redevelop the station and its environs while at the same time building a new metro line linking Amsterdam's city centre with the south of the city and stations across the IJ in the resurgent north. For the best part of eight years now

CENTRAL AMSTERDAM

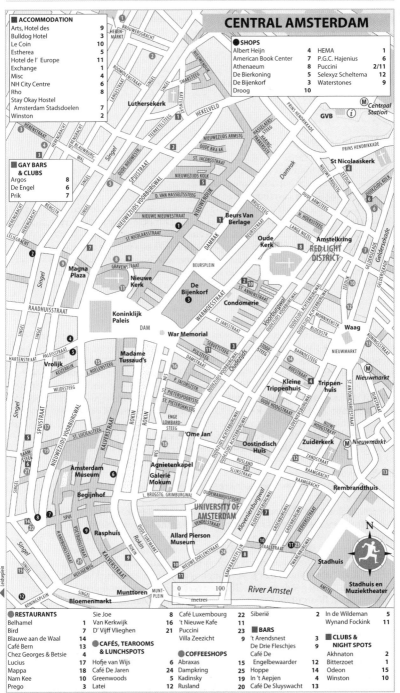

■ ACCOMMODATION

Arts, Hotel des	9
Bulldog Hotel	3
Le Coin	10
Estherea	5
Hotel de l' Europe	11
Exchange	1
Misc	4
NH City Centre	6
Rho	8
Stay Okay Hostel	
Amsterdam Stadsdoelen	7
Winston	2

● SHOPS

Albert Heijn	4	HEMA	1
American Book Center	7	P.G.C. Hajenius	6
Athenaeum	8	Puccini	2/11
De Bierkoning	5	Selexyz Scheltema	12
De Bijenkorf	3	Waterstones	9
Droog	10		

■ GAY BARS & CLUBS

Argos	8
De Engel	6
Prik	7

● RESTAURANTS

Belhamel	1	Sie Joe	8	Café Luxembourg	22
Bird	7	Van Kerkwijk	16	't Nieuwe Kafe	11
Blauwe aan de Waal	14	D' Vijff Vlieghen	21	Puccini	23
Café Bern	13			Villa Zeezicht	9
Chez Georges & Betsie	4	**● CAFÉS, TEAROOMS**			
Lucius	17	**& LUNCHSPOTS**		**● COFFEESHOPS**	
Mappa	18	Hofje van Wijs	6	Abraxas	15
Nam Kee	10	Café De Jaren	24	Dampkring	25
Prego	3	Greenwoods	5	Kadinsky	19
		Latei	12	Rusland	20

Siberië	2	In de Wildeman	5		
		Wynand Fockink	11		
■ BARS					
't Arendsnest	3	**■ CLUBS &**			
De Drie Fleschjes	9	**NIGHT SPOTS**			
Café De		Akhnaton	2		
Engelbewaarder	12	Bitterzoet	1		
Hoppe	14	Odeon	15		
In 't Aepjen	4	Winston	10		
Café De Sluyswacht	13				

the area around Stationsplein has been a massive construction site, and the chaos looks set to continue for some time, until completion of the project in 2015. There have been huge arguments over the plan: some question whether it's even possible to build a tunnel under a city centre that is mainly built on wooden stilts, and work was halted for a while in 2008 when a number of city-centre buildings began to collapse, but the authorities claim they will deliver not only better connections between the city centre and its outlying districts, but also a more pleasant, pedestrian-friendly Stationsplein and inner harbour.

St Nicolaaskerk

Prins Hendrikkade 73 • Mon & Sat noon–3pm, Tues–Fri 11am–4pm • Free • ☏ 020 624 8749, ⊛ nicolaas-parochie.nl

The whopping twin towers and heavy-duty dome of **St Nicolaaskerk**, the city's foremost Catholic church, peer out across the inner harbour towards Centraal Station. Dating back to the 1880s, the cavernous interior holds some pretty dire religious murals, mawkish concoctions that are only partly relieved by swathes of coloured brickwork. Above the high altar is the crown of the Habsburg Emperor Maximilian, very much a symbol of the city and one you'll see again and again. Amsterdam had close ties with Maximilian: in the late fifteenth century he came here as a pilgrim and stayed on to recover from an illness. The burghers funded many of his military expeditions and, in return, he let the city use his crown in its coat of arms – a practice that, rather surprisingly, survived the seventeenth-century revolt against Spain.

Damrak

A wide but unenticing avenue lined with tacky restaurants, bars and bureaux de change, **Damrak** slices south from Stationsplein into the heart of the city, first passing an inner harbour crammed with the bobbing canal boats of Amsterdam's considerable tourist industry. Just beyond the harbour is the imposing bulk of the **Beurs**, the old Stock Exchange – known as the "Beurs van Berlage" – a seminal work designed at the turn of the last century by the leading light of the Dutch Modern movement, **Hendrik Petrus Berlage** (1856–1934). It's used for concerts and occasional exhibitions these days, so you can't often get in to see the graceful exposed ironwork and shallow-arched arcades of the main hall, but you can pop into its café, round the corner on Beurssplein, to admire the tiled scenes of the past, present and future by Jan Toorop.

De Bijenkorf

Damrak 1 • Mon 11am–7pm, Tues & Wed 10am–7pm, Thurs & Fri 10am–9pm, Sat 9.30am–7pm & Sun 11am–7pm • ☏ 0800 0818, ⊛ debijenkorf.nl

Stretching along the Damrak, the long-established **De Bijenkorf** – literally "beehive" – department store posed all sorts of problems for the Germans when they first occupied the city in World War II. It was a Jewish concern, so the Nazis didn't really want their troops shopping here, but the store was just too popular to implement a total ban. The bizarre solution was to prohibit German soldiers from shopping on the ground floor, where the store's Jewish employees were concentrated, as they always had been, in the luxury goods section. These days it's a good all-round department store, with the usual floors of designer-wear and well-known brands.

Dam Square

Situated at the very heart of the city, **Dam Square** gave Amsterdam its name: in the thirteenth century the River Amstel was dammed here, and the fishing village that grew around it became known as "Amstelredam". Boats could sail down the Damrak into the square and unload right in the middle of the settlement, which soon prospered by trading herrings for Baltic grain. In the early fifteenth century, the building of Amsterdam's principal church, the Nieuwe Kerk, and thereafter the town hall (now the Royal Palace), formally marked the Dam as Amsterdam's centre, but since World War II it has lost much of its dignity. Today it's open and airy but somehow rather desultory, despite – or perhaps partly because of – the presence of the main municipal **war memorial**, a prominent stone tusk adorned by bleak, suffering figures and decorated with the coats of arms of each of the Netherlands' provinces (plus the ex-colony of Indonesia).

The Koninklijk Paleis

Dam Square • June–Aug daily 11am–5pm; Sept–May daily noon–5pm, but closed on royal occasions as detailed on the website • €7.50 • ☎ 020 620 4060, ⓦ paleisamsterdam.nl

Dominating Dam Square is the sturdy bulk of the **Koninklijk Paleis** (Royal Palace), although the title is deceptive, given that this vast sandstone structure was built as the city's Stadhuis (Town Hall), and only had its first royal occupant when Louis Bonaparte moved in during the French occupation (1795–1813). The **exterior** of the palace is very much to the allegorical point: twin tympani depict Amsterdam as a port and trading centre, the one at the front presided over by a female representation of the city with Neptune and a veritable herd of unicorns at her feet. Above these tympani are representations of the values that the city council espoused – at the front, Prudence, Justice and Peace, to the rear Temperance and Vigilance on either side of a muscular, globe-bearing Atlas. One deliberate precaution, however, was the omission of a central doorway – just in case the mob turned nasty (as they were wont to do) and stormed the place.

THE STADHUIS: FROM TOWN HALL TO ROYAL PALACE

At the time of the **Stadhuis**'s construction in the mid-seventeenth century, Amsterdam was at the height of its powers. The city was pre-eminent among Dutch towns, and the council craved a residence that was a declaration of the city's municipal power. They opted for a startlingly progressive design by **Jacob van Campen**, who proposed a Dutch interpretation of the classical principles revived in Renaissance Italy. Initially, there was opposition to the plan from the council's Calvinist minority, who pointed out that the proposed building would dwarf the neighbouring Nieuwe Kerk (see p.54). However, the Calvinists fell into line after being promised a new church spire (which was never built), and work started in 1648 on what was then the largest town hall in Europe. Supported by no less than 13,659 wooden piles driven into Dam Square's sandy soil – a number every Dutch schoolchild remembers by adding a "1" and a "9" to the number of days in the year – the new building was called "The world's Eighth Wonder/With so much stone raised high and so much timber under", by the poet Constantijn Huygens.

The Stadhuis received its **royal designation** in 1808, when Louis Bonaparte, who had recently been installed as "king of Holland" by his brother Napoleon, commandeered it as his residence. Louis took his new job seriously enough, but an initial gaffe set the scene when he declared himself the "Konijn van 'Olland" (Rabbit of 'Olland) rather than the "Koning van Holland" (King of Holland). Lonely and unpopular, Louis was deposed by his brother in 1810 and left the country, leaving the Netherlands to the despotic mercies of Napoleon himself. After Napoleon's final defeat, possession of the palace became something of a sore point between the Dutch royal family and the city: an initial compromise allowed the royals to keep the building provided they stayed here for part of the year. However, the Oranges failed to do this, which irritated many Amsterdammers, and in the 1930s the royal family offered the city fifteen million guilders to build a new city hall. Ownership of the Stadhuis passed to the state (as distinct from the city) in return for a new agreement allowing the Oranges to use the Palace whenever they wanted. A new town hall was built on Waterlooplein (see p.70), and finally completed in the 1980s. Today, the Dutch royals live elsewhere, and only use the Royal Palace for state occasions.

1

The interior

The palace **interior** proclaims the pride and confidence of Amsterdam's Golden Age, principally in its lavish **Citizen's Hall**, an extraordinarily handsome, arcaded marble chamber. Here, the enthroned figure of Amsterdam looks down on the earth and the heavens, which are laid out before her in three circular, inlaid marble maps, one each of the eastern and western hemispheres, the other of the northern sky. Other allegorical **figures** ram home the municipal point: flanking "Amsterdam" to the left and right are Wisdom and Strength, while the reliefs to either side of the central group represent good governance – on the left is the god Amphion, who plays his lyre to persuade the stones to pile themselves up into a wall, and to the right Mercury attempts to lull Argos to sleep, stressing the need to be vigilant. All this is part of a good-natured and witty symbolism that pervades the Hall and its surrounding galleries: in the top left gallery, cocks fight above the entrance to the Commissioner of Petty Affairs, while in the gallery to the right of the main hall, above the door of the Bankruptcy Chamber, a medallion shows the Fall of Icarus below marble carvings depicting hungry rats scurrying around an empty money chest and nibbling at unpaid bills.

The decorative whimsy fizzles out in the narrow and cramped **High Court of Justice** at the front of the building, close to the entrance. Inside this intimidating chamber, the judges sat on marble benches overseen by heavyweight representations of Righteousness, Wisdom, Mercy and so forth as they passed judgement on the hapless criminal in front of them; even worse, the crowd on Dam Square could view the proceedings through barred windows, almost always baying for blood. They usually went home contented; as soon as the judges had passed the death sentence, the condemned were whisked up to the wooden scaffold attached to the front of the building and promptly dispatched.

The Nieuwe Kerk

Dam Square • Daily 10am–5pm, Thurs till 10pm • Entrance fee varies according to the exhibition, but usually €15 • ☎ 020 626 8168, ⓦ nieuwekerk.nl

Vying for importance with the Royal Palace is the **Nieuwe Kerk** (New Church), which – despite its name – is an early fifteenth-century structure built in a late flourish of the Gothic style, with a forest of pinnacles and high, slender gables. Nowadays it's deconsecrated and used for temporary exhibitions, but its hangar-like interior is worth investigating for its decorative details, principally the seventeenth-century tomb of Dutch naval hero **Admiral Michiel de Ruyter**, complete with trumpeting angels, conch-blowing Neptunes and cherubs all in a tizzy. Ruyter trounced in succession the Spaniards, the Swedes, the English and the French, and his rise from deck hand to Admiral-in-Chief is the stuff of national legend. The church is still used for state occasions: the coronations of queens Wilhelmina, Juliana and, in 1980, Beatrix, were all held here.

Rokin and Kalverstraat

Rokin picks up where the Damrak leaves off, cutting south from Dam Square in a wide sweep that follows the former course of the River Amstel. This was the business centre of the nineteenth-century city, and although it has lost much of its prestige it is still flanked by an attractive medley of architectural styles incorporating everything from grandiose nineteenth-century mansions to more utilitarian modern buildings. Rokin culminates at the **Muntplein**, a dishevelled traffic junction overlooked by the sturdy, late medieval **Munttoren**, which was originally a strategic point in the old city wall. Later, the tower was adopted as the municipal mint – hence its name – and Hendrik de Keyser, in one of his last commissions, added a flashy spire in 1620. Running parallel to Rokin, pedestrianized **Kalverstraat** is a busy shopping street that has been a

1

commercial centre since medieval times, when it was used as a calf market; today, it's home to many of the city's chain stores – you could be anywhere in Holland really.

The Allard Pierson Museum

Oude Turfmarkt 127 • Tues–Fri 10am–5pm, Sat & Sun 1–5pm • €6.50 • ☎ 020 525 2556, ⓦ allardpiersonmuseum.nl

The **Allard Pierson Museum** is a good, old-fashioned archeological museum in a solid Neoclassical building. The collection is spread over two floors and although it is not a large museum, it covers a lot of ground. A particular highlight is the museum's Greek pottery, with fine examples of both the black- and red-figured wares produced in the sixth and fifth centuries BC. Look out also for the Roman sarcophagi, especially a marble whopper decorated with Dionysian scenes, several rare Etruscan funerary urns and a platoon of Egyptian 'mummies'.

Bloemenmarkt

Singel • Mon–Sat 9am–5pm, Sun 11am–5pm, though some stalls close on Sun

Amsterdam's floating **Bloemenmarkt** (Flower Market) extends along the southern bank of the Singel canal west from the Muntplein as far as Koningsplein. Popular with locals and tourists alike, the market is one of the main suppliers of flowers to central Amsterdam, though its blooms and bulbs now share stall space with souvenir clogs, garden gnomes and delftware.

Spui

One of Amsterdam's most appealing streets, the pedestrianized **Spui** begins as a narrow alley running west off the Rokin, but soon widens out into an aimiable wedge-shaped square. Dotted with bookshops and popular café-bars, it's home to an innocuous-looking statue of a young boy, known as **'t Lieverdje** ("Little Darling" or "Lovable Scamp"), a gift to the city from a cigarette company in 1960. It was here in the mid-1960s, with the statue seen as a symbol of the addicted consumer, that the playful Sixties pressure group, the **Provos** (see box, p.334) organized some of their most successful *ludiek* ("pranks").

The Begijnhof

Spui • There are two entrances: a side entrance on Spui, and the main entrance, 100m north of Spui on Gedempte Begijnensloot • Daily 8am–5pm • Free • ☎ 020 622 1918, ⓦ begijnhofamsterdam.nl

Accessed via a fancy little gateway on the north side of Spui, the **Begijnhof** consists of a huddle of immaculately maintained old houses looking onto a central green – their backs turned firmly against the outside world. The Begijnhof was founded in the fourteenth century as a home for the *beguines* – members of a Catholic sisterhood living as nuns, but without vows and with the right of return to the secular world. The original medieval complex comprised a series of humble brick cottages, but these were mostly replaced by the larger, grander houses of today shortly after the Reformation, though the secretive, enclosed design survived. A couple of pre-Reformation buildings remain, including the **Houten Huys**, at no. 34, whose wooden facade, the oldest in Amsterdam, dates from 1477 – before the city forbade the construction of timber houses as an essential precaution against fire.

Engelse Kerk

Mon & Thurs 11am–4pm, Tues 10.30am–3pm, Fri 1–5pm, Sat 11am–2.30pm; closed Wed & Sun • Free

Of the Begijnhof's two churches, the **Engelse Kerk** (English Reformed Church) is of medieval construction, but it was taken from the *beguines* and given to Amsterdam's

1

English community during the Reformation. Plain and unadorned, the church is of interest for its carefully worked pulpit panels, several of which were designed by a youthful Piet Mondrian (1872–1944), of De Stijl fame and fortune.

Begijnhofkapel

Mon 1–6.30pm, Tues–Fri 9am–6.30pm, Sat & Sun 9am–6pm • Free

After they had lost their original church, the Catholic *beguines* were allowed to celebrate Mass inconspicuously in the **Begijnhofkapel**, which they established in the house opposite their old church. It's still used today, a cosy little place with some terribly sentimental religious paintings, one of which – to the left of the high altar – depicts the miracle of the unburnable Host (see p.57).

Amsterdam Museum

Entrances at Sint Luciënsteeg 27 & Kalverstraat 92 • Daily 10am–5pm • €10; audio-tour €4 • ☎ 020 523 1822, ⓦ amsterdammuseum.nl

Occupying the rambling seventeenth-century buildings of a former municipal orphanage, the **Amsterdam Museum** traces the city's development from its origins as an insignificant fishing village to its present incarnation as a major metropolis and trading centre. It is divided into three main sections with the first providing an overview by means of a series of short films. The second (rather confusing) section has a series of thematic displays in roughly chronological order – Amsterdam in the Golden Age, maritime trade, municipal charity and so forth. The highlight of this section is the paintings, including a series showing the city's regents to best advantage, self-contented bourgeois giving succour to the grateful poor. Here also, in the medical care section, is Rembrandt's wonderful *Anatomy Lesson of Dr Jan Deijman*.

Attached to the main body of the museum is the third and final section, an open-air **courtyard**, with a set of wooden lockers where the orphans used to stow their kit. There's also a **glassed-in passageway**, which is used for temporary exhibitions of group portraits, featuring anything from Johan Cruyff and his footballing chums to paintings of the Amsterdam militia in their seventeenth-century pomp.

The Red Light District

The area to the east of Damrak, between Warmoesstraat, Nieuwmarkt and Damstraat, is the **Red Light District**, known locally as "De Walletjes" (Small Walls) on account of the series of low brick walls that contains its canals. The district stretches across the two narrow canals that once marked the eastern limits of medieval Amsterdam, **Oudezijds Voorburgwal** and **Oudezijds Achterburgwal**. The area is pretty seedy, although the legalized prostitution here has long been one of the city's most distinctive draws. It wasn't always so: the handsome facades of Oudezijds Voorburgwal in particular recall ritzier days when this was one of the wealthiest parts of the city, richly earning its nickname the "Velvet Canal".

Oudezijds Voorburgwal and Oudezijds Achterburgwal, with their narrow connecting passages, are thronged with "**window brothels**", and at busy times the crass, on-street haggling over the price of sex is drowned out by a surprisingly festive atmosphere – entire families grinning more or less amiably at the women in the windows or discussing the specifications of the sex toys in the shops. Nonetheless, there is a nasty undertow to the district, oddly enough sharper during the daytime, when the pimps hang out in shifty gangs and drug addicts wait anxiously, assessing the chances of scoring their next hit. Don't even think about taking a picture of one of the windows, unless you're prepared for some major grief from the camera-shy prostitutes and their minders.

Warmoesstraat

Soliciting hasn't always been the principal activity on sleazy **Warmoesstraat**. It was once one of the city's most fashionable streets, home to Holland's foremost poet, **Joost van den Vondel** (1587–1679), who ran his hosiery business from no. 110 in between writing and hobnobbing with the Amsterdam elite. Vondel is a kind of Dutch Shakespeare: his *Gijsbrecht van Amstel*, a celebration of Amsterdam during its Golden Age, is one of the classics of Dutch literature, and he wrote regular, if ponderous, official verses, including well over a thousand lines on the inauguration of the new town hall. He had more than his share of hard luck too. His son frittered away the modest family fortune and Vondel lived out his last few years as doorkeeper of the pawn shop on Oudezijds Voorburgwal, dying of hypothermia at what was then the remarkable age of 92. Vondel's Warmoesstraat house was knocked down decades ago, and the street holds few attractions apart, perhaps, from the **Condomerie Het Gulden Vlies**, at no. 141, which specializes in every imaginable design and make of condom, in sizes ranging from the small to the remarkable.

The Oude Kerk

Oudekerksplein 23 • **Oude Kerk** Mon–Sat 11am–5pm, Sun 1–5pm; €5 • **Oudekerkstoren** April–Sept Thurs–Sat 1–5pm; €7 • ☎ 020 625 8284, ⓦ oudekerk.nl

In the midst of the Red Light District, the Gothic **Oude Kerk** (Old Church) is the city's most appealing church. There's been a church on this site since the middle of the thirteenth century, but most of the present building dates from a century later, funded by the pilgrims who came here in their hundreds following a widely publicized **miracle**. The story goes that in 1345 a dying man regurgitated the Host he had received here at Communion and when it was thrown on the fire afterwards, it did not burn. The unburnable Host was placed in a chest and eventually installed there: although the Host itself disappeared during the Reformation, thousands of the faithful still come to take part in the annual commemorative **Stille Omgang** in mid-March, a silent nocturnal procession terminating at the Oude Kerk. Inside the church, you can see the unadorned memorial tablet of Rembrandt's first wife, Saskia van Uylenburgh, beneath the smaller of the organs and, beside the ambulatory, three beautiful sixteenth-century stained-glass windows. They depict, from left to right, the Annunciation, the Adoration of the Shepherds and the Dormition of the Virgin. Finally, the **Oudekerkstoren** (tower) offers great views in a city with relatively few such opportunities.

The Amstelkring

Oudezijds Voorburgwal 40 • Mon–Sat 10am–5pm, Sun 1–5pm • €8 • ☎ 020 624 6604, ⓦ museumamstelkring.nl

The northern reaches of **Oudezijds Voorburgwal** are home to the **Amstelkring**, formerly the city's principal Catholic place of worship, and now one of Amsterdam's most enjoyable museums. The Amstelkring – "Amstel Circle" – is named after the group of nineteenth-century historians who saved the building from demolition, but its proper name is **Ons Lieve Heer Op Solder** ("Our Dear Lord in the Attic"). The church dates from the early seventeenth century when, with the Protestants firmly in control, the city's Catholics were only allowed to practise their faith in private – such as here in this clandestine church (*schuilkerk*), which occupies the loft of an old merchant's house. The church's narrow nave has been skilfully shoehorned into the available space, and flanked by elegant balconies, there's just enough room for an ornately carved organ at one end and a mock-marble high altar, decorated with Jacob de Wit's mawkish *Baptism of Christ*, at the other. The rest of the house is similarly untouched, its original furnishings reminiscent of interiors by Vermeer or De Hooch.

The Zeedijk

Curving round the northern edge of the Red Light District is the **Zeedijk**, which was originally just that – a dyke to hold back the sea. A couple of decades ago this narrow, twisting thoroughfare was the haunt of drug addicts and very much a no-go area at night, but it's been spruced up and now forms a lively route from Stationsplein through to Nieuwmarkt as well as being the main hub of Amsterdam's small but vibrant Chinatown. Its seaward end is home to a couple of the oldest bars in the city and the jazz trumpeter **Chet Baker** famously breathed his last here in 1988, when he either fell or threw himself out of the window of the *Prins Hendrik Hotel* – an event remembered by an evocative plaque of the man in full blow.

Nieuwmarkt

Just clear of the Red Light District, **Nieuwmarkt** was long one of the city's most important market squares and the place where Gentiles and Jews from the nearby Jewish Quarter – just southeast along St Antoniebreestraat – traded. All that came to a traumatic end during World War II, when the Germans cordoned off the Nieuwmarkt with barbed wire and turned it into a holding pen. After the war, the square's old exuberance never quite returned and these days its focus is the sprawling multi-turreted **Waag**, dating from the 1480s and with a chequered history. Built as one of Amsterdam's fortified gates, the city's expansion soon made it obsolete and the ground floor was turned into a municipal weighing-house (*waag*), with the rooms upstairs taken over by the surgeons' guild. It was here that the surgeons held lectures on anatomy and public dissections, the inspiration for Rembrandt's *Anatomy Lesson of Dr Tulp*, displayed in the Mauritshuis collection in Den Haag. Abandoned by the surgeons and the weigh-masters in the nineteenth century, the building eventually fell into disuse, until being renovated to house a café-bar and restaurant, *In de Waag*.

Kloveniersburgwal

With Nieuwmarkt at its head, **Kloveniersburgwal** is one of the city's most charming canals, a long, dead-straight waterway framed by a string of old and dignified facades. One of the most imposing, the **Trippenhuis**, at no. 29, is a huge overblown mansion complete with Corinthian pilasters and a grand frieze built for the Trip family in 1662. Almost directly opposite, on the west bank of the canal, the **Kleine Trippenhuis**, at no. 26, is, by contrast, one of the narrowest houses in Amsterdam, albeit with a warmly carved facade. Legend asserts that Mr Trip's coachman was so taken aback by the size of the new family mansion that he exclaimed he would be happy with a home no wider than the Trips' front door – which is exactly what he got. His reaction to his new lodgings is not recorded.

Oostindisch Huis

Kloveniersburgwal 48, on the corner of Oude Hoogstraat

The former headquarters of the Dutch East India Company, the **Oostindisch Huis** is a monumental red-brick structure built in 1605 shortly after the founding of the company. It was from here that the company organized and regulated its immensely lucrative trading interests in the Far East, importing shiploads of spices, perfumes and exotic woods. This trade underpinned Amsterdam's Golden Age, but predictably the people of what is now Indonesia, the source of most of the raw materials, received little in return. Today, the building is occupied by university classrooms and offices.

The Zuiderkerk

Zuiderkerkhof 72 • **Zuiderkerk** Mon–Fri 9am–4pm, Sat noon–4pm; free • **Zuiderkerktoren** April–Sept Mon–Sat 1–5pm; €7 • ☏ 020 689 2565, ⓦ zuiderkerkamsterdam.nl

Dating from 1614, the **Zuiderkerk** was the first Amsterdam church built specifically for Protestants. It was designed by the prolific architect and sculptor Hendrick de Keyser

(1565–1621), whose distinctive – and very popular – style extrapolated elements of traditional Flemish design, with fanciful detail and frilly towers added wherever possible. The basic design of the Zuiderkerk is firmly Gothic, but the soaring **Zuiderkerktoren** (tower) is an especially fine example of de Keyser's work, complete with balconies and balustrades, arches and columns. Now deconsecrated, the church has been turned into a **municipal information centre**, with displays on housing and the environment, plus temporary exhibitions revealing the city council's future plans. The **tower**, which has a separate entrance, can be climbed during the summer and from the top there are sweeping views over the city centre.

The Grachtengordel

Medieval Amsterdam was enclosed by the **Singel**, part of the city's protective moat, but this is now just the first of five canals that reach right around the city centre, extending anticlockwise from Brouwersgracht to the River Amstel in a "girdle of canals" or **Grachtengordel**. This is without doubt the most charming part of the city, its lattice of olive-green waterways and dinky humpback bridges overlooked by street upon street of handsome seventeenth-century canal houses, almost invariably undisturbed by later development. It's a subtle cityscape – full of surprises, with a bizarre carving here, an unusual facade there – but architectural peccadilloes aside, it is the district's overall atmosphere that appeals rather than any specific sight – with the notable exception of the **Anne Frank Huis**. There's no obvious walking route

THE CANALS OF THE GRACHTENGORDEL

The three main **canals of the Grachtengordel** – Herengracht, Keizersgracht and Prinsengracht – were dug in the seventeenth century as part of a comprehensive plan to extend the boundaries of a city no longer able to accommodate its burgeoning population. Increasing the area of the city from two to seven square kilometres was a monumental task, and the conditions imposed by the council were strict: **Herengracht**, **Keizersgracht** and **Prinsengracht** were set aside for the residences and businesses of the richer and more influential Amsterdam merchants, while the radial cross-streets were reserved for more modest artisans' homes; meanwhile, immigrants, newly arrived to cash in on Amsterdam's booming economy, were assigned, albeit informally, the Jodenhoek (see p.69) and the Jordaan (see p.66). Of the three main canals, **Herengracht**, the "Gentlemen's Canal", was the first to be dug, followed by the **Keizersgracht**, the "Emperor's Canal", named after the Holy Roman Emperor and fifteenth-century patron of the city, Maximilian. Further out still, the **Prinsengracht**, the "Princes' Canal", was named in honour of the princes of the House of Orange.

In the Grachtengordel, everyone, even the wealthiest merchant, had to comply with a set of detailed **planning regulations**. In particular, the council prescribed the size of each building plot – the frontage was set at thirty feet, the depth two hundred – and although there was a degree of tinkering, the end result was the loose conformity you can see today: tall, narrow residences, whose individualism is mainly restricted to the stylistic permutations among the gables. The earliest extant **gables**, dating from the early seventeenth century, are crow-stepped but these were largely superseded from the 1650s onwards by neck gables and bell gables. Some are embellished, others aren't, many have decorative cornices, and the fanciest, which almost invariably date from the eighteenth century, sport full-scale balustrades. The plainest gables are those of former **warehouses**, where the deep-arched and shuttered windows line up on either side of loft doors, which were once used for loading and unloading goods, winched by pulley from the street down below. Indeed, outside **pulleys** remain a common feature of houses and warehouses alike, and are often still in use as the easiest way of moving furniture into the city's myriad apartments.

1

around the Grachtengordel, and indeed you may prefer to wander around as the mood takes you, but the description we've given below goes from north to south, taking in all the highlights on the way. On all three of the main canals – **Herengracht**, **Keizersgracht** and **Prinsengracht** – street numbers begin in the north and increase as you go south.

Brouwersgracht

Running east to west along the northern edge of the three main canals is leafy **Brouwersgracht**, one of the most picturesque waterways in the city. In the seventeenth century, Brouwersgracht lay at the edge of Amsterdam's great harbour. This was where ships returning from the East unloaded their silks and spices, and as one of the major arteries linking the open sea with the city centre it was lined with storage depots and warehouses. Breweries flourished here too, capitalizing on their ready access to shipments of fresh water. Today, the harbour bustle has moved elsewhere, and the warehouses, with their distinctive spout-neck gables and shuttered windows, formerly used for the delivery and dispatch of goods by pulley from the canal below, have been converted into apartments, some of the most expensive in Amsterdam. There are handsome merchants' houses here as well, plus moored houseboats and a string of quaint little swing bridges.

Blauwburgwal

The **Blauwburgwal**, one block south of Brouwersgracht, is a short and inordinately pretty slip of a canal, which had the misfortune to be hit by a random bomb during the German invasion of 1940. This was very much a one-off: the speed of the German victory meant that central Amsterdam was hardly damaged at all, though this incident alone cost 44 lives.

The Anne Frank Huis

Prinsengracht 263–267 • Mid-March to mid-Sept daily 9am–9pm, Sat till 10pm; July & Aug daily till 10pm; mid-Sept to mid-March daily 9am–7pm, Sat till 9pm; closed Yom Kippur • €9, 10- to 17-year-olds €4.50, under-10s free • ☎ 020 556 7100, ⓦ annefrank.org • Queues can be long, so either come early or book online

In 1957, the Anne Frank Foundation set up the **Anne Frank Huis** in the premises on Prinsengracht where the young diarist and her family were in hiding for two years (see box opposite). Since the posthumous publication of her diaries, Anne Frank has become extraordinarily famous, in the first instance for recording the iniquities of the Holocaust, and latterly as a symbol of the fight against oppression in general and racism in particular.

Anne Frank's **diary** was among the few things left behind in the annexe after the Gestapo raid. It was retrieved by one of the family's Dutch helpers and handed to Anne's father on his return from Auschwitz. In 1947, Otto decided to publish his daughter's diary and, since its appearance, Anne's *Diary of a Young Girl* has been translated into over sixty languages and sold millions of copies worldwide. The rooms the Franks lived in for two years have been left much the same as they were during the war, even down to the movie star pin-ups in Anne's bedroom and the marks on the wall recording the children's heights. Remarkably, despite the number of visitors, there is a real sense of intimacy here and only the coldest of hearts could fail to be moved. Apposite film clips on the family in particular and the Holocaust in general give the background. Anne Frank was only one of about 100,000 Dutch Jews who died during World War II, but this, her final home, provides one of the most enduring testaments to its horrors. Her diary has been a source of inspiration to many, including Nelson Mandela. Otto Frank died in 1980

THE STORY OF ANNE FRANK

The story of **Anne Frank**, her family and friends is well known. Anne's father, **Otto Frank**, was a well-to-do Jewish businessman, who fled Germany in December 1933 after Hitler came to power, moving to Amsterdam, where he established a successful spice-trading business on the Prinsengracht. After the German occupation of the Netherlands, he felt – along with many other Jews – that he could avoid trouble by keeping his head down. However, by 1942 it was clear that this was not going to be possible: Amsterdam's Jews were isolated and conspicuous, being confined to certain parts of the city and forced to wear a yellow star, and roundups were becoming increasingly commonplace. In desperation, Otto Frank decided to move the family into the unused back rooms of their Prinsengracht premises, first asking some of his Dutch office staff if they would help him with the subterfuge – they bravely agreed.

The Franks went into hiding in July 1942, along with a Jewish business partner and his wife and son, the van Pels (renamed the van Daans in the *Diary*). Their new "home" was separated from the rest of the building by a **bookcase** that doubled as a door. As far as everyone else was concerned, they had fled to Switzerland. So began a two-year incarceration in the **achterhuis**, or rear house, and the two families were joined in November 1942 by a dentist friend, Fritz Pfeffer (the *Diary's* Albert Dussel), bringing the number of occupants to eight. Otto's trusted office staff continued working in the front part of the building, regularly bringing supplies and news of the outside world. In her diary Anne Frank describes the **day-to-day lives** of the inhabitants of the annexe, frequent in such a claustrophobic environment, the celebrations of birthdays, or of a piece of good news from the Allied Front; and of her own, slightly unreal, growing up (much of which, it's been claimed, was later deleted by her father).

By 1944, the atmosphere was optimistic; the Allies were clearly winning the war and liberation seemed within reach; it wasn't to be. One day in the summer of that year, the Franks were **betrayed** by a Dutch collaborator and the Gestapo arrived and forced open the bookcase. The occupants of the secret annexe were arrested and dispatched to Westerbork – the transit camp in the north of the country where all Dutch Jews were processed before being moved to Belsen or Auschwitz. Of the eight who had lived in the annexe, only Otto Frank survived; Anne and her sister died of typhus within a short time of each other in **Belsen**, just one week before the German surrender.

at the age of ninety-one; the identity of the collaborator who betrayed his family has never been confirmed.

The Westerkerk

Prinsengracht 279 • **Westerkerk** Early April to Oct Mon–Sat 11am–3pm; free • **Westertoren** April–Oct Mon–Sat 10am–6pm; €6 • ⓣ 020 624 7766, ⓦ westerkerk.nl

Trapped in the *achterhuis*, Anne Frank liked to listen to the bells of the **Westerkerk** until they were taken away to be melted down for the German war effort. The church still dominates the district, its 85-metre tower – without question Amsterdam's finest – soaring imperiously above the gables of Westermarkt. On its top perches the crown of the Habsburg Emperor Maximilian, a constantly recurring symbol of Amsterdam and the finishing touch to what was only the city's second place of worship built expressly for Protestants. The church was designed by **Hendrik de Keyser** and completed in 1631 as part of the general enlargement of the city, but whereas the exterior is all studied elegance, the interior – as required by the Calvinist congregation – is bare and plain. The church is also the reputed resting place of **Rembrandt**, though the location of his pauper's tomb is not known. Instead, a small memorial in the north aisle commemorates the artist close to the spot where his son Titus lies buried. Rembrandt adored his son – as evinced by numerous portraits – and the boy's death dealt a final crushing blow to the ageing artist, who died just over a year later. In the summertime, you can clamber up the **Westertoren** (tower) for a view over this part of the city.

1

DESCARTES: SPY OR PHILOSPHER?

The French philosopher **René Descartes** (1596–1650) once lodged at **Westermarkt 6**. Apparently happy that the Dutch were indifferent to his musings – and that therefore he wasn't going to be persecuted – he wrote "Everybody except me is in business and so absorbed by profit-making that I could spend my entire life here without being noticed by a soul". However, this declaration may itself have been a subterfuge: it's quite possible that Descartes was spying on the Dutch for the Habsburg King Philip II of Spain, a theory explored in detail in A.C. Grayling's book, *Descartes: The Life and Times of a Genius*. In the event, Descartes spent twenty years in the Netherlands before accepting an invitation from Queen Christina to go to Stockholm in 1649. It was a poor choice: no sooner had he got there, than he caught pneumonia and died.

Westermarkt

Westermarkt, an open square in the shadow of the Westerkerk, is home to two evocative statues. The first of the two, standing just to the south of the church entrance, by Prinsengracht, is a small but beautifully crafted **statue of Anne Frank** by the gifted Dutch sculptor Mari Andriessen (1897–1979), who was also the creator of the dockworker statue outside Amsterdam's Esnoga (see p.71). The second, at the back of the church, beside Keizersgracht, consists of three pink granite triangles (one each for the past, present and future), which together comprise the **Homomonument**. The world's first memorial to persecuted gays and lesbians, commemorating all those who died at the hands of the Nazis, it was designed by Karin Daan and recalls the pink triangles that homosexuals were forced to display on their clothes during the occupation. The monument's inscription, by the Dutch writer Jacob Israel de Haan, translates as "Such an infinite desire for friendship".

De Negen Straatjes (The Nine Streets)

Westermarkt flows into **Raadhuisstraat**, the principal thoroughfare into the Old Centre, running east to Dam square. South of here, the narrow cross-streets of the Grachtengordel are named after animals whose pelts were used in the local tanning industry – Reestraat ("Deer Street"), Hartenstraat ("Hart Street") and Berenstraat ("Bear Street"), to name but three. The tanners are long gone, but they've been replaced by some of the most pleasant shopping streets in the city, known collectively as **De Negen Straatjes** ("The Nine Streets"), selling everything from carpets and handmade chocolates to designer toothbrushes and beeswax candles. The area's southern boundary is marked by **Leidsegracht**, a mostly residential canal, lined with chic townhouses and a medley of handsome gables.

The Bijbels Museum

Herengracht 366–368 • Mon–Sat 10am–5pm, Sun 11am–5pm • €8 • ☎ 020 624 2436, ⓦ bijbelsmuseum.nl

The graceful and commanding **Cromhouthuizen**, at Herengracht 364–370, consist of four matching stone mansions, embellished with tendrils, garlands and scrollwork, all finessed by charming little bull's-eye windows and elegant neck gables. Built in the 1660s for one of Amsterdam's wealthy merchant families, the Cromhouts, the houses were designed by **Philip Vingboons** (1607–78), the most inventive of the architects who worked on the Grachtengordel during the city's expansion.

Two of the houses have now been adapted to hold the **Bijbels Museum** (Bible Museum), which is named after the antique Bibles displayed in the cellar. The most important is the **Statenvertaling** (literally State's Translation), published in 1637. Key to the development of Dutch Protestantism, it was the result of years of study by leading scholars, who returned to the original Greek and Hebrew texts for this

HAN VAN MEEGEREN AND THE FORGED VERMEERS

Keizersgracht 321 looks innocuous enough today, but this was once the home of the Dutch art forger **Han van Meegeren** (1889–1947). During the German occupation of World War II, Meegeren sold a "previously unknown" Vermeer to a German art dealer working for Herman Goering; what neither the agent nor Goering realized was that Meegeren had painted it himself. A forger *par excellence*, Meegeren had developed a sophisticated ageing technique in the early 1930s. He mixed his paints with phenol formaldehyde resin dissolved in benzene and then baked the finished painting in an oven for several hours; the end result fooled everyone, including the curators of the Rijksmuseum, who had bought another "Vermeer" from him in 1941. The forgeries may well have never been discovered but for a strange sequence of events. In May 1945 a British captain by the name of Harry Anderson discovered Meegeren's "Vermeer" in Goering's art collection. Meegeren was promptly arrested as a collaborator and, to get himself out of a pickle, he soon confessed to this and other forgeries, arguing that he had duped and defrauded the Nazis rather than helping them – though he had, of course, pocketed the money. It was a fine argument and his reward was a short prison sentence – but in the event he died before he was locked up.

translation, which sold by the cartload. Much stranger, however, are the idiosyncratic models of **Solomon's Temple** and the **Jewish Tabernacle** on Floor 3. Attempts to reconstruct biblical scenes were something of a cottage industry in the Netherlands in the late 1800s, with scores of Dutch antiquarians beavering away: a Protestant vicar by the name of **Leendert Schouten** (1828–1905) was particularly prolific and several of his models get pride of place here.

Leidseplein and around

Lying on the edge of the Grachtengordel, **Leidseplein** is the bustling hub of Amsterdam's nightlife, a rather cluttered and disorderly open space that has never had much character. The square once marked the end of the road in from Leiden and, as horse-drawn traffic was banned from the centre long ago, it was here that the Dutch left their horses and carts – a sort of equine car park. Today, it's quite the opposite: continual traffic made up of trams, bikes, cars and pedestrians gives the place a frenetic feel, and the surrounding side streets are jammed with bars, restaurants and clubs in a bright jumble of jutting signs and neon lights. On a good night, however, Leidseplein can be Amsterdam at its carefree, exuberant best. Running northeast from the Leidseplan, busy **Leidsestraat,** a crowded shopping street full of fashion and shoe shops of little distinction, leads across the three main canals up towards the Singel.

Stadsschouwburg

Leidseplein 26 • ☎ 020 624 2311, ⓦ ssba.nl

The grandiose **Stadsschouwburg**, a neo-Renaissance edifice dating from 1894, was so widely criticized for its clumsy vulgarity that the city council of the day temporarily withheld the money for decorating the exterior. Formerly home to the National Ballet and Opera, it is now used for theatre, dance and music performances, but its most popular function is as the place where the Ajax football team gather on the balcony to wave to the crowds whenever they win anything – as they often do.

American Hotel

Leidsekade 97 • ☎ 020 556 3009, ⓦ edenamsterdamamericanhotel.com

The **American Hotel**, just off Leidseplein, is one of the city's oddest buildings, a monumental and slightly disconcerting rendering of Art Nouveau, complete with angular turrets, chunky dormer windows and fancy brickwork. Completed in 1902, the present structure takes its name from its demolished predecessor, which was adorned with statues

1

and murals of North American scenes. Inside the present hotel, the *Café Americain* was once the fashionable haunt of Amsterdam's literati, but today is a mainstream location for coffee and lunch. The Art Nouveau decor is well worth a peek – an artful combination of stained glass, shallow arches and geometric patterned brickwork.

The Golden Bend

At Leidsegracht, the elegant sweep of the main **Herengracht canal** reaches the so-called **De Gouden Bocht** (Golden Bend), where the canal is overlooked by a long sequence of double-fronted mansions, some of the most opulent dwellings in the city. Most of the houses here date from the eighteenth century, with double stairways leading to the main entrance – and the small door beneath reserved for servants. Classical references are common, both in form – pediments, columns and pilasters – and decoration, from scrolls and vases through to geometric patterns inspired by ancient Greece. One of the first buildings to look out for is **Herengracht 475**, an extravagant edifice surmounted by a slender French-style balustrade and decorated with twin caryatids. Typically, the original building was a much more modest affair, but in the 1730s, a new owner created the ornate facade of today. **Herengracht 493** is similarly grand, and completed with a carved pediment. Equally imposing is the nearby **Herengracht 507**: all Neoclassical pilasters and slender windows, it was once the home of Jacob Boreel, a one-time major whose attempt to impose a burial tax prompted a riot during which the mob ransacked his house.

The Stadsarchief

Vijzelstraat 32 • Tues–Fri 10am–5pm, Sat & Sun noon–5pm • Free • ☎ 020 251 1510, ⓦ stadsarchief.amsterdam.nl

The **Stadsarchief** (State Archives) are housed within one of Amsterdam's weirdest and most monumentally incongruous buildings, a mammoth edifice of broadly Expressionist design that stretches down Vijzelstraat from Herengracht to Keizersgracht. Dating from the 1920s, the building started out as the headquarters of a Dutch shipping company, the Nederlandsche Handelsmaatschappij, before falling temporarily into the hands of the ABN-AMRO bank, then becoming home to the city's archives in 2007. The building is commonly known as **De Bazel** after its architect Karel de Bazel (1869–1923), whose devotion to theosophy formed and framed his design. Founded in the late nineteenth century, theosophy combined metaphysics and religious philosophy, and every facet of de Bazel's building reflects the cult's belief in order and balance, from the pink and yellow brickwork of the exterior (representing male and female respectively) to the repeated use of motifs drawn from the Middle East, the source of much of its spiritual inspiration.

The Schatkamer

Much of de Bazel's building is out of bounds, but visitors can venture into the very heart of the edifice, to its **Schatkamer** (Treasury), a richly decorated, two-storey Art Deco extravagance that feels rather like a royal crypt. Here, you can view a regularly rotated selection of photographs and documents drawn from the city's archives – anything from 1970s squatters occupying City Hall to hagiographic tracts on the virtues of the Dutch naval hero, Admiral de Ruyter and, perhaps best of all, photos of miscreants (or rather the poor and the desperate) drawn from police archives.

FOAM

Keizersgracht 609 • Daily 10am–6pm, Thurs & Fri till 9pm • €8.50 • ☎ 020 551 6500, ⓦ foam.org

Occupying a large canal house, **FOAM** is devoted to photography, its top-ranking exhibitions including both installations and more traditional gallery-style displays. It has also won plaudits for its encouragement of young photographers from Amsterdam in particular and the rest of the Netherlands in general. Recent exhibitions have featured the work of Stéphanie Solinas and Bertien van Manen.

The Museum van Loon

Keizersgracht 672 • Daily except Tues 11am–5pm • €10 • ☎ 020 624 5255, ⓦ museumvanloon.nl

The **Museum van Loon** has perhaps the finest accessible canal house interior in the whole of Amsterdam. In the 1670s, the first tenant of the property was the artist Ferdinand Bol, who married an exceedingly wealthy widow and promptly hung up his easel for the rest of his days. The last owners were the van Loons, co-founders of the East India Company and long one of the city's leading families, though they came something of a cropper at the end of World War II. One of the clan, Thora van Loon-Egidius, the wife of Willem van Loon, was proud of her German roots and allegedly entertained high-ranking Nazi officials here during the occupation – a charge of collaboration that led to the van Loons being shunned by polite society.

In recent years, the house has been returned to something akin to its eighteenth-century appearance, with plenty of wood panelling and fancy stuccowork. Look out also for the ornate copper balustrade on the **staircase**, into which is worked the name "Van Hagen-Trip" (after a one-time owner of the house); the van Loons later filled the spaces between the letters with iron curlicues to prevent their children falling through. The **top-floor** landing has several pleasant paintings sporting classical figures, and one of the bedrooms – the "painted room" – is decorated with a Romantic painting of Italy, a motif favoured by Amsterdam's bourgeoisie from around 1750 to 1820. The oddest items are the **fake bedroom doors**: the eighteenth-century owners were so keen to avoid any lack of symmetry that they camouflaged the real bedroom doors and created imitation, decorative doors in the "correct" position instead.

The Tassenmuseum Hendrikje

Herengracht 573 • Daily 10am–5pm • €8.50 • ☎ 020-524 64 52, ⓦ tassenmuseum.nl

The delightful **Tassenmuseum Hendrikje** is home to a superb collection of handbags, pouches, wallets, bags and purses from medieval times onwards, exhibited on three floors of a sympathetically refurbished grand old mansion. Highlights include examples of several types of bag that preceded the purse – portefeuilles, chatelaines, frame-bags and stocking purses to name but four – as well as a number of beautiful Art Nouveau handbags. There is also a separate display on handbags made from animal skins – check out the eel, crocodile, python and lizard bags, though the armadillo bag is really rather gruesome. A final floor is given over to temporary displays usually featuring contemporary bags and purses.

The Museum Willet-Holthuysen

Herengracht 605 • Mon–Fri 10am–5pm, Sat & Sun 11am–5pm • €8 • ☎ 020 523 1822, ⓦ museumwilletholthuysen.nl

The **Museum Willet-Holthuysen** offers an insight into the life and tastes of one of Amsterdam's leading families, the coal-trading Holthuysens, who occupied this elegant, late seventeenth-century mansion until the last of the line, Sandra Willet-Holthuysen, gifted her home and its contents to the city in 1895. The museum is entered via the old servants' door, which leads into the basement, where there's a small collection of porcelain and earthenware on display. Above are the family rooms, most memorably the **Blue Room**, which has been returned to its eighteenth-century Rococo appearance – a flashy and ornate style that the Dutch merchants of the day held to be the epitome of refinement and good taste. The Ballroom, all creams and gilt, is similarly opulent and the Dining Room is laid out for dinner as of 1865 complete with the family's

1

original Meissen dinner set. The top floor displays the fine and applied art collection assembled by Sandra's husband, Abraham Willet, principally Dutch ceramics, pewter and silverware. Behind the house are the formal **gardens**, a neat pattern of miniature hedges graced by the occasional stone statue, and framed by the old coach house.

The Amstel

The main canals come to an abrupt halt beside the wide and windy **River Amstel**, long the main route into the interior, with goods arriving by barge and boat to be traded for the materials held in Amsterdam's many warehouses. Several bridges span the river, including the **Blauwbrug** ("Blue Bridge"), leading to the Old Jewish Quarter (see pp.69–72), and the **Magere Brug** ("Skinny Bridge"), arguably the cutest of the city's many swing bridges, which leads over to the Hermitage Amsterdam (see p.72). Near the Magere Brug are the **Amstelsluizen**, or Amstel locks, which play an integral part in refreshing the city's canal water nightly. Every night, the municipal water department closes these locks to begin the process of sluicing out the canals. A huge pumping station on an island to the east of the city then pumps fresh water into the canal system from the freshwater IJsselmeer lake; similar locks on the west side of the city are left open for the surplus to flow into the IJ and, from there, out to sea via the North Sea Canal.

The Jordaan

Lying to the west of the city centre and the Grachtengordel, its boundaries clearly defined by the Prinsengracht and the Lijnbaansgracht, the **Jordaan** is a likeable and easily explored area of slender canals and narrow streets flanked by an agreeable mix of architectural styles, from modern terraces to handsome seventeenth-century canal houses. In all probability the district takes its name from the French word *jardin* ("garden"), since the area's earliest settlers were Protestant Huguenots, who fled here to escape persecution in the sixteenth and seventeenth centuries. Another possibility is that it's a corruption of the Dutch word for Jews, *joden*. Whatever the truth, the Jordaan developed from open country – hence the number of streets and canals named

---

A SCENIC STROLL AROUND THE JORDAAN

The streets and canals extending north from **Rozengracht to Westerstraat** form the heart of the Jordaan and hold the district's prettiest moments. Beyond Rozengracht, the first canal is the **Bloemgracht** (Flower Canal), a leafy waterway dotted with houseboats and arched by little bridges, its network of cross-streets sprinkled with cafés and bars. There's a warm, relaxed community atmosphere here which is really rather beguiling, not to mention a clutch of old and handsome canal houses. Pride of architectural place goes to **Bloemgracht 89–91**, a sterling Renaissance building of 1642 complete with mullion windows, crow-step gable, brightly painted shutters and distinctive facade stones, representing a *steeman* (city-dweller), *landman* (farmer) and a *seeman* (sailor).

From Bloemgracht, it's a few metres north to **Egelantiersgracht** (Rose-Hip Canal), where, at no. 12, *Café 't Smalle* is one of Amsterdam's oldest cafés, opened in 1786 as a *proeflokaal* – a tasting house for the (long-gone) gin distillery next door. In the eighteenth century, when quality control was intermittent, each batch of *jenever* (Dutch gin) could turn out very differently, so customers insisted on a taster before they splashed out. As a result, each distillery ran a *proeflokaal* offering free samples, and this is a rare survivor. A narrow cross-street – Tweede Egelantiersdwarsstraat and its continuation Tweede Tuindwarsstraat and Tweede Anjeliersdwarsstraat – runs north from Egelantiersgracht, flanked by many of the Jordaan's more fashionable stores and clothing shops as well as some of its liveliest bars and cafés.

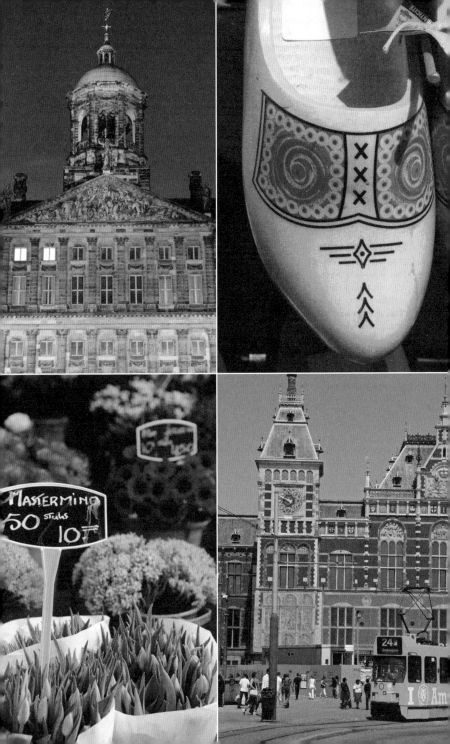

1

after flowers and plants – into a refugee enclave, a teeming, cosmopolitan quarter beyond the pale of bourgeois respectability. Indeed, when the city fathers planned the expansion of the city in 1610, they made sure the Jordaan was kept outside the city boundaries. Consequently, the Jordaan was not subject to the rigorous planning restrictions of the Grachtengordel, and its lattice of narrow streets followed the lines of the original polder drainage ditches rather than any municipal outline. This gives the district its distinctive, mazy layout, and much of its present appeal.

Traditionally the home of Amsterdam's working class, the Jordaan has in recent years been transformed by a middle-class influx, with the district now one of the city's most sought-after **residential neighbourhoods**. Before then, and until the late 1970s, the Jordaan's inhabitants were primarily stevedores and factory workers, earning a crust among the docks, warehouses, factories and boatyards that extended north beyond Brouwersgracht (see p.60), the Jordaan's northern boundary. Specific sights are few and far between but it's still a very pleasant area to wander.

Noordermarkt

Dominated by its hulking church, the **Noordermarkt** is a somewhat inconclusive square that nudges down to the Prinsengracht canal. Here, beside the church entrance, you'll see a **statue** of three figures bound to each other, a poignant tribute to the bloody Jordaanoproer riot of 1934, part of a successful campaign to stop the government cutting unemployment benefit during the Depression. The inscription reads: "The strongest chains are those of unity". The square also hosts one of Amsterdam's best open-air **markets**, the **Boerenmarkt** (Sat 9am–4pm; ⓦ boerenmarktamsterdam.nl), a lively affair selling organic fruit and vegetables, freshly baked breads and a plethora of oils and spices.

The Noorderkerk

Noordermarkt • Mon 10.30am–12.30pm, Sat 11am–1pm & April–Oct Sun 1.30–5.30pm • Free • ☏ 020 626 6436, ⓦ noorderkerk.org

Cramped and ungainly, the **Noorderkerk** was the architect Hendrik de Keyser's last creation and perhaps his least successful, finished two years after his death in 1623. Unsuccessful perhaps, but the church did represent a radical departure from the conventional church designs of the time, having a symmetrical Greek-cross floor plan, with four equally proportioned arms radiating out from a steepled centre. The design was an attempt to reformulate religious worship, making it more democratic with the

---

ARCHITECTURE AS SOCIAL UTOPIA: THE AMSTERDAM SCHOOL

At its peak from around 1910 to 1930, **the Amsterdam School** brought together the leading Dutch architects of the period in a loose alliance that was Expressionistic in style and politically committed: the School's leading practitioners were eager to build housing for the working class that was of the highest possible standard. Several of these utopian ventures have survived here in Amsterdam, but perhaps the most architecturally pleasing is the delightful **Het Schip** just west of the city centre. A municipal housing block designed by Michael de Klerk (1884–1923), it takes its name from its ship-like shape and is graced by all manner of decorative details, such as wavy brick facades and misshapen windows.

THE MUSEUM HET SCHIP

Housed inside the complex's former post office at Spaarndammerplantsoen 140, the **Museum Het Schip** (Tues–Sun 11am–5pm; €7.50; ⓦ hetschip.nl) explores the history of the Amsterdam School and details the building's principal features. Regular half-hour guided tours take you inside one of the restored residences – the block is still used as social housing today – and up to the main turret. It takes about 15min to get there from Centraal Station on **bus #22** – get off at the terminus and it's a short walk.

congregation sitting on sets of wooden pews that face inward rather than to any altar. The pews are also overseen by the pulpit, a fancy affair with a large carved canopy, from where the Calvinist preachers would sermonize away for several hours at a time.

The Old Jewish Quarter and the Eastern Docklands

Originally one of the marshiest parts of Amsterdam, prone to regular flooding, the narrow slice of land sandwiched between the curve of the Amstel, Kloveniersburgwal and the Nieuwe Herengracht was the home of Amsterdam's **Jews** from the sixteenth century up until World War II. By the 1920s, this **Old Jewish Quarter**, or **Jodenhoek** ("Jews' Corner"), was crowded with tenement buildings and smoking factories, but in 1945 it lay derelict – and postwar redevelopment has not treated it kindly either. Its focal point, **Waterlooplein**, has been overwhelmed by a whopping town hall and concert hall complex, and the once-bustling Jodenbreestraat – the "Broad Street of the Jews" – is now bleak and very ordinary, with Mr Visserplein, at its east end, one of the city's busiest traffic junctions. Picking your way round these obstacles is not much fun, but you should persevere – among all the cars and concrete are several moving reminders of the Jewish community that perished in the war, including the imposing **Esnoga** (Portuguese synagogue) and the fascinating **Joods Historisch Museum** (Jewish Historical Museum), as well as Rembrandt's former home, the **Rembrandthuis**.

Immediately east of the Old Jewish Quarter lies the **Plantagebuurt**, a well-heeled district centred around the **Plantage Middenlaan**, a wide boulevard that was constructed in the mid-nineteenth century as the first part of the creation of this leafy suburb – one of Amsterdam's earliest. The avenue borders the city's largest botanical gardens, the **Hortus Botanicus**, and runs close to both the **Artis Zoo** and the excellent **Verzetsmuseum** (Dutch Resistance Museum). Nearby, the reclaimed islands of the **Oosterdok** are home to the excellent children's science museum **NEMO** and the city's popular **Scheepvaartmusuem** (Maritime Museum).

The Rembrandthuis

Rembrandt House • Jodenbreestraat 4 • Daily 10am–5pm • €10 • ☎ 020 520 0400, ⓦ rembrandthuis.nl

One of the city's key attractions, the **Rembrandthuis** (Rembrandt House) boasts an intricate facade decorated by pretty wooden shutters and a small pediment. Rembrandt bought this house in 1639 at the height of his fame and popularity, living here for over twenty years and spending a fortune on furnishings – an expense that ultimately contributed to his bankruptcy (see box, p.340). An inventory made at the time details the huge collection of paintings, sculptures and art treasures he'd amassed, almost all of which were confiscated after he was declared insolvent and forced to move to a more modest house on Rozengracht in the Jordaan in 1658. The city council bought the Jodenbreestraat house in 1907 and has subsequently revamped the premises on several occasions.

The house

Entry is via a modern annexe, but you're soon into Rembrandt's old house, where a string of **period rooms** has been restored to something resembling their appearance when the artist lived here. The period furniture is appealing enough, especially the dinky box-beds, and the great man's studio is surprisingly large and well lit, but pride of place goes to the "**Art Cabinet**", which is jam-packed with objets d'art and miscellaneous rarities reassembled here in line with the original inventory. There are African spears and shields, Pacific seashells, Venetian glassware and even busts of

1

Roman emperors, all of which demonstrate Rembrandt's wide interests and eclectic taste. The rooms are also hung with **seventeenth-century Dutch paintings**, but most are distinctly second-rate and none of them is actually a Rembrandt. The most interesting paintings are those by Rembrandt's master in Amsterdam, Pieter Lastman (1583–1633) – not because of their quality, but rather because their sheer mawkishness demonstrates just how far Rembrandt soared above his artistic milieu.

Rembrandt's etchings and engravings

Beyond the Art Cabinet, the rest of the Rembrandthuis is usually given over to temporary exhibitions on the artist and his contemporaries. Here also, space permitting, is the museum's own collection of **Rembrandt's etchings**, as well as several of the original copper plates on which he worked. It's a large and varied collection, with the biblical illustrations usually attracting the most attention, though the studies of tramps and vagabonds are equally appealing. But to see Rembrandt's major paintings, you'll have to go to the Rijksmuseum (see p.75).

Waterlooplein

A rectangular parcel of land that was originally swampy marsh, **Waterlooplein** was the site of the **first Jewish Quarter**, but by the late nineteenth century it had become an insanitary slum, home to the poorest of the Ashkenazi Jews. The slums were cleared in the 1880s and thereafter the open spaces of the Waterlooplein hosted the largest and liveliest marketplace in the city, the place where Jews and Gentiles met to trade. In World War II, the Nazis used the square to round up their victims, but despite these ugly connotations the Waterlooplein was revived in the 1950s as the site of the city's main **flea market** and remains so to this day (see p.95). The market is nowhere as large as it once was thanks to the town hall and concert hall development, but nonetheless it's still the final resting place of many a pair of yellow corduroy flares and has some wonderful antique and junk stalls to root through.

Stadhuis en Muziektheater

Waterlooplein

Dominating Waterlooplein is the **Stadhuis en Muziektheater** (Town Hall and Theatre) a sprawling and distinctly underwhelming modern complex dating from the 1980s and incorporating the city hall and a large auditorium. The Muziektheater offers a varied programme of theatre, dance and ballet as well as opera from the first-rate Netherlands Opera (for ticket details, see p.95). One of the city's abiding ironies is that the title of the protest campaign aiming to prevent the development in the 1980s – "**Stopera**" – has passed into common usage to describe the finished building. Inside, there are a couple of minor attractions, beginning with the glass columns in the public passageway towards the rear of the complex. These give a salutary lesson on the fragility of the Netherlands: two contain water indicating the sea levels in the Dutch towns of Vlissingen and IJmuiden (below knee level), while another records the levels experienced during the 1953 flood disaster (way above head height). Downstairs a concrete pile shows what is known as "Normal Amsterdam Level" (NAP), originally calculated in 1684 as the average water level in the River IJ and still the basis for measuring altitude above sea level across the Netherlands. Metres away, in the Muziektheater's foyer, is a forceful and inventive **memorial** to the district's Jews, in which a bronze violinist bursts through the floor tiles.

Mr Visserplein

Just behind the Muziektheater, **Mr Visserplein** is a busy junction for traffic speeding towards the IJ tunnel. It takes its name from **Lodewijk Ernst Visser**, president of the

Supreme Court of the Netherlands in 1939. He was dismissed the following year when the Germans occupied the country, and became an active member of the Jewish resistance, working for the illegal underground newspaper *Het Parool* ("The Password") and refusing to wear the yellow Star of David. He died from a brain haemorrhage in 1942, a few days after publicly – and famously – denouncing all forms of collaboration.

The Esnoga

Mr Visserplein • April–Oct Sun–Fri 10am–4pm; Nov–March Sun–Thurs 10am–4pm & Fri 10am–2pm; closed Yom Kippur • €12 • ☎ 020 531 0380, ⓦ esnoga.com

Unmissable on the corner of Mr Visserplein is the brown, bulky brickwork of the **Esnoga** or **Portuguese synagogue**, completed in 1675 for the city's Sephardic Jews. One of Amsterdam's most imposing buildings, the central structure, with its grand pilasters and blind balustrade, was built in the broadly Neoclassical style that was then fashionable in Amsterdam. It's surrounded by a courtyard complex of small outhouses, where the city's Sephardim have fraternized for centuries. Barely altered since its construction, the synagogue's lofty interior follows the Sephardic tradition in having the *hechal* (the Ark of the Covenant) and *tebah* (from where services are led) at opposite ends. Also traditional is the seating, with two sets of wooden benches (for the men) facing each other across the central aisle – the women have separate galleries up above. A set of superb brass chandeliers holds the candles, which remain the only source of artificial light. When it was completed, the synagogue was one of the largest in the world, its congregation almost certainly the richest; today, the Sephardic community has dwindled to just 250 families, most of whom live outside the city centre. In one of the outhouses, a short film sheds light on the history of the synagogue and Amsterdam's Sephardim; the mystery is why the Nazis left it alone. No one knows for sure, but it seems likely that they intended to turn it into a museum once all the Jews had been polished off.

Jonas Daniel Meijerplein

Jonas Daniel Meijerplein, a scrawny triangle of gravel located beside the Esnoga, was named after the eponymous lawyer, who in 1796, at the age of just 16, was the first Jew to be admitted to the Amsterdam Bar. It was here in February 1941 that around 400 Jewish men were forcibly loaded up on trucks and taken to their deaths at Mauthausen concentration camp, in reprisal for the killing of a Dutch Nazi during a street fight. The arrests sparked off the **Februaristaking** (February Strike), a general strike in protest against the Germans' treatment of the Jews. It was organized by the outlawed Communist Party and spearheaded by Amsterdam's transport workers and dockers – a rare demonstration of solidarity with the Jews whose fate was almost always accepted without visible protest in occupied Europe. The strike was quickly suppressed, but is still commemorated by an annual wreath-laying ceremony on February 25, as well as by Mari Andriessen's statue of the **Dokwerker** (dockworker), which was actually modelled on a carpenter from Haarlem.

The Joods Historisch Museum

Nieuwe Amstelstraat 1 • Daily 11am–5pm; closed Yom Kippur • €12 • ☎ 020 531 0310, ⓦ jhm.nl

The **Joods Historisch Museum** (Jewish Historical Museum) is cleverly shoehorned into four adjacent Ashkenazi synagogues that date from the late seventeenth century. For years after World War II these buildings lay abandoned, but they were finally refurbished – and connected by walkways – in the 1980s, to accommodate a Jewish resource and exhibition centre. The first major display area, just beyond the reception desk on the ground floor of the Nieuwe Synagoge, features temporary exhibitions on Jewish life and culture with vintage photographs to the fore. Upstairs, also in the

Nieuwe Synagoge, are displays on the history of Dutch Jewry from 1900 to the present. Inevitably, the emphasis is on the fate of the Jews during the German occupation, but there is also a biting exhibit on the indifference, and even hostile, reaction of many Dutch men and women to liberated Jews in 1945.

On the ground floor of the adjacent **Grote Synagoge**, there's an engaging display on Jewish culture, with a fine collection of religious silverware, plus all manner of antique artefacts illustrating religious customs and practices, alongside a scattering of paintings and portraits. The gallery above holds a finely judged social history of the country's Jewish population from 1600 to 1900.

Hermitage Amsterdam

Amstel 51 • Daily 10am–5pm, Wed till 8pm • €15 • ☎ 020 530 74 88, ⓦ hermitage.nl

Backing onto the River Amstel, the stern-looking **Amstelhof** started out as a *hofje* or almshouse for the care of elderly women built in the 1680s on behalf of the Dutch Reformed Church. In time, it grew to fill most of the chunk of land between Nieuwe Herengracht and Nieuwe Keizersgracht, becoming a fully-fledged hospital in the process, but in the 1980s it became clear that its medical facilities were out of date and it went up for sale. Much municipal debate ensued until it was finally agreed to convert it into a museum, **Hermitage Amsterdam**, to display items loaned from the Hermitage in St Petersburg. It was – and is – a very ambitious scheme, with a substantial number of galleries now displaying prime pieces. Exhibitions, which usually last about five months, have included "Nicholas & Alexandra" and "Impressionism: Sensation & Inspiration".

Hortus Botanicus

Plantage Middenlaan • Daily 10am–5pm • €7.50 • ☎ 020 625 9021, ⓦ dehortus.nl

The lush **Hortus Botanicus**, the city's botanical gardens, were founded in 1682 for medicinal purposes after an especially bad outbreak of the plague. Thereafter, many of Amsterdam's merchants made a point of bringing back exotic plants from the East, the result being the 6000-odd species exhibited here today – both outside and in a series of hothouses. The gardens are divided into several distinct sections, each clearly labelled, its location pinpointed on a map available at the entrance kiosk. The outdoor sections are mainly devoted to temperate and Arctic plants, trees and shrubs, while the largest of the hothouses, the **Three-Climate Glasshouse**, is partitioned into separate climate zones: subtropical, tropical and desert. The gardens also hold a **butterfly house** and a capacious **palm house** with a substantial collection of cycad palms. It's all very low-key – and none the worse for that – and the gardens make a relaxing break on any tour of central Amsterdam, especially as the **café**, in the old orangery, serves tasty lunches and snacks.

The Hollandsche Schouwburg

Plantage Middenlaan 24 • Daily 11am–4pm; closed Yom Kippur • Free • ☎ 020 531 0340, ⓦ hollandscheschouwburg.nl

A sad relic of the war, **De Hollandsche Schouwburg** was a one-time Jewish theatre, which was turned into the main assembly point for Amsterdam Jews prior to their deportation in 1942. Inside, there was no daylight and families were interned in conditions that foreshadowed those of the camps they would soon be taken to. The front of the building has been refurbished to display a list of the dead and an eternal flame along with a small exhibition on the plight of the city's Jews, but the old auditorium out at the back has been left as an empty, roofless shell. A memorial **column** of basalt on a Star of David base stands where the stage once was, an intensely mournful monument to suffering of unfathomable proportions.

Artis Zoo

Plantage Kerklaan • April–Oct daily 9am–6pm; Nov–March daily 9am–5pm; June–Aug till dusk on Sat with special activities • €19, 3- to 9-year-olds €15.50, seniors (65+) €17.50 • ☎ 0900 278 4796 (premium line), ⓦ artis.nl

Opened in 1838, **Artis Zoo** has long been one of the city's top tourist attractions and its layout and lack of bars and cages mean that it never feels overcrowded. Highlights include an African savanna environment, a seventy-metre-long aviary, aquaria and a South American zone with llamas and the world's largest rodent, the capybara. **Feeding times** – always popular – include: 11am birds of prey; 11.30am and 3.45pm seals and sea lions; 2.50pm lions and tigers (not Thurs); and 3.30pm penguins. In addition, the on-site **Planetarium** has five or six shows daily, all in Dutch, though you can pick up a leaflet with an English translation from the desk.

The Verzetsmuseum

Plantage Kerklaan 61 • Tues–Fri 10am–5pm; Sat–Mon 11am–5pm • €8 • ☎ 020 620 2535, ⓦ verzetsmuseum.org

The excellent **Verzetsmuseum** (Dutch Resistance Museum) details the development of the Dutch Resistance from the German invasion of the Netherlands in May 1940 to the country's liberation in 1945. Thoughtfully presented, the main gangway examines the experience of the majority of the population, dealing honestly with the fine balance between cooperation and collaboration. Side rooms are devoted to different aspects of the resistance, from the brave determination of the Communist Party, who went underground as soon as the Germans arrived, to more ad hoc responses like the so-called **Melkstaking** (Milk Strike) of 1943, when hundreds of milk producers refused to deliver in protest at the Germans' threatened deportation of 300,000 former (demobilized) Dutch soldiers to labour camps in Germany. Fascinating old photographs illustrate the (English and Dutch) text along with a host of original artefacts, from examples of illegal newsletters to signed German death warrants and, perhaps most moving of all, farewell letters thrown from the Auschwitz train. Interestingly, the Dutch Resistance proved especially adept at forgery, forcing the Germans to make the identity cards they issued more and more complicated – but with little success. Aside from their treatment of the Jews, perhaps the most chilling feature of the occupation was the use of indiscriminate reprisals to terrify the population. The museum has dozens of little metal sheets providing biographical sketches of the members of the Resistance – and it's this mixture of the general and the personal that is its real strength.

The Oosterdok

The reclaimed islands of the **Oosterdok** were dredged out of the River IJ to accommodate warehouses and docks in the seventeenth century, and once formed part of a vast maritime complex that spread right along the River IJ. Industrial decline set in during the 1880s, but the area has recently been subject to a massive redevelopment programme, with the outer islands now dotted with upmarket housing and popular with the city's young professionals. The Oosterdokskade, near Centraal Station, is home to the city's brand-new library, with an elevated walkway spanning the greasy waters of the Oosterdok harbour.

Entrepotdok

A footbridge leads from the northern end of Plantage Kerklaan over the canal to **Entrepotdok**, the most interesting of the **Oosterdok** islands. Here, on the far side of the bridge, old brick warehouses stretch along much of the quayside, distinguished by their spout gables, multiple doorways and overhead pulleys. Built by the **Dutch East India Company** in the eighteenth century, they were once part of the largest warehouse complex in continental Europe, a gigantic customs-free zone established for goods in transit. On the ground floor, above the main entrance, each warehouse sports the name

1

of a town or island; goods for onward transportation were stored in the appropriate warehouse until there was enough to fill a boat or barge. The warehouses have been tastefully converted into offices and apartments, a fate they share with the central East India Company compound, whose chunky Neoclassical entrance is at the west end of Entrepotdok on Kadijksplein.

Nederlands Scheepvaartmuseum

Kattenburgerplein • Daily 9am–5pm • €15 • ☎ 020 523 2222, ⓦ hetscheepvaartmuseum.nl

One of the city's most popular attractions, **Het Scheepvaartmuseum** (Maritime Museum) occupies the old arsenal of the Dutch navy, a vast sandstone structure built on the Oosterdok in the seventeenth century. Remarkably, the rectangular arsenal is underpinned by no fewer than 18,000 wooden piles, each of which was driven deep into the riverbed at enormous expense – and at tremendous effort. Visitors get their bearings in the central **courtyard** from where you can enter any one of three display areas – labelled "West", "Noord" and "Oost". Of the three, the "**West**" displays are the most gimmicky and child-orientated, the "**Oost**" the most substantial, including garish ships' figureheads, examples of early atlases, globes and navigational equipment. There are many nautical paintings in this section too, some devoted to the achievements of Dutch trading ships, others showing heavy seas and shipwrecks and yet more celebrating the successes of the Dutch Navy. Honed by the long and bloody struggle with Habsburg Spain, the Navy was the most powerful fleet in the world for about thirty years from the 1650s to the 1680s. **Willem van de Velde II** (1633–1707) was the most successful of the Dutch marine painters of the period and there's a good sample of his work here – canvases that emphasize the strength and power of the Dutch warship, often depicted in battle.

The "**Noord**" section features a couple of short nautical films and also gives access to the 78-metre **De Amsterdam**, a full-scale replica of an East Indiaman merchant ship. The original vessel first set sail in 1748, but came to an ignominious end, getting stuck on the British coast near Hastings. Visitors can wander the ship's decks and galleys, storerooms and gun bays at their leisure.

NEMO

Oosterdok • Tues–Sun 10am–5pm; June–Aug & school hols also Mon 10am–5pm • €13.50, under-3s • ☎ 020 531 3233, ⓦ e-nemo.nl

Dominating its surroundings, the massive elevated hood that rears up above the entrance to the River IJ tunnel is home to **NEMO**, a kids' attraction *par excellence*, with all sorts of interactive science and technological exhibits spread over five floors. Moored beside NEMO is a collection of antique barges and boats, which together make an informal record of the development of local shipping; the earliest boats date from the middle of the nineteenth century, and plaques, in English and Dutch, give the historical lowdown on the more important vessels.

The Museum Quarter and the Vondelpark

During the nineteenth century, Amsterdam burst out of its restraining canals, gobbling up the surrounding countryside with a slew of new residential suburbs. Neither did the developers forget to impress for it was here in the 1880s, on the southern edge of the city centre, that Petrus Josephus Hubertus Cuypers, the creator of Centraal Station, built the city's **Rijksmuseum**, an imposing edifice designed in an inventive and especially attractive historic style. No mistake, the museum possesses one of the most comprehensive collections of Dutch paintings in the world and although it is in the throes of an extraordinarily long-winded revamp, the kernel of the collection – **Dutch paintings** from Amsterdam's seventeenth-century Golden Age – is still on display in the **Philips Wing**, the only part of the museum to remain open during the refurbishment, which is supposed to be completed in 2013. Equally enticing is the neighbouring **Van**

Gogh Museum, which boasts the most satisfying collection of van Gogh paintings in the world, with important works representative of all his artistic periods. Taken together, the two museums form one of Amsterdam's biggest draws – and they are supplemented by the modern and contemporary art of the newly reopened Stedelijk Museum. From the Stedelijk Museum, it's a brief walk northwest along van Baerlestraat to the sprawling greenery of the **Vondelpark**, Amsterdam's loveliest park. As an alcoholic counterblast to all this culture, the area is also home to the **Heineken Experience** – a hoppy hop round the old brewery with tasting included.

The Rijksmuseum

Jan Luijkenstraat • Daily 9am–6pm • €14, audioguide €5 • ☎ 020 674 7000, ⓦ rijksmuseum.nl • Summer weekend queues can be long, so either come early or book online

The **Rijksmuseum** is without question the country's foremost art museum, with an extravagant collection of Dutch paintings, as well as a vast hoard of applied art and sculpture. Although much of the museum is closed for refurbishment until 2013, you can still see some of its world-renowned collection of **Rembrandts** – with *The Night Watch* (see box below) and the exquisite *Jewish Bride* leading the way – but there's much, much else. One undoubted highlight is the paintings of **Johannes Vermeer** (1632–75), most memorably *The Love Letter*, which reveals a tension between servant and mistress – the lute on the woman's lap was a well-known sexual symbol – and *The Kitchen Maid*, an exquisitely observed domestic scene, right down to the nail, and its shadow, on the background wall. There are also paintings by Rembrandt's pupils – Ferdinand Bol, Gerard Dou, Carel Fabritius and Gabriel Metsu; the carousing peasants of Jan Steen; the cool interiors of Gerard ter Borch and Pieter Saenredam;

REMBRANDT'S 'DE NACHTWACHT'

Pride of place in the Rijksmuseum goes to Rembrandt's **De Nachtwacht** (*The Night Watch*). Dated to 1642, it's a group portrait of a **militia company**, the Kloveniersdoelen, one of the armed bands formed in the sixteenth century to defend the United Provinces (later the Netherlands) against Spain. As the Habsburg threat receded, so the militias became social clubs for the wealthy, who were eager to commission their own group portraits as signs of their prestige. Rembrandt charged the princely sum of one hundred guilders to each member of the company who wanted to be in the picture; sixteen – out of a possible two hundred – stumped up the cash, including the company's moneyed captain, **Frans Banningh Cocq**, whose disapproval of Rembrandt's live-in relationship with Hendrickje Stoffels (see box, p.340) was ultimately to tarnish their friendship. Curiously, *The Night Watch* is, in fact, a misnomer – the painting got the tag in the eighteenth century when the background darkness was misinterpreted. There were other misconceptions about the painting too, most notably that it was this work that led to the downward shift in Rembrandt's standing with the Amsterdam elite; in fact, there's no evidence that the militiamen weren't pleased with the picture, or that Rembrandt's commissions dwindled after it was completed. Though not as subtle as much of the artist's later work, *The Night Watch* is an adept piece, full of movement and carefully arranged. Paintings of this kind were collections of individual portraits as much as group pictures, and for the artist their difficulty lay in doing justice to every single face while simultaneously producing a coherent group scene. Abandoning convention in vigorous style, Rembrandt opted to show the company preparing to march off – a snapshot of military activity in which banners are unfurled, muskets primed and drums rolled. There are a couple of **allegorical figures** as well, most prominently a young, spotlit woman with a bird hanging from her belt, a reference to the Kloveniersdoelen's traditional emblem of a claw. Militia portraits commonly included cameo portraits of the artist involved, but in this case it seems that Rembrandt didn't insert his likeness, though some art historians insist that the pudgy-faced figure peering out from the back between the gesticulating militiamen is indeed the artist himself.

1

tonal river scenes by the Haarlem artist Salomon van Ruysdael; and several wonderful canvases by **Frans Hals** (1582–1666), most notably his expansive *Marriage Portrait of Isaac Massa and Beatrix Laen*.

The Van Gogh Museum

Paulus Potterstraat 7 • Daily 10am–6pm, Fri until 10pm • €14, audioguide €5 • ☎ 020 570 5200, ⓦ vangoghmuseum.nl • Summer queues can be long, so either come early or book online

Vincent van Gogh is arguably the most popular, most reproduced and most talked-about of all modern artists, so it's not surprising that the **Van Gogh Museum**, comprising a fabulous collection of the artist's work, is one of Amsterdam's top attractions. The museum occupies two modern buildings, with the kernel of the collection housed at the front in an angular structure designed by a leading light of the De Stijl movement, **Gerrit Rietveld**, and opened to the public in 1973. Well conceived and beautifully presented, this part of the museum provides an introduction to the man and his art, based on paintings that were mostly inherited from Vincent's art-dealer brother Theo. To the rear of Rietveld's building, and connected by a ground-floor escalator, is an ultramodern curved annexe, an aesthetically controversial structure built in 1998, that holds temporary exhibitions.

The collection

The **ground floor** of the main museum displays works by some of van Gogh's well-known friends and contemporaries, many of whom influenced his work

---

VAN GOGH'S EAR

In February 1888, **Vincent van Gogh** (1853–90) left Paris for Arles, a small town in the south of France, where he warmed to the open vistas and bright colours of the Provençal countryside. In September he moved into the house he called the "**Yellow House**", where he hoped to establish an artists' colony – though only **Gauguin**, who arrived in Arles in late October, stayed for any length of time. Initially the two artists got on well, hunkering down together in the Yellow House and sometimes painting side by side, but the bonhomie didn't last. They argued long and hard about art, with van Gogh complaining, "Sometimes we come out of our arguments with our heads as exhausted as a used electric battery". Later, Gauguin claimed that van Gogh threatened him during several of these arguments: whether this is true or not, Gauguin had certainly already decided to return to Paris by the time the two had a ferocious quarrel on the night of December 23. The argument was so bad that Gauguin left to stay at the local hotel, and when he returned in the morning, he was faced by the police. After Gauguin's hasty exit, a deeply disturbed van Gogh had taken a razor to his **ear**, severing part of it before presenting the selected slice to a prostitute at the local brothel – in van Gogh's addled state he may well have forged some sort of connection with bullfighting, where the dead bull's ears are cut off and given as a prize to the bullfighter. Hours after Gauguin's return, van Gogh was admitted to hospital, the first of several extended stays before, fearing for his sanity, he committed himself to the asylum of St Rémy in May 1889. Here, the doctor's initial assessment described him as suffering from "**acute mania**, with hallucinations of sight and hearing"; van Gogh attributed his parlous state to excessive drinking and smoking, though he gave up neither during his year-long stay.

In May 1890, feeling lonely and homesick, van Gogh discharged himself from St Rémy and headed north to Paris before proceeding on to the village of Auvers-sur-Oise. At first, his health improved and he even began to garner critical recognition for his work. However, his twin ogres of **depression and loneliness** soon returned to haunt him and, in despair, van Gogh shot himself in the chest. This wasn't, however, the end; he didn't manage to kill himself outright, but took 27 hours to die, even enduring a police visit when he refused to answer any questions, pronouncing: "I am free to do what I like with my own body".

– Gauguin, Millet, Anton Mauve, and Charles Daubigny all feature. Above, on the **first floor** are paintings by the artist himself, mostly displayed chronologically, starting with the dark, sombre works of the early years like *The Potato Eater*. The collection continues with the brighter palate he adopted in Arles, superbly represented by one of the artist's *Sunflowers* series, intensely – almost obsessively – rendered in the deepest oranges, golds and ochres. While van Gogh was in the asylum in St Rémy, his approach to nature became more abstract, as evidenced by his unsettling *Wheatfield with a Reaper*, the dense, knotty *Undergrowth* and his palpable *Irises*. Van Gogh is at his most expressionistic here, the paint applied thickly, often with a palette knife, a practice he continued in his final, tortured works painted at **Auvers-sur-Oise**, where he lodged for the last three months of his life. It was at Auvers that he painted the frantic *Wheatfield with Crows*, in which the fields swirl and writhe under weird, dark skies, as well as the deeply disturbing *Tree Roots*.

The two floors above provide backup to the main collection. The **second floor** hosts temporary exhibitions focusing on aspects of van Gogh's art and life, while the **third floor** has a conservation and restoration area, more drawings and sketches from the permanent collection and temporary exhibitions illustrating yet more of van Gogh's artistic influences.

The Stedelijk Museum

Paulus Potterstraat 13 • Tues & Wed 11am–5pm, Thurs 11am–10pm, Fri–Sun 10am–6pm • €15 • ☎ 020 573 2911, Ⓦ stedelijk.nl

The **Stedelijk Museum** has long been Amsterdam's number one venue for modern and contemporary art. The museum focuses on cutting-edge, **temporary exhibitions** of modern art, from photography and video through to sculpture and collage, and these are supplemented by a regularly rotated selection from the museum's large and wide-ranging **permanent collection**. Among many highlights, the latter includes a particularly large sample of the work of **Piet Mondriaan** (1872–1944), from his early, muddy abstracts to the boldly coloured rectangular blocks for which he's most famous. The Stedelijk is also strong on **Kasimir Malevich** (1878–1935), whose dense attempts at Cubism lead to the dynamism and bold, primary tones of his "Suprematist" paintings – slices, blocks and bolts of colour that shift around as if about to resolve themselves into some complex computer graphic. Other high spots include several **Marc Chagall** paintings and a number of pictures by American Abstract Expressionists Mark Rothko, Ellsworth Kelly and Barnett Newman, plus the odd work by Lichtenstein, Warhol, Robert Ryman, Kooning and Jean Dubuffet.

The Concertgebouw

Concertgebouwplein 10 • English-language guided tours Sun 12.15–1.15pm & Mon 5–6pm • €10 • Box office ☎ 020 671 8345, Ⓦ concertgebouw.nl

The **Concertgebouw** (Concert Hall) is home of the famed – and much recorded – **Koninklijk Concertgebouworkest** (Royal Concertgebouw Orchestra; Ⓦ concertgebouworkest.nl). When the German composer Brahms visited Amsterdam in the 1870s he was scathing about the locals' lack of culture and in particular their lack of an even halfway suitable venue for his music. In the face of such ridicule, a consortium of Amsterdam businessmen got together to fund the construction of a brand-new concert hall and the result was the Concertgebouw, completed in 1888. Since then it has become renowned among musicians and concertgoers for its marvellous acoustics, and after a facelift in the early 1990s it is looking and sounding better than ever. The **guided tour** takes in the Grote Zaal and Kleine Zaal auditoria, as well as various behind-the-scenes activities – control rooms, piano stores, artistes' dressing rooms and the like.

1

The Vondelpark

Several entrances off van Baerlestraat · Daily dawn to dusk · Free · ⓦ vondelpark.nl

Central Amsterdam is short of green spaces, which makes the leafy expanse of the **Vondelpark** doubly welcome. This is easily the largest and most popular of the city's parks, its network of footpaths used by a healthy slice of the city's population. The park dates back to 1864, when a group of leading Amsterdammers clubbed together to transform the soggy marshland that lay beyond the Leidseplein into a landscaped park. The group, who were impressed by the contemporary English fashion for natural (as distinct from formal) landscaping, gave the park commission to the Zocher family, big-time gardeners who set about their task with gusto, completing their work in 1865. Named after the seventeenth-century poet **Joost van den Vondel**, the park proved an immediate success and was expanded to its present size (45 hectares) in 1877. It's now home to over 100 species of tree, a wide variety of local and imported plants, and – among many incidental features – a **bandstand**, an excellent **rose garden** and a grand **statue** of a pensive Vondel, shown seated with quill in hand, near the park's main entrance. Neither did the Zochers forget their Dutch roots: the park is latticed with ponds and narrow waterways, home to many species of wildfowl, including numerous heron, though it's the large colony of (very noisy) bright green parakeets which grabs the attention. The Vondelpark has several different children's play areas and during the summer regularly hosts free concerts and theatrical performances, mostly in its **open-air theatre**.

The Heineken Experience

Stadhouderskade 78 · Daily 11am–7pm · €17 · ☏ 020 523 9222, ⓦ heinekenexperience.com · Tram #16 or #24 from Centraal Station

Overlooking the Singelgracht canal, the former Heineken brewery is a whopping modern building that now holds the **Heineken Experience**. The brewery was Heineken's headquarters from 1864 to 1988, when the company was restructured and brewing was moved to a more efficient location out of town. Since then, Heineken has developed the site for tourists with lots of gimmicky but fun attractions such as virtual reality tours and displays on the history of Heineken, from advertising campaigns to beer-making. The old brewing facilities with their vast copper vats are included on the self-guided tour (allow an hour or so) but for many the main draw is the free beer you get to quaff at the end in the bar – two drinks, and a souvenir glass.

ARRIVAL AND DEPARTURE   AMSTERDAM

Schiphol Amsterdam's international airport, is a quick and convenient train ride from Amsterdam Centraal Station, the city's international train station, which is itself just a 10min metro ride from Amstel Station, the terminus for long-distance and international buses. Centraal Station is also the hub of an excellent public transport network, whose trams, buses and metro combine to delve into every corner of the city and its suburbs.

BY PLANE

Schiphol airport (☏ 0900 0141, premium line reachable from within the Netherlands only, ⓦ schiphol.nl) is located about 15km southwest of the city centre. The taxi fare from the airport to the city centre is about €50.

TRAINS TO THE CITY

There are fast and frequent trains from the airport to Amsterdam Centraal Station (6am–midnight every 10min, midnight–6am hourly; 15min; one-way €3.80; ⓦ ns.nl).

SHUTTLE BUS TO THE CITY

The Connexxion Schiphol Hotel Shuttle runs a shuttle-bus service between the airport and most of the city's hotels (every 30min; 6am–9pm; €16 one-way, €26 return; ☏ 038 339 4741, ⓦ schipholhotelshuttle.nl). Tickets are available from the Connexxion desk in the arrivals hall and shuttle buses depart from the stops just outside; journey times vary considerably depending on the hotel.

BY TRAIN

Centraal Station (CS) is conveniently located right in the city centre, and has services to and from every other Dutch city as well as from several key cities in Germany, France and Belgium. Domestic trains are operated by NS (ⓦ ns.nl), international services by several companies (see Basics, p.25). The station has all the facilities you would expect, including ATMs, a bureau de change, coin-operated

PARKING IN AMSTERDAM

On-street parking in Amsterdam is limited and expensive. Every city-centre street where parking is permitted is **metered** between 9am and midnight from Monday to Saturday, from midday to midnight on Sunday, with a standard cost of €5 an hour, €30 a day, and €20 for the evening (7pm to midnight). **Tickets** are available from meters, which give instructions in several languages. If you overrun your ticket, you can expect to be clamped and fined. **Car parks** in the centre charge comparable rates to the metered street spaces, but those on the outskirts are a good deal less expensive and are invariably but a short journey from the centre by public transport. The city also operates a reasonably priced **Park and Ride scheme** (details on ⓦ iamsterdam.com), with regular bus connections into the centre. Note also that some of the better hotels either have their own parking spaces or offer special deals with nearby car parks.

luggage lockers and a staffed left-luggage office. Just outside the station on Stationsplein, where there is a taxi rank as well as the tourist office – the VVV (see below) – and the information office of GVB (see below), which operates Amsterdam's trams, metro and buses; Stationsplein is also the hub of the city's public transport system with multiple tram and bus stops.

DESTINATIONS

Alkmaar (every 15min; 35–45mins); Apeldoorn (every 30min; 1hr 10min); Arnhem (every 15min; 1hr 10min); Den Helder (every 30min; 1hr 15min); Dordrecht (every 20min; 1hr 20min); Eindhoven (every 20min; 1hr 20min); Enkhuizen (every 20min; 1hr); Groningen (every 30min; 2hr 20min); Haarlem (every 10min; 15min); The Hague/ Den Haag (every 15min; 50min); Hoorn (every 20min; 35min); Leeuwarden (every 30min; 2hr 20min); Leiden (every 15min; 35–45mins); Maastricht (every 30min; 2hr 30min); Nijmegen (every 15min; 1hr 30min); Rotterdam (every 15min; 1hr); Schiphol Airport (every 15min; 15min); Utrecht (every 15min; 30min); Vlissingen (every 30min; 2hr 45min); Zwolle (every 30min; 1hr 15min).

BY BUS
AMSTEL STATION

Long-distance, international buses to Amsterdam,

including services operated by Eurolines (ⓦ eurolines.nl), arrive at Amstelstation, about 3.5km to the southeast of Centraal Station. The metro journey from here to Centraal Station takes about 10min.

CENTRAAL STATION

Amsterdam's Centraal Station is the hub of the city's excellent public transport system, which is operated by GVB (ⓦ gvb.nl): trams and buses depart from Stationsplein, which is also the location of a metro station and a GVB public transport information office. Buses to Noord-Holland destinations, such as Edam (hourly; 40min); Marken (every 30min; 30min); Monnickendam (every 30min; 20min) and Volendam (hourly; 30min), run by several different companies, also leave from Stationsplein.

BY CAR

Arriving by car on either the A4/E19 from Den Haag (The Hague) or the A2/E35 from Utrecht, you should experience few traffic problems, and the city centre is clearly signposted as soon as you approach Amsterdam's southern reaches. Both roads feed onto the A10 ring road; on its west side, leave the A10 at either the Osdorp or Geuzenveld exits for the city centre. However, be warned that driving in central Amsterdam – never mind parking – is extremely difficult (see box above).

INFORMATION

Tourist office The main information desk of the VVV, Amsterdam's official tourist bureau, is located on Stationsplein, across from the entrance to Centraal Station (July to early Sept Mon–Sat 9am–7pm; rest of year Sun–Thurs 9am–5pm, Fri & Sat 9am–6pm; ☎ 020 201 8800, ⓦ iamsterdam.com). They take bookings in person (and online) for canal cruises and other organized excursions and operate an extremely efficient accommodation reservation service, though at peak times the wait can be long.

Tickets The Amsterdam Uitburo Ticketshop (Mon–Fri 10am–7pm, Sat 10am–6pm, Sun noon–6pm; ☎ 020 795

9950, ⓦ iamsterdam.com), in the Stadsschouwburg on Leidseplein, sells tickets for most upcoming performances, from rock and classical concerts through to theatre and opera. They also operate a last-minute ticket discount scheme, carry a range of promotional flyers and listings magazines (see p.93), and sell public transport cards (see p.82), but do not book accommodation.

Discount cards and passes The VVV's much-touted I Amsterdam City Card provides free and unlimited use of the city's public transport network, a complimentary canal cruise and free admission to the bulk of the city's museums and attractions. It costs €40 for 24hr, €50 for

1

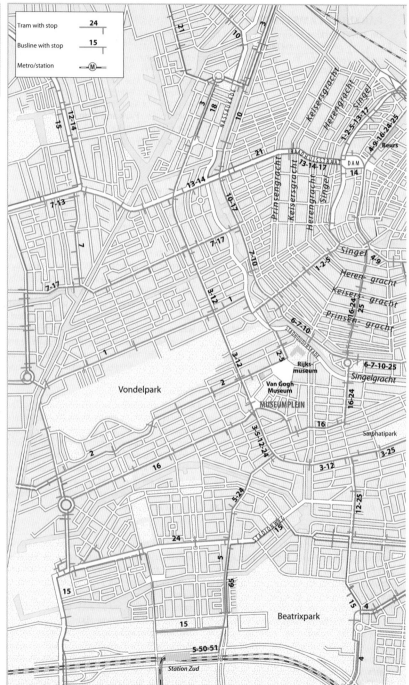

Tram with stop	24
Busline with stop	15
Metro/station	⟨M⟩

Beurs

DAM

Singel

Herengracht

Keisersgracht

Prinsengracht

Singelgracht

Rijks-museum

Van Gogh Museum

MUSEUMPLEIN

Vondelpark

Sarphatipark

Beatrixpark

Station Zud

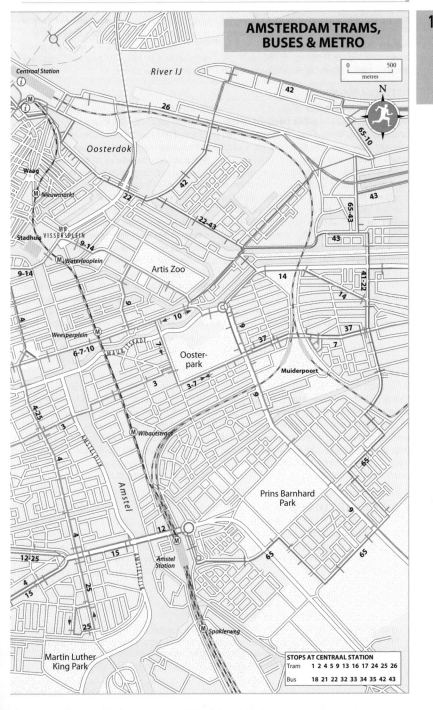

AMSTERDAM TRAMS, BUSES & METRO

STOPS AT CENTRAAL STATION	
Tram	1 2 4 5 9 13 16 17 24 25 26
Bus	18 21 22 32 33 34 35 42 43

1

48hr and €60 for 72hr. Altogether it's not a bad deal, but you have to work fairly hard to make it worthwhile. It's available in person and online from the VVV on Stationsplein and the Ticketshop on Leidseplein (see box, p.93). Another option is the Museumkaart (Museum Card; ⓦ museumkaart.nl), which gives free entry to most museums in the whole of the Netherlands for a year; it costs €40 (less if you're 18 or under) and you can purchase one at any participating museum – most major museums are in the scheme.

GETTING AROUND

BY PUBLIC TRANSPORT

Amsterdam has a first-rate **public transport system**, comprising trams, buses, a one-line metro and four passenger ferries across the River IJ to the northern suburbs. Centraal Station is the hub of this transit system. Trams, buses and the metro operate daily between 6am and midnight, supplemented by a limited number of night buses (*nachtbussen*) on major routes. Almost all tram and bus stops display a detailed map of the network. The whole system is operated by **GVB**, whose main information/ticketing office is opposite Centraal Station on Stationsplein (Mon–Fri 7am–9pm, Sat & Sun 10am–6pm; ☎ 0900 8011, ⓦ gvb.nl); here they also issue free transit maps.

TICKETS AND FARES

To travel on the GVB network, you will need an electronic OV-chipkaart of one type or another (see Basics, p.25). Bus and tram drivers issue disposable, paper OV-chipkaart that are valid for 1hr and cost €2.70. More economical are the disposable, paper OV-chipkaart that offer unlimited travel on the GVB system for 24hr (€7.50), 48hr (€12) or 72hr (€16). These are available from the GVB office on Stationsplein, at metro stations and at many hotels. In all cases, the OV-chipkaart must be scanned as you enter and leave the GVB network – if you forget your *chipkaart* will become invalid. Note that these paper OV-chipkaart are not valid on NS trains, where you'll need either a plastic OV-chipkaart or an ordinary (paper) ticket.

BY CANAL

Canal Bus (☎ 020 626 5574, ⓦ canal.nl). A good way to get around Amsterdam's waterways, the Canal Bus operates on three circular routes, coloured green, red and blue, which meet at various places, including the jetty outside Centraal Station and on the Singelgracht between the Rijksmuseum and Leidseplein. There are seventeen stops in all and together they give easy access to all the major sights. Boats leave from opposite Centraal Station every half an hour or so during high season between 9.30am and 6pm, and a day ticket for all three routes, allowing you to hop on and off as many times as you like, costs €22/adult, €12 for children (4–12 years old); it's also worth considering the 24hr ticket, which costs just €2 more.

Museum Line (☎ 020 530 5412, ⓦ lovers.nl), A similar boat service to Canal Bus, this calls at seven jetties located at or near several of the city's major attractions. It departs from outside Centraal Station (every 30min; 10am–5pm) and a day ticket costs €16, €8 for children (4–12 years old).

Canal Bikes (☎ 020 623 9886, ⓦ canal.nl). These are four-seater pedaloes which take a lifetime to get anywhere but are nevertheless good fun unless – of course – it's raining. You can rent them at four locations – on the Singelgracht opposite the Rijksmuseum; the Prinsengracht outside the Anne Frank Huis; on Keizersgracht at Leidsestraat; and behind Leidseplein. Rental prices per person per hour are €7 (3–4 persons) or €8 (1–2 persons), plus a refundable deposit of €20. Pedaloes can be picked up at one location and left at any of the others (daily 10am–6pm, July & Aug until 10pm).

CITY CANAL TOURS

No one could say the Amsterdam tourist industry doesn't make the most of its canals, with a veritable armada of glass-topped **cruise boats** shuttling along the city's waterways, offering everything from quick hour-long excursions to fully-fledged dinner cruises. There are several major operators and they occupy the prime pitches, either the jetties near Centraal Station on Stationsplein or beside the first part of the Damrak. Despite the competition, **prices** are fairly uniform with a one-hour tour costing around €14 per adult, €7 per child (4–12 years old). The big companies, for example **Lovers** (☎ 020 530 5412, ⓦ lovers.nl), also run a lot of different themed cruises – candlelight cruises, cocktail cruises, etc – with tickets costing in the region of €32–35, though dinner cruises will rush you about €75. All the basic cruises are extremely popular and long queues are common throughout the summer. One way of avoiding much of the crush is to walk down the Damrak from Centraal Station to the jetty at the near end of the Rokin, where **Reederij P. Kooij** (☎ 020 623 3810, ⓦ rederijkooij.nl), which also has a jetty beside Centraal Station, offers all the basic cruises at cheaper prices. For other types of canal transport, see above.

1

BY BIKE

One of the most agreeable ways to explore Amsterdam is **by bicycle**. The city has an excellent network of designated bicycle lanes (*fietspaden*) and for once cycling isn't a fringe activity – there are cyclists everywhere. Indeed, much to the chagrin of the city's taxi drivers, the needs of the cyclist take precedence over those of the motorist and by law if there's a collision it's always the driver's fault.

BIKE RENTAL

Bike rental is straightforward. There are lots of rental companies (*fietsenverhuur*), including Bike City, Bloemgracht 70 (☎020 626 3721, ⓦbikecity.nl); Damstraat Rent-a-Bike, Damstraat 20 (☎020 625 5029, ⓦrentabike.nl); Yellow Bikes, Nieuwezijds Kolk 29 (020 620 6940, ⓦyellowbike.nl); and MacBike (ⓦmacbike .nl) at Centraal Station, Stationsplein 5 (☎020 624 8391), Waterlooplein 199 (☎020 428 7005), Weteringschans 2 (☎020 528 7688), and Marnixstraat 220 (☎020 626 6964). Standard bicycles cost around €8 for three hours, €12/day, €20 for two days. All rental companies ask for some type of security, usually in the form of a cash deposit (some will take credit card imprints) or passport.

BY CAR

Driving Central Amsterdam is geared up for trams and bicycles rather than cars; motorists have to negotiate a convoluted one-way system, avoid getting boxed onto tram lines, and steer round herds of cyclists.
Car rental Europcar, Overtoom 197 ☎020 683 2123; Hertz, Overtoom 333 ☎020 612 2441.

BY TAXI

Taxi Taxi ranks are liberally distributed across the city centre and taxis can also be hailed on the street. If all else fails, call Taxicentrale on ☎020 777 7777.
Fares Taxi fares are tightly regulated with, for instance, a 2km trip costing €7.5, €10 for 3km, and €25 for 10km.

ACCOMMODATION

Despite a slew of new hotels, from chic designer places through to chain high-rises, hotel accommodation in Amsterdam can be difficult to find, and is often a major expense, especially at peak times of the year – July and August, Easter and Christmas. Indeed, such is the popularity of Amsterdam as a short-break destination that you'd be well advised to make an **advance reservation** at any time of the year – either direct or via the VVV's website (ⓦiamsterdam.com). That said, most hotels only charge the full quoted rates at the very busiest times, which means that you'll often pay less than the peak-season prices quoted in this book, and **breakfast** is included (unless otherwise indicated) as is, in most cases, free wi-fi. Another bonus is that the city's compactness means that you're pretty much bound to end up somewhere within easy reach of the centre. Amsterdam also does well for **hostels**, though they do vary in quality from the (very) rough and ready to the passable if frugal.

HOTELS

THE OLD CENTRE

Hotel des Arts Rokin 154–56 ☎020 620 1558, ⓦhoteldesarts.nl; map p.51. The 22 rooms here in this tall and slender, seventeenth-century canal house are cosy and well furnished, and the welcome is friendly. An excellent location, too. Canal-facing rooms attract a small premium. **€140**
Hotel de l'Europe Nieuwe Doelenstraat 2–14 ☎020 531 1777, ⓦleurope.nl; map p.51. One of the city's swankiest hotels and one that retains a wonderful *fin-de-siècle* charm, with large, well-furnished rooms and an attractive riverside terrace. This is about as luxurious as the city gets and although it's pricey, special deals and discounts are commonplace. **€500**
The Exchange Damrak 50 ☎020 523 0080, ⓦexchangeamsterdam.com; see map p.51. A second hotel from the guys who run the distinctive *Lloyd Hotel* in the Oosterdok (Eastern Docklands see p.85), and they've stayed true to their creative roots here, letting the students of the Amsterdam Fashion Institute loose on most of the guest rooms, which range from two- to five- star in quality and price. It's all pretty wacky, with a range of rooms decorated every which way – one of the best has bespoke wire furniture, in another you sleep in a giant tent – and at the low to moderate range it's one of the best hotels there is. **€150**
Le Coin Nieuwe Doelenstraat 5 ☎020 524 6800, ⓦlecoin.nl; map p.51. A good location opposite the swanky *Hotel de l'Europe*, but a quarter of the price, though breakfast is an extra €11.50. All rooms have kitchenettes and are kitted out in contemporary style. **€145**
★ **Misc** Kloveniersburgwal 20 ☎020 330 6241, ⓦhotelmisc.nl; map p.51. Very friendly hotel occupying a tastefully renovated canal house on the edge of the Red Light District. Has six good-sized rooms, each decorated with a different theme – Africa, Baroque and so forth – and half of them overlook the canal (for which there is a premium of about €20). Excellent value. **€155**
NH City Centre Spuistraat 288 ☎020 795 6088, ⓦnh-hotels.com; map p.51. This appealing chain hotel occupies a sympathetically renovated 1920s Art Deco former textile factory, and is well situated for the cafés and

1

bars of the Spui, and the Museum Quarter. Rooms vary in size, some have canal views, and all boast extremely comfy beds and good showers. The buffet breakfast is extra (€20), but will set you up for the day. **€150**

Rho Nes 5 ☎020 620 7371, ⓦrhohotel.com; map p.51. Built as a theatre in 1908, the lovely, high-ceilinged, *fin-de-siècle* lobby gives a slightly misleading impression: the rooms beyond are on the small side and have been unimaginatively modernized. Still, it's pleasant enough, and in a handy central location down a rather gloomy side street just off Dam Square. **€125**

Winston Warmoesstraat 129 ☎020 623 1380, ⓦwinston.nl; map p.51. This self-consciously young and cool hotel (doubles €44–55) and hostel (dorm beds €33–40) has funky, mostly en-suite rooms individually decorated with wacky art, as well as a busy ground-floor bar that has regular live music. It's a formula that works a treat; the *Winston* is popular and often full – though the bargain-basement prices are undoubtedly the main magnet. A ten-minute walk from Centraal Station. **€44**

THE GRACHTENGORDEL

★ **Ambassade** Herengracht 341 ☎020 555 0222, ⓦambassade-hotel.nl; map pp.48–49. Eminently appealing hotel that occupies a series of cleverly renovated seventeenth-century canal houses in one of the most beautiful corners of the city. There are 58 rooms, each decorated in period-meets-country-house style, mostly in pastel shades with top-notch furnishings and fittings including good, big beds and high-spec bathrooms. There's also a well-stocked library, a study room with modern art and guests get significant discounts at a "Float & Massage" centre just a few doors away. Breakfast is taken in the elegant, panelled room, where the original merchant-owners once surveyed the scene. **€230**

Dylan Keizersgracht 384 ☎020 530 2010, ⓦdylanamsterdam.com; map pp.48–49. This stylish, medium-sized boutique hotel is housed in a seventeenth-century mansion that centres on a beautiful courtyard and terrace. Its sumptuous rooms range in style from opulent reds or greens to minimal white and oatmeal shades, and all have flat-screen TVs. The ambience is hip without being pretentious, and that goes for the staff too, making the hotel extremely popular. Luxury suites overlooking the Keizersgracht canal will set you back at least €600, but standard doubles start at a more feasible **€350**

Estherea Singel 303–9 ☎020 624 5146, ⓦestherea .nl; map pp.48–49. A comfortable, four-star hotel occupying a pair of sympathetically modernized old canal houses in a great location, a brief stroll from the Spui. There's no minimalism here – the carpets are thick and plush, the public areas rich in browns and reds. The guest rooms are similar in style, with beds that you can sink into, and the pick of them overlook the canal. Rack rates are

around €330 excluding breakfast (an extra €16), but special deals are commonplace. **€330**

't Hotel Leliegracht 18 ☎020 422 2741, ⓦthotel.nl; map pp.48–49. Appealing, low-key hotel located in an old high-gabled house along a quiet stretch of canal. The eight spacious rooms – three with canal views – are decked out in a pleasant, unassuming modern style with large beds, TV, fridge and either bath or shower. Minimum three-night stay at weekends. **€150**

Prinsenhof Prinsengracht 810 ☎020 623 1772, ⓦhotelprinsenhof.com; map pp.48–49. In an old canal house, this small, family-run hotel is one of the city's top budget options, with great-value double rooms – both en suite (€89) and with shared facilities (€69). The public rooms are attractively decorated and kitted out with all manner of bygones and although the guest rooms beyond are quite small and plain at these prices you can't complain. Booking essential. **€69**

★ **Seven Bridges** Reguliersgracht 31 ☎020 623 1329, ⓦsevenbridgeshotel.nl; map pp.48–49. One of the city's most charming hotels – and excellent value for money too. Takes its name from its canal-side location, which affords a view of no less than seven dinky little bridges – though you'll pay extra for a room with a view. Beautifully decorated in antique style, its spotless rooms are regularly revamped, and it's small and popular, so advance reservations are pretty much essential. Breakfast is served in your room – and costs an extra €13. **€140**

★ **Toren** Keizersgracht 164 ☎020 622 6033, ⓦhoteltoren.nl; map pp.48–49. Cosy, retro-chic boutique hotel, converted from two elegant canal houses, where the emphasis is on intimacy and comfort. All rooms have been tastefully renovated, and there's an annexe if the main building is full. There's a nice bar/breakfast room downstairs and the staff are very friendly and attentive. **€200**

Wiechmann Prinsengracht 328–332 ☎020 626 3321, ⓦhotelwiechmann.nl; map pp.48–49. Family-run for over fifty years, this medium-sized hotel occupies an attractively restored canal house close to the Anne Frank Huis. The foyer, with its assortment of bygones and antique beamed ceiling, sets the tone and the guest rooms beyond are restrained and traditional in style. **€130**

TOP 5 CANAL-SIDE HOTELS

Staying in a renovated canal house, with a view over the water is one of the real treats of Amsterdam. Here's our favourite canal-side accommodation:

Ambassade See p.84
Estherea See p.84
The Posthoorn See p.85
Seven Bridges See p.84
Toren See p.84

1

THE JORDAAN

Van Onna Bloemgracht 104 ☎020 626 5801, ⓦhotelvanonna.nl; map pp.48–49. A quiet, well-maintained, one-star hotel on a tranquil canal. The building dates back over three hundred years and still retains some of its original fixtures, though the rooms themselves are rather modest, with basic furnishings and fittings. **€100**

THE OLD JEWISH QUARTER AND THE OOSTERDOK

Arena 's-Gravesandestraat 51 ☎020 850 2400, ⓦhotelarena.nl; map pp.48–49. In a handsomely renovated old convent on the edge of the Oosterpark, this hip four-star hotel comes complete with split-level rooms and minimalist decor. Despite the odd pretentious flourish, it manages to retain a relaxed vibe, attracting businesspeople and travellers alike. Lively bar, intimate restaurant, and late-night club (Fri & Sat) located within the former chapel. Breakfast an extra €20. Tram #9 from Centraal Station; get off at the Mauritskade stop. **€200**

Lloyd Hotel Oostelijke Handelskade 34 ☎020 561 3636, ⓦlloydhotel.com; map pp.48–49. In the flourishing Oosterdok district, east along the River IJ from Centraal Station, this ex-prison and migrant workers' hostel has been renovated to become one of Amsterdam's grooviest hotels – and a self-billed "Cultural Embassy". Uniquely, it serves all kinds of travellers, with rooms ranging from one-star affairs (€100) to five-star offerings (€280). Some rooms are great, others not, so don't be afraid to ask to change, and the location is better than you might think – just five minutes by tram #26 from Centraal Station. **€100**

THE MUSEUM QUARTER AND THE VONDELPARK

Bilderberg Hotel Jan Luyken Jan Luykenstraat 58 ☎020 573 0730, ⓦbilderberg.nl; map pp.48–49. One of a small chain, this medium-sized hotel inhabits a substantial nineteenth-century red-brick building near the Rijksmuseum. The guest rooms are fairly standard – modern and undistinguished – but comfortable for all that. Competitive rates. **€140**

★ **College** Roelof Hartstraat 1 ☎020 571 1511, ⓦthecollegehotel.com; map pp.48–49. Converted from an old schoolhouse, *College* is one of the most elegant and original recent additions to Amsterdam's hotel scene. It's original for being largely run by students from the city's catering school, and elegant because of the sheer class of the refurbishment. **€200**

Conservatorium Van Baerlestraat 27 ☎020 570 0000, ⓦconservatoriumhotel.com; map pp.48–49. This slick, supra-modern hotel is a five-star addition to the Amsterdam scene, its 129 deluxe rooms shoehorned into an older building directly opposite the Stedelijk Museum. Has every facility, including its own spa. **€300**

Fita Jan Luykenstraat 37 ☎020 679 0976, ⓦfita.nl; map pp.48–49. Handily located on a quiet side street near the Rijksmuseum, this agreeable family-run hotel has a small selection of reasonably priced, modern rooms. Great breakfasts – try the tasty pancakes. **€140**

JL 76 Jan Luykenstraat 76 ☎020 515 0453, ⓦvondelhotels.com; map pp.48–49. The latest addition to a small group of boutique hotels, this medium-sized hotel has cool, sleek and simple rooms, with great beds, iPod docks, coffee machines and DVD players – you can even watch TV in the bath. There's a pleasant lounge downstairs with an honesty bar and iPad for guests' use. One of the best options in the area. **€250**

Owl Hotel Roemer Visscherstraat 1 ☎020 618 9484, ⓦowl-hotel.nl; map pp.48–49. The reasonably priced doubles at this family-run hotel have rather bland decor, but the location – not far from the Leidesplein – is nice and quiet and the downstairs lounge opens out onto a pleasant garden. **€110**

Piet Hein Vossiusstraat 53 ☎020 662 7205, ⓦhotelpiethein.com; map pp.48–49. Five minutes' walk from Leidseplein, the guest rooms at this sleek and slick boutique hotel are decorated in sharp modern style with shades of black and white to the fore. Some of the rooms overlook the Vondelpark and there's a patio and garden too. **€175**

B&BS

Marcel's Creative Exchange Leidsestraat 87 ☎020 622 9834, ⓦmarcelamsterdam.com; map pp.48–49. Owned and operated by a graphic designer and artist, this popular B&B is a stylishly restored house with three attractive en-suite doubles. Relaxing and peaceful amid the buzz of the city, with regulars returning year after year, so you'll need to book well in advance in high season. Breakfast isn't included, but guests have access to the kitchen, where there are tea- and coffee-making facilities, a fridge and a microwave. **€120**

The Posthoorn Prinsengracht 7 ☎068 173 50 24, ⓦposthoornamsterdam.com map pp.48–49. Well-regarded B&B in a great location overlooking the Prinsengracht. It has three accomplished guest rooms, each decorated in engaging tones of cream and grey. Minimum two-night stay. **€120**

HOSTELS

Bulldog Hotel Oudezijds Voorburgwal 220 ☎020 620 3822, ⓦbulldoghotel.com; map p.51. Part of the *Bulldog* coffeeshop chain, with a newly renovated lounge for "chill'n, drink'n & puff'n", this laidback, low-budget hostel-cum-hotel has dorm beds (from €20 per person in a double bed), double rooms (€120) and apartments (from

1

€150). The decor is bright, modern and frugal, but all the rooms – including the dorms – are en suite and there are lockable lockers throughout. Doubles €120

Cocomama Westeinde 18 ☏020 627 2454, ⓦcocomama.nl; map pp.48–49. This relatively new hotel-hostel, in what was once a brothel, has a communal vibe, with a communal kitchen and sitting room on the lower ground floor, as well as a garden beyond. The upper levels have a nice mix of small dorms and private rooms, each with a different theme. Dorm beds €36, doubles €100

Flying Pig Uptown Vossiusstraat 46 ☏020 400 4187, ⓦflyingpig.nl; map pp.48–49. The better of the city's two *Flying Pig* hostels, facing the Vondelpark and close to the night-time frenzy of Leidseplein. Free use of kitchen facilities, no curfew and good tourist information, plus a bar and smoking room. Dorm beds in a fourteen-bunk room start at €36, doubles with shared facilities €80. Great value; lively vibe. €80

Shelter Jordaan Bloemstraat 179 ☏020 624 4717, ⓦwww.shelter.nl; map pp.48–49. Medium-sized Christian youth hostel with single-sex, four- to eighteen-bunk dorms with shared facilities. Each bed has a locker, there's a café, a lounge, free wi-fi and a courtyard garden.

Located in a particularly attractive and quiet part of the Jordaan, close to the Lijnbaansgracht canal. Prices include breakfast. Dorm beds €31

Stay Okay Hostel Amsterdam Stadsdoelen Kloveniersburgwal 97 ☏020 624 6832, ⓦstayokay .com; map p.51. Rather more basic than its sister hostel in the Vondelpark, but more centrally located, the *Stadsdoelen* has a laundry, a breakfast room, free wi-fi and bike storage. Most of the beds are in dorms holding between four and ten bunk beds, but there are a few double rooms too, and prices include breakfast. Dorm beds €33, doubles €86

Stay Okay Hostel Amsterdam Vondelpark Zandpad 5 ☏020 589 8996, ⓦstayokay.com; map pp.48–49. Pleasantly located on the perimeter of the Vondelpark, this is the more accomplished of the city's two HI hostels, with a good range of facilities, including a bar, restaurant, TV lounge, internet access and bike rental, plus various discounts on tours and museums. Rates vary, but in season expect to pay €33–38 for a dorm bed including breakfast in a six- to ten-bunk room – there are no singles or doubles. Secure lockers and no curfew. To be sure of a place in high season you'll need to book at least two months ahead. Dorm beds €33

EATING

Traditionally at least, Amsterdam has never been one of Europe's culinary hotspots, but there has been a resurgence of interest in Dutch cooking in recent years and the city has accumulated a string of excellent home-grown **restaurants**. It also boasts tremendous gastronomic diversity – as well as having some of the best Indonesian food outside Indonesia, at hard-to-beat prices, there are lots of ethnic restaurants, from French, Iberian and Italian, to Thai, Middle Eastern and Indian. Amsterdam also excels in the quantity and variety of its **eetcafés**, **cafés and lunch spots**, many of which serve increasingly adventurous and inexpensive food in a wide range of settings. These establishments are generally open all day, might serve alcohol (in which case they are often very similar to bars), but don't allow dope-smoking – and are not to be confused with the city's druggy "**coffeeshops**" (the signage is very different).

THE OLD CENTRE

CAFÉS, TEAROOMS AND LUNCH VENUES

Café de Jaren Nieuwe Doelenstraat 20 ☏020 625 5771, ⓦcafedejaren.nl; map p.51. Overlooking the River Amstel, next to the university, this large café, with three floors and two terraces, has a cool vibe and a laid-back clientele. A great place to read the Sunday papers – unusually you'll find English ones here. It serves reasonably priced food too, and there's a great salad bar. Daily 9.30am–1am, Fri & Sat till 2am.

Café Luxembourg Spui 24 ☏020 620 6264, ⓦluxembourg.nl; map p.51. Long and deep café-bar with a pleasant pavement terrace and an elegant, if faded, area at the back overlooking the Singel canal. Competent, reasonably priced food – and possibly the best hamburgers in town. Very popular. Daily 9am–midnight (Fri & Sat till 1am).

Hofje van Wijs Zeedijk 43 ☏020 624 0436,

ⓦhofjevanwijs.nl; map p.51. Lovely, cosy little place in an old courtyard, where the shop and café sell a truly international range of coffees and teas. The café also serves tasty home-made Dutch food – try the *hachee* (beef stew); a snip at just €9. Tues–Sun noon–6pm.

★ **Latei** Zeedijk 143 ☏020 6257485, ⓦlatei.net; map p.51. Homely shop and café that sells bric-a-brac as well as serving good coffee and decent lunches. Quite a find if you fancy something different from the Chinese restaurants that dominate this end of Zeedijk. Mon–Wed 8am–6pm, Thurs & Fri 8am–10pm, Sat 9am–10pm, Sun 11am–6pm.

't Nieuwe Kafe Eggerstraat 8 ☏020 6272830, ⓦnieuwe-kafe.nl; map p.51. Beside the Nieuwe Kerk, this straightforward modern café is popular with shoppers and tourists alike, serving reasonably priced breakfasts, lunches and light meals. Great pancakes too. Daily 8.30am–6pm.

1

★ **Puccini** Staalstraat 21 ☎ 020 620 84 58, ⊕ puccini .nl; map p.51. Lovely little café that serves great salads, sandwiches, cakes and pastries in bright modern premises. A few doors down from its sister chocolate shop (see p.98). Mon–Fri 8.30am–6pm, Sat & Sun 10am–6pm.

Villa Zeezicht Torensteeg 7 ☎ 020 626 7433; map p.51. In a handy central location, this laidback little café, with its boho-meets-ramshackle decor, serves up a good line in home-made food from breakfast in the morning to dinner at night. Bargain prices and great tomato soup. Daily 9am–9pm.

RESTAURANTS

★ **Bird** Zeedijk 77 ☎ 020 420 6289, ⊕ thai-bird.nl; map p.51. This Thai canteen is always packed, and rightly so, drawing people from far and wide for its cheap and authentic Thai fare. Its big brother across the road – also called *Bird* – serves much the same food in slightly more upmarket surroundings. Mains around €16. Daily 1–10pm.

Blauwe aan de Waal Oudezijds Achterburgwal 99 ☎ 020 330 2257, ⊕ blauwaandewal.com; map p.51. Quite a haven, situated down an alley in the heart of the Red Light District, with tremendous French-Dutch food and a wonderfully soothing environment after the mayhem of the streets outside. Not cheap – mains hover around €22 – but worth every cent. Tues–Sat 6–11pm.

Café Bern Nieuwmarkt 9 ☎ 020 622 0034; map p.51. Casual and inexpensive brown café patronized by a predominantly arty clientele. Run by a native of Switzerland, its speciality is, perhaps not surprisingly, excellent and alcoholic cheese fondue. Daily 6–11pm.

Hemelse Modder Oude Waal 11 ☎ 020 624 3203, ⊕ hemelsemodder.nl; map pp.48–49. Stylish restaurant serving a tasty menu of mainly Dutch dishes in an informal atmosphere. Service is very attentive and – despite the trendy environment – not at all precious, and the food is excellent and reasonably priced with main courses at €20. Try, for example, the beef braised in beer and plum with potatoes and carrots. Deservedly popular. Daily 6–11pm.

★ **Lucius** Spuistraat 247 ☎ 020 624 1831, ⊕ lucius.nl; map p.51. This long-established, bistro-style restaurant, with its high-varnish wooden panelling, is one of the best fish restaurants in town. The lemon sole, when it's on the menu, is excellent and so are the seafood platters. Attracts an older clientele. Mains €25, a tad less for the daily special. Daily 5pm–midnight.

Mappa Nes 59 ☎ 020 528 9170, ⊕ mappa.nl; map p.51. Classic Italian food with some inventive twists, incorporating good home-made pasta dishes and excellent service in an unpretentious and modern, café-style environment. Main courses €14–18. Tues–Sat 6–10pm (Fri & Sat till 11pm).

★ **Nam Kee** Zeedijk 111–113 ☎ 020 624 3470,

⊕ namkee.net; map p.51. Arguably the best of a number of Chinese diners along this stretch of the Zeedijk – and attracting a loyal clientele. Quick-fire service and great food at very affordable prices – reckon on €12 for a main course. Daily noon–11pm.

Sie Joe Gravenstraat 24 ☎ 020 624 1830, ⊕ siejoe.com; map p.51. Small Indonesian café-restaurant whose great value-for-money menu is far from extensive but comprises well-prepared, simple dishes such as *gado gado*, *sateh* and *rendang*. Mains average €9. Mon–Sat noon–7pm, Thurs until 8pm.

★ **Van Kerkwijk** Nes 41 ☎ 020 620 3316, ⊕ caferestaurantvankerkwijk.nl; map p.51. This looks like a bar but is more of a restaurant these days, serving steaks, fish and so on from an ever-changing menu that isn't written down but is heroically memorized by the waiting staff. Good food, and cheap too – mains from €15 or so. Daily 11am–10pm.

D' Vijff Vlieghen Spuistraat 294 ☎ 020 530 4060, ⊕ thefiveflies.com; map p.51. One of the city's smartest restaurants, "*The Five Flies*" spreads out over a series of small rooms each decorated in traditional Dutch style, from the tile- and wood-panelled walls to the beamed ceiling and antique embossed leather hangings. Intimate and very cosy, its enterprising menu features imaginative renditions of traditional dishes, with herring and suckling pig being two favourites. Prides itself on its wine cellar. Main courses €27–30. Daily 6–10pm.

THE GRACHTENGORDEL

CAFÉS, TEAROOMS AND LUNCH VENUES

★ **Buffet van Odette** Prinsengracht 598 ☎ 020 423 6034, ⊕ buffet-amsterdam.nl; map pp.48–49. Smart, modern and attractive café, where they do excellent light meals and salads, plus more substantial meals in the evening (after 5pm). The fresh pasta dishes are especially good (from €12). Sun & Mon 10am–5pm, Wed–Sat 10am–8.30pm; closed Tues.

Greenwoods Singel 103 ☎ 020 623 7071, ⊕ greenwoods.eu; map p.51. Cosy café serving up a tasty line in salads, omelettes and cakes. Look out for the daily specials and order an English-style pot of tea. Mon–Thurs 9.30am–5pm, Fri–Sun till 6pm.

M'Café Metz & Co, Leidsestraat 34 ☎ 020 520 7020, ⊕ metzco.eu; map pp.48–49. The location is the big deal here – for this smart café, situated on the top floor of the Metz & Co department store, offers grand views over the city centre – indeed there is no better vantage point. The menu is international, with a strong Asian influence, but they also serve Dutch-style salads and sandwiches. Mon 11am–6pm, Tues–Sat 9.30am–6pm & Sun noon–5pm.

Panini Vijzelgracht 3 ☎ 020 626 4939, ⊕ restaurant panini.nl; map pp.48–49. Formica may be a thing of the past almost everywhere else, but not here, giving this split-level, Italian café-cum-restaurant a vaguely beatnik air. Great coffee, sandwiches and pasta during the day; reasonably priced meat, fish and pasta dishes at night – try the ravioli stuffed with artichokes (€13). Mon–Sat 9.30am–11pm, Sun 11.30am–11pm.

Screaming Beans Hartenstraat 12 ☎020 626 0966, ⊛screamingbeans.nl; map pp.48–49. New kid on the block, this lively, modern café has a neighbourhood feel, great bread and tasty coffee. Mon–Sat 8.30am–5pm & Sun 10am–5pm.

Spanjer & van Twist Leliegracht 60 ☎020 639 0109, ⊛spanjerenvantwist.nl; map pp.48–49. Hip café-bar with an arty air and a pocket-sized outdoor terrace beside the canal. Serves up tasty snacks and light meals during the day and more substantial/filling meals from 6pm, when main courses are in the €15–18 range. Daily 10am–5pm & 6–10pm.

RESTAURANTS

★**Belhamel** Brouwersgracht 60 ☎020 622 1095, ⊛belhamel.nl; map p.51. Smashing restaurant where the Art Nouveau decor makes a delightful setting and the menu is short but extremely well chosen, mixing Dutch with French dishes. Try, for example, the guinea fowl with ham, prawns, mussels, aubergine and a sauce of roasted peppers. Main courses at around €20–25. Daily noon–4pm & 6–10pm.

Bolhoed Prinsengracht 60 ☎020 626 1803; map pp.48–49. Boho-meets-New Age café – dig the murals and the green-painted furniture – which has become something of an Amsterdam institution. Offers a daily changing menu featuring familiar vegan and vegetarian options, with organic beer to wash it down. Mains at around €15. Daily noon–10pm.

Chez Georges & Betsie Herenstraat 3 ☎020 626 3332; map p.51. Smart-to-formal, split-level, intimate restaurant offering highly rated, upmarket cuisine with an emphasis on meat dishes; Belgian owned and operated. Mains €23 and up. Daily except Wed & Sun 6–11pm.

De Luwte Leliegracht 26 ☎020 625 8548; map pp.48–49. This cordial restaurant is kitted out in attractive style with Art Nouveau flourishes, and the small but select menu offers first-rate Dutch/Mediterranean cuisine – the seafood is especially good. Mains from €20. Daily 6–10pm.

Piet de Leeuw Noorderstraat 11 ☎020 623 7181, ⊛pietdeleeuw.nl; map pp.48–49. Arguably Amsterdam's best steakhouse, an old-fashioned, darkly lit, wood-panelled affair dating back to the 1940s. Doubles as a local bar, but the steaks, served every which way and costing around €17, are excellent. Mon–Fri noon–11pm, Sat & Sun 5–11pm; closed for summer holidays two weeks in August.

★**Prego** Herenstraat 25 ☎020 638 0148, ⊛pregorestaurant.nl; map p.51. Appealing Mediterranean restaurant with sharp modern decor in one of the nicest parts of the Grachtengordel. Offers a short but inventive menu, including such delights as sea bass with smoked eel and spring onions. Mains €20. Daily 6–10pm.

Puri Mas Lange Leidsedwarsstraat 37 ☎020 627 7627 ⊛purimas.nl; map pp.48–49. Exceptionally good-value Indonesian restaurant near the Leidseplein. Friendly and informed service preludes excellent *rijsttafels*, both meat and vegetarian. Main courses from €17. Daily from 6pm.

Van de Kaart Prinsengracht 512 ☎020 625 9232, ⊛vandekaart.com; map pp.48–49. First-rate French/Mediterranean basement restaurant decorated in minimalist style and featuring a creative menu – try, for instance, the sautéed cod with spinach, oysters and caviar sauce. Main courses for around €28. There's a good cellar too. Mon–Sat 5.30–10.30pm.

THE JORDAAN

CAFÉS, TEAROOMS AND LUNCH VENUES

Arnold Cornelis Elandsgracht 78 ☎020 625 8585, ⊛cornelis.nl; map pp.48–49. Long-established confectioner and patisserie with a mouthwatering display of pastries and cakes. Take away or eat in the snug tearoom at the back. Mon–Fri 8.30am–6pm, Sat 8.30am–5pm.

Festina Lente Looiersgracht 40b ☎020 638 1412, ⊛cafefestinalente.nl; map pp.48–49. Relaxed, mezzanine neighbourhood café-bar with boho furniture and armchairs to laze about on. The outside tables overlooking the canal are a summer sun-trap and the interior is equally cosy in winter; a good selection of board games too. Mon noon–1am, Tues–Thurs 10.30am–1am, Fri & Sat 10.30am–3am, Sun noon–1am.

Winkel 43 Noordermarkt 43 ☎020 623 0223, ⊛winkel43.nl; map pp.48–49. Queue up along with the rest of Amsterdam (or so it seems) for mouthwatering, chunky apple pie, home-made in the basement of this laid-back and agreeable lunchroom-cum-restaurant. Great coffee and fresh mint tea to wash it all down. Mon 7am–1am, Tues–Thurs 8am–1am, Fri 8am–3am, Sat 7am–3am, Sun 10am–1am.

RESTAURANTS

Burger's Patio 2e Tuindwarsstraat 12 ☎020 623 6854, ⊛burgerspatio.nl; map pp.48–49. Despite the name (the place was once a butcher's), there isn't a burger in sight in this long-established convivial restaurant, which has managed to maintain its informal atmosphere without compromising on taste. Mediterranean-inspired dishes are wonderfully presented with a good choice of daily specials. All the

1

meat is free range and there are several vegetarian options daily. Mains from €16. Daily 6pm–late.

Cinema Paradiso Westerstraat 186 ☎020 623 7344, ⓦcinemaparadiso.info; map pp.48–49. Slick, fast-moving restaurant serving all the Italian classics with gusto. It's in a former moviehouse and very popular, so you may have to shout to be heard. Dress to kill/thrill. Pasta and pizzas kick off at around €13. Wed–Sun 6–11pm.

Duende Lindengracht 62 ☎020 420 6692, ⓦcafe-duende.nl; map pp.48–49. Wonderful and busy tapas bar with a tiled interior, mismatched wood furniture, and a warm and inviting feel. Also includes a small venue outside for live dance and music performances, including regular flamenco. Mon–Fri 5–11pm, Sat & Sun 4–11pm.

La Oliva Egelantiersstraat 122 ☎020 320 4316; map pp.48–49. This sleek Jordaan eatery specializes in *pinxtos*, the delectable Basque snacks on sticks that make Spanish bar-hopping such a delight. With a nod to Dutch tastes perhaps, this is more of a restaurant than a bar, and the *pinxtos* anything but bite-sized. Daily noon–10pm.

★ **Moeders** Rozengracht 251 ☎020 626 7957, ⓦmoeders.com; map pp.48–49. Incredibly cosy restaurant just across from the Singelgracht whose theme is obvious from the moment you step inside – Mothers ("*Moeders*"), photos of whom plaster the walls by the dozen. Traditional Dutch food, well presented and with the odd modern twist. Mains from €13 and three-course menus €25. Daily 5pm–1am, kitchen till 10.30pm.

Yam Yam Frederik Hendrikstraat 90 ☎020 681 5097, ⓦyamyam.nl; map pp.48–49. Top-ranking pizzeria and trattoria in a simple, traditional dining room, with wipe-clean table covers and an open kitchen. It attracts couples and all the hip young parents from the neighbourhood with its excellent pizza toppings. Booking recommended. Pizzas €9–15. Tues–Sun 6–10.30pm.

THE OLD JEWISH QUARTER AND THE OOSTERDOK

CAFÉS, TEAROOMS AND LUNCH VENUES

De Hortus Plantage Middenlaan 2a ☎020 625 9021, ⓦdehortus.nl; see map pp.48–49. This amenable café in the orangery of the botanical gardens – the Hortus Botanicus (see p.72) – serves a good range of tasty sandwiches and rolls plus the best cheesecake in the western world. Unfortunately, you have to pay to enter the gardens to get to the café. Daily 10am–4.30pm.

RESTAURANTS

éénvistwéévis Schippersgracht 6 ☎020 623 2894, ⓦeenvistweevis.nl; see map pp.48–49. An uncomplicated fish restaurant serving a prime selection of fish and seafood. Great place to try that Dutch favourite,

mussels and fries, here served up with a choice of sauces. Tues–Sat 6–10pm.

★ **Greetje** Peperstraat 23 ☎020 779 7450, ⓦrestaurantgreetje.nl; see map pp.48–49. A cosy, busy restaurant serving up Dutch staples with a modern flourish. A changing menu reflects the seasons and the favourite dishes of the owner's mother – a native of the southern Netherlands. Superb home cooking in a great atmosphere. Daily 6–10.30pm.

THE MUSEUM QUARTER AND VONDELPARK

CAFÉS, TEAROOMS AND LUNCH VENUES

't Blauwe Theehuis Vondelpark 5 ☎020 662 0254, ⓦblauwetheehuis.nl; map pp.48–49. In the middle of the Vondelpark, this tearoom-cum-café and bar may be a tad shabby, but the food is filling and inexpensive, the atmosphere very downbeat Amsterdam and the building, which dates from 1937, is a fine example of De Stijl. Upstairs, the circular bar hosts regular DJ nights. Café: Mon–Thurs 9am–5pm, Fri 9am–10pm, Sat & Sun 9am–8pm.

Pompa Willemsparkweg 6 ☎020 662 6206, ⓦpomp-restaurant.nl; map pp.48–49. A restaurant at night, and a café by day, this bright, modern place serves a good line in tapas from as little as €4. Daily 11am–11pm.

De Roos PC Hooftstraat 183 ☎020 689 0081, ⓦroos.nl; map pp.48–49. The unassuming downstairs café of this New Age centre on the edge of the Vondelpark is one of the most peaceful spots in the city, selling a range of drinks, organic snacks and light meals. There's also a bookshop and any number of courses in yoga and meditation. Mon–Fri 8.30am–9pm, Sat & Sun 8.30am–5.30pm.

RESTAURANTS

Café Loetje J. Vermeerstraat 52 ☎020 662 8173, ⓦcafeloetje.nl; map pp.48–49. Excellent steaks, hamburgers, fries and salads are the big deal at this eetcafé. The service can be touch and go, but the food is great and inexpensive with mains from as little as €8. The pleasant outdoor terrace is a summer bonus. Mon–Fri 11am–midnight, Sat & Sun 5pm–midnight, though the kitchen closes at 10pm.

Le Garage Ruysdaelstraat 54 ☎020 679 7176, ⓦrestaurantlegarage.nl; map pp.48–49. Fashionable restaurant, popular with a media crowd, that offers a top-notch French menu with all sorts of international flourishes – from Italian to Thai. Start off with the snails in butter (€12.50) followed by an excellent bouillabaisse (€32.50). Prices are less at lunch times. Reservations pretty much essential. Mon–Fri noon–2pm & 6–11pm; Sat & Sun 6–11pm only.

DRINKING

Amsterdam's selection of **bars and café-bars** is one of the real pleasures of the city. There are, in essence, two main kinds of bar: the traditional, old-style bar or brown café – a *bruin café* or *bruine kroeg* – cosy, intimate places so called because of the colour of their walls, stained by years of tobacco smoke; and the slick, self-consciously modern designer bars, some of them known as "grand cafés", which tend to be as un-brown as possible and geared towards a younger crowd. Another type of drinking spot – though there are very few of them left – is the tasting house (*proeflokalen*), originally the sampling rooms of small private distillers, now tiny, stand-up places that concentrate on selling spirits – mainly Dutch gin or *jenever*.

THE OLD CENTRE

Café De Engelbewaarder Kloveniersburgwal 59 ☎020 625 3772, ⓦcafe-de-engelbewaarder.nl; map pp.48–49. Once the meeting place of Amsterdam's bookish types, this is still known as a literary café. It's relaxed and informal, with live jazz on Sunday afternoons. Mon–Thurs & Sun 11am–1am, Fri & Sat 11am–3am.

De Drie Fleschjes Gravenstraat 18 ☎020 624 8443, ⓦdedriefleschjes.nl; map p.51. Tasting house for spirits and liqueurs, which once would have been made on the premises. Clients tend to be well heeled or well soused (often both). Mon–Sat 2–8.30pm, Sun 3–7pm.

Hoppe Spui 18 ☎020 420 4420, ⓦcafehoppe.com; map pp.48–49. Ancient pub with sawdust on its wooden floors, a long elevated bar, which makes the bar staff look like giants, one of the oddest (and worst) paintings you'll ever see (it's behind the bar), and cranky toilets. Frequented by the city's businessfolk on their long and wayward way home. It's especially good in summer, when the throng spills out onto the street. Sun–Thurs 8am–1am, Fri & Sat 8am–2am.

★ **In de Wildeman** Kolksteeg 3 ☎020 638 2348, ⓦindewildeman.nl; map p.51. This lovely old-fashioned bar has an ancient wood and tile interior that still boasts its original low bar and shelving. A peaceful escape from the loud, tacky shops of nearby Nieuwendijk, and one of the centre's most appealing watering holes. Mon–Thurs noon–1am, Fri & Sat noon till 2am.

★ **In 't Aepjen** Zeedijk 1 ☎020 428 8291, ⓦcafeintaepjen.nl, map p.51. This building has been a bar since the days when the Zeedijk was the haunt of sailors gambling away their last few guilder. Some of the indebted sailors left their precious pet monkeys behind as security on their debts, hence the name of the bar – literally "In the Monkeys". The monkeys are gone, but not much else has changed – and the place looks simply wonderful. Daily midday to 1am, Fri & Sat till 3am.

★ **Wynand Fockink** Pijlsteeg 31 ☎020 639 2695, ⓦwynand-fockink.nl; map pp.48–49. Small and incredibly cosy bar hidden just behind the *Krasnapolsky* hotel off Dam Square. One of the older *proeflokalen*, it offers a wide range of its own flavoured *jenevers* that used to be distilled down the street. Daily 3–9pm.

THE GRACHTENGORDEL

★ **'t Arendsnest** Herengracht 90 ☎020 421 20 57,

ⓦarendsnest.nl; map p.51. In a handsome old canal house, this bar boasts impressive wooden decor – from the longest of bars to the tall wood-and-glass cabinets – and specializes in Dutch beers, of which it has over one hundred varieties, twelve on tap. Attracts an older clientele. Mon–Thurs 4pm–midnight, Fri 4pm–2am, Sat 2pm–2am & Sun 2–11.30pm.

De Hegeraad Noordermarkt 34 ☎020 624 5565, ⓦcafehegeraad.nl; map pp.48–49. Lovingly maintained, old-fashioned brown café with a loyal clientele. The back room with red plush furnishings and paintings is the perfect place to relax with a hot chocolate – or something stronger. Mon–Sat 8am to midnight, Sun 11am–11pm.

Oosterling Utrechtsestraat 140 ☎020 623 4140; map pp.48–49. Intimate, family-owned, neighbourhood bar that's been plying its trade for donkey's years – since 1820 to be exact – and before that the building was occupied by the Dutch East India Company. It specializes in *jenever*, with dozens of brands and varieties. Mon–Sat noon–1am, Sun 1–8pm.

★ **Het Papeneiland** Prinsengracht 2 ☎020 624 1989, ⓦpapeneiland.nl; map pp.48–49. With its wood panelling, antique Delft tiles and ancient stove, this rabbit warren of a place is one of the cosiest bars in the Grachtengordel – and it attracts a garrulous, friendly clientele. In traditional Dutch style, cheese and sausages are on hand too. Mon–Thurs noon–1am, Fri & Sat noon till 3am.

De Pieper Prinsengracht 424 ☎020 6264775; map pp.48–49. Laidback neighbourhood brown bar, at the corner of Leidsegracht, with rickety old furniture and a mini-terrace beside the canal. Has a surprisingly large selection of liqueurs plus the most genial sometime inebriated atmosphere. Mon–Thurs 11am–1am, Fri & Sat 11am–2am.

De Prins Prinsengracht 124 ☎020 6249 382, ⓦdiningcity.nl/deprins; map pp.48–49. With its well-worn decor and chatty atmosphere, this popular and lively brown bar offers a wide range of drinks and a well-priced bar menu. Daily 10am–1am; food served from 10am to 10pm.

Walem Keizersgracht 449 ☎020 625 3544, ⓦwalem.nl; map pp.48–49. A chic bar-restaurant – cool, light and vehemently un-brown; eat in or chill out at the bar with a mojito. The clientele is stylish, and the food a hybrid of

1

French- and Dutch-inspired dishes. Breakfast in the garden in summer is a highlight. Often jam-packed. Mon & Tues 9.30am–7pm, Wed–Sun 9.30am–10.30pm.

THE JORDAAN

Chris Bloemstraat 42 ☎020 624 5942, ⓦ cafechris.nl; map pp.48–49. Proud of itself for being the Jordaan's (and Amsterdam's) oldest bar, dating from 1624, this brown bar has a comfortable, homely atmosphere – plus a wooden floor and oodles of wood panelling. Mon–Thurs 3pm–1am, Fri & Sat 3pm–2am, Sun 3–9pm.

De Kat in de Wijngaert Lindengracht 160 ☎020 622 4554; map pp.48–49. With the enticing name "The Cat in the Vineyard", this small bar is the epitome of the Jordaan local – and quiet enough for conversation. Sun–Thurs 10am–1am, Fri 10am–3am, Sat 9am–3am.

Nol Westerstraat 109 ☎020 624 5380, ⓦ cafenolamsterdam.nl; map pp.48–49. Raucous and jolly Jordaan singing bar, this luridly lit dive closes late, especially at weekends, when the back-slapping joviality and drunken sing-alongs keep you rooted until the small hours. Daily except Tues 9pm–3am.

De Reiger Nieuwe Leliestraat 34 ☎020 624 7426, ⓦ dereigeramsterdam.nl; map pp.48–49. Situated in the thick of the Jordaan, this is one of the area's prime meeting places, an old-style café filled with modish Amsterdammers, who eat and drink among a medley of Dutch bygones – and with faded portraits on the walls. A good range of beers on tap, too. Tues–Fri 5–10.30pm, Sat noon–10.30pm & Sun 5–10.30pm; closed Mon.

't Smalle Egelantiersgracht 12 ☎020 623 9617, ⓦ t-smalle.nl; map pp.48–49. One of Amsterdam's oldest cafés, 't Smalle opened in 1786 as a *proeflokaal* – a tasting house for the (long-gone) gin distillery next door. It still does a good line in *jenever*, but today it's as much a café as

a bar – candlelit and comfortable with a pontoon on the canal out front for relaxed summer afternoons. Wed–Sun 6–11pm.

THE OLD JEWISH QUARTER AND THE EASTERN DOCKLANDS

Brouwerij 't IJ De Gooyer windmill, Funenkade 7 ☎020 320 1786, ⓦ brouwerijhetij.nl; map pp.48–49. Well-established if somewhat frugal bar and mini-brewery in the old public baths adjoining the De Gooyer windmill. Serves up an excellent range of beers and ales, from the thunderously strong Columbus amber ale (9 percent) to the creamier, more soothing Natte (6 percent). Daily 3–8pm.

Café de Sluyswacht Jodenbreestraat 1 ☎020 625 76.11, ⓦ sluyswacht.nl; map p.51. This pleasant little bar occupies an old and now solitary gabled house, which stands sentry by the lock gates opposite the Rembrandthuis. A smashing spot to nurse a beer on a warm summer's night, gazing down the canal towards the Montelbaanstoren. Mon–Sat 11.30am–1am, Sun 11.30am–7pm.

De Druif Rapenburgerplein 83 ☎020 624 4530; map pp.48–49. Claims to be the city's oldest bar and is certainly one of its more beguiling, a neighbourhood joint that pulls in an easy-going crowd. Daily 11am to midnight.

THE MUSEUM QUARTER AND VONDELPARK

Wildschut Roelof Hartplein 1 ☎020 676 8220, ⓦ goodfoodgroup.nl; map pp.48–49. Not far from the Concertgebouw, this café-bar is well known for its Art Deco trimmings and congenial outside terrace, which gets jam-packed as soon as the sun comes out. Much the nicest place to drink in the neighbourhood, and with a decent menu too. Mon–Fri 9am to midnight, Sat & Sun 10am–1am.

COFFEESHOPS

In Amsterdam a "**coffeeshop**" is advertising just one thing: **cannabis**. You might also be able to get coffee and a slice of cake, but the main activity in a coffeeshop is, predictably enough, dope smoking. There are almost as many different kinds of coffeeshops as there are bars: some are neon-lit, with loud music and Day-Glo decor, but there are plenty of others that are quiet, comfortable places to have a relaxed smoke and take it easy. It's worth noting that the legal position of the coffeeshop is currently in a state of flux with plans to restrict their use to residents of Amsterdam who possess a "weed card" (see Basics, p.36).

★ **Abraxas** Jonge Roelensteeg 12 ☎020 6255763, ⓦ abraxas.tv; map p.51. This is the original *Abraxas* coffeeshop, a quirky – and quirkily decorated – mezzanine place with spiral staircases that are a real challenge after a spliff. The hot chocolate with hash is not for the susceptible. Daily 10am–1am.

Barney's Haarlemmerstraat 102 ☎020 612 3987, ⓦ barneys.biz; map pp.48–49. Something of an Amsterdam institution, this extremely popular

café-cum-coffeeshop is simply the most civilized place in town to enjoy a big hit with a big breakfast – at any time of the day. A few doors down, at no. 98, *Barney's Farm* affords a nice sunny spot in the morning and serves alcohol. Daily 7am–1am.

The Bulldog Leidseplein 15 ☎020 627 1908, ⓦ thebulldog.com; map pp.48–49. The biggest and most famous of the coffeeshop chains, and a long way from its poky Red Light District origins, the main branch of *The*

Bulldog is here on the Leidseplein, housed in a former police station. It has a large cocktail bar, coffeeshop, juice bar and souvenir shop, all with separate entrances. It's big and brash, not at all the place for a quiet smoke, though the dope they sell (packaged up in neat little brand-labelled bags) is reliably good. Thurs 10am–1am, Fri & Sat 10am–3am, Sun 10am–2am.

★ **Dampkring** Handboogstraat 29 ☎06 38 07 05, ⓦdampkring.mobi; map p.51. Appealing coffeeshop that looks every inch the brown bar with its highly varnished wooden interior – so much so that scenes from "*Ocean's Twelve*" were shot here. Offers groovy tunes and a laidback atmosphere; also known for its good-quality hash. Daily 10am–1am.

Kadinsky Rosmarijnsteeg 9 ☎020 624 7023, ⓦcoffeeshopmenus.org; map p.51. Small and central branch of this small chain. Strictly accurate deals are weighed out to a background of jazz and the chocolate chip cookies are to die for. Daily 10am–1am.

Paradox 1e Bloemdwarsstraat 2, Jordaan ☎020 623 5639, ⓦparadoxcoffeeshop.com; map pp.48–49. If you're fed up with the usual coffeeshop food offerings, *Paradox* satisfies the munchies with outstanding natural food, including spectacular fresh fruit concoctions and veggie burgers. Daily 10am–8pm.

Rusland Rusland 16 ☎020 627 9468, ⓦcoffeeshopmenus.org; map p.51. One of the first Amsterdam coffeeshops, a cramped but vibrant place that's a favourite with both dope fans and tea addicts (it has 40 different kinds). A cut above the rest. Daily 10am–1am.

★ **Siberië** Brouwersgracht 11 ☎020 623 5909, ⓦcoffeeshopsiberie.nl; map pp.48–49. Very relaxed, very friendly, and worth a visit whether you want to smoke or not, with a good selection of magazines and a chessboard. Daily 11am–11pm (Fri & Sat till midnight).

ENTERTAINMENT AND NIGHTLIFE

Amsterdam offers a broad range of **music, dance and film**, partly due to its relatively youthful population and partly to government subsidies. Indeed, the city is often at the cutting edge of the arts and its frequent **festivals** and fringe events provide plenty of offbeat/exciting entertainment. It's also something of a Mecca for **clubbers**, with numerous venues clustered around Leidseplein and its environs buzzing into the small hours, and more late-night haunts among the narrow lanes and alleys around Rembrandtplein.

ROCK, JAZZ AND FOLK VENUES

Amsterdam is a regular tour stop for many major artists, and something of a testing ground for current rock bands. Its largest venue is the 50,000-seat Amsterdam ArenA, out in the southeastern suburbs, while the nearby Heineken Music Hall also hosts some big-name acts. In the city centre, the *Paradiso* and the *Melkweg* are much smaller, with a daily programme of music to suit all tastes and budgets. Alongside the main venues, the city's clubs, bars and multimedia centres host performances by live bands on a regular basis.

Akhnaton Nieuwezijds Kolk 25 ☎020 624 3396, ⓦakhnaton.nl; see map p.51. Fashionable,

medium-sized club hosting a wide-ranging programme of events, from salsa nights to Turkish dance parties. On a good night, the place heaves.

Amsterdam ArenA ArenA Boulevard ☎020 311 1333, ⓦamsterdamarena.nl; Metro or train to Bijlmer station; map pp.48–49. The massive Ajax soccer stadium also plays host to world-class music acts such as the Rolling Stones and Madonna..

Bimhuis Piet Heinkade 3 ☎020 788 2188, ⓦbimhuis .nl; map pp.48–49. In 2004, the city's premier jazz and improvised-music venue moved to its spanking new building next to the Muziekgebouw (see p.95). It showcases gigs by both Dutch and international artists throughout the week, as well as jam sessions and

---

WHAT'S ON WHERE AND WHEN

For **information** about what's on, head for the Amsterdam Uitburo, or **AUB**, the cultural office of the city council, whose **Ticketshop** is housed inside the Stadsschouwburg theatre on Leidseplein (Mon–Fri 10am–7pm, Sat 10am–6pm & Sun noon–6pm; ⓦamsterdam suitburo.nl). It hands out all manner of flyers and promotional stuff, including two free and comprehensive, Dutch-language **listings magazines**, the monthly *Uitkrant* (ⓦamsterdamsuitburo.nl/extra/uitkrant) and *NL20* (ⓦnlagenda.com/Amsterdam): both are also widely available in the city's supermarkets, cafés, hotels and shops, as is *Time Out Amsterdam* (ⓦtimeout.com/amsterdam), a free English-language monthly magazine with extensive listings and reviews. **Tickets** for most performances can be bought at the Ticketshop or reserved by phone through the AUB Uitlijn (☎020 795 9950, 9am–8pm), though it's usually cheaper to buy tickets from the venue itself.

1

workshops. There's also a modern bar and restaurant for concert-goers with fantastic views over the water.

Heineken Music Hall ArenA Boulevard 590 ☎0900 68742 42, ⓦheineken-music-hall.nl; Metro or train to Bijlmer station; map pp.48–49. This simple but acoustically impressive black box is a hi-tech venue attracting international bands ranging from Pink Floyd to the Stone Roses and James Taylor.

Jazz Café Alto Korte Leidsedwarsstraat 115 ☎020 626 3249, ⓦjazz-cafe-alto.nl; map pp.48–49. It's worth hunting down this legendary little jazz bar just off Leidseplein for its quality modern jazz, performed every night from around 10pm until 3am (even later at the weekend). It's big on atmosphere, though slightly cramped, but entry is free. Daily 9pm–3am.

Maloe Melo Lijnbaansgracht 163 ☎020 420 4592, ⓦmaloemelo.nl; map pp.48–49. Dark, low-ceilinged bar where you can hear lively local blues and rock acts most days of the week. Daily 9pm–3am.

★ **Melkweg** Lijnbaansgracht 234a ☎020 531 8181, ⓦmelkweg.nl; map pp.48–49. Amsterdam's most famous entertainment venue, plus one of the city's prime multimedia arts centres, with a young, hip clientele. A former dairy (hence the name) just round the corner from Leidseplein, it has two separate halls for live music, and hosts a broad range of bands playing everything from reggae to rock, all of which lean towards the "alternative". There are excellent DJ sessions at the weekend, plus a monthly film programme, a theatre, gallery and café-restaurant (Marnixstraat entrance).

★ **Paradiso** Weteringschans 6–8 ☎020 626 4521, ⓦparadiso.nl; map pp.48–49. A converted church near the Leidseplein, revered for its atmosphere and excellent programme, featuring local and international bands ranging from the newly signed to the more established. Popular club nights draw in the crowds too – and look out for DJ sets featuring live performances on Saturdays. From time to time, it also hosts classical concerts as well as debates and multimedia events.

Winston Warmoesstraat 129 ☎020 623 1380, ⓦwinston.nl; map p.51. Adventurous small venue, part of the eponymous hotel (see p.84), which attracts an eclectic crowd and offers a mixed bag of live bands, electro, drum 'n' bass and cheesy pop nights. Bar: Sun–Thurs 10am–1am, Fri & Sat 10am–3am.

CLUBS

Amsterdam's full-throttle club scene ranges from standard-issue meat markets to the cool, the rough, the ready, the rough and ready and the super groovy. DJs, both domestic stars and big-name imports, have headline status and most play variations on house, trance, garage and techno. As you might expect, it's a late-night scene too – arrive before 11pm and you'll wonder where everyone is. Most clubs charge for entry, with ticket prices between €15 and €20 at weekends and around €10 during the week. A singular feature of Amsterdam clubbing, however, is that you should tip the bouncer if you want to return to the same place next week; €1 or €2 in the palm of his hand will do. Drinks are slightly more expensive than in cafés, though you'll usually pay a bit more for spirits.

Bitterzoet Spuistraat 2 ☎020 421 2318, ⓦbitterzoet .com; map p.51. Spacious but cosy two-floored bar and theatre hosting a mixed bag of events: DJs playing acid jazz, R&B, funk and disco, film screenings and occasional urban poetry nights. Times vary, but almost always include Thurs–Sat from 9pm.

Club Trouw Wibautstraat 127 ☎020 463 77 88, ⓦtrouwamsterdam.nl; map pp.48–49. Housed in an old large industrial building to the southeast of the city centre, this combined multi-arts venue offers some of the best club nights in town – and has been voted the best club in the Netherlands on a couple of occasions. Opening hours vary, but nearly always include Fri & Sat from 10pm.

Escape Rembrandtplein 11 ☎020 622 1111, ⓦescape.nl; map pp.48–49. This vast club has space enough to house 2000 people, but its glory days – when it was home to Amsterdam's cutting-edge Chemistry nights – are long gone and it now focuses on weekly club nights that pull in crowds of mainstream punters. Thurs–Sun from 11pm.

Jimmy Woo Korte Leidsedwarsstraat 18 ☎0202 626 3150, ⓦjimmywoo.com; map pp.48–49. Intimate and stylish club spread over two floors. Upstairs, the black lacquered walls, Japanese lamps and cosy booths with leather couches ooze sexy chic, while downstairs a packed dancefloor throbs under hundreds of oscillating lightbulbs. Popular with young, well-dressed locals so look smart if you want to join/fit in. Thurs–Sun 11pm–3/4am.

Melkweg Lijnbaansgracht 234a ☎020 531 8181, ⓦmelkweg.nl; map pp.48–49. After the bands have finished, excellent offbeat/downbeat club sessions go on well into the small hours, sometimes featuring the best DJs in town. Also plays host to some of the most enjoyable theme nights around. Wed–Sat from 8pm.

Odeon Singel 460 ☎020 521 8555, ⓦodeontheater.nl; map p.51. Originally a brewery, this modishly restored old canal house has been a theatre, cinema and concert hall until it was gutted by fire in 1990. Rescued and refurbished, it's now a stylish nightclub hosting Eighties parties and regular club nights with a splendid bar overlooking the canal. There's also a restaurant and a café.

Paradiso Weteringschans 6–8 ☎020 626 8790, ⓦparadiso.nl; map pp.48–49. One of the principal

AMSTERDAM'S ARTS FESTIVALS

The best multi-venue event is June's annual **Holland Festival** (ⓦhollandfestival.nl), which attracts the best domestic mainstream and fringe performers in all the performing arts, as well as an exciting international line-up. Otherwise, one of the more interesting, music-oriented events is the popular **Grachtenfestival** (ⓦgrachtenfestival.nl), held in the middle of August, a week-long classical music festival which concludes with a piano recital on a floating stage outside the *Pulitzer Hotel* on the Prinsengracht. Amsterdam's only regular film event is the top-ranking **International Documentary Film Festival**, held in November/December (ⓦidfa.nl), during which two hundred documentaries from all over the world are shown in ten days.

venues in the city, *Paradiso* hosts up to five club and/or themed nights/week, though Friday is the main night. For schedule, check the website: open from midnight onwards.

Studio 80 Rembrandtplein 17 ☎020 521 8333, ⓦstudio-80.nl; map pp.48–49. Right on the Rembrandtplein, this uber-cool club attracts the more fashionable underground scene with techno, soul, funk, minimal and electro. A creative breeding ground for young and upcoming DJs, bands and acts. Wed–Sat from 10pm.

CLASSICAL MUSIC AND OPERA

There's no shortage of classical music concerts in Amsterdam, with two major orchestras based in the city, plus regular visits by other touring orchestras. Amsterdam's Koninklijk Concertgebouworkest (Royal Concertgebouw Orchestra; ⓦconcertgebouworkest.nl) is one of the most dynamic in the world, and occupies one of Europe's finest concert halls to boot, sharing its premises with the other resident orchestra, the Nederlands Philharmonisch Orkest (Dutch Philharmonic; ⓦorkest.nl). There's also the internationally renowned De Nederlandse Opera (Dutch Opera; ⓦdno.nl), who perform at the Muziektheater, as does Het Nationale Ballet (National Ballet; ⓦhet-ballet .nl). Contemporary classical music is a major deal at the Muziekgebouw, overlooking the River IJ, and visiting orchestras sometimes appear here too, though they are just as likely to perform at either the Stadsschouwburg or the Carré Theatre.

Carré Theatre Amstel 115 ☎020 524 9452, ⓦcarre.nl; map pp.48–49. A splendid hundred-year-old structure (originally built for a circus) that has become the ultimate venue for Dutch folk artists and musicians. Hosts top international acts, anything from Swedish gospel to *Carmen*, with reputable touring orchestras and opera companies squeezed in between.

Concertgebouw Concertgebouwplein 10 ☎020 671 8345, ⓦconcertgebouw.nl; map pp.48–49. After a recent facelift, the Concertgebouw is looking – and sounding – better than ever. There are two halls here and both boast a star-studded international programme. Prices

are very reasonable, €15–50, and around €15 for Sunday-morning events.

Muziekgebouw Piet Heinkade 1 ☎020 788 2000, ⓦmuziekgebouw.nl; map pp.48–49. Amsterdam's bright new concert hall, with two medium-sized halls, a café, a bar and state-of-the-art acoustics, has given impetus to the redevelopment along the River IJ. Its top-quality programme of opera and orchestral music draws a highbrow crowd to this part of town. Worth a visit for the building alone; the café offers great views over the water.

Muziektheater Amstel 3 ☎020 625 5455 or ☎551 8100, ⓦhet-muziektheater.nl; map pp.48–49. Adjoining the Stadhuis (city hall), the Muziektheater is home to the city's ballet and opera companies. Tickets go very quickly – so advance booking is recommended.

Stadsschouwburg Leidseplein 26 ☎020 624 2311, ⓦssba.nl; map pp.48–49. Long-established concert hall in the thick of Amsterdam's nightlife offering a wide range of performances, including theatre, opera and dance by both Dutch and foreign troupes.

CABARET AND COMEDY CLUBS

Surprisingly for a city that functions so much in English, there is next to no English-language theatre – though English-speaking touring companies do regularly visit. English-language comedy, on the other hand, has become a big thing here, spearheaded by the resident and extremely successful Boom Chicago comedy company.

Boom Chicago Leidseplein 12 ☎020 423 0101, ⓦboomchicago.nl; map pp.48–49. Something of a phenomenon in Amsterdam, this rapid-fire improv comedy troupe hailing from the US performs at the Leidseplein Theater nightly to crowds of both tourists and locals, and regularly receives rave reviews. Inexpensive food, cocktails and beer served in pitchers.

Nachttheater Sugar Factory Lijnbaansgracht 238 ☎020 627 0008, ⓦsugarfactory.nl; map pp.48–49. Busy Leidseplein's "theatrical nightclub" hosts a stimulating programme of cabaret, live music, poetry and theatre, plus a late-night club that kicks off after the show. Pulls in a young and artistic crowd, and features up to two events per evening. Closed Mon & Tues.

FILM

Most of Amsterdam's cinemas are huge, multiplex picture palaces where you can watch a selection of general releases, but there is also a scattering of film houses (*filmhuizen*) showing revival and cult films along with occasional retrospectives and themed nights. All foreign movies playing in Amsterdam are shown in their original language and subtitled in Dutch.

Cinecenter Lijnbaansgracht 236 ☎020 623 6615, ⓦcinecenter.nl; map pp.48–49. Opposite the *Melkweg*, this cinema shows independent and quality commercial films, the majority originating from non-English-speaking countries.

EYE IJ promenade 1 ☎020 589 1400, ⓦeyefilm.nl; map pp.48–49. Recently rehoused in a splendidly equipped tower block on the north side of the River IJ from Centraal Station, the Netherlands Film Institute offers regular screenings of all kinds of movies from all corners of the world. As you might expect, Dutch films – and directors – get pride of cinematic place. To get there, catch the free Buiksloterweg ferry, which shuttles across the river from behind Centraal Station.

Melkweg Lijnbaansgracht 234a ☎020 531 8181, ⓦmelkweg.nl; map pp.48–49. As well as music, art and dance (see p.94), the *Melkweg* manages to maintain a consistently good monthly film programme, ranging from mainstream fodder through to obscure imports.

The Movies Haarlemmerdijk 161 ☎020 638 6016, ⓦthemovies.nl; map pp.48–49. A beautiful Art Deco cinema, and a charming setting for independent films. Worth visiting for the bar and restaurant alone, plus late shows most weekends.

Tuschinski Theater Reguliersbreestraat 26 ☎020 428 1060, ⓦpathe.nl; map pp.48–49. Fabulous Art Deco cinema, famous for the foyer's hand-woven carpet and hand-painted wallpaper. Shows the artier offerings from the mainstream list.

GAY AND LESBIAN AMSTERDAM

Amsterdam boasts one of the most dynamic **gay scenes** in Europe, with a liberal sprinkling of advice centres, bars and clubs. The city has four main gay areas, beginning with **Reguliersdwarsstraat**, where the bars and clubs tend to attract a young and trendy crowd, and quieter **Kerkstraat**, which is populated as much by locals as visitors. The streets just **north of Rembrandtplein** and along the Amstel are a camp focus, while **Warmoesstraat**, in the heart of the Red Light District, is cruisey and mainly leather- and denim-oriented. Many bars and clubs have **darkrooms**, which are legally obliged to provide safe-sex information and condoms. The **bars and clubs** listed below cater either predominantly or exclusively to a gay clientele. Some venues have both gay-only and mixed gay/straight nights; there are, however, very few **lesbian**-only nights or clubs and bars. The city also has its own gay and lesbian radio station, **MVS Radio** (ⓦmvs.nl).

GAY INFORMATION AND BOOKSHOPS

COC Rozenstraat 14 ☎020 626 3087, ⓦcocamsterdam .nl; map pp.48–49. COC (pronounced "say-oh-say"), the Netherlands' national gay and lesbian pressure group, is one of the oldest, and largest, groups of its kind in the world. Their Amsterdam branch offers advice and provides contacts. Mon–Fri 10am–4pm.

Gay and Lesbian Switchboard ☎020 623 6565, ⓦswitchboard.nl. An English-speaking phone service which provides help and advice. Mon–Fri noon–10pm, Sat & Sun 4–8pm.

Pink Point Westermarkt ☎020 428 1070, ⓦpinkpoint.org; map pp.48–49. Run by a team of volunteers, this free advice and information point on where to go and what to do in the city, is stocked with flyers and brochures, as well as a range of souvenirs and T-shirts. Metres from the Homomonument. Daily 10am–6pm.

Vrolijk Paleisstraat 135 ☎020 623 5142, ⓦvrolijk.nu; map p.51. Probably the largest gay and lesbian bookstore in Europe, with a vast stock of new and secondhand books and magazines, as well as music and videos. Mon–Fri 11am–6pm, Sat 10am–5pm & Sun 1–5pm.

GAY BARS AND CLUBS

Argos Warmoesstraat 95 ☎020 622 6595, ⓦargosbar .nl; map p.51. Europe's oldest gay leather bar, with two bars and a raunchy cellar. Not for the faint-hearted or whimsical. Mon–Thurs & Sun 10pm–3am, Fri & Sat 10pm–4am.

De Engel Zeedijk 21 ☎020 427 6381, ⓦengel amsterdam.nl; map p.51. Popular gay bar attracting a mixed crew, who join in the special events – Singalongs, Deal or No Deal – with vim and gusto. Daily 1pm–1am.

Entre Nous Halvemaansteeg 14 ☎020 623 1700; map pp.48–49. Camp and often outrageous bar. Can be packed at peak times, when everyone joins in the cheesy sing-alongs. Women welcome. Daily 9pm–3am (Fri & Sat till 4am).

Prik Spuistraat 109 ☎020 320 0002, ⓦprikamsterdam .nl; map p.51. Voted Amsterdam's best gay bar in 2011, with tasty cocktails, smoothies and snacks, plus DJs on weekends. Has its own T-shirts too. Daily 4pm–1am (Fri & Sat till 3am).

Vivelavie Amstelstraat 7 ☎020 624 0114, ⓦvivelavie .net; map pp.48–49. Small, campy bar, patronized mostly, but not exclusively, by gay women. Quiet during the week, it steams on the weekend. Daily 4pm–3am.

WHERE TO SHOP

Broadly speaking, the **Nieuwendijk/Kalverstraat** strip, and, to a lesser extent, **Koningsplein and Leidsestraat** are where you'll find the usual high-street fashion and mainstream department stores. Elsewhere, the expensive end of Amsterdam's renowned antiques trade is clustered around the smart and chic **Spiegelkwartier** (ⓦwww.spiegelkwartier.nl), with its string of bijou shops stretching out along Nieuwe Spiegelstraat and a few retail outposts on adjacent Spiegelgracht – it's a great district to browse with one local speciality being antique Dutch tiles. The **Grachtengordel** chips in with a string of lovely little independent shops selling everything from secondhand clothes to fancy chandeliers – head particularly to the area between Reestraat/Hartenstraat and Runstraat/Huidenstraat, known as "**De Negen Straatjes**", or more usually "**The Nine Streets**" (ⓦtheninestreets.com). There's a further pocket of interesting little shops – chocolatiers, bookshops and the like – on and around **Staalstraat**, near the Waterlooplein, and several more further out from the centre in the **Jordaan**.

SHOPPING

Amsterdam has some excellent and unusual **speciality shops** as well as a handful of great **street markets**. Where the city scores most though is in its convenience – the centre concentrates most of what's interesting within its tight borders – and, as an added bonus, the majority of shops are still individual businesses rather than chains, which makes a refreshing change from many big cities.

BOOKS AND MAGAZINES

American Book Center Spui 12 ☎020 625 5537, ⓦabc.nl; map p.51. This store has a vast stock of books in English, as well as lots of imported US magazines and books. Does a good line in discounts too. Mon 11am–8pm, Tues–Sat 10am–8pm, Thurs till 9pm, Sun 11am–6.30pm.

Athenaeum Spui 14 ☎020 514 1470, ⓦathenaeum .nl; map p.51. Excellent all-round bookshop with an adventurous stock, though mostly in Dutch, but also the best source of international newspapers and magazines. Mon 11am–6pm, Tues–Sat 9.30am–6pm, Thurs till 9pm, Sun noon to 5.30pm.

The English Bookshop Lauriergracht 71 ☎020 626 4230, ⓦenglishbookshop.nl; map pp.48–49. In the Jordaan, this independent bookshop stocks an extremely well-chosen collection of titles on a wide range of subjects, though its speciality is English-language literature, both original and in translation. Tues–Sat 11am–6pm.

Reisboekhandel Pied à Terre Overtoom 135 ☎020 627 4455, ⓦjvw.nl; map pp.48–49. The city's best travel bookshop, with knowledgeable staff and a huge selection of books and maps. Also sells inflatable and illuminated globes and hiking maps for the Netherlands and beyond, often in English. Mon 1–6pm, Tues–Fri 10am–6pm, Thurs till 9pm, Sat 10am–5pm.

Selexyz Scheltema Koningsplein 20 ☎020 523 1411, ⓦselexyz.nl; map p.51. Large and long-established bookshop with six floors of absolutely everything, though as you might expect, most of the stock is in Dutch. Mon 11am–7pm, Tues–Sat 10am–7pm & Sun noon–6pm.

Waterstones Kalverstraat 152 ☎020 638 3821, ⓦwaterstones.com; map p.51. Dutch branch of the UK high-street chain, with four floors of books and magazines. A predictable selection perhaps, but prices are sometimes cheaper here than elsewhere. Mon–Sat 9.30am–6.30pm, Thurs till 9pm, Sun 11am–6pm.

DEPARTMENT STORES

De Bijenkorf Dam 1 ☎0800 0818, ⓦdebijenkorf.nl; map p.51. Dominating the northern corner of Dam Square, this is the city's biggest and most diverse department store, a huge bustling place that sells a wide range of just about everything. Departments to head for include household goods, cosmetics and kids' wear. Sun & Mon 11am–7pm, Tues & Wed 10am–7pm, Thurs & Fri 10am–9pm, Sat 9.30am–7pm.

HEMA Nieuwendijk 174 ☎020 623 4176, ⓦhema.nl; map p.51. Nationwide chain that's good for stocking up on toiletries and other essentials, plus occasional designer delights. Surprises include wine and salami at the back of the shop, and a good bakery and cheese counter; great sweets too. Mon–Fri 9am–7pm, Thurs till 9pm, Sat 9am–6pm & Sun noon–6pm.

Metz & Co Keizersgracht 455 ☎020 520 7020, ⓦmetzco.eu; map pp.48–49. Classic department store with five floors of clothing, from shoes and overcoats to lingerie – and featuring every designer you can think of: Hugo Boss, Marc Jacobs et al. When it was built, Metz & Co was the tallest commercial building in the city, with a rooftop glass and metal showroom designed by Gerrit Rietveld, the leading architectural light of the De Stijl movement, added in 1933. The top-floor showroom is now home to M'Café, from where there are fabulous views over the city centre. Mon 11am–6pm, Tues–Sat 9.30am–6pm & Sun noon–5pm.

1

FOOD AND DRINK

Albert Heijn NZ Voorburgwal 226 ☎020 421 8344, ⊚ah.nl; map p.51. Located just behind Dam Square, this is the biggest of the city's forty-odd Albert Heijn supermarkets. Mon–Thurs & Sat 8am–10pm, Fri 8am–7pm; closed Sun.

★ **Bakkerij Paul Année** Runstraat 25 ☎020 623 5322, ⊚bakkerijannee.nl; map pp.48–49. The best wholegrain and sourdough breads in town, bar none – all made with organic grains. Mon–Fri 7.30am–6pm, Sat 8am–5pm & Sun 10am–3pm.

★ **De Bierkoning** Paleisstraat 125 ☎020 625 2336, ⊚bierkoning.nl; map p.51. The "Beer King" is aptly named: over one thousand different beers, with the appropriate glasses to drink them from – and 25 years of experience selling them. Mon 1–7pm, Tues–Fri 11am–7pm, Sat noon–6pm & Sun 1–6pm.

Jordino Haarlemmerdijk 25a ☎020 420 3225, ⊚jordino.nl; map pp.48–49. Tempting little shop where you can sample some of Amsterdam's best ice cream and chocolates, from the tasty and straightforward to the positively idiosyncratic. An Haarlemmerdijk institution. Sun & Mon 1–7pm, Tues–Sat 10am–7pm.

De Kaaskamer Runstraat 7 ☎020 623 3483, ⊚kaaskamer.nl; map pp.48–49. Friendly cheese shop, with both Dutch and international cheeses piled high up towards the rafters, and tapas and olives too. Mon

noon–6pm, Tues–Fri 9am–6pm, Sat 9am–5pm & Sun noon–5pm.

Oud-Hollandsch Snoepwinkeltje Tweede Egelantierdwarsstraat 2 ☎020 420 7390, ⊚snoepwinkeltje.com; map pp.48–49. Delightfully old-fashioned sweetshop, selling all sorts of mouthwatering Dutch sweets, piled up in glass jars – a great place to try Dutch liquorice (*drop*). Tues–Sat 11am–6.30pm, Sun noon–5pm.

Pompadour Chocolaterie Patisserie Huidenstraat 12 ☎020 623 9554, ⊚patisseriepompadour.com; map pp.48–49. Deluxe café-cum-shop selling delicious chocolates and lots of home-made pastries – usually smothered in or filled with chocolate. Mon–Fri 10am–6pm, Sat 9am–5pm & Sun noon–6pm.

★ **Puccini** Staalstraat 17 ☎020 626 5474, ⊚puccinibomboni.com; map p.51. Make no mistake about it, this is the best chocolate shop in town – all handmade, with an array of fantastic and imaginative fillings, and in all sorts of unusual shapes and sizes. Mon noon–6pm, Tues–Sat 9am–6pm, Sun noon–6pm.

Puccini Singel 184 17 ☎020 427 8341, ⊚puccinibomboni.com; map pp.48–49. Second outlet of the best chocolatier in town. Mon noon–6pm, Tues–Sat 11am–6pm, Sun noon–6pm.

AMSTERDAM MARKETS

Visiting one of Amsterdam's **open-air markets** is a must. There's a first-rate flea market on Waterlooplein, several lively street markets selling everything from fresh veg to clothes, plus smaller, specialist markets devoted to everything from books to flowers.

★ **Albert Cuypstraat market** De Pijp, ⊚albertcuypmarkt.nl. Long and slender, Albert Cuypstraat is the heart of De Pijp and it's here you'll find the city's biggest and best open-air general market stretching east for over a kilometre from Ferdinand Bolstraat to Van Woustraat. There are scores of stalls selling everything from cut-price carrots and raw-herring sandwiches to saucepans, Day-Glo thongs and eccentric bygones. Check out, too, the shops that flank the market on each side, and the Indian and Surinamese restaurants down the side streets – they're often cheaper than their equivalents in the city centre. Daily except Sunday 10am–5pm.

Bloemenmarkt Singel. Stretching out between Koningsplein and Muntplein, this very popular floating market specializes in flowers and plants, ostensibly for tourists, but locals congregate here too. Mon–Sat 9am–5pm, Sun 11am–5pm.

Boekenmarkt Spui ⊚deboekenmarktophetspui .org. The city's best secondhand book market, a

rambling affair with many an interesting find lurking in the unsorted boxes. Fri 10am–4pm.

★ **Boerenmarkt** Noordermarkt ⊚boerenmarkt amsterdam.nl. Next to the Noorderkerk, this farmers' market offers all kinds of organically grown produce, fresh bread, exotic fungi and fresh herbs. Sat 9am–4pm.

Flea Market Noordermarkt. A junk-lover's goldmine with of all kinds of bargains, tucked away beneath piles of useless – or semi-useless – rubbish. Get here early. Mon 9am–2pm.

Flea Market Waterlooplein. A real Amsterdam institution, sprawling and chaotic, this is the final resting-place of ancient clothes, antique junk and secondhand records. Mon–Sat 9am–5pm.

Kunstmarkt Spui, ⊚artplein-spui.nl. Low-key but good-quality fine and applied art market enabling mostly Dutch artists to sell their work direct to the public. Late March to Oct Sun 10am–5pm.

HOME

★ **Droog** Staalstraat 7B ☎020 523 5059, ⓦdroog
.com; map p.51. Founded in 1993, this super-cool shop
does a tasty line in designer lighting, tableware, furniture
and even bling. Most of the stuff they design themselves
and, at its best, it's strikingly original. Tues–Sat
11am–6pm, Sun noon–5pm.

★ **Eduard Kramer** Nieuwe Spiegelstraat 64 ☎020
623 0832, ⓦantique-tileshop.nl; map pp.48–49. The
Dutch have a long and distinguished history of tile making
and this excellent shop specializes in vintage tiles from the
fifteenth century onwards. In the heart of the
Spiegelkwartier. Mon 1–6pm, Tues–Sat 10am–6pm,
Sun 1–6pm.

Frozen Fountain Prinsengracht 645 ☎020 622 9375,
ⓦfrozenfountain.nl; map pp.48–49. Contemporary
furniture and interior design with the emphasis on all
things Dutch – all the leading designers make a showing.
Mon 1–6pm, Tues–Sat 10am–6pm & Sun 1–5pm.

Gerda's Bloemen Runstraat 16 ☎020 624 2912,
ⓦtheninestreets.com/gerda.html; map pp.48–49.
Amsterdam is full of flower shops, but this one is the most
imaginative and sensual. Designer pottery and glassware
too, plus expert advice. Mon–Fri 9am–6pm & Sat
9am–5pm.

MUSIC

Back Beat Records Egelantiersstraat 19 ☎020 627
1657, ⓦbackbeat.nl; map pp.48–49. Small and
independent specialist record shop with a great line in soul,
blues, jazz, funk, etc, both vinyl and CD. Opened in 1988 by
"Sweet Soul Music" Arthur Conley. Mon–Sat 11am–6pm.

Concerto Utrechtsestraat 52–60 ☎020 623 5228,
ⓦconcertomania.nl; map pp.48–49. New and used
records and CDs in all categories; equally good on Baroque

as on grunge. The best all-round selection in the city, with
the option to listen before you buy. Mon–Sat 10am–6pm,
Thurs till 9pm, Sun noon–6pm.

VINTAGE

★ **Lady Day** Hartenstraat 9 ☎020 623 5820,
ⓦladydayvintage.com; map pp.48–49. This spacious
store offers a wide-ranging selection of secondhand and
vintage fashion mostly dating from the fifties, sixties and
seventies. Caters for both men and women. Mon–Sat
11am–6pm, Thurs till 9pm, & Sun 1–6pm.

Laura Dols Wolvenstraat 7 ☎020 624 9066,
ⓦlauradols.nl; map pp.48–49. One of Amsterdam's
largest vintage stockists, Laura Dols has rails groaning with
countless dresses sorted according to colour as well as
printed fabrics from the 50s and 60s. Also does a good line
in party dresses and formal evening wear – for both men
and women. Mon–Sat 11am–6pm (Thurs till 9pm), Sun
1–6pm.

MISCELLANEOUS

P.G.C. Hajenius Rokin 96 ☎020 623 7494, ⓦhajenius
.com; map p.51. There was a time when no self-respecting
Netherlander would go anywhere without his pipe and
although those days are long gone, this old-fashioned
tobacconists, with its wood panelling and glass display
cabinets, sells top-quality pipe tobacco and an outstanding
range of cigars and cigarillos. Mon noon–6pm, Tues–Sat
9.30am–6pm & Sun noon–5pm.

Witte Tanden Winkel Runstraat 5 ☎020 623 3443,
ⓦdewittetandenwinkel.nl; map pp.48–49. The "White
Teeth Shop" sells wacky toothbrushes and just about every
dental hygiene accoutrement you could ever need – or
imagine. Good fun and orally sound. Tues–Fri 10am–5pm,
Sat 10am–5pm.

DIRECTORY

Doctor Your hotel/hostel or the VVV should be able to
provide the address of an English-speaking doctor.
Otherwise, call the Centraal Doktorsdienst ☎088 003
0600.

Left luggage Centraal Station has both coin-operated
luggage lockers (daily 7am–11pm) and a staffed left-
luggage office (daily 7am–11pm).

Library The city's new, deluxe library, the Amsterdam
bibliotheek is at the heart of a massive docklands
redevelopment programme at Oosterdokskade 143 (daily
10am–10pm; ⓦoba.nl).

Lost property For items lost on the trams, buses or metro,
contact GVB Head Office, Prins Hendrikkade 108–114
(Mon–Fri 9am–4pm; ☎020 460 5858). For property lost

on an NS train, first go to the service office at Centraal
Station (☎020 557 8544). Schiphol Airport's lost and found
desk is in the Arrivals Hall (☎020 649 1433).

Pharmacies You'll need a pharmacy (*apotheek*) for minor
ailments or to get a prescription filled. Pharmacies are
legion and are usually open Mon–Fri 9am–6pm, though
some are closed on Monday mornings.

Post The Dutch postal system is now operated by TNT, who
have opened dozens of mini-post offices in stores and
supermarkets. Opening times vary, but are at least Mon–Fri
9am–5pm & Sat 9am–noon. There's also a larger TNT post
office at Singel 250, on the corner with Raadhuisstraat
(Mon–Fri 8am–6pm, Sat 10am–5pm). Stamps are sold at
a wide range of outlets, including most hotels.

Noord-Holland

BEACH HUTS, TEXEL

Noord-Holland

Stretching north from Amsterdam to the island of Texel, the province of Noord-Holland is largely rural, its polder landscapes of green, pancake-flat fields intercepted by hundreds of drainage canals and ditches, and its wide horizons only interrupted by the odd farmhouse or windmill. The province's west coast is defended from the ocean by a long belt of sand dunes, which is itself shielded by long and broad sandy beaches, and it's these that attract holidaying Netherlanders. Much of the east coast has been reclaimed from what was once the saltwater Zuider Zee and is now, after the construction of two complementary dykes, the freshwater Markermeer and IJsselmeer. Here, along this deeply indented coast, lies a string of old seaports which flourished from the fourteenth to the eighteenth century on the back of the sea trade with the Baltic.

Noord-Holland's principal urban highlight is **Haarlem**, an easy-going town with more than its fair share of Golden Age buildings, the province's best art gallery, and ready access to some wild stretches of dune and beach in the **Nationaal Park Zuid-Kennemerland**. Northeast of the capital, the old Zuider Zee ports of **Marken**, **Volendam** and **Edam** are a bit touristy in summer, but have considerable charm if you visit off-season. Further north, **Hoorn** and **Enkhuizen** were once major Zuider Zee ports, and their historic wealth is reflected in a scattering of handsome old buildings. Enkhuizen, in particular, is very attractive and has one of the country's best open-air museums, the **Zuiderzeemuseum**. A short train ride north of Amsterdam is the **Zaanstad** conurbation, whose chief attraction is the antique windmills and canals of **Zaanse Schans**. Further up the line, the pleasant provincial town of **Alkmaar** has a much-touted summer cheese market, and makes a good base for exploring two protected coastal zones, the **Noordhollands Duinreservaat** (North Holland Dune Reserve) and the **Schoorlse Duinen Nationaalpark**. Beyond, in the far north of the province, the island of **Texel** is the most accessible of the Waddenzee islands. It can get crowded in summer, but don't be put off: with a bit of walking – or cycling – you can easily find some solitude.

Most of Noord-Holland is located north of Amsterdam, though the borders of the province also dip round the city, taking in an area known as **Het Gooi**, where the highlights are the small town of **Muiden** with its castle and the old fortified town of **Naarden**.

GETTING AROUND

By public transport Getting around Noord-Holland by public transport is easy, with trains linking all the major centres – Haarlem, Alkmaar, Hoorn, Enkhuizen and Den Helder (for Texel) – and buses filling in the gaps. Distances are small and frequencies regular so the majority of Noord-Holland is easily visited on day-trips from Amsterdam, but to make the most of the province you're better off staying over at least a couple of nights.

The painter with 27 kinds of black
p.108
Haarlem's hofjes p.109
Hans Brinker p.110

How the Zuider Zee became the IJsselmeer p.112
The Stoomtram p.120
Alkmaar's cheese market p.129

THE GROTE KERK, HAARLEM

Highlights

❶ Haarlem This good-looking old town is home to the outstanding Frans Hals Museum and makes a lovely base for exploring the southern part of the province and the nearby coast. **See p.105**

❷ Edam Archetypal Dutch country town of narrow canals and antique cottages. Once famous for its mermaids, it now has a couple of very enticing places to stay. **See p.116**

❸ Enkhuizen This handsome old Zuider Zee port of slender waterways is worth a visit in its own right, but it has the excellent Zuiderzeemuseum thrown in too. **See p.121**

❹ Dunes The dunes of Noord-Holland's west coast are the closest the country gets to hills, and exploring them by bike or on foot is one of the joys of this part of the country. **See p.129 & p.132**

❺ Texel Just twenty minutes from the mainland by regular ferry, but with a real island feel – not to mention, good places to stay and eat and some magnificent sandy beaches. **See p.134**

HIGHLIGHTS ARE MARKED ON THE MAP ON P.104

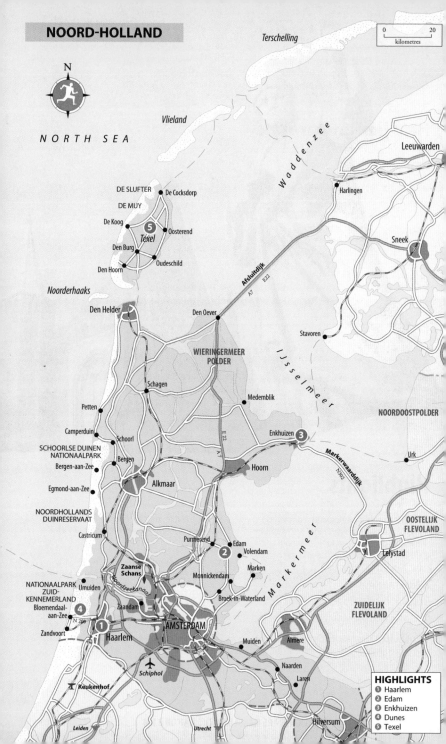

By car If you want to continue north or east, the two dykes that enclose the Markermeer and the IJsselmeer carry handy road links. The former, the Markerwaarddijk, connects Enkhuizen with Lelystad on the reclaimed Flevoland polders (see p.245), while the latter, the Afsluitdijk, makes the 30km trip from Den Oever to the province of Friesland (see Chapter 4).

Haarlem and around

It's only fifteen minutes from Amsterdam by train, but **HAARLEM** has a very different pace and feel from its neighbour. A former cloth-making centre, it's an easy-going, medium-sized town of around 150,000, with a good-looking centre that is easily absorbed in a few hours or on an overnight stay. In 1572, the townsfolk sided with the Protestant rebels against the Habsburgs, a decision they must have regretted when a large Spanish army besieged them in December of the same year. The siege was a desperate affair that lasted for eight months, but finally the town surrendered after receiving various assurances of good treatment – assurances which the Spanish commander, Frederick of Toledo, promptly broke, massacring over two thousand of the Protestant garrison. Recaptured five years later, Haarlem went on to enjoy its greatest prosperity in the seventeenth century and was home to a flourishing school of **painters**, whose canvases are displayed at the outstanding **Frans Hals Museum**, located in the almshouse where Hals spent his last, and according to some his most brilliant years.

Haarlem is also within easy striking distance of the **coast**: every half-hour trains make the ten-minute trip to the modern resort of **Zandvoort-aan-Zee**, while frequent buses serve the huddle of fast-food joints that make up **Bloemendaal-aan-Zee** just to the north. Neither is particularly endearing in itself, but both are redeemed by long sandy beaches and the pristine stretches of the dune and lagoon, crisscrossed by footpaths and cycling trails, that make up the nearby **Nationaal Park de Zuid-Kennemerland**.

Grote Markt

At the heart of Haarlem is the **Grote Markt**, an attractive open space flanked by an appealing ensemble of Gothic and Renaissance architecture, including an intriguing if garbled **Stadhuis**, whose turrets and towers, balconies and galleries were put together between the fourteenth and the seventeenth centuries. At the other end of the Grote Markt stands a **statue** of Laurens Coster (1370–1440), who, Haarlemmers insist, is the true inventor of printing. Legend tells of Coster cutting a letter "A" from the bark of a tree, dropping it into the sand by accident, and, hey presto, realizing how to create the printed word. The statue shows him earnestly holding up the wooden letter, but most historians agree that it was the German Johannes Gutenberg who invented printing, in the early 1440s.

The Hallen

Grote Markt 16 • **Archeologisch Museum** Wed–Sun 1–5pm; free • **Kunstcentrum De Hallen** Tues–Sat 11am–5pm, Sun noon–5pm; prices vary depending on the exhibition

Opposite the Stadhuis, the rambling **Hallen** is divided into two. In one half, the old meat market, the **Vleeshal**, which boasts a flashy Dutch Renaissance facade, houses the town's modest archeological museum in its basement. The other half is given over to a gallery, the Kunstcentrum, that provides additional exhibition space for the Frans Hals Museum as well as hosting temporary exhibitions of more modern art and photography.

The Grote Kerk

Grote Markt • **Church** Mon–Sat 10am–4pm; €2.50 • **Organ recitals** mid-May to mid-Oct Tues at 8.15pm; July & Aug also Thurs at 3pm; free

Dominating Haarlem's Grote Markt is the **Grote Kerk**, a soaring Gothic structure supported by mighty buttresses that dwarfs the surrounding clutter of ecclesiastical

2

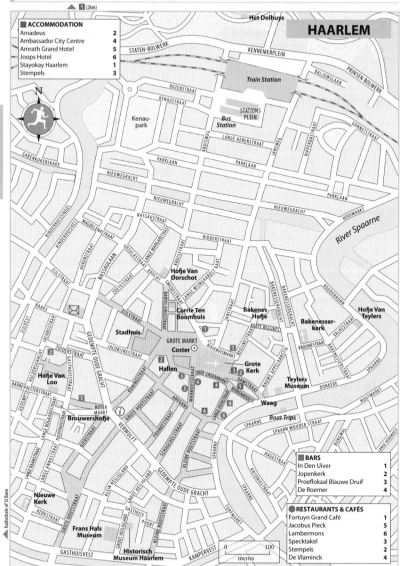

HAARLEM

Het Dolhuys

Train Station

River Spaarne

■ ACCOMMODATION
Amadeus	2
Ambassador City Centre	4
Amrath Grand Hotel	5
Joops Hotel	6
Stayokay Haarlem	1
Stempels	3

■ BARS
In Den Uiver	1
Jopenkerk	2
Proeflokaal Blauwe Druif	3
De Roemer	4

● RESTAURANTS & CAFÉS
Fortuyn Grand Café	1
Jacobus Pieck	5
Lambermons	6
Specktakel	3
Stempels	2
De Vlaminck	4

outhouses. Dedicated to St Bavo, the church was finished in 1538, after 150 years in the making, and is surmounted by a good-looking lantern tower, which perches above the transept crossing. Inside, the towering beauty of the nave is enhanced by the creaminess of the stone and the bright simplicity of the whitewashed walls. The Protestants cleared the church of most of its decoration during the Reformation, but the splendid wrought-iron **choir screen** has survived, as have the choir's wooden **stalls** with their folksy misericords. In front of the screen is the conspicuous Neoclassical **tomb** of Haarlem's own Christiaan Brunings (1736–1805), a much-lauded hydraulic engineer and director of Holland's water board.

The chapels

Next to the south transept is the **Brewers' Chapel**, where the central pillar bears two black markers – one showing the height of a local giant, the 2.64m-tall Daniel Cajanus, who died in 1749, the other the 0.84m-high dwarf Simon Paap from Zandvoort (1789–1828). In the middle of the nave, the pulpit's banisters are in the form of snakes – fleeing from the word of God – while on the other side the pocket-sized **Dog Whippers' Chapel** was built for the men employed to keep dogs under control in the church, as evidenced by the rings there to tether them to, and now separated from the nave by an iron grille.

The Christian Müller organ

At the west end of the church, the mighty Christian Müller **organ** is one of the biggest in the world, with over five thousand pipes and loads of snazzy Baroque embellishment. Manufactured in Amsterdam in the 1730s, it is said to have been played by both Handel and Mozart – you can still hear it at one of the free organ recitals held in the summer. Beneath it, Jan Baptist Xavery's lovely group of draped marble figures represent Poetry and Music offering thanks to the town, which is depicted as a patroness of the arts – in return for its generous support in the purchase of the organ.

The Corrie Ten Boomhuis Museum

Barteljorisstraat 19 • April–Oct Tues–Sat 10am–4pm; Nov–March Tues–Sat 11am–3pm • 1hr guided tours only • Free • ⓦ corrietenboom.com

Two minutes from the Grote Markt, the **Corrie Ten Boomhuis** is where a Dutch family – the Ten Booms – hid fugitives, resistance fighters and Jews alike above their jeweller's shop during World War II. There isn't actually much to look at in the house, but the guided tour is instructive and moving, if a tad drawn-out. The family, whose bravery sprang from their Christian faith, was betrayed to the Gestapo in 1944, and only one member, Corrie Ten Boom, survived – as does the jeweller's itself, still doing business at street level.

The Frans Hals Museum

Groot Heiligland 62 • Tues–Sat 11am–5pm, Sun noon–5pm • €10 • ⓦ franshalsmuseum.nl

Haarlem's biggest draw, the **Frans Hals Museum**, is a five-minute stroll south of the Grote Markt, housed in the almshouse complex where the aged Hals lived out his last destitute years. The collection comprises a handful of prime works by Hals along with a small but eclectic sample of Dutch paintings from the fifteenth century onwards, all immaculately presented and labelled in English and Dutch. There's also a small separate section consisting of a life-size replica of a seventeenth-century Haarlem street.

Sixteenth- and Seventeenth-century paintings

The museum has a small group of early sixteenth-century paintings, the most prominent of which is a triptych from the School of **Hans Memling**, but otherwise focuses on work by Haarlem artists. The most notable works are a couple of paintings by **Jan van Scorel** (1495–1562), and **Cornelis Cornelisz van Haarlem's** (1562–1638) giant *Wedding of Peleus and Thetis*, an appealing rendition of what was then a popular subject. This marriage precipitated civil war among the gods and was used by the Dutch as an emblem of warning against discord, a call for unity during the long war with Spain. Similarly, the same artist's *Massacre of the Innocents* connects the biblical story with the Spanish siege of Haarlem in 1572. Opposite, three accomplished pictures by **Hendrik Goltzius** (1558–1617) depict Hercules, Mercury and Minerva.

2

THE PAINTER WITH 27 KINDS OF BLACK

Little is known about **Frans Hals** (c.1580–1666), born in Antwerp, the son of Flemish refugees who settled in Haarlem in the late 1580s. His extant oeuvre is relatively small – some two hundred paintings, and nothing like the number of sketches and studies left behind by his contemporary, Rembrandt. His outstanding gift was as a portraitist, showing a sympathy with his subjects and an ability to capture fleeting expression that some say even Rembrandt lacked. Seemingly quick and careless flashes of colour characterize his work, but they are always blended into a coherent and marvellously animated whole. He is perhaps best known for his civic guard portraits – group portraits of the militia companies initially formed to defend the country from the Spanish, but which later became social clubs for the gentry. Getting a commission to paint one of these portraits was a well-paid privilege – Hals got his first in 1616 – but their composition was a tricky affair and often the end result was dull and flat. With great flair and originality, Hals made the group portrait a unified whole instead of a static collection of individual portraits, his figures carefully arranged, but so cleverly as not to appear contrived. Hals's later paintings are darker, more contemplative works, closer to Rembrandt in their lighting and increasingly sombre in their outlook, giving meaning to van Gogh's remark that "Frans Hals had no fewer than 27 blacks".

Look out also for *Adam and Eve* by **Marten van Heemskerck** (1498–1574), whose work dominates one room, in particular a brutal and realistic *Christ Crowned with Thorns* and a painting of St Luke with the Virgin and infant Jesus. There are also several rooms of paintings by the **Haarlem Mannerists**, including two tiny and precise works by **Karel van Mander** (1548–1606), leading light of the Haarlem School and mentor of many of the city's most celebrated painters, including Hals, genre works by **Adriaen** (1610–85) and **Isaac van Ostade** (1621–49); and depictions of the Grote Kerk by **Gerrit Berckheyde** (1638–98) and others. Look out also for **Pieter Brueghel the Younger**'s (1564–1638) berserk *Dutch Proverbs*, illustrating a whole raft of contemporary proverbs – a detailed key next to the painting gives the lowdown.

Frans Hals paintings

The **Hals paintings** begin in earnest in **Room 14** with a set of five "Civic Guard" portraits. For a time, Hals himself was a member of the Company of St George, and in the *Officers of the Militia Company of St George* he appears in the top left-hand corner – one of his few self-portraits. See also Hals's Haarlem contemporary Johannes Verspronck's (1600–62) *Regentesses of the Holy Ghost Orphanage* – one of the most accomplished pictures in the gallery, which echoes Hals's own *Regents of St Elizabeth Gasthuis*, a serious but benign work of 1641. Perhaps the museum's most valuable and impressive works, however, are Hal's famous twin portraits, *Regents* and *Regentesses of the Oudemannenhuis*, which depicts the people who ran the almshouse when Hals was there – a collection of cold, self-satisfied faces staring out of the gloom, the women reproachful, the men only marginally more affable. There are those who claim Hals had lost his touch by the time he painted these pictures, yet their sinister, almost ghostly, power suggests quite the opposite.

Historisch Museum Haarlem

Groot Heiligland 47 • Tues–Sat noon–5pm, Sun 1–5pm • €5 • ⓦ historischmuseumhaarlem.nl

Across the road from the Frans Hals Museum, the **Historisch Museum Zuid-Kennemerland** tracks through a fairly pedestrian history of Haarlem and its region, in premises that were once used as a women's almshouse. A short film illuminates things with the help of some spectacular dramatic effects, and there's a model of the town as it would have been in the early nineteenth century as well as various other displays of paintings, porcelain and silver.

The Teyler's Museum

Spaarne 16 • Tues–Sat 10am–5pm, Sun noon–5pm • €9 • ⓦ teylersmuseum.nl

It's a short stroll from the Grote Markt to the **River Spaarne**, whose wandering curves mark the eastern periphery of the town centre, and are home to the country's oldest museum, the **Teylers Museum**. Founded in 1774 by a wealthy local philanthropist, one **Pieter Teyler van der Hulst**, the museum is delightfully old-fashioned, its wooden cabinets crammed with fossils and bones, crystals and rocks, medals and coins, all displayed alongside dozens of antique scientific instruments of lugubrious appearance and uncertain purpose. The finest room is the **rotunda** – De Ovale Zaal – a handsome, galleried affair with splendid wooden panelling, and there is also a room of nineteenth-century and early twentieth-century Dutch paintings, featuring the likes of Breitner, Israëls, Weissenbruch and Wijbrand Hendriks (1774–1831), who was once the keeper of the art collection here.

Het Dolhuys

Schotersingerl 2 • Tues–Fri 10am–5pm, Sat & Sun noon–5pm • €8.50 • ⓦ hetdolhuys.nl

Perhaps Haarlem's strangest attraction is **Het Dolhuys**, an imaginative and thought-provoking museum of madness and psychiatric care throughout the ages, housed in a converted lunatic asylum. There are isolation cells, exhibits which tell the stories of "mad" people who have done extraordinary things, as well as displays which show different attitudes to mental illness over the years – from medieval imbalances to possession. The central Zorgzaal is the hub of the exhibition, with films, pictures and artefacts from asylums around Holland. Most of it is in Dutch, but a helpful booklet on loan from the reception translates the most important stuff. The museum is just a five-minute stroll from the train station.

Zandvoort-aan-Zee

The suburbs of Haarlem ramble out almost as far as **ZANDVOORT-AAN-ZEE**, a major seaside resort just 5km to the west. As Dutch resorts go, Zandvoort is pretty standard – packed in summer, dead and gusty in winter – and its agglomeration of modern apartment blocks hardly cheers the heart, but its **beach** is wide and sandy, it musters up

HAARLEM'S HOFJES

You could do worse than spend a day exploring Haarlem's **hofjes** – small, unpretentious complexes of public housing built for the old and infirm in the seventeenth century. The best known and perhaps most accessible is the one that was home to Frans Hals in the last years of his life and now houses the Frans Hals Museum. But there are others dotted around town, most of them still serving their original purpose but with their gardens at least open to the public. The most grandiose is the riverside **Hofje van Teylers,** a little way east of the museum of the same name around the bend of the Spaarne at Koudenhorn 64. Unlike many of the other *hofjes*, which are decidedly cosy, this is a Neoclassical edifice dating from 1787 with solid columns and cupolas. To the west, the elegant fifteenth-century tower of the **Bakenesserkerk** on Vrouwestraat is a flamboyant, onion-domed affair soaring high above the Haarlem skyline, that marks the nearby **Bakenes Hofje**, at Wijde Appelaarsteeg 11: founded in 1395, it is Haarlem's (and indeed the country's) oldest *hofje*, with a delightful enclosed garden. Five minutes' walk away, the **Hofje van Oorschot**, at the junction of Kruisstraat and Bartelijorisstraat, dates from 1769 and is also rather grand. To the south of here, the **Brouweshofje**, just off Botermarkt, is a small, peaceful terrace of housing with a courtyard behind, and windows framed by brightly painted red and white shutters, while the nearby **Hofje van Loo**, on nearby Barrevoetstraat, is equally diminutive, and open to view from the road.

2

HANS BRINKER

Given that the Dutch have spent most of their history struggling to keep the sea from flooding their land, it's hardly surprising that their folklore abounds with tales of watery salvation, either by luck or the bravery of its inhabitants. One well-known hero is **Hans Brinker**, a young lad who supposedly saved the Haarlem area from disaster by sticking his finger into a hole in the dyke. The village of **Spaarndam**, just north of Haarlem, has a statue in his honour, but in fact, although the tale has the ring of truth, it's all fictitious – invented by the American writer Mary Mapes Dodge in her 1873 children's book, *The Silver Skates*. The monument to the boy was unveiled in 1950, more, it seems, as a tribute to the opportunistic Dutch tourist industry than anything else.

---

a casino and a car-racing circuit and it is one of the few places in the Netherlands where the rail network reaches the coast: there's a half-hourly service from Haarlem, and Zandvoort train station is a mere five-minute walk (if that) from the beach. Bus #81 also runs hourly from Haarlem bus station, via Bloemnedaal-aan-Zee (see below), to Zandvoort bus station, on Louis Davidsstraat, a short, signposted walk from the train station.

Nationaal Park de Zuid-Kennemerland

The pristine woods, dunes and lagoons of the **NATIONAAL PARK DE ZUID-KENNEMERLAND** stretch north from Zandvoort up to the eminently missable industrial town of IJmuiden, at the mouth of the Nordzeekanaal. Bus #81 leaves Haarlem bus station every thirty minutes to cross the national park via the N200 before reaching the coast at the minuscule beachside settlement of **Bloemendaal-aan-Zee**. En route, several bus stops give access to the clearly marked **hiking and cycling trails** that pattern the national park, but the best option is to get off at the **Koevlak** entrance – ask the driver to let you off. Maps of the park are available at Haarlem tourist office (see below), and there are three colour-coded **hiking routes** posted at Koevlak (and indeed all entrances). The most appealing is the 4- to 5-kilometre (1hr) jaunt west through pine woods and dunes to the seashore, where the *Parnassia* café (April–Nov), provides refreshments with a view of the North Sea. From here, it's a 1.5km walk back to Bloemendaal-aan-Zee, where you can catch bus #81 back to Haarlem (or of course you can do the whole thing in reverse).

ARRIVAL AND DEPARTURE   HAARLEM

By train Haarlem's train station is on Stationsplein, just north of the city centre, about ten minutes' walk from the Grote Markt. Trains run between here and Amsterdam every ten minutes or so and take about fifteen minutes, and there

are also regular services up to Alkmaar and Hoorn.
By bus Buses stop on Stationsplein, just in front of the train station, with services roughly every thirty minutes to Bloemendaal (15min) and Zaandvoort (20min).

INFORMATION

Tourist office The VVV is at Verwulft 11 (April–Sept Mon–Fri 9.30am–5.30pm, Sat 10am–5pm, Sun 11am–3pm; Oct–March Mon–Fri 9.30am–5.30pm, Sat 10am–5pm;

☏ 0900 616 1600, ⓦ vvv.haarlem.nl), and issues free city maps and brochures. It also has details of a small number of rooms in private houses, mostly on the outskirts of town.

ACCOMMODATION

HOTELS
Amadeus Grote Markt 10 ☏ 023 532 4530, ⓦ amadeus-hotel.com. The town centre's cheapest option and right on Haarlem's main square. The rooms here are a bit tatty but nice enough and wi-fi is free. The downstairs restaurant serves a cheap international menu. €55
Ambassador City Centre Oude Groenmarkt 20–24

☏ 023 512 5300, ⓦ acc-hotel.nl. Haarlem's best budget option, this modern hotel couldn't be more central, with its eccentrically decorated lobby and heavy antique furniture. Double rooms are simply but well furnished, a few with four-posters, and although bathrooms are on the small side, wi-fi is free and the welcome warm. €60

Amrath Grand Hotel Frans Hals Damstraat 10 ☎023 518 1818, ⓦbestwestern.com. Plumb in the centre of town, this modern chain hotel has 79 good-sized rooms with bathrooms, decent enough, if a bit lacking in character. The lobby at least tries hard to be memorable, with its spiral steel staircase and stained-glass dome. **€145**

Joops Hotel Lange Veerstraat 36 ☎023 512 5300, ⓦacc-hotel.nl. Owned by the *Ambassador* (see p.110), with a mixture of large antique-filled and slightly more expensive rooms as well as good-value, functionally furnished apartments for up to four people. Check in at the *Ambassador*. Rooms **€85**, apartments **€100**

★ **Stempels** Klokhuisplein 9 ☎023 512 3910, ⓦstempelsinhaarlem.nl. Housed in a former printworks behind the Grote Kerk, Haarlem's best boutique hotel has a variety of rooms, all of them simply and comfortably furnished, with a contemporary restraint that suits the building. The nicest tend to be in the grander end, where the printing family lived, and which dates from the 1700s; try the first-floor corner room, or the large junior suite above. The restaurant is excellent and there's an allday brasserie too. **€112.50**

HOSTELS

Stayokay Haarlem Jan Gijzenpad 3 ☎023 537 3793, ⓦstayokay.com. Spick-and-span modern HI hostel near the sports stadium about 3km north of the town centre. To get there, take bus #2 from the station – a 10min journey. Dorm beds **€29**, rooms **€75**

EATING AND DRINKING

BARS, CAFÉS AND TAKEAWAYS

Fortuyn Grand Café Grote Markt 21, ⓦgrandcafefortuyn.nl. A popular café-bar with charming 1930s decor, including a tiled entrance and quaint glass cabinets preserved from its days as a shop. Lunch (served 10am–5pm) consists of a good selection of substantial sandwiches for around €8, while at dinner main courses – steak, salmon, fondues – hover around €20. Sun–Wed 10am–midnight, Thurs–Sat 10am–1am.

In den Uiver Riviervismarkt 13 ☎023 532 5399 ⓦindenuiver.nl. Just off the Grote Markt, this lively and extremely appealing brown bar, housed in an old fish shop, is decked out in traditional Dutch-café style; it has occasional live music too. Mon–Wed 4pm–1am, Thurs–Sat 4pm–2am, Sun 2–10pm.

Jopenkerk Vestestraat ☎023 533 411, ⓦjopen.nl. Haarlem used to be known for its beer, and this converted old church is home to the Jopen microbrewery which is successfully reviving the old traditions. It's a brewery, bar and restaurant rolled into one, and is very nicely done, with long benches, comfy sofas and its own cloudy, unfiltered beer. The food is simple rather than splendid, but you should at least try one of the dozen or so Jopen brews at the bar. Daily 10am–1am; lunch noon–3pm; dinner 5.30–8pm.

Proeflokaal Blauwe Druif Lange Veerstraat 7. Just off the main square, this is an intimate and amiable bar – that is typically Dutch. Mon–Thurs 4pm–midnight, Fri & Sat 4pm–1am, Sun 4–9pm.

De Roemer Botermarkt 17 ☎023 532 5267, ⓦcafederoemer.nl. Cosy bar with a covered outside terrace, tucked away on Botermarkt on the edge of the old centre. It serves excellent, mainly Dutch food, with sandwiches and salads (€5–8) at lunchtime (11am–4.45pm), and a great-value evening menu, including decent burgers and excellent steaks at dinner (5–9pm). Mon–Thurs 10am–1am, Fri & Sat 10am–2am, Sun noon–1am.

De Vlaminck Warmoesstraat 3 ☎023 532 1084. It may just be a takeaway, but this is a decent and very central *friterie*, if you fancy lunch on the go. It serves excellent frites, with all the usual toppings. Tues–Fri 11.30am–6pm, Sat 11.30am–5pm, Sun noon–5pm.

RESTAURANTS

Jacobus Pieck Warmoesstraat 18 ☎023 532 6144, ⓦjacobuspieck.nl. Welcoming café-restaurant that's a good bet for either lunch or dinner, with sandwiches for €6.75, burgers and salads for €8.75, and a short menu of more substantial main courses in the evenings for €16.50–17.50: the *dagschotel* is €12.50. Mon 11am–4pm, Tues–Sat 11am–4pm & 5.30–10pm.

Lambermons Korte Veerstraat 51 ☎023 542 7804, ⓦlambermons.nl. Large, old-fashioned French restaurant that focuses on classic French food – everything from bouillabaisse to *pot au feu* and oysters and seafood. Meat and fish mains around €25, big seafood sharing platters €125. Mon–Thurs noon–3pm & 6–10pm.

Specktakel Spekstraat 4 ☎023 532 3841, ⓦspecktakel.nl. Inventive little place that tries its hand at an international menu, dishing up everything from kangaroo through to antelope – it's better than you might think. Starters cost €12.50, main courses €20, though if you're hungry enough it's better to choose three courses for €32.50. Daily 5–10pm, Sat also noon–4pm.

★ **Stempels** Klokhuisplein 9 ☎023 512 3910, ⓦstempelsinhaarlem.nl. Not a cheap option by any means, but you do feel you're eating in one of the grander spaces in the city, and the four-course daily menu at €38.50 has to be one of Haarlem's (if not the country's) greatest food bargains: very high-quality cooking, with great fish and meat laced with innovative blends of flavours and ingredients. Daily 5.30–10pm.

2

2

HOW THE ZUIDER ZEE BECAME THE IJSSELMEER

The towns and villages that string along the east coast of **Noord-Holland** flourished during Amsterdam's Golden Age, their economies buoyed up by shipbuilding, the Baltic Sea trade and the demand for herring. They had access to the open sea via the waters of the **Zuider Zee** (Southern Sea) and, to the north, the connecting **Waddenzee** (Mud Sea). The business was immensely profitable and its proceeds built a string of prosperous seaports – most notably Volendam, Hoorn and Enkhuizen – and nourished market towns like Edam, while the Zuider Zee itself supported a batch of fishing villages such as Marken and Urk. In the eighteenth century, however, the Baltic trade declined and the harbours silted up, leaving the ports economically stranded.

The Zuider Zee continued to provide a livelihood for local fishermen, but most of the country was more concerned by the danger of flooding it posed, as time and again storms and high tides combined to breach the east coast's defences. The first plan to seal off and reclaim the Zuider Zee was proposed in 1667, but the rotating-turret windmills that then provided the most efficient way of drying the land were insufficient for the task and matters were delayed until suitable technology arrived – in the form of the steam-driven pump. In 1891, **Cornelis Lely** (1854–1929) proposed a retaining dyke and his plans were finally put into effect after devastating floods hit the area in 1916. Work began on this dyke, the **Afsluitdijk**, in 1920 and, on May 28, 1932, the last gap in it was closed and the Zuider Zee simply ceased to exist, replaced by the freshwater **IJsselmeer**.

The original plan was to reclaim all the land protected by the Afsluitdijk, turning it into farmland for settlers from the country's overcrowded cities, starting with three large-scale land-reclamation schemes that were completed over the next forty years: the **Noordoostpolder** in 1942 (480 square kilometres), **Oostelijk Flevoland** in 1957 (540 square kilometres) and **Zuidelijk Flevoland** in 1968 (440 square kilometres). In addition, a second, complementary dyke linking Enkhuizen with Lelystad was finished in 1976, thereby creating lake **Markermeer** – a necessary prelude to the draining of another stretch of the IJsselmeer. The engineers licked their contractual lips, but they were out of sync with the majority of the population, who were now opposed to any further draining of the lake. Partly as a result, the grand plan was abandoned and, after much governmental huffing and puffing, the Markermeer was left alone and thus most of the old Zuider Zee remained water.

There were many economic benefits to be had in the closing of the Zuider Zee, not least great chunks of new and fertile farmland, while the roads that were built along the top of the two main retaining dykes brought Noord-Holland within twenty minutes' drive of Friesland. The price was the demise of the old Zuider Zee **fishing fleet**, and today these placid, steel-grey lakes are popular with day-tripping Amsterdammers, who come here in their droves to sail boats, observe the waterfowl, and visit a string of dinky towns and villages that pretty much rely on tourism to survive. These begin on the coast just a few kilometres north of Amsterdam with the picturesque old fishing village of **Marken** and the former seaport of **Volendam**, just up the coast. From here, it's a couple of kilometres further to **Edam**, the pick of the local bunch, a small and infinitely pretty little town of narrow canals and handsome old houses.

Marken

Until its road connection to the mainland in 1957, **MARKEN** was an island in the Zuider Zee, and pretty much a closed community, supported by a small fishing industry. Today, it mainly lives off its tourist industry, and can get pretty busy on summer weekends, though it's of the day-tripping, coach-driven variety, and when the crowds have left, or out of season, it's a rather special place, very peaceful and remote, despite being within just a few miles of Amsterdam's urban sprawl.

The village

There's no denying the picturesque charms of the island's one and only village, also called Marken, where the immaculately maintained houses, mostly painted in deep green with white trimmings, cluster on top of artificial mounds raised to protect them from the sea. There are two main parts to the village: **Havenbuurt**, around and behind the harbour, is the bit you see in most of the photographs, where many of the waterfront houses are raised on stilts. Although these are now panelled in, they were once open, allowing the sea to roll under the floors in bad weather, enough to terrify most people half to death. One or two of the houses are open to visitors, proclaiming themselves to be typical of Marken, and the waterfront is lined by snack bars and souvenir shops, often staffed by locals in traditional costume. Still you do get a hint of how hard life used to be – both here and in **Kerkbuurt**, five minutes' walk from the harbour around the **church**, an ugly 1904 replacement for its sea-battered predecessor. Kerkbuurt is quieter and less touristy than Havenbuurt, its narrow lanes lined by ancient dwellings and a row of old eel-smoking houses, one of which is now the **Marker Museum** at Kerkbuurt 44 (April–Oct Mon–Sat 10am–5pm, Sun noon–4pm; Oct Mon–Sat 11am–4pm & Sun noon–4pm; €2.50; ◍markermuseum.nl), furnished as an old fishermen's cottage and devoted to the history of the former island and its fishing industry.

2

ARRIVAL AND DEPARTURE   MARKEN

By bus Marken is accessible direct from Amsterdam on bus #111, departing from outside Centraal Station every 30min; the journey takes forty minutes. The bus drops passengers beside the car park on the edge of Marken village, from where it's a five-minute walk to the lakeshore.

By ferry The Marken Express ferry, Haven 39, Volendam (☎029 936 3331, ◍markenexpress.nl) runs between Volendam and Marken every 30–45min (March–Oct daily 11am–5pm; 25min; €8 return, €5.50 one-way, €6.75 with bike, children €4.50 return).

ACCOMMODATION AND EATING

★**Hof van Marken** Buurt II 15 ☎0299 601 300, ◍hofvanmarken.nl. This small hotel-restaurant, tucked away in the backstreets from Marken's harbour, has seven simple but stylish rooms, with a homely yet contemporary feel. Its elegant dining room serves great food with a choice of three-, four- or five-course menus (for €36, €44 and €52 respectively), featuring things like beef tartare with potato confit and horseradish, followed by steamed turbot, sea

bass, or leg of lamb with aubergine couscous. Wed–Fri dinner only, Sat & Sun lunch and dinner. **€95**
Land en Zeezicht Havenbuurt 6 ☎0299 601 302. Right on the north side of the harbour, this old-fashioned place serves a decent smoked eel sandwich as well as more substantial, mainly traditional Dutch dishes. Mon–Thurs 11am–8pm, Fri 11am–8.30pm, Sat & Sun 11am-9pm.

Monnickendam

The former port of **MONNICKENDAM** was named by a group of Benedictine monks, who built a dam here in the fourteenth century. There's not much to it now, but it has the same sleepy charm of the other old Zuider Zee ports, and one or two attractions to divert you on your way to Volendam and Edam. The harbour repays a wander too. It has a more rough-and-ready air than that of its neighbours and a more authentically nautical one too, with herring smokehouses and lots of rugged sailing barges alongside the pleasureboats of its marina – all pleasingly not spruced up for tourists.

ARRIVAL AND DEPARTURE   MONNICKENDAM

By bus Monnickendam is pretty easy to reach, with regular buses between Amsterdam and the Zuider Zee towns of

Volendam and Edam stopping on the outskirts of town – principally the #110, #111 and #118.

ACCOMMODATION

★**De Posthoorn** Noordeinde 43 ☎0299 654 598, ◍posthoorn.eu. This boutique hotel brilliantly mixes the traditional and contemporary in its five large rooms and suites, with flat-screen TVs, DVD players, sumptuously

equipped bathrooms and wi-fi throughout merging seamlessly with the beams, old-fashioned beds, paintings and fabrics that show off this seventeenth-century mansion at its best. Very comfy, and the service is charming. **€155**

EATING AND DRINKING

De Koperen Vis Havenstraat 1 ☎ 0299 650 627, ⓦ dekoperenvis.nl. It means the "brazen fish" and this cosy bar right by the water is maybe Monnickendam's friendliest place for a drink and a bite to eat. You can sit outside on sunny days and watch the boats coming and going; and they serve a good menu of hot and cold sandwiches for around €5, *uitmijters* (€7 or so) and delectable Dutch bar snacks. Sun–Thurs 10am–1am, Fri & Sat 10am–2am. Closed Tues.

★ **De Posthoorn** Noordeinde 43 ☎ 0299 654 598, ⓦ posthoorn.eu. With one Michelin star, this refined hotel restaurant has a lovely dining room, with a terrace out the back in the summer, and service that is impeccable without being showy. You can choose a la carte – starters are €18–22, mains €30, or from one of three menus which range from €55 to €85, or you can mix and match as much as you like. The food won't disappoint, whether you choose succulent veal roulade with Russian salad and piccalilli – sounds ordinary, definitely isn't – creamy Zeeland oysters with fingers of bread and butter, or the slate full of rocks you get for dessert (challenge is to pick out the edible ones), it's all delicious. Sure, there are the hushed tones of any high-end restaurant, but the service is so nice, the sommelier so engaging and the food so fantastic, that it's a feast for all the senses. Tues–Sat 6–10pm, Sun 12.30–10pm.

Volendam

The former fishing village of **VOLENDAM** is the largest of the Markermeer towns and has had, by comparison with its neighbours, some rip-roaring times. In the early years of the twentieth century it became something of an artists' retreat, with both Picasso and Renoir spending time here, along with their assorted acolytes. Evidence of the town's artistic connections can be seen in the antique-filled public rooms of the **Hotel Spaander** on the waterfront, whose collection of paintings and sketches were given to the hotel by various artists in lieu of their lodgings. The hotel opened in 1881 and its first owner, Leendert Spaander, had seven daughters, quite enough to keep a whole bevy of artists in lust for a decade or two. The artists are, however, long gone and today Volendam is more or less a tourist target, crammed in season with day-trippers running the gauntlet of the souvenir stalls arranged along the length of the cobbled main street, whose perky gables line the picturesque yet workaday harbour.

Volendams Museum

Zeestraat 41 • Mid-March to mid-Nov daily 10am–5pm • €3 • ⓦ volendamsmuseum.nl

While it's pleasant enough to wander the harbour and the streets behind, Volendam's only real sight is the **Volendams Museum** which has displays of paintings by the artists who have come here over the years. Exhibits also include mannequins in local costumes and several interiors – a shop, school, and living room – although the museum's crowning glory is a series of mosaics made from 11 million cigar bands: the bizarre lifetime project of a local artist.

ARRIVAL AND INFORMATION · VOLENDAM

By bus Buses #110 and #118 from Amsterdam and Monnickendam drop passengers on Zeestraat, just across the street from the tourist office. From here, it's a five-minute walk to the waterfront.

By ferry The Marken Express passenger ferry, Haven 39, Volendam (☎ 0299 363 331, ⓦ markenexpress.nl), links Volendam and Marken every 30–45min (March–Oct daily 11am–5pm; 25min; €8 return, €5.50 one-way, €6.75 with a bike, children €4.50 return).

Tourist office The VVV is at Zeestraat 37 (mid-March to Oct Mon–Sat 10am–5pm; Nov to mid-March Mon–Sat 10am–3pm; ☎ 0299 363 747, ⓦ vvv-volendam.nl).

ACCOMMODATION AND EATING

Spaander Haven 15–19 ☎ 0299 363 595, ⓦ hotelspaander.com. If you want to stay In Volendam, there's no better place than this wonderfully old-fashioned hotel, whose maze of corridors and creaking old floor harbour a range of decently furnished rooms, the nicest of which overlook the water. Choose

from "classic" or "luxury" – the latter are larger and with bathtubs. **€110**

Van den Hogen Haven 106 ☎0299 363 775, ⓦhogen.nl. Five simply furnished but good-value rooms above an enticing restaurant and bar. This is the best of Volendam's harbourside restaurants, with a good

selection of local fish specialities, like sole, mussels and cod. Try the three small fried Volendam soles for €20, mussels for €18.50, or the cod with mustard sauce for €22. Or if you're feeling more adventurous, the stewed pike with shrimps is very good. Daily 11am–9pm, Sat & Sun till 9.30pm. **€92**

Edam

You might expect **EDAM** to be jammed with tourists, considering the international fame of the rubbery red balls of cheese that carry its name. In fact, Edam usually lacks crowds and remains a delightful, good-looking and prosperous little town of neat brick houses, high gables, swing bridges and slender canals. Founded by farmers in the twelfth century, it experienced a temporary boom in the seventeenth as a shipbuilding centre with river access to the Zuider Zee. Thereafter, it was back to the farm – the excellent pastureland surrounding the town is still grazed by large herds of cows, though nowadays most Edam cheese is produced elsewhere, even in Germany ("Edam" is the name of a type of cheese and not its place of origin). This does, of course, rather undermine the authenticity of Edam's open-air **cheese market**, held every Wednesday morning in July and August, but it's still a popular attraction and the only time the town heaves with tourists. From here, it's a couple of hundred metres south to the fifteenth-century **Speeltoren**, an elegant, pinnacled tower that is all that remains of Edam's second most important medieval church, and roughly the same distance again – south along Lingerzijde – to the impossibly picturesque **Kwakelbrug** bridge.

Damplein

At the heart of Edam is **Damplein**, a pint-sized main square. Alongside it, an elongated, humpbacked bridge vaults the Voorhaven canal, which now connects the town with the Markermeer and formerly linked it to the Zuider Zee. The bridge stopped the canal flooding the town, which occurred with depressing regularity, but local shipbuilders hated the bridge, as it restricted navigation, and on several occasions they launched night-time raids to break it down, though eventually they bowed to the will of the local council.

Edams Museum

Damplein • April–Oct Tues–Sat 10am–4.30pm, Sun 1–4.30pm • €3 • ⓦedamsmuseum.nl

Facing the bridge is the **Edams Museum**, which occupies an attractive old house whose crow-stepped gables date back to 1530. Inside, a series of cramped and narrow rooms holds a modest display on the history of the town as well as an assortment of local bygones, including a couple of splendid box beds. The museum's pride and joy is, however, its **floating cellar**, supposedly built by a retired sea captain who couldn't bear the thought of sleeping on dry land, but actually constructed to stop the house from flooding.

The museum is housed in two buildings, with the second part being in Edam's eighteenth-century **Stadhuis**, which lies across the Damplein – over the bridge. A severe Louis XIV-style structure whose plain symmetries culminate in a squat little tower, the Stadhuis is home to the tourist office (see p.117) on its ground floor, while upstairs, the Edams Museum (same times & ticket) comprises a handful of old Dutch paintings; the most curious is the portrait of **Trijntje Kever** (1616–33), a local girl who grew to over 2.5m tall – displayed in front of the portrait is a pair of her specially made shoes.

The Grote Kerk

Kerkepad • April–Oct daily 2–4.30pm • Free

From Damplein, it's a short walk to the rambling **Grote Kerk**, on the edge of the fields to the north of town. This is the largest three-ridged church in Europe, a handsome, largely Gothic structure whose strong lines are disturbed by the almost comically stubby spire, which was shortened to its present height after lightning started a fire in 1602. The church interior is distinguished by its magnificent stained-glass windows – which date from the early seventeenth century and sport both heraldic designs and historical scenes – and by its whopping **organ**.

2

The Cheese Market

Jan Niuewenhuizenplein • July to mid-Aug Wed 9.30am–12.30pm

Stroll back from the church along Matthijs Tinxgracht, just to the west of Grote Kerkstraat, and you soon reach Jan Niuewenhuizenplein, site of the summer **cheese market**. It's overlooked by the **Kaaswaag**, where they used to weigh the cheese, whose decorative panels feature the town's coat of arms, a bull on a red field with three stars. It's a good deal humbler than Alkmaar's market (see p.129), but follows the same format, with the cheeses laid out in rows before buyers sample them. Once a cheese has been purchased, the cheese porters, dressed in traditional white costumes and straw boaters, spring into action, carrying them off on their gondola-like trays.

ARRIVAL AND DEPARTURE

EDAM

By bus Edam's bus station is on the southwest edge of town, on Singelweg, a 5–10min walk from Damplein. Buses #110, #116 and #118 run between Amsterdam Centraal Station and Edam every 30 minutes or so; the journey takes forty minutes.

By bike Bikes can be rented from Ronald Schot, at Grote Kerkstraat 7 in the town centre (Tues–Fri 8.30am–6pm & Sat 8.30am–4pm; ☎0299 372 155, ⓦronaldschot.nl); one-day bike rental costs €6.50, and customers get free parking on Kaasmarkt or by the Grote Kerk.

INFORMATION

Tourist office The VVV is in the Stadhuis on Damplein (mid-March to Nov Mon–Sat 10am–5pm, also Sun 1–4.30pm in July & Aug; Nov to mid-March Mon–Sat 10am–3pm; ☎0299 315 125, ⓦvvv-edam.nl). They have details of – and take bookings for – local boat trips, both

along the town's canals and out into the Markermeer, and have a small supply of rooms in private houses (averaging €40–50 for a double), which they will book on your behalf for no extra charge.

ACCOMMODATION

Damhotel Keizersgracht 1 ☎0299 371 766, ⓦdamhotel.nl. Edam is a great place to spend a night or two, and this is perhaps the nicest place to do it – a boutique-style hotel with an emphasis on old-style opulence, with bunched curtains, statues of angels and luxuriant fabrics. Each room is different, but all have up-to-date facilities and there's free wi-fi throughout. **€125**
De Fortuna Spuistraat 3 ☎0299 371 671, ⓦfortuna -edam.nl. Just round the corner from the Damplein and butting a narrow canal, this attractive three-star hotel is the epitome of cosiness, its 23 guest rooms distributed

among two immaculately restored old houses and three cottage-like buildings round the back. The rooms are simply but very nicely furnished, all with baths, and there's free wi-fi throughout. It's a lovely spot with chairs and tables set out by the canal to take the evening air. **€97.50**
Camping Strandbad Zeevangszeedijk 7a ☎0299 371 994, ⓦcampingstrandbad.nl. East of town on the way to the lakeshore, Edam's nearest campsite is a 20min walk along the canal from the north side of Damplein. Also has cabins, sleeping two, for €38.50 a night. April–Sept. **€12.45**

EATING AND DRINKING

L'Auberge Damhotel Keizersgracht 1 ☎0299 371 766, ⓦdamhotel.nl. The bar here is a cosy place for a drink, and it has a terrace in an outside loggia facing the town hall, where you can get a decent lunch of

sandwiches, salads and pancakes for €6.75–10 and light mains for €16–18. There's also the upmarket but excellent-value *Auberge* restaurant, which serves a fantastic and quite ambitious menu; reckon on paying around €15 for starters like braised oxtail with lobster or duck liver three ways, and €25–30 for saddle of roe, pheasant with herb crust or beef tenderloin with bacon rosti and veal gravy. Yum. Daily noon–10pm.

De Fortuna Spuistraat 3 ☎ 0299 371 671, ⓦ fortuna -edam.nl. This first-rate restaurant is a lively and eminently agreeable spot decorated in traditional style and serving a slightly fussy, French-Dutch menu featuring local ingredients; starters go for €10–12, main courses €20–25. Reservations, especially at the weekend, are essential. Daily lunch noon–3pm; dinner from 6pm, Sun from 5.30pm.

Hoorn

The old Zuider Zee port of **HOORN**, 15km north of Edam, "rises from the sea like an enchanted city of the east, with its spires and its harbour tower beautifully unreal". So wrote the English travel writer E.V. Lucas, who passed through here in 1905, and Hoorn is still a place that is best approached from the water. During the seventeenth century this was one of the richest of the Dutch ports, referred to by the poet Vondel as the "trumpet" of the Zuider Zee, handling the important Baltic trade and that of the Dutch colonies. The Dutch East India Company had one of its centres of operation here; *The Tasman* left Hoorn to "discover" Tasmania and New Zealand; and in 1616 William Schouten sailed out of Hoorn to navigate a passage around South America, calling its tip "Cape Hoorn" after his native town. The good times ended in the early eighteenth century when the harbour silted up, strangling the trade on which the town was reliant and turning Hoorn into one of the so-called "dead cities" of the Zuider Zee – a process completed with the creation of the IJsselmeer in 1932 (see p.112).

Rode Steen

The centre of Hoorn is **Rode Steen**, literally "red stone", an unassuming square that used to hold the town scaffold and now zeroes in on a swashbuckling **statue** of Jan Pieterszoon Coen (1587–1629), founder of the Dutch East Indies Empire and one of the town's big shots in its seventeenth-century heyday. Coen was a headstrong and determined leader of the Dutch imperial effort and under him the country's Far East colonies were consolidated, and rivals, like the English, kept at bay. His settling of places like the Moluccas and Batavia was something of a personal crusade, and his austere, almost puritanical way of life was in sharp contrast to the wild and unprincipled behaviour of many of his fellow colonialists. On one side of Rode Steen stands the early seventeenth-century **Waag**, whose handsome stone symmetries were designed by Hendrik de Keyser (1565–1621), one of the leading architects of his day. The Waag now houses a café-bar, which is enjoyable for its setting amid the ponderous wood and iron appliances that once weighed the cheese here – and is in fact a good place to watch the summer **cheese market** from. The market has made a comeback recently and now takes place on Thursday lunchtimes and evenings (end of May to end of July 12.30pm & 8.30pm), though like Alkmaar's it's basically laid on for tourists.

The Westfries Museum

Rode Steen 1 • Mon–Fri 11am–5pm, Sat & Sun 1–5pm • €5 • ⓦ wfm.nl

On the opposite side of the square from the Waag, the **Westfries Museum** is housed in the former West Friesland government building of 1632, an imposing stone structure whose facade is decorated with the coats of arms of the house of Orange-Nassau and the region's towns. Now a district within the province of Noord-Holland, West Friesland incorporates the chunk of land between Alkmaar, Hoorn and Enkhuizen, but its origins were much grander. The **Frisians**, who speak a distinctive German dialect, once controlled a narrow sliver of seaboard stretching west from Bremerhaven in Germany to Belgium. Charlemagne conquered them in the 780s and incorporated

2

Museum van de Twintigste Eeuw

their territory into his empire, chopping it down in size and dividing the remainder into seven regions, two of which – West Friesland and Friesland – are now in the Netherlands.

The ground floor

Inside the museum (where the labelling is only in Dutch) the ground floor holds a string of period rooms that re-create the flavour of the seventeenth- and eighteenth-century seaport, with paintings, silverware, antique furniture and other objects. Most notable of the numerous paintings are the militia portraits of **Jan Rotius** (1624–66) in the old Council Chamber – walk past the figure in the far right of the central painting opposite the fireplace and you'll see his foot change position from left to right, a nifty little trick that was much admired by Rotius's contemporaries.

The upper floors

Upstairs, the **Chirurgijnskamer** (literally Surgeon's Room, but also, in medieval times, the barber's, the alchemist's and the pharmacist's), holds a mock-up of a medieval "medical" workshop, complete with skeletons, skulls and pickled specimens, while another room has a splendid wooden fireplace carved with tiny scenes of a whaling expedition – Hoorn was once a whaling port of some importance. On the next floor there's a focus on Coen and the Dutch East India Company, while the loft has exhibits on local trades and a gruesome holding cell from its time as a prison.

2

THE STOOMTRAM

Hoorn is the home of the **Stoomtram Museum**, across the rail tracks from the town's main station, which is the starting point for the **Stoomtram**, an antique steam train that chugs north out of Hoorn across open countryside to Medemblik, 14km away (see p.125). It's a popular family excursion and you can pick up a leaflet from the tourist office for the rather complicated schedule, or contact the Stoomtram direct on ☏0229 214 862, ⓦmuseumstoomtram.nl; advance booking is recommended. There are between one and three departures a day in late July and early August, and one departure a day (Tues–Sun) the rest of the year. The journey takes 1hr 15min and a return ticket costs €20 (children 4–12 years, €15), including an optional excursion by passenger ferry to Enkhuizen (see p.121), from where you can either come back the same way or take the half-hourly train service directly back to Hoorn (an additional €3.60).

Around the harbour

East of Rode Steen, **Grote Oost** is shadowed by fine, decorated old mansions, some of which house antique shops and art galleries, and one of which, the **Affiche Museum**, just off Rode Steen at Groot Oost 2–4 (Tues–Fri 11am–5pm, Sat & Sun noon–5pm; €3.50), sports a frieze of the cheese market as well as housing a modest permanent display of political and commercial posters – a treat for students of graphic design. At the far end of Groot Oost, on the corner of Slapershaven, the **Bossuhuizen** has a facade decorated with a long and slender frieze depicting a sea battle of 1573 – which Admiral Bossu actually lost. **Slapershaven** itself has some of the most comfortable houseboats imaginable and leads to Hoorn's inner harbour, the **Binnenhaven**, with its clutter of sailing boats and antique barges alongside **Oude Doelenkade**.

Veermanskade

Just over the swing bridge, **Veermanskade** is fringed by elegant merchants' houses mostly dating from the seventeenth century: look out, in particular, for the birthplace of **Willem Ysbrantzoon Bontekoe** (1587–1657), set back from the quay at Veermanskade 15, whose stone facade shows a particularly ugly spotted cow, as in *bonte* ("spotted") and *koe* ("cow"). A sea captain with the East India Company, Bontekoe published his journals in 1646, a hair-raising and very popular account of his adventures in which he portrayed himself as astute and brave in equal measure. Almost at the end of Veermanskade, the solid brick **Hoofdtoren**, a defensive watchtower from 1532, is now a bar-restaurant and has nearby a realistic bronze sculpture of 1968 of three little boys looking out to sea that also recalls Bontekoe – it's based on the 1924 classic Dutch novel by Johan Fabricius, *The Cabin Boys of Bontekoe*.

Museum van de Twintigste Eeuw

Krententuin 24 • Tues–Fri 10am–5pm, Sat & Sun noon–5pm • €6 • ⓦwww.museumhoorn.nl

The **Museum van de Twintigste Eeuw** (Museum of the Twentieth Century) is the centrepiece of a spanking new development of what used to be a prison on Oostereiland, at the end of Veermanskade. It's a museum of nostalgia basically, that documents life during the twentieth century with products and objects set up in engaging tableaux of everyday life. There are living rooms from the 1940s, 1950s and 1960s, a mock-up of Jacob Blokker's first housewares store at Breed 14 (it's now a nationwide chain) along with a number of other shops and businesses, an old school-room, various collections of household appliances, including some fantastic old radios, and a room full of Barbies and Kens in all their various incarnations. The café downstairs serves drinks and snacks and is decorated with photos that tell the story of the last century, and a rather out-of-context scale model of Hoorn as it would have looked during the seventeenth-century Golden Age.

ARRIVAL AND DEPARTURE

By train Hoorn's train station is on the northern edge of the town centre about ten minutes' walk from Rode Steen. Regular trains serve Hoorn from Amsterdam (every 30min; 40min).

By bus Regional buses stop just outside the train station to the right. Buses run from Medemblik to Hoorn every 30min–1hr, and the journey takes 30–40min; bus #114 runs from Edam bus station to Hoorn every 30min (hourly on Sun), and takes 30min.

INFORMATION

Tourist office The VVV is across the road from the train station at Veemarkt 4 (May–Aug Mon 1–6pm, Tues, Wed & Fri 9.30am–5.30pm, Thurs 9.30am–6pm & 7–9pm, Sat 9.30am–5pm; Sept–April Mon 1–5pm, Tues–Sat 10am–5pm; ☏ 072 511 4284, ✆ www.vvvhoorn.nl), and has the usual info plus a small supply of rooms to rent in private houses.

ACCOMMODATION

Keizerskroon Breed 33 ☏ 0229 212 717, ✆ keizerskroonhoorn.nl. Probably Hoorn's best hotel choice, with mostly large and bright rooms, recent refurbished with wi-fi and flat-screen TVs. Nicely situated midway between the station and Rode Steen and with a busy bar-restaurant downstairs. No elevator, but there are only two floors of rooms. **€90**

De Magneet Kleine Oost 5 ☏ 0229 215 021, ✆ hoteldemagneet.nl. Friendly long-established small hotel that's the best option if you want to stay down by the harbour. Well-kept if slightly characterless rooms in both the main building and a series of annexes in the garden behind. Free wi-fi is a plus. **€100**

Petit Nord Kleine Noord 53–55 ☏ 0229 212 750, ✆ hotelpetitnord.nl. Very well-kept and decently furnished rooms, most of which have baths. There's wi-fi (though you have to pay), but the major plus is that it's only two minutes from the station. **€80**

EATING AND DRINKING

Brasserie aan Het West West 27 ☏ 0229 210 574, ✆ aanhetwest.nl. Just off Rode Steen, this sleek, modern café-restaurant has a deliberately simple menu featuring half a dozen starters and main courses – good for steaks, tuna and other fish dishes. It's reasonably priced too: starters go for €10–12, mains €20–25. Mon–Thurs 2–10pm, Fri & Sat noon–10pm.

Charlie's Dubbele Buurt 4 ☏ 0229 217 798, ✆ charlies .nl. One of several places on this short yet lively street, just off Grote Noord, this is a great, very friendly bar, where there's always something going on. They serve a good selection of Belgian and Dutch beers, and a cheap two-course menu on Wed nights, when they also show films. Wed–Sat 4pm–1am, Sun 2–10pm.

De Hoornse Kogge Nieuwendam 2 ☏ 0229 219 309, ✆ dehoornsekogge.nl. In a sympathetically revamped old building right on the harbour, this relatively upscale restaurant offers first-rate French cuisine, with main courses hovering around €20 and three-course menus for around €30. It is strong on seafood and has a good range of vegetarian dishes too. Wed–Sun 5–10.30pm.

De Korenmarkt Korenmarkt 1 ☏ 0229 279 826, ✆ dekorenmarkt.nl. Mainly Dutch staples at this relaxed and informal brasserie with lots of outside seating right on the harbour quay. It serves everything from lunchtime salads and toasted sandwiches (from €5), to good fish soup, usually a catch of the day, and the standard steak, chicken and spare ribs options for €15–20. Wed–Sun noon–10pm.

De Oude Waegh Rode Steen 8 ☏ 0229 215 195, ✆ oudewaegh.nl. Café-restaurant fashioned out of the antiquated paraphernalia of the old municipal weigh-house, and with tables outside to watch the action on the square. All-day food, from club sandwiches, burgers and pasta dishes for €7.50–10.50, to beef bourgignon and steaks for €16–20. Mon–Thurs 11am–midnight, Fri–Sun 11am–1am.

Enkhuizen

Like Hoorn, **ENKHUIZEN**, just 19km to the east, was once one of the country's most important seaports. From the fourteenth to the early eighteenth century, when its harbour silted up, it prospered from both the Baltic sea trade and the North Sea herring fishery – and indeed its maritime credentials were second to none: Enkhuizen was home to Holland's largest fishing fleet and its citizens were renowned for their seamanship, with the Dutch East India Company always keen to recruit here.

2

Enkhuizen was also the first town in Noord-Holland to rise against Spain, in 1572, but unlike many of its Protestant allies it was never besieged – its northerly location kept it safely out of reach of the Habsburg army. Subsequently, Enkhuizen slipped into a long-lasting economic lull, becoming a remote and solitary backwater until tourism revived its fortunes. It's not a big place – about twenty minutes' walk from end to end – but the town centre, with its ancient streets, slender canals and pretty harbours, is wonderfully well preserved, a rough circle with a ring of bastions and moat on one side, and the old sea dyke on the other. It also has a major attraction in the excellent **Zuiderzeemuseum** and is a good place to visit for its summer passenger **ferry** connections across the IJsselmeer to Stavoren (see p.210) and Urk (see p.245).

The Oude Haven

A good place to start an exploration of Enkhuizen's compact centre is the **Oude Haven**, which stretches east in a gentle curve to the conspicuous **Drommedaris**, a heavy-duty brick watchtower built in 1540 to guard the harbour entrance. On the green by the tower there's a modern statue of the seventeenth-century artist **Paulus Potter**, who was a native of Enkhuizen, painting one of the farm animals he was most famous for. Beyond the Drommedaris is the picturesque Buitenhaven, a jangle of sailing boats and barges, while immediately to the east is the oldest part of town, an extraordinarily pretty lattice of alleys, quays, canals and antique houses.

ENKHUIZEN

RESTAURANTS, CAFÉS & BARS
't Ankertje	5
Die Drie Haringhe	4
De Mastenbar	2
De Smederij	6
Theo Schilder	3
Van Bleiswijk	1

ACCOMMODATION
De Koepoort	4
Recuer Dos	3
Suydersee Driebanen	1
Het Wapen van Enkhuizen	2

Flessenscheepjesmuseum

Zuiderspui 1 • Tues–Sun noon–5pm • €3.50

The pocket-sized **Flessenscheepjesmuseum** is built above the lock gates at the end of the Zuiderhaven canal – ask and they'll show you the water flowing beneath the house. The museum itself is devoted to that ubiquitous maritime curiosity, the ship-in-a-bottle, and is a well-presented and -labelled collection, with vessels ranging from East Indiamen to steamboats, and containers from light bulbs, even fuses, to a thirty-litre wine flagon. There's also a short film introducing you into the ingenious mysteries of how it's done.

Westerstraat and around

Walk north from the Flessenscheepjesmuseum along Zuider Havendijk and turn left at the end of the canal to get to the **Zuiderkerk**, a hulking Gothic pile with a massive brick tower that was erected in 1518 – the octagon and then the cupola on top were added later. Close by, just to the east, is the solid, classically styled mid-seventeenth-century **Stadhuis**, an elegant and imposing Neoclassical edifice that still houses the city council. From here stroll up to the end of Enkhuizen's main street, **Westerstraat**, the town's spine, and a busy pedestrianized street that is home to most of its shops and stores. About halfway along stands the **Westerkerk**, an early fifteenth-century, red-brick Gothic church with a free-standing wooden tower. The bare interior of the church, with its three naves of equal height, is distinguished by its **rood screen**, a mid-sixteenth-century extravagance whose six intricately carved panels show biblical scenes in dramatic detail – Moses with the Tablets, St John on Patmos and so forth.

Sprookjeswonderland

Kooizandweg 9 • April–Oct daily 10am–5.30pm • €9 • ☎ 0228 317 853

Just five to ten minutes' walk from the eastern end of Westerstraat, there's a little stretch of sandy **beach**; a shallow spot that's perfect for kids. Right by here, you'll also find **Sprookjeswonderland**, a modest theme park with gnome houses, rides, a mini railway, boats and a children's farm.

The Zuiderzeemuseum

Wierdijk 12–22 • Daily 10am–5pm; Museumpark April–Oct only • €14.50, children €8.70 • ⓦ zuiderzeemuseum.nl

It's a short walk from the centre of Enkhuizen to the landbound part of the **Zuiderzeemuseum**, around a dozen rooms devoted to changing annual exhibitions on different aspects of the Zuider Zee. At its heart is the impressive ship hall, where you can get up close and personal with a number of traditional sailing barges and other craft. There is an ice-cutting boat from Urk, once charged with the responsibility of keeping the shipping lanes open between the island and the mainland; a dinghy for duck-hunting, complete with shotgun; and some wonderful fully rigged and highly varnished sailing vessels.

Museumpark

The main event, however, is the so-called **Museumpark**, whose main entrance is about 100m to the north along Wierdijk, and which stretches north along the seaward side of the old dyke that once protected Enkhuizen from the Zuider Zee. It's a fantastically well-put-together collection of over 130 dwellings, stores, workshops and even streets that have been transported here from every part of the region, and which together provide the flavour of life hereabouts from 1880 to around 1932. There are many highlights, and just about everything is worth seeing, but the best include a reconstruction of Marken harbour as of 1900, a red-brick chapel and assorted cottages from Den Oever, old fishermen's houses from Urk, a post office and a pharmacy, which

2

has a marvellous collection of "gapers" – painted wooden heads with their tongues out, which were the traditional pharmacy's sign. The museum works very hard to be authentic: sheep and goats roam the surrounding meadows and its smokehouses smoke (and sell) real herring and eels, the sweetshop sells real old-fashioned sweets, the beautifully kept schoolrooms offer geography and handwriting classes, and there's even a woman in a 1930s furnished house who will make you a traditional Dutch lunch. There's also a **nature reserve**, where you can take a picnic and walk through the woods for some great views over the water. All in all not be missed, especially if you have children.

ARRIVAL AND DEPARTURE ENKHUIZEN

By train Enkhuizen is at the end of the line, and the station is right opposite the head of the main harbour – the Buitenhaven – at the southern end of town. There are regularly connections to Hoorn (25 min) and to Amsterdam (1hr).

By bus Buses stop beside the train station, with connections roughly every thirty minutes to Hoorn (20min) and Medemblik (1hr).

By ferry In summer, passenger ferries run east across the IJsselmeer to and from Stavoren (mid-April Tues–Sun 1 daily; May–Sept 3 daily; Oct 2 daily; 1hr 30min; €10.60, children €6.80; day-return €14.40, children €8.20; ☏ 0228 326 667, ⓦ veerboot.info). There are also summer sailings to Urk on a three-masted schooner (mid-July to end Aug 2 daily; 2hr 30min; €20, children €16; day-return €30, children €24; bikes €7, €10 return; ⓦ veerdienst-urk -enkhuizen.nl). Ferries arrive and depart from the jetty behind the train station, and you can buy tickets from the tourist office, which also has timetables.

INFORMATION

Tourist office The VVV is opposite the train station, on the harbourfront at Tussen Twee Havens 1 (daily 9am–5pm; ☏ 0228 313 164, ⓦ vvvenkhuizen.nl). They sell maps and town brochures and have details of local boat trips and rooms to rent in private houses.

ACCOMMODATION

HOTELS

De Koepoort Westerstraat 294 ☏ 0228 314 966, ⓦ dekoepoort.nl. On the edge of the centre, but its wide range of rooms are handy if everywhere else is full. There's a pleasant bar and restaurant downstairs, though the welcome is businesslike rather than friendly. **€90**

★ **Recuer Dos** Westerstraat 217 ☏ 0228 562 469, ⓦ recuerdos.nl. Enkhuizen's best accommodation option, this immaculate Victorian house has three doubles and one single in a series of chalets in a peaceful and elegant garden. The rooms are clean and comfortable, with well-appointed showers, and there are regular Spanish guitar and other concerts in the hotel's purpose-built music salon – reflecting the owner's occupation as a classical guitar teacher. **€80**

Suydersee Dreinbanen Driebanen 59 ☏ 0228 316 381, ⓦ suyderseehotel.nl. Right on the canal, in a very peaceful location, this has good-sized if plainly furnished rooms in a slightly faded 1960s building. Quite a large hotel – 37 rooms – but it's a friendly place and many of the rooms have been recently refurbished. **€96**

Het Wapen van Enkhuizen Breedstraat 59 ☏ 0228 313 434, ⓦ wapenvanenkhuizen.nl. Comfortable if slightly uninspiring rooms in a friendly town-centre location, with a downstairs bar and restaurant. Nothing fancy, but very handy for the harbour and Zuiderzeemuseum. **€72.50**

CAMPSITES

Enkhuizer Zand Kooizandweg 4 ☏ 0228 317 289, ⓦ campingenkhuizerzand.nl. The closest of Enkhuizen's two campsites, on the far side of the Zuiderzeemuseum, a 10- to 15-minute walk from the station, and very handy for the beach. Facilities include a well-stocked shop, snack bar and indoor swimming pool. April–Sept. **€15**

De Vest Noorderweg 31 ☏ 0228 321 221, ⓦ campingdevest.nl. The slightly plainer of Enkhuizen's two campsites, fitting snugly onto an old bastion. To get there, follow Vijzelstraat north off Westerstraat, continue along Noorderweg, and turn left by the old town ramparts – a fifteen-minute walk; or bus #138 from the station drops you nearby. April–Oct. **€16**

EATING AND DRINKING

't Ankertje Dijk 6 ☏ 0228 315 767, ⓦ cafe-ankertje .nl. An atmospheric, old-fashioned kind of place for a drink, with nautical knick-knacks hanging on the walls and lots of tables outside on the quay. It serves food too, from simple lunchtime menus of soup and sandwiches, a few mains at dinner, like spare ribs, satay pork or catch of the day for around €15, and a short list of tapas. Daily 10am–2am.

★ **Die Drie Haringhe** Dijk 28 ☎0228 318 610, ⓦ drieharinghe.nl. Housed in an immaculately renovated seventeenth-century building on the harbour, with tables in the courtyard garden outside and by the canal, this is perhaps the town's best restaurant, with a menu that's strong on seafood and local specialities. Main courses are in the region of €25 – though their three-course set dinner menu is worth trying at €42.50 (four courses €47.50); lunch menus are from €32.50 for two courses. Daily except Mon & Tues noon–2pm & 5–10pm.

De Mastenbar Compagnieshaven 3 ☎0228 313 691, ⓦ demastenbar.nl. Down in the marina, this place is great both for a drink or a full meal, lunch or dinner, with sandwiches, burgers and *uitsmijters*, soups and big salads for lunch and a nice shortish dinner menu of meat and fish dishes for €18–20, along with three-course menus for €29.95. It's cosy enough inside, but the outside terrace, from which you can watch the yachts chugging by after a long day on the IJsselmeer, is about as good an end to a summer's day in Enkhuizen as it gets. Daily 10am–11.30pm.

De Smederij Breedstraat 158–160 ☎0228 314 604. Inventive, modern French-Mediterranean cuisine in a smartly renovated building a block back from the harbour, with starters for €10–12, main courses around €20–25. Daily except Wed 5–10pm; Oct–March closed Thurs also.

Theo Schilder Dijk 48 ☎0228 317 809. A great fish shop with a pint-sized café attached and tables outside. Serves a wide variety of fish and seafood snacks. Mon–Sat 9am–7pm, Sun noon–7pm.

Van Bleiswijk Westerstraat 84–86 ☎0228 325 909, ⓦ vanbleiswijk.nl. Grand café with two large rooms that stay open all day for drinks, lunch and dinner. The lunch menu takes in basic sandwiches, soup, salads and more (good burgers and club sandwiches), while the dinner menu features fairly standard Dutch staples for €15–20. Mon 11am–11pm, Tues–Thurs 10am–midnight, Fri & Sat 10am–1am, Sun noon–11pm.

Medemblik and around

Nautical **MEDEMBLIK**, just over 20km north along the coast from Enkhuizen is one of the oldest towns in the Netherlands, a seat of Frisian kings until the seventh century and later a Zuider Zee port of some importance. Unfortunately, there's not a great deal to entice you here nowadays unless you're into yachts: the town's several waterways, harbour and marina are jam-packed with leisure craft. The main drag, **Nieuwstraat**, is wide and bustling, with the dinky Kasteel Radboud, perched at the end of the harbour.

Kasteel Radboud

Oudevaartsgat 8 • May to mid-Sept Mon–Thurs & Sat 11am–5pm, Sun 2–5pm; mid-Sept–April Sun 2–5pm • €5 • ⓦ kasteelradboud.nl

A handsome, gabled, fortified manor house, **Kasteel Radboud**, is named after the last Frisian king to hold sway here, although the structure that survives is not his at all, but a much-modified thirteenth-century fortress built by a count of Holland, **Floris V** (1254–96), one of the most celebrated of the country's medieval rulers. Nicknamed "God of the Peasants" (Der Keerlen God) for his attempts to improve the lot of his humbler subjects, Floris spent most of his time fighting his enemies, both the nobles within his territories and his archenemy, the duke of Flanders. In the end, it was his own nobles who did for him, capturing Floris when he was out hunting and then murdering him during a skirmish when the peasantry came to the rescue. As for the castle itself, it owes much of its present appearance to Petrus J.H. Cuypers (1827–1921), who repaired and rebuilt what had by then become a dilapidated ruin; Cuypers was a leading architect of his day, who was also responsible – among many other commissions – for Amsterdam's Centraal Station and the Rijksmuseum. Inside the castle, exhibits outline the fort's turbulent history and there's a ragbag of archeological finds from local sites.

The Wieringermeer Polder and the Afsluitdijk

North of Medemblik, the **Wieringermeer Polder** was reclaimed in the 1920s, filling in the gap between the former Zuider Zee island of Wieringen and the mainland. Towards the end of World War II, just three weeks before their surrender, the Germans

2

flooded the polder, boasting they could return the Netherlands to the sea if they so wished. After the war, it was drained again, leaving a barren, treeless terrain that had to be totally replanted. Almost sixty years later, it's indistinguishable from its surroundings, a familiar landscape of flat, geometric fields highlighted by neat and trim farmhouses. The polder leads north to the **Afsluitdijk** highway over to Friesland (see Chapter 4). The sluices on this side of the Afsluitdijk are known as the **Stevinsluizen**, after **Hendrick Stevin**, the seventeenth-century engineer who first had the idea of reclaiming the Zuider Zee. At the time, his grand plan was impracticable – the technology wasn't up to it – but his vision lived on, to be realized by **Cornelis Lely** (see box, p.112), though he too died before the dyke was completed. There's a **statue** of Lely by the modern Dutch sculptor Mari Andriessen at the west end of the dyke. Further out along the dyke, at the point where the barrier was finally closed, there's an observation point on which an inscription reads "A nation that lives is building for its future" – a linking of progress with construction that read well in the 1930s, but seems rather more dubious today.

ARRIVAL AND INFORMATION

MEDEMBLIK

By bus Buses to Medemblik, as well as the Stoomtram from Hoorn (see p.120), pull in on the Dam, at the north end of the town centre, and at the top of Nieuwstraat.

Tourist office The VVV is at the foot of Nieuwstraat at

Dam 2 (April–June, Sept & Oct Mon–Sat 10am–4pm; July & Aug Mon–Sat 9.30am–5pm; ☎0229 548 000, ⓦmedemblik.nl). It sells town maps and has a small supply of rooms in private houses.

ACCOMMODATION AND EATING

Medemblik Oosterhaven 1 ☎0227 543 844, ⓦhetwapenvanmedemblik.nl. This central hotel is the obvious place to stay in Medemblik, with comfortable if characterless rooms and a decent restaurant downstairs.

There's a simple lunch menu of sandwiches and *uitsmijters* from €6.95, while the short dinner menu features steaks and fish mains from about €22. Daily 9am–5pm & 5.30–9pm. **€105**

Zaandam

Largely a dormitory suburb of Amsterdam, the modern town of **ZAANDAM** is not especially alluring, though it does deserve a brief stop. The town was a popular tourist hangout in the nineteenth century, when it was known as "La Chine d'Hollande" for the faintly oriental appearance of its windmills, canals and row upon row of brightly painted houses. Monet spent some time here in the 1870s and, despite being under constant police surveillance as a suspected spy, went on to immortalize the place in a series of paintings.

The Czaar Peterhuisje

Krimp 23 • Tues–Sun 10am–5pm • €3 • From Zaandam train station, cross the main road and walk south to Hogendijk, where you turn left by the garage; follow this for 300m then take the fourth turning on the left

Zaandam's one historical curiosity is the **Czaar Peterhuisje**, where the Russian Tsar Peter the Great stayed incognito in 1697. Earlier that year, Peter had attached himself to a Russian trade mission to Holland as an ordinary sailor, Peter Mikhailov. The Russians came to Zaandam, which was then an important shipbuilding centre, and the tsar bumped into a former employee, one Gerrit Kist. Swearing Kist to the utmost secrecy, the tsar moved into Kist's simple home and worked at a local shipyard where he learnt as much as he could about shipbuilding – although he was, in fact, only here for just over a week. Kist's old home is these days a tottering wooden structure, enclosed within a brick museum erected in 1822, and comprises just two small rooms, decorated with a handful of portraits of a benign-looking emperor and the graffiti of tourists going back to the mid-nineteenth century. You can see the cupboard bed in which the tsar is supposed to have slept, together with the calling cards of various visiting Russian delegations, while around the outside of the house displays tell the story of Peter and his Western aspirations, and give background on the shipbuilding industry in Zaandam and the modest house itself. As Napoleon is said to have remarked on visiting the building, "Nothing is too small for great men".

Zaanse Schans

Schansend 7 • Information desk daily 9am–5pm; hours of attractions vary, but most, including the museum, are open 10am–5pm • The Zaanse Schans Pass includes entry to the museum and at least one windmill €11, children €7.50, or you can pay per attraction; museum €9; windmills €3 each • ☎ 075 681 0000, ⓦ zaanseschans.nl • Pleasant 50-minute-long boat trips on the River Zaan leave hourly on the hour from 11am–4pm from the jetty near the De Huisman spice windmill (April–June & Sept Tues–Sun; July & Aug daily) • €6

About 4km north of Zaandam, **Zaanse Schans** is a re-created Dutch village whose antique houses, shops, warehouses and windmills, mostly dating from the eighteenth century, were brought here from all over the region half a century ago and re-erected amid a network of narrow canals. It's a popular day-trip from Amsterdam and can get very crowded in summer, but it's a real village too – all the businesses are real, even though they derive most of their income from tourists, and all the houses are lived in year-round by people who have opted to move and work here. It's also the closest place to Amsterdam to see fully functioning windmills.

The museum and Verkade Paviljoen

The main building beside the car park houses an information and ticket desk, shop and the **Zaanse Schans Museum**, which has well-displayed and engaging collections relating to the history of the area, including pictures of all the folk who live in the village and some information in English; it also incorporates the **Verkade Paviljoen**, a separate space devoted to the history of the local manufacturing company, who made chocolate and biscuits in Zaandam until the 1990s, when the company was sold to a conglomerate (their mostly female workforce was famously known for years as the "Verkade Girls"). There are lots of buttons for kids to press as they watch the chocolate biscuits coming out of the 1950s-era machines.

The village and windmills

The village itself, across the car park from the museum, is very quaint, basically a string of attractions, focused on old **crafts** – a clog-making workshop, bakery and cheese farm – and throwback nostalgia: there's a museum of old clocks, an old-style Albert Heijn grocery, and even a B&B. But the real highlight of Zaanse Schans is the **windmills** themselves, eight in all, strung along the River Zaan, giant, insect-like affairs still used – among other things – to cut wood, grind mustard seeds and produce oil.

ARRIVAL AND DEPARTURE   **ZAANDAM**

By train Zaandam is just a 10- to 15-minute train ride from Amsterdam CS, while the nearest train station to Zaanse Schans is Koog-Zaandijk, two stops up the line from Zaandam. From the station, it's a 15min walk east to the river, where regular ferries take you across to Zaanse Schans. **By bus** Bus #91 runs twice an hour direct to Zaanse Schans

from Amsterdam CS, and takes 50 minutes. **By ferry** The Zaanhopper ferry runs every 2 hours between 10am and 4pm on Fri, Sat & Sun May–Oct between Wilhelminahuis in Zaandam to Zaans Schanse and beyond to Wormermeeer (5 stops in all, €1.25 per stop); ☎ 075 614 567, ⓦ varenopdezaan.nl.

Alkmaar

The engaging and attractive little town of **ALKMAAR** has preserved much of its medieval street plan, its compact centre surrounded by what was once the town moat and laced with spindly canals. The town is also dotted with fine old buildings, but is best known for its much-touted **cheese market**, an ancient affair that these days ranks as one of the

2

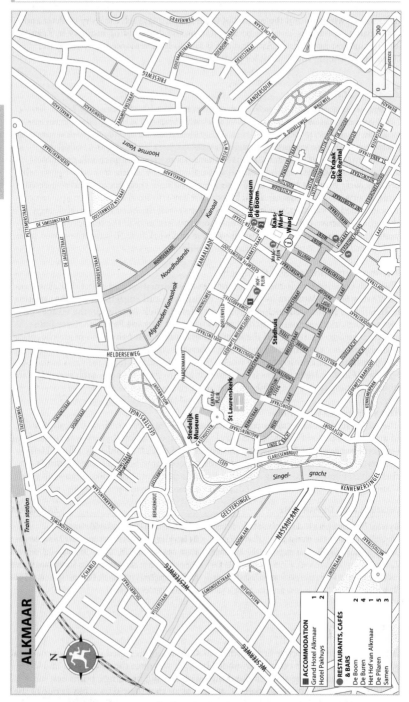

ALKMAAR

N

Train station

ACCOMMODATION
Grand Hotel Alkmaar   1
Hotel Pakhuys   2

RESTAURANTS, CAFÉS & BARS
De Boom   2
De Buren   4
Het Hof van Alkmaar 1
De Pilaren   5
Samen   3

most extravagant tourist spectacles in Noord Holland. Alkmaar was founded in the tenth century in the middle of a marsh – hence its name, which is taken from the auk, a diving bird which once hung around here in numbers, as in *alkeen meer*, or auk lake. Just like Haarlem, the town was besieged by Frederick of Toledo, but heavy rain flooded its surroundings and forced the Spaniards to withdraw in 1573, an early Dutch success in their long war of independence. At the time, Alkmaar was small and comparatively unimportant, but the town prospered when the surrounding marshland was drained in the 1700s and it received a boost more recently when the northern part of the old moat was incorporated into the Noordhollandskanaal, itself part of a longer network of waterways running north from Amsterdam to the open sea. Alkmaar is also within easy striking distance of **Bergen**, a pretty little village halfway between Alkmaar and the North Sea coast, whose immediate hinterland, with its woods and dunes, is protected in the **Noordhollands Duinreservaat** (North Holland Dune Reserve) and, just to the north, the **Schoorlse Duinen Nationaalpark** (Schoorl Dunes National Park). Both the reserve and the park are latticed by hiking and cycling routes, with bike rental available at Alkmaar and Bergen.

Waagplein and around

Alkmaar's main square is Waagplein, where the **Waag** or Weigh House was originally a chapel – hence the imposing tower – dedicated to the Holy Ghost; it was converted shortly after the town's famous victory against the Spanish, when it was given its delightful **gable** – an ostentatious Dutch Renaissance affair bedecked with allegorical figures and decorated with the town's militant coat of arms. The Waag holds the tourist office and the **Hollands Kaasmuseum** (April–Oct Mon 1–5pm; Tues–Sat 10am–5pm; Nov–March Sat 10am–4pm; €3; ⓦwww.kaasmuseum.nl) with displays on – predictably enough – the history of cheese, cheese-making equipment and the like. At the far end of the Waagplein, the **Biermuseum de Boom** (Mon–Sat 1–4pm; April–Sept Fri 10am–6pm; €4; ⓦbiermuseum.nl) above the *De Boom* bar, has three floors devoted to the art of making and distributing beer – no great shakes, but no worse than the cheese museum.

In the other direction, at the south end of Mient, the open-air **Vismarkt** (Fish Market) marks the start of the **Verdronkenoord** canal, whose attractive medley of facades and gables leads east to the spindly **Accijenstoren** (Excise Tower), part harbour master's office, part fortification built in 1622 during the long struggle with Spain. Turn left at the tower along Bierkade and you'll soon reach **Luttik Oudorp**, another attractive corner of the old centre, its slender canal jammed with antique barges.

Langestraat and the St Laurenskerk

One block south of Waagplein, pedestrianized **Langestraat** is Alkmaar's main and mundane shopping street, whose only notable building is the **Stadhuis**, a florid edifice,

ALKMAAR'S CHEESE MARKET

Cheese has been sold on Alkmaar's main square since the 1300s, and although it's no longer a serious commercial concern, the **kaasmarkt** (cheese market; Fri 10am–12.30pm, from the first Friday in April to the first Friday in Sept) continues to pull the crowds – so get there early if you want a good view. The ceremony starts with the buyers sniffing, crumbling and finally tasting each cheese, followed by intensive bartering. Once a deal has been concluded, the cheeses – golden discs of Gouda mainly, laid out in rows and piles on the square – are borne away on ornamental carriers by groups of four **porters** (*kaasdragers*) for weighing. The porters wear white trousers and shirt plus a black hat whose **coloured bands** – green, blue, red or yellow – represent the four companies that comprise the cheese porters' guild. Payment for the cheeses, tradition has it, takes place in the cafés around the square.

half of which (the Langestraat side) dates from the early sixteenth century. At the west end of Langestraat lurks **St Laurenskerk**, a de-sanctified Gothic church from the late fifteenth century whose pride and joy is its **organ**, commissioned at the suggestion of the diplomat and political bigwig Constantijn Huygens in 1645. The case was designed by Jacob van Campen, the architect who was later to design Amsterdam's town hall (see box, p.53), and decorated with paintings by **Caesar van Everdingen** (1617–78). The artist's seamless brushstrokes – not to mention his willingness to kowtow to the tastes of the burgeoning middle class – were to make van Everdingen a wealthy man. In the apse is the **tomb** containing the intestines of the energetic Count Floris V of Holland (1254–96), who improved the region's sea defences, succoured the poor and did much to establish the independence of the towns hereabouts, until his untimely demise at the hands of his own nobles; the rest of him ended up in Rijnsburg, near Leiden.

The Stedelijk Museum

Canadaplein 1 • Tues–Sun 10am–5pm • €8 • ⓦ stedelijkmuseumalkmaar.nl

Across from St Laurenskerk, Alkmaar's cultural centre holds a theatre, offices and a mildly diverting local museum, the **Stedelijk Museum**, whose three floors focus on the history of the town. Well displayed, but almost entirely labelled in Dutch only, the collection has a short film on the history of the town (in English), paintings, maps and models of Alkmaar during its seventeenth-century glory years. The many paintings include a typically precise interior of Alkmaar's St Laurenskerk by Pieter Saenredam (1597–1665), a striking *Holy Family* by the Mannerist Gerard van Honthorst (1590–1656) and a huge canvas by the medievalist Jacobus Hilverdink (1809–64) depicting the bloody siege of 1573. The top floor explores the history of the town during the twentieth century and hosts a large and well-displayed collection along with pictures by local artist Charley Toorop, daughter of the Dutch impressionist Jan Toorop.

ARRIVAL AND DEPARTURE ALEMAAR

By train There are trains every thirty minutes from Amsterdam, Haarlem and Hoorn to Alkmaar's train station, which is a 10min walk from the centre of town: outside the station head straight along Spoorstraat, turn left at the end onto Geestersingel and then turn right over the bridge to get to Kanaalkade; keep going along here until you reach Houttil Pieterstraat.

By bus All buses stop outside the train station, with departures to Bergen every 30min (hourly on Sun).

INFORMATION AND TOURS

Tourist office The VVV is housed in the Waag on Waagplein (Mon 1–5pm, Tues–Sat 10am–5pm; ☏ 072 511 4284, ⓦ www.vvvalkmaar.nl). They sell a useful town brochure, have details of the area's walking and cycling routes, and plenty of rooms in private houses for around €40 per double per night, including breakfast, though most places are on the outskirts of town.

Bike rental Bikes can be rented from the train station and in the centre of town at De Kraak, Verdronkenoord 54 (☏ 072 512 5840, ⓦ dekraak.nl; May Wed–Fri 11am–6pm, Sat & Sun 10am–8pm; June–Aug daily 10am–9pm). They also rent canoes and rowing boats.

Canal trips Boats leave from the jetty on Mient for a quick zip round the town's central waterways – an enjoyable way to spend 45 minutes (hourly 11am–5pm: April Mon–Sat; May–Sept; €5.30); tickets are on sale at the VVV or on board.

ACCOMMODATION

Grand Hotel Alkmaar Gedempte Nieuwsloot 36 ☏ 072 576 0970, ⓦ grandhotelalkmaar.nl. This new boutique-style hotel has been stylishly converted from a former post office and has sleek modern rooms, with free internet. It also has an inviting bar, which serves a brasserie menu and as well as a posher restaurant the other side of the reception. **€112.50**

Hotel Pakhuys Peperstraat 1 ☏ 072 520 2500, ⓦ inonshuys.nl. Just off Waagplein, this has lovely canalside doubles, both in the main building and in the annexe down the street: some come with jacuzzis and kitchenettes, and free wi-fi. **€89**

CLOCKWISE FROM TOP ENKHUIZEN (P.121); NATIONAL PARK ZUID-KENNEMERLAND (P.110); GABLES, VOLENDAM (P.114)

2

EATING AND DRINKING

De Boom Houttil 1, ☎072 511547, ⓦproeflokaaldeboom.nl. Right in the centre of town, this small unpretentious bar has a museum of beer upstairs (see p.129). Sun & Mon 2pm–midnight, Tues & Wed 1pm–midnight, Thurs–Sat 1pm–2am.

De Buren Mient 37 ☎072 512 0308, ⓦrestaurant -deburen.nl. Busy and fashionable restaurant that makes the most of its position on the corner of two canals, with the Vismarkt right outside. Food ranges from sandwiches, salads and *uitsmijters* at lunchtime to a dinner menu that incorporates a bit of everything, such as pork satay, burgers, cannelloni and Keralan chicken: mains start at €14.50 and go up to €25. Daily 10am–10pm.

Het Hof van Alkmaar Hof van Sonoy 1 ☎072 512 1222, ⓦhofvanalkmaar.nl. A delightfully restored medieval nunnery just off Nieuwesloot, this is pretty good for both lunch and dinner, with inexpensive omelettes, sandwiches and pancakes at lunch, and tasty Dutch cuisine at night with main courses averaging €15–20; there's an outside terrace too. Daily noon–10pm.

De Pilaren Verdronkenoord 129 ☎072 511 4997, ⓦcafedepilaren.nl. A youthful spot catering to a lively crowd, some of whom take refuge in the *Café Stapper* next door if the music gets too much. Daily 2pm–2am.

Samen Houttil 34 ☎072 511 3283, ⓦgrandcafe samen.nl. Nice, relaxed, child-friendly bar-café with an array of well-priced lunch options and a slightly rowdier feel at night. Mon & Tues 10.30am–midnight, Wed & Thurs 10am–1am, Fri & Sat 10.30am–2am, Sun noon–midnight.

Bergen and Bergen-aan-Zee

Out towards the coast, just 5km northwest of Alkmaar, the village of **BERGEN** is a cheerful sort of place that has been something of a retreat for artists since the late nineteenth century. Its centre is a pleasant place for a wander, with a leafy church square and plenty of cafés and restaurants, all focused on the amiable main square – intersection, really – of Plein. With a nod to the village's artistic heritage, the local council organizes all sorts of cultural events in Bergen, including open-air sculpture displays and concerts, and the village also boasts a scattering of chi-chi commercial galleries.

Museum Kranenburgh

Hoflaan 26 • Closed for renovation until 2013 • ☎072 589 8927, ⓦmuseumkranenburgh.nl

Bergen's main sight, the **Museum Kranenburgh**, in a Neoclassical villa five minutes' walk from the Plein, features the work of the Expressionist Bergen School, which was founded here in 1915. The group was greatly influenced by the Post-Impressionists, especially Cézanne, and though none of the group is original enough to stand out, taken as a whole it's a delightful collection and one that is supported by an imaginative programme of temporary exhibitions. These often focus on the two contemporaneous Dutch schools that were to have much more artistic impact – De Ploeg and De Stijl (see p.345).

Gemeentemuseum Het Sterkenhuis

Oude Prinsweg 21 • May–Oct Tues–Sat 1–5pm • €2 • ⓦmuseumhetsterkenhuis.nl

Bergen's other museum of note is the **Gemeentemuseum Het Sterkenhuis**, housed in a step-gabled manor house dating from 1655 right by the church. It holds regular exhibitions of work by contemporary Dutch artists, has a string of period rooms and features a local history section, including a display on a largely forgotten episode in the Napoleonic Wars, when a combined army of 30,000 English and Russian soldiers were defeated by a Franco-Dutch force here in 1799.

Bergen-aan-Zee and the dunes

It's just 5km across the dunes from Bergen to **BERGEN-AAN-ZEE**, a sprawling, modern resort that's of little interest beyond its first-rate **beach**, a strip of golden sand extending both north and south as far as the eye can see, and a small **aquarium** on the seafront at Van der Wijkplein 16 (April–Sept daily 10am–6pm; Nov–March daily 10am–5pm; €9, children €7; ☎072 581 2928, ⓦzeeaquarium.nl). The village also marks the northerly limit of the **Noordhollands Duinreservaat** (North Holland Dune

Reserve), whose bumpy sand dunes stretch north from the suburbs of IJmuiden, and the southern boundary of the **Schoorlse Duinen Nationaalpark** (Schoorl Dunes National Park), where a band of sweeping, wooded dunes, up to 5km wide, extends north as far as Camperduin – one of the widest undeveloped portions of the whole Dutch coastline. The dune reserve and the national park are both crisscrossed by footpaths and cycling trails, but the most lauded is the well-signposted, 42-kilometre-long **De Brede Duinen route** that takes cyclists on a loop through Alkmaar, Bergen, Bergen-aan-Zee, Schoorl and Camperduin, passing the highest of the national park's sand dunes (54m) on the way. Both Bergen and Alkmaar tourist offices sell detailed **maps** of local hiking and cycling routes but if you just want a taster of the landscape, there's a car park and access to marked trails halfway between Bergen and Bergen-aan-Zee on Uilenvangersweg.

2

ARRIVAL AND INFORMATION BERGEN AND BERGEN-AAN-ZEE

By bus Bus #6 leaves Alkmaar train station every thirty minutes or so – hourly on Sunday – for the 10min ride to Bergen, dropping passengers in the centre on Plein, a few metres from the tourist office.

Tourist office The Bergen VVV is in a kiosk at Plein 1 (Mon 1–5pm, Tues–Fri 10am–5pm, Sat 9.30am–4pm; July & Aug Mon–Fri 10am–5.30pm, Sat 9.30am–4pm; ☎072

581 3100, ⓦ vvvbergen.com). They sell maps of hiking and cycling routes in the Noordhollands Duinreservaat and the Schoorlse Duinen Nationaalpark.

Bike rental There are several places in Bergen to rent bikes, and it's much the best way to get around – try Fietsverhuur Bergen, just north of Plein at Breelaan 46 ☎072 589 8248.

Den Helder

The gritty port, oil supply centre and naval base of **DEN HELDER**, some forty minutes north from Alkmaar by train, was little more than a fishing village until 1811, when Napoleon, capitalizing on its strategic position at the very tip of Noord-Holland, built a fortified dockyard here. It's still the principal home of the Dutch navy, and **national fleet days**, or Vlootdagen, are held in the harbour on one weekend during the summer – usually in July – when, should you so desire, you can check out the bulk of the Dutch navy. Otherwise, the town holds little of interest beyond its ferry connections to the island of Texel (see p.134), and the recent development of the old dockyard complex of Willemsoord, which stretches down to the ferry terminal for Texel. Probably the most interesting part of Den Helder, it's a decent place to spend an hour or two while waiting for a ferry, and is home to a few places to eat, the tourist office and the excellent **Marinemuseum**, right by the ferry port.

The Marinemuseum

Hoofdgracht 3 • Mon–Fri 10am–5pm, Sat & Sun noon–5pm • €6 • ☎0223 657 534, ⓦ defensie.nl/marinemuseum

If you visit nowhere else in Den Helder, go to the **Marinemuseum**, which does justice to the town's role as home of the Dutch navy in a series of buildings and craft scattered around the seaward end of the Willemsoord complex. The original building by the ferry terminal houses a series of well-presented and entertaining exhibits tracking the history of the Dutch navy – in particular look out for the stuff on the naval heroes of yesteryear, especially Admiral Michiel de Ruyter (1607–76), who trounced in succession the Spaniards, the Swedes, the English and the French. His most daring exploit was a raid up the River Thames to Medway in 1667 and the seizure of the Royal Navy's flagship, *The Royal Charles*, an act that drove Charles II almost to distraction. There's lots of technical information too – on shipbuilding techniques and the like – and, perhaps most interestingly, several decommissioned vessels, including the 1960s submarine, the *Tonijn*, and the veteran World War II minesweeper, the *Abraham Crijnssen*, which famously escaped the Japanese by disguising itself as a tropical island and hotfooting it to Australia. You can also clamber around the bridge and radar turret of a warship.

ARRIVAL AND INFORMATION   DEN HELDER

By train Den Helder train station is a 5min walk from Willemsoord – follow Beatrixstraat and then Boerhaavestraat – and around 10min from the ferry terminal; alternatively, there's a direct bus between the train station and the ferry dock. There are two trains an hour to Amsterdam (1hr 15min).

By ferry Car and passenger ferries run to Den Helder from the nearby island of Texel hourly, and the journey takes 20min.

Tourist office There's a branch of the VVV in the Willemsoord complex at Willemsoord 47 (Mon–Sat 10am–4pm; ☎ 0223 616 100, ⓦ www.vvvkopvannoordholland.nl).

Texel

Stuck out in the Waddenzee, **Texel** (pronounced "tessel") is the westernmost of the string of islands that band the northern coast of the Netherlands. Some 25km long and up to 9km wide, Texel is a mixture of natural island – in its southeast reaches – and reclaimed polder, mostly on the western side. Overall it's a flat landscape of green pastureland dotted with chunks of woodland, speckled with small villages and protected by long sea defences. The west coast boasts magnificent stretches of sand that reach from one end of the island to the other, its numbered markers (*paal*) – from 6 in the south to 33 in the north – distinguishing one section from another. Behind the beach, a belt of sand dunes widens as it approaches both ends of the island. In the north it spreads out into two nature reserves – **De Muy** and **De Slufter** – the latter incorporates Texel's finest scenery in a tidal inlet where a deep cove of salt marsh, lagoon and dune has been left beyond the sea defences, exposed to the ocean. It's this landscape, and of course the beaches, combined with the island's laidback rural charms, that attracts holidaying Dutch and Germans by the ferryload in summer, and the island has scores of holiday bungalows and cottages, plus a scattering of hotels and campsites. The island's **villages** are fairly humdrum places, though the "capital", Den Burg, has its lively moments. **Den Hoorn**, is probably the prettiest place on the island, while **Oudeschild** still boasts a working harbour with a small fishing fleet. Overall, for UK visitors at least, it's a bit of an untouched gem.

Den Burg

DEN BURG is the island's main village and home to the tourist office, a Monday morning market and the island's best range of shops. There's little else of interest, the only sight being the **Oudheidkamer** local museum (Mon–Fri 11am–5pm, Sat 2–4pm; €3), whose period interiors show how life was on Texel in times gone by.

Wezenspyk Cheese Farm

Hoornderweg 29 Den Burg · **Tours** Tues & Fri at 2pm; July & Aug also on Thurs at 2pm · €5 · **Shop** April–Oct Tues–Sat 9.30am–5pm; Nov–March Tues, Thurs, Fri, Sat 9.30am–5pm · ☎ 0222 315 090, ⓦ wezenspyk.nl

To the southwest of Den Burg, the **Wezenspyk Cheese Farm** has been going for around thirty years, having revived the island's ancient sheep's milk cheese. Today, they make cheese using milk from both the island's many sheep and the farm's own Frian-Holsten herd of cows. The farm tour takes half an hour and includes the cowshed and milking parlour, the cheese-making room and the storeroom beyond, filled with the yellow discs of the different varieties of cheese they make here, which you can taste (and buy) in the shop. They are all variations on the basic Dutch cheese you see everywhere, but the Texel soil is said to import a special flavour, engendered by the saltiness of its soil, and certainly the cheese they make here is especially delicious.

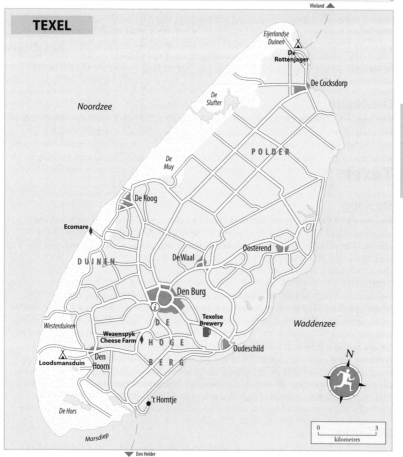

Kaap Skil Museum van Jutters & Zeelui

Heemskerckstraat 9 Oudeschild • April–Oct Tues–Sat 10am–5pm, Sun noon–5pm • €7.50, joint ticket with Ecomare and Oudheidkamer €15 • ☎ 0222 314 956, ⓦ kaapskil.nl

Right by the harbour in the village of **OUDESCHILD**, 3km from Den Burg, is the brand-new **Kaap Skil Museum van Jutters & Zeelui**. A wonderfully ramshackle collection of maritime junk, which was its core collection in days gone by, is still its most interesting feature – a shed full of beachcombed items from around the island, including an amazing collection of bottled stuff stacked as high as the ceiling (the lifetime obsession of one man). Next door is a windmill, which provides the flour you can buy in the museum shop, and a series of cottages done out as old-style shops and houses. In the main building is a model of Oudeschild in the seventeenth century, when its offshore waters were an important stopping-off point for merchant shipping, together with displays on various local individuals and their stories. There's also a café on the ground floor.

Texelse Brewery

Schilderweg 214 Oudeschild • Tues–Fri 2pm & 3pm, Sat 2pm, 3pm & 4pm • €7.50 • ☎ 0222 313 229, ⓦ speciaalbier.com

Just outside Oudeschild on the road to Den Burg, the **Texelse Microbrewery** offers

2

regular tours of its premises, starting with a short film and finishing up in the cosy *proeflokaal* to taste its unique and excellent brews. It's a great small business, and produces around ten so-called "special" beers (it doesn't do straight lager), from its popular Schumkoppe to an award-winning Bock. You can also try them in the bottle or on draft all over the island but you might just want to buy a case to take home.

Den Hoorn

The hamlet of **DEN HOORN** is the nearest village to the ferry dock on the southern side of the island. It's a leafy little place whose rustic cottages, some of which date back to the eighteenth century, string along the main street, Herenstraat, and out towards the dunes, just 2km away to the west: the beach is a further 2km (at *paal* 10). There's nothing to see in the village, but it does have a couple of good places to stay and to eat (see opposite).

De Koog

Northwest of Den Burg, **DE KOOG** is Texel's busiest resort, equipped with lots of restaurants and hotels and a small army of campsites stretching either side of the village. The village is entirely given over to shops and places to eat and the only sight as such is the Ecomare complex, 1.5km south of the village.

Ecomare

Ruijslaan 92 De Koog • €9.75, joint ticket with Oudeheidkamer & Kaap Skil €15 • ☎ 0222 317 741, ⓦ ecomare.nl

Just a couple of kilometres outside De Koog, amid the dunes, the **Ecomare** is a sealife and marine centre devoted to the wildlife and history of Texel. There are tanks of seals and porpoises, displays on the history of the island that sport some great skeletons of locally found turtles and humpback whales, and tanks devoted to the island's various habitats. It's also the headquarters of the Dunes national park, which oversees pretty much all of the west side of the island, and you can follow some guided paths through the surrounding dunes. The road leads beyond Ecomare to the beach, where there's a café and, of course, unlimited opportunities for duney walks.

De Slufter

North of De Koog, the coastal road north leads after about 4km past the first of two turnings that cut down to the sea wall behind **De Slufter** nature reserve, a beautiful tidal inlet whose assorted lagoons, marshes and dunes are exposed to the ocean's tides. Steps enable visitors to clamber up and over the sea wall to the footpaths beyond: it is perhaps the prettiest spot on the island.

De Cocksdorp

Near the northern tip of Texel, **DE COCKSDORP** is a middling sort of village (named after the Belgian banker De Cock, who funded the draining of these northwestern polders), whose wedge of mostly modern houses trail along a slender inlet, protected by a sea wall. Across the sea wall is a lighthouse, whose red shape is the iconic image of Texel. Ferries to the island Vlieland leave from the jetty about 1km north of the village, with an hourly **bus** running between De Cocksdorp, De Koog and the ferry dock.

ARRIVAL AND DEPARTURE   TEXEL

By ferry Car ferries, run by Teso (Mon–Sat 6.30am–9.30pm, Sun 7.30am–9.30pm; ☎ 0222 369 600, ⓦ teso.nl), leave Den Helder for Texel hourly on the half-hour, and the journey takes about 20min. Return tickets cost €3 for foot passengers, plus €2.50 for a bike or moped; cars cost €35 at peak times, which includes most weekend sailings, €24.50 at other times. Ferries dock at the southern end of the island, pretty much in the middle of nowhere, but there is a good island bus service to – and between – all Texel's main villages, and connections with each ferry arrival. There's also a seasonal passenger ferry to Vlieland, the next island along, which docks just outside De Cocksdorp, at the northern tip of the island. Operated by De Vriendschap (**☎** 0222 316 451, **⊛** waddenveer.nl), the ferry runs between May and September, with two services daily every day in July and August, and two services daily on Tuesday, Wednesday, Thursday and Sunday in May, June and September. The journey takes 30min and a return ticket costs €22.50 per person. Note that Vlieland is car-free.

INFORMATION

Tourist office Texel VVV is on the southern edge of Den Burg at Emmalaan 66 (Mon–Fri 9am–5.30pm, Sat 9am–5pm; **☎** 0222 314 741, **⊛** vvv.texel.net). It has a wide range of island information, including booklets detailing cycling routes as well as the best places to view the island's many bird colonies – for example De Slufter and the De Hors area south of the ferry terminal. The VVV operates an accommodation service, which is especially useful in the height of the summer when spare rooms can be thin on the ground, and it also has a substantial supply of rooms in private houses all over the island.

GETTING AROUND

By bus Pick up an island bus timetable at the Den Helder foot passenger ticket window, where you can also buy a one-day, island-wide bus pass for €4.50, though passes are also sold by the island's bus drivers.

By taxi There are also usually plenty of taxis, or at the foot passenger ticket window in Den Helder you can arrange for a Telekomtaxi (**☎** 0222 322 211) to take you anywhere on the island once you get there.

By bike The best way to get around the island is by bike – Texel has about 130km of cycle paths. Bike rental is available at a number of locations across the island at about €4.50–5.50/day, or €20 a week, but there is a very convenient outlet beside the Texel ferry dock – Fietsenverhuur Veerhaven Texel (daily 8.30am–6pm; **☎** 0222 319 588); reservations aren't necessary. Alternatively, you can rent bikes in Den Hoorn at Vermeulen Bikes, Herenstraat 69 (**☎** 0222 319 213), for €4.50 a day or €20 a week (Mon & Wed–Fri 9.30am–12.30pm & 1.30–5pm, Sat 9am–4pm).

ACCOMMODATION AND EATING

DEN BURG

★**De Smulpot** Binnenburg 5 **☎** 0222 312 756, **⊛** desmulpot.nl. You couldn't be more central in Den Burg, and Dave's cosy bar-restaurant has seven rooms upstairs, nicely finished in a boutiquey style, with driftwood furniture and headboards decorated with images of Texel's iconic lighthouse. The food served downstairs is tasty and plentiful, with most mains under €20, including excellent steaks, pork satay, ribs and other classic Dutch dishes. There's also an impressive breakfast included. **€105**

OUDESCHILD

't Pakhuus Haven 8 **☎** 0222 313 581, **⊛** pakhuus.nl. Right on the fishing harbour, this is one of the nicest restaurants on this side of the island, serving a lovely lunch menu of fish soup, open sandwiches and more substantial offerings (a three-course lunch fixed-price menu costs €32.50) and an array of great fish dishes in the evening – reckon on paying €25–50 for a main course. They also have three beautifully designed and very comfortable contemporary suites upstairs. Tues & Wed 5–9.30pm, Thurs–Sun noon–9.30pm.

Van der Star Heemskerckstraat 15 **☎** 0222 312 441, **⊛** vispaleistexel.nl. A good alternative to the posh fish restaurants down by Oudeschild's harbour, a seafood and fish café with lots of baked and smoked marine delights, fish soup and salads – all delicious. Daily noon–8pm.

DEN HOORN

Bij Jef Herenstraat 34 **☎** 0222 319 623, **⊛** bijjef.nl. In an old building right on the main street, this place is one of the island's most enticing prospects, with stylish and very comfortable rooms. The restaurant is one of Texel's best, all crisp white tablecloths and white leather chairs, and with an excellent reputation for its excellent Franco-Dutch cuisine: three- and four-course menus cost €75 and €90. Mon–Sat noon–2pm & 6–10pm, Sun noon–9pm. **€195**

Klif 23 Klif 23 **☎** 0222 319 515. On the west side of the village on the road that runs towards the dunes, this is a simple café that specializes in pancakes: it serves up more than 150 varieties, along with Texel lamb dishes. Daily 11am–9pm.

Loodman's Welvaren Herenstraat 12 **☎** 0222 319 228, **⊛** welvaarttexel.nl. Nine spick-and-span, modern double rooms, all decorated with naval scenes, in a sympathetically modernized old building. There's free wi-fi, and a decent restaurant downstairs that continues the nautical theme. **€105**

Loodsmansduin Rommelpot 19 **☎** 0222 317 208, **⊛** rsttexel.nl. Large campsite with plenty of space for tents and caravans on the edge of the dunes just to the southwest of Den Hoorn – about a 10min walk. April–Oct. **€24**

DE COCKSDORP

't Anker Kikkertstraat 24 **☎** 0222 316 274,

Ⓦ t-anker.texel.com. An unassuming little place in a pair of oldish cottages on the main street. It has a cosy downstairs sitting room and rooms that have a vaguely Scandinavian feel. €90

Pangkoekehuis Kikkertstraat 9 Ⓣ 0222 316 441, Ⓦ pangkoekehuus.nl. They serve a great line in pancakes here – both sweet and savoury – and you can sit outside on their large terrace and watch the world go by, while they deliver your bill to the table inside a tiny clog. Prices start at around €4. Daily noon–8.30pm, until 9pm in July and August.

2

Het Gooi

Known collectively as **Het Gooi**, the sprawling suburbs that spread southeast from Amsterdam towards Amersfoort and Utrecht (see p.186) are interrupted by open heaths, lakes, canals and woods, reminders of the time when this was a sparsely inhabited district largely devoted to sheep farming. The turning point was the construction of the Amsterdam–Amersfoort railway in 1874, which allowed hundreds of middle-class Amsterdammers to build their country homes here, nowhere more so than in well-heeled **Hilversum**, long the area's main settlement and nowadays pretty much a dormitory town despite the best efforts of the Dutch media, much of which has decamped here. Hilversum is a possible target for a day-trip on account of its modern architecture, most notably the work of Willem Dudok, although Het Gooi's two other prime attractions, the immaculate star-shaped fortifications of **Naarden** and the handsome medieval castle at **Muiden**, are frankly more appealing.

GETTING AROUND

HET GOOI

By train The most useful train line across Het Gooi passes through Weesp, where there are connecting buses onto Muiden, and then onto Naarden-Bussum (for Naarden) and Hilversum.

Muiden

Just to the north of the A1 motorway about 10km southeast of Amsterdam, **MUIDEN** straddles the River Vecht as it approaches the Markermeer, its several waterways crowded with pleasure boats and yachts. At the far end of the town on the old ramparts is the **Muiderslot**, one of the country's most visited castles.

The Muiderslot
Herengrach 1 • April–Oct Mon–Fri 10am–5pm, Sat & Sun noon–5pm; Nov–March Sat & Sun noon–5pm • €12.50 • Ⓣ 0294 256 262, Ⓦ muiderslot.nl

The **Muiderslot** is a handsome red-brick structure whose imposing walls are punctuated by mighty circular towers, all set behind a reedy moat. Originally built by Count Floris V of Holland (1254–96), it has been rebuilt or remodelled on several occasions, most recently after World War II when the interior was returned to its seventeenth-century appearance in honour of the poet Pieter Hooft, one of its most celebrated occupants. Hooft was chatelain here from 1609–47, a sinecure that allowed him to entertain a group of artistic and literary friends who became known as the Muiderkring or Muiden Circle.

In order to see certain parts of the castle, you have to join one of the half-hourly guided tours, which take you through a series of period rooms, among them a small dining room and kitchen, and the large Ridderzaal, which has a painting showing Hooft and his most famous cronies – Vondel, Huygens, Jacob Cats, Maria Tesselschaede and others – although the painting is something of a fake in that not all the people in the painting were alive at the same time. But really the best bits of the building can be seen on your own, whether it's the chapel which shows a short film about Muiden, Hooft's study and en-suite loo, which enjoys good views over what would have been the Zuider Zee, or the suits of armour and various knightly bits and pieces in one of the towers. Kids may also enjoy the chance to joust or dress in a jester's suit, but the best thing is the wonderful view over the Markerwaard from the bastions. Bear in mind that the entrance ticket also include the gardens, and the regular falconry displays that take place nearby.

ARRIVAL AND DEPARTURE	MUIDEN

By train and bus To get to Muiden, take the train from Amsterdam Centraal Station to Weesp (every 15min; 15min) where you catch the hourly local bus #110 to Muiden: it's a 5min journey. In Muiden, the bus drops you on the edge of town, a short, signposted walk from the centre and the Muiderslot.

EATING AND DRINKING

Ome Ko Herengracht 71. Right by the big lock gates in the centre of Muiden, this is a pleasant bar with an outside terrace overlooking the canal – it's a good lunch or drink stop, serving *uitsmijters*, sandwiches and the like. Mon–Thurs & Sun 8am–2am, Fri & Sat 8am–3am.

Naarden

Look at a postcard of **NAARDEN**, about 8km east along the A1 from Muiden, and it seems as if the old town was created by a giant pastry-cutter, its gridiron of streets encased within a double ring of ramparts and moats that were engineered with geometrical precision between 1675 and 1685 to defend the eastern approaches to Amsterdam. Within the ramparts, Naarden's attractive and architecturally harmonious centre mostly dates from the late sixteenth century, its small, low houses erected after the Spanish sacked the town in 1572, including the elaborately step-gabled **Stadhuis**, built in 1601 and still in use by the town council today. Naarden's old town is readily explored on foot – it's only 1km long and about 800m wide.

Nederlands Vestingmuseum

Westwalstraat 6 • Tues–Fri 10.30am–5pm, Sat & Sun noon–5pm • €6 • ☏ 035 694 5459, Ⓦ vestingmuseum.nl

Naarden's formidable defences were used right up until the 1920s, and one of the fortified spurs is now the wonderful **Nederlands Vestingmuseum**, on whose grassy forks you can clamber around among the cannons. It's great to explore and its claustrophobic casemates demonstrate how the garrison defended the town for nigh-on 300 years.

The Grote Kerk

Markstraat 15 • Free • ☏ 035 694 9873, Ⓦ grotekerknaarden.nl

One building that was spared by the Spaniards was the late Gothic **Grote Kerk**, whose superb vault paintings, based on drawings by Dürer, are the town's other main sight. These 22 rectangular wooden panels were painted between 1510 and 1518 and show Old Testament scenes on the south side, New Testament scenes on the north; there are also five triangular panels at the east end of the church. To study the paintings without cricking your neck, borrow a mirror at the entrance. The church is also noted for its wonderful acoustics: every year there are several acclaimed performances of Bach's *St Matthew Passion* in the Grote Kerk in the days leading up to Easter – details from the tourist office. A haul up the 235 steps of the Grote Kerk's massive square **tower** gives the best view of the fortress.

Comenius Museum

Kloosterstraat 33 • Tues–Sun noon–5pm • €5 • ☏ 035 694 3045, Ⓦ comeniusmuseum.nl

The mildly absorbing **Comenius Museum** is the third of Naarden's trio of sights. Jan Amos Komenski, his name latinized as Comenius, was a seventeenth-century philosopher, cartographer and educational reformer who was born in Moravia, today part of the Czech Republic. A Protestant, he was expelled for his religious beliefs in 1621 and spent the next 36 years wandering round Europe preaching and teaching before finally settling in

2

Amsterdam. The museum outlines Comenius' life and times and takes a stab at explaining his views, notably his plan to improve the Swedish educational system and his 1658 *Orbis Pictus* ("The World in Pictures"), the first-ever picture-book for children. Comenius was buried here in Naarden, and the museum incorporates his **mausoleum**, a remarkable affair with an ornamental screen and engraved glass panels decorated with scenes from his life, in what was once the chapel of a Franciscan convent. In the 1930s the Dutch authorities refused the Czech government's request for the repatriation of the philosopher's remains, and instead sold them the building (and the land it stood on) for the symbolic price of one guilder: the mausoleum remains a tiny slice of Czech territory to this day.

ARRIVAL AND INFORMATION   NAARDEN

By train and bus There are three trains hourly from Amsterdam Centraal Station to Naarden-Bussum train station, about 4km from the old town – Naarden has spread well beyond its original fortifications – with local buses linking the train station with the old town.

Tourist office The VVV is at the south end of the main Marktstraat at Ruijsdaelplein 9 (mid-March to Oct Tues–Sun 11.30am–3pm; Nov to mid-March noon–3pm; ☎ 035 694 2673, ⓦ vvvnaarden.nl), and provides maps of the town.

EATING AND DRINKING

Het Arsenaal Kooltjesbuurt 1 ☎ 035 694 9148 ⓦ paulfagel.nl. Housed in the old arsenal shopping complex across the canal from Naarden's main street, this is without doubt the town's best restaurant, home base of the well-known Dutch chef Paul Fagel, who cooks excellent French food for both the restaurant and a more informal brasserie. Restaurant Mon–Fri noon–4pm & daily from 6pm; Brasserie Mon–Fri 10am–5pm.

Café de Doelen Markstraat 7 ☎ 035 694 2720, ⓦ doelennaarden.nl. You can sit inside, in the darkish, pubby interior, or on the terrace outside at this café near the Grote Kerk. It serves good *uitsmijters*, sandwiches and pancakes at lunch (starting at about €6.50), as well as more substantial meals in the evening, with Dutch dinner classics like chicken satay, spare ribs, etc from about €14.50. Wed–Sun 11.30am–10pm.

Hilversum

Sprawling, leafy **HILVERSUM** is the main town of Het Gooi and a prosperous, commuter suburb with a population of around 90,000. Many locals love the place, but for the casual visitor, Hilversum is mainly of interest for its modern architecture – or to be precise the work of **Willem Marinus Dudok** (1884–1974), the director of public works and town architect for over thirty years. Hilversum possesses several dozen buildings by Dudok, who was much influenced by the American Frank Lloyd Wright.

Raadhuis

Dudokpark 1 • Tours Fri & Sun at 1.30pm; €7.50 • Dudok Centrum Wed & Sun noon–4.30pm; €3

Pride of place among Hilversum's Dudok buildings goes to the **Raadhuis**, about 700m northwest of the train station – follow Stationsstraat and then Melkpad from the station; it's a ten-minute walk. Dating from 1931, the design of the building was based on a deceptively simple progression of straw-coloured blocks rising to a clock tower, with long, slender bricks giving it a strong horizontal emphasis. The interior is well worth seeing too: essentially a series of lines and boxes, its marble walls are margined with black, like a monochrome Mondrian painting, all coolly and immaculately proportioned. Dudok also designed the interior decorations, and though some have been altered, his style prevails, right down to the ashtrays and lights. The **Dudok Centrum**, in the basement of the Raadhuis, presents an overview of Dudok's life and work.

Singer Museum

Oude Drift 1, Laren • Tues–Sun 11am–5pm • €15 • ⓦ singerlaren.nl • Bus #109 runs here every thirty minutes from Hilversum station and from outside Naarden-Bussum station

It's a short trip from Hilversum to the nearby village **OF LAREN**, where the **Singer Museum** houses an impressive collection of mainly late nineteenth-century paintings by both local artists and the Hague School, as well as the French Barbizon painters and American Impressionists – in a beautiful, well-lit modern space. It was established in the 1950s by the widow of the American artist William Henry Singer and is well worth the fifteen-minute bus journey from Hilversum.

ARRIVAL AND INFORMATION   HILVERSUM

By train Trains leave Amsterdam's Centraal Station twice an hour for Hilversum, and take about 30min to get there. Hilversum also has regular train connections with the nearby towns of Amersfoort (every 30min; 15min) and Utrecht (every 20min; 20min).

Tourist office It's a 10min walk from the train station to the VVV at Kerkbrink 6 (Mon–Sat 10am–5pm, Sun noon–5pm; ☏035 629 2810, ⓦvvvgooivecht.nl) – take Stationsstraat to the main Groest, turn left and then right onto Kerkstraat and follow it for around 200m. The VVV has the usual information and maps and a small supply of rooms in private houses, though with Amsterdam so close, and connections to more interesting towns so easy, there's little reason to stay overnight.

2

Zuid-Holland and Utrecht

WINDMILLS AT KINDERDIJK

Zuid-Holland and Utrecht

Zuid-Holland (South Holland) is the most densely populated province of the Netherlands, incorporating a string of towns and cities that make up the bulk of what is commonly called the Randstad (literally "Rim-Town"). By and large, careful urban planning has succeeded in stopping this from becoming an amorphous conurbation, however, and each town has preserved a pronounced identity.

A short hop from Amsterdam is **Leiden**, a university town *par excellence*, with an antique centre latticed by canals and dotted with fine old buildings. **Den Haag** (The Hague) was once a humdrum government town, but has jazzed itself up and is now a very likeable city with a string of good museums and an appealing bar and restaurant scene. Neighbouring **Delft** is a much smaller place, with just 100,000 inhabitants, but it possesses an extremely pretty centre replete with handsome seventeenth-century buildings, in stark contrast to the rough and tumble of big-city **Rotterdam**, the world's largest port, where an adventurous city council has stacked up a string of first-rate attractions, from fine art through to harbour tours. It's a short journey inland from here to **Gouda**, a good-looking country town historically famed for its cheese market, and to the somnambulant charms of rural **Oudewater**. Back on the coast, **Dordrecht** marks the southern edge of the Randstad and is of mild interest as an ancient port and for its location, within easy striking distance of the windmills of the **Kinderdijk** and the creeks and marshes of the **Biesbosch**. Finally, the province of **Utrecht** is distinguished by its capital city, Utrecht, a sprawling city with a dramatic history and a bustling, youthful centre.

The region's coastal cities – especially Leiden and Den Haag – are only a short bus or tram ride from the wide sandy **beaches** of the North Sea coast, while the pancake-flat Randstad landscape is brightened by rainbow flashes of **bulbfields** in spring with the **Keukenhof gardens**, near Leiden, having the finest display. A fast and efficient rail network makes travelling around Zuid-Holland extremely easy, and where the trains fizzle out, buses take over.

Brief history

Historically, Zuid-Holland is part of what was once simply **Holland**, the richest and most influential province in the country. Throughout the Golden Age, Holland dominated the political, social and cultural life of the Republic, overshadowing its neighbours, their economies dwarfed by its success. There are constant reminders of this pre-eminence in the province's buildings: elaborate town halls proclaim civic importance and even the usually sombre Calvinist **churches** allow themselves decorative excesses – the later windows of Gouda's Janskerk being a case in point. Many of the great Dutch **painters** either came from, or worked here, too – Rembrandt, Vermeer, Jan Steen – a tradition that continued into the nineteenth century with the paintings of the Hague School. All the towns offer good **museums** and galleries, most notably The Hague's Mauritshuis and Rotterdam's Boijmans van Beuningen.

CANAL, UTRECHT

Highlights

❶ Den Haag The political capital of the Netherlands and home of the Dutch royal family is an enjoyable city, which boasts the impressive Mauritshuis art gallery and has an extensive coastline. **See p.152**

❷ Delft A lovely little town and one-time home of Vermeer, with one of the prettiest market squares in the Netherlands and picture-perfect canals flanked by old mansions. **See p.163**

❸ Rotterdam This gritty and boisterous port city has resurrected itself in flash modern style after extensive war damage, complete with its own Museumpark and a vibrant nightlife. **See p.168**

❹ Gouda Archetypal Dutch country town, home of the famous round cheese and a splendid set of stained-glass windows in St Janskerk. **See p.177**

❺ Utrecht Lively university town wound around a tight skein of narrow canals, with the Domtoren – the highest Gothic church tower in the Netherlands – dominating the city skyline. **See p.186**

HIGHLIGHTS ARE MARKED ON THE MAP ON P.146

Leiden and around

Just twenty minutes by train from Amsterdam's Schiphol airport, **LEIDEN** is a lively and energetic city of around 120,000 souls that makes for an enjoyable day-trip or overnight stay. At its heart, the city's antique, sometimes careworn, centre is a maze of narrow lanes that wriggle and worm their way around a complicated network of canals, one of which marks the line of the medieval walls. It's all very appealing and unfussy, with Leiden's multitude of bars and cafés kept afloat by the thirsty students of the city's one great institution, its **university** – one of Europe's most prestigious seats of learning. The obvious place to start an exploration of the city centre is the **Beestenmarkt**, a large and really rather plain open space that's long been the town's major meeting point. As for specific sights, top billing goes to the magnificent ancient Egyptian collection at the **Rijksmuseum van Oudheden** (National Museum of Antiquities) and the seventeenth-century Dutch paintings of the **Stedelijk Museum de Lakenhal**, though, perhaps surprisingly, given that this was his home town, the museum is very short of Rembrandts. Leiden is also within easy striking distance of the Dutch bulbfields and the showpiece **Keukenhof gardens** as well as the pleasant North Sea resort of **Katwijk-aan-Zee** and its long sandy beach.

Brief history

It may well have been the **Romans** who founded Leiden as a forward base on an important trade route running behind the dunes, but, whatever the truth, it was certainly fortified in the ninth century when a local lord built a castle here on an artificial mound. Flemish weavers migrated to Leiden in the fourteenth century and thereafter the town prospered as a minor cloth-making centre, but things didn't really take off until the foundation of its university in 1575. It was **William the Silent** who chose Leiden to be the home of the university as a reward for the city's bravery during the rebellion against Spain: Leiden had declared for William in 1572, but a Habsburg army besieged the city in October 1573. The siege, which lasted a whole year, was a desperate affair during which hundreds of city folk starved to death, but William the Silent finally sailed to the rescue on October 3, 1574, cutting through the dykes around the town and vanquishing the Spaniards in one fell swoop. The event is still commemorated with an annual fair, fireworks and the consumption of two traditional dishes: herring and white bread, which the fleet brought with them, and *hutspot*, a vegetable and potato stew, a cauldron of which was found simmering in the abandoned Spanish camp outside the walls.

Rijksmuseum van Oudheden

Rapenburg 28 • Tues–Sun 10am–5pm, plus Mon 10am–5pm in school hols • €9 • Ⓦ rmo.nl

A gentle, curving canal lined by some of Leiden's grandest mansions, the Rapenburg is also home to the town's most important museum, the **Rijksmuseum van Oudheden** (National Museum of Antiquities). Its three floors display extensive Egyptian and Classical collections as well as hosting an ambitious programme of temporary exhibitions.

The Ground Floor

On the ground floor, the museum kicks off in style with the squat and sturdy **Taffeh Temple**, a present from the Egyptian government. It was gifted in gratitude for Dutch help with the 1960s UNESCO excavations that saved scores of ancient monuments from the rising waters of the Nile following the construction of the Aswan dam. Dating back to the first century AD, the Taffeh Temple was originally part of a fortress that guarded the southern border of the Roman province of Egypt. Initially, it was dedicated to Isis, the goddess of love and magic, but in the fourth century it was turned into a Christian church.

3

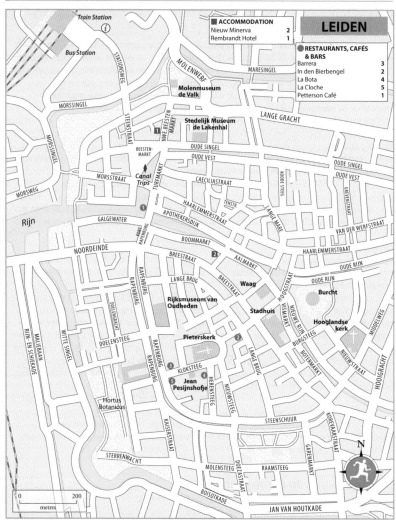

On the same floor is the rest of the **Egyptian collection**, which includes wall reliefs, statues, stele and sarcophagi from a variety of tombs and temples, plus a set of mummies as complete as you're likely to see outside Egypt. Particular highlights include magnificent stele from the temple at Abydos and the exceptionally well-preserved double sculpture of Maya and Merit, Maya being the minister of finance under Tutankhamen, Merit his wife.

The Upper Floors

The next floor up exhibits oodles of classical **Greek and Roman sculptures**, including stolid busts, statues and friezes from imperial Rome as well as a scattering of Etruscan artefacts. Moving on, the top floor displays a **Netherlands archeological section**, which has a first-rate selection of Roman stone altars and inscribed tombstones retrieved from the waters of Zeeland in the 1970s.

Hortus Botanicus

Rapenburg 73 • April–Oct daily 10am–6pm; Nov–March Tues–Sun 10am–4pm • €6 • ⓦ hortusleiden.nl

Just beyond the Rijksmuseum van Oudheden on Rapenburg, a three-sided courtyard complex includes – on the left – the building that became the university's first home, after previously being part of a medieval monastery. Through the courtyard is the **Hortus Botanicus**, lushly planted and subtly landscaped botanical gardens that stretch along the Witte Singel canal. Planted in 1587, this is one of the oldest botanical gardens in Europe, a mixture of carefully tended beds of shrubs, ancient gnarled trees and hothouses full of tropical foliage.

Pieterskerk

Pieterskerkhof 1a • April–Oct Mon–Fri 10am–4pm, Sat & Sun 1.30–4pm; Nov–March daily 1.30–4pm • Free

On the east side of Rapenburg, across from the botanical gardens, lies the network of narrow streets that once constituted the medieval town and now converges on the Gothic **Pieterskerk**, Leiden's principal church. Deconsecrated now, it has an empty warehouse-like feel, but among the fixtures that remain are a simple and beautiful Renaissance rood screen and a host of memorials to the sundry notables buried here – including one to John Robinson (1575–1625), leader of the Pilgrim Fathers. Robinson lived in a house on the site of what is now the **Jean Pesijnshofje** at Kloksteeg 21, right beside the church – look out for the plaque. A curate in England at the turn of the seventeenth century, he was suspended from preaching in 1604, later fleeing with his congregation to pursue his Puritanism in the more amenable atmosphere of Calvinist Holland. Settling in Leiden, Robinson acted as pastor to growing numbers, but even here he found himself at odds with the religious establishment. In 1620, one hundred of his followers – the **Pilgrim Fathers** – sailed via Plymouth for the untrammelled wilderness of America, though Robinson died before he could join them; he's buried in the church.

The Stadhuis and the Waag

From the **Pieterskerk**, it's a short stroll east to **Breestraat**, which marks the southern edge of Leiden's present commercial centre, but is undistinguished except for the **Stadhuis**, an imposing edifice whose Renaissance facade is a copy of the late sixteenth-century original destroyed by fire in 1929. Behind the Stadhuis, the canals that cut Leiden's centre into pocket-sized segments converge at the busiest point in town, tiny **Hoogstraat**, the focus of a vigorous general **market** on Wednesdays and Saturdays (9am–5pm). Around Hoogstraat, a tangle of narrow bridges is flanked by a number of fetching buildings, ranging from overblown Art Nouveau department stores to modest terrace houses. Here also, on Vismarkt, is the **Waag**, built to a design by Pieter Post (1608–69) and fronted with a naturalistic frieze showing a merchant watching straining labourers.

The Hooglandsekerk

Middelweg 2 • Mid-May to mid-Sept Mon 1–5pm, Tues–Fri 11am–3.30pm, Sat 11am–4pm • Free

Stretching southeast from Vismarkt, the Nieuwe Rijn is one of the town's prettiest canals, the first of its several bridges topped off by a matching pair of Neoclassical porticoes dating from 1825. Nearby, the **Hooglandsekerk** is a light and lofty Gothic structure built in stages over a couple of hundred years. The church holds a monument to Pieter van der Werff, the heroic burgomaster of Leiden at the time of the 1573–74 siege. When the situation became so desperate that the people were all for giving up, the burgomaster, no doubt remembering the massacre at Haarlem (see p.105), offered up his own body to be eaten. The invitation was declined, but it inspired new determination in the town's flagging citizens.

The Burcht

Burgsteeg 14 • Daily 10am–10pm • Free

At the end of Burgsteeg, go through a gateway and you'll soon pass the steps up to the top of the **Burcht**, the artificial mound where Leiden's first castle stood. The castle is long gone and the circular stone wall which occupies the site today is disappointingly paltry, but the view over the city centre is first-rate. At the far end of the alley is the **Oude Rijn** canal, on the other side of which lies the blandly pedestrian **Haarlemmerstraat**, the town's main shopping street.

The Stedelijk Museum de Lakenhal

Oude Singel 32 • Tues–Fri 10am–5pm, Sat & Sun noon–5pm • €7.50 • ⓦ lakenhal.nl

It's a short walk north from Haarlemmerstraat to Leiden's **Stedelijk Museum de Lakenhal** housed in the former Cloth Hall. The museum's ground floor holds mixed rooms of furniture, silver, tiles, glass and ceramics as well as a healthy sample of local sixteenth- and seventeenth-century paintings, including examples of the work of Jacob van Swanenburgh (first teacher of the young Rembrandt), Jan Lievens (with whom Rembrandt shared a studio), and Gerrit Dou (1613–75), who is well represented by his exquisite *Astrologer*. Rembrandt's first pupil, Dou began by imitating his master but soon developed his own style, pioneering the Leiden tradition of small, minutely detailed pictures of enamel-like smoothness. There's also Lucas van Leyden's (1494–1533) alarming and spectacularly unsuccessful *Last Judgement* triptych, several paintings devoted to the siege of 1574 and the heroics of burgomaster van der Werff, plus two canvases by the earthy Jan Steen (1626–79) and a splendid *View of Leiden* by Jan van Goyen (1596–1656). **Rembrandt** (1606–69) himself, though a native of Leiden, is poorly represented; he left his home town at the tender age of 14, and although he returned in 1625, he was off again six years later, this time to settle permanently in Amsterdam. Only a handful of his Leiden paintings survive, but there's one here, *Agamemnon before Palamedes*, a stilted and rather unsuccessful rendition of the classical tale, painted in 1626.

The other floors of the museum are of cursory interest only: the first floor is devoted to Leiden textiles, the next floor up is used for temporary exhibitions, while the top floor houses a series of modest displays on the town's history.

The Molenmuseum de Valk

2e Binnenvestgracht 1 • Tues–Sat 10am–5pm, Sun 1–5pm • €3 • ⓦ molendevalk.leiden.nl

The **Molenmuseum de Valk** (Falcon Windmill Museum), a restored grain mill, is the last survivor of the twenty-odd windmills built on the town's outer fortifications in the eighteenth century. On the ground floor are the miller's musty living quarters, furnished in simple late nineteenth-century style, and then it's up the stairs for a short video recounting the history of Dutch windmills. Up yet more stairs are a series of displays that give the lowdown on the hard life of the average Dutch miller, who had to be incredibly nimble to survive if the cramped conditions here are anything to go by. The miller was rarely paid in cash, but took a scoop from each sack instead. He was supposed to pay tax on this – some windmills even had a taxman's kiosk next door – but evasion was widespread and many windmills, including this one, had a so-called smuggler's cupboard where the miller could hide the proceeds.

The Keukenhof gardens

Stationsweg 166, Lisse • Mid-March to mid-May daily 8am–7.30pm • €14.50 • ⓦ keukenhof.com • Bus #54 runs from Leiden bus station direct to the main entrance (every 15min; 30min)

If you're after bulbs, then make a beeline for the bulb growers' showcase, the **Keukenhof gardens**, located on the edge of the little town of **LISSE**, beside the N208 about 15km

THE BULBFIELDS

The pancake-flat fields stretching north from Leiden towards Haarlem (see p.105) are the heart of the Dutch **bulbfields**, whose bulbs and blooms support a billion-euro industry and some ten thousand growers, as well as attracting tourists in their droves. Bulbs have flourished here since the late sixteenth century, when one **Carolus Clusius**, a Dutch botanist and one-time gardener to the Habsburg emperor, brought the first **tulip bulb** over from Vienna, where it had – in its turn – been brought from Asia Minor by an Austrian aristocrat. The tulip flourished in Holland's sandy soil and was so highly prized that it fuelled a massive **speculative bubble**. At the height of the boom – in the mid-1630s – bulbs were commanding extraordinary prices: the artist Jan van Goyen paid 1900 guilders and two paintings for ten rare bulbs, while a bag of one hundred bulbs was swapped for a coach and horses. When the government finally intervened in 1636, the industry returned to reality with a bang, leaving hundreds of investors ruined – much to the satisfaction of the country's Calvinist ministers, who had long railed against such excesses.

Other types of bulbs apart from the tulip have also been introduced, and nowadays the spring flowering season begins in mid-March with **crocuses**, followed by **daffodils** and yellow **narcissi** in late March, **hyacinths** and **tulips** from mid-April through to May, and **irises** and **gladioli** in August. The views of the bulbfields from any of the trains heading southwest from Schiphol airport can often be sufficient in themselves, the fields divided into stark geometric blocks of pure colour, but, with your own transport – either bicycle or car – you can take in their particular beauty by way of special routes marked by hexagonal signposts; local tourist offices sell pamphlets describing the routes in detail. You could also drop by the bulb growers' showpiece, the **Keukenhof** gardens. Bear in mind also that there are any number of local flower festivals and parades in mid- to late April; every local VVV has the details of these too.

north of Leiden. The largest flower gardens in the world, dating back to 1949, the Keukenhof was designed by a group of prominent bulb growers to convert people to the joys of growing flowers from bulbs in their own gardens. Literally the "kitchen garden", its site is the former estate of a fifteenth-century countess, who used to grow herbs and vegetables for her dining table. Several million flowers are on show for their full flowering period, complemented, in case of especially harsh winters, by thousands of square metres of glasshouse holding indoor displays. You could easily spend a whole day here, swooning with the sheer abundance of it all, but to get the best of it you need to come early, before the tour buses descend on the place. There are several restaurants in the grounds, and a network of well-marked footpaths explores every horticultural nook and cranny.

Katwijk-aan-Zee

Katwijk is a 30min bus ride from Leiden bus station (every 15min, Sat & Sun every 30min); buses #36 and #37 drop you off right at the beach

Leiden is just a few kilometres from the North Sea coast, where the prime target is **KATWIJK-AAN-ZEE**, a pleasant little resort whose low-slung houses string along behind a wide sandy beach, with a pristine expanse of beach and dune beckoning beyond – and stretching south towards Scheveningen (see p.159). Here and there, a row of cottages recalls the time when Katwijk was a busy fishing village, but there are no real sights as such with the possible exception of a chunky, old **lighthouse** by the beach on the southern edge of the resort, and the Katwijk sluices, on the north side of Katwijk. Completed in 1807, this chain of sluice gates regulates the flow of the Oude Rijn as it approaches the sea. Around high tide, the gates are closed, and when they are reopened the pressure of the accumulated water brushes aside the sand deposited at the mouth of the river. This simple system has effectively fixed the course of the Oude Rijn, which for centuries had been continually diverted by its sand deposits, flooding the surrounding area with depressing regularity.

ARRIVAL AND DEPARTURE

By train Leiden's ultramodern train station is on the northwest edge of town on Stationsplein 3, a 5min walk from the Beestenmarkt at the west end of the centre. Regular trains connect Leiden to Amsterdam (every 10min; 35min), Den Haag CS (every 10min; 15min) and Rotterdam (every 15min; 35min).

INFORMATION AND TOURS

Tourist offices Leiden's Visitor Centre is at Stationsweg 41 (Mon–Fri 8am–6pm, Sat 10am–4pm, Sun 11am–3pm; ☎071 516 6000, ⊕vvvleiden.nl). It has all manner of local information, including city maps and brochures, as well as an excellent range of walking and touring maps covering most of the country. Katwijk-aan-Zee's VVV is on the main street, a short walk from the beach at Voorstraat 41 (Mon 1.30–5.30pm, Tues–Fri 10am–5.30pm, Sat

LEIDEN AND AROUND

By bus Leiden's bus station is next to the train station on Stationsplein. Although most major towns can be easily reached by train, you might need to catch a bus when going to the smaller seaside resorts such as Katwijk-aan-Zee (buses #36 and #37) or Noordwijk (buses #40 and #44).

9.30am–5pm; ☎071 407 5444, ⊕vvvkatwijk.nl). They have a supply of rooms in private houses, as well as a list of hotels and pensions, but may struggle to find a vacancy in July and August.

Canal trips The Beestenmarkt is the starting point of canal trips around the centre – an enjoyable way to spend fifty minutes (March–Oct hourly between 11am–4pm; €10).

ACCOMMODATION

Nieuw Minerva Boommarkt 23 ☎071 512 6358, ⊕nieuwminerva.nl. Easily the most appealing hotel in town – a cosy, very Dutch place that occupies a sequence of old canal-side houses in the centre. The tiled breakfast room is particularly pleasant and all the guest rooms are spacious and comfortable, in an undemanding sort of way, though the "honeymoon room" is up a notch, boasting a

four-poster bed and fancy drapes. **€106**

Rembrandt Hotel Nieuwe Beestenmarkt 10 ☎071 514 4233, ⊕rembrandthotel.nl. Obviously drawings and sketches of Rembrandt dominate this conveniently located hotel with a pleasant café downstairs and great views of the Falcon Windmill. The 20 rooms are plain but perfectly adequate, some with balcony. **€130**

EATING AND DRINKING

Leiden's crowded centre heaves with inexpensive cafés and café-bars, and there's a cluster of top-flight restaurants too. Many of the more interesting places are concentrated in the immediate vicinity of Pieterskerk, among the ancient brick houses that make up this especially pretty part of the city.

Barrera Rapenburg 56 ☎071 514 6631. A fashionable café-bar and student favourite, with a good beer menu and a pavement terrace. Also many wines by the glass and corpulent meal salads for €10. Opposite the entrance to the Hortus Botanicus. Mon–Sat 10am–1am, Sun 11am–1am.

In den Bierbengel Langebrug 71 ☎071 514 8056, ⊕indenbierbengel.nl. Inhabiting an old building in an attractive corner of the town centre, this popular, informal restaurant has a short but well-chosen menu covering all the Dutch basics. Mains such as grilled butterfish or steak with Calvados go for around €18. Daily from 5–10pm.

La Bota Herensteeg 9 ☎071 514 6340, ⊕labota.nl. Popular, very informal restaurant serving up some of the

best-value Dutch food in town as well as an excellent range of beers. Mains from €12 and a three-course meal for a mere €13.50. Daily 5–10pm.

La Cloche Kloksteeg 3 ☎071 512 3053, ⊕laclocheleiden.nl. Small and smart French restaurant with a well-chosen menu featuring local ingredients – try the Texel lamb. Mains €20–25 and a daily changing three-course menu for €35. Tues–Sat 5.30–10.30pm.

Pettersson Café Turfmarkt ☎071 512 1279, ⊕pettersonleiden.nl. Modern, floating café, where the food is routine, if perfectly OK, but the view of the boats and barges on the busy Galgewater compensate. Many Swedish specialties and lunch is served until 9pm. Daily 9am–10pm.

Den Haag

DEN HAAG (The Hague) is markedly different from any other Dutch city. In a country built on municipal independence and munificence, it's been the focus of national institutions since the sixteenth century, but is not – curiously enough – the capital, which is Amsterdam. Frequently disregarded until the development of central government in the 1800s, Den Haag's older buildings are a comparatively subdued and modest collection, with little of Amsterdam's flamboyance. Indeed, the majority of the canal houses are demurely classical and exude that sense of sedate prosperity which prompted Matthew Arnold's harsh estimation of 1859: "I never saw a city where the well-to-do classes seemed to have given the whole place so much of their own air of wealth, finished cleanliness, and comfort; but I never saw one, either, in which my heart would so have sunk at the thought of living".

The city centre

The prettiest spot in Den Haag – and the logical place to start a visit – is the north side of the **Hofvijver** (Court Pond), a placid lakelet that mirrors the attractive, vaguely Ruritanian symmetries of the extensive **Binnenhof** (Inner Court), the one-time home of the country's bicameral parliament. The Binnenhof is the very heart of the city and it's also metres from what will be the prime attraction when it reopens in 2014, the **Mauritshuis** art gallery. A string of other, lesser museums occupy the handsome mansions that spread north of the Binnenhof, the pick of them being the **Bredius Museum**, with a second superb collection of fine art. To the west of the Binnenhof, by contrast, are the narrow streets of the old centre, where the key building is the **Grote Kerk**.

The Binnenhof

The **Binnenhof** (open access) occupies the site of the medieval castle where Den Haag began. The first fortress was raised by William II, Count of Holland (1227–56) – hence the city's official name, 's Gravenhage, literally "Count's Hedge", but more precisely "Count's Domain". William's descendants became the region's most powerful family, simultaneously acting as Stadholders (effectively provincial governors) of most of the seven United Provinces, which rebelled against the Habsburgs in the sixteenth century. In due course, one of the family, Prince Maurice of Orange-Nassau (1567–1625), established his main residence in Den Haag, which had effectively become the country's political capital. As the embodiment of central rather than municipal power, the Binnenhof was at times fêted, at others virtually ignored, until the nineteenth century when Den Haag officially shared political capital status with Brussels during the uneasy times of the United Kingdom of the Netherlands (1815–30). Thereafter it became the seat of government and home to a functioning legislature.

The lack of prestige in the low-slung brick buildings of the Binnenhof long irked Dutch parliamentarians and finally, in 1992, they moved into a flashy new extension next door. Without the politicians, the original Binnenhof became somewhat redundant, but it's still an eye-pleasing architectural ensemble, comprising a broadly rectangular complex built around two connecting courtyards.

The Ridderzaal

Guided tours leave from the ProDemos visitor centre on Hofweg 1 • €4 • Check the website for hours and reservations • ⓦ binnenhofbezoek.nl

The Binnenhof's main sight as such is the **Ridderzaal** (Knights' Hall), an imposing twin-turreted structure that looks distinctly church-like, but was built as a banqueting hall for Count William's son, Floris V, in the thirteenth century. Now used for state occasions, it's been a courtroom, market and stable, and so often renovated that little of the original remains.

The Mauritshuis

Korte Vijverberg 8 • Closed for major refurbishment until mid-2014 • ☏ 070 302 3435, ⓦ mauritshuis.nl

The **Mauritshuis** is located in an elegant seventeenth-century mansion, immediately east of the Binnenhof. The gallery is famous for its eclectic collection of Flemish and

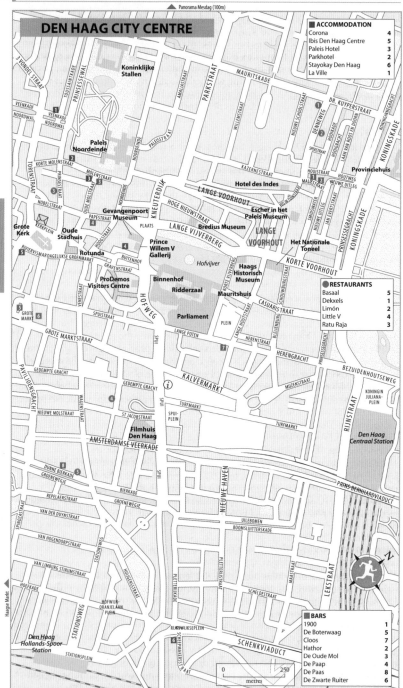

DEN HAAG CITY CENTRE

Panorama Mesdag (100m)

ACCOMMODATION

Corona	4
Ibis Den Haag Centre	5
Paleis Hotel	3
Parkhotel	2
Stayokay Den Haag	6
La Ville	1

RESTAURANTS

Basaal	5
Dekxels	1
Limón	2
Little V	4
Ratu Raja	3

BARS

1900	1
De Boterwaag	5
Cloos	7
Hathor	2
De Oude Mol	3
De Paap	4
De Paas	8
De Zwarte Ruiter	6

Dutch paintings from the fifteenth to the eighteenth century, based on the hoard accumulated by Prince William V of Orange (1748–1806). Its permanent collection has examples of work by all the major Dutch artists, but the Mauritshuis also runs an ambitious programme of temporary exhibitions. At the time of writing, the museum is closed for major renovation of the old mansion and expansion of the adjacent **Sociëteit de Witte** in which a new museum wing will be housed. An underground foyer will connect both buildings, almost doubling the museum's exhibition space. During the construction period, highlights from its permanent collection will be on display at the Gemeentemuseum (see p.158), while the museum's most famous painting **Johannes Vermeer**'s *Girl with a Pearl Earring* will travel the world.

The Haags Historisch Museum

Korte Vijverberg 7 • Tues–Fri 10am–5pm, Sat & Sun noon–5pm • €7.50 • Ⓦ haagshistorischmuseum.nl

The **Haags Historisch Museum** (City Historical Museum) occupies a handsome Neoclassical mansion that was originally home to the city's leading militia company, the so-called Archers of St Sebastian. The museum's ground floor gives a clear and concise history of the city, illustrating its various twists and turns by means of a fine sequence of paintings. In particular, look out for Jan Steen's charmingly droll *The Merry Homeward Journey* and a lovely, tonal landscape, *River View with Sentry Post* by that pioneer of realistic landscape painting, Jan van Goyen. Here also is a portrait of a lantern-jawed Johan de Witt in all his magisterial pomp and, by way of contrast, a mummified piece of his tongue, rescued from the mob that chopped him and his brother to pieces in 1672 (see p.329). Upstairs are ninety Golden Age paintings, with pride of place going to another canvas by Jan van Goyen, a large and simply wonderful *View of Den Haag*.

Lange Voorhout

Just north of the Binnenhof are the trees and cobblestones of **Lange Voorhout**, a wide L-shaped street-cum-square overlooked by a string of ritzy Neoclassical mansions, many of which are now embassies and consulates. Most conspicuous is the *Hotel des Indes*, an opulent hotel where the ballerina Anna Pavlova died in 1931 and where today you stand a fair chance of being flattened by a chauffeur-driven limousine.

Escher in het Paleis Museum

Lange Voorhout 74 • Tues–Sun 11am–5pm • €8.50 • Ⓦ escherinhetpaleis.nl

The leafy Lange Voorhout is also home to the **Escher in het Paleis Museum** occupying a grand mansion that was once a favourite royal residence from 1901 to 1934. Nowadays, it's devoted to the work of the Dutch graphic artist, Maurits Cornelis Escher (1898–1972), who churned out dozens of very precise, often disconcerting, lithographs and engravings. The most enjoyable part of the museum is the top floor, which is given over to several hands-on **optical illusions**, all based on Escher's work.

Museum Bredius

Lange Vijverberg 14 • Tues–Sun 11am–5pm • €6 • Ⓦ museumbredius.nl

The delightful **Museum Bredius** displays the collection of paintings bequeathed to the city by art connoisseur and one-time director of the Mauritshuis, Abraham Bredius, in 1946. Squeezed together in this fine old house, with its stuccowork and splendid staircase, are some exquisite paintings, notably **Rembrandt**'s *Head of Christ*, all smooth browns and yellows with the face of Jesus serene and sensitive; interestingly, Rembrandt was the first Dutch artist to use a Jewish model for a portrait of Christ. Among the genre paintings is a characteristic *Boar Hunt* by **Roelandt Savery** (1576–1639), all green foliage and fighting beasts, and the careful draughtsmanship of **Aert van de Neer** (1603–77) in his *Winter Landscape*. There are also two noteworthy paintings by **Jan Steen**, the fruity *Couple in a Bedchamber* and the curious *Satyr and the Peasant*, a representation of a well-known Aesop fable in which the satyr, sitting at the table with his hosts, is bemused by human behaviour. The creature's confusion is symbolically represented by the surrounding figures – the man blowing on his soup to cool it down, the woman with the basket of fruit on her head.

Museum Gevangenpoort

Buitenhof 33 • Tues–Fri 10am–5pm, Sat & Sun noon–5pm • €7.50, combination ticket with the Galerij Prins Willem V €10 • ⓦ gevangenpoort.nl

The **Museum Gevangenpoort** (Prison Gate Museum) on the west side of the Hofvijver, is sited in the old town prison, which is itself squeezed into one of Den Haag's medieval, fortified gates. The big pull here is the museum's collection of instruments of torture, interrogation and punishment, which goes down a storm with visiting school parties. Several of the prison's old cells have survived too, including the *ridderkamer* for the more privileged captives. Here Cornelis de Witt, burgomaster of Dordrecht, was imprisoned before he and his brother Johan, another staunch Republican and leader of the States of Holland, were dragged out and murdered by an Orangist mob in 1672. The brothers were shot, beheaded and cut into pieces that were then auctioned to the crowd; Johan's tongue can be seen in the Haags Historisch Museum, along with the toe of poor old Cornelis.

Galerij Prince Willem V

Buitenhof 35 • Tues-Sun noon–5pm • €5, combination ticket with the Prison Gate Museum €10 • ⓦ mauritshuis.nl

The **Galerij Prins Willem V**, sharing its entrance with the Museum Gevangenpoort, was created in 1773 as the private picture gallery of the eponymous prince and Stadholder of the United Provinces. It holds a diverting collection of seventeenth-century paintings exhibited in the style of an eighteenth-century "cabinet" gallery, with the paintings crowded together from floor to ceiling.

The Oude Stadhuis and the Paleis Noordeinde

The cobweb of narrow, mostly humdrum streets and squares stretching west of the Buitenhof zeroes in on the flamboyant Dutch Renaissance facade of the **Oude Stadhuis** (Old City Hall), a good-looking, sixteenth-century affair complete with mullioned windows, shutters and decorative carvings. It's a short walk north from here to the sixteenth- and seventeenth-century **Paleis Noordeinde** (no public access), the grandest of several royal buildings, which also houses the Queen's office. Outside the palace's main entrance, on Noordeinde, is a jaunty equestrian statue of Holland's principal hero, William the Silent.

Grote Kerk

Rond de Grote Kerk 12 • July & Aug Mon–Fri noon–4pm; also open for exhibitions & concerts • Free • ⓦ www.grotekerkdenhaag.nl

To the rear of the Oude Stadhuis are the plodding symmetries of a later extension, and next door rises the deconsecrated mass of St Jacobskerk, or the **Grote Kerk** easily the pick of Den Haag's old churches. Dating from the middle of the fifteenth century, the building's cavernous interior, with its three naves, has an exhilarating sense of breadth and handsome timber vaulting. Like most Dutch churches, it's short on decoration, but there are one or two highlights, notably the **stained-glass windows** of the choir. Of the two windows right at the back of the church, one depicts the Nativity, while the other shows the Virgin descending from heaven to show the infant Jesus to a kneeling Emperor Charles V, who footed the glaziers' bill. The latter may well have been the work of Dirk Crabeth, one of the craftsmen responsible for the windows in Gouda's St Janskerk (see p.178). To either side are three other key windows, an Annunciation, a Christ in the Temple with the Pharisees and a modern Prophet Zachariah in the Temple. Also at the back of the church stands a memorial to a bewigged Admiral Jacob van Opdam, who was blown up with his ship during the little-remembered naval battle of Lowestoft in 1665.

North of the city centre

Den Haag's suburbs canter north towards Scheveningen and the North Sea, an apparently haphazard sequence of long boulevards intercepted by patches of woodland. For the most part, this is a prosperous part of town and embedded in it are a string of museums, the most important of which are the **Panorama Mesdag**, a tribute to the endeavours of the nineteenth-century landscape painter Hendrik Mesdag, and the **Gemeentemuseum Den Haag**, with its enormous collection of fine and applied art. The area's attractions are widely dispersed, but it's easy to get around by **tram**.

Panorama Mesdag

Zeestraat 65 • Mon–Sat 10am–5pm, Sun noon–5pm • €7 • ⓦ panorama-mesdag.com • The Panorama is a 10min walk north of the Paleis Noordeinde, and accessible by tram #10 from Centraal Station and trams #1 and #10 from the Buitenhof

The **Panorama Mesdag** was designed in the late nineteenth century by Hendrik Mesdag (1831–1915), banker-turned-painter and local citizen-become-Hague School luminary. For the most part, Mesdag painted unremarkable seascapes tinged with bourgeois sentimentality, but there's no denying the achievement of his panorama, a delightful depiction of Scheveningen in 1881. Completed in four months with help from his wife and George Hendrik Breitner (1857–1923), the painting is so naturalistic that it takes a few moments for the skills of lighting and perspective to become apparent. Before you get to the Panorama, you pass through three small rooms showing the best of Mesdag's other **paintings**,

3

including a veritable battery of boats on Scheveningen beach beneath cotton-wool skies.

The Mesdag Collection

Laan van Meerdervoort 7f • Wed–Sun noon–5pm • €7.50 • ⓦ demesdagcollectie.nl • Take tram #10 from Centraal Station or trams #1 and #10 from the Buitenhof

It's a ten-minute walk from the Panorama north to the **Mesdag Collection**, the house Mesdag bought as a home and gallery. At the time, Mesdag had a view over the dunes, the inspiration for many of his canvases, but the house and its environs were gobbled up by the city long ago and today it is visited for its easily assimilated collection of nineteenth- and early twentieth-century paintings, especially those of the Hague School, whose artists – like Mesdag – took local land and seascapes as their favourite subject. The Dutch canvases are supplemented by a modest collection of French paintings from the likes of Corot, Rousseau, Delacroix and Millet, though none of them represent the artists at their peak.

3

The Peace Palace

Carnegieplein 2 • **Visitor centre** May–Oct Tues–Sun 10am–5pm; Nov–April Tues–Sun 10am–4pm • Free • Check the website for details of guided tours • ⓦ vredespaleis.nl • Tram #10 from Centraal Station or trams #1 and #10 from the Buitenhof

Flanking the Carnegieplein, round the corner from the Mesdag Museum, the **Vredespaleis** (Peace Palace) is home to the **International Court of Justice**, the principal judicial organ of the United Nations and, for all the wrong reasons, a monument to the futility of war. Towards the end of the nineteenth century, Tsar Nicholas II called an international conference for the peaceful reconciliation of national problems. The result was the First Hague Peace Conference of 1899, whose purpose was to "help find a lasting peace and, above all, a way of limiting the progressive development of existing arms". This in turn led to the formation of a **Permanent Court of Arbitration** housed obscurely in Den Haag until the American industrialist Andrew Carnegie gave $1.5 million for a large new building – the Peace Palace. These honourable aims came to nothing with the onset of World War I: just as the donations of tapestries, urns, marble and stained glass were arriving from all over the world, so Europe's military commanders were preparing their offensives. Backed by a massive law library, fifteen judges still sit at the court today, conducting trade matters in English and diplomatic affairs in French. Widely respected and generally considered neutral, their judgments are nevertheless not binding.

The Gemeentemuseum Den Haag

Stadhouderslaan 41 • Tues–Sun 11am–5pm • €12.50 • ⓦ gemeentemuseum.nl • The museum is easy to reach on tram #17 from Centraal Station and the Buitenhof

The **Gemeentemuseum Den Haag** is easily the largest and most diverse of Den Haag's many museums. Designed by Hendrik Petrus Berlage (1856–1934) and completed in 1935, the building itself is often regarded as his masterpiece, an austere but particularly appealing structure with brick facings superimposed on a concrete shell. Inside, the museum displays a regularly rotated selection from its vast permanent collection and also offers an ambitious, headline-making programme of temporary exhibitions. Among much else, the museum's permanent collection includes a large and diverting array of **Delft pottery**, a platoon of period rooms, a fashion section and a wide selection of drawings, prints and posters from the nineteenth and twentieth centuries. The **modern art** section outlines the development of painting since the early nineteenth century and although the bulk of the paintings are Dutch, there's a liberal sprinkling of international artists too. The museum is especially strong on the land and seascape painters of the **Hague School**, which flourished here in the city from 1860 to 1900, and until mid-2014 it also houses some of the Mauritshuis' fine collection: highlights include *View of Delft* by **Johannes Vermeer**, the *Anatomy Lesson of Dr Tulp* by **Rembrandt** and *Young Bull* by **Paulus Potter** (see p.159).

THE MAURITSHUIS MASTERPIECES

More than one hundred paintings from the permanent collection of the Mauritshuis are currently on display at the Gemeentemuseum during the Mauritshuis' renovation (see p.153). Expect to see the fine canvas by **Hans Holbein the Younger** (1497–1543): a striking *Portrait of Robert Cheseman*, where all the materials – the fur collar, the falcon's feathers and the cape – seem to take on the appropriate texture. Of **Peter Paul Rubens** (1577–1640), the acclaimed painter and diplomat, *Old Woman and a Boy with Candles*, is an intriguing canvas with dappled, evocative shades and light. Another of his highlights is *The Garden of Eden with the Fall of Man*, a collaboration between himself and **Jan Brueghel the Elder** (1568–1625). Rubens painted the figures and Brueghel the landscape and animals, from monkeys to deer and lions coexisting peacefully. The Mauritshuis owns no fewer than twelve paintings by **Rembrandt** (1606–69). Pride of place among them goes to the *Anatomy Lesson of Dr Tulp*, the artist's first commission in Amsterdam, dating from 1632. The peering pose of the students who lean over the corpse solved the problem of emphasis falling on the body rather than the subjects of the portrait, who were members of the surgeons' guild. Hopefully Tulp's skills as an anatomist were better than his medical advice, which included the recommendation that his patients drink fifty cups of tea a day. Also look out for *Young Bull* by **Paulus Potter** (1625–54), a massive canvas that includes the smallest of details, from the exact hang of the testicles to the dung at the rear end.

Although **Johannes Vermeer**'s (1632–75) most famous painting, *Girl with a Pearl Earring*, is not on display here, his superb and somehow thrilling *View of Delft* can be seen. A deceptive canvas: the fine lines of the city are pictured beneath a cloudy sky, a patchwork of varying light and shade, but all is not quite what it seems. The painting may look like the epitome of realism, but in fact Vermeer doctored what he saw to fit in with the needs of his canvas, straightening here, lengthening there, to emphasize the horizontal. Interestingly, the detached vision implicit in the painting has prompted some experts – like Wilenski – to suggest that Vermeer viewed his subject through a fixed reducing lens or maybe even a mirror.

3

The De Stijl Movement

The museum has a fine collection of works by the **De Stijl** movement, that loose but influential group of Dutch painters, sculptors, designers and architects who developed their version – and vision – of modern art and society between the two world wars. On display is the world's largest collection of paintings from the most famous member of the group, **Piet Mondrian** (1872–1944), and although much of it consists of unfamiliar early works, painted before he evolved the abstraction of form into geometry and pure colour for which he's best known, it does include *Victory Boogie Woogie*, his last and – some say – finest work.

The Gemeentemuseum campus

Stadhouderslaan 43 **GEM** Tues–Sun noon–6pm; €6, including Fotomuseum; Ⓦ gem-online.nl • **Fotomuseum** Tues–Sun noon–6pm; €6, including GEM; Ⓦ www.fotomuseumdenhaag.nl • **Museon** Tues–Sun 11am–5pm; €10; Ⓦ museon.nl

There are three other museums on the Gemeentemuseum campus. First up is **GEM**, **Museum voor Actuele Kunst**, a gallery of contemporary art featuring an enterprising programme of temporary exhibitions. In the same building, the **Fotomuseum** puts on a minimum of four exhibitions a year and in between times displays photographs from the Gemeentemuseum's permanent collection. Nearby is the **Museon**, a sequence of non-specialist exhibitions dealing with human activities and the history of the earth – everything from rock formations to the use of tools. Self-consciously internationalist, it's aimed principally at school parties.

Scheveningen

Scheveningen is best visited on a day-trip from Den Haag; take tram #9 from Central Station or tram #1 from the Spui in the city centre – it's a 10min journey

Wedged against the seashore about 4km north of the centre of Den Haag, the old

A BEACH WITHOUT THE CROWDS

If the crowded seaside antics of Scheveningen don't appeal, then head about 3km south to the **Zuiderstrand**, a long, sandy beach that is often deserted. Even at peak times there's oodles of space – and you can watch the ships pulling through the waters of the North Sea. To get there, take tram #12 from The Hague HS train station to its Duindorp terminus and it's a 5min walk through the dunes of the **Westduinpark** to the beach.

fishing port and harbour of **SCHEVENINGEN** is now the Netherlands' biggest coastal resort, a sometimes tacky, often breezy place that attracts more than nine million visitors a year. It also has one curious claim to fame: during World War II, resistance groups tested suspected Nazi infiltrators by getting them to say "Scheveningen" – an impossible feat for Germans, apparently, and not much easier for English-speakers (try a throaty *s-khay-ve-ning-uh*). A thick strip of forested dune once separated Den Haag from Scheveningen, but nowadays it's hard to know where one ends and the other begins. There is, however, no mistaking Scheveningen's principal attraction, its **beach**, a long expanse of golden sand that is hard to resist on a warm day. Scheveningen also hosts a lively programme of special events, most memorably an international **sand sculpture** competition held in early May.

The Kurhaus and around

Scheveningen's handiest tram stop (Kurhaus) is a couple of hundred metres from its most impressive building, the **Kurhaus**, a grand hotel of 1885, built when this was one of the most fashionable resorts in Europe. Pop inside for a peek at its central hall, a richly decorated affair with pendulous chandeliers and rich frescoes bearing mermaids and semi-clad maidens cavorting high above the diners and coffee-drinkers.

Most of Scheveningen's attractions are within easy walking distance of the *Kurhaus*: the **casino** is across the street; it's east along the seashore to the **pier** and its amusement arcades; and west to **Sea Life** at Strandweg 13 (daily: 10am– 6pm; July & Aug 10am–8pm; €15.50, children 3–11 years €10.50; ⓦvisitsealife.com), a glorified aquarium complete with a sea-bed walkway and coral reef.

Museum Beelden-aan-Zee

Harteveltstraat 1 • Tues–Sun 11am–5pm • €9.50 • ⓦ beeldenaanzee.nl

Scheveningen's most original attraction is the **Museum Beelden-aan-Zee**, which features an intriguing assortment of modern sculptures arranged around a pavilion built by King William I for his ailing wife, Wilhelmina, in 1826. There are examples of the work of many leading sculptors, including Karel Appel and Wim Quist, Man Ray and Fritz Koenig, and although there is supposed to be a unifying theme – the human experience – it's the variety of forms and materials that impresses.

ARRIVAL AND DEPARTURE   DEN HAAG

By train The city has two train stations: Den Haag HS (Hollands Spoor) on Stationsplein 41 and Den Haag CS (Centraal Station) on Koningin Julianaplein 10. Of the two, Den Haag CS is the more convenient, a 5–10min walk from the town centre; Den Haag HS is 1km to the south. There are frequent rail services between the two or you can catch tram #1 from Den Haag HS direct to the centre.

Destinations Den Haag CS to Amersfoort (every 30min; 1hr); Amsterdam CS (every 30min; 50min); Delft (every 15min; 12min); Dordrecht (every 30min; 35min); Gouda (every 20min; 20min); Leiden (every 30min; 20min); Rotterdam (every 15min; 25min) and Utrecht (every 15min; 40min).

INFORMATION

Tourist offices Den Haag's main VVV is bang in the centre of the city, a 5–10min walk west from Den Haag CS at Spui 68 inside the public library (Mon noon–8pm, Tues–Fri 10am–8pm, Sat 10am–5pm, Sun noon–5pm; ☎ 070 361 8860, ⓦdenhaag.com). They provide a wide range of information on the city and its surroundings, sell public transport tickets and passes, will reserve accommodation and stock several free listings magazines. There's also a small information booth in Scheveningen, right at the entrance of the Pier (April–Oct Sat & Sun 11am–5pm; July & Aug daily 11am–5pm), which can help with accommodation.

GETTING AROUND

By tram and bus Most of the city's principal sights are in – or within easy walking distance of – the centre, but this is the country's third-largest city and you may need to catch a tram or bus if you're visiting the more outlying attractions. The twin hubs of the tram system, which covers most of where you're likely to want to go, are Centraal Station and the Spui, in the centre of town just south of the VVV; there's also a mini-metro, where some of the trams go underground, to the west of Centraal Station underneath Grote Marktstraat and Prinsegracht.

Tickets and passes You can buy a ticket valid for either 30min (€2.50) or 60min (€3.50) from the bus or tram driver. If you're planning to do more travelling, consider buying a *dagkaart* (day-card; €7.50) at the VVV or the train station.
By bike Cycle rental is available at both train stations for around €7.50 a day.
By car There are plenty of car rental companies in town, including Europcar, Binckhorstlaan 297 (☎ 070 381 1811) and Hertz, Binckhorstlaan 318 (☎ 070 381 8989).
Taxi HTMC ☎ 070 390 7722.

ACCOMMODATION

Den Haag has a good supply of central **hotels**, with many of the more comfortable (and sometimes luxurious) ones dotted near the Binnenhof, to the west of Den Haag CS. Advance reservations are a good idea especially during the week, when business folk arrive in numbers, pushing up hotel prices; weekend rates are usually around thirty percent cheaper. The VVV can help you find a hotel room either in Den Haag or the neighbouring resort of Scheveningen (see p.159) for a small fee; they have a dedicated accommodation booking line ☎ 070 361 8860. Out of season, there's no shortage of vacant rooms in Scheveningen but in the summer it's best to use the VVV's accommodation booking service.

HOTELS

Carlton Ambassador Hotel Sophialaan 2 ☎ 070 363 0363, ⓦ carlton.nl/ambassador. Deluxe, executive four-star hotel with every mod con you can imagine and then some, located in an immaculately maintained nineteenth-century mansion in a smart residential avenue about 1km north of the centre. The rooms are large, well appointed and all decorated in plush, period style. The breakfasts are banquet-like and there's an open-air terrace. **€129**
Corona Buitenhof 39 ☎ 070 363 7930, ⓦ corona.nl. In a great location just across the street from the Binnenhof, this smart hotel has large and extremely comfortable double rooms and a great recently revamped restaurant downstairs. It's not cheap, but weekend discounts and special deals can reduce the rate from €230 to below €100. **€100**
Ibis Den Haag Centre Jan Hendrikstraat 10 ☎ 070 318 4318, ⓦ ibishotels.com. Few would say that Ibis hotels have much character, but they are reliable and inexpensive – and this one, with 200 rooms, is in a handy central location too: breakfast is served until noon. **€99**
La Ville Veenkade 5 ☎ 070 346 3657, ⓦ hotellaville.nl. Small and unassuming two-star hotel in a three-storey terrace house just west of the Paleis Noordeinde. All the rooms are en suite and decorated in a neat modern style. They also have a couple of apartments, complete with kitchenette. **€95**, apartments **€105**
★ **Paleis Hotel** Molenstraat 26 ☎ 070 362 4621, ⓦ paleishotel.nl. This charming, privately owned hotel is in an old, mostly eighteenth-century townhouse. Each of

the twenty bedrooms is decorated with style and panache – antique furniture, French fabrics and so forth. Great central location as well. **€135**
★ **Parkhotel** Molenstraat 53 ☎ 070 362 4371, ⓦ parkhoteldenhaag.nl. Smart and immaculately maintained hotel in a handy central location. From the outside it doesn't look anything special, but the interior is graced by all sorts of superb Art Deco flourishes. The hotel has over one hundred well-appointed rooms decorated in brisk modern style. Some rooms overlook the Paleis Noordeinde gardens next door. **€135**
Residenz Sweelinckplein 35 ☎ 070 364 6190, ⓦ residenz.nl. In a creatively remodelled, late nineteenth-century villa, this boutique hotel is slick and smart in equal measure with shades of grey, brown and white to the fore. Sweelinckplein itself is an attractive garden square to the north of the centre near the Laan van Meerdervoort boulevard. **€160**

HOSTELS

Jorplace Beach Hostel Keizerstraat 296 ☎ 070338 3270, ⓦ jorplace.nl. Scheveningen's only beach hostel is located in the old centre of the fishermen's village and within walking distance of the beach and the Scheveningen nightlife. A camper van in the garden has been converted into a double room, and it's a great location to practise your kitesurfing skills. Dorm beds **€19**, doubles **€54**
Stayokay Den Haag Scheepmakersstraat 27 ☎ 070 315 7888, ⓦ stayokay.com. This large and comfortable

HI hostel is located just 400m east of – and across the canal from – Den Haag HS station. A good range of facilities includes luggage and bicycle storage, bike rental, a café, internet terminals and a small library. Dorm beds €26.50, doubles €74

EATING AND DRINKING

Den Haag has an excellent range of **restaurants**, and although some are aimed squarely at the expense account, many more are very affordable, with main courses hovering between €20 and €25. There is a cluster of first-rate places just beyond Lange Voorhout along and around Denneweg and Frederikstraat, and another on Molenstraat, near the Paleis Noordeinde: frankly, you need look no further. These two areas are good for cafés and café-bars too, though the liveliest **bars** are concentrated on and around the Grote Markt, south of the Grote Kerk, and on the Plein, near the Mauritshuis.

RESTAURANTS

Basaal Dunne Bierkade 3 ☎ 070 427 6888, ⓦ basaal .net. With its crisp, modern decor, this smashing restaurant has a short but sharp menu featuring local ingredients – like the catch of the day. Main courses – for example lemon dab and saffron potatoes – average €22. Wed–Sun 6–11pm.

Da Sebastiano Javastraat 138 ☎ 070 345 5291, ⓦ dasebastiano.nl. The interior is sober, but the food is superb. Owner Sebastiano has a daily changing menu where you can choose from five different dishes, some prepared at your table. Being a typical Italian, he can be chaotic but that adds to the atmosphere. Daily 5–10pm.

Dekxels Denneweg 130 ☎ 070 365 9788, ⓦ dekxels.nl. This highly recommended, coolly decorated, chic restaurant serves a superb range of international and Dutch dishes. All dishes – such as truffle risotto or Peking-style duck – are starter-sized and average around €12. Daily 5.30–10/11pm.

Limón Denneweg 39a ☎ 070 356 1465, ⓦ limon.nl. Pastel-painted Spanish tapas restaurant catering to a fashionable, youngish crowd. Good food – though admittedly not all the tapas turn out as well as each other; a very popular spot. Tapas from as little as €4. Mon–Sat 4.30–11pm.

Little V Rabbijn Maarsenplein 21 ☎ 070 392 1230, ⓦ littlev.nl. Incredibly trendy Vietnamese restaurant located near The Hague's Chinatown. Mains such as caramelized sea bass or chicken in curry-coco sauce average between €8 and €14. Tues & Wed 5–10pm, Thurs 5–10.30pm, Fri 4–10.30pm, Sat noon–10.30pm, Sun noon–9.30pm.

Ratu Raja Prinsestraat 30 ☎ 070 356 3366, ⓦ raturaja .com. Smooth, richly decorated Franco-Indochinese restaurant that has proved a real Den Haag hit. With mains that average €24, it's not a cheap option, but worth the splurge. Also has an extensive whisky collection. Wed–Sat 6–10pm.

CAFÉ-BARS AND BARS

1900 Maliestraat 10 ⓦ 1900.nu. Intimate little wine bar in the cosy Denneweg area with many wines by the glass, best enjoyed with a tasty farmers cheese platter. For a bigger appetite, a daily *plat du jour* should fill you up. Occasional live music. Wed–Sat 6pm–midnight.

De Boterwaag Grote Markt 8a ☎ 070 365 9686, ⓦ gmdh.nl. Immensely appealing café-bar housed in an old and cavernous brick-vaulted weigh house. It's very popular with a youthful crowd and offers a wide range of beers as well as inexpensive bar food, though this hardly inspires the palate. Large terrace, which fills up quickly when the sun comes out. Wednesday night is salsa night. Daily 10am–1.30am.

Cloos Plein 12a ☎ 070 363 9786, ⓦ eetcafecloos.nl. If you thought Den Haag might be demure, wander down to the Plein, and see the locals getting stuck into the sauce. *Cloos* is one of several large and youthful bars on this square. Tues–Sun 10am–1am, Sat & Sun until 2am.

Hathor Maliestraat 22 ☎ 070 346 4081, ⓦ hathor.nl. This old-time local favourite quickly fills up after work with young professionals enjoying the floating terrace on one of The Hague's most picturesque canals. Also a good spot for a quick bite, although it becomes loud later at night. Mon–Fri noon–1am, Sat 4pm–2am.

⭐ **De Oude Mol** Oude Molstraat 61 ☎ 070 345 1623. Good old traditional bar and neighbourhood joint down a narrow side street. Oodles of atmosphere and an enjoyable range of beers. Upstairs is a tiny tapas bar. Daily from 5pm; kitchen Wed–Sat from 5.30pm.

De Paap Papestraat 32 ☎ 070 365 2002, ⓦ depaap.nl. Dark and raucous bar with live music every night showcasing the best of local talent, many of which have made it to the bigger venues. A locals' favourite. Thurs 7pm–4am, Fri 5pm–5am, Sat 7pm–5am.

De Paas Dunne Bierkade 16a ☎ 070 360 0019, ⓦ depaas.nl. Traditional brown bar with lots of zip and over one hundred and fifty beers to sample. Canal-side with an inviting boat-terrace in summer and a central location near The Hague's Chinatown. Also has an ample whisky collection. Daily 3pm–1am, Sat & Sun until 1.30am.

⭐ **De Zwarte Ruiter** Grote Markt 27 ☎ 070 364 9549, ⓦ gmdh.nl. This fashionable bar boasts a good selection of beers and ales, and positively heaves at the weekend. There's a large terrace too, with picnic tables under a comfortable heater for chilly evenings. Daily 11am–1am, Sat & Sun until 1.30am.

DIRECTORY

Cinema Filmhuis Den Haag, Spui 191 (☎070 365 6030, ⓦfilmhuisdenhaag.nl) is the best independent cinema in the city, while Omniversum, at President Kennedylaan 5 (Mon 10am–3pm, Tues & Wed 10am–5pm, Thurs & Sun 10am–8pm, Fri & Sat 10am–9pm; €10; ⓦomniversum .nl), is an IMAX cinema in all but name.

Embassies and consulates Australia, Carnegielaan 4 ☎070 310 8200; Canada, Sophialaan 7 ☎070 311 1600; Ireland, Dr Kuyperstraat 9 ☎070 363 0993; New Zealand, Eisenhowerslaan 77 ☎070 346 9324; UK, Lange Voorhout 10 ☎070 427 0427; US, Lange Voorhout 102 ☎070 310 2209.

Markets Antiques, books and curios markets are on Lange Voorhout (mid-May to late Sept Thurs & Sun 10am–6pm) and on Plein (Oct–May Thurs 10am–6pm). Europe's largest outdoor market, the Haagse Markt, is a bit off the beaten track in the multicultural part of town: here you'll find everything from cheap veggies to colourful clothing (Mon, Wed, Fri & Sat 8am–5pm; trams #6, #11 and #12 to the Hobbemaplein stop).

Pharmacy Hofstad Apotheek, right in the centre at Korte Poten 7a (Mon–Fri 8.30am–6pm, Sat 10am–4pm).

Delft

DELFT, in between Den Haag and Rotterdam, has a beguiling centre, a medley of ancient red-tiled houses set beside tree-lined canals interrupted by the cutest of bridges. With justification, it's one of the most visited spots in the Netherlands, but most tourists come here for the day, and in the evening, even in the summer, the town can be surprisingly – and mercifully – quiet. Delft boasts a clutch of fascinating old buildings, one of them – the **Prinsenhof** – holding an enjoyable collection of Golden Age paintings. Nevertheless it's the general flavour of the place that appeals rather than any specific sight. That said, the two big pulls as far as day-trippers are concerned are the **Delftware factories**, stuffed with the blue and white ceramics for which the town is famous, and **Vermeer** (see box below), the town's best-known son.

Markt

The obvious place to start an exploration of Delft is the **Markt**, a handsome square and central point of reference with the Stadhuis at one end and the Nieuwe Kerk at the other, and with cafés and restaurants and a **statue** of Delft's own Hugo Grotius lined up in between. A well-known scholar and statesman, **Grotius** (1583–1645) was sentenced to life imprisonment by Maurice of Orange-Nassau during the political turmoil of the 1610s, but was subsequently rescued by his wife who smuggled him out of jail in a chest. Unfortunately, it didn't save Grotius from a sticky end – he died of exposure after being shipwrecked near Danzig.

JOHANNES VERMEER

Precious little is known about **Johannes Vermeer** (1632–75), but he was certainly born in Delft and died here too, leaving a wife, eleven children and a huge debt to the local baker. He had given the baker two pictures as security, and his wife subsequently bankrupted herself trying to retrieve them. Vermeer's most celebrated painting is his 1661 *View of Delft*, now belonging to the Mauritshuis collection in Den Haag (see p.153), but if you're after a townscape that even vaguely resembles the picture, you'll be disappointed – it doesn't exist and in a sense it never did, no matter how many "Vermeer walks" Delft lays on. Vermeer made no claim to be a realist and his *View* accorded with the landscape traditions of his day, presenting an idealized Delft framed by a broad expanse of water and dappled by a cloudy sky. There is a cool detachment here that Vermeer also applied to those scenes of contemporary domestic life which are more typical of his oeuvre – though only 37 Vermeers survive – as exemplified by *The Love Letter*, in Amsterdam's Rijksmuseum (see p.75).

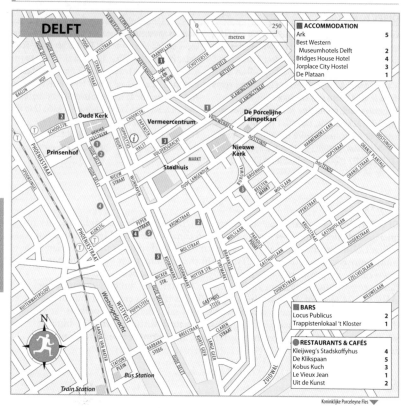

DELFT

0 _____ 250
metres

Koninklijke Porceleyne Fles ▼

The Nieuwe Kerk

Markt 80 • Mon–Sat: April–Oct 9am–6pm; Nov–March 11am–4pm • €3.50, including Oude Kerk; spire €3.50 extra

The **Nieuwe Kerk** is new only in comparison with the Oude Kerk, as there's been a church on this site since 1381. Most of the original structure was destroyed in the great fire that swept through Delft in 1536, and the remainder in an explosion a century later – a disaster, incidentally, which claimed the life of the artist Carel Fabritius, Rembrandt's greatest pupil and (debatably) the teacher of Vermeer. The most striking part of the rebuilding is one of the most recent, the church's 100-metre **spire**, replaced in 1872 and from whose summit there's a great view over the town. Otherwise, apart from the sheer height of the nave, the interior is mainly distinguished by the **mausoleum of William the Silent**, a prodigiously elaborate marble structure built on the orders of the States General between 1614 and 1623. The mausoleum holds two effigies of William, one in his pomp, seated and dressed in his armour, the other showing him recumbent on his deathbed. This second carving is exquisite, down to the finest details of his face, and at his feet is his faithful dog, who – so legend has it – refused to eat or drink after William's death, thereby rejoining his master. The two effigies are surrounded by bronze allegorical figures, representing the likes of Liberty and Justice. The statue of **Fame**, standing on tiptoe behind the recumbent William, caused all sorts of problems: it fell over and the cost of the repairs pushed the whole project way over budget. Look out also for the attractive Art Deco **stained-glass windows** in the north transept and chancel. Inserted between 1927 and 1936, they are a mixed bunch, some illustrating biblical themes, but most singing the praises of the House of Orange, many of whom are interred in the **burial vault** beneath the nave (no public access).

The Stadhuis

Directly opposite the Nieuwe Kerk, across the Markt, is the **Stadhuis**, whose delightful facade of 1618 is equipped with dormer windows, shutters, fluted pilasters and shell decoration. Most of its medieval predecessor was incinerated in the fire of 1536, but the stern stone tower of the earlier building survived and was incorporated – none too successfully – into the later design.

The Vermeercentrum

Voldersgracht 21 • Daily 10am–5pm • €7 • ⓦ vermeerdelft.nl

Just a few metres from the Markt, the **Vermeercentrum** is Delft's attempt to cash in on its most famous native son, the painter Vermeer. The problem is that the centre doesn't actually own any of the great man's paintings, so it has been forced to bluff its way through, beginning in the basement where a short film introduces the artist and there are copies of all his paintings. A second floor has a mock-up of his studio, making an attempt to explore Vermeer's technique.

The Oude Kerk

Heilige Geestkerkhof 25 • Mon–Sat: April–Oct 9am–6pm; Nov–March 11am–4pm • €3.50 • including Nieuwe Kerk

It's a short but pretty walk from the Markt north to the **Oude Kerk**, a rambling Gothic pile whose discordant lines are redeemed by the most magnificent of church towers – a soaring cluster of turrets rising high above the town. Despite its dense buttressing, the tower has long been subject to subsidence and the angle of its lean has been measured by generations of worried town architects. Indeed, there have been periodic panics about its safety, not least in the 1840s when the council almost decided to pull it down; the last repairs were undertaken in the 1990s. Inside, the church boasts a splendid vaulted timber ceiling and a fine set of modern **stained-glass windows** which mostly depict biblical scenes, the key exception being the intense "Liberation Window", installed in the transept in 1956 to celebrate the Expulsion of the German army at the end of World War II. Also of interest is the **pulpit**, whose five intricately carved panels depict John the Baptist and the four Evangelists in false perspective; dating from 1548, the pulpit did well to survive the attentions of the Protestants when they ransacked the church in the Iconoclastic Fury of 1565.

The tombs

Among the assorted **tombs** there is a plain floor plaque in honour of Vermeer just to the west of the pulpit and a flashy marble memorial to **Admiral Maarten Tromp** (1598–1653) close by, next to the transept. One of the country's most successful admirals, Tromp was captured twice at sea – once by the English and once by Tunisian Arabs – but survived to lead the Dutch fleet at the start of the First Anglo-Dutch War (1652–54). Tromp famously hoisted a broom at his masthead to "sweep the seas clear of the English", but the Royal Navy had its revenge, shooting him down during a sea battle off Scheveningen in 1653. It's this last battle that is depicted on Tromp's tomb alongside an effigy of the man himself, dressed up in his armour beneath a flock of bawling, trumpeting cherubs. The marble carving depicting the battle, which shows the British fleet burning away, was much admired by no less than Samuel Pepys, who wrote "the smoke [was] the best expressed that ever I saw".

3

DELFTWARE DELIGHTS

The origins of the clunky ceramics known as **delftware** can be traced to the Balearic island of Mallorca, where craftsmen had earlier developed **majolica**, a type of porous pottery that was glazed with bright metallic oxides. During the Renaissance, these techniques were exported to Italy from where they spread north, first to Antwerp and then to the United Provinces. Initially, delft pottery designs featured Dutch and Italian landscapes, portraits and biblical scenes, but the East India Company's profitable import of Chinese ceramics transformed the industry. Delft factories freely copied Chinese designs and by the middle of the seventeenth century they were churning out blue-and-white tiles, plates, panels, jars and vases by the boatload – even exporting to China, where they undercut Chinese producers.

From the 1760s, however, the delft factories were themselves undercut by British and German workshops, and by the time Napoleon arrived they had all but closed down. There was a modest revival of the industry in the 1870s and there are several local producers today, but it's mostly mass-produced stuff of little originality.

BUYING DELFTWARE

Koninklijke Porceleyne Fles Rotterdamseweg 196 (Mon–Sat 9am–5pm; April–Oct also Sun 9am–5pm; frequent guided tours €12; ⓦ www.royaldelft.com). Although Delft's souvenir shops are jam-packed with delftware, it's worth heading for the factory of the leading local manufacturer, where they still produce hand-painted pieces. It's located a good twenty minutes' walk south of the centre, or take bus #121 or #40 from Delft train station and get off at Jaffalaan, from where it's a five-minute walk.

De Porcelijne Lampetkan Just behind the Nieuwe Kerk at Vrouwenregt 5 (Mon–Sat 10.30am–5.30pm; ⓣ 015 212 1086, ⓦ antiquesdelft.com). Conveniently located, this appealing little shop sells a good range of antique delftware at (comparatively) reasonable rates.

Het Prinsenhof

Sint Agathaplein 1 • Tues–Sun 11am–5pm • €7.50 • ⓦ prinsenhof-delft.nl

Down a passageway opposite the Oude Kerk, in what was originally a convent, is **Het Prinsenhof**, which served as the main residence of William the Silent of Orange-Nassau from 1572 to 1584. A sprawling, somewhat confusing building spread over two floors, it was here that William coordinated the Dutch resistance to the Habsburgs and it was here too that he was assassinated. Today, the building has displays celebrating the William connection and also holds the **municipal art collection**, an appealing jumble of works mostly dating from the sixteenth and seventeenth centuries. Free **plans** are issued at reception.

The ground floor

At the beginning, Rooms 3–8 concentrate on the life and turbulent times of **William the Silent** with portraits of some of the protagonists. In Room 7, the bottom of the old wooden staircase marks the spot where William the Silent was **assassinated** on July 10, 1584. A former army commander of both Charles V and Philip II, William turned against the Habsburgs during Alva's persecution of the Protestants in 1567. He went on to lead the Protestant revolt against Philip, mustering a series of armies and organizing the Watergeuzen, guerrilla units that played a key role in driving back the imperial army. In return, Philip put a bounty of 25,000 gold crowns on William's head, but in the event the man who shot him was not a professional assassin but a fanatical Catholic, Balthazar Gerard, who did the deed for his religion. Gerard's two bullets passed right through William and the **bullet holes** are now protected by a glass sheet, put there to stop curious fingers enlarging them.

The first floor

Upstairs, Room 16 holds a selection of **militia paintings**, the pick of which is *The Officers of the White Company* by Jacob Willemsz (1619–61). During the long war with Spain, every Dutch city had its own militia, but as the Habsburg threat diminished so the militias devolved into social clubs, each of them keen to immortalize their particular company in a group portrait like these on display here. Nearby, Rooms 17, 18 and 19 also exhibit paintings from Delft's **seventeenth-century heyday**, including a pair of superbly executed anatomy paintings, with *The Anatomy Lesson* by Cornelis de Man (1621–1706) being especially striking.

ARRIVAL AND INFORMATION   DELFT

By train Delft train station is conveniently located at Van Leeuwenhoeksingel 41, a 5–10min walk from the market square. Be prepared to step over some hurdles though, due to major renovations of the train station and the construction of an underground passage for passing trains. Frequent trains connect Delft to both of Den Haag's stations (every 10min; 10min) as well as Amsterdam (every 15min; 1hr), Rotterdam (every 5min; 10min) and Dordrecht (every 10min; 25min).

By bus Delft bus station is in front of the train station, a 5–10min walk from Delft's main square, Markt. However, with Delft being so well connected by train, you're unlikely to arrive by bus.

By tram You can also make the trip from Den Haag on tram #1, which runs south from Scheveningen to the centre of Den Haag before proceeding onto Den Haag HS station and Delft, where it rattles along Phoenixstraat/Westvest between the train station and the centre; for the centre of Delft, get off at the Prinsenhof tram stop. Allow 20min to get from Den Haag to Delft by tram.

Tourist office Delft's Toeristen Informatie Punt (TIP) is located just north of the Markt at Hippolytusbuurt 4 (April–Sept Mon & Sat 10am–5pm, Tues–Fri 9am–6pm, Sun 10am–4pm; Oct–March Mon 11am–4pm, Tues–Sat 10am–4pm; Sun 10am–3pm ☎ 015 215 4051, ⓦ delft .com). They issue free city maps, offer free internet access and can help with accommodation.

ACCOMMODATION

HOTELS

Ark Koornmarkt 65 ☎ 015 215 7999, ⓦ deark.nl. Attractive four-star hotel occupying three tastefully restored seventeenth-century canal houses. The bedrooms are perhaps more spartan than you might expect from the public areas, but they are comfortable and well appointed all the same. **€147**

Best Western Museumhotels Delft Phoenixstraat 50 ☎ 015 215 3070, ⓦ museumhotel.nl. There are two separate sections to this four-star hotel – one in an eighteenth-century building, the other in its grander, seventeenth-century neighbour. Great location, backing onto the Oude Delft canal just along from the Prinsenhof, though the bedrooms themselves are uninspiringly modern. **€105**

★ **Bridges House Hotel** Oude Delft 74 ☎ 015 212 4036, ⓦ bridges-house.com. This medium-sized, privately owned hotel occupies an old townhouse that was once the home of the artist Jan Steen. There's no chain-hotel standardization here and the best guest rooms are large, well equipped and have good views of the Oude Delft canal. It's in an ideal location, too, the shortest of walks from the Markt. **€112**

De Plataan Doelenplein 10 ☎ 015 212 6046, ⓦ hoteldeplataan.nl. A little off the beaten track, but still within easy walking distance of the Markt, this three-star hotel has really pushed the decorative boat out, from the cheerful colours of the regular rooms through to the four themed rooms, including a "Garden of Eden" and a "Desert Island" – great fun. **€115**

HOSTEL

Jorplace City Hostel Voldersgracht 16–18 ☎ 015 887 5088, ⓦ jorplace.nl. Only recently opened but already has a real laidback hostel feel to it, with 124 beds located on the charming Voldersgracht smack in the centre of town. Free wi-fi, darts and a funky bar downstairs. Dorm beds **€19**

EATING AND DRINKING

Many of Delft's cafés, bars and restaurants are geared up for day-trippers and serve up some pretty routine stuff, but there are also several excellent places dotted within easy strolling distance of the Markt.

RESTAURANTS AND CAFÉS

★ **Kleijweg's Stadskoffyhus** Oude Delft 133 ☎ 015 212 4625, ⓦ stads-koffyhuis.nl. Appealing café near the Markt, that serves the best pancakes in town, for €5–10. Very popular with tourists both inside, in a cosily kitted-out old terrace house, and outside, on a patio barge. Mon–Fri 9am–8pm & Sat 9am–6pm.

De Klikspaan Koornmarkt 85 ☎ 015 214 1562, ⓦ klikspaandelft.nl. Smart and polished restaurant in an old canal-side townhouse just south of the Markt. The food is broadly French, though Dutch dishes do pop up now and then, and you can eat outside on their patio-barge in summer. Mains €23–27. Wed–Sun 5.30–11pm.

Kobus Kuch Beestenmarkt 1 ☎ 015 212 4280, ⓦ kobuskuch.nl. Located on Delft's most atmospheric square, this café is famous for its home-baked apple pie with whipped cream – an absolute hit – served in an old-fashioned wood-panelled setting. Great terrace too. Mon–Thurs 9.30am–1am, Fri & Sat 9.30am–2am, Sun 10am–1am.

Le Vieux Jean Heilige Geestkerkhof 3 ☎015 213 0433, ⓦlevieuxjean.nl. Smart but informal French restaurant in old, vaguely rustic premises serving nouvelle cuisine (read: small portions) with care and precision. Main courses are around €23–27, and there's an excellent cellar too. Tues–Fri noon–2.30pm & 6–10.30pm, Sat 6–10.30pm.

★ **Uit de Kunst** Oude Delft 140 ☎015 212 1319, ⓦuitdekunstdelft.nl. Cute little coffee bar with an inviting canal-side terrace away from the tourist crowds. Scrumptious sandwiches and great coffee, as well as a nice covered courtyard patio overlooked by two parrots. Wed–Sat 10am–5.30pm, Sun 11am–5.30pm.

BARS

Locus Publicus Brabantse Turfmarkt 67 ☎015 213 4632, ⓦlocuspublicus.nl. You don't come to Delft for the nightlife, but this is one of the town's busiest and most youthful bars – and it offers a wide range of beers as well as some simple bar food. Mon–Thurs 11am–1am, Fri & Sat 11am–2am, Sun noon–1am.

Trappistenlokaal 't Klooster Vlamingstraat 2 ☎015 212 1013, ⓦtrappistenlokaal.nl. Smashing little bar with traditional decor and an excellent range of beers, mainly Belgian but also from Scandinavia, Germany and the US, both on tap and bottled. They often organize beer tastings and have a great whisky selection too. Sun–Thurs 4pm–1am, Fri 4pm–2am, Sat 2pm–2am.

Rotterdam

Home to the largest port in the world, **ROTTERDAM** is a no-nonsense working-class city lying at the heart of a maze of rivers and artificial waterways that together form the outlet of the rivers Rijn (Rhine) and Maas (Meuse). After devastating damage during World War II, Rotterdam has grown into a vibrant, forceful city dotted with first-division cultural attractions. Redevelopment hasn't obliterated its earthy character though: its tough grittiness is part of its appeal, as are its boisterous bars and clubs.

In terms of sights, Rotterdam's attractions are enticing, most notably the **Kunsthal**, exhibiting contemporary art, and the **Museum Boijmans van Beuningen**, which has an outstanding art collection including representative works from almost all the most important Dutch painters: both are in the city's designated culture zone, the **Museumpark**. Other city highlights include **Oude Haven**, the city's oldest harbour, ravaged during World War II but sympathetically redeveloped, and **Delfshaven**, an antique harbour that managed to survive the bombs pretty much intact. Rotterdam also boasts a string of first-rate **festivals**, including the much-lauded **North Sea Jazz Festival** (see p.175) and the colourful **Summer Carnival**.

Brief history

An important **port** as early as the fourteenth century, Rotterdam was one of the major cities of the United Provinces and shared its periods of fortune and decline until the nineteenth century when it was caught unawares. The city was ill-prepared for the industrial expansion of the Ruhr, the development of larger ships and the silting up of the Maas, but prosperity did finally return in a big way with the digging of an entirely new ship canal (the "Nieuwe Waterweg") between the city and the North Sea in the 1860s. Rotterdam has been a major seaport ever since, though it has had difficult times, especially during World War II, when the Nazis **bombed** the city centre in 1940 and, in retreat, destroyed much of the harbour four years later, with Allied bombing doing much damage in between.

The postwar period saw the rapid reconstruction of the **docks** and, when huge container ships and oil tankers made the existing port facilities obsolete, Rotterdammers promptly built an entirely new deep-sea port, the **Europoort**, jutting out into the North Sea some 25km to the west of the old town. Completed in 1968, the Europoort can accommodate the largest of ships, handling some 350 million tonnes of goods a year, with more than half of all goods heading into Europe passing through it. The same spirit of enterprise was reflected in the council's plans to rebuild

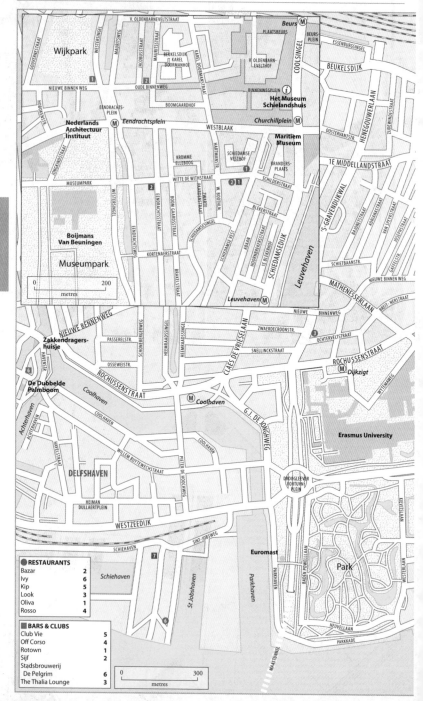

3

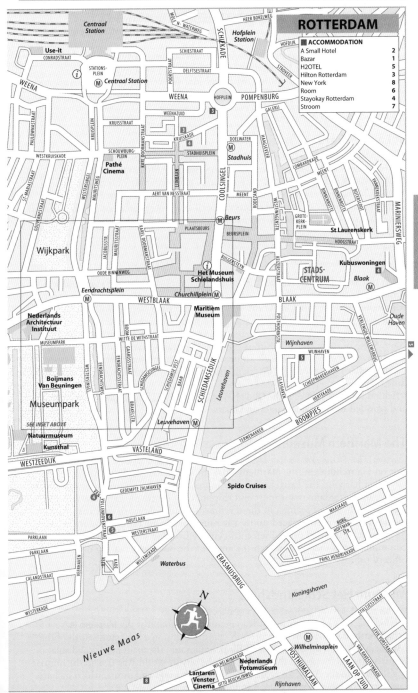

ROTTERDAM

ACCOMMODATION

A Small Hotel	2
Bazar	1
H2OTEL	5
Hilton Rotterdam	3
New York	8
Room	6
Stayokay Rotterdam	4
Stroom	7

Centraal Station

Hofplein Station

Use-it
CONRADSTRAAT
STATIONS-PLEIN
Centraal Station

WEENA
PAULOWNASTRAAT

SCHIESTRAAT
POORTSTRAAT
DELFTSESTRAAT

HEER BOKELWEG
SCHIEKADE
HOFDIJK
STROVEER

WEENA

HOFPLEIN
POMPENBURG

WEENAZUID
KRUISSTRAAT
KRUISPLEIN
WESTKRUISKADE

GALERIJ

KRUISKADE

SCHOUWBURG-PLEIN
Pathé Cinema

DOELWATER
STADHUISPLEIN
Stadhuis

LOMBARDKADE
BINNENROTTE
BUIZENGAT

AERT VAN NESSTRAAT

MEENT

RODEZAND
WESTEWAGENSTR.

GROTE-KERK-PLEIN
St Laurenskerk

MARINIERSWEG

ST MARIASTRAAT

WESTERSINGEL
MAURITSWEG
KARL DOORMANSTRAAT

Beurs
PLAATSBEURS
BEURSPLEIN

BULGERSTEYN

KEIZERSTRAAT

HOOGSTRAAT

Wijkpark
JACOBUSSTR.
MAURITSSTRAAT
KARL DOORMANSTRAAT

OUDE BINNENWEG

Het Museum
Schielandshuis

STADS-CENTRUM
Blaak

Kubuswoningen

Eendrachtsplein

Churchillplein

WESTBLAAK

Maritiem Museum

BLAAK

BLAAK

Oude Haven

Nederlands Architectuur Instituut

BOOMPJES
GAARDSTRAAT
WITTE DE WITHSTRAAT

MUSEUMPARK

WESTERSINGEL
EENDRACHTSWEG
EENDRACHTSSTRAAT

SCHIEDAMSESINGEL
SCHIEDAMSE VEST
BAAN

SCHIEDAMSEDIJK

Leuvehaven

POSTHOORNSTR.

Wijnhaven
WIJNHAVEN

GLASHAVEN

SCHEEPMAKERSHAVEN

HERTEKADE

Boijmans Van Beuningen

Museumpark

BRAKELSTR.

Leuvehaven

SEE INSET ABOVE

Natuurmuseum
Kunsthal

VASTELAND

WESTZEEDIJK

GEDEMPTE ZALMHAVEN

HOUTLAAN
WESTERSTRAAT

Spido Cruises

MAASKADE

BURG. HOFFMAN-STR.

PRINS HENDRIKKADE

PARKLAAN
PARKLAAN

VEERHAVEN

WILLEMSKADE

ERASMUSBRUG

Waterbus

Koningshaven

CALANDSTRAAT

WESTERKADE

Nieuwe Maas

N

Wilhelminaplein

POSTHUMALAAN

LAAN OP ZUID

STIELTJESSTRAAT

LEUVE VORSTSTR.

Lantaren Venster Cinema

WILHELMINAKADE
OTTO REUCHLINWEG

Nederlands Fotomuseum

Rijnhaven

3

5

the devastated **city centre**. There was to be no return to the crowded terrace houses of yesteryear; instead the centre was to be a modern extravaganza of concrete and glass, high-rise and pedestrianized areas. Decades in the making, parts of the plan work very well indeed – such as the *kubuswoningen* ("cube houses") of the Blaak district – but others, such as the Lijnbaan shopping precinct, look tired and sad. Construction seems never-ending, with high-rise skyscrapers soaring from around the city's Central Station, itself in the process of reconstruction – a project which should be completed by 2014.

St Laurenskerk

Grote Kerkplein 15 • **Church** Tues–Sat 11am–5pm ; €1 • **Tower** April–Oct Wed at 2pm, Sat at 1pm & 3pm; €3.50

To the east of Coolsingel, just north of Hoogstraat, the fifteenth-century **St Laurenskerk** or Grote Kerk, is a mighty brick pile rebuilt after bomb damage in 1940. With its splendid bronze doors – the work of Giacomo Manzu in the 1960s – the church now hosts cultural events and well as the occasional house party. You can also climb the tower for great views of the city on a clear day, though its opening hours are limited.

Blaak

From the back of St Laurenskerk it's a short walk south along the wide and windy Binnenrotte to **Blaak**, a compact, one-time working-class district that was comprehensively levelled in World War II, but has since been rebuilt in a full flush of modern design. The architectural high point is a remarkable series of cube-shaped houses, the *kubuswoningen*, completed in 1984 to a design by the architect Piet Blom. One of them, the **Kijk-Kubus** (Show Cube; daily 11am–5pm; €2.50; ⓦkubuswoning.nl) at Overblaak 70 near Blaak train and metro station, is open to visitors, offering a somewhat disorientating tour of what amounts to an upside-down house.

Behind the cube houses is the **Oude Haven**, built in 1325, and now flanked by cafés and crowded with antique barges and boats.

The Maritiem Museum

Leuvehaven 1 • Tues–Sat 10am–5pm, Sun 11am–5pm; July & Aug also Mon 10am–5pm • €7.50 • ⓦ maritiemmuseum.nl

Just off Churchillplein, the **Maritiem Museum** is situated beside the waters of the city's first harbour, the Leuvehaven. The museum has an interesting display on the history of Rotterdam as a seaport and shipbuilding centre plus an entertaining section on the life of seamen in the seventeenth and eighteenth centuries. The outside area has been spruced up for the museum's prime exhibit, the *Buffel*, an immaculately restored mid-nineteenth-century ironclad ship, complete with communal sinks shaped to match the angle of the bows and a string of luxurious officers' cabins.

Museum Het Schielandshuis

Korte Hoogstraat 31 • Tues–Sun 11am–5pm • €6 • ⓦ hmr.rotterdam.nl

A good overview of the history of Rotterdam can be found at the **Museum Het Schielandshuis**, housed in a seventeenth-century mansion a brief stroll north of the Maritiem Museum on the far side of Blaak boulevard. The main historical display features original footage of the bombing of the city in World War II, and the museum is also home to the Atlas van Stolk collection of drawings and prints, which includes fascinating sketches of pre-colonial Indonesia.

SPIDO CRUISES

The shape and feel of the Leuvehaven, Rotterdam's first artificial harbour, has been transformed by the Boompjes freeway, which scoots along the top of the old enclosing sea dyke. Beside the Boompjes, at the south end of the Leuvehaven, is the departure point for **Spido cruises** (☎010 275 9988, ⊛spido.nl). They have several different tours of the surrounding waterways and port facilities, heading off past the wharves, landings, docks and silos of the world's largest port, but the standard **harbour tour** costs just €10.50 (April–Oct 5–11 daily; Nov–March Mon–Wed 1 daily, Thurs–Sun 4 daily; 1hr 15min). In July and August, there are also longer trips to several destinations, most notably the series of colossal dams that make up the Delta Project (see box, p.317) along the seaboard southwest of Rotterdam (July & Aug 1 weekly on Wed; 7hr; €55).

Museumpark

Tram #8 (direction Spangen) links Centraal Station and Coolsingel/Schiedamsedijk with the southern edge of the park

The Museumpark is a designated cultural zone where a string of museums fringe a wide, open area. In the south, bordering Westzeedijk, are the **Natuurmuseum** (Tues–Sat 10am–5pm, Sun 11am–5pm; €6; ⊛nmr.nl), where all sorts of stuffed animals are displayed, and the excellent **Kunsthal** (Tues–Sat 10am–5pm, Sun 11am–5pm; €11; ⊛kunsthal.nl), which showcases first-rate exhibitions of contemporary art, photography and design. On the park's eastern side, the **Nederlands Architectuur Instituut** (Dutch Architecture Institute; Tues–Sat 10am–5pm, Sun 11am–5pm; €8; ⊛nai.nl) is housed in a modern glass building and showcases sketches, models and photos by prominent Dutch architects from 1800 onwards in an ambitious programme of temporary exhibitions. Highlight of the park, however, is the wonderful Museum Boijmans van Beuningen, Rotterdam's top attraction.

Museum Boijmans van Beuningen

Museumpark 18 • Tues–Sun 11am–5pm • €9 • ⊛boijmans.nl

A few minutes' walk from the Kunsthal, on the northern edge of Museumpark near Eendrachtsplein metro stop, is, the **Museum Boijmans van Beuningen**. The museum spreads over two floors with the ground floor used for temporary exhibitions, the first floor for the vast permanent collection. The older paintings are in one wing of the first floor, and those from the late nineteenth century onwards in the other. The information desk provides an updated and simplified diagrammatic outline of the museum, necessary because the exhibits are frequently rotated.

Flemish and Netherlandish paintings

Among the museum's earlier paintings is an excellent **Flemish and Netherlandish** section, where one highlight is the sumptuous *Christ in the House of Martha and Mary* by Pieter Aertsen (1508–75). There are also four exquisite works by Hieronymus Bosch (1450–1516). Usually considered a macabre fantasist, Bosch was actually working at the limits of oral and religious tradition, where biblical themes were depicted as iconographical representations, laden with explicit symbols. In his *St Christopher*, the dragon, the hanged bear and the broken pitcher lurk in the background, representations of danger and uncertainty, whereas the Prodigal Son's attitude to the brothel behind him in *The Peddler* is deliberately ambivalent. Bosch's technique never absorbed the influences of Renaissance Italy, and his figures in the *Marriage Feast at Cana* are static and unbelievable, uncomfortably arranged around a distorted table. Other works in this section include paintings by Jan van Scorel (1495–1562), who was more willing to absorb Italianate styles as in his *Young Scholar in a Red Cap*; the mysterious, hazy *Tower of Babel* by Pieter Brueghel the Elder; and Geertgen tot Sint Jans' (1460–90) beautiful, delicate *Glorification of the Virgin*.

The Golden Age

A fascinating selection of **Dutch genre** paintings reflects the tastes of the emergent seventeenth-century middle class. The idea was to depict real-life situations overlaid with a symbolic moral content as typified by Jan Steen's (1625–79) *The Doctor's Visit* and *Sick Woman*. There's also *The Quack* by Gerrit Dou (1613–75), ostensibly just a passing scene, but littered with small cameos of deception – a boy catching a bird, the trapped hare – that refer back to the quack's sham cures. In this section also are a number of **Rembrandts**, including two contrasting canvases: an analytic *Portrait of Aletta Adriaensdr*, her ageing illuminated but softened by her white ruff, and a gloomy, powerfully indistinct *Blind Tobias and his Wife* painted twenty years later. His intimate *Titus at his Desk* is also in marked contrast to the more formal portrait commissions common to his era. Most of the work of Rembrandt's pupil Carel Fabritius (1622–54) was destroyed when he was killed in a Delft gunpowder explosion in 1654; an exception is his *Self-Portrait*, reversing his master's usual technique by lighting the background and placing the subject in shadow.

Modern paintings

The museum's collection of **modern paintings** is perhaps best known for its **Surrealists**. It's difficult to appreciate Salvador Dalí's *Spain*, de rigueur for students' bedrooms in the 1970s, as anything more than the painting of the poster, but other works by the likes of René Magritte, Max Ernst and Giorgio de Chirico still have the power to surprise. Surrealism was never adopted by Dutch artists, though the **Magic Realism** of Carel Willink (1900–83) has its similarities in the precise, hallucinatory technique he uses to distance the viewer in *Self-Portrait with a Pen*. *Three Generations* by Charley Toorop (1891–1955) is also Realism with an aim to disconcert: the huge bust of her father, Jan, looms in the background and dominates the painting. In this section, look out also for paintings from many of Europe's most famous artists, including Monet, van Gogh, Picasso, Gauguin, Cézanne and Munch, as well as a representative sample of the Barbizon and Hague schools, notably *Strandgezicht* by J.H. Weissenbruch (1822–80), a beautiful gradation of radiant tones.

Nederlands Fotomuseum

Wilhelminakade 332 • Tues–Fri 10am–5pm, Sat & Sun 11am–5pm • €7 • Ⓦ nederlandsfotomuseum.nl

Within easy walking distance of the Museumpark – cross the Erasmusbrug and take the first right – is a further museum, the **Nederlands Fotomuseum** (Dutch Museum of Photography) at Wilhelminakade 332. It hosts frequently rotated exhibitions of both big-name and up-and-coming photographers.

Delfshaven

2km southwest of Centraal Station • From the train station, catch tram #8 (direction Spangen) and get off at Spanjaardstraat tram stop, or take the metro to Delfshaven

If little in Rotterdam city centre can exactly be called picturesque, **Delfshaven**, goes part of the way there. Once the harbour that served Delft, it was from here that the **Pilgrim Fathers** set sail in 1620, changing to the more reliable *Mayflower* in Plymouth before continuing onward to the New World. Nevertheless, despite this substantial claim to fame, Delfshaven was long a neglected corner of the city until finally, in the 1970s, the council recognized its tourist potential and set about conserving and restoring it. Most of the buildings lining the two narrow canals that comprise Delfshaven are eighteenth- and nineteenth-century warehouses, with the more fetching facades on the more westerly Voorhaven.

THE NORTH SEA JAZZ FESTIVAL

The North Sea Jazz Festival (W northseajazz.nl), held every year in mid-July, is the country's most prestigious jazz event, attracting international media coverage and the world's most famous jazz musicians. For many years, the festival was held in Scheveningen near Den Haag, but in 2006 it transferred to Rotterdam's Ahoy' centre, about 4km south of the city centre at Ahoy'-weg 10. To get there by metro, take the Erasmuslijn and get off at Zuidplein. Details of performances are available online and from the VVV, which will also reserve accommodation – virtually impossible to find after the festival has begun. Various tickets can be purchased; a *dagkaart*, for example, valid for an entire day, costs €89.

ARRIVAL AND DEPARTURE   ROTTERDAM

By plane Rotterdam has its own (rapidly expanding) airport (W rotterdam-airport.nl), just 10km or so northwest of Centraal Station on Airportplein 60; bus #33 (every 10–20min; 20min) links the two. A taxi from the airport to the station costs about €20.

By train Most visitors arrive by train: Rotterdam has several train stations, but the one you want for the centre is Centraal Station, which adjoins Stationsplein, the hub of

the RET public transport system, whose metro, trams and buses serve all parts of the city. Be warned, however, that Centraal Station and its immediate surroundings can be intimidating late at night and is currently under major reconstruction, making it a grim area indeed.

Destinations Delft (every 5min; 10min); Den Haag CS (every 10min; 25min); Dordrecht (every 10min; 15min); Gouda (every 10min; 25min); and Utrecht (every 15min; 45min).

INFORMATION

Tourist offices There's a VVV Info Café on the right as you leave the train station at Stationsplein 45 (Mon–Sat 9am–5.30pm, Sun 10am–5pm), where you can plan your route over coffee and use free internet terminals. The main VVV located in a large glass building is a 10min walk southeast of Centraal Station, at Coolsingel 195-197 (Mon–Fri 10am–7pm, Sat 9.30am–6pm, Sun 10am–5pm; ☎ 010 271 0120, W rotterdam.info). They have all the usual tourist information, supply a useful and free mini-guide to the city, issue free city and public transport maps and operate an accommodation booking service. There's also a first-rate youth information office too, Use-it, in a red-painted building a couple of minutes'

walk from the west side of the train station at Schaatsbaan 41 (at the time of writing, Use-it had plans to relocate: check the website for its current location and opening hours, W use-it.nl); they specialize in budget stuff – from accommodation to cafés and beyond – and offer free internet access as well.

Discount cards If you plan on visiting many cultural sights, you might want to consider the Rotterdam Welcome Card, giving you up to fifty-percent discount on many key attractions and unlimited access to the city's public transport. The card comes in three versions: 1 day (€10), 2 days (€13.50), or 3 days (€17.50).

GETTING AROUND

By public transport Operated by RET (☎ 0900 9292, W ret.nl), Rotterdam's public transport system is fast, comprehensive and efficient and comprises an extensive bus, tram and metro network. It was the first city in the Netherlands to introduce the OV-chipcard, a rechargeable card the size of a credit card that gives you unlimited travel on the city's buses, trams and metro. Most regulars using

public transport in the Netherlands have a personalized card, but you can buy disposable ones for 1 hr (€3), 2 hr (€3.50), 1 day (€7), 2 days (€10.50) or 3 days (€14) at any metro station or at the tourist office.

By car Europcar, Rotterdam Airportplein 60 ☎ 010 437 1826; Hertz, Weena 699 ☎ 010 404 6088.

Taxi RTC ☎ 010 462 6060.

THE WATERBUS

Leaving from beside Rotterdam's Erasmusbrug, the **Waterbus passenger ferry** (☎ 0900 9292, W waterbus.nl) takes an hour to zip down the rivers Nieuwe Maas and Noord bound for Dordrecht (see p.181). It's a great way to see this part of the country and fares are very reasonable – a single to Dordrecht costs just €6 or opt for a day card with unlimited use for €12.50; boats leave every half-hour from 7am to 8pm on weekdays, 8am to 8pm on Saturdays and 11am to 7.30pm on Sundays. Furthermore, connecting ferries make side journeys to – among several places – the Dordrecht Biesbosch (see p.185).

ACCOMMODATION

As you might expect of an important industrial city, Rotterdam has a slew of big chain **hotels**. It also possesses a clutch of much less expensive places, occasionally in – or at least near – the centre, including an HI **hostel** in one of Rotterdam's distinctive *kubuswoningen* (see p.172). Conferences and congresses mean that rooms can sometimes be in short supply, which is one good reason to use the VVV's efficient accommodation service, the cost of which is minimal.

HOTELS

★ **A Small Hotel** Witte de Withstraat 94 ☎010 414 0303, ⓦasmallhotel.nl. Incredibly stylish boutique hotel located at the up-and-coming Witte de Withstraat with just six themed rooms, such as Tex, Coco and Zen, all well equipped and spacious. Free use of minibar included. No reception so you have to check yourself in. **€125**

Bazar Witte de Withstraat 16 ☎010 206 5151, ⓦbazarrotterdam.nl. Lively, very agreeable two-star hotel in a central location near the Museumpark, with great rooms decorated in African, South American and Eastern style. There's also an excellent café-restaurant downstairs (see below). Great value for money. **€80**

H2OTEL Wijnhaven 20a, ☎010 444 5690, ⓦh2otel.nl. Rotterdam's only floating hotel with 49 rooms, all decorated by artists in different styles; from funky to Baroque or nautical. They also have a picnic boat which you can rent out for €65 (with guide) taking you though the Rotterdam canals while enjoying breakfast, lunch or drinks. **€95**

Hilton Rotterdam Weena 10 ☎010 710 8000, ⓦrotterdam.hilton.com. Luxurious four-star hotel with large and extremely well-appointed rooms. Occupies a classic early 1970s tower block with a wide sweeping foyer that comes complete with oceans of marble and a broken mirror motif on the walls. The hotel is currently being updated, and special weekend deals are abundant. **€79**

★ **New York** Koninginnenhoofd 1 ☎010 439 0500, ⓦhotelnewyork.nl. This prestigious four-star hotel occupies the grand nineteenth-century former head office of a shipping line. All the rooms are extremely well appointed and most have smashing river views. It's situated across from the city centre on the south bank of the Nieuwe Maas, and accessible via water taxi from the centre or on the metro – the hotel is a 5min walk from Wilhelminaplein station. **€115**

Stroom Lloydstraat 1 ☎010 221 4060, ⓦstroomrotterdam.nl. Twenty-three hi-tech studios – all varying in size – located in a former power station, which gives them an urban-industrial feel. All the studios on the second floor are split-level and there's also a modish bar-lounge downstairs. Take tram #8 in the direction of Spangen (Pieter de Hooghweg stop) or it's a 5min walk from Coolhaven metro. **€112**

HOSTELS

★ **Room** Van Vollenhovenstraat 62 ☎010 282 7277, ⓦroomrotterdam.nl. Funky hostel in bright orange and purple colours, accommodating up to 100 people in dorms with themes such as art, festival, port and zoo. There's free wi-fi and a vibrant bar downstairs. Dorm beds **€23.50**, doubles **€57**

Stayokay Rotterdam Overblaak 85 ☎010 436 5763, ⓦstayokay.com. It was an inspired idea to run an HI hostel in one of Rotterdam's cube houses – the *kubuswoningen*. It opened in 2009, with good facilities – there's bike storage and bike rental plus a launderette. Dorm beds **€26**, doubles **€70**

EATING AND DRINKING

Handy for many of the sights, the Oude and Nieuwe Binneweg are two of Rotterdam's grooviest streets, lined with decent cafés, café-bars and **restaurants**. Similarly enticing is Witte de Withstraat, where you'll also find one of the city's more pleasant cannabis **coffeeshops**, the *Witte de With*, at no. 92. The Oude Haven is also a lively spot in summer, where outdoor terraces line up overlooking the old harbour, while the Westelijk Handelsterrein, an old warehouse area, now holds a dozen very fashionable restaurants, bars and art galleries.

RESTAURANTS

Bazar Witte de Withstraat 16 ☎010 206 5151, ⓦbazarrotterdam.nl. Big and bustling North African restaurant with a good variety of vegetarian dishes. Mains such as couscous or chicken kebab cost around €13, but you can also opt for the daily special for a mere €8.50. Laidback (some would say cool) atmosphere. Daily 9am–11pm; Fri & Sat till midnight.

Ivy Lloydstraat 294 ☎010 425 0520, ⓦrestaurantivy .nl. Much lauded and incredibly popular with the in-crowd, this pricey restaurant specializes in molecular cooking, inspired by the masters of *El Bulli* and *The Fat Duck*. Be sure to book and check the limit on your credit card before splashing out: the five-course menu will set you back a whopping €88. Tues–Sat noon–2.30pm & 6.30–10.30pm.

Kip Van Vollenhovenstraat 25 ☎010 436 9923, ⓦkip-rotterdam.nl. This smooth and chic restaurant in classy premises has won all sorts of gastronomic awards. Kitted out in a modern version of Golden Age style, it serves up food at its finest with mains such as grated cod fish or veal with duck liver from €25. Daily 6–10pm.

Look's Gravendijkwal 140 ☎010 436 7000, ⓦrestaurantlook.nl. As the name would suggest, garlic is the big deal here (*look* is Flemish for "garlic"), in everything from the creamy garlic soup to the garlic-vanilla ice cream. Tasty surprises at affordable prices, with a three-course set menu costing just €26. Wed–Sun 5.30–10pm.

Oliva Witte de Withstraat 15 ☎010 412 1413, ⓦgustoliva.nl. All the ingredients in this relaxed restaurant are directly imported from Italy and most are organic. The main courses are written out on a blackboard, guaranteeing you the freshest seasonal produce, and a three-course meal will set you back just €34. Daily 5.30–10pm.

Rosso Van Vollenhovenstraat 15 ☎010 225 0705, ⓦrossorotterdam.nl. Located in the happening Westelijk Handelsterrein, this is one of the best of the several fashionable restaurants here, attracting a lively crowd. The menu changes frequently, but if you pick the surprise three-course menu (€39) you can bet on the freshest ingredients with delicacies such as raw marinated tuna or beef from one of the country's top butchers. It also serves many wines by the glass. Tues–Sat 6–11pm.

CAFÉ-BARS AND BARS

Rotown Nieuwe Binnenweg 17 ☎010 436 2669, ⓦrotown.nl. Lively café-bar attracting an alternative crew and serving up a wide variety of snacks and light meals from as little as €3.50. Regular live music too with both local talent as well as the occasional international artist. Mon–Wed & Sun 11am–2am, Thurs–Sat 11am–3am.

Sijf Oude Binnenweg 115 ☎010 433 2610, ⓦsijf.nl. Downbeat café-bar with entertaining Art Deco decor; serves filling Dutch snacks and light meals such as wild salmon or satay for around €14. Intimate little French-style terrace, great for people-watching. Daily 10am–midnight, Fri & Sat till 2am.

Stadsbrouwerij De Pelgrim Aelbrechtskolk 12 ☎010 477 1189, ⓦpelgrimbier.nl. Rotterdam's only brewery is located in the old council hall, which dates back to 1580 and has an attractive terrace overlooking Delfshaven. Their Mayflower Triple beer with a hint of caramel is especially tasty. Wed–Sun noon–midnight.

NIGHTLIFE AND ENTERTAINMENT

Rotterdam has a vibrant **club** scene as well as several **music venues** that host regular live performances. Tickets for gigs and concerts are on sale at the VVV (see p.175), which is an authorized outlet for Ticket (ⓦticketmaster.nl). For an up-to-date overview of all nightlife, pick up the free *NL10* magazine, which can be found in stores, cafés and supermarkets around town.

Club Vie Maasboulevard 300 ☎010 280 0238, ⓦclubvie.nl. A stylish venue hosting regular R&B, hip-hop and dance-classics nights as well as many international DJs. On Saturday the focus is Latin house, while every other Monday they host a club night especially for people working at weekends, your best bet for some night-time entertainment. Every other Monday 10pm–5am, Fri & Sat 10.30pm–4/5am.

Off Corso Kruiskade 22 ☎010 411 3897, ⓦcorsorotterdam.nl. Large and funky venue near Centraal Station, with top DJs, groovy visuals and even art exhibitions. Their occasional 1980s & 1990s dance night is an absolute hit. Usually Thurs–Sat 11pm–4/5am, but also check the website for current events.

The Thalia Lounge Kruiskade 31 ☎010 214 2547, ⓦwww.thaliarotterdam.nl. Housed in an old cinema in front of *Off Corso*, this style-conscious club is best known for its frequent Latin house nights. Dress to impress. Fri & Sat 11pm–4/5pm.

DIRECTORY

Cinema Lantaren Venster at Otto Reuchlinweg 996 (☎010 277 2277, ⓦlantarenvenster.nl) offers the best independent cinema in the city. For mainstream cinema, head for Pathé on Schouwburgplein 101 (☎0900 1458, ⓦpathe.nl).

Markets The largest market is at Binnenrotte in the centre of town (Tues & Sat 8am–5pm), with almost 500 stalls selling everything from food to cheap clothing.

Pharmacy Apotheek Erasmus can be found at West-Kruiskade 21a (Mon–Fri 8.30am–5.30pm).

Gouda and around

GOUDA, a pretty little place some 20km northeast of Rotterdam, is everything you'd expect of a Dutch country town, with its ring of quiet canals encircling ancient buildings set amid a tangle of narrow lanes and alleys. More surprisingly, its **Markt** is the largest in the Netherlands, a wide and airy piazza that remains an attractive reminder of the town's prominence as a centre of the medieval cloth trade, and later of its success in the manufacture of cheeses and that old Dutch favourite, the clay pipe.

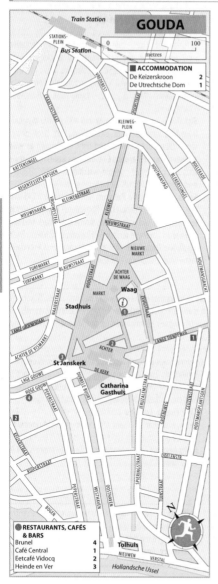

The weekly cheese market held here is mercilessly milked by tour operators who herd their crowds here – but don't let this put you off, since Gouda's charms lie elsewhere, especially in the splendid stained-glass windows of **St Janskerk**, and the winsome jumble of old canal-side buildings along **Westhaven** which rambles off towards the old **Tolhuis** (toll house) beside the Hollandsche IJssel River, on the southern edge of the town centre.

The Stadhuis and Kaaswaag

Slap-bang in the middle of the Markt, the **Stadhuis** is an elegant Gothic structure whose soaring stonework, with its spiky towers and dinky dormer windows, dates from 1450. Statues of Burgundian counts and countesses decorate the building's facades and on its east side is the cheeriest of carillons, where the tiny figures play up and around every half-hour. Opposite, on the north side of the square at Markt 35, is the **Waag**, a tidy seventeenth-century building adorned by a detailed relief of cheese-weighing and now holding a moderately interesting **Kaaswaag** (Cheese Weigh House museum; April–Oct daily 10am–5pm; Nov–March Thurs–Sun 1–5pm; €4).

St Janskerk

Achter de Kerk 16 • Mon–Sat: March–Oct 9am–5pm; Nov–Feb 10am–4pm • €3.50 • ⓦ sintjan.com

Just to the south of the Markt, the lumpy **St Janskerk** was founded in 1280, though the present structure mostly dates from the second half of the sixteenth century, when it was rebuilt following a fire. The church is famous for its magnificent and stunningly beautiful **stained-glass windows**, which bear witness to the move from Catholicism to Calvinism. All the windows are numbered and a detailed guide and audioguide are available at the entrance.

The biblical themes executed by **Dirk and Wouter Crabeth** between 1555 and 1571, when Holland was still Catholic, are traditional in content, but they have an amazing clarity of detail and richness of colour. Their last work, Judith Slaying Holofernes (Window no. 6), is perhaps the finest, the story unfolding in intricate perspective – and a gruesome tale it was too. The Assyrian general Holofernes made the mistake of

GOUDA'S CHEESE

Gouda's main claim to fame is its **cheese market**, held on the Markt every Thursday morning (10am–12.30pm) from the middle of June to late August. Traditionally, a thousand or so local farmers brought their home-produced cheeses here to be weighed, tested and graded for moisture, smell and taste. These details were marked on the cheeses and formed the basis for negotiation between buyer and seller, the exact price confirmed by an elaborate code of handclaps. Today, however, the cheese market is a shadow of its former self, comprising a few locals in traditional dress standing outside the Waag with their cheeses, all surrounded by modern, open-air stands.

sharing his tent with Judith, a Jewish woman from Bethulia, the town he was besieging; he made things worse by drinking himself into a stupor and Judith, not one to look a gift horse in the mouth, lopped off his head and carried it back to Bethulia in triumph.

By comparison, the **post-Reformation windows**, which date from 1594 to 1603, adopt an allegorical and heraldic style typical of a more secular art. A prime illustration is The Relief of Leiden (Window no. 25), which shows William the Silent retaking the town from the Spanish, though Delft and its burgomasters take prominence – no doubt because they footed the bill for the window's manufacture.

3

Catharina Gasthuis

Achter de Kerk 14 • Tues–Fri 11am–5pm, Sat & Sun noon–5pm • €7 • ⓦ museumgouda.nl

By the south side of St Janskerk, the fancily carved **Lazarus Gate** of 1609 was once part of the town's leper hospital, until it was moved here to form the back entrance to the **Catharina Gasthuis**, a hospice till 1910 and now a fine art museum. The collection, which spreads over two floors, is really rather confusing and short of major paintings, but the Gasthuiskapel does hold a pleasant assortment of sixteenth- and seventeenth-century Dutch paintings, notably a sterling biblical triptych by Dirck Barendsz (1534–92), and, in the corridor between Rooms 10 and 11, a set of four striking Civic Guard group portraits. Upstairs, a modest selection of Hague and Barbizon School canvases is given a bit of artistic sparkle by four small paintings of rural idylls by Anton Mauve (1838–88).

ARRIVAL AND INFORMATION

By train Gouda's train and bus stations are to the immediate north of the town centre at Stationsplein 11. Gouda is well connected by train from Den Haag Centraal (every 10 min; 20min); Utrecht (every 10 min; 20min); and Rotterdam (every 10 min; 20min).

Tourist office Gouda currently has no VVV, though there are plans to open a new tourist information centre: until then, you can get tourist information at the Kaaswaag (see p.178).

ACCOMMODATION

De Keizerskroon Keizerstraat 11–13 ☎ 0182 528 096, ⓦ hotelkeizerskroon.nl. An unassuming family-run hotel in a terrace house to the west of Westhaven. Facilities include free wi-fi and bike rental. On weekdays the downstairs restaurant serves a reasonable *daghap*. €60 with shared facilities, €85 en suite

De Utrechtsche Dom Geuzenstraat 6 ☎ 0182 528 833, ⓦ hotelgouda.nl. Located in an airy and pleasantly renovated building five minutes' walk from the Markt, this is Gouda's most enjoyable hotel and excellent value. In summer, breakfast is served in a lovely little garden. €65 with shared facilities, €85 en suite

EATING AND DRINKING

Brunel Hoge Gouwe ☎ 0182 518 979, ⓦ restaurantbrunel .nl. The best restaurant in town, this smart Franco-Dutch split-level joint serves up main courses such as deer steak or guinea fowl for around €22; alternatively, opt for the four-course meal for €35. Daily 5–10pm.

Café Central Markt 23 ☎ 0182 512 576, ⓦ grandcafecentral.nl. All old-time favourite, where they rustle up a tasty and filling range of home-made Dutch staple dishes in resolutely old-fashioned premises – there's been no tacky modernization here, witness the wood panelling. Main

courses average around €17, salads and snacks €8, and they serve great pancakes too. Daily 9am–midnight.
Eetcafé Vidocq Koster Gijzensteeg 8 ☎0182 522 819, ⓦeetcafevidocq.nl. Tucked away in a little alley, this café serves up good-quality Dutch cuisine: the menu is unpretentious featuring mains such as rib-eye or salmon for around €12. It's also a pleasant place for a drink. Daily 5–10.30pm.

Heinde en Ver Wijdstraat 13 ☎0182 551 221, ⓦheinde-ver.nl. An eclectic mix of local produce and dishes from all over the world (hence its name "near and far") served in a pleasant and airy setting. A three-course surprise menu will set you back €26.50 and main courses are around €19. There's a nice terrace in summer. Tues–Sun 5–10pm.

Oudewater

Pocket-sized **OUDEWATER**, about 11km east of Gouda, deep in the countryside, is a compact and delightful town that holds a unique place in the history of Dutch witchcraft (see box below). Apart from the Heksenwaag, there's not much else to see in Oudewater, but it is a pleasant place, whose old brick houses spread out along the River Hollandsche IJssel as it twists its way through town.

Heksenwaag

Leeuweringerstraat 12 • April–Oct Tues–Sun 11am–5pm • €4.25 • ⓦheksenwaag.nl

Pride of place in Oudewater goes to the town's sixteenth-century Waag, which has been turned into the curious **Heksenwaag** (Witches' Weigh House), where many medieval women were weighed and saved from certain death when it was "proved" they were not

---

WITCH HUNTS AND OUDEWATER

It's estimated that over one million European women were burned or otherwise murdered in the widespread **witch hunts** of the sixteenth century – and not just from quasi-religious fear and superstition: anonymous accusation to the authorities was an easy way of removing a wife, at a time when there was no divorce. Underlying it all was a virulent misogyny and an accompanying desire to terrorize women into submission. There were three main methods for investigating accusations of witchcraft: in the first, **trial by fire**, the suspect had to walk barefoot over hot cinders or have a hot iron pressed into the back or hands. If the burns blistered, the accused was innocent, since witches were supposed to burn less easily than others; naturally, the (variable) temperature of the iron was crucial. **Trial by water** was still more hazardous: dropped into water, if you floated you were a witch, if you sank you were innocent – though those deemed innocent were more than likely to drown before being rescued from the water. The third method, **trial by weight**, presupposed that a witch would have to be unduly light to fly on a broomstick, so many Dutch towns – including Oudewater – used the Waag (town weigh house) to weigh the accused. If the weight didn't accord with a notional figure derived from a person's height, the woman was burned. The last Dutch woman to be burned as a witch was a certain Marrigje Ariens, a herbalist from Schoonhoven in Zuid-Holland, whose medical efforts, not atypically, inspired mistrust and subsequent persecution. She was killed in 1597.

The Emperor Charles V (1516–52) made Oudewater famous after seeing a woman accused of witchcraft in a nearby village. The weigh-master there, who'd been bribed, stated that the woman weighed only a few pounds, but Charles was dubious and ordered the woman to be weighed again in Oudewater, where the officials proved unbribable, pronouncing a normal weight and acquitting her. The probity of Oudewater's weigh-master impressed Charles, and he granted the town the privilege of issuing certificates, valid throughout the empire, stating: "The accused's weight is in accordance with the natural proportions of the body." Once in possession of the certificate, a woman could never be brought to trial for witchcraft again. Not surprisingly, thousands of women came from all over Europe for this life-saving piece of paper, and, much to Oudewater's credit, no one was ever condemned here.

witches. Today, it's a family-run affair where you can be weighed on the original rope and wood balance, while the owners dress up in national costume and issue a certificate in olde-worlde English.

ARRIVAL AND INFORMATION OUDEWATER

By bus Oudewater is readily reached on bus #180 linking Gouda with Utrecht (every 30min, hourly on Sun; 25min from Gouda). Get off at the Molenwal stop, a 5min walk from the centre – just follow the signs.

Tourist office There is a Tourist Information Centre at Leeuweringerstraat 10 (April–Oct Tues–Sat 10am–4pm; June–Aug also Sun 11am–3pm; Nov–March Tues–Sat 10am–1pm).

EATING

Lumière Eetcafé Markt Westzijde 7 ☎ 0348 560 004, ⓦ eetcafe-lumiere.nl. An extremely cosy old place with a tiled fireplace and oodles of wood panelling just opposite the Heksenwaag. They serve traditional, home-made

Dutch food here – and very tasty it is too; mains average €19 at dinner, less at lunch. Daily except Wed 10am–10pm; kitchen from noon.

3

Dordrecht and around

Some 20km southeast of Rotterdam, the ancient port of **DORDRECHT**, or "Dordt" as it's often called, sits beside one of the busiest waterway junctions in the world, where tankers and containers from the north pass the waterborne traffic of the Maas and Rijn. Eclipsed by the expansion of Rotterdam – and barely touched by World War II – Dordrecht's old centre has survived in excellent nick, its medley of eighteenth- and nineteenth-century warehouses, townhouses and workers' terraces strung along its innermost canals and harbours. It takes about three hours to cover all the town's main sights, and it's the obvious base from which to explore the sprawling marshes and tidal flats of the wilderness **Nationaal Park de Biesbosch** just south of town. The other main pull hereabouts is the windmills of the **Kinderdijk**.

Brief history

Granted a town charter in 1220, **Dordrecht** was the most important and powerful town in Holland until well into the sixteenth century. One of the first cities to declare against the Habsburgs in 1572, it was the obvious site for the first meeting of the Free Assembly of the United Provinces, and for a series of doctrinal conferences that tried to solve a whole range of theological differences among the various Protestant sects. The Protestants may have hated the Catholics, but they inherited the medieval church's enthusiasm for theological debate; in 1618, at the **Synod of Dordt**, the Remonstrants argued with the Calvinists over the definition of predestination – pretty weighty stuff compared with the Synod of 1574, when one of the main rulings demanded the dismantling of church

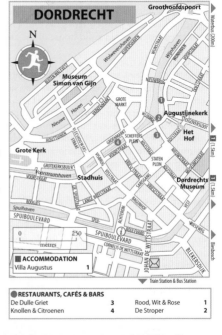

organs. From the seventeenth century, Dordrecht lost ground to its great rivals to the north, slipping into comparative insignificance, though it did manage to hold on to enough trade and shipbuilding to keep its economy afloat.

The Town

Jutting out into the River Maas, the old part of Dordrecht is interrupted by the three concentric waterways that once protected it from assault. The middle canal runs beside the **Voorstraat**, today's main shopping street, and here, at the junction of Voorstraat and Visstraat, sitting pretty on the **Visbrug**, is a clunky **monument** to the de Witt brothers, Johan and Cornelius, prominent Dutch Republicans who paid for their principles when they were torn to pieces by an Orangist mob in Den Haag in 1672. To the right of the Visbrug, Voorstraat wends its way northeast, a chaotic mixture of the old, the new and the restored, intersected by a series of tiny alleys that once served as the town's docks. About halfway along Voorstraat the Wijnbrug bridge crosses the **Wijnhaven**, the harbour used by the city's merchants to control the import and export of wine when they held the state monopoly from the fourteenth to the seventeenth century. At the end of Voorstraat, the **Groothoofdspoort** was once the main city gate, its grand brick facade of 1618, complete with a bronze-green cupola, staring down at the barges and boats that shuttle across the adjacent waterways. From the Groothoofdspoort, it's a few metres to the slender **Wolwevershaven**, the first of the two small harbours that together make up the town's innermost canal.

The Museum Simon van Gijn

Nieuwe Haven 29 • Tues–Sun 11am–5pm • €7 • Ⓦ simonvangijn.nl

The Wolwevershaven is home to an eye-catching mixture of old boats and barges, some of which date back to the 1880s, and is framed by several fine old mansions, one of which has been turned into the **Museum Simon van Gijn**, whose collection of local memorabilia and period rooms is of moderate interest. Its highlights are some eighteenth-century Brussels tapestries and a fine Renaissance chimneypiece of 1550, transferred from the old guild house of the arquebusiers.

The Grote Kerk

Lange Geldersekade 2 • **Church** April–Oct Tues–Sat 10.30am–4.30pm, Sun noon–4pm; Nov & Dec Tues, Thurs & Sat 2–4pm; free • **Tower** April–Oct Tues–Sat 10.30am–4.30pm, Sun noon–4pm; Nov–March Sat 1–4pm; €1 • Ⓦ grotekerk-dordrecht.nl

Lording it over the Nieuwe Haven, the Gothic **Grote Kerk** is visible from all over town, its truncated, fourteenth-century **tower** topped with incongruous seventeenth-century clocks. One of the largest churches in the country, it was built to emphasize Dordrecht's wealth and importance, but it's heavy and dull, despite its attractive environs, and there's only an elaborately carved choir inside to hold your interest. Climb the tower for a great view over the town and its surrounding waterways.

Dordrechts Museum

Museumstraat 40 • Tues–Sun 11am–5pm • €10 • Ⓦ dordrechtsmuseum.nl

A ten-minute walk east of the Stadhuis, the **Dordrechts Museum** is the town's premier art gallery, with a lively programme of temporary exhibitions and a strong permanent collection focused on local artists from the seventeenth century onwards. High points include a couple of finely drawn portraits by Jacob Cuyp (1594–1651), specifically pictures of a very young Michiel Pompe and of the eminently bourgeois Anthonis Repelaer, and four romanticized land and seascapes by Jacob's son, Aelbert (1620–91). Jan van Goyen (1596–1656), one of the country's finest landscape painters, is well represented by the detailed realism of his exquisite *View of*

Dordrecht, the city flat and narrow beneath a wide, cloudy sky. Goyen's vision of Dordrecht bears interesting comparison with Adam Willaertz's (1577–1664) massive *Gezicht op Dordt* ("View of Dordt"), in which the painter abandons proper scale to emphasize the ships in front of the city. More curiously, *De Dordtse Vierling* ("The Dordt Quadruplets") is an odd, unattributed seventeenth-century painting of a dead child and her three swaddled siblings, a simple, moving tribute to a lost daughter.

There's also a selection of work by the later and lesser Ary Scheffer (1795–1858), who was born in Dordrecht, but lived in Paris from 1811. His much-reproduced *Mignon Pining for her Native Land* struck a chord in the sentimental hearts of the nineteenth-century bourgeoisie. Lastly, Jozef Israëls' (1824–1911) *Midday Meal at the Inn*, a scream against poverty, and G.H. Breitner's (1857–1923) *Amsterdam's Lauriergracht* are among a small collection of Amsterdam and Hague School paintings.

ARRIVAL AND INFORMATION   DORDRECHT

By train Dordrecht's train station is a 10min walk from the town centre on Stationsplein 1: to get there, head straight down Stationsweg/Johan de Wittstraat and left at the end along Bagijnhof/Visstraat. Regular trains run to Delft (every 10min; 25min); Den Haag Centraal (every 20min; 45min); and Rotterdam (every 10min; 15min).

By bus The bus station is next to the train station on Stationsplein 1, with hourly services to the Biesbosch (bus #801, though you'll need to call at least an hour in advance to confirm the bus at ☎ 0900 1961 or bus #4 during school holidays which you do not need to confirm), and Kinderdijk (bus #19; hourly; 45min).

By boat The Waterbus passenger ferry service from Rotterdam (see p.175) drops passengers within easy walking distance of the old centre, a couple of hundred metres from the Groothoofdspoort.

Tourist office The VVV is at Spuiboulevard 99 (Mon noon–5.30pm, Tues, Wed & Fri 9am–5.30pm, Thurs 9am–9pm, Sat 10am–5pm; ☎ 0900 463 6888, ⓦ vvvdordrecht.nl). It carries a good range of information about the town and its surroundings – including the Biesbosch – and operates an accommodation booking service.

ACCOMMODATION

HI Hostel Baanhoekweg 25 ☎ 078 621 2167, ⓦ stayokay.com. Dordrecht's nearest hostel is way out of town, about 6km east, on the edge of the Biesbosch. To get there, take bus #4 from the station, which will drop you off at the hostel in high season, otherwise it's a fifteen-minute walk from the Baanhoekweg stop. There's also a small campsite at the hostel. Dorm beds €29, doubles €75

★ **Villa Augustus** Oranjelaan 7 ☎ 078 639 3111, ⓦ villa-augustus.nl. About 1.5km east of the centre, this hotel is located in an old, converted watermill with 37 rustic but smart rooms, some with great views. They also have a huge canteen-like restaurant overlooking the kitchen garden. €125

EATING AND DRINKING

De Dulle Griet Nieuwstraat 25 ☎ 078 614 5995, ⓦ dedullegriet.nl. Groovy and inexpensive eetcafé with an international menu including everything from Thai fish curry to Indian vegetable curry and Mexican steak, priced between €9–14 for a main dish: side dishes have to be ordered separately. There's also a garden terrace in the summer. Tues–Sat 6–9.30pm, Fri & Sat also noon–3pm.

Knollen & Citroenen Groenmarkt 8 ☎ 078 614 0500, ⓦ knollen-citroenen.nl. Traditional Dutch stews, soups and veggie dishes from – as they say – grandma's kitchen, with decor to match. Main courses average around €20. Wed–Fri 6–10pm, Sat 5–10pm, Sun 5–9pm.

Rood, Wit & Rose Voorstraat 227, ⓦ roodwitenrose.nl.

An original *vinoteca* specializing in European wines, and serving fifty wines by the glass, many more by the bottle. Little appetizers such as wild salmon, cheese or farmer's pâté are matched perfectly with each wine. Try the Champagne brunch (€22.50) for a truly decadent experience. Thurs, Fri & Sun noon–7pm, Sat noon–10.30pm.

De Stroper Wijnbrug 1 ☎ 078 613 0094, ⓦ destroper .com. A smart seafood restaurant in modern, well-turned-out premises; main courses such as halibut, cod or bouillabaisse (rich fish soup) cost €20–25. The four-course menu is made using the freshest of ingredients, and is good value for money at €27.50. Mon–Fri 11am–2pm & 6–10pm, Sat & Sun 6–10pm.

The Nationaal Park de Biesbosch

Located on the border of the provinces of Noord-Brabant and Zuid-Holland, the **Biesbosch** (Reed Forest) is one of the Netherlands' larger national parks and one of the few remaining freshwater tidal areas in Europe. The park covers around fifteen square kilometres of river, creek, marsh and reed to the south and east of Dordrecht and divides into two main sections, north and south of the Nieuwe Merwede waterway. The undeveloped heart of the park is the **Brabantse Biesbosch**, the chunk of land to the south, while almost all the tourist facilities have been carefully confined to the north on a strip just east of Dordrecht, along the park's perimeter. Being a wetland habitat, the park offers a perfect breeding ground for all species of birds such as kingfishers, bluethroats and waterfowls. Best explored by boat, the park makes for a pleasant day-trip from Dordrecht.

Inundated twice daily by the tide, the Biesbosch produced a particular **reed culture**, its inhabitants using the plant for every item of daily life, from houses to baskets and boats, and selling excess cuttings at the local markets. It was a harsh existence that lasted well into the nineteenth century, when machine-manufactured goods largely rendered the reeds redundant. Although protected as a national park, its delicate ecosystem is threatened by the very scheme that aims to protect the province from further flooding. The dams of the Delta Project (see p.317) have controlled the rivers' flow and restricted the tides' strength, forcing the reeds to give ground to other forms of vegetation incompatible with the area's bird and plant life. Large areas of reed have disappeared, and no one seems to know how to reconcile the nature reserve's needs with those of the seaboard cities, but vigorous attempts are being made.

3

ARRIVAL AND DEPARTURE
NATIONAAL PARK DE BIESBOSCH

By bus Bus #801 runs hourly to the Biesbosch from Dordrecht bus station, though you'll need to call at least an hour in advance to confirm the bus at ☎0900 1961. During summer school holidays, bus #4 runs regularly from Dordrecht bus station and you do not need to confirm.

By bike The other way to visit the park is by cycling: bikes are available to rent for approx €7.50 a day from Dordrecht train station. The VVV sells detailed maps of the park and brochures with suggested cycle routes. The cycle from town to the Kop van 't Land dock, where ferries shuttle over to the Brabantse Biesbosch, takes about half an hour.

INFORMATION AND TOURS

Information The Biesboschcentrum Dordrecht is at the entrance to the park, 7km or so east of Dordrecht at Baanhoekweg 53 (Visitor Centre: Jan–April & Oct–Dec Tues–Sun 10am–5pm; May–Sept daily 9am–6pm; free; ⓦhollandsebiesbosch.nl). It has some pretty dull displays on the flora and fauna of the region and a beaver observatory, as well as being the departure point for the boat trips that are the best way of seeing the park.
Boat trips Exploring by boat takes you to the untouched

reaches of the park, where deep and dense tracts of forest are crisscrossed by narrow waterways inhabited by all manner of wildfowl. Prices vary according to the itinerary, starting at €7.20 for an hour-long excursion ("Rondvaarten"): check what's on offer – and make an advance booking – at Dordrecht VVV (see opposite) before you set out. If you fancy doing it under your own steam, there is boat and kayak rental here too.

ST ELIZABETH DAY FLOOD

On November 18, 1421, Zuid-Holland's sea defences gave way and the **St Elizabeth Day flood** formed what is now the **Hollands Diep** sea channel and the **Biesbosch** (Reed Forest). It was a disaster of major proportions, with seventy towns and villages destroyed and a death toll of around 100,000. The effect on the region's economy was catastrophic, too, with the fracturing of links between Zuid-Holland and Flanders accelerating the shift in commercial power to the north. Those villages that did survive took generations to recover, subjected as they were to raids by the wretched refugees of the flood.

The Kinderdijk

Some 12km north of Dordrecht, the **Kinderdijk** (Child's Dyke) sits at the end of a long drainage channel that feeds into the River Lek. Sixteenth-century legend suggests it takes its name from the time when a cradle, complete with cat and kicking baby, was found at the precise spot where the dyke had held during a particularly bad storm. Encompassing a mixture of symbols – rebirth, innocence and survival – the story encapsulates the determination with which the Dutch fought the floods for hundreds of years. Today, the Kinderdijk is famous for its picturesque, quintessentially Dutch **windmills**, all nineteen lining the main channel and its tributary beside the Molenkade for some 3km. Built around 1740 to drive water from the Alblasserwaard polders, the windmills are put into operation every Saturday afternoon in July and August, while one of the windmills is also open to visitors (April–Oct daily 9.30am–5.30pm; Nov–March Sat & Sun 11am–4pm; €6; ⍟kinderdijk.nl).

ARRIVAL AND DEPARTURE
KINDERDIJK

By bus Arriva bus runs here from Dordrecht station (bus #19: hourly; 45min); Utrecht (bus #90: every 30min; 1hr 30min); and Rotterdam's Lombardijen station (bus #190: every 20min; 40min).

By waterbus It is possible to travel here on the Waterbus passenger ferry from Rotterdam and Dordrecht (see p.175).

By bike Easily the best way to get to – and get around – the Kinderdijk is by bike; rent one at Dordrecht station, then follow signs to the Kinderdijk or rent one at the shop at Kinderdijk itself for €2.50 for two hours.

Utrecht and around

First impressions of **UTRECHT** are rarely positive: the mammoth shopping centre that encloses the city's train station is not encouraging and neither is its tangle of busy dual carriageways. But persevere: much of Utrecht's old centre has survived intact, with its network of canals, cobbled lanes and old gabled houses at their prettiest around the **Domkerk**, the city's cathedral. Domkerk apart, it's the general appearance and university atmosphere of the place that is its appeal rather than any specific sight – and indeed Utrecht's two key museums, the **Centraal** and the **Catharijne Convent**, both of which have an enjoyable collection of old Dutch paintings, are out of the immediate centre to the south. Utrecht was also the long-time home of the De Stijl luminary **Gerrit Rietveld**, whose assorted furniture decorates the Centraal Museum, which pays further tribute to the man by organizing bus trips to the house that Rietveld built – the **Rietveld Schröderhuis**. Further De Stijl treasures can be seen at the **Mondriaanhuis** in the nearby town of Amersfoort.

As you might expect of a university town, Utrecht has a vibrant café, bar and restaurant scene and the presence of students ensures that prices are kept down. One of the best times to visit is during the **Netherlands Film Festival**, ten days of cinematic inspiration held every year at the end of September (⍟filmfestival.nl).

Brief history

Founded by the **Romans** in the first century AD, Utrecht only came to prominence in the eighth century after the consecration of its first **bishop**. Thereafter, a long line of powerful bishops made Utrecht an independent city-state, albeit under the auspices of the German emperors, extending and consolidating their control over the surrounding region. In 1527, the bishop, seeing which way the historical wind was blowing, sold off his secular rights to the Habsburg Emperor Charles V, and shortly afterwards the town council enthusiastically joined the revolt against Spain. Indeed, the **Union of Utrecht**, the agreement that formalized the opposition to the Habsburgs, was signed here in 1579. The seventeenth century witnessed the foundation of **Utrecht University** and the eighteenth saw Utrecht pop up again as the place where the **Treaty of Utrecht** was signed in 1713, thereby concluding decades of dynastic feuding between Europe's rulers. Fifty years later,

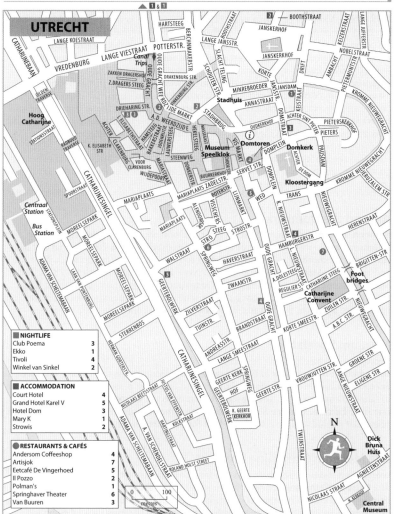

UTRECHT

■ **NIGHTLIFE**
Club Poema	3
Ekko	1
Tivoli	4
Winkel van Sinkel	2

■ **ACCOMMODATION**
Court Hotel	4
Grand Hotel Karel V	5
Hotel Dom	3
Mary K	1
Strowis	2

● **RESTAURANTS & CAFÉS**
Andersom Coffeeshop	4
Artisjok	7
Eetcafé De Vingerhoed	5
Il Pozzo	2
Polman's	1
Springhaver Theater	6
Van Buuren	3

it was also the source of one of James Boswell's harsher judgements: "I groaned with the idea of living all winter in so shocking a place," he moaned, which said more about his homesickness – he had just arrived here from England to study law – than it did about the city. Today, with a population of around a quarter of a million, Utrecht is one of the country's most important cities, its economy buoyed by light industry, academia and IT.

The Domtoren and Domkerk

The logical place to start a visit to the city is the **Domtoren**, Domplein 9, at over 112 meters the highest church bell tower in the country. It's one of the most beautiful, too, its soaring columns and arches rising to a delicate, octagonal lantern, which was added in 1380 some sixty years after the rest of the tower was completed. Beginning at the adjacent VVV, hour-long guided tours (April–Sept hourly between 11am–4pm;

Oct–March Mon–Fri & Sun at noon, 2pm and 4pm, Sat hourly between 11am–4pm; €9; ⓦ domtoren.nl) take you unnervingly near to the top, from where on a clear day you can see Rotterdam and Amsterdam. Below, the empty space on the east side of the tower was where the nave of the cathedral stood until a storm brought it tumbling down in 1674. However, the monumental transepts and chancel survived and these comprise today's **Domkerk**, Achter de Dom 1 (May–Sept Mon–Fri 10am–5pm, Sat 10am–3.30pm & Sun 2–4pm; Oct–April Mon–Fri 11am–4pm, Sat 10am–3.30pm & Sun 2–4pm; free; ⓦ domkerk.nl), which is distinguished by its strong Gothic lines and funerary monuments. Among the latter, the high point is the exquisitely carved marble sarcophagus of Admiral Willem Joseph van Gendt, who came a cropper at the long-forgotten sea battle of Solebay in 1672.

Next to the Domkerk stands the fifteenth-century **Kloostergang** (cloisters), whose good-looking gables sport low reliefs illustrating the life of the city's fourth-century patron saint, St Martin of Tours.

Around the Domkerk

Kromme Nieuwegracht, just to the east of the Domkerk, is one of the city's most delightful streets, its medley of fine old buildings overlooking a slender canal and its string of mini-footbridges. Follow the canal round and eventually you reach Jansstraat, and the nearby **Stadhuis**, whose grandiose, Neoclassical facade dates from 1826. The Stadhuis stands on a bend of the pretty **Oude Gracht**, where, most unusually, a long series of brick cellars, which once served as warehouses and are now bars, cafés and restaurants, are down by the canal and the street level is one storey up.

Museum Speelklok

Steenweg 6 • Tues–Sun 10am–5pm • €9.50 • ⓦ museumspeelklok.nl

Right in the town centre, a 3min walk west of the Domtoren is the unusual **Museum Speelklok**, a collection of fairground organs and ingenious musical boxes worth an hour of (almost) anyone's time. The museum is housed in the **Buurkerk**, once the home of one sister Bertken, who was so ashamed of being the illegitimate daughter of a cathedral priest that she hid away in a small cell here for 57 years, until her death in 1514.

The Museum Catharijne Convent

Lange Nieuwstraat 38 • Tues–Fri 10am–5pm, Sat & Sun 11am–5pm • €12 • ⓦ catharijneconvent.nl

The **Museum Catharijne Convent**, 500m south of the Domtoren, displays a mass of paintings and church ornaments dating from the ninth century onwards, all superbly exhibited in an imaginatively recycled former convent. The museum's labelling is almost exclusively in Dutch, though there is an audioguide available in English. A visit begins in the basement **Schatkamer** (Treasury), which is stuffed with gold and silver chalices, reliquaries, communion cups, ecclesiastical rings, vestments and crucifixes. The next floor up (Floor 0) is divided into two main sections – pre-Reformation and post-Reformation – and both hold statues of the saints and apostles, a battery of retables and several striking paintings, most memorably a *Man of Sorrows* by Geertgen tot Sint Jans. The top floor – Floor 1 – is devoted to temporary displays.

Centraal Museum

Nicolaaskerkhof 10 • Tues–Sun 11am–5pm • €9 including Dick Bruna Huis; €12 including Dick Bruna Huis and Rietveld Schröderhuis (see opposite) • ⓦ centraalmuseum.nl

The **Centraal Museum**, about 500m south of the Catharijne Convent along Lange Nieuwestraat, has an extensive fine art collection with the paintings of local sixteenth- and seventeenth-century artists playing a star role. One of the most interesting of these painters is **Jan van Scorel** (1495–1562), who lived in Utrecht before and after he visited Rome, from where he brought the influence of the Renaissance back home to his fellow painters. A prime example of this mix of native Dutch observation and Renaissance style is Scorel's vivid *Portraits of Twelve Members of Utrecht's Jerusalem Brotherhood*, in which, incidentally, the fifth figure from the right is the artist himself. Scorel is also thought to have made a trip to Jerusalem sometime in the 1520s and this may well account for his unusually accurate drawing of the city in the Lokhorst Triptych: *Christ's Entry into Jerusalem*.

The Utrecht School

A later generation of city painters known as the **Utrecht School** fell under the influence of Italian art in general and Caravaggio (1572–1610) in particular. One of the group's leading practitioners was **Gerrit van Honthorst** (1590–1656), whose *Procuress* adapted Caravaggio's chiaroscuro technique to a genre subject and also developed an erotic content that would itself influence later genre painters like Jan Steen and Gerrit Dou. Even more skilled and realistic is **Hendrick Terbrugghen**'s (1588–1629) *The Calling of St Matthew*, a beautiful balance of gestures dramatizing Christ summoning the tax collector to become one of the twelve disciples.

Gerrit Rietveld

Gerrit Rietveld (1888–1964), the celebrated De Stijl architect and designer, lived and worked in Utrecht, and the museum has a fine collection of his furniture, especially the brightly coloured geometrical chairs for which he is perhaps best known. The chairs are quite simply beautiful, but although part of the De Stijl philosophy stressed the need for universality, they are undoubtedly better to look at than to actually sit on.

Dick Bruna Huis

Agnietenstraat 2 • Tues–Sun 11am–5pm • €9 including Centraal Museum • ⓦ dickbrunahuis.com

A few metres from the Centraal Museum, the **Dick Bruna Huis** celebrates the life and work of the Dutch graphic designer, illustrator and writer Dick Bruna (b.1927), who has established an international reputation for his children's picture-books in general and for his star creation, *Miffy*, in particular. Created in 1955, the books have been translated into over fifty languages, making Miffy one of the world's best-known rabbits. The books' appeal lies in the simplicity of the illustrations, using primary colours and simple lines. Mainly aimed at children, the museum displays an ample collection of Bruna's work, and often puts on activities and workshops for kids.

The Rietveld Schröderhuis

Prins Hendriklaan 50 • Fixed entry times: Wed–Sun at 11am, noon, 2pm, 3pm & 4pm • €12 including audio tour plus entry to the Centraal Museum and Dick Bruna Huis • Reservations recommended on ☎ 030 236 2310, ⓦ rietveldschroderhuis.nl

A twenty-minute walk east of the Centraal Museum, the **Rietveld Schröderhuis** was designed and built by Rietveld in 1924 for one Truus Schröder and her family. It's hailed as one of the most influential pieces of modern architecture in Europe, demonstrating the organic union of lines and rectangles that was the hallmark of the De Stijl movement. The ground floor is the most conventional part of the building, since its design had to meet the rigours of the building licence; however, Rietveld was able to let his imagination run riot with the top floor living space, creating a flexible environment where only the outer walls are solid – indeed the entire top floor can be subdivided in any way, simply by sliding the modular walls. The admission fee also covers the low-slung modernist **terrace** Rietveld designed nearby at Erasmuslaan 5–11.

The Mondriaanhuis

Kortegracht 11, Amersfoort • Tues–Fri 11am–5pm, Sat & Sun noon–5pm • €6 • ⓦ mondriaanhuis.nl • It's fifteen minutes by train from Utrecht to Amersfoort: the museum is located on the south side of Amersfoort, about 1.2km east of the train station

The **Mondriaanhuis** comprises the house where the artist **Piet Mondrian** (1872–1944), the leading light of De Stijl, was born and raised, along with the adjacent school where his father was the head teacher. The museum holds an enjoyable retrospective of the artist's life and work, and although the exhibits are regularly rotated, you can expect to see prime examples of the geometric, non-representational paintings for which Mondrian was internationally famous. There is also an interesting reconstruction of the five-sided studio Mondrian had built for himself in Paris in the 1920s.

ARRIVAL AND INFORMATION
UTRECHT

By train Utrecht's train and bus stations are both enmeshed within the sprawling and extremely ugly Hoog Catharijne shopping centre, on the western edge of the city centre. From Utrecht regular trains run to Amersfoort (every 15min; 15min); Amsterdam CS (every 15min; 30min); Arnhem (every 30min; 40min); Den Haag (every 15min; 40min); Leeuwarden (hourly; 2hr); Rotterdam (every 15min; 45min); and Zwolle (every 30min; 1hr).

By bus The only bus you're likely to use is bus #90 between Utrecht and Kinderdijk (every 30min; 1hr 30min).
Tourist office The VVV is beside the Domtoren (cathedral tower) at Domplein 9 (Mon & Sun noon–5pm, Tues–Sat 10am–5pm, ☎ 0900 128 8732, ⓦ bezoek-utrecht.nl). It has a range of information on the city and its surroundings, sells city maps and operates an accommodation booking service.

GETTING AROUND

Bike rental The best way to explore the city centre is on foot, but bikes can be rented from the train station for around €7.50 a day.
Canal trips Throughout the summer, Schuttevaer (☎ 030

272 0111, ⓦ schuttevaer.com) runs enjoyable, hour-long canal trips (daily 11am–5pm; €9.20) around the centre of the city. Departures are from Oude Gracht, just south of the Lange Viestraat/Potterstraat junction.

ACCOMMODATION

As you might expect of a big city, Utrecht has a battery of chain hotels, some in big modern blocks, but one or two are rather more distinctive and a couple of recent additions to the hotel scene have improved the city's somewhat dull image.

HOTELS
Court Hotel Korte Nieuwstraat 14 ☎ 030 233 0033, ⓦ courthotel.nl. The city's former courthouse has been transformed into an incredibly stylish hotel with 27 well-appointed rooms, all decorated in warm purple shades and with pictures of famous "inmates" on the walls. Also has a busy restaurant, serving excellent seafood such as *fruits de mer* and a scrumptious crab platter, and there's a large terrace in summer. **€135**
Hotel Dom Domstraat 4 ☎ 030 232 4244, ⓦ hoteldom .nl. Newly opened, this luxurious and happening hotel is located above a trendy cocktail bar and restaurant, and offers the city's best views of the Dom tower from its eleven suites. Regular DJs at weekends make this the place to be for style-conscious visitors, while lonely sleepers can even rent a goldfish for some company. **€170** at weekends, **€190** on weekdays
★ **Grand Hotel Karel V** Geertebolwerk 1 ☎ 030 233 7555, ⓦ karelv.nl. This delightful five-star hotel occupies the site of what was, in medieval times, the headquarters of the Knights of the Teutonic Order. The main building has been cleverly modernized and there's a contemporary wing

– the Roman wing – too; in between are attractive gardens. All the rooms are well appointed and extremely comfortable, but the mostly split-level suites in the Roman wing are somewhat larger and more luxurious. **€135**
Mary K Oudegracht 25 ☎ 030 230 4888, ⓦ marykhotel .com. A funky little art hotel located in an eighteenth-century canal house, with only nine rooms, all decorated in different styles. The concept is simple, making guests feel like they're staying with relatives, and being part of a cosy household. The hotel is eco-friendly, so breakfast, coffee and bed linen are all organic. **€145**

HOSTEL
Strowis Boothstraat 8 ☎ 030 238 0280, ⓦ strowis.nl. This pleasant hostel, in a seventeenth-century townhouse, has a good range of facilities including a small library, bike rental, a self-catering kitchen and free internet access. The good-value bedrooms, which range from single rooms to 14-bed dorms, are well kept and painted in cheerful colours. The *Strowis* is situated in the old centre near St Janskerk, 1km east of the station. Dorm beds **€18**, doubles **€65**

EATING AND DRINKING

The old centre of Utrecht literally heaves with inexpensive cafés, bars and restaurants, especially along the Oudegracht canal. There are several pricier/smarter restaurants too, but these are very much in the minority and for the most part lack the atmosphere of their more informal competitors.

Andersom Vismarkt 23 ☎ 030 232 8665. One of the few cannabis coffeeshops in Utrecht that is fairly central – most of the thirty or so others are located out of the centre. Mon–Sat 10am–11pm, Sun noon–11pm.

Artisjok Nieuwegracht 33 ☎ 030 231 7494, ⓦ deartisjok.nl. Cosy little place with an imaginative menu featuring variations on a Dutch theme. Main courses such as duck breast in Japanese herbs or monkfish with cauliflower hover around €20. In a nice location on the canal. Daily 5–10pm.

Eetcafé De Vingerhoed Donkere Gaard 11 ☎ 030 231 9659, ⓦ eetcafedevingerhoed.nl. Near the Domtoren, this bustling, brown eetcafé offers a wide range of Dutch dishes, not haute cuisine perhaps but certainly filling. Daily specials cost €13.50, regular main courses such as lamb chops or steak go for around €16. Mon–Fri 5–9.30pm.

Il Pozzo Oude Gracht 136 ☎ 030 231 1861, ⓦ ilpozzo .nl. Fantastically popular Italian place with a large canal-side terrace. Covers all the Italian classics, as well as serving fresh bread from its own bakery. Prices start at €9.50 for a simple Margherita pizza to €14.75 for a pizza with Parma ham. Tues–Sun 5–10pm.

Polman's Keistraat 2 ☎ 030 231 3368, ⓦ www .polmanshuis.nl. Arguably the pick of Utrecht's smarter restaurants, *Polman's* occupies a large, rather grand nineteenth-century building – and has its waiters in bow ties to match. The menu mixes Italian and Dutch dishes and mains average €25. Mon–Sat noon–10pm.

Springhaver Theater Springweg 50 ☎ 030 231 3789, ⓦ springhaver.nl. Groovy, pint-sized cinema-cum-bar-cum-restaurant that attracts an interesting, arty crew. The food isn't brilliant, but the atmosphere is – and there's a pavement terrace too. Sun–Wed 5–9pm, Thurs–Sat 5–9.30pm.

Van Buuren Drieharingstraat 16 ☎ 030 321 7503, ⓦ vanbuurenutrecht.nl. Popular restaurant where you can order half-portions of two different main courses (labelled "samsam" on the menu), to give you a chance to sample more dishes such as tiger prawn with coriander pasta or rack of lamb with port sauce. Usually jam-packed so book ahead. Daily 4–10pm.

NIGHTLIFE

Club Poema Drieharingstraat 22 ☎ 030 232 2673, ⓦ clubpoema.nl. For a city not known for its heavy clubbing, *Poema* might be your only bet for some serious dancing with well-known Dutch DJs spinning the wheel in an up-to-the-minute setting. Usually Thurs–Sat 11pm–3/4am, but check the website.

Ekko Bemuurde Weerd WZ 3 ☎ 030 231 7457, ⓦ ekko .nl. Alternative rock and dance venue with live performances by international artists and DJs. The café serves a well-priced veggie three-course meal for €12.50 on Thurs & Fri. Check the website for the schedule of gigs.

Tivoli Oude Gracht 245 and Helling 7 ☎ 030 231 1491, ⓦ tivoli.nl. The city's main underground music venue is in two locations – one not so conveniently located out of the city centre, the other near the Catharijne Convent. It hosts many international artists as well as regular dance nights such as Nineties alternative and 40up. Check the website for the schedule of gigs.

Winkel van Sinkel Oude Gracht 158 ☎ 030 230 3030, ⓦ dewinkelvansinkel.nl. One of the city's best and most distinctive bars with a spacious interior, whose gallery and mirrors date from its previous incarnation as a ballroom. There's a canal-side terrace too and the occasional club night hosted by, for example, Hed Kandi or Latin Lover. Open daily for coffee and drinks 11am–midnight/1am: check the website for details of club nights and events.

The North and the Frisian Islands

HINDELOOPEN, FRIESLAND

The North and the Frisian Islands

Until the early twentieth century, the north of the Netherlands was a remote area, a distinct region of small provincial towns far removed from the mainstream life of the Randstad. Yet, in 1932, the opening of the Afsluitdijk, a 30-kilometre-long sea wall bridging the mouth of the Zuider Zee, changed the orientation of the country once and for all: the Zuider Zee, once a corridor for great trading ships, became the freshwater IJsselmeer and the cultural gap between the north and west narrowed almost immediately.

One of the three northern provinces, **Friesland**, is a deservedly popular tourist stopover, with its cluster of dune-swept **islands**, a likeable capital in Leeuwarden, and a chain of eleven immaculate, history-steeped "cities" (villages really), each with a distinct charm: **Harlingen** is noted for its splendid merchant houses; **Hindeloopen**, with its cobbled streets and pin-neat canals, encapsulates the antique prettiness of the region;while **Makkum** was a centre of tile manufacture and is still known for ceramics and its role as a sailing centre. As for the islands, each is barely more than an elongated sandbank, parts of which can be reached by indulging in **wadlopen**, hearty walks along (or ankle-deep in) the mud flats that flank the islands to the south. In the north stretches kilometre after kilometre of hourglass-fine sandy beach and a network of cycleways. Like much of the Netherlands, the scenery of the mainland is predominantly green, bisected by canals and dotted with black-and-white cattle – Friesians, of course – and pitch-black Frisian horses. Breaking the pancake-flat monotony of the landscape, sleek wind turbines make the most of the strong westerlies, a modern counterpart to the last working windmills in the area.

East of Friesland, the province of **Groningen** has comparatively few attractions, but the university town of Groningen more than makes up for this with a vibrant ambience, contemporary fashions, range of affordable bars and restaurants, a growing international performance-art festival and the best nightlife in the region. It's also home to the **Groninger Museum**, a striking and controversial vision of urban architecture and art, and a definite highlight of the region.

South of Groningen lies **Drenthe**, little more than a barren moor for much of its history. During the nineteenth century, the face of the province was changed by the founding of peat colonies, whose labourers drained the land and dug the peat to expose the subsoil below. As a result, parts of Drenthe are given over to prosperous farmland, with agriculture the dominant industry. Sparsely . and the least visited of the Dutch provinces, Drenthe is now popular with home-grown tourists, who are drawn by its quiet natural beauty, swathes of wood, wide cycling paths and abundant walking trails, although many come here to visit Drenthe's most original feature – its *hunebeds*, or megalithic tombs.

SNEEK WEEK REGATTA

Highlights

❶ The Eleven Towns Touring this historic chain of towns in southwest Friesland is really one of the best introductions to the region – and overall they are as enticing a group of places as you'll find anywhere in the country. **See p.205**

❷ Sneek Week This prosperous shipbuilding town of old is now famous as the location of the annual Sneek Week sailing regatta, held every August. **See p.205**

❸ The Frisian Islands The most popular spots can be busy in high summer, but for much of the year these offshore dunescapes can feel as remote and unspoilt as anywhere in Europe. **See p.214**

❹ Groningen Dynamic university town in the far north, with a great nightlife and the memorable Groninger Museum of art and culture. **See p.221**

❺ Wadlopen The best way to experience the northern landscapes is to copy the Dutch and take a guide for *wadlopen* – mud-flat walking. **See p.221**

HIGHLIGHTS ARE MARKED ON THE MAP ON P.196

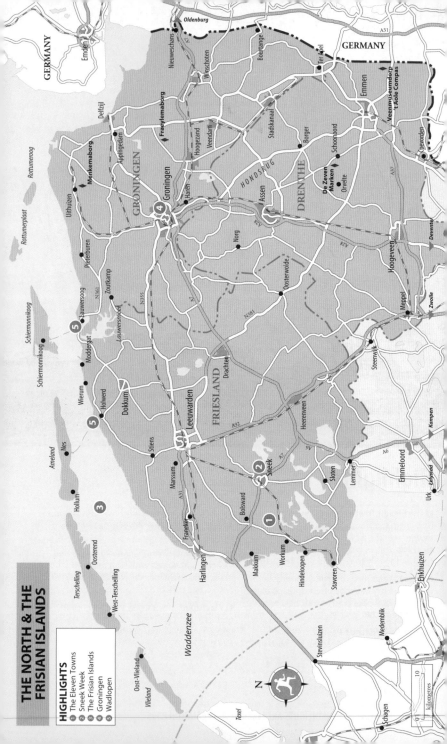

THE NORTH & THE FRISIAN ISLANDS

HIGHLIGHTS

1. The Eleven Towns
2. Sneek Week
3. The Frisian Islands
4. Groningen
5. Wadlopen

FRIESLAND: A LAND APART?

A region that prospered during the sixteenth-century heyday of the Zuider Zee trade, **Friesland** is focused around eleven historic cities and seven lakes, the latter symbolized by the seven red hearts on the region's flag, which proudly flutters in many a back garden. Friesland once occupied a much larger chunk of the north and, in the eighth century, Charlemagne recognized three parts: West Frisia, equivalent to today's West Friesland, across the IJsselmeer; Central Frisia, today's Friesland; and East Frisia, now Groningen province. From earliest times, much of the region was prey to inundation by the sea and the inhabitants built their settlements on artificial mounds (*terpen*) in a frequently forlorn attempt to escape the watery depths. It was a tough existence, but over the centuries the Frisians finessed their skills, extending their settlements by means of a complex network of dykes. You can still see what's left of some of the mounds around the area, though in large settlements they're mostly obscured. Always a maverick among Dutch provinces, the area that is now Friesland proper remained independent of the rest of Holland until it was absorbed into the Habsburg Empire by Charles V in 1523.

Since the construction of the Afsluitdijk, Friesland has relied on holidaymakers drawn to its rich history, picturesque lakes and immaculate villages to replace the trading routes and fishing industries of yesteryear. Grand old farmhouses define the region: their thatched roofs slope almost to the ground and are crowned with *úleboerden,* white gables in the form of a double swan once used as a deterrent to evil spirits. Boating is one way of getting around and Friesland is also an ideal province to visit by bicycle. The best loop, which takes in all of the Eleven Towns, follows the 220-kilometre-long route of the **Elfstedentocht**, a marathon ice-skating race held during winters cold enough for the canals to freeze over (see p.205). Most tourist offices stock maps and guides for cycling, in-line skating, driving or sailing the route all year round.

Finally, the Frisians have several unusual **sports and traditions** that can still raise eyebrows in the rest of the country. Using a large pole to jump over wet obstacles was once a necessity in the Frisian countryside, but the Frisians turned it into a sport: **fierljeppen**. Today Frisian and Dutch pole jumpers compete during the annual Frisian championships held in Winsum, on the second Saturday of August.

Skûtjesilen, a fourteen-day sailing race held throughout Friesland in July or August, is another regional oddity. *Skûtjes* are large cargo vessels, but they went out of use after World War II and are now only used for contests and recreational purposes: the tourist office in Sneek can give information on where to see the races. Last but not least is **kaatsen**, a Frisian version of tennis, with over 2000 contests held every year. Instead of a racket a *kaatser* uses a handmade glove to hit the handmade ball; a team of *kaatsers* comprises three players. There's a small museum devoted to *kaatsen* in Franeker, p.202.

Leeuwarden

An old market town lying at the heart of an agricultural district, **LEEUWARDEN** was formed from the amalgamation of three *terpen* that originally stood on an expanse of water known as the Middelzee. Later it was the residence of the powerful Frisian Stadholders, who vied with those of Holland for control of the United Provinces. These days it's Friesland's capital, a university town with a laidback provincial air, its centre a haphazard blend of modern glass and traditional gabled terraces overlooking canals. It perhaps lacks the concentrated historic charm of many other Dutch towns, but it's an amiable old place, with a couple of decent museums. Its most appealing feature is its compact and eminently strollable old centre, almost entirely surrounded and dissected by water. Leeuwarden is a real student town too, so it has a bit of life about it, not to mention a decent array of good-value places to eat and drink.

Waagplein and around

The southern part of Leeuwarden's centre, near the station, is an indeterminate and careless mixture of the old and new, high-rise blocks and shopping centres lining

LEEUWARDEN

RESTAURANTS & CAFÉS
Eetcafé Spinoza	1
Eindeloos	3
Humphrey's	5
De Kleine Wereld	4
De Lachende Koe	2
De Vliegende Hollander	6

BARS
Fire Palace	2
De Oranje Bierhuis	1
Paddy O'Ryan	3

ACCOMMODATION
Hotel 't Anker	1
Grand Hotel Post Plaza	3
Oranje Leeuwarden	4
Stadhouderlijk Hof	2

Wirdumerdijk as far as the central **Waagplein**, a long, narrowing open space cut by a canal and flanked by cafés and large department stores. There's a Friday and Saturday market here, and on modern **Wilhelminaplein**, just to the south, home to the brand-new **Zaailand** shopping and cultural complex. The **Waag** itself, now converted into a restaurant, dates from 1598. Walking west, **Nieuwestad** is Leeuwarden's main shopping street, from where Kleine Kerkstraat leads to the featureless **Oldehoofster Kerkhof**, a large and recently refurbished square near the old city walls, at the end of which stands the precariously leaning **Oldehove**. Something of a symbol for the city, this is part of a cathedral started in 1529 but never finished because of subsidence, the end result being a lugubrious mass of disproportion that defies all laws of gravity and geometry. To the right stands a statue of the Frisian politician and trade unionist P.J. Troelstra, who looks on impassively, no doubt admonishing the city fathers for their choice of architects. For a better view, climb the 40-metre-high tower (May–Sept Tues–Sat 1–5pm; €3).

Boomsma Beerenburg

Bagijnestraat 42a • Tues–Sat 10am–5pm • Free • ⓦ boomsma.net

Tucked away near the Princessehof Museum, the delightful small **Boomsma Beerenburg** museum is housed in the old distillery where they used to make the herb-flavoured gin that is a regional speciality. The distillery is still owned by the original family, although the liquor is made in a modern building on the outskirts of town these days. You can taste the gin, which includes a number of other more conventional *jenevers*, in the *proeflokaal* out the back, and if you like it buy a bottle from the museum shop.

Het Princessehof

Grote Kerkstraat 11 • Tues–Sun 11am–5pm • €8, joint ticket with the Fries Museum €10 • ⓦ princessehof.nl

Just off Oldehoofster Kerkhof, following the line of the track that once connected two of Leeuwarden's original *terpen*, Oldehove and Nijehove, **Het Princessehof** was the birthplace of the graphic artist M.C. Escher. Dating from 1650, the house is now home to Leeuwarden's destination **museum of ceramics**, with an outstanding collection. On the ground floor, you can see the largest collection of tiles in the world, with good examples of all the classic designs – soldiers, flowers, ships and so forth – framed by uncomplicated borders, and a fine array of European ceramics: highlights here include earthenware and majolica from Spain, Delftware naturally, lots of fine porcelain, the creamware of Josiah Wedgwood in Staffordshire, incorporating a nice collection of teapots, and a spectacular collection of Art Nouveau pieces.

On the first floor, the collection of **Chinese**, **Japanese** and **Vietnamese ceramics** is similarly impressive, devoted to the development of **Chinese porcelain** from prehistory to the Ming Dynasty (1368–1644), and from the Ming to the nineteenth century, with powerful open-mouthed dragons, billowing clouds and sharply drawn plant tendrils. Next door is a room of **Middle Eastern ceramics**, mostly tiles from Iran, Central Asia, Syria and Turkey, beautiful pieces dating from the eleventh to sixteenth centuries.

Hofplein

The town's most central square, **Hofplein**, lies just a short stroll from the Princessehof museum. This enclosed open space is home to the sedate eighteenth-century Stadhuis, topped with a clock tower and, opposite, the **Stadhouderlijk Hof**, the original seat of the Frisian Stadholders, now a hotel.

The Grote Kerk

Bredeplaats 4 • June Sat 11am–4pm; July & Aug Tues–Thurs & Sat 11am–4pm, Fri 1–4pm • Free

Though restored in recent years, the **Grote** or **Jacobijner Kerk** remains an unremarkable Gothic construction. A victim of subsidence, the whole place tilts slightly toward the newer south aisle, where you can see some fragmentary remnants of sixteenth-century frescoes and a Muller organ dating back to 1727. In front of the church, a modernistic monument remembers Leeuwarden's wartime Jewish community – deliberately placed in front of a building that was until 1943 the Jewish School, it's based on the classroom registers of the previous year.

The Fries Museum

Zaailand • Tues–Sun 11am–5pm • €6 • ⓦ friesmuseum.nl

As you might expect from the country's proudest and most distinct region, the **Fries Museum** is one of the Netherlands' best regional museums, housed in a spectacular new building on Wilhelminaplein. Founded by a society that was established in the nineteenth century to develop interest in the language and history of Friesland, the museum traces the development of Frisian culture from prehistoric times up until the present day. It also incorporates the Frisian Resistance Museum, with its story of the local resistance to Nazi occupation.

MATA HARI

Leeuwarden's most famous daughter, **Mata Hari** (1876–1917) was born Gertrud Zelle. Hari became a renowned "exotic" dancer after an early but unsuccessful marriage to a Dutch army officer. Although the Netherlands was neutral during World War I, Hari seems to have accepted a German bribe to spy for the kaiser. The French intelligence service soon got wind of the bribe – partly because she was also supposed to be working for them – and she was subsequently arrested, tried and shot. What she actually did remains a matter of some debate, but in retrospect it seems likely that she acted as a double agent, gathering information for the Allies while giving snippets to the Germans. Whatever the truth, there's a small statue commemorating her at her partially clad best on Over de Kelders, erected on the hundredth anniversary of her birth in 1976.

Among the museum's many highlights is an extensive collection of **silver** – silversmithing was a flourishing Frisian industry throughout the seventeenth and eighteenth centuries, with most of the work being commissioned by the local gentry, who were influenced by the fashions of the Frisian Stadholder and his court. There's also a chronological exhibition tracing the early days of the **Nazi invasion**, through collaboration and resistance and on to the Allied liberation. A range of photographs, Nazi militaria, Allied propaganda and moving personal stories illustrate the text, but the emphasis is very much on the local struggle rather than the general war effort. There are also rooms devoted to the painted **furniture** of Hindeloopen: rich, gaudy and intense, patterned with tendrils and flowers on a red, green or white background.

Popta Slot

Slotleane 1, Marssum • Guided tour only: April–June & Sept & Oct Mon–Sat by appointment; July & Aug Mon–Sat hourly 11am–4pm • €6 • ⓦ poptaslot.nl • Bus #71 leaves hourly from Leeuwarden station

On the western outskirts of Leeuwarden, in the tiny village of Marssum, **Popta Slot** is a trim, onion-domed eighteenth-century manor house that sits prettily behind its ancient moat. There are fruit trees and formal gardens outside, while inside the period rooms are furnished in the style of the local gentry. Dr Popta was an affluent lawyer who spent some of his excess wealth on the neighbouring **Popta Gasthuis**, neat almshouses cloistered behind an elaborate portal of 1712.

ARRIVAL AND INFORMATION

LEEUWARDEN

By train Leeuwarden's train and bus stations virtually adjoin each other, five minutes' walk south of the town centre, with regular services to Amsterdam, usually via Zwolle, (every 30min; 2hr 30min); Franeker (every 30min; 15min); Groningen (every 30min; 1hr); Harlingen (every 30min; 25min); Hindeloopen (hourly; 45min); Sneek (every 30min; 20min); and Stavoren, for Enkhuizen ferries (hourly; 55min).

By bus Buses leave from the bus station just outside the train station, and there are regular connections to Dokkum (30–50min); Holwerd (bus #66: hourly; 50min) for boats to

Ameland, and Lauwersoog (bus #50: 6 daily; 1hr 30min) for boats to Schiermonnikoog.

Tourist office The VVV is on the ground floor of the Achmea Tower, two minutes' walk from the train station at Sophialaan 4 (Mon noon–5.30pm, Tues–Fri 9.30am–5.30pm, Sat 10am–3pm; June–Aug Sat until 4pm; ☎ 0900 202 4060, ⓦ vvvleeuwarden.nl). They publish a map detailing walking tours of the centre and have a short list of private rooms that covers the whole of Friesland; they also dispense information on guided boat trips to the Frisian lakes and canal trips through Leeuwarden.

ACCOMMODATION

HOTELS

Hotel 't Anker Eewal 69–75 ☎ 058 212 5216, ⓦ hotelhetanker.nl. This popular and central hotel has a cosy downstairs bar and is one of the cheapest options in the centre of town. Its 23 rooms are nothing special

but they're pretty cheap. And there's free wi-fi too. **€69.50**

Grand Hotel Post Plaza Tweebaksmarkt 25–27 ☎ 058 215 9317, ⓦ post-plaza.nl. Shoehorned behind an eighteenth-century facade, this boutique hotel, with spruce rooms finished in a contemporary style, all greys and blacks, is probably Leeuwarden's best place to stay. The rooms are comfortable, and it has a restaurant and a downstairs bar that's a bit of a hub on busy nights. **€79**

Oranje Leeuwarden Stationsweg 4 ☏058 212 6241, ⊚hampshire-hotels.com. A neat and trim four-star chain hotel right in front of the train station with spacious and comfortable rooms, fairly recently refurbished. It won't win any prizes for originality but the service is great and there's free wi-fi throughout, plus a large bar and restaurant downstairs. Excellent value. **€85**

Stadhouderlijk Hof Hofplein 29 ☏0347 750 424, ⊚hotelstadhouderlijkhof.nl. This place enjoys the best location in town and is housed in a former palace with a beautiful inner courtyard, which makes it all the more of a shame that the interior is so weary-looking, with drab public areas and rooms that are urgently in need of updating. The good news is that its run-down condition has been priced into the rates. **€59.50**

CAMPSITE

De Kleine Wielen De Groene Ster 14 ☏0511 431 660, ⊚dekleinewielen.nl. About 5km west of Leeuwarden, this is a really nice campsite, beautifully situated by a lake with a shop, bar and snack bar, and with plenty of watersports opportunities nearby. It costs €8 for a tent and one person, and €4 for each extra adult. Electricity hook-ups available for an additional €4. Take bus #10 or #51 from the train station. April–Sept. **€12**

EATING AND DRINKING

RESTAURANTS AND CAFÉS

Eetcafé Spinoza Eewal 50–52 ☏058 212 9393, ⊚eetcafespinoza.nl. One of the most popular places to eat in Leeuwarden, this is a youthful, reasonably priced restaurant with a wide-ranging menu of mainly hearty Dutch food cunningly disguised by the names of philosophers. Main courses run around €15–20 but they always have a daily special for €7.95 and there's a good choice of veggie dishes too. The hidden inner courtyard is a well-kept treasure. Daily 10am–10pm.

Eindeloos Korfmakersstraat17 ☏058 213 0835. You get what you're given in this sleek, modern restaurant, with changing set menus featuring things like hake ceviche and Friesland lamb. Great food, always seasonal, usually locally sourced, with none of the stress of having to make up your mind – though probably not a place to come if you're in a hurry. Menus start at €30 for three courses. Wed–Fri lunch noon–3pm, Tues–Sat dinner 6–10pm.

Humphrey's Nieuwestad 91 ☏058 216 4936. Although part of a chain, *Humphrey's* offers great value for money in a cosy atmosphere to enjoy steaks, mixed grills or veggie options like spinach and ricotta lasagne. Three-course menus go for €23.90, and there are usually around eight choices for each course. Daily 5–10pm.

De Kleine Wereld Weerd 18 ☏058 216 5151, ⊚dekleinewereld.eu. The place to come if you're arguing about what to eat, with a round-the-world-in-eighty-courses menu that serves up everything from Moroccan tagines to Yankee burgers, Argentine grills and veggie Greek moussaka – it's affordably priced, with most mains €12–15. Housed in a grand old mansion, it's a nice place for a drink too, with great music and lovely bar snacks, and a courtyard for summer eating and drinking. Tues–Thurs 5–10pm, Fri 4–10pm, Sat 11am–10pm; Sun & Mon closed.

De Lachende Koe Grote Hoogstraat 16–20 ☏058 215 8245, ⊚dekoeleeuwarden.nl. A long-time favourite among students, this youthful and unpretentious place has a menu that caters for everyone except die-hard foodies, with all the Dutch staples – satay royal, spare ribs, schnitzels, a decent mixed grill and a couple of veggie and fish dishes, all for €15–18. There's a kids' menu too that doesn't try too hard to convert your little ones to healthy eating. Great outside yard in summer. Tues–Sun 5–10pm.

De Vliegende Hollander Berlikumermarkt 9 ☏058 212 1717, ⊚vliegendehollanderlwd.nl. Big place with wooden floorboards and a relaxed eetcafé ambience, a good option for both lunch or dinner, or just a drink, which you can sip on the small terrace that opens on to the secluded alley behind. Decent lunch specials for €8.50, otherwise mains go for €15–20. Mon–Thurs 4–11.30pm, Fri & Sat 11am–11.30pm.

BARS

Fire Palace Nieuwestad 47–49 ☏058 213 9900, ⊚fire-palace.nl. Housed in a former police station, this comfortable bar has wooden floors and cosy chairs out in the back room and a front terrace that overlooks the canal. There's a laidback vibe during the day that perks up later with DJs that spin sounds at its next-door venue. Music venue Thurs & Fri 11pm–4.30am, Sat 11pm–5.30am; bar daily 10am–1am.

★**De Oranje Bierhuis** Auckamastraatje 2 ☏058 213 0131. Right on the Stadhuis square, this is the old centre's oldest bar, and a thoroughly welcoming place it is too, with a little corner bar and a mixed crowd who have been making themselves at home in this classic brown café for years. Mon–Wed 4pm–midnight, Thurs–Sun 4pm–1am.

Paddy O'Ryan Tweebaksmarkt 49 ☏058 212 2047, ⊚paddy.nl. OK, it's an Irish bar, but you wouldn't especially know it apart from some of the beers on tap and the fact that it serves Irish Stew alongside its other pubby staples. Its grandish main room is very convivial, and it's got a little glassed-in booth for those dying for a cigarette. Its excellent-value mains go for €12–15, mainly consisting of burgers, fish and chips, steaks and the like. All good, and there's live music on Wed nights, pub quizzes on Mon. Mon–Fri 11.30am–1am, Sat noon–2am, Sun noon–1am.

DIRECTORY

Bike rental You can rent bikes from the Fietspoint next to the train station at Stationsweg 3 (☎058 213 9800, ⓦfietspointleeuwarden.nl) from €7.50 a day.
Books Van der Velde, Nieuwestad 57–59 (☎058 213 2360), has a good stock of English-language titles.
Car rental AutoRent, Celsiusweg 1b (☎085 273 3631, ⓦautorent.nl).

Police Holstmeerweg 3 ☎0900 8844.
Post office Oldehoofster Kerkhof 4 (Mon–Fri 7.30am–6pm, Thurs 7.30am–8pm, Sat 7.30am–1.30pm).
Taxi Taxi Leeuwarden (☎0645 606 616. ⓦtaxi-leeuwarden.nl).

Franeker

FRANEKER, about 17km west of Leeuwarden, was the cultural hub of the northern Netherlands until Napoleon closed its university in 1810. Today, it's a quiet country town with a spruce old centre, the highlight of which is an intriguing eighteenth-century planetarium.

Voorstraat and around

All Franeker's key sights are beside or near the main street, **Voorstraat**, which runs east–west and ends in the **Sternse Slotland** park – site of a medieval castle. Near the park is the **Waag** of 1657 and, east along Voorstraat, the **Museum Martena** (Tues–Fri 10am–5pm, Sat & Sun 1–5pm; €5; ⓦmuseummartena.nl) in the old **Martenahuis** of 1498, with bits and pieces relating to the former university and its (obscure) alumni. Past the Martenahuis, on the left, the **Stadhuis** (Wed–Fri 1–5pm; free), with its twin gables and octagonal tower, is a magnificent mixture of Gothic and Renaissance styles built in 1591 and is worth a peek upstairs for the leather-clad walls – all the rage until French notions of wallpaper took hold in the eighteenth century. Further up Voorstraat, on the corner of Breedeplaats, the **Kaatsmuseum** (May–Sept Tues–Sat 1–5pm; €2) is devoted to the uniquely Frisian sport of *kaatsen* (see p.197 for more on this).

The Planetarium

Eise Eisingastraat 3 • Tues–Sat 10am–5pm, Sun 1–5pm; April–Oct also Mon 1–5pm • €4.50 • ☎0517 393 070, ⓦplanetarium-friesland.nl

Most people visit Franeker for its fascinating eighteenth-century **planetarium** opposite the town hall. Now the oldest working planetarium in the world, it was built by a local woolcomber, Eise Eisinga. Born in 1744, Eisinga was something of a prodigy: he taught himself mathematics and astronomy, and published a weighty arithmetic book when aged only 17. In 1774, the unusual conjunction of Mercury, Venus, Mars and Jupiter under the sign of Aries prompted a local paper to predict the end of the world. There was panic in the countryside, and an appalled Eisinga embarked on the construction of his planetarium, completed in 1781, in order to dispel superstition by demystifying the workings of the cosmos.

The planetarium isn't of the familiar domed variety but was built as a false ceiling in the family's living room, a series of rotating dials and clocks indicating the movement of the planets and associated phenomena, from tides to star signs. The whole apparatus is regulated by a clock, driven by a series of weights hung in a tiny alcove beside a half-size cupboard-bed. Above the face of the main dials, the mechanisms – hundreds of handmade nails driven into moving slats – are open for inspection. Beyond, a series of rooms in both the original house and the building next door have displays on Eisinga's work – you can see reproductions of his notebooks as well as the works of other venerable astronomers in the lovely garden room. A detailed guidebook explains every aspect of the place, and there are regular tours and an explanatory film (sometimes in English).

ARRIVAL AND INFORMATION
FRANEKER

By train Franeker is on the Harlingen–Leeuwarden line and there are usually two trains an hour in each direction. The train station is five minutes' walk southeast of the centre: follow Stationsweg round to the left and over the bridge, first left over the second bridge onto Zuiderkade and second right along Dijkstraat to reach the town.

By bus There are regular buses to Leeuwarden and Harlingen, and they drop off passengers on Kleijenburg, at the northwest corner of the old town centre.

Tourist office Franeker's VVV is inside the Museum Martena on Voorstraat (Tues–Fri 10am–5pm, Sat & Sun 1–5pm; ☎ 0517 392 192, ⓦ beleeffriesland.nl).

ACCOMMODATION AND EATING

Bloemketerp Burg. J. Dijkstraweg 3 ☎ 0517 395 099, ⓦ bloemketerp.nl. Ten minutes' walk north of the station – head up Stationsweg, Oud Kaatsveld and Leeuwarderweg, then turn left – Franeker's campsite is a nice waterside site with lots of facilities, including a pool, tennis courts and canoes and bikes for rent. It also has a number of chalets if you're not actually camping. **€20**

De Doelen Breedeplaats 6 ☎ 0517 383 256, ⓦ dedoelen-franeker.nl. The rooms upstairs don't reflect the cool makeover this place has received downstairs, but it couldn't be more central or more cheap, and the young owners plan to start upgrading the accommodation any day now. There's free wi-fi in the downstairs bar and restaurant, where you can choose from a wide-ranging menu that has sandwiches, salads and burgers for lunch and main courses at dinner for €15–20 (steaks, spare ribs, schnitzels, a couple of fish dishes). Mon–Thurs & Sun 11am–11pm, Fri 11am–1am, Sat 9.30am–1am. **€60**

De Grillerije Groenmarkt 14 ☎ 0517 395 7044, ⓦ degrillerije.nl. This upmarket, canal-side, mainly French restaurant offers main courses like lamb racks, catch of the day and mixed grill for around €19 in a lovely, electically decorated modern interior. Tues–Sun 5–10pm.

Planetarium Café Eise Eisingastraat 2 ☎ 0517 382 106. Beside the planetarium, the building dates back to 1745 and has fine wooden counters, a mosaic floor and original coffee cabinets from 1910, as well as an attractive back garden. And its short menu of soups, salads and sandwiches is always good. Tues–Sat 10am–5pm, Sun 11am–5pm; April–Sept also Mon noon–5pm.

De Stadsherberg Oude Kaatsveld 8 ☎ 0517 392 686, ⓦ stadsherbergfraneker.nl. Situated next to the canal on the continuation of Stationsweg, this is the pick of Franeker's small choice of hotels, a friendly place with ten neat and trim rooms, and a decent restaurant downstairs. **€97.50**

Harlingen

Thirty kilometres west of Leeuwarden and just north of the Afsluitdijk, **HARLINGEN**, is a more compelling stop than nearby Franeker. An ancient and salty old port that serves as the ferry terminus for the islands of Terschelling and Vlieland, it's something of a centre for traditional Dutch **sailing barges**, a number of which are usually moored in the harbour. It was a naval base from the seventeenth century onwards, and abuts the Vliestroom channel, once the easiest way for shipping to pass from the North Sea through the shallows that surround the Frisian islands and on into the Zuider Zee. Before trade moved west, this was the country's lifeline, where cereals, fish and other foodstuffs were brought in from the Baltic to feed the expanding Dutch cities, and it was also once a centre for the ceramics industry. Its historic importance is reflected in a fine old centre of sixteenth- to eighteenth-century houses, sandwiched between the pretty Noorderhaven and the more functional Zuiderhaven canals. However, Harlingen is too busy to be a twee tourist town: there's a fishing fleet, a small container depot and a shipbuilding yard.

Voorstraat

The heart of Harlingen is **Voorstraat**, a long, tree-lined avenue in between Harlingen's two main harbours, Zuiderhaven and Noorderhaven – the latter home to the elegant eighteenth-century **Stadhuis** which faces the water.

Harlinger Aardewerk en Tegelfabriek

Voorstraat 84 • Mon–Fri 8am–6pm, Sat 9am–5pm • ☎ 0517 415 362, ⊛ harlinger.nl

This workshop is worth a peek for its modern-day ceramics, examples of Harlingen's traditional and now resurgent ceramics business, which flourished until tiles were undermined by the rise of wallpaper. The last of the old factories closed in 1933, but the demand for traditional crafts led to something of a recovery, and the opening of new workshops during the 1970s.

The Hannemahuis Museum

Voorstraat 56 • Tues–Fri 11am–5pm, Sat & Sun 1.30–5pm • €3.50 • ☎ 0517 413 658, ⊛ hannemahuis.nl.

Sited in an eighteenth-century merchant's house, the **Hannemahuis** museum concentrates as you would expect on Harlingen's long and distinguished, mostly maritime history, and includes some interesting displays on shipping. It also displays seascapes and other paintings by local artists, as well as a lovely array of locally produced tiles.

ARRIVAL AND INFORMATION

By train Trains from Leeuwarden stop on the south side of town at Harlingen's main train station, a 5–10min walk from Voorstraat; there's a second station, Harlingen Haven, right next to the docks.

By ferry Ferries leave for the islands of Vlieland and Terschelling from the dock at the seaward end of Noorderhaven 2–3 times a day during summer. Cars are not allowed on Vlieland: see p.215 for more details or check ⊛ rederij-doeksen.nl.

Tourist office Harlingen's VVV is at Grote Bredeplaats 17, a westerly extension of Voorstraat (May–Oct Mon 1–5pm, Tues–Fri 10am–5pm, Sat 10am–4pm; Nov–April Tues–Fri 1–4pm, Sat 10am–2pm; ☎ 0517 430 207, ⊛ harlingen -friesland.nl): it has a sizeable list of rooms and pensions, many of which are on Noorderhaven.

ACCOMMODATION

HOTELS

Hotel Almenum Harlingen Kruisstraat 8–14 ☎ 0625 031 173, ⊛ hotelalmenum.nl. Converted from a seventeenth-century warehouse, this has a comfortable and nicely furnished range of budget rooms and apartments, and is a five-minute walk from the end of Voorstraat. **€80**

Anna Caspari Noorderhaven 67–71 ☎ 0517 412 065, ⊛ annacasparii.nl. Located in three historical buildings, with a cosy lobby, classy restaurant and canal-side terrace (see below), this place has one of the best locations in town: the rooms are large and comfortable if blandly furnished, with the best ones boasting views over the Noorderhaven. **€95**

De Zeezicht Zuiderhaven 1 ☎ 0517 412 536, ⊛ hotelzeezicht.nl. A friendly place, right on the harbour, best of whose 27 rooms are those at the top, which have been refurbished and have nice sea views. **€95**

CAMPSITES

Popta Zathe Kimswerd ☎ 0517 641 205. A delightful mini-campsite close to the sea wall, about 4km south of town, with a small plot of grass, a beautiful garden and bike rental; the sunsets are great and it's a lovely bike ride along the top of the dyke into town. **€10.50**

De Zeehoeve Westerzeedijk 45 ☎ 0517 413 465, ⊛ zeehoeve.nl. Harlingen's nearest campsite is a twenty-minute walk along the sea dyke to the south of town – follow the signs from Voorstraat. April–Sept. **€20**

EATING AND DRINKING

Anna Caspari Noorderhaven 67–71 ☎ 0517 412 065, ⊛ annacasparii.nl. Perhaps the best restaurant in town, with a great range of fish dishes – Dover sole, perch, monkfish – along with steaks, lamb rumps, etc, for €21–25. Daily noon–2pm & 5–9pm.

't Noorderke Noorderhaven 17–19 ☎ 0517 415 043. At the seaward end of Noorderhaven, this place does good-value daily specials – herring in season, plus baked mussels, sole fillets, as well as steaks, goulash, spare ribs, etc – and a view of the boats passing by from the terrace. Mains go for €17–20. Mon–Thurs 10am–midnight, Fri & Sat 10am–1am, Sun 11am–midnight.

De Tjotter Romnmelhaven 2 ☎ 0517 414 691, ⊛ detjotter.nl. Right on one corner of Noorderhaven, this is both a café and a smarter restaurant, with fish snacks and *broodjes* in the café for upwards of €2.80, as well as fried fish, sole and mussel plates for €8.95. Next door in the restaurant, the more expensive dinner menu features wonderful oysters, fish soup and cod and monkfish mains for €20–25. There are a few meat and veggie options too. Tues–Sat noon–10.30pm, Sun & Mon 1–10.30pm.

THE ELFSTEDENTOCHT

The **Elfstedentocht** ("Eleven Towns Race") is Friesland's biggest spectacle, a gruelling **ice-skating** marathon around Friesland that dates back to 1890, when one Pim Muller, a local sports journalist, skated his way around the eleven official towns of the province, simply to see whether it was possible. It was, and twenty years later the first official Elfstedentocht was launched, contested by 22 skaters. Weather – and ice – permitting, it has taken place just fifteen times in the last hundred years, most recently in 1997, attracting skaters from all over the world.

The race is organized by the Eleven Towns Association, of which you must be a member to take part; the high level of interest in the race means that membership is very difficult to obtain. The route, which measures about 200km in total, takes in all the main centres of Friesland, starting in Leeuwarden in the town's Expo Centre, from where the racers sprint – skates in hand – 1500m to the point where they get onto the ice. The first stop after this is Sneek, after which the race takes in Hindeloopen and the other old Zuider Zee towns, plus Dokkum in the north of the province, before finishing back in Leeuwarden. The event is broadcast live on national TV, the route lined with spectators. Of the 17,000 or so people who take part, usually no more than three hundred are professional skaters. Casualties are inevitably numerous; the worst year was 1963, when 10,000 skaters took part and only seventy finished, the rest beaten by the fierce winds, extreme cold and snowdrifts along the way. Generally, however, something like three-quarters of the competitors make it to the finishing line.

If you're not around for the race itself, the route makes a popular bike ride and is signposted by the ANWB as one of their national cycling routes; four or five days will allow enough time to sightsee as well as cycle.

Sneek

Twenty minutes by train from Leeuwarden, **SNEEK** (pronounced *snake*) was an important shipbuilding centre as early as the fifteenth century, a prosperous maritime town protected by an extensive system of walls and moats. Postwar development has robbed the place of some of its charm but there are still some buildings of interest, notably the grandiose **Waterpoort** at the end of Koemarkt, all that remains of the seventeenth-century town walls. At the beginning of August, crowds flock in for **Sneek Week**, an annual regatta, when the flat green expanses around town are thick with the white of slowly moving sails – and accommodation is almost impossible. The town is also known for its regional speciality, Beerenburg, a herb-flavoured gin, that you can buy at the **Weduwe Joustra shop**, at Kleinzand 32, which retains its original nineteenth-century interior, with the old barrels and till.

Martiniplein and around

Sneek's main square is **Martiniplein**, whose ponderous sixteenth-century **Martinikerk** (mid-June to mid-Sept Tues–Sat 2–4.30pm; July also Wed & Thurs 7.30–9pm) is edged by an old wooden belfry, though it's a grand, in-the-round space inside. Around the corner, the **Stadhuis**, Marktstraat 15, is all extravagance, from the Rococo facade to the fanciful outside staircase; inside there's an indifferent display of ancient weapons in the former guardroom.

The Scheepvaart Museum en Oudheidkamer

Kleinzand 16 • Mon–Sat 10am–5pm, Sun noon–5pm • €6 • ☎ 0515 414 057, ⓦ friesscheepvaartmuseum.nl.

Expanded over the years to fill several adjoining canal houses, with a modern entrance hall at its centre, this museum has a large and well-displayed collection of maritime miscellany. A film – in English – gives you a potted history of Sneek and its role in the maritime history of the country, while the same room also displays a model of the town as it would have looked in the seventeenth century. Other rooms exhibit old maps, including a lovely one of Friesland in the eighteenth century, artefacts pertaining to ice-skating and the Elfstedentocht (see p.205), lots of beautiful wooden models of sailing ships, paintings of local scenes and various recreations of domestic settings, including that of a local timber merchant.

ARRIVAL AND INFORMATION

SNEEK

By train Sneek's train and bus stations are five minutes' walk from the old centre, with regular services to Leeuwarden (every 20min; 20min), and in the other direction to Stavoren (hourly; 30min).

By bus Bus #98 runs four times an hour (less at weekends) between Sneek and Bolsward (20min) then on to Makkum. Bus #99 runs slightly less frequently between Sneek and Harlingen (30min).

Tourist office The central VVV, is near the Stadhuis at Marktstraat 18 (Mon–Fri 9.30am–6pm, Sat 9.30am–5pm; summer Thurs till 9pm; T 0515 414 096, W vvvsneek.nl). They can arrange private rooms for a small fee and give out a free map with an overview of the best ways to explore southwest Friesland, either by foot, in-line skate, horse or canoe – W routezuidwestfriesland.nl.

ACCOMMODATION

De Domp Domp 4 T 0515 412 559, W dedomp.nl. Sneek's nearest campsite is 2km northeast of the centre, a right turn off the main road to Leeuwarden; no buses run near, but it's a nice waterside site with decent facilities and its own yacht-filled marina. Tents cost around €5 plus €6 per person. April–Oct. €17

4

Hostel Sneek Oude Oppenhuizerweg 17 T 0515 412 132, W stayokay.com. Located on the edge of town, a 5- to 10-minute walk from the centre, this is a bright, modern, purpose-built hostel with clean public spaces and a mixture of functional dorms and private rooms.To get there on foot, head east to the end of Kleinzand, turn right down Oppenhuizerweg, and it's the first major road on the left – or take bus #99 from the station. Dorm beds €18, doubles €50

Nieuw Hanenburg Wijde Noorderhoorne 2 T 0515 412 570, W hotelhilverda.nl. The slightly cheesy 1960s-style lobby here belies the comfy lounge beyond, full of books, a piano and stuff to occupy the kids, not to mention the nice rooms upstairs, which have been refurbished fairly recently in a contemporary style. Free wi-fi throughout. €97.50

De Wijnberg Marktstraat 23 T 0515 412 421, W hoteldewijnberg.nl. The twenty-odd rooms are large and decent enough at this lively pub and restaurant, though the ones at the front can be a little noisy. Free wi-fi. €95

EATING AND DRINKING

Kastanje Grote Kerkstraat 12 T 0515 422 387. Steaks, brill fillets and venison all feature on the menu here, with starters around €9, mains around €20. Daily except Tues 5–10pm.

Klein Java Wijde Noorderhorne 18 T 0515 432 498, W kleinjava.nl. Indonesian food served in a pleasant round, light-filled space, with a large terrace outside. Excellent and authentic food, with *rijstaffels* from €18.75 per person and most other mains €16; 8-course menus start at €28.75. Tues–Sun 5–10pm.

Bolsward

Some 10km west of Sneek, **BOLSWARD** (pronounced *bozwut*) was founded in the seventh century and became a bustling and important textile centre in the Middle Ages, though its subsequent decline was prolonged and deep. It's less touristy than the surrounding towns, with a busy and attractive central street, Marktstraat, bisected by a canal, and a couple of especially handsome old buildings.

The Stadhuis

Jongemastraat 2 • April–Oct Mon–Thurs 9am–noon & 2–6pm, Fri 9am–12.30pm • Free

Your first stop should be the **Stadhuis**, a magnificent red-brick, stone-trimmed Renaissance edifice of 1613. The facade is topped by a lion holding a coat of arms over the head of a terrified Turk, and below a mass of twisting, curling carved stone frames a series of finely cut cameos, all balanced by an extravagant external staircase. Inside there's a small **museum** holding local historical bits and pieces.

The Martinikerk

Groot Kerkhof • May–Sept Mon–Fri 10am–noon & 2–4pm; Oct–April Mon–Fri 2–4pm

Five minutes' walk away from Bolsward's main street, the fifteenth-century **Martinikerk** was originally built on an earthen mound for protection from flooding. Some of the woodcarving inside is quite superb, particularly the choir with its rare misericords from 1470 and the seventeenth-century pulpit, carved from a single oak tree. Its panels depict the four seasons: the Frisian baptism dress above the young eagle symbolizes spring and the carved ice skates, winter. The stone font dates from around 1000, while the stained-glass windows at the back depict the German occupation of World War II and subsequent liberation by the Canadians.

The Friese Bierbrouwerij

Snekerstraat 43 • Thurs & Fri 3–6pm, guided tour at 4pm; Sat 10am–6pm, guided tours hourly • €6.50, drink included • ☎ 0515 577 449, ⓦ bierbrouwerij-usheit.nl

A ten-minute walk from the centre of town, Bolsward is also home to the **Friese Bierbrouwerij**, one of the smallest breweries in the country, producing eight different kinds of "Us Hei" beer and several "Frysk" whiskies. There are regular tours of the building, taking you through a small museum and introducing you to the basics of the production process before allowing you to sample the product in the clubby *proeflokaal* upstairs.

ARRIVAL AND INFORMATION

BOLSWARD

By bus Buses stop on Bolsward's main street. Services include bus #99 from Sneek train station, which runs on to Harlingen, and bus #98 from Makkum, which runs on to Sneek (every 30min).

Tourist office Bolsward's VVV is located in the small Gysbert Japicxhus museum at Wipstraat 6 (April–Sept Mon 1.30–5pm, Tues–Fri 9am–12.30pm & 1.30–5pm, Sat 1.30–4pm; hours vary out of season; ☎ 0515 577 701). They have details of a handful of private rooms.

ACCOMMODATION, EATING AND DRINKING

Hid Hero Hiem Kerkstraat 53 ☎ 0515 575 299. Housed in a former orphanage, and with a pleasant garden and courtyard, this is a great-value and very peaceful hotel, five minutes' walk from Bolsward's main street, near the church. Rooms are small apartments really, with a sitting room, kitchenette and separate bedrooms. There's free parking and wi-fi throughout, and it also has a decent restaurant – *Het Weehuys* – with menus from €20. €85

De Wijnberg Marktplein 5 ☎ 0515 572 220, ⓦ wijnbergbolsward.nl. You can't get more central than this big, busy bar with a terrace right on Marktplein. There are 29 rooms upstairs, free wi-fi throughout, and all are nicely furnished and reasonably up to date decor-wise; and if there's a slightly institutional feel upstairs it's more than offset by the lively bar and restaurant on the ground floor, which serve an all-day menu of tapas, croquettes, sandwiches and burgers from around €7.50, plus steaks for €15. €75

Makkum

Just 10km west of Bolsward, **MAKKUM** is a very agreeable place, a collection of immaculate houses, church towers, and canals, cobbled streets and wooden boats that's saved from postcard-prettiness by a working harbour. It's long been a centre for the manufacture of traditional, high-end Dutch **ceramics**, and the town is a bit of a magnet for coach parties during the summer, as well as a year-round sailing centre. But it never feels overwhelmed, and the Tichelaar **workshops**, Turfmarkt 65 (Mon–Fri 9am–5.30pm, Sat 10am–5pm; ☎ 0515 231 341, ⓦ tichelaar.nl), are worth a visit during your wander around the centre. You can have a look at the workshop out the back or just browse through the gallery-like shop, which is full of beautiful objects priced way beyond the reach of most people, before taking the weight off in its small *Bakkerswinkel* café.

MUSEUMROUTE ALDFAERSERF

Choosing the scenic route south from Makkum to Workum takes you along the **Museumroute Aldfaerserf**, in which the villages of Allingawier, Exmorra and others serve as open-air museums illustrating Frisian life in the eighteenth and nineteenth centuries. Historical buildings have been restored and refurbished, regaining their historical functions as bakeries, carpenters' shops, farms and smithies, and the 25km route can be done by car or bicycle. Bikes can be rented at the museum route's base at Meerweg 4 in Allingawier (April–Oct Tues–Sun 10am–5pm; €5; ☎0515 231 631, ✆aldfaerserf.nl).

ARRIVAL AND INFORMATION

MAKKUM

By bus Makkum is served by bus #102 from Workum train station and Hindeloopen beyond (Mon–Fri every 2hr), as well as by the much more frequent bus #98 from Bolsward.

Tourist office Makkum's VVV is in the old Waag at

Pruikmakershoek 2 (April–May & Sept–Oct Mon, Tues, Thurs & Fri 10am–noon & 1–3pm; June–Aug Mon–Fri 10am–noon & 1–5pm, Sat 10am–3pm; ☎0900 540 0001, ✆hetfriesehart.nl.nl), and can arrange private rooms for free.

ACCOMMODATION AND EATING

★ **It Posthus** Plein 15 ☎0515 231 153, ✆itposthus .nl. Housed in an old post office, this is basically an Italian restaurant, but oddly one with no pasta on the menu. Instead the food is Italian in style with local ingredients, and pretty good; choose from beef or salmon carpaccio, prawns with zucchini or Mediterranean fish soup to start, for €8–12, followed by saltimbocca, steak or a couple of good fish options as mains for around €20. Or just go for the excellent-value €29.50 menu. The setting is bright and contemporary, service very friendly and the terrace outside is a lovely place to eat if it's warm enough. Only drawback is the somewhat limited opening hours. Wed–Sun 6–10pm.

★ **Villa Mar** DL Touwenlaan 5 ☎0515 232 469, ✆villa -mar.com. There's probably no better place to stay in Makkum than this tastefully renovated old villa with large, beautifully furnished rooms that have nice bathrooms, classic rooms, a huge kitchen for communal use with a roaring fire that's lit most nights in winter and a lush garden. There's free wi-fi too, and the lovely German lady owner rustles up a decent breakfast. **€80**

De Waag Markt 13 ☎0515 231 447, ✆hoteldewaagmakkum.nl. Right in the centre of Makkum, this is a welcoming place that has 14 plainish but fairly recently renovated rooms and a nice bar and restaurant downstairs. **€70**

Workum

Heavily protected by its sea defences, the town of **WORKUM**, ten minutes southwest of Sneek by train, is a very pleasant place that was until the early eighteenth century a busy seaport. It has a bustling main street and a pretty central square anchored by a seventeenth-century **Waag**, at Merk 4. This is now home to both the tourist office and a small museum exhibiting a standard nautical-historical collection (April–Oct Mon & Sun 1.30–5pm, Tues–Sat 10am–5pm; June–Aug also Mon morning; Nov–March Thurs–Sun 1.30–5pm; €2). Immediately behind is Friesland's largest medieval church, the **St Gertrudiskerk** (April–Oct Mon–Sat 11am–5pm), with its enormous stand-alone bell tower and small collection of mostly eighteenth-century odds and ends inside.

Jopie Huisman Museum

Noard 6 • April–Oct Mon–Sat 10am–5pm, Sun 1–5pm; mid-Feb to March & Nov–Dec daily 1–5pm • €6 • ✆jopiehuismanmuseum.nl

On the opposite side of the square from the church, the likeable **Jopie Huisman Museum** is a sleek modern space devoted to the work of the eponymous local artist who died in 2000. The art on display includes ink drawings, watercolours and paintings – graphic depictions of local people, landscapes and most uniquely the discarded objects of everyday life. Perhaps best is his self-portrait rolling a cigarette.

By train Workum's station is 2km from the town's main square and it's on the main Sneek to Stavoren line, with trains roughly every hour.

By bus Bus #102 runs between Workum, Makkum and Hindeloopen every 2 hours during the week.

Tourist office The VVV is located in the old Waag at Merk 4 (April–Oct Mon & Sun 1.30–5pm Tues–Sat 10am–5pm; June–Aug also Mon morning; Nov–March Thurs–Sun 1.30–5pm; ☎ 0515 541 045, ⓦ vvvworkum.nl), and has a list of private rooms in the area.

ACCOMMODATION AND EATING

Aan de Wymerts Noard 37 ☎ 0515 540 004, ⓦ hotelaandewymerts.nl. Tucked away off Workum's main street, this is very convenient and very well run, with a cool, contemporary feel and spick-and-span modern rooms with free wi-fi. **€105**

Gulden Leeuw Merk 2 ☎ 0515 542 341, ⓦ deguldenleeuw.nl. Nice decent-sized rooms, fairly recently redecorated, with refurbished bathrooms. There's also a convivial bar and restaurant on the ground floor that serves mainly fish specialities. **€60**

It Pottebakkershûs Merk 18 ☎ 0515 541 900, ⓦ itpottebakkershus.nl. One of the most appealing places to eat in the centre of Workum, right opposite the

main square, with short menus of tasty veggie and fish dishes for €18–20, good coffee and high teas. The place doubles as a ceramics factory with a permanent exhibition of antique local pottery. July & Aug daily 10am–9pm; Sept–June Mon & Tues 10am–6pm & Wed–Sun 10am–9pm.

It Soal Suderséleane 29 ☎ 0515 541 443, ⓦ itsoal .nl. This beautifully situated campsite is located right on the IJsselmeer, 3km south of the centre, and has its own beach, marina and lots of opportunities for watersports. Pitches start at about €18 for one or two people plus a tent, and they also rent small bungalows. April–Oct. **€18**

Hindeloopen

The exquisitely pretty village of **HINDELOOPEN** juts into the IJsselmeer, and is very much on the tour-bus trail. Outside high summer, however, and in the evening when most visitors have gone home, it's peaceful and very enticing, a tidy jigsaw of old streets, canals and wooden bridges that are almost too twee to be true.

Its attractive **church**, a seventeenth-century structure with a wonky medieval tower, has some graves of British airmen who perished in the Zuider Zee, while the small village museum beside the church, the **Museum Hindeloopen** (April–Oct Mon–Fri 11am–5pm, Sat & Sun 1.30–5pm; €3; ⓦ museumhindeloopen.nl), displays examples of Hindeloopen's unusual furniture (see box, p.210), although the largest display is at the Fries Museum in Leeuwarden (see p.199).

Schaats Museum

Kleine Wiede 1 • Mon–Sat 10am–6pm & Sun 1–5pm • €2.50 • ⓦ schaatsmuseum.nl

The small **Schaats Museum** is the best kind of local museum, packed full of stuff, lovingly presented, that's utterly unique to its location. It displays skating mementoes relating to the great Frisian ice-skating race "De Friese Elfstedentocht" (see box, p.205), as well as further exhibits on skating in general. Upstairs is plenty of Hindeloopen's unique painted furniture, which is also for sale in the museum shop.

By train Hindeloopen is the next stop down from Workum on the Leeuwarden–Stavoren line, with connections roughly hourly: its train station is 20 minute's walk east of the village centre.

By bus Bus #102 runs to Workum and on to Makkum (Mon–Fri every 2 hr).

By bike From Workum, it's just 6km to Hindeloopen, a pleasant, well-signposted bike ride across fields, past a

windmill and along a dyke. It's a popular route with families as it steers clear of busy roads.

Tourist office Hindeloopen VVV is at Nieuwstad 26 (April & May Mon, Wed & Sat 11am–4pm; June also Fri 11am–4pm; July & Aug Mon–Sat 10am–12.30pm & 1–5pm; Sept & Oct Mon, Wed & Sat 10.30am–4pm; ☎ 0514 851 223, ⓦ vvvhindeloopen.nl), and can organize the odd private room.

THE PAINTED FURNITURE OF HINDELOOPEN

Until the seventeenth century, Hindeloopen prospered as a Zuider Zee **port**, concentrating on trade with the Baltic and Amsterdam. The combination of rural isolation and trade created a specific culture within this tightly knit community, with a distinctive dialect (Hylper–Frisian with Scandinavian influences) and sumptuous local **dress**. Adopting materials imported into Amsterdam by the East India Company, the women of Hindeloopen dressed in a florid combination of colours where dress was a means of personal identification: caps, casques and trinkets indicated marital status and age, and the quality of the print indicated social standing. Other Dutch villages adopted similar practices, but nowhere were the details of social position more precisely drawn. However, the development of dress turned out to be a corollary of prosperity, for the decline of Hindeloopen quite simply finished it off. Similarly, the local **painted furniture** showed an ornate mixture of Scandinavian and Oriental styles superimposed on traditional Dutch carpentry. Each item was covered from head to toe with painted tendrils and flowers on a red, green or white background, but the town's decline resulted in the collapse of the craft. Tourism has revived local furniture-making, and countless shops now line the main street selling modern versions, though even the smallest items aren't cheap, and the florid style is something of an acquired taste.

ACCOMMODATION

HOTELS

★ **Likhus** 5–7 ☎ 0514 523 208, ⊛ hylperhuis.nl. By far the most charming option is to sleep in this old tiny house that once served as a residence for the wives and children of ships' captains when they were at sea; the entire place is decorated in old Hindeloopen style. It may seem pricey, but the rate includes champagne, flowers and a DIY breakfast. **€200–250**

De Stadsboerderij Nieuwe Weide 7–9 ☎ 0514 521 278, ⊛ destadsboerderij.nl. Part of the *De Brabander* restaurant (see below), this place is right in the centre of Hindeloppen and has simply furnished double rooms at excellent prices that include breakfast and wi-fi. They also run sailing trips and rent out sailing boats. **€72**

Pension de Twee Hondjes Paardepad 2 ☎ 0514 522 873, ⊛ detweehondjes.nl. Right in the heart of the village, this cosy place has free wi-fi and bikes to rent; it also offers the option to sleep in an original *bedstee* (an elevated Frisian-style closet). It has five rooms including two family-sized options. **€78**

CAMPSITE

Camping Hindeloopen Westerdijk 9 ☎ 0514 521 452, ⊛ campinghindeloopen.nl. Just a kilometre or so south of the village near the coast, this site is set back from the IJsselmeer behind the sea dyke. It's got lots of facilities – shop, restaurant, bike rental, tennis and other sports, and you can go windsurfing on the lake too. April–Oct. **€23.50**

EATING

De Brabander Nieuwe Wiede 7–9 ☎ 0514 521 278, ⊛ hcrdebrabander.nl. Very friendly bar and restaurant that has rooms attached (see above), a garden out the back and serves drinks and a plain but wholesome menu of Dutch dishes for under €20 – *dagschotels* for around €10 – and a wide array of excellent pancakes for under €5. Live music occasionally too. April–Sept daily noon–2pm & 4–9pm; Oct–March Tues–Sat 4–9pm.

Oost Achterom Kalverstraat 13 ☎ 0514 522 053. This is a lovely and quite intimate place to enjoy Italian fare on the terrace in the evening, just off the harbour. Pizzas €6–10, pasta dishes from €8. Wed–Sun 5–9pm.

De Steur Buren 5 ☎ 0514 522 012. Right by the church, this is the place for fishy treats for lunch, either in its small café or to take away and eat by the harbour. Daily 10am–6pm.

Stavoren

Named after the Frisian god Stavo, **STAVOREN** is the oldest town in Friesland and was once a prosperous port; it's now both the end of the train line and the departure point for **ferries** to Enkhuizen (see pp.221–225). Strung out along the coast, Stavoren is an eclectic mix of the old and new: the harbour is flanked by modern housing while the shipyards are linked by cobbled backstreets. Popular with yachty types, it's a great place

CYCLING AROUND STAVOREN

Stavoren is a good base for cycling. Options include following the coastal cycleway 10km north to **Hindeloopen**, or 5km south to **Laaksum**, past dark green and marine-blue lagoons with banks of reeds rustling in the wind. For a longer ride, continue through Laaksum and pick up the signposts to **Oudemirdum**, with its swathes of forest crisscrossed by cycleways and wooden bridges spanning pea-soupy canals. This 40-kilometre loop makes a pleasant day-trip, but bear in mind the winds can be forceful along the coast, and generally blow from the southwest.

---

to admire the carefully restored seventeenth- to nineteenth-century vessels that once plied the Zuider Zee, now moored up and awaiting rental. On a sunny day, watching the old wooden ships go by and listening to the clink of halyards is as an enjoyable pastime as any. At the southern end of town, massive, squat turbines encased in glass can be seen pumping water out of Friesland and into the IJsselmeer.

ARRIVAL AND INFORMATION   STAVOREN

By train Stavoren's train station is by the harbour and is the terminus of the line that runs to Sneek and Leeuwarden: trains run roughly hourly.

By ferry In season there are three ferry sailings daily between Stavoren and Enkhuizen at 10.05am, 2.05pm and 6.05pm (2 out of season), and the journey takes 1hr 20min. Fares are €10.40 one-way, day returns €14 (at 10.05am and 6.05pm); €5.20 for bikes. See ⓦveerboot .info for more information.

Tourist office The VVV is on the harbour at Stationsweg 7, two minutes' walk from the train station (mid-April to Oct Mon–Sat 9.15am–noon & 1.30–6pm, Sun 9.15am–10.30am, 1.30–2.30pm & 5.30–6pm; ☎0514 682 424, ⓦstavoren.nl): it has details of pensions and private rooms.

ACCOMMODATION AND EATING

Doede's Vishandel Smidstraat 21. Takeaway with a few indoor seats that dishes up tasty fish and chips and lots of other fishy favourites for €5 or less. Mon–Sat 11am–6pm, Sun noon–6pm.

De Vrouwe van Stavoren Havenweg 1 ☎0514 681 202, ⓦhotel-vrouwevanstavoren.nl. Attractively sited right on the harbour, this is Stavoren's best place to stay, with twenty rooms in a variety of shapes and sizes. The furnishings are simple but comfortable, and there's free wi-fi throughout. The restaurant downstairs is excellent and well priced, with a good menu of sandwiches, salads and pancakes served 10am–6pm and a dinner menu comprising good steaks and excellent fish dishes weighing in at about €20 for main courses. Restaurant daily 10am–10pm. **€70–115.**

Sloten

With its thicket of boat masts poking out above the rooftops, it's easy to spot **SLOTEN** from afar. It's something of a museum piece, and the village's 1000 inhabitants are proud to call Sloten one of Friesland's eleven "cities", and a medieval one at that. Encircled by water, it's a popular spot with Dutch and German tourists alike – the delightful central canal, **Heerenwal** is flanked by plane trees and pavement cafés. On the bastion at Heerenwal's far end, the **De Kaai** windmill provides a sort of focus, a working mill open on Saturdays for visits (April–Sept Sat 1–5pm; Oct–March Sat 10am–noon). There's also a small **museum**, in the town hall on Heerenwal (April–Oct Tues–Fri 11am–5pm, Sat & Sun 1–5pm; €3; ⓦmuseumsloten.nl), but otherwise it's just a case of wandering the cobbled alleyways and encircling bastions and admiring the gabled facades.

ARRIVAL AND INFORMATION   SLOTEN

By bus Reaching Sloten by public transport can be a little awkward; the easiest way is to take bus #42 from Sneek train station to the bus changeover point on the motorway at Spannenburg (takes 35min), where connecting bus #41 continues west to Sloten, while bus #44 runs to Sloten and Bolsward. Alternatively, it's a 19km bike ride from Sneek.

Tourist office The VVV is located with the museum in the town hall at Heerenwal 48 (April–Oct Tues–Fri 11am–5pm, Sat & Sun 1–5pm; ☎ 0514 531 541, ⓦ gaasterlandpromotion .nl), and can suggest a few places to stay.

ACCOMMODATION AND EATING

't Bolwerk Voorstreek 116–117 ☎ 0514 531 405, ⓦ restauranthetbolwerk.nl. Right on the canal in the centre of Sloten, with tables overlooking the water, this is a lovely spot for lunch, with a light menu of sandwiches, salads, *uitsmijters* and pancakes. The short and simple evening dinner menu features dishes like salmon or cod, and there's always a veggie option: three courses cost €23.50, two courses €19.50. Summer daily 10am–9pm; winter Wed–Sun noon–9pm.

De Tjasker Iwert 17, Wijkel ☎ 0514 605 869, ⓦ campingdetjasker.nl. If you have your own transport, it's worth striking out 2km to neighbouring Wijckel and this friendly mini-camping with its own thatched barn and spotless lawn. Turn left opposite the church, bear right at the first fork, follow the road round, and it's just past the cow postbox. €14.50

Dokkum

The one significant settlement hereabouts, the town of **DOKKUM**, about 12km northeast of Leeuwarden, made a name for itself when its early pagan inhabitants murdered the English missionary St Boniface and 52 of his companions here in 754. In part still walled and moated, Dokkum has kept its shape as a fortified town, and is best appreciated by the side of the Het Grootdiep canal, which cuts the town into two distinct sections. This was the commercial centre of the old town and is marked by a series of ancient gables, including that of the **Admiraliteitshuis** which serves as the town's **museum** (Tues–Sat 1–5pm; €4; ⓦ museumdokkum.nl). There's not much else to see beyond a couple of windmills, quiet walks along the old ramparts and all sorts of things named after St Boniface as penance for the locals' early misdeeds. But there are a couple of nice places to stay, and it makes a good base for some *wadlopen* (see p.221), or if you just want to experience small-town Dutch life in one of Friesland's pleasantest provincial centres.

ARRIVAL AND INFORMATION   DOKKUM

By bus Bus #50 runs between Dokkum and Leeuwarden (every 30min; 30min), and there are also buses to Wierum and Moddergat (Mon–Sat hourly; Sun 5 daily; 25–35min).

Tourist office The VVV is at Op de Fetze 13 (Mon 11am–5.30pm, Tues–Fri 9am–5.30pm, Fri also 7–9pm, Sat 9am–5pm; ☎ 0519 293 800, ⓦ vvvlauwersland.nl).

ACCOMMODATION

★ **De Abdij van Dokkum** Markt 30 ☎ 0519 220 422, ⓦ abdij.nl. The top hotel choice in Dokkum, with lovely rooms in the main building – a former abbey – and slightly cheaper ones in the modern annexe next door; many of them are themed according to the eleven Frisian "cities". There's a great bar and restaurant downstairs too. €75–100

Harddraverspark Harddraversdijk 1a ☎ 0519 294 445, ⓦ campingdokkum.nl. Dokkum's closest campsite is just five minutes' walk east of the centre, and is a

well-organized site, with good shelter. Not big on facilities though, so just as well it's so near town. €13

De Posthoorn Diepswal 21 ☎ 0519 293 500, ⓦ hotel -deposthoorn.nl. This hotel enjoys the town's best position, right on the canal. The rooms are decent enough, good-sized with large bathrooms, and pretty good value, either in the main building or the annexe two doors down. Note that the rooms at the front can be a bit noisy on summer weekends. There's also a restaurant with a terrace overlooking the water. €85

EATING AND DRINKING

Pizzeria Romana Koornmarkt 8 ☎ 0519 297 756, ⓦ pizzeria-romana.nl. A simple place with a huge selection of pizzas for €6–10, and a few pasta dishes too. The service could be better and the decor is uninspiring, but the food is good. Wed–Sun 4–10pm.

't Raedhus Koningstraat 1 ☎ 0519 294 082,

ⓦ raedhus.nl. Friendly restaurant that serves excellent food from a simple lunch menu of toasties, *uitsmijters* and sandwiches. The evening menu features delicious Dutch classics – schnitzels, spare ribs, steaks, pork medallions; starters go for €6–9 and main courses for €15–20. Daily noon–2pm & 5–9pm; Oct–June closed Sun.

Moddergat and Wierum

Of all the tiny hamlets in north Friesland, two of the most interesting lie on the Waddenzee. **MODDERGAT**, the more easterly of the two, spreads out along the road behind the sea wall 10km northeast of Dokkum, merging with the village of **Paesens**. At its western edge, a memorial commemorates the 1883 tragedy when seventeen ships sank during a storm, with the loss of 83 lives. Opposite, **'t Fiskerhuske Museum**, Fiskerpad 4–8 (end Feb to Oct Mon–Sat 10am–5pm; July & Aug Mon closed but Sun 1–5pm; €4; ⑩museummoddergat.nl), comprises three restored fishermen's cottages with displays on the history and culture of the village and details of the disaster: as such small museums go, it's pretty good.

Huddled behind the sea dyke 5km to the west, **WIERUM** has one main claim to fame, its twelfth-century church with a saddle-roof tower and (as in Moddergat) a golden ship on the weather vane. The dyke offers views across to the islands and holds a monument of twisted anchors to the fishermen who died in the 1883 storm and the dozen or so claimed in the century after.

ARRIVAL AND DEPARTURE	MODDERGAT AND WIERUM
By bus Moddergat and Wierum are on the same hourly bus #52 route from Dokkum. **By bike** If you've rented a bicycle from Leeuwarden and	ridden to Dokkum, follow the signposted cycleway; it's around 8km to Moddergat and a few kilometres more to Wierum.

ACCOMMODATION

Recreatiebedrijf Meinsma Meinsmaweg 5 Moddergat ☎0519 589 396, ⑩recreatiebedrijf-meinsma.nl. This farmhouse pension has six double rooms and a small adjacent campsite with twelve pitches as well as three self-contained four-person bungalows. It's very friendly and in a great location, too. Rooms €65, bungalows €55, tents €11

The Frisian Islands

The four **Frisian islands** preserve an unexpected sense of wilderness in so populated a country, low-lying sandbanks with mile upon mile of hourglass-fine sandy beaches and well-developed networks of cycleways. A tourist magnet in summertime, busy and developed **Terschelling** is large enough to swallow the holiday crowds, while car-free **Vlieland** resembles a grass-covered dunescape and is popular with young families. Both can be reached from Harlingen, while the access point for busy **Ameland** is the port of Holwerd. The smallest of the four islands is **Schiermonnikoog**; this can be reached from Leeuwarden and Dokkum, but the shorter route there is from neighbouring Groningen. One way of reaching the islands is by indulging in **wadlopen**, a hearty walk at low tide across – and often knee-deep in – the mud flats that lie between the islands and the mainland. See p.221 for ways to do this, but don't attempt it without a qualified guide. The islands have a wide range of **accommodation**, particularly Terschelling and Ameland, but prices rise dramatically in summer, when vacant rooms can be thin on the ground, and you should also always reserve ahead if you're visiting in July or August, or indeed at anytime during the summer.

Vlieland

Compared with its closest neighbour, Terschelling, **VLIELAND** is very low-key. All but car-free, it has just one settlement, **Oost-Vlieland**, which has most of the amenities you might need: in fact, it's little more than a tree-lined street with a string of pavement cafés, bike rental agencies and a few hotels and B&Bs. Historically isolated by a complex pattern of sandbanks, the island was of minor importance during the Zuider Zee trade; indeed its only other village was swept away by the sea in the eighteenth century and never rebuilt. These days, there's not much to do but enjoy the country walks and relax along the 12km of sandy beach – a sedate lifestyle that is popular with Dutch families, who load up their bikes with panniers, tents, children and animals, and head for one of the island's campsites. To explore the island's woods and dunes, follow one of the many **bike** routes that run the length of the island, passing close to the wide sandy beach that runs along the north shore. The tourist office can provide you with details in English of two main cycle routes, and there are also plenty of marked **walking** trails.

Centrum "De Noordwester"

Dorpsstraat 150, Oost-Vlieland • July & Aug Mon–Fri 10am–5pm, Sat 2–5pm & Sun 1–4pm; hours vary out of season • €3 • ⓦ denoordwester.nl

Oost-Vlieland is home to a maritime centre mainly geared towards children and displaying an assortment of shells, an explanation of dune formation, and a couple of aquariums housing crabs and rays. It also boasts an unexpected elf forest, though information is in Dutch only.

ARRIVAL AND DEPARTURE VLIELAND

By bus A limited bus service runs along the southern shore from near the ferry terminus.

By ferry Ferries from Harlingen (see p.203) dock at the east end of the island in the village of Oost-Vlieland. There are crossings at least three times a day in summer and twice daily in winter; the journey takes 1hr 45min. A return fare is €15, plus around €8/bike. There's also a fast hydrofoil service from Harlingen (May–Sept 2 daily; Oct–April 1 daily), which costs €21.50 one-way but saves you an hour each way in travelling time – perfect for day-trips. In addition, a ferry runs between Terschelling and Vlieland, twice a day in summer, for which tickets cost €7.75 one-way (plus roughly the same

again for a bike). Check ⓦ rederij-doeksen.nl for the latest schedules and information. You can also travel between Texel and Vlieland twice daily in July and August, 3 times a week the rest of the year (€15.50 one-way, plus €8.50 for bikes); see ⓦ waddenveer.nl for more information.

By bike Visitors' cars are not allowed on Vlieland, but in any case the best way to explore is by bike. There are rental companies near the ferry terminal, and you can also rent bikes, tandems and trailers – for kids as well as canines – all over town. Given the sometimes steep, stony hills, it's worth shelling out a bit more for a machine with decent gears.

INFORMATION AND TOURS

Tourist office The VVV, Havenweg 10 (Mon–Fri 9am–12.30pm & 1.30–5pm, also open for brief periods daily to coincide with ferry arrivals; ☏ 0562 451 111, ⓦ vlieland .net), does its best with the island's few private rooms, and will help groups rent apartments and "dune houses"; it also has information on birdwatching expeditions.

Day-trips Private operators organize day-trips to the northern tip of the neighbouring island of Texel (see p.134) by means of a tractor-like lorry, which crosses the great expanse of sand (the "Vliehors") on Vlieland's western extremity to connect with a boat (May–Sept; €22.50 for a return trip to Texel; ⓦ waddenveer.nl).

ACCOMMODATION AND EATING

Badhotel Bruin Dorpsstraat 88 ☏ 0562 452 828, ⓦ badhotelbruin.nl. This comfortable boutique hotel is a lovely option, with sleek rooms and an excellent restaurant. It's very child-friendly too – unusual for places like this. The restaurant in particular is excellent, perhaps the best place to eat on the island. **€80**

Duin en Dal Dorpsstraat 163 ☏ 0562 451 684, ⓦ pensionduinendal.vlie.nl. This small pension has just three simply furnished rooms and is right in the middle of town. It's not the most glamorous option, but probably the cheapest. **€60**

Lange Paal Postweg 1a ☏ 0562 451 639, ⓦ langepaal .com. A really lovely and very peaceful place to camp, set in the forest clearing of a nature reserve. Facilities are simple but clean and there's a relaxed, friendly atmosphere. Bring some insect repellent though: the mosquitoes here can be ruthless. €5 per person plus €5 for a pitch. **€15**

De Stortemelk Kampweg 1 ☏ 0562 451 225, ⓦ stortemelk.nl. Nicely situated campsite on the dunes behind the beach, about half an hour's walk or a ten-minute bike ride northeast of the village. €6.60/person per night plus around €5 for a tent. April–Sept. **€18.20**

De Wadden Dorpsstraat 61 ☎0562 452 626, �🌐westcordhotels.nl. There are 222 nicely furnished rooms, some faintly marine in style, in this smartish hotel in Oost-Vlieland. There is free wi-fi throughout, and a cosy bar and restaurant downstairs, as well as a lovely outdoor terrace. **€100**

Terschelling

Of all the Frisian Islands, **TERSCHELLING** is both the largest – some 30km long and 3.5km wide – and the easiest to reach. Despite its reputation as a summer teenage hangout, it does offer wilderness, peace and tranquillity – you just have to head away from main centres to get it. Quite simply, the further east you go the more attractive the island becomes; eighty percent of the island is a nature reserve, dominated by beach, dunes, forest and polder. Although summer temperatures can soar, out of season Terschelling's wild weather seems to mirror its wild landscape, with storms lending it a brooding air.

Most of Terschelling's villages are on the south side of the island, sheltered from winter storms by the sand dunes and occasional patches of forest that lie to the immediate north. Cycle routes are almost always traffic-free hereabouts and you can aim to stay in one of the pensions between the villages of Formerum and Oosterend, far enough east to escape most of the crowds.

West-Terschelling

The ferry docks next to the fishing harbour of **WEST-TERSCELLING**, a tourist resort in its own right that's packed throughout the summer with visitors sampling the restaurants and bars that line the main streets, Torenstraat in particular. West-Terschelling today is a rather unappealing sprawl of chalets, bungalows and holiday complexes that spreads out from what remains of the old village, belying its past importance as a port and safe anchorage on the edge of the Vliestroom channel, the main shipping lane to and from the Zuider Zee. This strategically positioned town boomed throughout the seventeenth century as a centre for the supply and repair of ships and had its own fishing and whaling fleets; it paid the price for its prominence when the British razed it in 1666. The islanders were renowned sailors, much sought after by ships' captains who also needed them to guide vessels through the treacherous shallows and shifting sandbanks that lay to either side of the Vliestroom. All the same, **shipwrecks** were common all along the island's northern and western shores, the most famous victim being the *Lutine*, which sank while carrying gold and silver to British troops stationed here during the Napoleonic Wars. The wreck still lies at the bottom of the sea, and only the ship's bell was recovered; it's now in Lloyd's of London and is still rung whenever a big ship goes down.

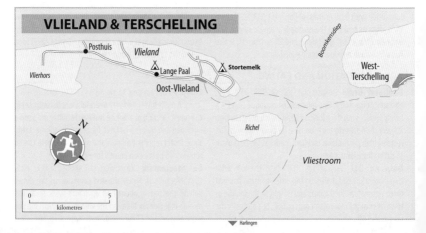

Museum 't Behouden Huys

Commandeurstraat 30–32, near the ferry terminus • April–Oct Mon–Fri 10am–5pm & Sat 1–5pm; July–Sept also Sun 1–5pm • €3 • ⓦ behouden-huys.nl

The best place to investigate West Terschelling's past is at the excellent **Museum 't Behouden Huys**, near the ferry terminus. Prime exhibits here include maps of the old coastline illustrating Terschelling's crucial position, various items from the whaling fleet, lots of sepia photos of bearded islanders and a shipwreck-diving room.

West-Aan-Zee

From West-Terschelling, plenty of visitors cycle off for the day to the beach 5km away at **WEST-AAN-ZEE**. There's a beach café here, *WestAanZee*, and as much empty beach as you're prepared to look for. There are two cycle routes to get here, the more northerly passing through a cemetery in a wood, with a small Commonwealth forces graveyard; as ever, the inscriptions make sad reading, with few of the downed airmen aged more than 25.

Formerum

Definitely worth a visit in the village of **FORMERUM** is the delightful **Wrakken-museum "De Boerderij"** at Formerum Zuid 13 (March–Nov daily 10am–5pm; €3; ⓦ wrakkenmuseum.nl), whose ground floor is an atmospheric bar decked out with all things nautical. Upstairs you can browse a collection of items salvaged from the island's beaches and shipwrecks, including cannons and coins, relics from the *Lutine*, and the Netherlands' largest collection of diving helmets. Another Formerum attraction is the **cranberry factory** at Formerum 51a near the windmill (May–Oct presentation and sampling Mon–Fri at 2pm; €3; shop May–Oct Mon–Fri 10.30am–5pm, Sat 10.30–4pm), where you can sample and buy all things cranberry. Cranberries are a major island crop, harvested from September until the first frost.

Hoorn and Oosterend

The island's two final settlements, **HOORN** and **OOSTEREND**, are particularly pleasant and within easy reach of empty tracts of beach and the nature reserve **De Boschplaat**, where thousands of birds, including gulls, oystercatchers, green plovers and spoonbills, congregate in the marshy shallows of the southeastern shore. To help protect the birds, De Boschplaat is closed during the breeding season (mid-March to mid-Aug), although the tourist office runs guided tours for bird enthusiasts.

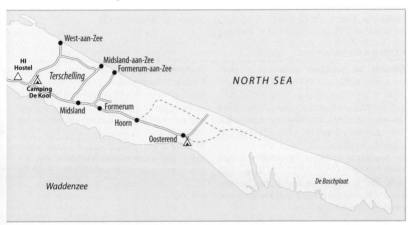

ARRIVAL AND INFORMATION

By ferry Ferries from Harlingen (see p.203) run to West-Terschelling at least three times a day in summer and twice daily in winter and the journey takes 1hr 45min. A return fare is €15, plus around €8/bike. There's also a fast hydrofoil service from Harlingen (May–Sept 2 daily; Oct–April 1 daily; 45min), which costs €21.50 one-way. In addition, a ferry runs between Vlieland and Terschelling twice a day in summer; tickets cost €7.75 one-way, plus €8/bike. See ⓦ rederij-doeksen.nl for up-to-date information.

Tourist office The VVV is near the ferry port at Willem Barentszkade 19a (summer Mon–Sat 9.30am–5.30pm; winter Mon–Fri 9.30am–5pm, Sat 10am–3pm; ☎ 0562 443 000, ⓦ vvvterschelling.nl). It can provide a full list of pensions and rooms and operates a booking service for the whole island. It also offers a variety of walking tours, sells a good island map that includes towns, beaches and cycleways, and dispenses information on cycling routes and seal-watching excursions.

Environmental information For information about Terschelling's natural environment, visit the Centrum voor Natuur en Landschap, at Burgemeester Reedekerstraat 11 just east of West-Terschelling (April–Oct Mon–Fri 9am–5pm, Sat & Sun 2–5pm; Nov–March Tues, Sat, Sun 2–5pm; €5.50; ⓦ natuurmuseumterschelling.nl), which also has a decent aquarium.

ISLAND TRANSPORT AND ACTIVITIES

By bus The island's bus service leaves from right next to the ferry terminus (every 1hr 10min), taking thirty minutes to travel along the south coast to Oosterend.

By bike Haantjes, 50m to the right of the ferry terminal, beyond the VVV (☎ 0562 448 883, ⓦ fietsenopterschelling .nl) rents out bikes for €5–7 a day, €25–30 a week: they also rent tandems and have various drop-off points around the island, and a handy cycling map. There are more bike rental shops down by the harbour and at the ferry terminal.

Horseriding Rijpaarden Verhuur Lok, 2km west of Formerum in tiny Landerum (☎ 0562 448 188, ⓦ rijpaardenverhuurlok.nl), arranges horseback rides: an hour's ride through the woods for beginners costs €22.50, but if you're an experienced rider you can set out for the beach (2hr; €33).

ACCOMMODATION

Pension Altijd Wad Trompstraat 6, West-Terschelling ☎ 0562 442 050, ⓦ altijdwad.nl. Close to the ferry terminal, this is a lovely, bright B&B with five rooms, a cosy studio and small private house to choose from. The furnishings are deliberately marine and minimalist and very nicely done. **€100**

Hotel Buren Burgemeester Mentzstraat 20, West-Terschelling ☎ 0562 442 226, ⓦ hotel-buren.nl. Within easy walking distance from the ferry terminus, this small hotel has eleven rooms, all distinctively decorated in different colour schemes and tastefully furnished. **€78**

Camping de Kooi Heester Kooiweg 20, Terschelling-Hee ☎ 0562 442 743, ⓦ campingdekooi.nl. There are a number of shoreside campsites east of town that are popular with the hordes of partying teenagers who descend on the island in summer, and this is one of the best, about a kilometre inland but near a small lake, with a decent café, free wi-fi, bike rental, etc – €3.50 for a small tent plus €6.50 per person. **€16.50**

Hostel Terschelling 't Land 2, West-Terschelling ☎ 0562 442 338, ⓦ stayokay.com. HI hostel overlooking the harbour with dorm beds and en-suite doubles: it's a 1.5km walk eastwards along the coast from the centre of the village, or you can take any bus to the Dellewal stop. Dorm bed **€23**, double room **€50**

EATING AND DRINKING

Brasserie De Brandaris Boomstraat 3 West-Terschelling ☎ 0562 442 554, ⓦ brasserie-brandaris .nl.One of Terschelling's best places to eat, with a suitably nautical atmosphere. It serves *uitsmijters*, sandwiches and pancakes at lunchtime and at dinner main courses such as steak, satay, pork and spare ribs for around €17.50. Daily noon–4pm & 6–10pm.

De Boschplaat Oosterend 14 ☎ 0562 448 821, ⓦ eetcafedeboschplaat.nl. Hefty Dutch cuisine – lamb shanks, ribs, steaks – at this long-standing Oosterend stalwart. Eat in the cosy interior or on the outside terrace. Daily noon–3pm & 5–10pm.

Heartbreak Hotel Strandpaviljoen Oosterender Badweg 71, Oosterend ☎ 0562 448 634, ⓦ heartbreak -hotel.nl. In a superb location overlooking kilometres of white sand and sea, this American-style diner is decorated with wall-to-wall 1950s memorabilia. Live music Fri and Sat. Daily 10am–2am.

De Walvis Groene Strand, ⓦ walvis.org. On the western edge of West-Terschelling, this beach-facing shack is a perfect place to enjoy snacks and drinks while taking in the sea view. Mon–Fri noon–2.30pm & 6–9.30pm, Sat 6–9.30pm.

THE OEROL FESTIVAL

Every year around the middle of June, Terschelling celebrates the beginning of the warmer season with the **Oerol Festival** (W oerol.nl). Oerol – meaning "everywhere" in the Terschelling dialect – is the name of a rural tradition in which the island's cattle were released from their winter stables to frolic and graze in the open fields, an event that marked the changing of the seasons. Today, over 50,000 people head out to the island for the Oerol, transforming Terschelling into a big festival area, with the island serving as both inspiration and stage for theatre producers, musicians and graphic artists. Finding accommodation is almost impossible during the ten-day festival, so book ahead.

Ameland

Easy to reach from the tiny port of **HOLWERD**, a few kilometres west of Wierum, the island of **Ameland** is one of the major tourist resorts of the north Dutch coast, with a population that swells from 3000 to a staggering 35,000 during summer weekends. Not that the sun is always shining: at times, clouds jostle for position and the colour of the sky can mirror that of the water. It's during the storms that the island is at its moodiest, the flatness of the land accentuating the action in the sky above.

Ameland is just 2km wide and 25km long, its entire northern shore made up of a fine expanse of **sand** and **dune** laced by foot-and cycle paths. The east end of the island is the most deserted, and you can cycle by the side of the marshy shallows that once made up the whole southern shore before the sea dyke was built.

Nes

NES is a tiny place that nestles among the fields behind the dyke. Once a centre of the Dutch whaling industry, it has more than its fair share of cafés, hotels and tourist shops, though quite a bit of the old village has also survived. Mercifully, high-rise development has been forbidden, and there's a focus instead on the seventeenth- and eighteenth-century captains' houses, known as *commandeurshuizen*, which line several of the streets. Perhaps surprisingly, the crowds rarely seem to overwhelm the village, but rather to breathe life into it – which is just as well as there's not a lot to do other than wander the streets and linger in cafés. Even if you do hit peak season, it's fairly easy to escape the crowds and you can **rent bikes** at a number of shops in the village. If it's raining, you might consider the **Natuurcentrum**, Strandweg 38 (April–Oct Mon–Fri 10am–5pm, Sat & Sun 11am–5pm; Jan, Nov & Dec Wed–Sat 1–5pm; €6; W amelandermusea.nl), an aquarium and natural history museum – look out for the life-size whale – although there's no information in English.

Hollum

Of the smaller villages that dot the island, the prettiest place to stay is **HOLLUM**, a sedate settlement of old houses and farm buildings west of Nes. There are a couple of small museums here, if you're into all things marine: the **Sorgdragermuseum**,

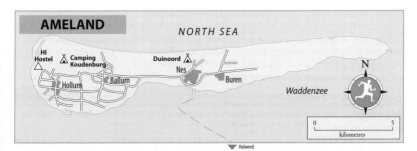

Herenweg 1 (April–June & Sept & Oct Mon–Fri 10am–5pm, Sat & Sun 1.30–5pm; July & Aug Mon–Fri 10am–5pm; €3.75; ⓦamelandermusea.nl), in an old *commandeurshuis*; and the **Vuurtoren**, or lighthouse, dating from 1880, which offers great views over the island (April–Oct Mon & Sun 1–5pm, Tues–Sat 10am–5pm; Nov–March Wed, Sat & Sun 1–5pm; €4.25; ⓦamelandermusea.nl).

ARRIVAL AND DEPARTURE   AMELAND

By ferry From Leeuwarden, bus #66 runs to Holwerd (30min), from where the connecting **ferry** departs to Ameland (6–14 ferries daily; 45min); tickets cost €11.50 one-way (April–Sept €13.65), plus €7.25–8.75 for a bike:

see ⓦwpd.nl for detailed information. Ferries dock near Nes, the main village, and there's a summer bus service from the ferry to the island's other villages.

INFORMATION AND TOURS

Tourist office There are two VVVs on the island: one is at Bureweg 2 in Nes (Mon–Fri 9am–5pm, Sat 10am–3.30pm; ☏0519 546 546, ⓦvvvameland.nl); the other in Hollum, at O.P. Lapstraat 6 (April–Aug Mon–Fri 9am–noon & 1.30–5.30pm, Sat 10am–noon; Sept–March Mon–Fri 9am–noon, Sat 10am–noon; ☏0519 546 546, ⓦvvvameland

.nl). Both offer the same services and can fix you up with a pension or private room anywhere on the island.
Boat trips A variety of boat trips leave Nes, including excursions to the islands of Terschelling (see p.216) and Schiermonnikoog (see p.220), and to the sandbanks to watch seals: details from the VVV or tour operators in Nes.

ACCOMMODATION AND EATING

Pension Ambla Westerlaan 33a, Hollum ☏0519 554 537, ⓦambla.n.l Hollum's best-value place to stay is this homely pension, which has a mixture of ordinary rooms and large studios, some with kitchenettes. **€80**
Duinoord Jan van Eijckweg 4 Nes ☏0519 542 070, ⓦcampingduinoord.eu. Ameland's best-appointed campsite is a sprawling affair, 1km north of Nes – head out of town and then follow Strandweg all the way to the sea, bearing left to enter the camping complex. Facilities include a supermarket, restaurant, bike rental and wi-fi. It costs €13.40 for a pitch, plus €4.70 per person. April–Oct. **€22.80**
De Jong Reeweg 29 Nes ☏0519 542 016, ⓦhoteldejong. nl. Central and family-run hotel with comfortable double rooms right in the heart of Nes. There's also a handy café and restaurant on the ground floor, which serves food all day – everything from lunchtime soups and sandwiches to a full

dinner menu that includes an inventive array of meat and fish dishes – lamb curry, steak, veal, fish – for €16.50–22. **€84**
Koudenburg Oosterhiemweg 2, Hollum ☏0519 554 367, ⓦkoudenburg.nl. This well-equipped campsite by the heath to the north of the island is very welcoming and has lots of facilities, including a snack bar and pub, bike rental and wi-fi, Pitches vary in size and cost from €5, plus €4.40 per person. **€13.80**
Waddencentrum Ameland Oranjeweg 59 ☏0519 555 353, ⓦstayokay.com. Dramatically located at the tip of the island, beyond the lighthouse and between pine forest and dunes, this is a great hostel, with rooms in three different buildings: facilities include basketball, bike rental and a playground – good for kids. To reach it, take bus #130 from West-Terschelling to the last stop. Dorm beds **€13.75**, doubles **€36**

Schiermonnikoog

At 16km long and 4km wide, **Schiermonnikoog** is the smallest of the Frisian islands, and, once you're clear of the main village, it's a wild, uncultivated place, crisscrossed by cycle paths – a popular spot for day-trippers. Until the Reformation, the island belonged to the monastery of Klaarkamp on the mainland; its name means literally "island of the grey monks". Nothing remains of the monks, however, and these days Schiermonnikoog's only settlement is a prim and busy village, fringed by weekend homes and bordering long stretches of muddy beach and sand dune to the north and farmland and mud flats to the south. At low tide, these motionless pools of water reflect the colours in the sky, particularly atmospheric at dawn and dusk.

ARRIVAL AND INFORMATION   SCHIERMONNIKOOG

By ferry Ferries to Schiermonnikoog leave from the port of Lauwersoog, reached by bus #163 from Groningen (7 daily; 1hr), or bus #50 (6 daily) from Dokkum (30min) or

Leeuwarden (1hr 30min). Ferries (Mon–Sat; 5 daily, Sun 4 daily; 45min) cost €11.80 one-way (April–September €13.95) plus €7.25–8.75 for a bike; see ⓦwpd.nl for more

WADLOPEN

Wadlopen, or mud-flat walking, is a popular and strenuous Dutch pastime, and the stretch of coast on the northern edge of the provinces of Friesland and Groningen is one of the best places to do it: twice daily, the receding tide uncovers vast expanses of mud flat beneath the Waddenzee. It is, however, a sport to be taken seriously, and far too dangerous to do without an experienced guide: the depth of the mud is variable and the tides inconsistent. In any case, channels of deep water are left even when the tide has receded, and the currents can be perilous. The **timing of treks** depends on weather and tidal conditions, but most start between 6am and 10am. It's important to be properly equipped; **recommended gear** includes shorts or a bathing suit, a sweater, wind jacket, knee-high socks, high-top trainers and a complete change of clothes stashed in a watertight pack. In recent years, *wadlopen* has become extremely popular, and as excursions are infrequent, between May and August it's advisable to book a place at least a month in advance. The VVVs in Leeuwarden, Dokkum and Groningen can provide details, or you could contact one of the *wadlopen* organizations direct.

Prices and trips vary according to location, and how long (and far) you choose to go. You can do a **full trip** crossing to one of the islands – Ameland or Schiermonnikoog – and coming back by ferry, or just do a **circular trip** across the mud flats and back again. **Pieterburen** is a popular place to start: a circular trip from there costs €16.50 per person, and takes three and a half hours; while a full trip to Schiermonnikoog and back by ferry costs €75 a head.

WADLOPEN GUIDED WALK COMPANIES

Dijkstras Wadlopencentrum Hoofdstraat 118, Pieterburen ☎ 0595 528 345, ✆ wadloop-dijkstra.nl.

Stichting Wadloopcentrum Pieterburen Hoofdstraat 105, Pieterburen ☎ 0595 528 300, ✆ wadlopen.com.

Wadloopcentrum Fryslân ✆ wadlopen.net.

information. Only residents' cars are allowed on the island. Ferries dock at the island jetty, some 3km from the village; a connecting bus drops you off outside the VVV in the centre.

On foot It's possible to walk to the island across the mud flats from Kloosterburen, a distance of about 8km, but you must do this accompanied by a guide (see box above).

Tourist office Schiermoonikoog's VVV is at Reeweg 5 (Mon–Fri 9am–5pm, Sat 10am–4pm; ☎ 0519 531 233, ✆ vvvschiermonnikoog.nl) and offers the usual services, including booking private rooms around the island.

ACCOMMODATION AND EATING

HOTELS

Herberg Rijsbergen Knuppeldam 2 ☎ 0519 531 257, ✆ rijsbergen.biz. On the east side of the village, fifteen minutes' walk from the tourist office, this is an excellent-value and very peaceful hotel, located in a historical building with lovely gardens and a sun terrace. €95

De Tjattel Langestreek 94 ☎ 0519 531 133, ✆ detjattel.nl. Two-star hotel in the heart of the village, with decent but unspectacular rooms. It also has a large restaurant and bar, which serves meat and fish mains for €17.50–20 at dinner and a variety of *uitsmijters*, salads, sandwiches, etc, at lunch for €5–10. Restaurant daily noon–3pm & 4.30–9pm. €110

Van der Werff Reeweg 2 ☎ 0519 531 203, ✆ hotelvanderwerff.nl. This large hotel is the most pleasant place to stay in town, housed in a landmark building with comfortable rooms. Its wood-panelled bar is one of the island's cosiest places for a drink, and there's also a rather grand restaurant. €105

CAMPSITE

Seedune Seeduneweg 1 ☎ 0519 531 398, ✆ seedune .nl. Schiermonnikoog's campsite is in a lovely location, to the north of the main village in the woods just east of Badweg. Facilities include bike rental and wi-fi. €7 per person, plus €3 for a tent. April–Sept. €17

Groningen

The most exciting city in the northern Netherlands, **GRONINGEN** comes as something of a surprise in the midst of its namesake province's quiet, rural surroundings. It's a hip, rather cosmopolitan place for the most part, with a thriving student life that imbues the city with vim and gusto. Competitively priced restaurants dish up exotic curries and fresh falafel alongside the standard Dutch staples, and the arts scene is particularly vibrant,

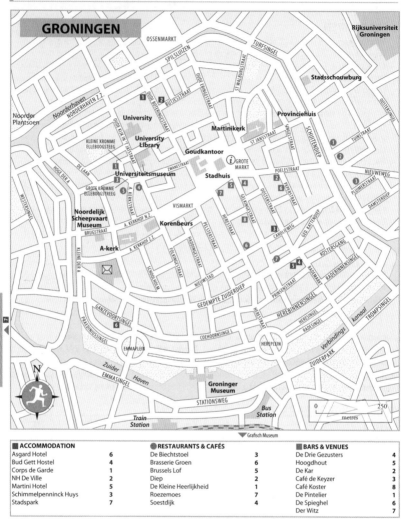

■ ACCOMMODATION		● RESTAURANTS & CAFÉS		■ BARS & VENUES	
Asgard Hotel	6	De Biechtstoel	3	De Drie Gezusters	4
Bud Gett Hostel	4	Brasserie Groen	6	Hoogdhout	5
Corps de Garde	1	Brussels Lof	5	De Kar	2
NH De Ville	2	Diep	2	Café de Keyzer	3
Martini Hotel	5	De Kleine Heerlijkheid	1	Café Koster	8
Schimmelpenninck Huys	3	Roezemoes	7	De Pintelier	1
Stadspark	7	Soestdijk	4	De Spieghel	6
				Der Witz	7

especially during the academic year. Virtually destroyed during the Allied liberation in 1945, the city focuses on two enormous squares and is now a jumble of styles, from traditional canal-side townhouses to bright Art Deco tilework along the upper facades of the shopping streets – an eclecticism that culminates in the innovative **Groninger Museum** sitting on its own island near the station. Finally, one of the nice things about Groningen is that the centre is almost **car-free**, the result of huge investment in traffic-calming measures and a network of cycle paths and bus lanes. Today two-thirds of residents travel regularly by **bike**, the highest percentage in the country.

Grote Markt

Still encircled by what was once a moat, Groningen's compact city centre is the enjoyable part of town with all the main sights within easy walking distance of each other. The effective centre of town is **Grote Markt**, a wide-open space that was badly damaged by wartime bombing and has been rather unimaginatively reconstructed. It's home to the tourist office at one end and the Neoclassical **Stadhuis** at the other, tucked in front of the mid-seventeenth-century **Goudkantoor** (Gold Office); look out for the shell motif above the windows, a characteristic Groningen decoration.

Martinikerk

Martinikerkhof 3 · **Church** Late March to early Nov Tues–Sat 11am–5pm, Sun 2–5pm; July & Aug Mon–Sat 11am–5pm, Sun 2–5pm; €1 · **Tower** April–Oct Mon–Sat 11am–5pm; July & Aug also Sun 11am–5pm; Nov–March Mon–Sat noon–4pm; €3 · ☎ 050 311 1277, ⓦ martinikerk.nl

At the northeast corner of the Grote Markt, the tiered tower of the **Martinikerk** is perhaps Groningen's most significant landmark, and is worth peeking into for its impressive interior. Alhough the oldest parts of the church were built in around 1180, most of it dates from the mid-fifteenth century, the nave being a Gothicized rebuilding undertaken to match the added choir. Adjoining the church, the essentially seventeenth-century **Martinitoren** can be climbed and offers a view that is breathtaking in every sense of the word. Behind the church is the lawn of the **Kerkhof**, an ancient piece of common land that's partly enclosed by the **Provinciehuis**, a rather grand neo-Renaissance building of 1915, seat of the provincial government.

The Universiteitsmuseum

Oude Kijk in 't Jatstraat 7a · Tues–Sun 1–5pm · €5 · ☎ 050 363 5083, ⓦ rug.nl/museum

Northwest of Grote Markt are the main buildings of Groningen's prestigious **university**, one of the oldest and largest in the country, with over 25,000 students at any one time. Founded in the early seventeenth century, its gabled main building is topped with a bulbous clock tower and normally has a sea of student bikes in front. Around the corner the **Universiteitsmuseum** gives a taste of the university's history, with exhibits ranging from scientific equipment to photos of derby-hatted students clowning around at the turn of twentieth century.

The Vismarkt

Almost as large an open space as the Grote Markt, the neighbouring Vismarkt is anchored at its far end by the **Korenbeurs** (Corn Exchange) of 1865. The statues on its facade represent, from left to right, Neptune, Mercurius (god of commerce) and Ceres (goddess of agriculture), while you can enjoy its wrought-iron-and-glass interior while browsing the aisles of the Albert Heijn supermarket inside. Just behind, the **A-kerk** is a fifteenth-century church with a Baroque steeple, attractively restored in tones of yellow, orange and red. The church's full name is Onze Lieve Vrouwekerk der A ("Our Dear Lady's Church of the A"), the A being a small river which forms the moat encircling the town centre.

Noordelijk Scheepvaart Museum

Brugstraat 24–26 · Tues–Sat 10am–5pm, Sun 1–5pm · €4 · ☎ 050 312 2202, ⓦ noordelijkscheepvaartmuseum.nl

Just west of the A-kerk, the **Noordelijk Scheepvaart Museum** is one of the best-equipped and most comprehensive maritime museums in the country, tracing the history of north Holland's shipping from the sixth to the twentieth centuries. Housed in a warren of steep stairs and timber-beamed rooms, each of the museum's twenty displays deals with a different aspect of shipping, including trade with the Indies, the development of peat canals and a series of reconstructed nautical workshops. The museum's particular appeal is its imaginative combination of models and original artefacts, which are themselves a mixture of the personal (seamen's chests, quadrants) and the public (figureheads, tile designs of ships).

The Groninger Museum

Museumeiland 1 · Tues–Sun 10am–5pm · €10 · ☏ 050 3666555, ⓦ groningermuseum.nl

The town's main draw is the excellent **Groninger Museum**, set on its own island on the southern edge of the centre, directly across from the train station. Aside from a very cool information lounge with computers and touch screens, the museum is mostly given over to temporary exhibitions and what you see really depends on when you're here. If you're lucky, a rare work by the seventeenth-century Dutch painter Carel Fabritius – *Man in a Helmet* (probably the museum's most prized possession) – will be on display, or Rubens' energetic *Adoration of the Magi* and Isaac Israëls' inviting *Hoedenwinkel* from a modest sample of Hague School paintings.

Most people, however, visit as much for the building itself as for what's inside, which consists of **six pavilions**, each designed in a highly individual style: think Gaudí on holiday in Miami, and you'll have some idea of the interior decor. Once inside, between the stylish café and museum shop, the striking mosaic stairwell sweeps downwards, depositing you among bulbous lemon-yellow pillars and pink walls, from where moat-level corridors head off to pavilions either side: east to Mendini, Mendini 1 and Coop Himmelb(l)au, west to Starck and De Ploeg.

De Ploeg and the Starck Pavilion

The museum's collection includes a number of works by the Expressionists of the Groningen De Ploeg school, housed in their own pavilion, a trapezium constructed from red bricks. The De Ploeg movement is characterized by intense colour contrasts, exaggerated shapes and depiction of landscapes – often of the countryside north of Groningen. As founding member Jan Altink put it: "There wasn't much going on in the way of art in Groningen, so I thought of cultivation and thus also of ploughing. Hence the name De Ploeg." As well as Altink, look out for the paintings of Jan Wiegers. Upstairs from De Ploeg, the **Philippe Starck pavilion** is a giant disc clad in aluminium plating and houses the museum's wonderful collection of **Chinese and Japanese porcelain**, beautifully displayed in circular glass cases, softened by gauzy drapes.

The Mendini Pavilions and Coop Himmelb(l)au

On the other side of the mosaic stairway, the **Mendini pavilions** are dedicated to temporary exhibitions, while a large concrete stairway links Mendini 1 to the final, and most controversial, pavilion. Designed by Wolfgang Prix and Helmut Swiczinsky, who together call themselves **Coop Himmelb(l)au**, it's a Deconstructivist experiment: double-plated steel and reinforced glass jut out at awkward angles, and skinny aerial walkways crisscross the exhibition space. It all feels – probably deliberately – half-built. Look out for the glass-walk holes, where the concrete floor stops and suddenly between your feet the canal gapes, two storeys below. This pavilion is also given over to temporary exhibitions.

The train station

Across the water from the Groninger Museum, Groningen's train station was built in 1896 at enormous cost. It was one of the finest stations of its day, decorated with the strong colours and symbolic designs of Art Nouveau tiles from the Rozenburg factory in The Hague. The grandeur of much of the building has disappeared under a welter of concrete, glass and plastic suspended ceilings, but the old first- and second-class waiting rooms have survived pretty much intact, and have been refurbished as restaurants.

ARRIVAL AND DEPARTURE   GRONINGEN

By train Groningen's grand train station is on the south side of the town centre and is very well connected to the rest of the Netherlands, with services to Amsterdam (hourly; 2hr 20min); Assen (every 20min; 20min); Leeuwarden, (every 30min; 50min); Uithuizen (every 30min; 35min); and Zwolle (every 30min; 1hr 10min).

LIQUOR FIT FOR A QUEEN?

Although Groningen does not have a rich culinary tradition, the **Hooghoudt brewery** (wwwhooghoudt.nl) is known throughout the country and dates back to 1888. It's best known for its Graanjevever, but they also produce Beerenburg and other liquors like the Wilhelmus Orange Liquor, which is traditionally served on Queen's Day.

By bus The bus station is right next to the train station, with regular buses to and from Lauwersoog for boats to Schiermonnikoog (bus #163: 7 daily; 1hr); to Zoutkamp (Mon–Fri every 30min, Sat hourly; 1hr); and Emmen (every 20min; 1hr 10min).

INFORMATION

Tourist office The VVV is housed in a hideous building on the main square at Grote Markt 25 (Mon noon–6pm, Tues–Fri 9.30am–6pm, Sat 10am–5pm; July & Aug also Sun 11am–4pm; www0900 202 3050, wwwtourism.groningen.nl). It offers information on the town and province, online accommodation reservations, tickets for visiting bands, theatre groups and orchestras, and information on exploring Groningen by boat (wwwrondvaartbedrijfkool.nl) or canoe. It also sells a brochure of city walks for €1.50, and has a short list of private rooms in both Groningen and the surrounding area, though hardly any are near the centre.

ACCOMMODATION

HOTELS

Asgard Hotel Ganzevoortsingel 2 www050 368 4810, wwwasgardhotel.nl. Very handy for both the train station and the centre of town, this eco-hotel tries very hard, with its untreated Scandinavian wood and bright, simple and contemporary rooms. The rooms could be a bit larger, and a bit cosier, but they have comfortable beds, nice bathrooms and there's free wi-fi throughout, so whose complaining. **€115**

★ **Corps de Garde** Oude Boteringestraat 72–74 www050 314 5437, wwwcorpsdegarde.nl. A lovely hotel, probably the city's best choice, with a beautiful bright breakfast room downstairs and a variety of rooms in a sixteenth-century mansion. The cheaper beamed rooms are on the top floor, with more contemporary rooms below, recently refurbished with large showers and a modern look and feel that sits well with the ancient building. There's a cosy bar in the basement and the welcome is always warm. Breakfast, though, is extra – €14.50. **€94.50**

NH de Ville Oude Boteringestraat 43 www050 318 1222, wwwdeville.nl. Although it's now part of a chain, this hotel has maintained its intimate feel with friendly staff and a fine Baroque interior. The cosy courtyard is also a great location for a romantic dinner, and the downstairs lounge is lovely, very well designed in the context of the old building. **€120**

Martini Hotel Gedempte Zuiderdiep 8 www050 312 9919, wwwmartinihotel.nl. A large and central 100-room hotel in an attractive and quite imposing nineteenth-century building. The rooms vary from standard – darker, less recently renovated – to the more recently updated "comfort" rooms on the upper floors, which are much lighter and include free wi-fi. Breakfast costs extra (€11.50) whichever room you choose. There's a large bar and reception downstairs, and a restaurant – *Weeva* – next door. **€74.50**

Schimmelpenninck Huys Oosterstraat 53 www050 318 9502, wwwschimmelpenninckhuys.nl. This place likes to think of itself as the poshest place in town, and its faded elegance certainly looks the part, with a lovely downstairs bar and lobby, part of which overlooks a pretty inner courtyard. The rooms vary from grand antique-filled affairs with large bathrooms in the original old mansion, to simpler, more up-to-date affairs in the back annexe. There's a relentlessly old-fashioned restaurant at the front, where a three-course dinner menu costs €32.50. **€100**

HOSTEL

Bud Gett Hostel Rademarkt 3 www050 588 6558, wwwbudgetthostels.nl. A relatively new, cheekily named (geddit?) hostel, smack in the centre of town and offering well-equipped dorm beds as well as simple but functional twin rooms with private facilities. Dorm beds **€25**, twins **€50**

CAMPSITE

Stadspark Campinglaan 6 www050 525 1624, wwwwww.campingstadspark.nl. Groningen's most obvious option if you're camping, and a pleasant waterside site to boot. It's within a twenty-minute walk of the centre, and located in the city's nicest and largest park. Mid-March to mid-Oct. **€18**

EATING

De Biechtstoel Schuitendiep 88 www050 313 8246, wwwdebiechtstoel.com. Cosy restaurant hidden in a small alley and crammed with holy relics (hence the name "confession chair"). The menu offers everything from stew to scallops for €16–20. Wed–Sun 5.30–10pm.

Brasserie Groen Carolieweg 16 www050 311 3962,

ⓦ brasseriegroen.nl. Agreeable multi-level lunchroom-cum-restaurant with fresh green accents and very decent coffee. A seasonal three-course menu sets you back €22.50. Tues–Sat 11am till late.

Brussels Lof A-Kerkstraat 24 ☎050 312 7603, ⓦ brusselslof.com. Serves a wide range of vegetarian dishes and good fondues, but also known for its fresh fish; pure, simple and excellent cooking, with veggie mains from €15.50, and fish mains for €21.50. Tues–Sat 5.30–9.30pm.

★ **Diep** Schuitendiep 44 ☎050 589 0009, ⓦ dinercafediep.nl. Once a residence for monks, now a stylish restaurant with lime-green hues and a hidden inner courtyard. The friendly staff serve mains such as salmon fillet, steak Japanese-style and goat's cheese salad for around €18. Daily 5–10pm.

De Kleine Heerlijkheid Schuitendiep 42 ☎050 313 1370, ⓦ dekleineheerlijkheid.nl. Located in one of the town's oldest buildings just outside the city walls, the smallest restaurant in Groningen serves mains such as barramundi or lamb shoulder for around €16.95, in an agreeable atmosphere. Daily 5.30–9.30pm.

Roezemoes Gedempte Zuiderdiep 15 ☎050 314 8854, ⓦ eetcafe-roezemoes.nl. If all you want is an original *stamppot* (mashed potatoes with veggies and meat) you're in the right place – they even serve this typical Dutch winter dish in summer, for €11.50 a pop. There are also non-mashed mains on the menu for around €13–15. Tues–Sun 11am–3pm & Sun–Wed 5–9.30pm, Thurs–Sat 5–10pm.

★ **Soestdijk** Grote Kromme Elleboog 6 ☎050 314 5050, ⓦ cafesoestdijk.nl. Groningen's closest thing to a gastropub, where you can just as easily sit at the bar and nurse a drink as eat. There are specials on the board from around €14.50 and a handful of other dishes on the menu – steaks, port satay, a couple of fish options – for €15–20. A really nice feel, and good food too – like all good gastropubs, simple but well cooked and delicious; and they do portions of cheese and various bar snacks, if you don't want a full meal. Mon–Thurs 4pm–1am, Fri & Sat 3pm–3am, Sun 5pm–midnight.

BARS AND VENUES

Café de Keyzer Turftorenstraat 4 ☎050 312 9194. A likeable brown café – very popular with local students – with many beers on draught and free peanuts in the shell. Mon–Sat 4pm–2am.

Café Koster Hoogstraat 7–9 ☎050 314 5217, ⓦ cafekoster.nl. With a dancefloor overlooked by pious figures of Christ, this is central Groningen's old rockers' bar with loud music most nights, and live sounds on Sundays from 4pm. Always fun. Wed 8pm–late, Thurs–Sun 4pm–late.

De Drie Gezusters Grote Markt 39 ☎050 312 7041, ⓦ driegezustersgroningen.nl. Perhaps the most historic watering hole in the centre of Groningen, a beautiful *fin-de-siécle* bar and restaurant with a reading bench down the middle and covered booths at the side – quite a Groningen institution, with many of its original fixtures and fittings still in place. Walk through to the rooms at the back, fitted out with old railway seats and luggage racks. Daily 10am–midnight.

Hoogdhout Grote Markt 42 ☎050 542 0000, ⓦ hooghoudt.nl. Located in the old Lloyds Insurance building, this is a convivial bar with the *Bij den Boven* restaurant on the first floor: there's a huge terrace and attractively priced daily specials. It's at its best in summer. Daily 11.30am–9pm, Fri & Sat until 10pm.

De Kar Peperstraat 15, ☎06 8709 6112, ⓦ dekar-groningen.com. A popular bar among students, on the lively Peperstraat: it stays open late on weekdays and has dancing. Wed–Sun 10pm–late.

De Pintelier Kleine Kromme Elleboog 9 ☎050 318 5100, ⓦ pintelier.nl. A great long bar with loads of Belgian beers on tap, and a very large selection of whiskies. Sun–Thurs 3pm–2am, Fri & Sat 3pm–3am.

De Spieghel Peperstraat 11 ☎050 312 6651, ⓦ jazzcafedespieghel.nl. This jazz café has live performances most nights, including some reasonably big names, and a nice terrace in summer. Mon–Wed, Fri, Sat open from 8pm, music from around 10.30pm.

★ **Der Witz** Grote Markt 47 ☎050 314 1417, ⓦ derwitz.nl. Cosy, narrow old bar, very comfy and the pick of the many places on the Grote Markt. Even the smokers' booth is better than usual. They serve a good range of German and Belgian beers on draft and strong chilled *korns* (the German version of *jenever*). Mon noon–midnight, Tues–Fri from 10am–midnight, Sat from 9am–1am, Sun from 1pm–midnight.

FESTIVAL NOORDERZON

Every year in mid-August, Groningen hosts the increasingly popular **Festival Noorderzon** (ⓦ noorderzon.nl), a ten-day blend of theatre, music, film and performance art. About a third of the events are free, many of them staged in the Noorderplantsoen park, a fifteen minute walk north along Nieuwe Kijk in 't Jatstraat. Come night-time, food stalls and drinking-holes surround the lake in the park, while folk stroll along the lantern-lit paths or chill on the lake's stone steps to the sound of Afrobeat, Latin, funk, rock, jazz or ambient music. Other entertainment includes circuses, mime, puppetry, videos and installations. Hotels get busy, so if you're planning to visit around this time you'd do well to book in advance.

DIRECTORY

Bike rental At the train station (€6.50/day, €32.50/week; ☎ 050 312 4174).

Boat trips Kool, Stationsweg 1012 (☎ 050 312 8379, ⓦ rondvaartbedrijfkool.nl), runs regular trips around the old town moat; tickets cost €11 for a 1hr tour.

Books There's a good range of English-language titles at Selexyz Scholtens at Guldenstraat 20 (☎ 050 317 2500).

Markets Vegetables, fruit, flowers, fish and fabrics at A-Kerkhof (Tues, Fri & Sat 9am–5pm). Organic food market at Vismarkt (Wed 9am–5pm). Non-food general market at the Grote Markt (Thurs 1–9pm).

Police Rademarkt 12 ☎ 0900 8844.

Post office By the A-kerk at Munnekeholm 1 (Mon 10am–6pm, Tues–Fri 9am–6pm, Sat 10am–1.30pm).

Taxi TaxiCentrale ☎ 050 549 7676, ⓦ taxicentrale -groningen.nl.

Around Groningen

Once known as East Frisia, the province of **Groningen** does not have the high tourist profile of many of the country's other regions, but it does boast a large slab of empty coastline where the **Lauwersmeer National Park** is home to extensive wildlife, the **seal sanctuary** of Pieterburen, and the pick of the old manor houses that dot the province, **Menkemaborg** in **Uithuizen**. To the southeast of Groningen, the old frontier village of **Bourtange** has been painstakingly restored, offering an insight into eighteenth-century life in a fortified town, while nearby **Ter Apel** holds a rare survivor from the Reformation in the substantial remains of its monastery.

Menkemaborg

March–May Tues–Sun 10am–5pm; July & Aug daily 10am–5pm; Oct–Dec Tues–Sun 10am–4pm • €6 • ⓦ menkemaborg.nl

The most agreeable day-trip from Groningen is to the village of **Uithuizen**, 25km northeast, where the moated manor house of **Menkemaborg** is a signed ten-minute walk from the station. Dating from the fifteenth century and surrounded by formal gardens in the English style, the house has a sturdy, compact elegance and is one of the very few mansions, or *borgs*, of the old landowning families to have survived. The interior consists of a sequence of period rooms furnished in the style of the seventeenth century, displaying some of the Groninger Museum's applied art and history collection.

The Pieterburen Seal Sanctuary

Hoofdstraat 84a • Daily 9am–6pm • €10 • ☎ 0595 526 526, ⓦ zeehondencreche.nl

Founded almost 40 years ago by Lenie 't Hart, a local animal welfare heroine, the **Pieterburen Seal Sanctuary** rescues abandoned or weak seals with the purpose of releasing them back into the wild. You can view seals – lots of them – in the outside tanks, or on their own in quarantine quarters inside; the best time to see seal pups is

WALKS AROUND UITHUIZEN

The trip to Uithuizen can be combined with *wadlopen* (see p.221) – a guided walk across the coastal mud flats to the uninhabited sand-spit island of **Rottumeroog**, the most easterly of the Dutch Wadden islands. Excursion buses head out to the coast from Menkemaborg at weekends two or three times a month(June–Sept); the trip costs from €32.50 per person and lasts four hours: booking is essential – contact Stichting Uithuizer Wad (ⓦ wadlopen.nl). Without a guide, it's too dangerous to venture onto the mud flats, but it is easy enough to **walk** along the enclosing dyke that runs behind the shoreline for the whole length of the province. There's precious little to see, but when the weather's clear, the browns, blues and greens of the surrounding land and sea are unusually beautiful. From Uithuizen, it's a good hour's stroll north to the nearest point on the dyke, and you'll need a large-scale map for directions.

> **THE PIETERPAD**
>
> Pieterburen is also the start and end point for the longest unbroken walking route in the Netherlands, the 464-kilometre-long **Pieterpad** to Maastricht. More information and a map of the walking route can be obtained at Pieterburen VVV (see opposite) or at Ⓦ pieterpad.nl.

during the summer, when many will be nursed and fed until they are strong enough to make it on their own. Look in also on the "kitchen" where they prepare the seals' fish, and take in a permanent exhibition on the work of the centre (info is in Dutch but there is an English booklet), plus naturally there's a shop selling all manner of cuddly seal-related merchandise. It's not cheap, but is great for kids – and in a very good cause.

The Lauwersmeer Nationaal Park

Lauwersmeer Nationaal Park, some 35km northwest of Groningen, comprises a broken and irregular lake that spreads across the provincial boundary into neighbouring Friesland. Once an arm of the sea, it was turned into a freshwater lake by the construction of the Lauwersoog dam, a controversial 1960s project that was vigorously opposed by local fishermen, who ended up having to move all their tackle to the coast. Spared intensive industrial and agricultural development because of the efforts of conservationists, it's a quiet and peaceful region with a wonderful variety of sea birds, and is increasingly popular with anglers, windsurfers, sailors and cyclists. The local villages are uniformly dull. At the mouth of the lake, the desultory port of **LAUWERSOOG** is where **ferries** leave for the fifty-minute trip to the island of Schiermonnikoog (see p.220). The most convenient base for exploring the park is **ZOUTKAMP**, near the southeast corner of the lake on the River Reitdiep.

Bourtange

W Lodewijstraat 33 • Mid-March to Oct daily 10am–5pm • Entry is free but a €6 ticket gives admission to specific buildings and exhibitions • ☏ 0599 354 600, Ⓦ bourtange.nl

Some 60km southeast of Groningen, just a kilometre or so from the German frontier, **BOURTANGE** is a superbly restored fortified village. Founded by William of Orange in 1580 to help protect the eastern approaches to Groningen, Bourtange fell into disrepair during the nineteenth century, only to be entirely refurbished as a tourist attraction in 1964. The design of the village is similar to that of Naarden (see p.139) and is best appreciated as you walk around the old bastions of the star-shaped fortress. There are regular events throughout the summer, including mock battles, markets and guided walks, and you can even get married here if you want. Otherwise just turn up: it's tremendously atmospheric, there are usually folk attired in period dress and a cannon is fired at 3pm every Sunday.

Klooster Ter Apel

Boslaan 3–5 Ter Apel • Tues–Sat 10am–5pm, Sun 1–5pm • €7.50 • ☏ 0599 581370, Ⓦ museumklooster-terapel.com

Some 30km to the south of Bourtange, in the small town of **TER APEL**, the **Museum Klooster** is a highlight of this part of the country. This was the monastery of the Order of the Holy Cross – or Croziers – dating back to the Middle Ages and probably unique among rural Dutch monasteries in surviving the ravages of the Reformation. The chapel, superbly restored, preserves a number of unusual features, including the tripartite sedilia, where the priest and his assistants sat during Mass, and a splendid rood screen that divides the chancel from the nave. Elsewhere, the east wing is a curious hybrid of Gothic and Baroque styles, the cloister has a small herb garden and the other rooms are normally given over to temporary exhibitions of religious art. The monastery is surrounded by extensive beech woods and magnificent old horse chestnut trees; follow one of the marked walks or simply ramble at your leisure.

ARRIVAL AND INFORMATION
AROUND GRONINGEN

By train There are regular trains to Uithuizen from Groningen, and Menkemaborg is a ten-minute walk from Uithuizen station.

By bus Zoutkamp, for the Lauwesmeer National Park, is served by bus #65 approx hourly from Groningen. Bus #73 runs from Groningen to Ter Apel hourly during the week and every two hours at weekends: the journey takes about thirty minutes. Getting to Bourtange by public transport is more difficult: take the train from Groningen to Winschoten, a half-hour journey, and then bus #12 to Vlagtwedde and change to bus #35 for the short hop to Bourtange.

Tourist offices Pieterburen VVV, at Hoofdstraat 83 (April–June & Sept & Oct Tues–Sun 1–5pm; July & Aug daily 1–5pm ☎0595 528 522, ⓦvvvlauwersland.nl), has information on everything in the surrounding area, including *wadlopen* and the Pieterpad. Zoutkamp VVV, Reitdiepskade 11 (April–Sept Mon–Fri 9am–5pm, Sat 10am–4pm; Nov–March Mon–Fri 10am–noon & 1–3pm; ☎0595 401 957, ⓦvvvlauwersland.nl) has a limited supply of private rooms, which can be reserved here or at Groningen VVV (see p.225).

ACCOMMODATION AND EATING

PIETERBUREN

Bij de Buren van Pieter Hoofdstraat 82 ☎0595 528 203. Right in the centre of the village, this cosy joint does sandwiches, *uitsmijters* and bar snacks, plus pizzas from €6.50 – ideal before or after a spot of *wadlopen*. Daily noon–2am; more limited hours out of season.

De Kromme Raake Molenstraat 5 Eenrum ☎0595 491 600, ⓦhoteldekrommeraake.nl. Just 5km from Pieterburen, the village of Eenrum hosts what is officially (according to the *Guinness Book of Records*) the smallest hotel in the world, an old grocery shop that was transformed into a one-room hotel in 1989 by a former governor of Groningen. The room itself is very nice, if rather eccentrically decorated, but needless to say you have to book a fair way in advance. €150

TER APEL

Hotel Boschhuis Boslaan 6 ☎0599 581 208, ⓦhotelboschhuis.nl. Right opposite the Ter Apel monastery, this is a lovely place to stay if you fancy spending a quiet night in the country. The rooms are comfortable with slightly boutiquey aspirations and there's an excellent restaurant with both atmosphere and good, seasonal food. €82.50

BOURTANGE

't Plathuis Bourtangekanaal Noord 1 ☎0599 354 383, ⓦplathuis.nl. Great campsite spread across several tree-fringed fields, with a café and bar, a small lake and canal. There are also a few wooden cabins in the trees in case you don't fancy pitching your tent. April–Oct. €17.50

NOORDPOLDERZIJL

't Zielhoes Zijlweg 4 Noordpolderzijl ☎0595 423 058, ⓦzielhoes.nl. This must be the country's remotest café in an amazing spot, where you can climb onto the dike and look out over the Wadden Sea. It serves a fairly basic but always delicious menu of sandwiches, *uitsmijters*, soup and pancakes at really good prices. April & May Tues–Fri noon–6pm, Sat & Sun 10am–6pm; June–Sept daily 10am–8pm; Oct–March Fri & Sat noon–6pm, Sun 10am–6pm.

Drenthe

Until the early nineteenth century, the sparsely populated province of **Drenthe**, by the German border, was little more than a flat expanse of empty peat bog, marsh and moor. In recent decades, it's accumulated a scattering of small towns, but it remains the country's least populated province, whose main pull is its woods and countryside. Its only conspicuous geographical feature is a ridge of low hills that runs northwest for some 50km from Emmen, its largest town, toward Groningen. This ridge, the **Hondsrug**, was high enough to attract prehistoric settlers whose *hunebeds* (megalithic tombs) have become Drenthe's main tourist attraction. Otherwise, **Assen**, the provincial capital, is a dull place with a good museum, and **Emmen**, its only real rival, can only be recommended as a convenient base for visiting some of the *hunebeds* and three neighbouring open-air folk culture museums.

Assen

About 16km south of Groningen, **ASSEN** is the capital of Drenthe, though you're unlikely to want to stay here long. Its main square, **Brink** is a big, green open space, which was once home to the monastery that gave rise to the town in the Middle Ages, and there are a few scattered remains of this. Off to the left, **Marktstraat** is the town's main shopping street.

Drents Museum

Brink 1 • Tues–Sun 11am–5pm • €12 • ☎ 0592 377773, ⓦ drentsmuseum.nl

On the southern edge of Brink, spread over a pleasant group of old houses, the **Drents Museum** is perhaps the only thing that makes a stop in Assen worthwhile. The museum's most important exhibit is its collection of prehistoric skeletons brought here from the neighbouring *hunebeds*. There is also the much-vaunted Pesse Canoe, the oldest water vessel ever found: dating from about 6800 BC, it looks its age.

Herinneringscentrum Kamp Westerbork

Oosthalen 8 Hooghalen • Mon–Fri 10am–5pm, Sat & Sun 1–5pm; April–Sept Sat & Sun also 11am–1pm • €6.50 • ☎ 0593 592 600, ⓦ kampwesterbork.nl

Assen's other main sight is a sad one, the **Herinneringscentrum Kamp Westerbork**, a little south of town on the road between the villages of Amen and Hooghalen. It commemorates Holland's only concentration camp, which was based 3km away and was where the Nazis assembled Dutch Jews before transporting them to the death camps in the east, mainly Auschwitz and Sobibor. The documents and artefacts on display here are deeply affecting, and buses run every twenty minutes to the camp itself. Not much remains of the camp – there is just a watchtower and a stretch of rail line, together with a number of monuments, one to the Dutch Resistance in the trees and another a series of coffin-shaped stones remembering those who spent time here before being transported to their deaths.

ARRIVAL AND INFORMATION

By train Assen's train station is on the eastern edge of the city centre, five minutes' walk from Brink. There are regular – usually hourly – services to Amersfoort, Hilversum and Amsterdam, and every thirty minutes to Groningen and Zwolle.

Tourist office Assen's VVV is at Marktstraat 8–10 (Mon 1–6pm, Tues–Thurs 9am–6pm, Fri 9am–9pm, Sat 9am–5pm; ☎ 0592 243 788, ⓦ ditisassen.nl).

ACCOMMODATION AND EATING

City Hotel de Jonge Brinkstraat 85 ☎ 0592 312 023, ⓦ hoteldejonge.nl. The only hotel in the centre of town, and a large, fairly corporate affair, with 61 rooms that are nice enough, if a bit short on home comforts. There's also a reasonable restaurant and terrace. **€70**

Emmen and around

To all intents and purposes **EMMEN** is a new town, a twentieth-century amalgamation of strip villages that were originally peat colonies. The centre is a modern affair, mixing the remnants of the old with lumpy boulders, trees and shrubs and a job lot of concrete

---

MOTOR RACING IN ASSEN

Pretty much the only time Assen is the centre of attention is during the **Assen TT** (ⓦ tt-assen .com), the only Grand Prix motorcycle race in the Netherlands, and the British Superbike championships in September. The last TT drew a crowd of around 130,000, making it the largest one-day sports event in the Netherlands. On the three nights leading up to the event, Assen's centre is packed with people enjoying live music and lots of beer. If you are visiting while it's on (the last Saturday in June), make sure you book accommodation well in advance.

and glass. Emmen is known for two things: its *hunebeds* and its zoo, while the nearby Veenpark is also worth a visit for its giant open-air museum-village.

The Zoo

Hoofdstraat 18 • Daily 10am–5pm; March–May & Oct closes 5pm, Sept closes 5.30pm, Nov–Feb closes 4.30pm • €20.50, children (3–9) €18 • ☎ 0591 850 855, ⊛ dierenparkemmen.nl

Emmen's **zoo**, right in the middle of town, is the reason most people visit, and unusually for a city centre zoo boasts an imitation African savanna, where the animals roam relatively freely. It also has a massive sea-lion pool and a giant hippo house, and in the newer part of the park you can find Humboldt penguins.

The Hunebeds

The best of Emmen's *hunebeds* is **Emmerdennen Hunebed**, in the woods 1km or so east of the station along Boslaan. This is a so-called passage-grave, with a relatively sophisticated entrance surrounded by a ring of standing stones. The largest *hunebed* in Drenthe, however, lies twenty kilometres northwest of Emmen, in the village of Borge, which takes the *hunebed* theme seriously, from street names and pancakes to special menus. On the northeast edge of the village, the **Hunebedcentrum** at Bronnegerstraat 12 (Mon–Fri 10am–5pm, Sat & Sun 11am–5pm; €7.10; ☎ 0599 236 374, ⊛ hunebedcentrum.nl) explains the origins of the massive *hunebed*, which, at 22.5m long, is an extraordinary feat (in prehistoric terms at least).

The Veenpark

Berkenroede 4 Barger-Comapscum • Daily Easter to Oct 10am–5pm; July & Aug until 6pm • €13.25 (under-5s free) • ☎ 0591 324 444, ⊛ veenpark.nl

About 11km east of Emmen, not far from the German border, the **Veenpark** is a massive open-air museum-village that traces the history and development of the peat colonies of the moors of southern Groningen and eastern Drenthe. The colonies were established in the nineteenth century, when labour was imported to cut the thick layers of peat that lay all over the moors. Isolated in small communities, and under the thumb of the traders who sold their products and provided their foodstuffs, the colonists were harshly exploited and lived in abject poverty until well into the 1930s. Built around some old interlocking canals, the museum consists of a series of reconstructed villages that track through the history of the colonies. It's inevitably a bit folksy, but very popular, with its own narrow-gauge railway, a canal barge, and working period bakeries, bars and shops. A thorough exploration takes a full day.

ARRIVAL AND INFORMATION

EMMEN AND AROUND

By train and bus Emmen's train and bus stations adjoin each other, five minutes' walk north of the town centre: head straight down Stationsstraat into Boslaan and turn left down Hoofdstraat, the main drag. There are trains to Zwolle every 30min, and the journey takes an hour. Bus #59 runs to Borger on its way between Emmen and Groningen.

The Veenpark is served by hourly bus #26 from Emmen station (25min).

Tourist office Emmen VVV, at Hoofdstraat 22 (Mon 1–5pm, Tues–Sat 10am–5pm; ☎ 0591 649 712, ⊛ drenthe.nl), can arrange accommodation at pensions, private rooms and hotels.

ACCOMMODATION AND EATING

EMMEN

Stadshotel Boerland Hoofdstraat 57 ☎ 0591 613 746, ⊛ stads-hotelboerland.nl. Probably Emmen's nicest place to stay, across the street from the zoo, and with a decent restaurant, serving main courses like schnitzel, steaks and cod fillets for around €16. **€87.50**

BORGER

Nathalia Hoofdstraat 87 Borger ☎ 0599 234 791, ⊛ hotelpensionnathalia.nl. Pin-neat 2-, 3- and 4-bedded rooms in a delightful shuttered Dutch cottage in the middle of Borger, every one with cable TV and en-suite facilities. There's a lovely welcome, a cosy sitting-room, a garden terrace – and parking too. **€60**

4

The eastern Netherlands

BLOKZIJL HARBOUR

5

The eastern Netherlands

The three provinces that make up the eastern Netherlands –Flevoland, Overijssel and Gelderland – are home to a string of lovely country towns, whose long and often troubled history is recalled by a slew of handsome old buildings. Among them, Zwolle, Deventer and Zutphen are perhaps the pick, but there are intriguing former Zuider Zee ports as well, most memorably Kampen and Elburg. For British visitors at least, the most famous town hereabouts is Arnhem, site of the "bridge too far" when the Allies tried unsuccessfully to shorten the war with a lightning strike. Art lovers, meanwhile, won't want to miss the outstanding Kröller-Müller Museum set among the sandy heaths and woodland of the Nationaal Park de Hoge Veluwe.

Heading east from Amsterdam, the first province you reach is **Flevoland**, whose three pancake-flat, reclaimed polders – the twin Flevoland polders and the Noordoostpolder – incorporate two former Zuider Zee islands, **Urk** and **Schokland**, both of which are of considerable interest. The boundary separating Flevoland from the province of **Overijssel** runs along the old Zuider Zee shoreline and it's here that the region comes up trumps with a string of one-time seaports, most strikingly the pretty little towns of **Elburg** (in Gelderland), **Kampen** and **Blokzijl**. These three, along with nearby **Zwolle**, the capital of Overijssel, enjoyed a period of immense prosperity from the fourteenth to the sixteenth centuries, but the bubble burst in the seventeenth when the great merchant cities of Zuid- and Noord-Holland simply outplayed and undercut them. Later, these four towns – along with neighbouring **Deventer** and **Zutphen** – were bypassed by the Industrial Revolution, one happy consequence being that each of them boasts a medley of handsome late medieval and early modern houses and churches. Blokzijl also shares part of the province with the lakes and waterways that pattern the postcard-pretty hamlet of **Giethoorn**.

Further south, **Gelderland** spreads east from Utrecht to the German frontier, taking its name from the German town of Geldern, its capital until the late fourteenth century. As a province it's a bit of a mixture, varying from the uninspiring agricultural land of the **Betuwe** (Good Land), south of Utrecht, to the more distinctive – and appealing – **Veluwe** (Bad Land), an expanse of heath, woodland and dune that sprawls down from the old Zuider Zee coastline to **Arnhem**, incorporating the **Nationaal Park de Hoge Veluwe**. Anchoring Gelderland is the ancient town of **Nijmegen**, a fashionable university city, with a lively contemporary feel.

Zwolle

ZWOLLE, the compact capital of **Overijssel** about 85km from Amsterdam, is on the up. Not so long ago, it was a dowdy sort of place, but it has recently attracted

HOGE VELUWE NATIONAL PARK

Highlights

❶ Zwolle Encased within its old fortifications, this engaging old town boasts a distinguished cityscape not to mention several fine restaurants and bars. **See p.234**

❷ Kampen Lovely little town and former Zuider Zee port perched on the edge of moors and wetlands. **See p.241**

❸ Giethoorn Oh-so-pretty hamlet set amid lakes, canals and wetlands; an ideal place for pottering around on the water. **See p.250**

❹ Zutphen Quintessential Dutch country town tucked up against the River IJssel. **See p.253**

❺ Hoge Veluwe National Park Spacious area of heath and forest, crossed by footpaths and with cycle routes galore. **See pp.257–260**

❻ Kröller-Müller Museum Top-notch museum of modern European art, with a large sculpture garden and an impressive collection of works by van Gogh. **See p.257**

❼ Arnhem This industrious, riverside city may have a searing wartime history, but it's a smashing place to hunker down for a few days and it makes a perfect base for exploring the rest of Gelderland. **See pp.260–265**

HIGHLIGHTS ARE MARKED ON THE MAP ON PP.236–237

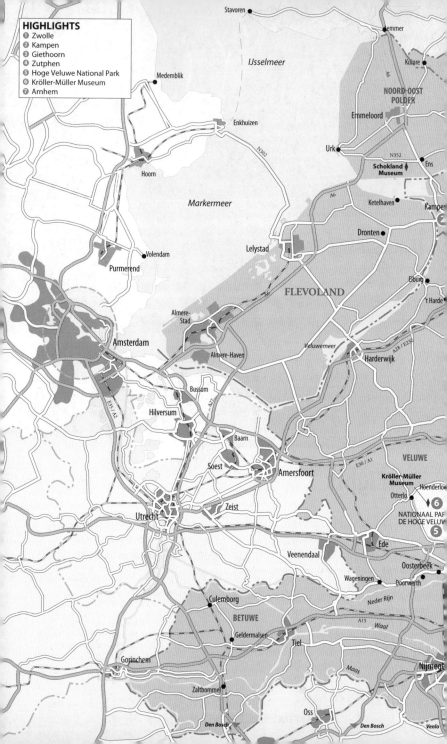

HIGHLIGHTS

1. Zwolle
2. Kampen
3. Giethoorn
4. Zutphen
5. Hoge Veluwe National Park
6. Kröller-Müller Museum
7. Arnhem

Stavoren

Lemmer

IJsselmeer

Kuinre

Medemblik

NOORD-OOST POLDER

Enkhuizen

Emmeloord

N302

Urk

N352

Ens

Hoorn

Schokland Museum

Ketelhaven

Kampe ❷

Markermeer

Dronten

Elburg

Lelystad

't Harde

Volendam

FLEVOLAND

Purmerend

Almere-Stad

Veluwemeer

A28 / E232

Harderwijk

Amsterdam

Almere-Haven

Bussum

Hilversum

Baarn

VELUWE

Soest

E30 / A1

Kröller-Müller Museum

Hoenderlo

Amersfoort

Otterlo

❻

Utrecht

Zeist

NATIONAAL PARK DE HOGE VELUW ❺

Veenendaal

Ede

Oosterbeek

Wageningen

Doorwerth

Culemborg

Neder Rijn

BETUWE

Geldermalsen

A15

Waal

Tiel

Gorinchem

Maas

Nijmege

Zaltbommel

Oss

Den Bosch

Den Bosch

Venlo

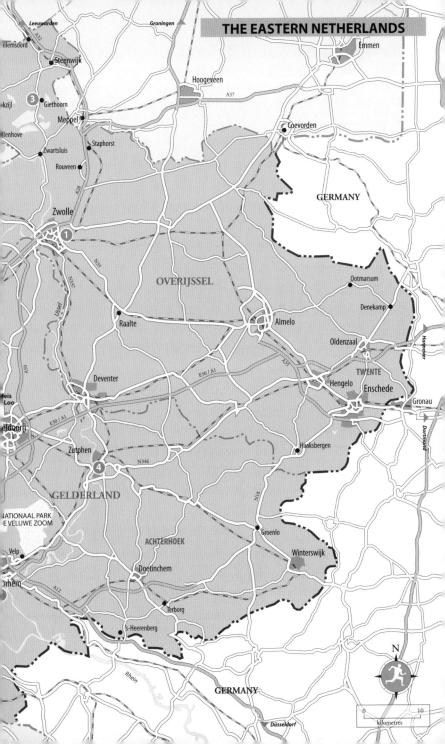

THE EASTERN NETHERLANDS

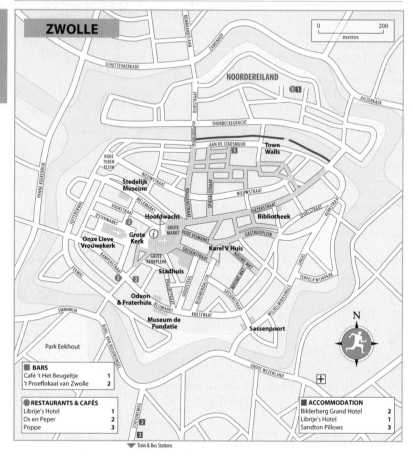

ZWOLLE

0 ——— 200
metres

NOORDEREILAND

Town Walls

RODE TOREN PLEIN

Stedelijk Museum

Hoofdwacht

Bibliotheek

Onze Lieve Vrouwekerk

Grote Kerk

Karel V Huis

Stadhuis

Odeon & Fraterhuis

Museum de Fundatie

Sassenpoort

Park Eekhout

BARS
Café 't Het Beugeltje   1
't Proeflokaal van Zwolle   2

RESTAURANTS & CAFÉS
Librije's Hotel   1
Os en Peper   2
Poppe   3

ACCOMMODATION
Bilderberg Grand Hotel   2
Librije's Hotel   1
Sandton Pillows   3

N

▼ Train & Bus Stations

substantial investment and the results are plain to see in a flush of modern buildings and the revival of its old harbour, which is now jammed with sailing boats and vintage canal barges.

An ancient town, Zwolle achieved passing international fame when Thomas à Kempis settled here in 1399. Thereafter, it went on to prosper as one of the principal towns of the **Hanseatic League**, its burghers commissioning an extensive programme of public works designed to protect its citizens and impress their rivals. Within the city walls, German textiles were traded for Baltic fish and grain, or more exotic products from Amsterdam like coffee, tea and tobacco. The boom lasted some two hundred years, but by the middle of the seventeenth century the success of Amsterdam and the general movement of trade to the west had undermined its economy – and Zwolle slipped into a sort of provincial reverie from which it is now emerging with much of its old centre intact and well preserved. Unusually, Zwolle's **moat** has survived in fine fettle, encircling the centre and overlooked by nine, seventeenth-century earthen **bastions** that once protected the city. These bastions are seen to fine advantage on the walk in from the train station with fountains playing in the moat and the fortifications clearly visible among the trees.

Grote Kerk

Grote Markt • May–Oct Tues–Fri 11am–4.30pm, Sat 1.30–4.30pm • Free • ☎ 038 421 2512, ⓦ grotekerkzwolle.nl

Right in the middle of Zwolle, the **Grote Markt** is a large and somewhat discordant square that surrounds the sandstone mass of the **Grote Kerk,** one of the unluckiest churches in Overijssel: the townsfolk were once inordinately proud of the church's soaring bell tower, but after it had been hit by lightning no fewer than three times (in 1548, 1606 and 1669), they gave up and sold the bells. Inside, you'll find the familiar austerity of Dutch Protestantism, with the cavernous nave bare of decoration and the seats arranged on a central pulpit plan. The pulpit itself is an intricate piece of Renaissance carving, but it's the Baroque organ of 1721 that really catches the eye, a real musical whopper with no less than four thousand pipes.

Hoofdwacht

Grote Markt 20

Attached to the outside of the Grote Kerk is the **Hoofdwacht**, an ornately gabled building of 1614, which once served as the municipal guardhouse. Public executions took place in front of the Hoofdwacht and the building bears the inscription *Vigilate et Orate* ("Watch and Pray"), a stern warning to the crowds who gathered to witness the assorted mutilations. The locals of Zwolle once had a reputation for being preoccupied more with money than civic justice, earning them the nickname Blauwvingers (Bluefingers), after they spent ages counting the pile of copper coins the neighbouring town of Kampen gave them for the bells of the Grote Kerk. It was all rather petty: since the bells were faulty, Kampen paid for them with the lowest denomination of coin possible.

The Stedelijk Museum

Melkmarkt 41 • Tues–Sun 11am–5pm • €7.50 • ☎ 038 421 4650, ⓦ stedelijkmuseumzwolle.nl

The **Stedelijk Museum**, on the west side of the city centre, is divided into two halves – a modern wing, which hosts temporary exhibitions, some of which are very good indeed, and the old wing in the eighteenth-century Drostenhuis. The latter mainly consists of a string of period rooms, enlivened by a modest selection of Golden Age paintings – the highlights being the finely detailed genre scenes of Gerard ter Borch (1617–81) and Hendrick ten Oever (1639–1716).

Onze Lieve Vrouwekerk

Ossenmarkt • **Church** April–Oct Mon–Sat 11am–4.30pm; Nov–March Mon–Sat 1.30–4.30pm; free • **Tower (Toren)** April Mon–Sat 1.30–3.30pm; May–Oct Mon 1.30–3.30pm, Tues–Sat 11am–3.30pm; €3 • ⓦ olvbasiliek-zwolle.org

The prim-and-proper **Onze Lieve Vrouwekerk**, down an alley off the Grote Markt, has had some hard times: in the sixteenth century, the congregation stuck to their Catholic faith, so the Protestants closed the place down and the last priest had to hotfoot it out of town after he delivered a final sermon in 1580. Thereafter, the church was used for all sorts of purposes – including a cart shed and a musket range – until it was returned to the Catholics in 1809 during the far more tolerant days of the Batavian Republic (see p.330). Today, the interior is firmly neo-Gothic, all ornate paintings and painted walls, but the church does boast an unusual – and especially attractive – tower, called **De Peperbus** (The Pepper Mill) after its distinctive shape.

Museum de Fundatie

Blijmarkt 20 • Tues–Sun 11am–5pm • €7.50 • ☎ 0572 388 188, ⓦ museumdefundatie.nl

Zwolle's premier art museum, the **Museum de Fundatie**, occupies a grand Neoclassical building from 1841 that began life as the municipal courts. Inside, the ground floor

5

displays a regularly rotated selection from the museum's wide-ranging permanent collection, which includes works by the likes of Turner, Bernini and Canova alongside a large collection of modern Dutch art – Mondrian, Israëls, Toorop and Appel to name but four. Upstairs, the top floor is devoted to temporary exhibitions.

The old town walls

Like many other towns in the Netherlands, Zwolle was encircled by high **brick walls** until the seventeenth century, when the development of artillery rendered such fortifications obsolete: within the space of a few decades, they became all too easy to flatten, hence the earthen bastions that replaced them here as elsewhere. Most of Zwolle's medieval wall disappeared centuries ago, but one stretch has survived, complete with defensive parapets and a couple of fortified towers: it stretches out along **Aan de Stadsmuur**, on the south side of the old harbour. The wall is, however, small architectural beer in comparison with the massive **Sassenpoort**, a mighty brick construction whose spiky turrets stand guard over the southern entrance to the old town. Dating from 1409 but extensively restored in the 1890s, this is the town's only surviving medieval gate and Zwolle's main landmark.

ARRIVAL AND DEPARTURE   ZWOLLE

By train From Zwolle train station, it's a 10min walk to the Grote Markt in the centre of town: head north along Stationsweg and then proceed east round the old moat.
Destinations Amsterdam CS (1–2 hourly; 1hr 15min); Arnhem (1–2 hourly; 1hr); Deventer (1–2 hourly; 25min); Emmen (1–2 hourly; 55min); Groningen (3 hourly; 1hr–1hr 10min); Kampen (Mon–Fri every 30min, Sat & Sun hourly; 10min); Leeuwarden (1–2 hourly; 55min–1hr 5min); Nijmegen (1–2 hourly; 1hr 30min); Schiphol airport (1–2 hourly; 1hr 25min); Steenwijk (1–2 hourly; 25min); and Zutphen (1–2 hourly; 40min).

By bus Adjacent to the train station, Zwolle bus station is something of a transport hub with buses run by two main bus companies, Syntus (ⓦ syntusoverijssel.nl) and Connexxion (ⓦ connexxion.nl), serving most of Overijssel's larger towns and villages.
Destinations Elburg (Mon–Sat every 30min, Sun hourly; 40min); Giethoorn (every 1–2 hour; 1hr); Urk (Mon–Fri 2 hourly; 1hr 40min); Vollenhove (Mon–Fri every 30min, Sat & Sun hourly; 50min); and Zwartsluis (Mon–Sat every 30min, Sun hourly; 30min).

INFORMATION

Tourist office Zwolle VVV is in the Hoofdwacht, beside the Grote Kerk in the centre of town at Grote Markt 20 (Mon 1–5pm, Tues–Fri 10am–5pm, Sat 10am–4pm; ☎ 038 421 6198, ⓦ vvvzwolle.nl). They have oodles of information on the city and its surroundings, plus bus timetable books.
Transport information There is a train and bus

information kiosk at the train station or check the easy-to-use, English and Dutch journey planner (ⓦ http://9292.nl/) or telephone helpline (☎ 0900 9292; €0.70/minute). For bus information, the two main companies, Syntus (ⓦ syntusoverijssel.nl) and Connexxion (ⓦ connexxion.nl) both carry timetables on their Dutch-only websites.

ACCOMMODATION

Bilderberg Grand Hotel Wientjes Stationsweg 7 ☎ 038 425 4254, ⓦ bilderberg.nl. Housed in a substantial early twentieth-century house near the train station, this chain hotel offers routine modern bedrooms at competitive prices. It has a pleasant terrace to shoot the breeze on a summer's evening. **€125**
Librije's Hotel Spinhuisplein 1 ☎ 038 853 0000, ⓦ librijeshotel.nl. One of the region's – if not the country's – most unusual deluxe hotels, the *Librije's* has been shoehorned into Zwolle's old prison, a stern, square stone building dating from the mid-eighteenth century. Many of the prison's original features have been left intact – from the thick wooden doors through to the bars on the

windows – and one of the old cells has been left untouched, but 19 high-spec guest rooms have been added too, each with a large comfy bed, a top-of-the-range bathroom and designer furnishings. Breakfast is taken in the cobbled courtyard, which is covered in the winter, and it's no mean breakfast either – with a series of courses designed to tickle the most jaded of palates. **€300**
Sandton Pillows Stationsweg 9 ☎ 038 425 6789, ⓦ sandton.eu. Part of a medium-sized chain, this well-maintained hotel has 45 guest rooms with high-spec furnishings and fittings, notably Coco-mat-brand beds and flat-screen TVs. It's in a handy location and competitively priced. **€90**

5

EATING AND DRINKING

RESTAURANTS

Librije's Hotel Spinhuisplein 1 ☎ 038 853 0000, ⓦ librijeshotel.nl. This luxury hotel has two award-winning restaurants – one formal, one more relaxed – but at both the menu is almost self-consciously inventive, featuring such dishes as oxtail with wild mushrooms and piccalilli. Set meals are the order of the day – a three-course lunch costs €60, a four-course dinner €75 – and you are expected to linger, dilly and dally. They also have an "atelier" where groups can cook their own meals under a chef's supervision – an extremely popular activity. Reservations are well-nigh essential. Tues–Sun noon–1.30pm & daily 6–8.30pm.

Os en Peper Ossenmarkt 7 ☎ 038 421 1948, ⓦ osenpeper.nl. Attractively chic restaurant in a lovely old building, and with a finely judged menu of both French and Dutch dishes. A three-course set menu costs around €45, but there is à la carte too – try, for example, the halibut with basil risotto, fried mushrooms, tomato and *beurre blanc* (€24). Tues–Sat 6–10.30pm.

Poppe Luttekestraat 66 ☎ 038 421 3050, ⓦ poppezwolle.nl. This popular and extremely cosy restaurant, in antique premises with a tiled floor and old Dutch photos on the wall, offers a Franco-Dutch menu featuring dishes like lamb with polenta and aubergine. Mains hover around €25. Reservations recommended – or arrive early. Mon–Fri noon–2.30pm & 5–10.30pm, Sat & Sun 5–10.30pm.

BARS

Café 't Het Beugeltje Krabbestraat 63 ☎ 038 423 6410, ⓦ hetbeugeltje.nl. Cleverly shoehorned into a slice of the medieval city wall, this amiable neighbourhood bar looks a bit like a cave – dark, mysterious but still somehow rather cosy. When the sun is out, customers migrate to the adjacent terrace, which overlooks the harbour. Daily 5–11.30pm.

't Proeflokaal van Zwolle Blijmarkt 3 ☎ 038 421 7808, ⓦ pfk.nl. Neighbourhood bar, which looks rather like a shop from the outside, but don't let that fool you – the interior is cosy and very brown. Offers five beers on draft plus over 30 *jenevers*, many of which are from the Zwolle region. Sun–Thurs 4pm–1am, Fri & Sat 4pm–3am.

ENTERTAINMENT

Cinema Zwolle's art-house cinema, the Fraterhuis, Blijmarkt 25 (☎ 038 422 0475, ⓦ filmtheaterfraterhuis.nl) offers the best in independent films, both Dutch and foreign, in a handy town-centre location. Tickets cost in the region of €9.

Theatre Zwolle's main centre for the performing arts is the Odeon, Blijmarkt 25 (☎ 038 428 8280, ⓦ odeondespiegel.nl), which offers a lively and varied programme, everything from cabarets and musicals through to contemporary theatre. It shares the same premises as the Fraterhuis cinema.

Kampen

Pocket-sized **KAMPEN**, just ten minutes by train from Zwolle, strings along the River IJssel, its bold succession of towers and spires recalling headier days when the town was a bustling seaport with its own fleet. The good times came to an abrupt end in the sixteenth century when rival armies ravaged its hinterland and the IJssel silted up – and then Amsterdam mopped up what was left by undercutting its trade prices. Things have never been the same since and, although Kampen did experience a minor boom on the back of its **cigar factories** in the nineteenth century, it remains, in essence, a sleepy provincial town. It only takes a couple of hours to explore central Kampen: its medley of handsome old buildings spread over six streets that run parallel to the river – and are themselves bisected by the Burgel canal. The logical place to start exploring is the **IJssel bridge**, which crosses the river from beside the train station to hit the town centre about halfway along.

Stedelijk Museum

Oudestraat 133 • Tues–Sat 10am–5pm, Sun 1–5pm • €5 • ☎ 038 331 7361, ⓦ stedelijkemuseakampen.nl

From the IJssel bridge, it's a few metres to the **Raadhuis**, which is divided into two: the red-brick Oude Raadhuis, dating from 1543 and topped by a distinctive onion-shaped dome, and the Neoclassical Nieuwe Raadhuis, which was built in the eighteenth century. Together, the two buildings comprise the **Stedelijk Museum**, which is devoted to the history of Kampen with a particular focus on its most prosperous days. The highlight is, however, the **Schepenzaal** ("Magistrates' Hall") in the Oude Raadhuis, a claustrophobic medieval affair with dark-stained walls capped by a superbly preserved barrel-vault roof. The hall's magnificent stone **chimneypiece** – a grandiloquent, self-assured work – was carved by Colijn de Nole in tribute to the Habsburg Charles V in 1545, though the chimney's typically Renaissance representations of Justice, Prudence and Strength speak more of municipal pride than imperial glory. To the right, the magistrate's bench is the work of an obscure local carpenter, a Master Frederik, who didn't get on with de Nole at all: angry at not getting the more important job of the chimneypiece, his legacy can be seen on the left-hand pillar, where a minute, malevolent satyr laughs maniacally at the chimney.

The Nieuwe Toren

Oudestraat 146

Just across the street from the Oude Raadhuis is a second tower, the seventeenth-century **Nieuwe Toren**, which becomes Kampen's main attraction for one morning each year, usually in mid-July (check the exact date and time with the VVV), when the "**Kampen cow**" is pulled up to its top. The story goes that when grass began growing at the top of the tower, a local farmer asked if he could graze his cattle up there. To commemorate this daft request, an animal has been hoisted up the tower every year ever since, though thankfully it's now a plastic model rather than a real one.

The Bovenkerk

Koornmarkt • Early May to mid-Sept Mon & Tues 1–4pm, Wed–Fri 10am–4pm; mid–Sept to Oct Mon–Fri 1–4pm • Free • ☎ 038 331 3608, ⓦ debovenkerk.nl

Kampen's innocuous main street, pedestrianized **Oudestraat**, runs south from near the IJssel bridge to the **Bovenkerk**, a huge albeit finely proportioned Gothic structure with a mighty spire and an unusual – and architecturally influential – choir with no fewer than thirteen radiating chapels. The choir was the work of Rotger of Cologne, a member of the Parler family of masons who was subsequently to work on Cologne Cathedral. Inside, the nave is light and spacious and although the Protestants jettisoned most of the furnishings and fittings, the fancy sixteenth-century **choir screen** has survived as has the late Gothic limestone **pulpit**. In the south transept, look out also for the urn containing the heart of **Admiral Willem de Winter**, a native of Kampen who loathed the House of Orange. A staunch Republican, he helped the French during the invasion of 1795 and played a leading role in the Batavian Republic thereafter; the rest of him lies in the Pantheon in Paris.

The Old Town Gates

Beside the Bovenkerk is the earliest of Kampen's three surviving **gates**, the fourteenth-century **Koornmarktspoort**, an imposing affair that looks as if it could withstand a fair old battering. It wasn't put to the test, though, when a Habsburg army showed up here in 1572: aware of the massacre at Zutpen (see p.253), the town burghers surrendered in double-quick time. The other two gates – the **Cellebroederspoort** and the **Broederpoort** – are of a later, more ornamental design and lie on the west side of town. They are best reached via Vloeddijk, which runs along the west side of the Burgel canal.

ARRIVAL AND INFORMATION   KAMPEN

By train Kampen train station is the terminus of a branch line from Zwolle, with regular services connecting the two towns (Mon–Sat every 30min, Sat & Sun hourly; 10min).

From the station, it's a 5min walk over the bridge to the town centre.

By bus Kampen bus station is next to the train station,

with regular services to Emmeloord (1–2 hourly; 30min); Museum Schokland (Mon–Fri 4 daily, change at Ens; 20min–1hr 30min); and Urk (Mon–Sat hourly; 1hr).

Tourist office The VVV is on the main street, a two-minute walk north of the IJssel bridge at Oudestraat 151 (Tues–Fri 10am–5pm, Sat 10am–4pm; ☎038 331 3500, ⓦ vvvijsseldelta.nl).

ACCOMMODATION AND EATING

Hotel van Dijk IJsselkade 30 ☎038 331 4925, ⓦ hotelvandijk.nl. Appealing, family-run, three-star hotel in a well-maintained, two-storey modern building just along the riverfront from the IJssel bridge. There are eighteen guest rooms, most of which are quite spacious and the better ones overlook the river. **€90**

De Bottermarck Broederstraat 23 ☎038 331 9542, ⓦ debottermarck.nl. The best restaurant in Kampen, this is a smart little place with the emphasis on local, seasonal ingredients, especially seafood – try, for example, the halibut with lobster sauce (€30). Broederstraat begins a few metres from the IJssel bridge, running west from the main street, Oudestraat. Mon–Fri noon–10.30pm, Sat 5–10.30pm.

Elburg

Once a Zuider Zee port of some renown, tiny **ELBURG**, 17km southwest of Zwolle, abuts the **Veluwemeer**, the narrow waterway separating the mainland from the Oostelijk Flevoland polder. In recent years, the town has become a popular day-trip destination, awash with visitors who come here to wander the old streets, a handsome collection of brick cottages bleached ruddy-brown by the elements beneath dinky pantile roofs. Elburg is also full of cafés and restaurants, some of whom serve the local delicacy, **smoked eel**.

Elburg was a successful port with its own fishing fleet from as early as the thirteenth century, but the boom times really began in the 1390s when the governor, a certain **Arent thoe Boecop**, redesigned the whole place in line with the latest developments in town planning, imposing a **central grid** of streets encircled by a protective wall and moat. Not all of Elburg's citizens were overly impressed – indeed the street by the museum is still called Ledige Stede, literally "Empty Way" – but the basic design, with the notable addition of sixteenth-century ramparts and gun emplacements, survived the decline that set in when the harbour silted up, and can still be observed today. Elburg's two main streets are **Beekstraat**, which forms the northeast–southwest axis, and **Jufferenstraat/Vischpoortstraat**, which runs southeast–northwest; they intersect at right angles to form the main square, the **Vischmarkt**.

Museum Elburg

Jufferenstraat 6–8 • Tues–Sat 11am–5pm • €4.50, including Kazematten (see p.244) • ☎ 0525 681 341, ⓦ museumelburg.nl

Entering Elburg from the southeast, it's a few metres from the town moat to the **Museum Elburg**, which is housed in a severe-looking, old brick convent and displays a rambling collection focused on the town's history. Of particular interest is the collection of silverware that was once the prized possession of the local sailors' guild, and a small display on the town's maritime hero, **Vice Admiral J.H. van Kinsbergen** (1735-1819). Kinsbergen spent years in the Russian navy before returning to the Netherlands, where he promptly became a hero by defeating an English fleet at the Battle of Dogger Bank in 1781.

St Nicolaaskerk

Zuiderkerkstraat • June–Aug Mon–Fri 2–4.30pm, Tues also 10am–noon • Free

From the Museum Elburg, it's a couple of minutes' walk north to **St Nicolaaskerk**, a lumpy fourteenth-century structure that dominates its immediate surroundings even without its spire, which was destroyed by lightning in 1693: the city fathers huffed and puffed about replacing it, but there wasn't enough money.

5

The Vischpoort and around

Northwest of St Nicolaaskerk, just down Van Kinsbergenstraat, is the three-storey, balconied **Stadhuis**, which once served as Boecop's home. From here it's just a few paces to Beekstraat, which leads to the town's main square, **Vischmarkt**, a pleasant little piazza, overlooked by pavement cafés. Vischpoortstraat leads off the square to the best preserved of the medieval town gates, the **Vischpoort**, a much restored brick rampart tower dating from 1594. Behind the Vischpoort, the pattern of the sixteenth-century defensive works is clear to see – from interior town wall to dry ditch, to earthen mound and moat. At the Vischpoort, one of the subterranean artillery casements, the **Kazematten**, is sometimes open to the public in summer: the entrance fee is included in the Museum Elburg ticket (see p.243), but you'll need to check the opening times with the tourist office (see below). It's easy to see why the Dutch called such cramped and poorly ventilated emplacements Moortkuijl, literally "Pits of Murder". From the Kazematten, a lovely, leafy, one-hour stroll takes you right round the old **ramparts**.

ARRIVAL AND INFORMATION ELBURG

By bus Elburg is not on the train network, but bus #100S (1–2 hourly) links it with both Zwolle train station (45min) and Nunspeet train station (on the Amersfoort/Zwolle line) to the southwest (20min). In Elburg, buses drop passengers just outside the southern

entrance to the old town near the tourist office.
Tourist office Elburg VVV is at Jufferenstraat 8 (Tues–Sat 11am–4pm; ☎ 0525 681 520, ⓦ vvvelburg.nl). They have details of boat trips along the Veluwemeer, as well as information about renting your own sailing boat.

ACCOMMODATION AND EATING

The tourist office has a list of **private rooms and B&Bs** and will phone around to make a booking on your behalf; try to get a room in the old centre and come early in the day in high season, when accommodation can get tight. Expect to pay around €80 for a double, en-suite room. In summer, the town's favourite nibble, **smoked eel in jelly**, is available at any number of pavement stalls and is sold by weight – a *pond* is 500g.

Le Papillon Vischpoortstraat 15 ☎ 052 568 1190, ⓦ restaurantlepapillon.nl. The best of Elburg's many cafés and restaurants that cater for day-trippers. It's a smart, split-level place with a Franco-Dutch menu: try, for example, the tasty coq au vin (€17). Wed–Sun 10.30am–11pm; June–Sept also Tues 10.30am–11pm. Kitchen noon–9pm.

Rose Garden Kamperweg 1 ☎ 052 568 5849, ⓦ rose-garden.nl. Of the town's several B&Bs, this one is in a particularly pleasant location just outside (and facing back onto) the old town walls. The rooms are nothing fancy, but they are well kept and well equipped. **€80**

The Noordoostpolder

Nudging out into the IJsselmeer about 20km northeast of Zwolle, the pancake-flat **Noordoostpolder** was the first large segment of Flevoland to be reclaimed from the

WIND TURBINES

A small army of **wind turbines** strings out along the shores of the IJsselmeer and the Veluwemeer, but they also pop up on many other rural horizons from Friesland to Zeeland. In the countryside, solitary turbines provide electricity for farmers, while on the coast and out to sea, banks of turbines harness the incoming weather systems, providing electricity for thousands of households. Erected in the 1930s, the first wind turbines provided electricity for remote communities in the US and the Australian outback. However, their full potential wasn't realized until research into cleaner forms of energy, carried out in Denmark and Germany during the 1970s, produced mechanisms that were both more efficient and more powerful. Ideally suited to the flat, windswept polders of the Netherlands, the first Dutch turbines generated 40 kilowatts of electricity; output is now a beefier 600 kilowatts – enough for a single wind farm of 50 turbines to provide power to 6500 households.

FLEVOLAND RISES FROM THE DEEP

Following the damming of the Zuider Zee and the formation of the IJsselmeer (see box, p.112), the coastline east of Amsterdam was transformed by the creation of the Netherlands' twelfth and newest province, **Flevoland**, which was reclaimed from the sea in two major phases. Drained in the early 1930s, the **Noordoostpolder** was the first major chunk of land to be salvaged and during the process two old Zuider Zee islands – Urk and Schokland – were joined to the mainland. The original aims of the Noordoostpolder scheme were predominantly agricultural, with the polder providing 500 square kilometres of new farmland, which the government handed out to prospective smallholders. Yet it soon became apparent that there were issues: very few trees were planted, so the land was subject to soil erosion, and both the polder and the adjacent mainland dried out and started to sink – problems that persist today. The Dutch did, however, learn from their mistakes when they came to drain the next large slice of Flevoland in the 1950s and 1960s: they created an encircling waterway, which successfully stopped the land from drying out and sinking, and the government tried hard to make the new polders more attractive to potential settlers, planting mini-forests and setting aside parkland. Together, these two newer polders, the **Zuidelijk Flevoland** and **Oostelijk Flevoland**, now form one large chunk of reclaimed land in front of the old shoreline, effectively a polder-island that comprises the bulk of Flevoland. The new polders were also used to house urban over spill with the creation of two new medium-sized towns, **Almere** and **Lelystad**, the latter named after Cornelis Lely (1854–1929), the pioneering engineer who had the original idea for the Zuider Zee scheme.

ocean (see box, p.112). It has the wide skies that characterize the polders, and these can indeed be breathtaking especially at sunrise and sunset, but – and this is where it really scores – it also incorporates two former Zuider Zee islands. One is home to the engaging fishing village of **Urk** while the other, **Schokland** has been a UNESCO World Heritage Site since 1995 and boasts a particularly fascinating museum.

Urk

Easily the most interesting town on the Noordoostpolder is **URK**, a burgeoning harbour, shipyard and fishing port, where a series of narrow lanes – and tiny terraced houses – indicate the extent of the **old village** before it was topped and tailed by new housing estates. Before it became part of the mainland, centuries of hardship and isolation had bred a tight-knit island community, one that had a distinctive dialect and its own version of the national costume. Most of Urk's individuality may have gone, but its earlier independence does still resonate, rooted in a **fishing industry** that marks it out from the surrounding agricultural communities. One Urk peculiarity that remains today is its addresses: traditionally the village was divided into areas called "Wijks", though nowadays the streets also have names – the tourist office, therefore, is at both Raadhuisstraat 2 and/or Wijk 2-2.

The old village

Wandering around the **old village** of Urk, which cuddles up to the north side of the harbour, is a pleasant way to pass an hour or two. Look out for the lakeshore **Vissersmonument** (Fisherman's Monument), where a plaque commemorates local seamen lost at sea and a statue of a woman gazes westward, presumably awaiting the return of her man. There are handsome views out across the IJsselmeer from here, too, with a small sandy **beach** below. Nearby, the conspicuous **lighthouse** marks the southwesterly tip of the old village – with another, larger sandy beach just along the lakeshore back towards the harbour. From the lighthouse you can see an insignificant-looking rock sticking out of the water about seventy metres offshore – this is the **Ommelebommelestien**, a rock from where, according to legend, all newly born Urkers spring: all the prospective dad has to do is row out to the rock and pick up a baby – very handy.

5

The Museum Het Oude Raadhuis

Wijk 2-2/Raadhuisstraat 2 • April–Oct Mon–Fri 10am–5pm, Sat 10am–4pm; Nov–March Mon–Sat 10am–4pm • €4.20 • ☎ 0527 683 262, ⓦ museum.opurk.nl

In the former town hall, in the centre of the old village, the **Museum Het Oude Raadhuis** is an enjoyably folksy affair with a series of displays devoted to all things Urk-ian. There are examples of the islanders' distinctive traditional costume, down to the fancily painted clogs; a recreated fisherman's home from the 1930s; an old barber's shop, where the men once met to shoot the breeze as confirmed by a set of old photos; fishing tackle; landscape paintings – the best are by Ernst van Leyden (1892–1969); and a small cabinet devoted to Pieter Hoekman, the village policeman who joined the Resistance in World War II, but was betrayed and subsequently shot by the Germans in 1943.

ARRIVAL AND INFORMATION   URK

By bus Buses to Urk cut a circuitous route through the village's sprawling outskirts. The stop to get off at is just north of the traffic roundabout on the Singel, from where it's a three-minute walk to the harbour and the old village. Buses serve Kampen (Mon–Sat hourly; 1hr); Museum Schokland (Mon–Fri 2 daily; 15min); and Zwolle (Mon–Fri 2 hourly; 1hr 40min).

By boat In summer there's a limited sailing boat service across the IJsselmeer from Urk to Enkhuizen on the *Willem Barentsz* (mid-July to late Aug Mon–Sat 2 daily; 2hr 45min; €20 one-way; €30 day-return; ⓦ willem-barentsz.nl). A

passenger ferry, *De Zuiderzee*, also covers the same route (late June to Aug 2 daily; 1hr 45min; €12.50 one-way; €17.50 day-return; ⓦ de-zuiderzee.nl). For both boats, tickets and departure times are available from Urk's tourist office (see below).

Tourist office Urk VVV is in the same building as the Museum Het Oude Raadhuis, in the centre of the old village at Wijk 2-2 (April–Oct Mon–Fri 10am–5pm & Sat 10am–4pm; Nov–March Mon–Sat 10am–4pm; ☎ 0527 684 040, ⓦ touristinfourk.nl).

ACCOMMODATION AND EATING

There are no hotels in Urk, but the tourist office has a list of B&Bs with double rooms costing between €65 and €80. The village is also home to several seafood restaurants, supplemented by a cluster of seafood kiosks on and around the main street, Raadhuisstraat.

Pension het Anker Wijk 4–13/Prins Hendrikstraat 13 ☎ 0527 685 307. Among Urk's handful of B&Bs, this is perhaps the pick, a cosy little place in an old fisherman's cottage a couple of minutes' walk from the tourist office. **€65**

Restaurant de Boet Wijk 1–61/Westhavenkade 61 ☎ 0527 688 736, ⓦ restaurantdeboet.nl. In an old harbourside building, this is the smartest restaurant in Urk, a neat and modern place where they serve the freshest of

---

URK IRKED

The damming of the Zuider Zee (see box, p.42) posed special problems for the **deep-sea fishermen of Urk** and it's hardly surprising that they opposed the IJsselmeer scheme from the beginning. Some villagers feared that the disappearance of their island enclave would spell the end of their distinctive way of life (by and large they were right), but it was the **fishermen** who were most annoyed by the loss of direct access to the North Sea. After futile negotiations at national level, the fishermen of Urk decided to take matters into their own hands: the larger ships of the fleet were sent north to fish from ports above the line of the Afsluitdijk, particularly Delfzijl, and transport was organized to transfer the catch straight back for sale at the Urk fish auctions. In the meantime, other fishermen decided to continue to fish locally and adapt to the freshwater species of the IJsselmeer. These were not comfortable changes for the islanders and the whole situation deteriorated after the Dutch government passed new legislation banning trawling in the IJsselmeer in 1970. When the inspectors arrived in Urk to enforce the ban, years of resentment exploded in ugly scenes of dockside violence and the government moved fast to sweeten the pill by offering substantial subsidies to compensate those fishermen affected. This arrangement continues today and the focus of conflict has moved to the attempt to impose EU quotas on the catch of the deep-sea fleet.

seafood with main courses averaging around €20. Tues–Fri noon–2pm; daily 5.30–10pm.

Visrestaurant de Kaap Wijk 1–5/Staverse Kade 5 ☎ 0527 681 509, ⓦ restaurantdekaap.nl. The Urk fishing fleet specializes in sole, plaice and eel, and the best place to sample them is here at this long-established restaurant, near the west end of the harbour on the way to the lighthouse. It's an informal, laidback place with a mini-terrace looking out over the IJsselmeer, and main courses from €15. Daily 10am–10pm, 8pm in winter.

Schokland

The southern reaches of the Noordoostpolder incorporate the former Zuider Zee islet of **Schokland**, a slender sliver of land that was finally abandoned in 1859 by royal decree – the government decided it was just too dangerous for the islanders to soldier on. Given the turbulent waters of the Zuider Zee, it's a wonder that the islanders stayed for as long as they did: approaching from the east or west along the N352, you can only just spot the gentle ridge that once kept the islanders out of the ocean. Neither did their heroic efforts win the respect of their fellow Netherlanders – they were nicknamed *schokker* (literally cow dung) – nor breed a sense of community: the north end of the island was Catholic, the south Protestant and relations were strained, verging on the positively hostile. Schokland's intriguing history is explored at the Museum Schokland (see below) and you can extend your visit by taking the combined **footpath and cycleway** that follows the old Schokland shoreline, a loop trail about 10km long. There's not much to see as such – the islanders didn't leave much behind – but it's a pleasant way to spend a few hours.

Museum Schokland

Middelbuurt 3, 300m south of the N352 • April–June & Sept–Oct Tues–Sun 11am–5pm; July & Aug daily 10am–5pm; Nov–March Fri–Sun 11am–5pm • €5 • ☎ 0527 25 13 96, ⓦ schokland.nl

The main reminder of Schokland's precarious existence is the **Museum Schokland**, a huddle of buildings lying just to the south of the N352 on the site of what was once the island's largest village. The museum kicks off with an excellent film tracking the history of the island and continues with a display of all sorts of bits and pieces found during the draining of the Noordoostpolder – tools, a rusty cannon, pottery and even mammoth bones. Footsteps away from the main museum building, is the old village **church**, a plain, rather dour building dating from 1834, and a portion of the old stockade, which once protected the village from the sea.

ARRIVAL AND DEPARTURE   SCHOKLAND

By bus There are buses from Urk (Mon–Fri 2 daily; 15min) and Kampen (Mon–Fri 4 daily, change at Ens; 20min to 1hr 30min), but you need to tell the driver your destination, or the bus won't stop here.

By road Between the hamlets of Ens and Nagele, the former island of Schokland runs north/south and is bisected by the N352.

Northwest Overijssel

The closing of the Zuider Zee and the draining of the Noordoostpolder transformed **northwest Overijssel**: not only were the area's seaports cut off from the ocean, but they were placed firmly inland with only a narrow channel, the **Vollenhover Kanaal**, separating them from the new polder. As a result, **Vollenhove** and more especially **Blokzijl**, the two main seaports concerned, reinvented themselves as holiday destinations and today hundreds of Dutch city folk come here to sail and cycle.

Traditionally, both Vollenhove and Blokzijl looked firmly out across the ocean, doing their best to ignore the moor and marshland villages that lay **inland**. They were not alone: for many centuries this was one of the most neglected corners of the country and things only began to pick up in the 1800s, when the "Society of Charity" established a series of agricultural colonies here. The Dutch bourgeoisie were, however, as wary of the pauper as their Victorian counterparts in Britain and the 1900 *Baedeker*, when surveying the colonies, noted approvingly that "the houses are visited almost daily by the superintending officials and the strictest discipline is everywhere observed". The villagers were reliant on **peat** for fuel and their haphazard diggings, spread over several centuries, created the canals, lakes and ponds that now lattice the area, attracting tourists by the boatload. The big pull is picture-postcard **Giethoorn**, whose mazy canals are flanked by splendid thatched cottages, but try to avoid visiting in the height of the season, when the crowds can get oppressive.

Vollenhove

The N331 heads north from Zwolle via the old Zuider Zee coastline at Zwartsluis, once the site of an important fortress, then west for 11km to **VOLLENHOVE**. Its former role as a flourishing seaport is recalled by the remains of its bastions and ramparts, which now nudge up against the Vollenhover Kanaal, as does its old **harbour**, a cramped, circular affair encased within steep grassy banks. Overlooking the harbour, **St Nicolaaskerk** is a large, rambling Gothic church that started out as a small chapel in the eleventh century. It backs onto Kerkplein, once the heart of the old seaport and now home to several handsome old buildings, most notably the elegant, arcaded **Raadhuis** and the seventeenth-century **Latin School**, now an antique shop, which boasts charming crow-stepped gables.

ARRIVAL AND DEPARTURE
VOLLENHOVE

By bus Buses stop on Clarenberglaan, a five-minute walk from Kerkplein – straight up Doelenstraat and then Kerkstraat – and serve Blokzijl (Mon–Sat hourly; 35min, change at Marknesse); Giethoorn (1–2 hourly; 1hr 15min, change at Zwartsluis); Zwartsluis (1–2 hourly; 25min); and Zwolle (1–2 hourly; 1hr).

EATING

Restaurant Seidel Kerkplein 3 ☏0527 241 262, ⓦseidel.nl. At the very heart of Vollenhove, this is the best restaurant in town, a smart and fairly formal place in the old Raadhuis with charming antique decor. The menu is classic Dutch, featuring such delights as calf liver with bacon and onions. Main courses average €23 at dinner, less at lunch. Tues–Sat noon–2pm & 5–10.30pm, Sun 2–10pm.

Blokzijl

Tiny **BLOKZIJL**, some 5km north of Vollenhove, is the prettiest of the area's former seaports, its cobweb of narrow alleys and slim canals surrounding a trim little harbour, which is now connected to the Vollenhover Kanaal. The town once prospered from the export of peat and boasts dozens of seventeenth-century buildings, dating from its heyday. The most conspicuous is the **Grote Kerk**, which, with its splendid wooden pulpit and ceiling, was one of the country's first Protestant churches.

ARRIVAL
BLOKZIJL

By bus Buses to Blokzijl drop passengers beside the N333 on the western edge of town, a five-minute walk from the harbour, with regular services to Vollenhove (Mon–Sat hourly; 35min, change at Marknesse); Giethoorn (Mon–Fri hourly; 50min, change at Steenwijk); and Zwolle (Mon–Sat hourly; 1hr, change at Marknesse).

ACCOMMODATION AND EATING

Auberge aan Het Hof Kerkstraat 9 ☏0527 291 844, ⓦaubergeaanhethof.nl. In the centre of Blokzijl, this restaurant and hotel has four bedrooms, decorated in a spick-and-span modern style. The restaurant serves a well-considered French menu using seasonal ingredients as much as possible. Main courses average €24 and advance reservations are advised. Thurs–Mon 6–10pm. **€80**

5

Giethoorn

GIETHOORN's origins are really rather odd. No one gave much thought to this marshy, infertile chunk of land until the thirteenth century, when the local landowner gifted it to an obscure religious sect. Perhaps to his surprise, the colonists made a go of things, eking out a living from local **peat** deposits and discovering, during their digs, the horns of hundreds of **goats**, which are presumed to have been the victims of the great St Elizabeth's Day flood of 1170; duly impressed, the residents named the place Geytenhoren ("goats' horns"). Later, the settlers dug canals to transport the peat and the diggings flooded, thus creating the watery network that has become the number one tourist attraction hereabouts – and no wonder: Giethoorn is extraordinarily picturesque, its slender brown-green waterways overseen by lovely thatched cottages, shaded by mature trees and crisscrossed by pretty humpbacked footbridges. The only fly in the ointment is Giethoorn's popularity: avoid the centre of the village in the summer, when the place heaves with tour groups.

The village's unusual origins account for its shape: Giethoorn is about 4km from top to bottom and never more than 900m wide – and it runs parallel to (and just east of) the N334 between Zwartsluis and Steenwijk. Most visitors make a beeline for the centre of Giethoorn, which spreads out along **Ds. Hylkemaweg**, between the N334 and Lake Bovenwijde, but this is in fact the least appealing section. Much more agreeable, with little tourist congestion even in summer, is **northern Giethoorn**, where you'll find pristine thatched cottages, immaculate gardens, the cutest of wooden bridges and the first-rate *Hotel de Harmonie* (see opposite).

There's more of the same along **Dwarsgracht**, on the other side of the N334, about 4km west of Giethoorn, which is in the middle of the **Nationaal Park Weerribben-Wieden** (ⓦnp-weerribbenwieden.nl), that conserves and protects a large area of canal and marshland.

ARRIVAL AND INFORMATION

By bus Running between the train stations at Zwolle and Steenwijk, Connexion bus #70 (ⓦconnexion.nl) travels the length of Giethoorn, pulling in at several stops, including Ds. Hylkemaweg and the *Hotel De Harmonie*. Regular buses link Giethoorn with Blokzijl (Mon–Fri hourly; 50min, change at Steenwijk); Steenwijk (1–2 hourly; 20min); Vollenhove (1–2 hourly; 1hr 15min, change at Zwartsluis); and Zwolle (1–2 hourly; 1hr 10min).

Tourist office The VVV is at Eendrachtsplein 1 (April–June & Sept–Oct Mon–Sat 9am–5pm; July & Aug Mon–Sat 9am–6pm, Sun 10am–4pm; Nov–March Mon & Wed–Sat 9am–5pm; ☎0521 362 124, ⓦervaarhetwaterrijk.nl), just off the N334 and a few metres from the Ds. Hylkemaweg bus stop. They have all sorts of local information, including several dozen leaflets detailing suggested cycling routes.

GETTING AROUND

The only way to get the real flavour of Giethoorn and its watery surroundings is by **boat or bike** – and fortunately almost every business hereabouts, from petrol stations to hotels, will be able to assist.

Boat rental Boats in Giethoorn come in a variety of shapes and sizes and although prices vary, reckon on paying around €18/hr for a whisper boat (a quiet, environmentally friendly, electric-powered motorboat) down to €28/day for a kayak.

Covered water taxis are similarly commonplace and a trip round the village costs about €5/hr.
Bike rental Bicycles start at about €7.50/day. Cycle route leaflets are on sale at the tourist office (see above).

ACCOMMODATION AND EATING

Giethoorn tourist office has a long list of **private rooms** (€50–100), though only a few of them are in the north part of Giethoorn, which is really where you want to stay. Accommodation can get very tight between June and August.

Botel Giethoorn Binnenpad 49 ☎0521 361 332, ⓦwaterreijkgiethoorn.nl. Short and fat, Lake Bovenwijde lies immediately to the east of Giethoorn, and its western shore is dotted with campsites and

holiday complexes. One of the best equipped is the *Botel* in a prime spot just north of the village centre, and a short stroll from the east end of Ds. Hylkemaweg. The campsite is right beside a canal, and there are also chalets and cottages to rent (three-night minimum). April to mid-Oct. Tent €16

★ **Hotel de Harmonie** Beulakerweg 55 ☎ 0521 361 372, ⓦ harmonie-giethoorn.nl. Giethoorn's best hotel by a long chalk, the four-star *De Harmonie* is a warm and friendly modern place at the north end of the village. The hotel consists of two, two-storey buildings, one of which is thatched, and although the rooms are not especially stylish, they are attractive, simple and spacious: some have their own canal-side balconies. The hotel also rents out bikes and boats and organizes boat trips from its own jetty.

Its attractively decorated restaurant is first-rate, serving a tasty range of Dutch dishes with main courses costing about €22. This is *the* place to try a local delicacy, perch and pike (*snoekbaarsfilet*) from the IJsselmeer. €95

Hotel de Dames van De Jonge Beulakerweg 30 ☎ 0521 361 360, ⓦ dedamesvandejonge.nl. Across the street from the *Hotel de Harmonie* in the northern part of Giethoorn, this appealing canal-side hotel occupies several intelligently converted old buildings and its restaurant has a pleasant terrace. The hotel rooms are modern and smart (verging on the plush) and there's cycle and boat rental here too. €90

Deventer

Glued to the east bank of the River IJssel, **DEVENTER**, some 30km from Zwolle, is an intriguing and – in tourist terms – rather neglected town, whose origins can be traced back to the missionary work of the eighth-century Saxon monk, Lebuinus. An influential centre of medieval learning, it was here in the late fourteenth century that Gerrit Groot founded the **Brotherhood of the Common Life**, a semi-monastic collective that espoused tolerance and humanism within a philosophy known as *Moderne Devotie* ("modern devotion"). This progressive creed attracted some of the great minds of the time, and Thomas à Kempis and Erasmus both studied here. Today, Deventer makes for a pleasant stop, with a handful of fine old buildings and a good bar and restaurant scene.

The Brink and around

Enclosed by the river and the remains of its moat, Deventer's engaging, broadly circular centre has kept its medieval street plan, which zeroes in on the **Brink**, a surprisingly large, cobbled marketplace running roughly north to south. On the west side of the Brink, where it widens out, is the distinctive **Penninckshuis**, whose florid Renaissance frontage is decorated with statuettes of six virtues. The inscription *Alst Godt behaget beter*

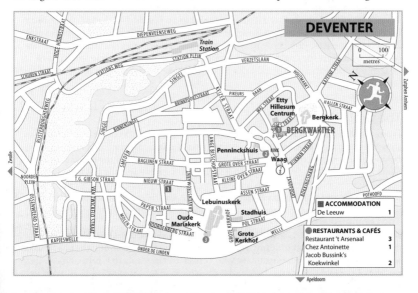

5

> ## CYCLING ALONG THE IJSSEL
> Beginning at the Wilhelminabrug in Deventer, a signposted **cycleway** follows the banks of the IJssel 20km south to Zutphen. It's a gentle ride through farmland and along quiet, winding lanes, with plenty of places to stop for a picnic and some fine views of the river and the weeping willows that thrive along its banks. Once in Zutphen, the return journey can be made either along the opposite shore, bringing the total distance to around 45km, or direct by train. You can **rent bikes** for the day from both Deventer and Zutphen train stations.

benyt als beclaget is smug indeed: "If it pleases God it is better to be envied than to be pitied". Nearby, at the square's southern end is the **Waag**, a late Gothic red-brick structure of 1528, whose good-looking medley of wobbly towers and turrets is fronted by a stone portico that was added a century later. Curiously, the large **pan** nailed to the outside of the Waag's western wall was left there as a warning: when the city council learnt that the mint master was debasing the town's coins, he was put in the pan and boiled alive. The bullet holes weren't an attempt to prolong the agony, however, but the work of idle French soldiers garrisoned here, who were taking, quite literally, "pot shots".

The Bergkwartier
From the east side of the Brink, near the Waag, **Rijkmanstraat** leads in to the **Bergkwartier**, an area of old housing that was tastefully refurbished during the 1960s in one of the region's first urban renewal projects. Centrepiece of the Bergkwartier is the medieval **Bergkerk**. Fronted by two tall towers, the church is a serious-looking affair whose two main stages of construction are clearly indicated by the differences in the colouring of the brickwork.

Etty Hillesum Centrum
Roggestraat 3 • Sept–May Wed, Sat & Sun 1–4pm; June–Aug daily 1–4pm • Free • ☎ 0570 641 003, ⓦ ettyhillesumcentrum.nl

On the edge of the Bergkwartier, just off the Brink, the **Etty Hillesum Centrum** is named after the eponymous Jewish woman (1914–1943), who lived in Deventer from 1924 to 1932, before ultimately perishing in Auschwitz. The centre has two permanent displays, one on Etty, the other on Jewish life in Deventer, and also features temporary exhibitions on related topics – racism, religious persecution and the like. A remarkable woman by any standard, Etty Hillesum refused to go into hiding during the German occupation and volunteered to work for the Jewish Council instead. Fully aware of the likely consequences, Etty chose to work at the Westerbork transit camp, assisting her fellow Jews as best she could before they were taken to the concentration camps of eastern Europe. Etty's wartime diaries and letters have survived – and are still in print (see p.349).

The Grote Kerkhof
From the Waag, it's a short walk along L-shaped Polstraat to the **Grote Kerkhof**, a large square flanked by shops and cafés. Towering over the square is the Lebuinuskerk (see below), whose southern end is attached to the bruised remains of the fourteenth-century **Oude Mariakerk**. Services haven't been held here since 1591 and the town council considered demolishing the church as early as 1600, but in the event it survived as the town's arsenal and now houses a smart restaurant – the *Arsenaal* (see opposite).

The Lebuinuskerk
Grote Kerkhof • April–Oct Mon–Sat 11am–5pm; Nov–March Mon–Sat 11am–4pm • Free • ☎ 0570 612 548, ⓦ lebuinuskerk.nl

A vast Gothic edifice built during Deventer's fifteenth-century pomp, the **Lebuinuskerk** is named after an English missionary who converted the locals to Christianity in the middle of the eighth century. Inside, the church's soaring, three-aisled nave, with its high-arched windows and slender pillars, rises to a vaulted ceiling adorned by intricate tracery. Look out also for the medieval murals on the walls of the nave – they may be faded, but enough remains to see the skill of their original execution.

ARRIVAL AND INFORMATION
DEVENTER

By train Deventer's train station is on the north side of the town centre, with the bus station adjacent. It's a 5–10min walk from here to the Brink: veer left out of the train station and go over the footbridge straight down Keizerstraat. Regular trains serve Apeldoorn (every 30min; 15min); Arnhem (every 30min; 40min); Nijmegen (every 30min;

1hr); Zutphen (every 30min; 15min); and Zwolle (every 30min; 25min).

Tourist office The VVV is bang in the centre of town, inside the Waag on the Brink (Sun & Mon 1–5pm, Tues–Sat 10am–5pm; ☎0570 710 120, ⓦvvvdeventer.nl).

ACCOMMODATION AND EATING

Restaurant 't Arsenaal Nieuwe Markt 33 ☎0570 616 495, ⓦrestaurantarsenaal.nl. At the back of the Lebuinuskerk, this smart little restaurant offers a short but well-selected, modern menu featuring the likes of prime steak with *pommes fondants* and seasonal vegetables; mains average €25. Sat & Mon 5.30–10pm, Tues–Fri noon–3pm & 5.30–10pm.

Chez Antoinette Roggestraat 10 ☎0570 616 630, ⓦchezantoinette.nl. Appealing Franco-Portuguese restaurant down a side street just east off the Brink. Authentic, tasty dishes – try, for example, the Setubal sardines. After the kitchen closes at 10pm, the places morphs into a bodega – with a first-rate wine cellar. Main courses average €20. Tues–Sun 5pm–1am.

Jacob Bussink's Koekwinkel Brink 84 ☎0570 614 246, ⓦdeventerkoekwinkel.nl. Among the platoon of

cafés that line up along the Brink, this is perhaps the most distinctive. It's a lovely old-fashioned place – the oldest cake shop in town – where they serve a tasty cup of coffee along with the local speciality, *Deventer koek*, a spiced and very chewy gingerbread biscuit; mind your fillings. Mon 1.30–5.30pm, Tues–Fri 9am–5.30pm & Sat 9am–5pm.

★ **De Leeuw** Nieuwstraat 25 ☎0570 610 290, ⓦhoteldeleeuw.nl. Deventer is short of places to stay, but this lovely family-run hotel has nine cosy rooms occupying an old terrace house whose stepped gable facade dates back to the 1640s. All the guest rooms are en suite and decorated in an unassuming but pleasant style, and the downstairs breakfast room doubles as a deli-cum-sweet shop (Wed–Sat 11am–5pm) with all manner of regional specialities displayed among the assorted antiques and bygones. **€160**

Zutphen

ZUTPHEN, 13km south of Deventer, is everything you might hope for in a Dutch country town: there's no crass development here and the centre musters dozens of old buildings set amid a medieval street plan that revolves around three long and very appealing piazzas – **Groenmarkt**, **Houtmarkt** and **Zaadmarkt** – with the disjointed seventeenth-century clock tower, the **Wijnhuis** marking the junction of the first two piazzas. Much of the centre is pedestrianized and, without a supermarket in sight, the town's old-fashioned shops still flourish, as do its cafés and, in a quiet sort of way, its bars.

Zutphen was founded in the eleventh century as a fortified settlement at the confluence of the Berkel and IJssel rivers. It took a hundred years for the town to become an important trading post, but thereafter its very success brought torrid times. **Habsburg armies** sacked Zutphen on several occasions, but the worst came in 1572, when Spanish troops massacred its citizens, an outrage that became part of Protestant folklore, strengthening their resolve against Catholic absolutism right across Europe.

SIR PHILIP SIDNEY: OR HOW TO DIE HEROICALLY

It was here at Zutphen that **Sir Philip Sidney**, the English poet, soldier and courtier, met his end while fighting the Spanish in 1586. Every inch the Renaissance man, Sidney even managed to die in style: mortally wounded in the thigh – after having loaned his leg-armour to a friend – he offered his last cup of water to a wounded chum, protesting "thy need is greater than mine".

5

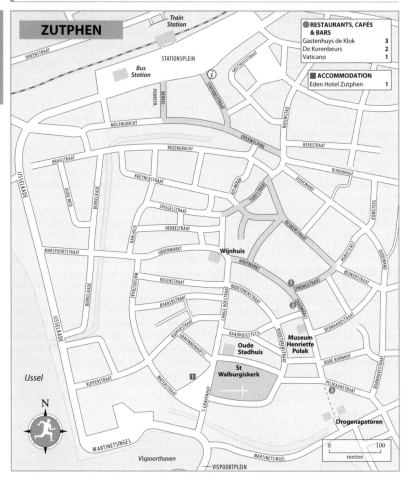

ZUTPHEN

RESTAURANTS, CAFÉS & BARS	
Gastenhuys de Klok	3
De Korenbeurs	2
Vaticano	1

ACCOMMODATION	
Eden Hotel Zutphen	1

St Walburgiskerk

Kerkhof • June Tues–Sat 1.30–4.30pm; July to early Sept Tues–Sat 10.30am–4.30pm • €2, €4 with library • ☏ 0575 514 178, ⓦ walburgiskerk.nl

On the south side of the town centre, **St Walburgiskerk** is an immense, Gothic church whose massive, square tower rises high above its surroundings. Inside, the most impressive features are the extravagant brass baptismal font and a remarkable medieval **library**, sited in the sixteenth-century chapterhouse. The library boasts a beautiful low-vaulted ceiling that twists around in a confusion of sharp-edged arches above the original wooden reading desks. It has all the feel of a medieval monastery, but it was in fact one of the first Dutch libraries to be built for the general public, a conscious effort by the Protestant authorities to dispel ignorance and superstition. The library owns over 700 items, ranging from early illuminated manuscripts to sixteenth-century books, a selection of which are still chained to the lecterns on which they were once read. Curiously, the tiles on one side of the floor are dotted with **paw marks**, which some contemporaries attributed to the work of the Devil. Across from St Walburgiskerk is the **Oude Stadhuis**, an elegant Neoclassical building whose main portal is decorated with military carvings in the style of ancient Rome.

The Drogenapstoren

5

From St Walburgiskerk, cross the old town moat to Martinetsingel, which curves east to the **Drogenapstoren** – offering delightful views of the town centre en route. One of the old city gates, the Drogenapstoren takes its name from the time when the town trumpeter, one Thomas Drogenap, lived here. A fine example of a brick rampart tower, it has had some high times, not least during World War II when the Resistance stored ammunition here until an explosion revealed the hideaway to the Germans.

Museum Henriette Polak

Zaadmarkt 88 • Tues–Sun 11am–5pm • €3.50 • ☎ 0575 439 470, ⓦ museazutphen.nl

A short stroll from the Drogenapstoren, the **Museum Henriette Polak**, features temporary displays of modern, usually Dutch, art. The house itself looks nineteenth-century, but is in fact much older, as evidenced by the tiny chapel on the top floor. When the Protestants took control of the Netherlands in the sixteenth century, Catholics were allowed to hold services in any private building providing that the exterior revealed no sign of their activities – hence the development of clandestine churches (*schuilkerken*) all over the country, of which this is one of the few to have survived.

ARRIVAL AND INFORMATION   ZUTPHEN

By train Zutphen's train station is on Stationsplein on the north side of the town centre: from here, it's a couple of minutes' walk south along Stationsstraat to the narrow passageway that leads through the old city wall to the town centre.

Destinations Apeldoorn (every 30min; 20min); Arnhem (every 30min; 25min); Deventer (every 30min; 15min); Nijmegen (every 30min; 50min); and Zwolle (every

30min; 40min).

By bus The bus station is adjacent to the train station on Stationsplein, with a range of local services.

Tourist office The VVV is across from the train station at Stationsplein 39 (Mon 11am–5.30pm, Tues–Fri 9am–5.30pm, Sat 10am–4pm; ☎ 0900 269 2888 (premium line only from within the Netherlands), ⓦ vvvzutphen.nl).

ACCOMMODATION AND EATING

Zutphen is a quiet country town, so don't expect too much in the way of **nightlife**. Hotels, too, are in short supply, though the VVV does have around a dozen **B&Bs** on its books, which will cost €60 or so for a double room.

Eden Hotel Zutphen 's Gravenhof 6 ☎ 0575 596 868, ⓦ edenhotelzutphen.com. In a fine old, eighteenth-century mansion across from St Walburgiskerk, this hotel could be a tad better than it actually is – most of the rooms are disappointingly routine in terms of both furnishings and fittings – though the location is excellent, and prices are competitive. **€90**

Gastenhuys de Klok Pelikaanstraat 6 ☎ 0575 517 035, ⓦ gastenhuysdeklok.nl. In antique, wood-panelled premises at the foot of Zaadmarkt, this appealing café-restaurant serves up tapas and salads during the day and French and Dutch dishes at night – try the beef medallions

in a red-wine sauce (€20). Wed–Sun noon–9pm.

De Korenbeurs Houtmarkt 84 ☎ 0575 512 423. Endearing, old-fashioned neighbourhood bar, with well-worn decor, a good range of brews both on tap and in the bottle – and a splendid wooden stairway. Daily from noon till late.

Vaticano Houtmarkt 79 ☎ 0575 542 752, ⓦ vaticano .nl. New kid on the gastronomic block, this large Italian restaurant has certainly made a splash in quiet Zutphen, not least on account of its decor – the red velvet seats and the open kitchen set the tone. The menu covers all the classics, including pizzas and pastas, with main courses from €16, pizzas €11. Daily 11am–11.30pm.

Apeldoorn

Workaday **APELDOORN**, about 20km west of Zutphen, was no more than a village a century ago, but it's grown rapidly to become an extensive garden city – a rather characterless modern place that spreads languidly into the surrounding countryside. Yet, as the one-time home of the Dutch royal family, Apeldoorn is now a major tourist

5

magnet, particularly popular with Dutch senior citizens who flock here to visit the town's star turn, the **Paleis Het Loo**, and with families heading for the **Apenheul monkey reserve**.

The Paleis Het Loo

Amersfoortseweg • Tues–Sun 10am–5pm • €12.50 • ☎ 055 577 2400, ⓦ paleishetloo.nl • Bus #102 from Apeldoorn train station (every 30min), or a 15min bike ride

Located on the northern edge of Apeldoorn, and looking something like a glorified military academy, the **Paleis Het Loo** was designed in 1685 by Daniel Marot for William III and his queen, Mary, shortly before they acceded to the thrones of England and Scotland. Later the palace was the favourite residence of Queen Wilhelmina, who lived here until her death in 1962. No longer used by the Dutch royal family – they moved out in 1975 – it was opened as a national museum in the early 1980s to illustrate three hundred years of the history of the **House of Orange-Nassau**. Years of repair work have restored a seemingly endless series of bedrooms, ballrooms, living rooms and reception halls to their former glory. A self-guided tour, with information in English, leads you along a warren of passageways with each room packed with displays of all things royal, from lavish costumes and silk hangings to documents and medals, via roomfuls of sombre dynastic portraits. If you are partial to royalty, it's a fascinating and infinitely detailed snapshot of Orange-Nassau life, and you can view the rooms of William and Mary, including their colourful individual bedchambers, as well as the much later study of Queen Wilhelmina.

Outside, the formal **gardens** (both William and Mary were apparently keen gardeners) are a relaxing place to wander. A maze of miniature hedgerows and a series of precise and neatly bordered flowerbeds are accessible by long walkways ornamented in the Dutch Baroque style, with tiered fountains, urns, statuettes and portals. The other part of the palace, the **Royal Stables** of 1906, has displays of some of vintage royal cars and carriages, including a baby carriage that's rigged up against gas attack.

Apenheul monkey reserve

J.C. Wilslaan • Late March to June & Sept to late Oct daily 10am–5pm; July & Aug daily 10am–6pm; €19, children (3–9) €16 • ☎ 055 357 5700, ⓦ apenheul.com • Bus #3 from Apeldoorn train station (3 hourly; 15min)

Apeldoorn's second major draw is the **Apenheul monkey reserve** just west of town. The highlight here is the **gorillas** – one of the world's largest captive colonies – living on wooded islands that isolate them from both visitors and the dozen or so species of monkey that roam around the rest of the park. It's best to go early to catch the young gorillas fooling around and antagonizing their elders; as the day warms up they all get a bit more slothful. The park is well designed, with a reasonable amount of freedom for most of the animals (at times it's not obvious who is watching whom), and you'll see other wildlife including otters, deer and capybara.

ARRIVAL AND INFORMATION   APELDOORN

By train From Apeldoorn train station, it's a 10–15min walk to the town centre straight down Stationsstraat. Regular trains serve Deventer (every 30min; 10min); Zutphen (every 30min; 20min); and Zwolle (every 30min; 40min; change at Deventer).

Bike rental Bikes can be rented from the train station

(€7.50/day).

Tourist office The VVV is in the centre of town at Deventerstraat 18 (Mon 1–5pm, Tues–Fri 10am–5pm & Sat 10am–4pm; ☎ 055 526 0200, ⓦ vvvapeldoorn.nl). They have information on walking trails and cycle routes in the forests around the Paleis Het Loo.

ACCOMMODATION AND EATING

There's no strong reason to overnight in Apeldoorn, though the town does have a reasonable spread of hotels. The main hive of evening activity is on and around the **Caterplein**, where Hoofdstraat meets Nieuwstraat.

Abbekerk Canadalaan 26 ☏ 055 522 2433, ⓦ hotelabbekerk.nl. Reasonably priced, centrally located hotel with straightforward modern rooms in a good-looking older building. On a leafy street a ten-minute walk north of the train station – head up Stationsstraat and Canadalaan is the fourth turn on the left after the Marktplein. **€85**

Central Park Kapelstraat 1 ☏ 055 578 6296, ⓦ central -park.nl. Excellent lunchroom serving tasty smoothies, bagels and coffees – plus snacks, such as tapas and light meals. Kapelstraat runs between Hoofdstraat and Nieuwstraat just south of the Caterplein. Mon–Sat 9am–6pm, Thurs till 11pm, Sun 11am–6pm.

Eetcafé 't Pakhuys Beekpark 9 ☏ 055 578 8006, ⓦ eetcafepakhuys.nl. Popular café-cum-restaurant just west off the Caterplein that serves up substantial portions of traditional Dutch food with mains costing €14–22. Also does a sideline in Asian/Indonesian dishes. Wed–Sun 4pm–1am; kitchen closes at 10pm.

Hostel Apeldoorn Asselsestraat 330 ☏ 055 355 3118, ⓦ stayokay.com. In a school-like complex in a wooded setting on the western edge of Apeldoorn, this all-year HI hostel has a café and a bar, bicycle rental and free wi-fi. All the rooms are en suite and range from doubles to nine-bunk dorms. To get there from the train station, take bus #3 (1–3 hourly; 10min) to the Waltersingel stop, from where it's a 10min walk. Dorm beds **€30**, doubles **€80**

The Veluwe

Stretching west of the River IJssel, Gelderland's **Veluwe** (literally "Bad Land") is an expanse of heath, woodland and sandy dune that lies sandwiched between **Apeldoorn** in the east, Amersfoort to the west, **Arnhem** in the south and the Veluwemeer waterway to the north. For centuries these infertile lands lay pretty much deserted, but today they make up the country's busiest holiday centre, dotted with a profusion of campsites, bungalow parks and second homes. The only part of the Veluwe to have survived aesthetically intact is the **Nationaal Park de Hoge Veluwe**, a slab of protected land lying just to the north of Arnhem – and home to one of the country's most vaunted art galleries, the **Kröller-Müller Museum.**

Nationaal Park de Hoge Veluwe

There are three main entrances to the Nationaal Park de Hoge Veluwe: one in the northwest corner of the park at the village of Otterloo (on the N310); a second in the northeast corner of the park at Hoenderloo (N804); and a third in the south at Schaarsbergen (N311) • Daily: April 8am–8pm; May & Aug 8am–9pm; June & July 8am–10pm; Sept 9am–8pm; Oct 9am–7pm; Nov–March 9am–6pm • Park €8.20; cars €6; bikes free

One of the region's most popular attractions, the **NATIONAAL PARK DE HOGE VELUWE** is an expanse of sandy heaths, lakes, dunes and woodland crisscrossed by cycle trails, with a number of hides from which you can observe its varied fauna. The park was formerly the private estate of the Kröller-Müllers: born near Essen in 1869, Hélène Kröller-Müller came from a wealthy family who made their money in the manufacture of blast furnaces, while her husband, the ever-so-discreet Anton came from a Rotterdam shipping family. Super-rich, the couple had a passionate desire to leave a grand bequest to the nation: a mixture of nature and culture, which would, Héléne felt, "be an important lesson when showing the inherent refinement of a merchant's family living at the beginning of the century". She collected the art, Anton the land and its animals – the *moufflons* (wild sheep) were, for example imported from Corsica – and in the 1930s ownership of the whole estate was transferred to the nation on the condition that a museum was built inside the park. The resulting **Kröller-Müller Museum** opened in 1938 with Hélène acting as manager until her death in 1939, and a **Sculpture Garden** was added a few years later.

The Kröller-Müller Museum

Houtkampweg • Tues–Sun 10am–5pm • €8.20, plus €8.20 park admission • ☏ 031 859 1241, ⓦ kmm.nl

At the heart of the Hoge Veluwe National Park, the **Kröller-Müller Museum** houses the private art collection of the Kröller-Müllers. It's one of the country's finest art

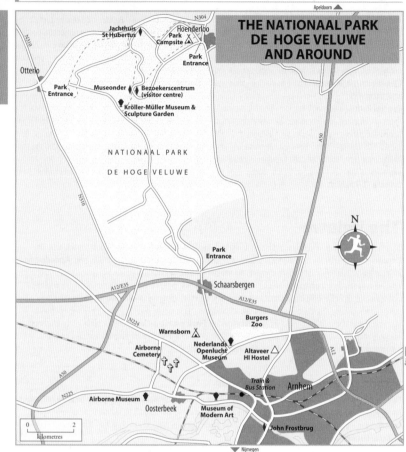

THE NATIONAAL PARK
DE HOGE VELUWE
AND AROUND

museums, comprising a wide cross section of modern European art from Impressionism to Cubism and beyond. It's housed in a low-slung building that was built for the collection in 1938 by the much-lauded Belgian architect van de Velde with a new wing added in the 1970s to create a T-shape: the bulk of the collection is displayed in the original wing. There's not enough space to exhibit all the museum's paintings at any one time, so what's on show is regularly rotated – though key works by the likes of Mondrian and van Gogh are pretty much guaranteed to be on display – and there's also a lively programme of temporary exhibitions. The works of individual artists are not necessarily exhibited together, which can be frustrating if you are keen to see the work of a particular painter: to help you navigate, the museum supplies a free information booklet with museum plans entitled "*12 Masterpieces*".

Vincent van Gogh

Hèléne Kröller-Müller's favourite artist was **Vincent van Gogh**, whom she considered to be one of the "great spirits of modern art", and the collection reflects her enthusiasm: the museum owns 91 of his paintings and 180 drawings, representing the largest collection of his works in the world bar the Van Gogh Museum in Amsterdam (see p.76). Of the earlier canvases, look out for *The Potato Eaters* and *Head of a Peasant with*

a Pipe, both rough, unsentimental paintings of labourers from around his parents'
home in Brabant. His penetrating *Self-Portrait* from 1887 is a superb example of his
work during his years in Paris, the eyes fixed on the observer, the head and background
a swirl of grainy colour and streaky brushstrokes. One of his famous sunflower
paintings also dates from this period, an extraordinary work of alternately thick and
thin paintwork in dazzlingly sharp detail and colour. The joyful *Café Terrace at Night*
and *Bridge at Arles*, with its rickety bridge and disturbed circles of water spreading from
the washerwomen on the riverbank, are from his months in Arles in 1888, one of the
high points of his troubled life (for more on which, see box on p.76).

The Tooraps and Mondrian

Other highlights of the museum's collection include several revealing self-portraits by
Charley Toorop (1891–1955), one of the most skilled and sensitive of twentieth-
century Dutch artists, as well as a number of key works by her father, **Jan Toorop**,
(1858–1928), from his early pointillist studies to later, turn-of-the-century works more
reminiscent of Aubrey Beardsley and the Art Nouveau movement. **Piet Mondrian** is well
represented, too: his 1909 *Beach near Domburg* is a good example of his more stylized
approach to landscape painting, a development from his earlier sombre-coloured scenes
in the Dutch tradition. In 1909 Mondrian moved to Paris, and his contact with
Cubism transformed his work, as illustrated by his *Composition* of 1917: simple flat
rectangles of colour with the elimination of any identifiable object, the epitome of the
De Stijl approach. One surprise is an early Picasso, *Portrait of a Woman*, from 1901, a
classic post-Impressionist canvas very dissimilar from his more famous works.

The Sculpture Garden

Houtkampweg • Tues–Sun 10am–4.30pm • Entrance included in Kröller-Müller Museum ticket • ☎ 031 859 1241, ⓦ kmm.nl • Free maps
of the Sculpture Park are available at the Kröller-Müller Museum entrance

Outside the Kröller-Müller Museum, the **Sculpture Garden** is one of the largest in Europe.
Some frankly bizarre creations reside within its 25 hectares, as well as works by Auguste
Rodin, Jacob Epstein and Barbara Hepworth. In contrast to the carefully conserved
paintings of the museum, the sculptures are exposed to the weather and you can even
clamber all over Jean Dubuffet's *Jardin d'email*, one of his larger and more elaborate jokes.

Museonder

Houtkampweg • April–Oct daily 9.30am–6pm; Nov–March 9.30am–5pm • Free with national park ticket • ☎ 0900 464 3835,
ⓦ hogeveluwe.nl

Great for kids, the **Museonder**, across from the Hoge Veluwe Park visitor centre and
about 1km from the Kröller-Müller Museum, is an engrossing exploration of the park's
subterranean ecosystems. With an array of interactive presentations, the museum also
displays such treats as giant beetle-mites, a rabbit morgue and a 23-metre-long beech
tree banister.

The Jachthuis St Hubertus

Hertjesweg • Guided tours only: Jan–March Tues–Sun 2–4 daily; April–Dec 2–8 daily • €3 • Tickets from the visitor centre or at any of the
park's entrances • ☎ 0900 464 3835, ⓦ hogeveluwe.nl

The **Jachthuis St Hubertus**, on the northern edge of the national park, about 3km from
the visitor centre, is a hunting lodge and country home built in 1920 for the Kröller-
Müllers by the modernist Dutch architect H.P. Berlage. Dedicated to the patron saint
of hunters, it's an impressive Art Deco monument, with lots of plays on the hunting
theme. The floor plan – in the shape of branching antlers – is representative of the stag
bearing a crucifix that allegedly appeared to St Hubert, the patron of hunters, and each
room of the sumptuous interior symbolizes an episode in the saint's life: all in all, a
somewhat unusual commission for a committed socialist who wrote so caustically
about the haute bourgeoisie.

5

Tegel Museum

Eikenzoom 12, Otterlo • Tues–Fri 10am–5pm, Sat & Sun 1–5pm • €5 • ☎ 031 859 1519, ⓦ nederlandstegelmuseum.nl

A ten-minute walk from the park's northwestern entrance, in the village of Otterlo, the small **Nederlands Tegel Museum** (Dutch Tile Museum), traces the development of the Dutch tile from the sixteenth to the twentieth century. Some of the displays are arranged chronologically, others thematically, featuring tiles with biblical scenes, shipping and sea monsters.

ARRIVAL AND INFORMATION   NATIONAAL PARK DE HOGE VELUWE

By bus There are frequent buses from Arnhem train station (see p.264) to the park's northwest entrance at Otterloo bus #105; Mon–Fri every half-hour, Sat & Sun hourly; 30min). These connect with a bus that runs from Otterlo to the Kröller-Müller Museum bus #106; Mon–Fri every half-hour, Sat & Sun hourly; 7min).

Information The Bezoekerscentrum (Visitor Centre; daily: April–Oct 9.30am–6pm; Nov–March 9.30am–5pm; ☎ 0900 464 3835, ⓦ hogeveluwe.nl) is in the middle of the park, about 1km from the Kröller-Müller Museum.

GETTING AROUND

By bike Visitors can help themselves to free white bicycles at each of the three park entrances and at the visitor centre. Maps of the park are available at all the entrances and at the visitor centre – and there also are several leaflets suggesting possible cycle routes. Most of the park's roads are also open to vehicles.

ACCOMMODATION

Nationaal Park de Hoge Veluwe Campsite Hoenderloo ☎ 0900 464 3835, ⓦ hogeveluwe.nl. The park's only campsite is set amid the woods, close to the Hoenderloo entrance. It comprises a car-free tent site, with three areas for caravans and campers. There's also a children's playground plus power hook-ups. Reservations are not available – you just have to turn up on spec. April–Oct. A tent pitch for two, including park admission €30

Arnhem and around

On the south side of the Nationaal Park de Hoge Veluwe, about 25km from Apeldoorn, **ARNHEM** was once a wealthy resort, a watering hole to which the merchants of Amsterdam and Rotterdam would flock to idle away their fortunes. All seemed set fair until World War II, when, in what was an unmitigated disaster for the town, hundreds of British and Polish troops died here during the failed Allied airborne operation codenamed **Operation Market Garden** (see box, p.262). Much of Arnhem took a pasting and although some of the key buildings were subsequently rebuilt, today's **city centre** can't but help seem a little dreary: only on its leafy outskirts do you get much of a sense of what Arnhem was like before the war. Perhaps inevitably, the city is still something of a place of pilgrimage for British visitors, who congregate here every summer to visit the crucial sites of the battle, including Arnhem's **John Frostbrug**. Despite this, it's also a lively town with a good selection of restaurants, bars and hotels. What's more, Arnhem makes a first-rate base for visiting a number of neighbouring attractions, most memorably the Airborne Museum Hartenstein at **Oosterbeek**, the **Nederlands Openluchtmuseum**, the country's largest open-air museum, and **Burgers' Zoo**, with its sizeable menagerie of animals housed in sensitively re-created habitats.

John Frostbrug

Battle of Arnhem Information Centre • Rijnkade 155 • April–Oct Mon–Sat 10am–5pm & Sun noon–5pm; Nov–March Mon–Sat 11am–5pm & Sun noon–5pm • Free

Named after the British commander who defended it for four days (see box, p.262), the **John Frostbrug** – the fabled "Bridge Too Far" – is a plain modern bridge, but it remains a symbol of people's remembrance of the battle, Dutch and British alike. Right beneath the north side of the bridge, the **Battle of Arnhem Information Centre** is a

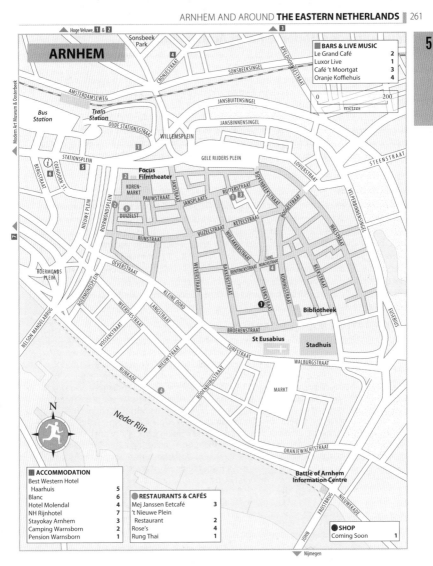

ARNHEM

Modern Art Museum & Oosterbeek

■ BARS & LIVE MUSIC	
Le Grand Café	2
Luxor Live	1
Café 't Moortgat	3
Oranje Koffiehuis	4

0   200
metres

Bus Station

Train Station

Focus Filmtheater

KOREN-MARKT

DUIZELST

ROERMONDS PLEIN

N

Neder Rijn

Bibliotheek

St Eusabius   Stadhuis

MARKT

Battle of Arnhem Information Centre

Nijmegen

■ ACCOMMODATION	
Best Western Hotel Haarhuis	5
Blanc	6
Hotel Molendal	4
NH Rijnhotel	7
Stayokay Arnhem	3
Camping Warnsborn	2
Pension Warnsborn	1

● RESTAURANTS & CAFÉS	
Mej Janssen Eetcafé	3
't Nieuwe Plein Restaurant	2
Rose's	4
Rung Thai	1

● SHOP	
Coming Soon	1

modest, one-room affair where the emphasis is on the individuals who participated in the battle – Germans, Allies and Dutch – with a large number of potted biographies.

Kerkstraat and the Korenmarkt

The north end of the John Frostbrug abuts that part of Arnhem which took the worst punishment in 1944 – and the replacement buildings are singularly unappetizing, mostly clumsy tower blocks that only give way to a more pleasant cityscape as you proceed along **Kerkstraat** with its medley of old shops and stores. From the north end of Kerkstraat, it's a brief stroll to the **Korenmarkt**, a small square that escaped much of the destruction and is now something of a social hub, flanked by several of the city's busiest bars.

5

Museum voor Moderne Kunst Arnhem (MMKA)

Utrechtseweg 87 • Tues–Sun 11am–5pm • €9 • ☎ 026 377 5300, ⓦ mmkarnhem.nl • The museum is a 15min walk west of the train station, or take trolleybus #1 (direction Oosterbeek)

The **Museum voor Moderne Kunst Arnhem** (Modern Art Museum) specializes in temporary exhibitions of modern Dutch art, many of which feature prime pieces drawn from the museum's permanent collection, whose forte is the work of the Magic Realists. It was the Amsterdam-born artist Carel Willink who popularized the style in the Netherlands in the 1930s, though Pyke Koch was perhaps the most talented practitioner – look out for his *Vrouwen in de Straat*, a typically disconcerting canvas, where the women's eyes look out from the picture in a medley of contrasting emotions.

Oosterbeek

Now a prosperous suburb of Arnhem, leafy **OOSTERBEEK** was a target for Operation Market Garden (see box below) on account of its rail bridge over the Lower Rhine. After the failure of the attempt to seize the bridge at Arnhem, it was also where the remains of the Allied forces held out within an ever-shrinking perimeter before their dramatic withdrawal south across the river. The Allied command post at Oosterbeek was in the *Hotel Hartenstein*, which now houses the excellent **Airborne Museum Hartenstein**, whose various displays examine the course of the battle. You might also consider a visit to the **Airborne Cemetery** (open access; free), a neat, symmetrical

---

OPERATION MARKET GARDEN

By September 1944, most of France and much of Belgium had been liberated from German occupation. However, fearing that an orthodox campaign to roll back the German army further would take many months and cost many lives, **Field Marshal Montgomery** decided that a pencil-thrust north through the Netherlands and subsequently east into the Ruhr, around the back of the heavily fortified Siegfried Line, offered a good chance of ending the war early. To speed the advance of his land armies, Montgomery needed to cross several major rivers and canals in a corridor of territory stretching from Eindhoven, just north of the front, to Arnhem. The plan, codenamed **Operation Market Garden**, was to parachute three Airborne Divisions behind enemy lines, each responsible for taking and holding particular bridgeheads until the main army could force their way north to join them. On Sunday, September 17, the 1st British Airborne Division parachuted into the fields around Oosterbeek, their principal objective being to seize the bridges over the Rhine at neighbouring Arnhem. Meanwhile, the 101st American Airborne Division was dropped in the area of Veghel to secure the Wilhelmina and Zuid-Willemsvaart canals, while the 82nd Division was dropped around Grave and Nijmegen, for the crossings over the Maas and the Waal.

The Americans were successful, and by the night of September 20, sections of the British army had reached the American bridgehead across the River Waal at Nijmegen. But the landings around Arnhem ran into serious problems: Allied Command had estimated that opposition was unlikely to exceed three thousand troops, but, as it turned out, the entire 2nd SS Panzer Corps was refitting near Arnhem just when the 1st Division landed. Taking the enemy by surprise, 2nd Parachute Battalion, under **Lieutenant-Colonel John Frost**, did manage to capture the north end of the road bridge across the Rhine, but it proved impossible to capture the southern end. Surrounded, outgunned and outmanned, the 2nd Battalion held their position from September 17th to the morning of the 21st, a feat of extraordinary courage and determination. Meanwhile, other British and Polish battalions had concentrated around the bridgehead at Oosterbeek, which they held at tremendous cost under the command of **General Urquhart**. By the morning of the 25th it was apparent that reinforcements in sufficient numbers would not be able to get through in support, so under cover of darkness, a dramatic and supremely well-executed withdrawal saved 2163 soldiers out of an original force of 10,005. There has been controversy about the plan ever since, with many arguing that it was poorly conceived, while others claim that it might have worked but for a series of military mishaps.

tribute to nearly two thousand paratroopers, mostly British and Polish, whose bodies were brought here from the surrounding fields. It's a quiet, secluded spot and the personal inscriptions on the gravestones are especially poignant. The cemetery is just a ten-minute walk east of Oosterbeek train station on van Limburg Stirumweg: cross the bridge over the train lines, then turn right.

The Airborne Museum Hartenstein

Utrechtseweg 232 Oosterbeek • April–Oct Mon–Sat 10am–5pm & Sun noon–5pm; Nov–March Mon–Sat 11am–5pm & Sun noon–5pm • €8 • ☎ 026 333 7710, ☯ airbornemuseum.com • Trains run from Arnhem station to Oosterbeek station (every 30min to 1hr; 5min), from where it's a 10min walk south along Stationsweg to the museum • Trolleybus #1 from Arnhem train station (every 20–30min; 20min) stops outside the museum

Given the intensity of the battle, it's perhaps surprising that the *Hotel Hartenstein*, the one-time Allied HQ, wasn't razed to the ground, but survive it did and it now makes an appropriate home for the **Airborne Museum**, lying just to the west of the centre of the village. The museum kicks off with a first-rate film of the battle, which makes skilful use of original footage – including the chilling scene where German machine gunners blaze away at paratroopers dropping from the sky. Ensuing rooms hold a series of small exhibitions on some of the individuals who took part, perhaps most memorably Private Albert Willingham who died protecting a Dutch woman from a German grenade. Here too, is a piece of wallpaper, salvaged from the hotel, where British snipers marked up the score of their hits, inscribing it "Fuck the Gerrys". A further display in the basement recreates the scene in the hotel as the Germans closed in – the British were besieged here for a week before finally retreating across the river. The Army Film and Photographic Unit landed with the British forces, and it's their photographs that perhaps stick in the memory most of all: grimly cheerful soldiers hauling in their parachutes; tense, tired faces during the fighting; and shattered Dutch villages.

The Nederlands Openluchtmuseum

Schelmseweg 89 • Daily: April–Oct 10am–5pm & Dec to mid-Jan 11am–7pm • €15, children (aged 4–12) €10.50 • ☎ 026 357 6111, ☯ openluchtmuseum.nl • From Arnhem train station, take bus #3 (direction Alteveer; every 20min), or direct bus #13 (July & Aug only; every 20min)

Located immediately to the north of Arnhem, the **Nederlands Openluchtmuseum** (Dutch Open-Air Museum) comprises an impressive collection of old Dutch buildings. One of the first of its type, the museum was founded in 1912 in order to "present a picture of the daily life of ordinary people in this country as it was in the past and has developed in the course of time". Over the years, original buildings have been taken from all over the country and assembled here in a large area of the Veluwe forest. Wherever possible, buildings have been placed in groups that represent the different regions of the Netherlands – from the farmsteads of Friesland to the peat colonies of Drenthe. There are about eighty buildings in all, including examples of every type of Dutch windmill, most sorts of farmhouse, a variety of bridges and several working craftshops, demonstrating the traditional skills of papermaking, milling, baking, brewing, bleaching and so forth. Other parts of the museum include one of the most extensive regional costume exhibitions in the country and a modest herb garden. Altogether, it's an imaginative attempt to re-create the rural Dutch way of life over the past two centuries.

The Burgers' Zoo

Antoon van Hooffplein 1 • April–Oct 9am–7pm; Nov–March 9am–5pm • €19, children (aged 4–9) €17 • ☎ 26 442 45 34, ☯ burgerszoo .nl • Bus #3 from Arnhem train station

Founded in 1913, **Burgers' Zoo** is now one of the largest zoos in the Netherlands, occupying a sizeable chunk of land just to the north of downtown Arnhem. Care has

5

been taken to re-create the habitats of the resident animals as closely as possible with, for example, separate desert, savanna and jungle areas.

ARRIVAL AND INFORMATION   ARNHEM

By train Arnhem's recently upgraded train station is on Stationsplein at the northern edge of the city centre – a 5–10min walk from the river.
Destinations Amsterdam CS (every 30min to 1hr; 1hr 10min); Deventer (every 30min; 40min); Nijmegen (every 30min; 20min); Oosterbeek (every 30min to 1hr; 5min); Zutphen (every 30min; 20min); and Zwolle (every 30min; 1hr).

Tourist office The VVV is across from the train station at Stationsplein 13 (Mon–Fri 9.30am–5.30pm & Sat 9.30am–5pm; ☎0481 366 250, ⓦarnhemexperience .nl). They have a good selection of Dutch maps, books on Operation Market Garden, and brochures on local cycling routes.

CITY TRANSPORT

By bus and trolleybus The bus station adjoins the train station on Stationsplein, and is the focus for the city's excellent public transport system comprising buses and trolleybuses operated by Breng (ⓦbreng.nl). The trolleybuses follow figure-of-eight routes around town. This means there'll often be two buses at the train/bus station with the same number and different destinations, so it's important to get the direction as well as the number right.

ACCOMMODATION

The VVV operates an **accommodation booking service**, which is especially useful in July and August when the best of Arnhem's pensions and hotels can fill up fast.

HOTELS

Best Western Hotel Haarhuis Stationsplein 1 ☎026 442 7441, ⓦhotelhaarhuis.nl. Mid-sized hotel with pleasantly modernized public areas, and the guest rooms that are of a good size and well appointed. The fly in the ointment can be the noise from fellow guests (the hotel is popular with partying weekenders). In a handy location, opposite the train station, with tasty breakfasts. **€150**

Blanc Coehoornstraat 4 ☎026 442 8072, ⓦhotel -blanc.nl. This small hotel has just 22 guest rooms, each decorated in a sort of homely-meets-kitsch style. Some of the rooms have mini-balconies and breakfast is served in the attractive next-door café. **€125**

★ **Hotel Molendal** Cronjéstraat 15 ☎026 442 4858, ⓦhotel-molendal.nl. In a beautifully renovated Art Nouveau villa, this delightful hotel has sixteen guest rooms decorated in soothing tones of white and cream with a selection of antique furniture. Just north of the train station, in a lovely, leafy residential part of Arnhem awash with fine old mansions, the hotel overlooks a slender canal near the assorted greenery of Sonsbeek Park. **€90**

NH Rijnhotel Onderlangs 10 ☎026 443 4642, ⓦ.nh-hotels.com. Medium-sized, four-star chain hotel where the guest rooms are decorated in attractive modern style, though the building itself is a bit of a clumpy eyesore. The best rooms have smashing views over the Rhine. Located just ten minutes' walk from the

train station in the direction of Oosterbeek. **€100**

★ **Pension Warnsborn** Schelmseweg 1 ☎026 442 5994, ⓦpensionwarnsborn.nl. This family-run B&B occupies an attractive old house in a leafy suburb just to the north of the city centre – and within easy reach of the Hoge Veluwe National Park. The guest rooms are homely and distinctly cheerful, most are spacious and some have private balconies. Very competitive prices, too, both en suite (an extra €10) and with shared facilities. **€55**

HOSTELS

Stayokay Arnhem Diepenbrocklaan 27 ☎026 442 0114, ⓦstayokay.com. In a modern complex on the edge of the Nationaal Park de Hoge Veluwe, some 5km north of central Arnhem, this well-equipped HI hostel has a laundry, a bar, a restaurant, free internet access, bicycle storage and bicycle rental. Take bus #3, direction Altaveer, to the Ziekenhuis Rijnstate stop, and then follow the signs. Bunk beds are in 4- to 9-bedded rooms **€27**

CAMPING

Camping Warnsborn Bakenbergseweg 257 ☎026 442 3469, ⓦcampingwarnsborn.nl. Large and well-appointed caravan and campsite in a forested setting on the approaches to the Nationaal Park de Hoge Veluwe, 6km northwest of central Arnhem. Electrical hook-up is included in the price. April–Oct. **€20**

EATING AND DRINKING

Arnhem has an especially good range of reasonably priced café-bars and restaurants plus a platoon of busy bars particularly down on the **Korenmarkt**. There's a further cluster of bars and restaurants beside the river on **Rijnkade**, though things only get going here if the weather is reasonable. There's often **live music** at one bar or another: for details of what's on where, pick up the listings magazine *Uit Loper*, which is widely available at bars, cafés and at the tourist office.

CAFÉS AND RESTAURANTS

★ **Mej Janssen Eetcafé** Duizelsteeg 6 ☎ 026 351 4069, ⓦ mej-janssen.nl. Outstanding café-restaurant with a dark and cosy interior, and a creative Dutch menu featuring tasty and substantial main courses from as little as €12. The Dover sole (*slibtongetjes*) is particularly delicious. Tues–Sun 5–10pm.

't Nieuwe Plein Restaurant Nieuwe Plein 22 ☎ 026 702 4010, ⓦ nieuweplein.nl. Smart but informal restaurant, decorated in shades of white and grey, that offers a short but select menu – try, for example, the pork medallions topped with brie and roasted pine nuts (€18). Tues–Sun 4.30–10.30pm.

Rose's Rijnkade 49 ☎ 026 351 9491, ⓦ roseslounge .com. Lounge bar and restaurant overlooking the River Rhine with kitsch velvet sofas, Chesterfields and an intimate fireplace where you can choose from a large selection of mixed platters and a creative à la carte menu (mains around €15). Occasional salsa and 1970s/1980s dance nights. Mon–Sat 5pm to midnight, Sun noon–midnight.

Rung Thai Ruiterstraat 43 ☎ 026 445 0032. Authentic Thai food in this fashionable, cheerily decorated little place with bright pink walls. Does a wicked *Tom Yam Kai* (spicy clear soup). Takeaway also. Main dishes around €16. Daily noon–11pm.

BARS AND LIVE MUSIC

Café 't Moortgat Ruiterstraat 35 ☎ 026 445 0393, ⓦ moortgat.nl. This brown-style café, with beer memorabilia on the walls and over 100 beers to choose from, caters to an older crowd. There's also a billiards table to pass the time on a rainy day. Mon–Sat noon–1am, Sun 4pm–1am.

Le Grand Café Korenmarkt 16 ☎ 026 442 6281. Probably the most popular drinking spot on the Korenmarkt, complete with fake palm trees and tacky lampshades – if, that is, you can actually get inside: dense crowds spill out onto the pavement terrace whenever the weather is half decent. Daily noon–1/2am.

Luxor Live Willemsplein 10 ☎ 026 351 1660, ⓦ luxorlive.nl. Arnhem's live music hot spot with turns from a wide range of bands and solo artists from jazz, soul and funk through to hip-hop and reggae. Times and opening nights vary – see website – but core hours are Thurs–Sat 8pm till late.

★ **Oranje Koffiehuis** Arke Noachstraat 7 ☎ 026 351 4081, ⓦ oranjekoffiehuis.nl. Tiny café with charming Art Deco interior that, despite its name (coffeehouse), also serves stronger drinks. A nice detail is the miniature glass of liquor that they serve with their coffee. Live music twice a week. Tues–Thurs 2pm–1am, Fri & Sat noon–2am & Sun 2pm–midnight.

ENTERTAINMENT

Cinema Right in the centre of Arnhem, the Focus Filmtheater, Korenmarkt 42 (☎ 026 442 4283, ⓦ focusarnhem.nl), features both mainstream and more alternative films, both domestic and international, as well as late-night showings.

Shopping In recent years, Arnhem's fashion academy, ArtEZ, has established an excellent reputation, producing a number of young and very successful designers. Selected work from some of these students is on sale at the city-centre store, Coming Soon, Kerkstraat 23 (☎ 026 370 3044, ⓦ arnhemcomingsoon.nl; Tues–Sat 10am–5pm).

Nijmegen

Almost certainly the oldest town in the Netherlands, **NIJMEGEN** sits on the southern bank of the River Waal some 20km from Arnhem. The town's medieval core was flattened in World War II, though key buildings – like the Grote Kerk – were subsequently rebuilt in imitation of the originals, and modern Nijmegen is a lively and appealing place, with a congenial street life. If the weather is good, join the locals down by the River Waal, where there is a pleasant **riverside promenade** and you can observe the barges and boats churning along on what is one of the region's busiest waterways.

Brief history

Nijmegen was built on the site of the Roman frontier fortress of Novio Magus, from which it derives its name, and was used by the Romans both as a buffer against the unruly tribes to the east and to awe the locals. In 69 AD, however, the Netherlanders took advantage of the confusion in Rome following the death of the Emperor Nero,

5

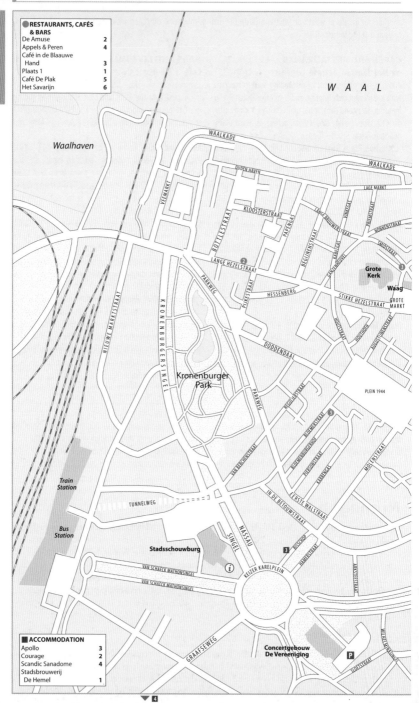

● RESTAURANTS, CAFÉS
  & BARS
De Amuse   2
Appels & Peren   4
Café in de Blaauwe
  Hand   3
Plaats 1   1
Café De Plak   5
Het Savarijn   6

Waalhaven

WAAL

WAALKADE

WAALKADE

OUDEN HAVEN

LAGE MARKT

KLOOSTERSTRAAT

VEEMARKT

BOTTELSTRAAT

PAPENGAS

LANGE BROUWERSTRAAT

REGULIERSTRAAT

GANZENHEUVEL

KERKGAS

NONNENSTRAAT

SMIDSTRAAT

LANGE HEZELSTRAAT

PIJKESTRAAT

PARKWEG

HESSENBERG

STIKKE HEZELSTRAAT

**Grote
Kerk**

Waag

GROTE
MARKT

HOUTSTRAAT

HOUTHOEK

AUGUSTIJNENSTRAAT

DODDENDAAL

KRONENBURGERSINGEL

*Kronenburger
Park*

PARKWEG

REGULIERSTRAAT

PLEIN 1944

NIEUWE MARKTSTRAAT

BERCHENSTRAAT

VAN BERCHENSTRAAT

KRONENBURGERHOF

BLOEMERSTRAAT

DIESCHSTRAAT

KARREGAS

EERSTE WALSTRAAT

MOLENSTRAAT

IN DE BETOUWSTRAAT

*Train
Station*

TUNNELWEG

*Bus
Station*

Stadsschouwburg

SINGEL

NASSAU

BISSCHOP

HAMERSTRAAT

ARCHITEKTSTRAAT

VAN SCHAECK MATHONSINGEL

KEIZER KARELPLEIN

VAN SCHAECK MATHONSINGEL

GRAAFSEWEG

**Concertgebouw
De Vereeniging**

P

WILHELMINASINGEL

SLOTEMAKERSTRAAT

■ ACCOMMODATION
Apollo   3
Courage   2
Scandic Sanadome   4
Stadsbrouwerij
De Hemel   1

▼ 4

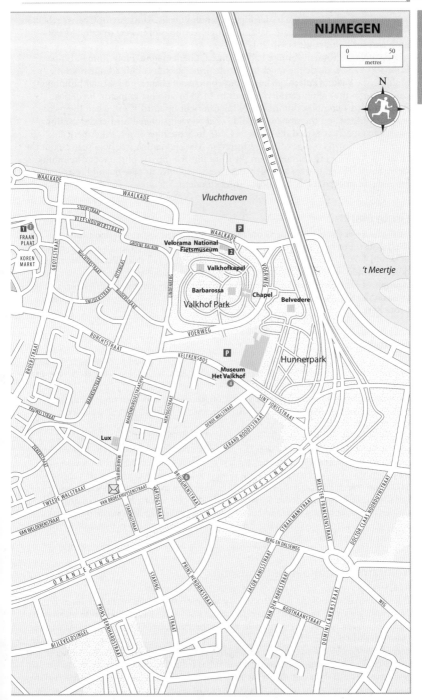

NIJMEGEN

0 — 50
metres

N

WAALBRUG

Vluchthaven

't Meertje

WAALKADE
WAALKADE
STEENSTRAAT
VLEESHOUWERSTRAAT
GROENE BALKON
WAALKADE

FRAAN PLAAT

KOREN MARKT

GROTESTRAAT
HOLLESTRAAT
OOYEVAAR
SNIJDERSTRAAT
RODDESTRAAT
LINDENBERG

Velorama National Fietsmuseum

Valkhofkapel

Barbarossa
Chapel
Belvedere

Valkhof Park

VOERWEG
VOERWEG

BURCHTSTRAAT

KELFKENSBOS

Hunnerpark

BROERSTRAAT
MARIKENSTRAAT
PAUWELSTRAAT

MARIENBURGSESTRAAT NIEUW
HERTOGSTRAAT

Museum Het Valkhof

DERDE WALSTRAAT

SINT JORISSTRAAT

GERARD NOODTSTRAAT

Lux

MARIENBURG
BRUGCHENSTRAAT
HERTOGSTRAAT

HEKELSTRAAT

TWEEDE WALSTRAAT
VAN BROECKHUYSENSTRAAT
STAMINGSTRAAT

VAN WELDERENSTRAAT

SINT CANISIUSSINGEL

STRAALMANSTRAAT
MEESTER FRANCKENSTRAAT
DOCTOR CLAAS VOORDUINSTRAAT

BERG EN DALSEWEG

ORANJESINGEL

STARING
PRINS HENDRIKSTRAAT

STRAAT

PRINS BERNHARDSTRAAT
BIJLEVELDSINGEL

JACOB CANISSTRAAT
VAN DEN HAVESTRAAT
ROOTHAANSTRAAT
DOMINICANENSTRAAT
WEG

5

and rose in revolt under the leadership of **Claudius Civilis**. The story of Civilis's rebellion became a staple of Dutch nationalism, though paintings of it were to cause lots of problems for Rembrandt (see p.75).

Long after the Roman Empire had collapsed, **Charlemagne**, Holy Roman Emperor from 800 to 814, made the town one of the principal seats of his administration, building the **Valkhof Palace**, an enormous complex of chapels and secular buildings completed in the eighth century. Rebuilt in 1155 by another emperor, Frederick Barbarossa, the complex dominated Nijmegen right up until 1769, when the palace was demolished and the stonework sold; what was left suffered further deprivations when the French occupied the town in 1796. In September 1944, the Americans captured the town's bridges during Operation Market Garden (see box, p.262), but the failure at Arnhem put Nijmegen on the front line for the rest of the war. The results are clear to see: the old town was largely destroyed, and, give or take the odd recreated building, Nijmegen today is almost entirely modern.

Grote Markt

At the heart of the town is the **Grote Markt**, a busy open square overlooked by a handsome set of high gabled buildings that somehow managed to survive the fighting of World War II. The most conspicuous structure is the red-brick **Waag**, which, with its dormer windows, nifty shutters, decorative gables and double-stairway, is a fine example of Dutch renaissance style dating from 1612. From the Grote Markt, a vaulted passage, the **Kerkboog**, leads through to the precincts of the much-renovated Gothic **Grote Kerk**.

Grote Kerk

St Stevenskerkhof • **Church** April–Oct Mon 10.30am–1pm, Tues–Sat 10.30am–4.30pm & Sun noon–4.30pm; Nov to late Dec & March Sat 10.30am–4.30pm & Sun noon–4.30pm; free • **Tower** April–Oct Mon 10.30am–12.30pm, Wed & Sat 2–4pm; €4 • ☎ 024 360 4710, Ⓦ stevenskerk.nl

Known as Stevenskerk until the Reformation, the **Grote Kerk** is of unusual design, without a nave but with a long and lofty, fifteenth-century choir and a chunky transept. Key features of its interior include a massive Baroque organ and a large and ornately carved, semicircular dignitary's bench, built by the Protestant merchants to demonstrate their importance over the ejected Catholic priesthood. The Protestants whitewashed the church when they took it over, but some of the medieval **wall paintings** survived and have now been uncovered. The most charming tells the tale of **St Ontcommer**, a Portuguese princess who refused the marital advances of a pagan king, her resistance helped by divine intervention – she grew a long beard overnight. It didn't do her much good, however: her father was so angry he had her crucified. In the summer, you can climb the church **tower**, from where there is a commanding vista over the surrounding landscape.

Velorama Nationaal Fietsmuseum

Waalkade 107 • Mon–Sat 10am–5pm, Sun 11am–5pm • €5 • ☎ 024 322 5851, Ⓦ velorama.nl

Bike enthusiasts shouldn't miss the **Velorama Nationaal Fietsmuseum** (National Bicycle Museum), down by the River Waal. The museum has the largest collection of bicycles and other human-powered vehicles in the Netherlands, over 200 contraptions dating from the early nineteenth century and displayed over three floors. There are delicately carved wooden bicycles, a bicycle seating five people, penny-farthings, recumbents and quadricycles – anything and everything that has helped shape bicycle design in the last few centuries. All the exhibits are lovingly restored and beautifully displayed – making this the perfect museum to visit in a country where the bicycle rules.

The Valkhof

5

Lindenberg • Open access • Free

In a small park on a hillock overlooking the River Waal lie the scant remains of the Holy Roman Emperor's **Valkhof Palace**. It's hard to imagine just how imposing the palace once was, but you can view a ruined fragment of the Romanesque choir of the twelfth-century palace chapel and, just to the west, a sixteen-sided chapel built around 1045, in a similar style to the palatinate church at Charlemagne's capital, Aachen. Perhaps more rewarding are the wide views over the river from the vantage point behind the ruins.

Museum Het Valkhof

Kelfkensbos 59 • Tues–Sun 11am–5pm • €8 • ☏ 024 360 8805, ⓦ museumhetvalkhof.nl

Housed in an attractive modern building a few metres from the ruins of the Valkhof Palace is Nijmegen's main museum, the **Museum Het Valkhof**. The museum's permanent collection is strong on Roman Nijmegen with a wide range of artefacts from helmets, swords and figurines through to grave monuments, coins and glassware. It also displays lots of paintings of Nijmegen and its environs, most notably Jan van Goyen's wonderful *Valkhof Nijmegen*, which used to hang in the town hall. Painted in 1641, it's a large, sombre-toned picture – pastel variations on green and brown – in which the Valkhof shimmers above the Waal, almost engulfed by sky and river. Supplementing these older paintings are more modern works by the likes of Carel Willink, Pyke Koch and Raoul Hynckes as well as a lively programme of temporary exhibitions of modern art.

ARRIVAL AND INFORMATION

NIJMEGEN

By train Nijmegen's train station is on Stationsplein, a ten-minute walk from the town centre.
Destinations Amsterdam CS (hourly; 1hr 30min); Arnhem (every 30min to 1hr; 20min); Deventer (every 30min to 1hr; 1hr); Zutphen (every 30min to 1hr; 50min); and Zwolle (every 30min to 1hr; 1hr 30min).

By bus The bus station is on Stationsplein too, in front of the train station, with regular local services.
Tourist office The VVV is housed in the Stadsschouwburg at Keizer Karelplein 32, halfway between the train station and the town centre (Mon–Fri 9.30am–5.30pm, Sat 10am–4pm; ☏ 0481 366 250, ⓦ nijmegenexperience.nl).

ACCOMMODATION

Apollo Bisschop Hamerstraat 14 ☏ 024 322 3594, ⓦ apollo-hotel-nijmegen.nl. If you can ignore the gloomy entrance, this straightforward three-star hotel is a decent option: it's in a handy central location, with eighteen spick-and-span, modern guest rooms. €105
Courage Waalkade 108 ☏ 024 360 4970, ⓦ hotelcourage.nl. In a prime location, overlooking the River Waal, the *Courage* does itself proud with its distinctively decorated guest rooms, the pick of which have fancy wall paintings. You'll pay €20 extra for a river view. €110
Scandic Sanadome Weg door Jonkerbos 90 ☏ 024 359 7280, ⓦ sanadome.nl. Sleek modern hotel with one

hundred guest rooms in a glassy, curved building about 4km southwest of the town centre. Apart from its woodland setting, the hotel's main selling point is its thermal waters, which bubble up from deep underground at 23°C, and are then heated up to 34°C. Hotel guests have use of the indoor and outdoor thermal baths at no extra charge. €100
Stadsbrouwerij de Hemel Franse Plaats 1 ☏ 024 360 6167, ⓦ brouwerijdehemel.nl. Near the Grote Markt, one of Nijmegen's oldest and grandest buildings is the Commanderie van St Jan, once a medieval hospital. Today, the building houses several restaurants and bars, as well as the De Hemel brewery which has two guest rooms, with a self-service breakfast. €95

EATING AND DRINKING

Nijmegen has a wide range of places to eat and drink at sensible prices. **Kelfkensbos** and **Lange Hezelstraat** are good areas for restaurants, while the Waalkade turns into one big riverside terrace on sunny, summer evenings.

De Amuse Lange Hezelstraat 64 ☏ 024 324 5570, ⓦ deamuse.nl. With a menu comprising over fifty small bites (all under €10), this is the ideal finger-food

restaurant – and is as trendy as anything you'll find in Amsterdam. Tues–Sun 5pm to midnight; kitchen closes at 10pm.

5

Appels & Peren Kelfkensbos 29 ☎024 324 1627, ⓦappelsenperen.nl. Groovy little place decorated to match its name and offering a creative Dutch-meets-Italian menu. Try, for example, the lemon sole with celeriac and asparagus. Main courses average around €15. Daily 5pm to midnight; kitchen closes at 10pm.

Café de Plak Bloemerstraat 90 ☎024 322 2757, ⓦcafedeplak.nl. A health-food collective operates this laidback, organic eetcafé, where the menu offers a large selection of vegetarian dishes at very affordable prices. Daily noon–4pm & 5.30–9.30pm.

Café in de Blaauwe Hand Achter de Hoofdwacht 3 ☎024 323 2066. Footsteps from the Grote Kerk, this is the oldest bar in town, a typical brown café with a lovely wooden facade and offering a wide array of beers and *jenevers*. Has a mini-pavement terrace, too. Sun–Fri

2pm–1am, Sat 1pm–2am.

Plaats 1 Franseplaats 1 ☎024 365 6708, ⓦplaats1 .com. This is the pick of the bars and restaurants that inhabit the Commanderie van St Jan, being a smart and well-organized restaurant with a delightful tree-shaded terrace. Creative dishes such as poached wolffish and a *confit* of duck go for the amazingly low price of €10. Tues–Fri 11am–11pm, Sat & Sun 10am–11pm.

Het Savarijn Van der Brugghenstraat 14 ☎024 323 2615, ⓦsavarijn.nl. Smart but unpretentious restaurant on a side street and with a pleasant pavement terrace. The focus is on French cuisine, with the short but extremely inventive menu featuring dishes such as snails with tapenade, mustard and parsley as a starter. Mains cost €20–25, and reservations are essential. Mon–Fri noon–2pm, Mon–Sat 5–11pm.

ENTERTAINMENT

Cinema The Lux, Marienburg 38–39 (☎0900 5894636, ⓦlux-nijmegen.nl) is the best mainstream cinema in town, with a good international programme and regular late-night shows. A second branch, **Villa Lux**,

Oranjesingel 42 (☎0900 5894636, ⓦlux-nijmegen.nl), is Nijmegen's new art-house cinema, a fashionable and popular spot offering an adventurous programme of independent movies.

Enschede

East of the River IJssel, the flat landscapes of the west give way to the lightly undulating, wooded countryside of **Twente**, an industrial region within the province of Overijssel whose principal towns – Almelo, Hengelo and Enschede – were once dependent on the textile industry. Hit hard by Asian imports, all three have been forced to diversify their industrial base, with mixed success. The largest of the three is **ENSCHEDE**, some 50km east of Zutphen, whose desultory modern centre is partly redeemed by **St Jacobuskerk**, built in 1933 in neo-Byzantine-meets-Art Deco style with angular copper-green roofs, huge circular windows and a lumpy main tower. The main reason to visit, however, is to see the outstanding collection of fine art gifted to the city by a wealthy mill-owning family, the van Heeks, and now housed in the **Rijksmuseum Twente**.

Rijksmuseum Twente

Lasondersingel 129 • Tues–Sun 11am–5pm • €7 • ☎053 435 8675, ⓦrijksmuseumtwenthe.nl • The museum is a 15min walk north of the train station

Housed in an Art Deco mansion of 1930 on the northern edge of town, the **Rijksmuseum Twente** contains two key sections – fifteenth- to nineteenth-century art and modern and contemporary art, primarily Dutch with the emphasis on Expressionism. Among a fine sample of early religious art, three particular highlights are a set of brilliant blue and gold fragments from a French hand-illuminated missal; a primitive twelfth-century woodcarving of Christ on Palm Sunday, and a delightful cartoon strip of contemporary life entitled *De Zeven Werken van Barmhartigheid* ("The Seven Acts of Charity").

Of later canvases, Hans Holbein's *Portrait of Richard Mabott* is typical of his work, the stark black of the subject's gown offset by the white cross on his chest and the face so finely observed it's possible to make out the line of his stubble. Pieter Brueghel the Younger's *Winter Landscape* is also fastidiously drawn, down to the last twig, and contrasts with the more loosely contoured figures and threatening clouds of his brother Jan's *Landscape*. Moving on, Jan Steen's *The Alchemist* is all scurrilous satire, from the skull on the chimneypiece to the lizard suspended from the ceiling and the ogre's whispered advice. Steen also mocks sex, most memorably here in his *Lute Player*, which features a woman with bulging breasts and flushed countenance in the foreground, while on the wall behind is the vague outline of tussling lovers.

High points of the modern and contemporary section include Monet's volatile *Falaises près de Pourville*; a characteristically unsettling canvas by Carel Willink, *The Actress Ank van der Moer*; and examples of the work of less well-known Dutch modernists like Theo Kuypers, Jan Roeland and Emo Verkerk.

ARRIVAL AND INFORMATION   ENSCHEDE

By train Enschede train station is on Stationsplein on the northwest edge of the town centre, about 500m from the Markt – just follow the signs. Regular trains serve Amsterdam CS (hourly; 2hr); Apeldoorn (hourly; 1hr 10min); Deventer (hourly; 1hr); and Zwolle (hourly; 1hr 10min).

By bus Enschede bus station is by the train station on Stationsplein.
Tourist office The VVV is at the train station, at Stationsplein 1 (Mon 1–6pm, Tues–Fri 10am–6pm, Sat 10am–5pm; ☎ 053 432 3200, ⊛ uitinenschede.nl).

ACCOMMODATION

Amadeus Oldenzaalsestraat 103 ☎ 053 435 7486, ⊛ amadeushotel.nl. Competent, rather traditional, three-star hotel in the centre of town with just twelve guest rooms. It wouldn't win any prizes for its decor, but the welcome is friendly and the breakfasts filling. **€105**

The south and Zeeland

MIDDELBURG STADHUIS

The south and Zeeland

Look at a map and you'll see that the southern part of the Netherlands doesn't make much geographical sense at all: in the west it's all islands and rivers, while in the east a dangling sliver of land hooks deep into Belgium, its shape defined by centuries of dynastic wrangling. The west, which comprises the province of Zeeland, is classically Dutch, the inhabitants of its small towns and villages spending much of their history either at sea or keeping the sea away from hearth and home. Zeeland suffered its last major flood in 1953 and it was this disaster that kick-started the Delta Project, whose complex network of dykes, dams and sea walls, completed in 1986, has prevented any watery repetition. Zeeland has mile upon mile of sandy beach and wide-open landscapes, but many of its old towns and villages have been badly mauled by the developers. Two have, however, survived – Middelburg, with its splendid old centre, and Veere, every inch a nautical, seafaring port.

Inland lies **Noord-Brabant**, whose arc of industrial towns long bore the brunt of the string of invading armies who marched up from the south. Each of these towns has lots of history but not much else, though both **Breda** and **'s-Hertogenbosch** have fine churches. Noord-Brabant's largest town is **Eindhoven**, home to the multinational electrical company Philips, and from here it's just a few kilometres to the region's third province, **Limburg**, which was badly damaged in World War II. Limburg's capital and principal attraction is **Maastricht**, a city of vitality and virtuosity, which comes complete with a lively restaurant and bar scene as well as a set of first-rate medieval buildings.

Maastricht

MAASTRICHT is one of the most vibrant cities in the Netherlands. With its cobbled streets and fashionable boutiques in the old town, contemporary architecture in the Céramique district, a fantastic art fair and excellent cuisine, the city literally buzzes with excitement and its multilingual, multinational population epitomizes the most positive aspects of the European Union.

Though its claim to be the oldest town in the Netherlands is disputed by Nijmegen, Maastricht was certainly settled by the **Romans**, who took one look at the River Maas and dubbed the town Mosae Trajectum or "Crossing of the Maas". An important stopoff on the trading route between Cologne and the North Sea, the town boasted a Temple of Jupiter, whose remains are now on view in a hotel basement. A millennium later, **Charlemagne** beefed up the city too, though his legacy is ecclesiastical, his two churches representing some of the finest extant Romanesque architecture in the whole of the country.

THE ONZE LIEVE VROUWE BASILIEK, MAASTRICHT

Highlights

❶ **Maastricht** Alluringly cosmopolitan city in the far south, squeezed between the Belgian and German borders, and known for its mouthwatering regional specialties. **See pp.274–283**

❷ **Eindhoven** Leading city in modern architecture and design with a vibrant student nightlife and the Netherlands' longest bar street. **See p.291**

❸ **'s Hertogenbosch** This bustling market town has a picturesque old quarter of alleys and little bridges. **See pp.297–299**

❹ **Breda** Pretty little town with a stunning Gothic cathedral, lively bar scene and great shopping. **See pp.301–304**

❺ **Carnival at Bergen-op-Zoom** If you're around in February, don't miss the country's most exuberant carnival. **See p.305**

❻ **Middelburg** Attractive maritime town, capital of the watery province of Zeeland and the best place to taste fresh mussels. **See p.306**

❼ **The Walcheren coast** Zeeland's windswept coast has some dramatic footpaths and cycle routes as well as pristine beaches. **See p.311**

❽ **Delta Expo** The Delta Project – a monumental engineering project to protect the Netherlands from flooding – is commemorated in this outstanding exhibition. **See p.317**

HIGHLIGHTS ARE MARKED ON THE MAP ON P.276

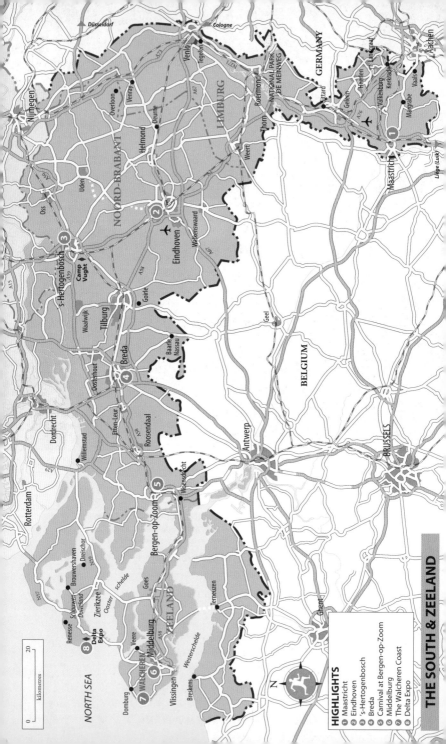

THE SOUTH & ZEELAND

HIGHLIGHTS
1. Maastricht
2. Eindhoven
3. 's-Hertogenbosch
4. Breda
5. Carnival at Bergen-op-Zoom
6. Middelburg
7. The Walcheren Coast
8. Delta Expo

Maastricht has also had its hard times, hitting the economic skids in the 1970s after the last of the region's coal mines closed, but its fortunes have been revived by a massive **regeneration** scheme, which has pulled in foreign investors by the busload. The town is now popular as a day-trip destination with the Dutch, the Germans and the Belgians, and it is also home to students from around the world studying at over forty international institutes, including the European Journalism Centre and the University of the United Nations. Redevelopment continues apace today with the addition of **'t Bassin**, a spruced-up inland harbour north of the Markt, with a handful of restaurants, cafés and galleries. The most recent construction in the centre of town is the **Mosae Forum**, a shopping centre with an attractive blend of classical and modern architecture. Finally, Maastricht is especially appealing during **Carnival**, with colourful parades and locals and visitors alike dressed up in the most creative outfits, mostly handmade.

Stadhuis

Mon–Fri 9am–12.30pm & 2–5pm • Free

The busiest of Maastricht's squares is the **Markt**, which hosts a general market on Wednesday and Friday mornings. At the centre of the square is the seventeenth-century **Stadhuis**, a square, grey limestone building that is a typical slice of Dutch civic grandeur. Its double staircase was constructed so that the rival rulers of Brabant and nearby Liège didn't have to argue about who should go first on the way in. Inside, the building has an imposing main hall which leads to an octagonal dome supported by heavy arches.

Vrijthof

Vrijthof, just west of the Markt, is the second of the town's main central squares. It's a large, rather grand open space flanked by a couple of churches on one side and a line of cafés on the other, with tables taking over the wide pavement in summer. During the Middle Ages, Vrijthof was the scene of the so-called "Fair of the Holy Relics", a seven-yearly showing of the bones of St Servaas, the first bishop of Maastricht, which brought plenty of pilgrims into the town but resulted in such civil disorder that it was eventually banned.

The Basiliek van St Servaas

Keizer Karelplein 3 • Mon–Sat 10am–5pm, Sun 12.30–5pm • €4 • ⓦ sintservaas.nl

Dominating the west side of Vrijthof is the church that holds the relics of St Servaas today, the **Basiliek van St Servaas**. Dating from 950, it was built on the site of an earlier shrine, which marked the spot where the saint was supposedly buried in c.384. Only the crypt remains of the tenth-century church, containing the tomb of the saint himself, and the rest is mostly of medieval or later construction. You enter on the north side, where a fifteenth-century Gothic cloister leads into the **treasury**, which holds a large collection of reliquaries, goblets and liturgical accessories. Among them a bust reliquary of St Servaas is decorated with reliefs telling the saint's story, which is carried through the town in Easter processions. There's also a coffin-reliquary of the saint, the so-called "Noodkist", dating from 1160 and bristling with saints, stones and ornate copperwork, as well as a jewelled crucifix from 890 and a twelfth-century Crucifixion in ivory. Beyond the treasury is the entrance to the rich and imposing interior, the round-arched nave supporting freshly painted Gothic vaulting. Don't miss the mid-thirteenth-century **Bergportaal** on the south side of the church, the usual entrance during services.

St Janskerk

Vrijthof 24 • April–Oct Mon–Sat 11am–4pm • Free • Church tower €1.50

The less prominent religious building on Vrijthof is Maastricht's main Protestant church, the fourteenth-century **St Janskerk**. It was originally built as the baptistery of

6

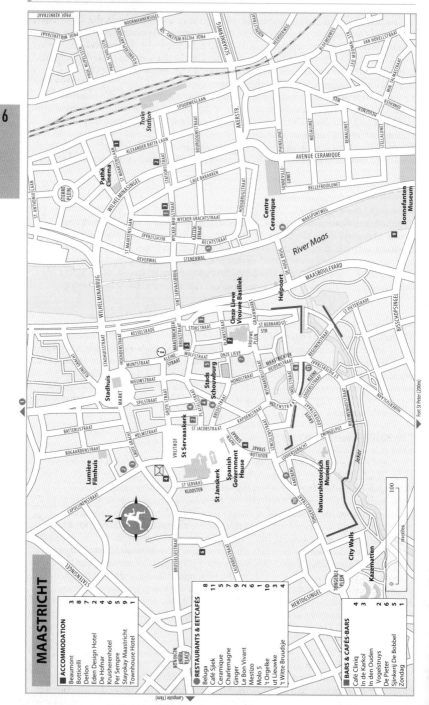

MAASTRICHT

■ ACCOMMODATION

Beaumont	3
Botticelli	8
Derlon	7
Eden Design Hotel	2
De Hofnar	4
Kruisherenhotel	6
Per Sempre	5
Stayokay Maastricht	9
Townhouse Hotel	1

● RESTAURANTS & EETCAFÉS

Beluga	8
Café Sjiek	11
Ceramique	5
Charlemagne	7
Ginger	9
Le Bon Vivant	2
Mestizo	6
Molo 5	1
't Orgelke	10
ut Lieuwke	3
't Witte Bruudsje	4

■ BARS & CAFÉS-BARS

Café Cliniq	4
In de Karkol	3
In den Ouden Vogelstruys	2
De Pieter	6
Sjinkerij De Bobbel	5
Zondag	1

the church of St Servaas when it was a cathedral and now comes complete with its own late-medieval Gothic tower. The church has some medieval murals, but a climb up the tower is the church's main appeal.

Museum aan het Vrijthof

Vrijthof 18 • Tues–Sun 10am–6pm • €8 • ⓦ museumaanhetvrijthof.nl

On the south side of the Vrijthof square, the sixteenth-century Spanish Government House holds the **Museum aan het Vrijthof**, which has a number of period rooms furnished in Dutch, French and the more local Liège–Maastricht style. Among various exhibits are statues and figurines, porcelain and applied arts and a handful of seventeenth-century paintings.

The Onze Lieve Vrouwe

The **Onze Lieve Vrouweplein** is a small, shady square crammed with café tables in summer, and dominated by the large Onze Lieve Vrouwe Basiliek. The square is also home to the statue of **Stella Mare**, an object of pilgrimage for centuries and one which attracts as many devotees as the church itself. Just north of the square is a small district of narrow streets, the **Stokstraat Kwartier**, named after its main gallery- and boutique-lined spine Stokstraat. This quarter has an intimate feel, with its vermilion townhouses, scattered sculptures and Maasland-Renaissance-style houses in warm Namur stone.

The Onze Lieve Vrouwe Basiliek

Onze Lieve Vrouweplein 7 • **Church** Daily 7.30am–5pm; free • **Treasury** Easter to mid-Oct Mon–Sat 11am–5pm, Sun 1–5pm; €3

The prominent **Onze Lieve Vrouwe Basiliek** is unusual for its fortified west front, with barely more than one or two slits for windows. First built around the year 1000, it's a solid, dark and deeply devotional place after the relative sterility of St Servaaskerk. The Gothic vaulting of the nave springs from a Romanesque base, while the galleried choir is a masterpiece of proportion, raised under a high half-dome, with a series of capitals exquisitely decorated with Old Testament scenes. Off the north aisle, the **treasury** holds the usual reliquaries and ecclesiastical garments, most notably the dalmatic of St Lambert – the evangelical bishop of Maastricht who was murdered at Liège in 705, allegedly by a local noble whom he had rebuked for adultery. Entrance to the church is through a side chapel on the Onze Lieve Vrouweplein.

The city walls and the Natuurhistorisch Museum

On the south side of Onze Lieve Vrouweplein lies another of Maastricht's most appealing quarters, with narrow streets winding out to the remains of the town battlements alongside the River Jeker. The best surviving part of the walls is the **Helpoort** of 1229, close to a stretch overlooking the river at the end of St Bernadusstraat. From here you can walk along the top of the walls almost as far as the **Natuurhistorisch Museum** at De Bosquetplein 6–7 (Natural History Museum; Tues–Fri 11am–5pm, Sat & Sun 1–5pm; €6; ⓦ nhmmaastricht.nl), where there's a small collection on the geology, flora and fauna of the surrounding area, along with a compact lush garden.

The Kazematten

Tongerseplein 9 • Tours July & Aug daily at 12.30pm and 2.30pm; Sept–June check opening hours with the VVV • €5.50 • ⓦ maastrichtunderground.nl

A short walk southwest of the Vrijthof square, in the Waldeck Park, the **Kazematten** (Casemates) provide further evidence of Maastricht's once-impressive fortifications.

Built between 1575 and 1825, these subterranean galleries are all that remain of a whole network which once protected the garrison from enemy attack and housed a string of complimentary gun batteries. The tour takes you through a string of damp passages, a mildly interesting way to spend an hour. Trivia buffs might be interested to know that the famous fourth "musketeer", d'Artagnan, was killed here, struck down while engaged in an attack on the town as part of forces allied to Louis XIV in 1673.

Bonnefanten Museum

Avenue Céramique 250 • Tues–Sun 11am–5pm • €9 • ⓦ bonnefanten.nl

Ten minutes' walk south of the St Servaas bridge, the **Bonnefanten Museum** is one of Maastricht's highlights. Named after the Bonnefanten monastery where it used to be housed, the museum now inhabits an impressive modern building on the banks of the Maas. Its space-rocket-style cupola is instantly recognizable, zooming skywards, and is usually devoted to a single piece of art. Inside is a permanent collection of old masters and contemporary fine art, including works from the Minimal Art and Arte Povera movements. The rest of the museum is given over to various temporary exhibitions, superbly displayed: you could find anything from giant spider installations to Titians.

Centre Céramique

Avenue Céramique 50, at the corner of Plein 1992 • Tues & Thurs 10.30am–7pm, Wed & Fri 10.30am–5pm, Sat 10am–3pm, Sun 1–5pm • ⓦ centreceramique.nl

With its low horizons and euro symbols impressed into the paving stones, the **Centre Céramique** is a huge modern building that houses the European Journalism Centre, the city archives and the library (which has free internet access). The permanent collection here consists of eighteenth- and nineteenth-century glass and crystal, locally produced ceramics as well as archeological artefacts, among others. The centre also frequently hosts temporary exhibitions and occasional concerts.

St Pietersberg

Zonneberg cave Buitengoed Slavante; tours in English July & Aug daily at 1.50pm; €5.50 • **Grotten Noord cave** Chalet Bergrust; tours in English May–June & Sept–Dec Sat & Sun at 2pm; €5.50 • ⓦ maastrichtunderground.nl

There are dank passageways to explore fifteen minutes' walk from the Casemates on the southern outskirts of Maastricht, where the flat-topped hill of **St Pietersberg** rises to a height of about 110m. The galleries here were hollowed out of the soft sandstone, or marl, that makes up the hill – an activity that has been going on here since Roman times. There are more than 20,000 passages, but nowadays only 8000 of them are accessible. The galleries used to claim the lives of people (usually children) who never found their way out, but these days it's almost impossible to enter the caves without guidance. Of the two cave systems, the **Zonneberg** is probably the better, situated on the far side of the St Pietersberg hill at Casino Slavante. These caves were intended to be used as air-raid shelters during World War II and were equipped accordingly, though they were in fact only used during the final days of the German occupation. There is some evidence of wartime usage, plus what everyone claims is Napoleon's signature on a graffiti-ridden wall. Also on the walls are recent charcoal drawings, usually illustrating a local story and acting as visual aids for the guides, not to mention the ten varieties of bat that inhabit the dark (and cold) corridors.

The other, more northerly system of caves, the **Grotten Noord**, is easier to reach (a 15min walk from the centre of town). There are panoramic views over the town and surrounding countryside from its entrance on the near side of St Pietersberg. Nearby is **Fort St Pieter**, a low brick pentagonal structure, built in 1702.

TEFAF ART AND ANTIQUES FAIR

Once a year, art and antique lovers gather at the **TEFAF** fair (ⓦtefaf.com), held in the congress centre (MECC) in Maastricht. From its modest beginnings in 1975 when it specialized in old master paintings, the TEFAF now claims to be the world's leading fine art and antiques fair, attracting visitors from all over the world. It usually takes place in March, but check the exact dates on the website. Even if you're not an art lover it's worth noting the dates, as finding accommodation is almost impossible when it's on.

6

ARRIVAL AND DEPARTURE   MAASTRICHT

The centre of Maastricht is on the west bank of the River Maas and most of the town spreads out from here towards the Belgian border. You're likely to arrive, however, on the east bank, in the district known as Wyck, that's home to the train and bus stations and many of the city's hotels. All local buses run from both the bus and train stations to the Markt, though it's easy enough to walk.

By plane Maastricht airport (ⓦwww.maa.nl) is 12km north of the city at Beek; from here it's a twenty-minute ride on bus #59 to the Markt and the train station; a taxi costs about €25.

By train The train station is about ten minutes' walk from the St Servaas bridge, which takes you across the river into the centre. Regular trains connect Maastricht to Amsterdam (every 30min; 2hr 25min); Den Haag/The Hague (every 30min; 2hr 45min) and Roermond (every 30min; 40min).

By bus The bus station is right in front of the train station, on Stationsplein, with services to smaller, local destinations such as Margraten and Vaals (bus #50; Mon–Sat every 15min, Sun every 30min).

By car Arriving by car, follow signs for Q-Parking; there's no free parking in the town centre. The VVV has a detailed "Parking in Maastricht" leaflet.

INFORMATION AND TOURS

Tourist office The VVV (May–Oct Mon–Sat 10am–6pm Nov–April Mon–Fri 10am–6pm, Sat 10am–5pm; ☎043 325 2121, ⓦvvvmaastricht.nl) is housed on the west side of the river in the Dinghuis, a tall, late fifteenth-century building at Kleine Staat 1, at one end of the main shopping street. As well as information on the city and on film, theatre and music events around town, they have decent maps and good walking guides. In July and August they organize walking tours in English, which leave from the office daily at 1.30pm (€5.50) and last about an hour and a half.

City tours From March to November, City Tour Maastricht offers a ride through the historical centre of town by horse carriage, departing from the Onze Lieve Vrouweplein (Tues–Sun from noon; 45min; €10; ⓦcitytourmaastricht. com).

Cruises Between May and September, Stiphout runs hourly cruises from the bottom of Graanmarkt down the Maas (daily 10am–5pm; check hours out of season; 50min; €7.75; ☎043 351 5300, ⓦstiphout.nl), as well as trips to the St Pietersberg caves (3hr; €13.25): phone first to check which cruises run each day, or ask at the VVV.

ACCOMMODATION

For a small city, Maastricht has a wide range of central hotels, though they do tend to be a tad pricey. Alternatively, the VVV has a list of private rooms, which they will either book on your behalf for a small fee or sell you the list. There are also several good pensions and a modern HI hostel, overlooking the River Maas.

HOTELS

Beaumont Wyckerbrugstraat 2 ☎043 325 4433, ⓦbeaumont.nl. This classic example of a contemporary designer hotel combines wooden floors, natural colours and chandeliers with modern elements. Its 121 rooms are divided over two buildings, and come with all mod cons. **€155**

★ **Botticelli** Papenstraat 11 ☎043 352 6300, ⓦhotelbotticelli.nl. In a former wine warehouse right in the heart of town, this luxurious hotel, decorated in Italian style, has plenty of atmosphere with an intimate inner courtyard, cosy *salotto* and wine cellar. **€143**

Derlon Onze Lieve Vrouweplein 6 ☎043 321 6770, ⓦderlon.com. Posh, plush and pricey, with 48 stylish designer rooms and a retro-chic restaurant. It's in a great location on the city's most atmospheric square and there's even a museum of Roman antiquities in its cellar, including the remains of a temple to Jupiter and a well. **€195**

Eden Design Hotel Stationsstraat 40 ☎043 328 2525, ⓦedenhotelgroup.com. The Netherlands' first design hotel still hasn't lost its spunk. Funky colours and daring art make this one of the trendiest spots in the Wyck area. The adjacent restaurant *Flo* is a great spot for drinks or dinner. Special deals are abundant so check in advance. **€135**

6

Kruisherenhotel Kruisherengang 19–23 ☎043 329 2020, ⊛chateauhotels.nl. A fifteenth-century monastery and Gothic church which have been transformed into a luxurious design hotel with sixty well-equipped rooms, an inviting wine bar in the former chancel and intimate inner courtyard. Pricey, but worth every penny. **€200**

★ **Townhouse Hotel** Sint Maartenslaan 5 ☎043 321 1111, ⊛townhousehotels.nl. This centrally located hotel combines modern design with old-fashioned cosiness with 69 well-equipped rooms in warm beige shades kitted out with flat-screens, comfortable beds and free wi-fi. Prices vary according to availability, so it pays off to book well in advance. **€102**

B&B, GUESTHOUSE AND HOSTEL

De Hofnar Capucijnenstraat 35 & Keizer Karelplein 13

☎043 351 0396, ⊛hofnarmaastricht.nl. Cosy B&B divided over two buildings with reasonable rooms, all varying in size and shape. Some rooms have shared facilities and it can be a bit noisy. A very homely atmosphere right in the heart of the city. **€75**

Per Sempre Maastrichter Smedenstraat 28 ☎043 321 9969, ⊛persempre.nl. This smart guesthouse, located above a store with the same name, is great value for money, with large rooms and a friendly owner. At the time of writing, major refurbishment was taking place to transform the rooms into more luxurious apartments. **€65**

Stayokay Maastricht Maasboulevard 101 ☎043 750 1790, ⊛stayokay.com. Modern hostel sleeping around 200, right on the banks of the River Maas and within walking distance of the Onze Lieve Vrouweplein. There's a great terrace overlooking the water in summer. Dorm beds **€34**.

EATING

Maastricht has some of the best cooking in the Netherlands, so options for good eating abound. Regional delicacies include asparagus, cave mushrooms, *Limburgse Vlaai* (fruit tart) and Rommedou cheese. Limburg is also the only wine-producing province in the Netherlands, although not everyone will enjoy its slightly sour taste.

EETCAFÉS

★ **Café Sjiek** Sint Pieterstraat 13 ☎043 321 0158, ⊛cafesjiek.nl. Anyone from a carpenter to a top lawyer will feel at home in this pleasant eetcafé, which serves a wide selection of regional dishes at affordable prices. Their cheese platter is a must for connoisseurs. It's also the best place in town to try *zuurvlees* (traditional meat stew). Mon–Fri 5–11pm, Sat & Sun noon–11pm.

Céramique Rechtstraat 78 ☎043 325 2097, ⊛eetcafeceramique.nl. Located in the Wyck, a burgeoning area with many restaurants, this eetcafé serves no-nonsense dishes, with main courses such as salmon, steak and sea bass for around €20. The interior has recently been revamped without losing its homely feel. Daily 5.30–10pm.

Charlemagne Onze Lieve Vrouweplein 24 ☎043 321 9373, ⊛cafecharlemagne.nl. An old favourite which has been serving reasonably priced steaks, stews, satay, salads and a wide variety of beers for over a hundred years. Great leaf-covered terrace in summer and attentive staff. Daily 9am–midnight.

't Witte Bruudsje Platielstraat 12 ☎043 321 0057. Late-night snack attacks can be assuaged here from their choice of baguettes, salads and hot staples such as chilli con carne and fish and chips. Sun–Thurs 10am–2am, Fri & Sat 10am–3am.

RESTAURANTS

Beluga Plein 1992 12 ☎043 321 3364, ⊛rest-beluga .com. A top-notch restaurant, with two Michelin stars, offering exquisite cuisine in a contemporary setting. A seven-course meal will set you back a whopping €160, but

it's worth the splurge. Tues–Fri noon–1.30pm & 7–9.30pm, Sat 7–9.30pm.

Ginger Tongersestraat 7 ☎043 326 0022, ⊛restaurantginger.nl. Contemporary Asian fusion cuisine in a retro-chic setting. Abundant sushi and sashimi as well as main courses such as stir-fried beef or green curry for around €17. Their home-made green tea rice crème brûlée is a must. Mon–Fri noon–11pm, Sat & Sun 5–11pm.

Le Bon Vivant Capucijnenstraat 91 ☎043 321 0816, ⊛lebonvivant.nl. Pure French cuisine such as foie gras, scallops, pigeon and fish soup. A three-course meal in this seventeenth-century vault starts at €35, with main dishes around €25. It also serves an ample selection of regional wines. Tues–Sat from 5.30pm.

Mestizo Bredestraat 18 ☎043 327 0874, ⊛mestizo.nl. A funky little place offering tasty Latin cuisine. Great starters such as raw tuna with lemon mayonnaise or piri-piri shrimps for around €11. Main dishes such as *zarzuela* or burritos will set you back around €18. Tues–Sun 5–10.30pm.

Molo 5 Bassinkade 5 ☎043 327 0033, ⊛molo5.nl. There are a few good restaurants and art galleries situated in this inland harbour; *Molo 5* serves Italian food in an intimate setting with prices starting at €15 for a pasta dish and €24 for a main course. Great terrace. Mon 5–10pm, Tues–Sun noon–2.30pm & 6–10pm.

't Orgelke Tongersestraat 40 ☎043 321 6982, ⊛www .orgelke.nl. This restaurant is famous for its satay and stews, but they also serve a wide variety of fish and meat dishes for around €18. If you beat the record holder in satay-eating (currently standing at 13 skewers), your name will be added to the wall of fame. Mon, Wed, Thurs & Sun 5–9pm, Fri & Sat 5–10pm.

PREUVENEMINT

Maastricht is known as the culinary capital of the Netherlands, and never more so than during **Preuvenemint**, an annual four-day culinary event held on the last full weekend in August (ⓦpreuvenemint.nl), when Vrijthof square is filled with over thirty stands functioning as restaurants. "Preuvenemint" is a contraction of the Maastricht words "*preuve*" (to taste) and "*evenemint*" (event), and it's a great way to explore the richness of Dutch cuisine. The main attraction, though, has to be the crowd the event attracts. Posh Maastricht comes out to show off its latest purchases, but also to contribute to a good cause, since all the proceeds go to charity.

6

★ **Ut Lieuwke** Grote Gracht 62 ☎043 321 0459, ⓦlieuwke.nl. Great classic Dutch/French cuisine, such as halibut with truffle sauce or lamb stew, in an informal setting with very amenable owners. Make sure you book as the tiny restaurant fills up fast with regulars. Mon & Thurs–Sat 5–10pm.

DRINKING AND NIGHTLIFE

For drinking, head to the bars on the east side of the Vrijthof, particularly in summer when the pavement cafés are jam-packed. A more intimate environment can be found around the Onze Lieve Vrouweplein, while heavy night-time entertainment is concentrated around the Platielstraat.

CAFÉS AND BARS

Café Cliniq Platielstraat 9a ☎043 350 0499, ⓦcafecliniq.nl. This trendy café turns into a vibrant club at night with DJs spinning up-to-the-minute beats and a young and good-looking crowd enjoying a cocktail or two. Tues & Wed 5pm–2am, Thurs 4pm–2am, Fri 4pm–3am, Sat noon–3am.

★ **In de Karkol** Stokstraat 5 ☎043 321 7035. For a true authentic Maastricht experience, this tiny café has music in dialect by regional artists, which is loudly sung along to by the local crowd. Their cosy little inner courtyard makes a pleasant hangout in summer. Mon–Wed noon–midnight, Thurs–Sun noon–2am.

In den Ouden Vogelstruys Vrijthof 15 ☎043 321 4888. One of the nicest bars on the otherwise touristy Vrijthof, just on the corner of Platielstraat, with a dark brown interior and oodles of atmosphere. Many beers on draft plus regional delicacies to accompany your drink. Try the specialties; nut bread with Rommedou cheese or waffle with cherries. Daily 9.30am–2am, Sat & Sun till 3am.

De Pieter Sint Pieterstraat 22 ☎043 321 2002. Popular with locals, this typical brown café has sand on the floor and a good array of beers. Also serves a simple lunch menu consisting of sandwiches and hefty *uitsmijters* (fried eggs on bread). It hosts occasional live *chanson* music and has a nice summertime terrace facing the city walls. Daily 10.30am–2am, Fri & Sat till 3am, Sun from noon.

Sjinkerij De Bobbel Wolfstraat 32 ☎043 321 7413. Just off Onze Lieve Vrouweplein, this is a bare-boards place, lively in the early evening. Classy Jugendstil interior, waiters in uniform and no music so great for an intimate conversation. A favourite with locals. Sun–Wed 10am–9pm, Thurs–Sat 10am–10pm.

Zondag Wyckerbrugstraat 42 ☎043 325 9653, ⓦcafezondag.nl. A trendy little lunchroom-cum-bar, great for a coffee and grandma's apple pie but also suitable for a quick lunch or tapas platter with drinks. Jam-packed at weekends when the DJ takes over. Try their stiff cocktails, if you dare. Daily 10am till late.

DIRECTORY

Bike rental Aon de Stasie, Stationsplein (Mon–Fri 5.15am–1.15am, Sat 6am–1.15am, Sun 7.15am–1.15am; ☎043 321 1100) rents out bikes from €10/day, plus a €50 deposit.

Books Maastricht's largest and best bookstore is Selexyz, inside the thirteenth-century Dominicanerkerk, at Dominicanerkerkstraat 1, just off Helmstraat: it has a good selection of new English-language titles, and you get a great view of the old restored frescoes, while you browse. There's also a branch of De Slegte at Grote Straat 53, for secondhand English-language paperbacks and much else besides.

Bureau de change There's a GWK office at the train station, (Mon–Fri 9am–7pm, Sat 9am–5pm, Sun 10am–5pm).

Car rental Europcar, Sibemaweg 1 ☎043 361 2310. The major companies also have desks at the airport.

Cinema The Lumière Cinema, Bogaardenstraat 40b (☎043 321 4080, ⓦlumiere.nl), regularly shows interesting art-house movies, while mainstream cinema can be found at Pathé, Wilhelminasingel 39 (☎0900 1458, ⓦpathe.nl).

Markets General market on Markt (Wed & Fri 8am–1pm). Antique and curiosities market on Stationsstraat (Sat 8am–4pm).

Taxis Crals, Posthoornstraat 75 ☎043 362 2222.

Limburg

Pressed between Belgium and Germany, **Limburg**, the Netherlands' southernmost province, is shaped like an hourglass and is only 13km across at its narrowest. By Dutch standards, this is a geographically varied province: the north is a familiarly flat landscape of farmland and woods until the town of **Roermond**, where the River Maas loops and curls its way across the map; in the south, and seemingly out of nowhere, rise rolling hills studded with vineyards and châteaux. The people of Limburg are as distinct from the rest of the Netherlands as their landscape – their dialects incomprehensible to "Hollanders", their outlook more closely forged by Belgium and Germany than the distant Randstad. Nowhere is this international flavour more apparent than in the main city of Maastricht (see p.274), while **South Limburg's** distinctive, and notably un-Dutch, atmosphere makes it popular with tourists from the rest of the Netherlands, who head to its many caves and scenic cycle routes, and visit its resorts such as **Valkenburg**. North and central Limburg are less colourful, but still have some places that are well worth visiting. **Venlo**, with its stunning Stadhuis, is a good starting point for heading on to the **National War and Resistance Museum**, and **Roermond** makes a good base to explore the **National Park de Meinweg**.

South Limburg

The hilly landscape of **South Limburg** makes a popular holiday destination for Netherlanders who are keen to escape the pancake-flat landscapes of the north. Several long-distance **walking routes** converge on Maastricht, including the popular and scenic Grand Randonné 5 "Traject der Ardennen", the Pieterpad (from St Pietersberg to Groningen's Pieterburen), and the Krijtlandpad, which winds its way to the German border. The countryside is green and rolling, studded with castles (many of which have been converted into hotels), seamed with river valleys and dotted with the crooked timber-framed houses that are unique to this area. **Valkenburg** is the region's main resort, and an easy place to get to as it's on the main train line from Maastricht to Aachen, though it does get packed throughout the summer.

Margraten American War Cemetery

Amerikaanse Begraafplaats 1 • Daily sunrise to sunset • Free • Bus #50 from Maastricht train station to Aachen stops right outside the cemetery

Just outside the town of Margraten, the **American War Cemetery** is a moving memorial to over eight thousand American servicemen who died in the Dutch and Belgian campaigns of late 1944 and 1945. The centrepiece is a stone quadrangle recording the names of the soldiers, together with a small visitors' room and a pictorial representation and narrative describing the ebb and flow of the local campaign; beyond the quadrangle, the white marble crosses that mark the burial places of the soldiers cover a depressingly huge area.

PINKPOP FESTIVAL

What started as a small gathering over forty years ago is now in the *Guinness Book of Records* as the oldest unbroken festival in Europe. Limburg's **Pinkpop** (ⓦ pinkpop.nl), a three-day event starting on Whitsun, has its roots in Geleen but soon moved to **Landgraaf**, close to the German border, where it grew into a festival attracting more than 90,000 alternative pop and rock fans. It's hosted many big names, from Elvis Costello to Lenny Kravitz and from the Counting Crows to Bruce Springsteen, and has always been a trendsetter for other festivals in the country. Traditionally Monday is the busiest day. Die-hards who don't want to miss a thing can stay on the purpose-built campsite on the premises; if that's not your thing, be sure to book accommodation ahead. During the festival, frequent trains connect Maastricht and Heerlen to Landgraaf station, from where a shuttle service will take you to the festival site.

A SCENIC CYCLE IN SOUTH LIMBURG

On a leisurely cycle route east from Maastricht to Vaals, right on the German border, scenic villages nestle among vineyards and orchards, linked by quiet lanes dotted with shrines. Cycling is a perfect way to appreciate this rolling landscape and its un-Dutch hills. Pick up a Limburg province map from Maastricht tourist office, and allow a day for this seventy-kilometre round trip.

From Maastricht train station, follow the river south to **Gronsveld**, picking up signs to the eleventh-century village of St Geertruid. The road snakes over hills draped with vineyards before swooping into the villages of **Mheer**, **Noorbeek** and **Slenaken** – all very pretty and popular. At Slenaken, the road develops some hairpin tendencies as it climbs the valley side above. Continue through **Eperheide** and **Epen**, with sweeping views across to the rolling valleys of Belgium on the right. Between Epen and **Vaals**, there's a gradual eight-kilometre climb on narrow roads, winding between woods of red oaks. From Vaals, you can do an extra six-kilometre round trip to the highest point in the Netherlands (a lofty 321m): follow the signs to the **Drielandenpunt**, where three flags in a graffiti-covered concrete block mark the meeting of the borders of Belgium, Germany and the Netherlands. Otherwise, follow the main road out of Vaals (there's a dedicated cycle lane), turning left to **Vijlen**. Surrounding you is a panoramic view over Belgium, Germany and the Netherlands, beautiful on a clear day. From **Mechelen** and **Gulpen**, you're within striking distance of **Valkenburg** to the north, approached through the old town. Climb the steep but brief Cauberg hill to return to Maastricht, enjoying a speedy descent between orchards and farmland with the city locked in your sights. Once on the outskirts, follow the cycle route signs to bring you back to the station.

An alternative (and shorter) return route is to continue from Gulpen to Maastricht on a straight route via **Margraten** and **Cadier-en-Keer**.

Valkenburg

Set in the gently wooded valley of the River Geul, **VALKENBURG**, ten minutes northeast of Maastricht by train, is southern Limburg's major tourist resort. A medieval castle, its ruins starkly silhouetted on crags above the town, surveys the ersatz castle train station and the garish centre, where busloads of tourists arrive every day throughout the summer. While you probably wouldn't want to stay here, it's certainly a change from the rest of the Netherlands, with a feel more akin to a Swiss or Austrian alpine resort. Valkenburg is famed for its Christmas markets, held in Fluweelengrot and Gemeentegrot, with all manner of special foodstuffs, decorations and street entertainment. It is also where the **Amstel Gold Race** (Ⓦ amstelgoldrace.nl), one of the country's leading cycle events, finishes sometime each April.

Theodoor Dorrenplein, five minutes' walk from the train station, is the centre of town, fringed with cafés and home to the tourist office. From here, the main Grotestraat leads up through the pedestrianized old centre to the old **Grendelpoort** arch beyond which is the town's second focal point, **Grendelplein**. Streets lead off from here to Valkenburg's main attractions, many of which are aimed at children, including a bobsleigh run, a fairy-tale wood and a hopeful reconstruction of Rome's catacombs.

Valkenburg castle and caves

Castle Entrance off Grendelplein; daily: Feb–June 10am–5pm; July–Aug 10am–6pm; Oct–Dec 10am–5pm; €4 • **Caves** Daalhemerweg 27; guided tours only: check website for hours; €6 • Joint ticket for both caves and castle €8.50 • Ⓦ kasteelvalkenburg.nl

Dating from the eleventh century, **Valkenburg castle** was blown up in 1672 on the orders of William III, after he had recaptured it from the French. Repair and restoration began in 1921 and continue still; in the process a series of long-forgotten underground passages has been discovered. These passages form part of the **Fluweelengrot**, a series of caves that were formed – like those of St Pietersberg in Maastricht – by the quarrying of marl, which has long been used for much of the building hereabouts. On the whole they're a damp, cold way to spend an hour, the most interesting features being the signatures and silhouettes of American soldiers who wintered here from 1944 to 1945 and a clandestine chapel that was used during the late eighteenth-century French occupation.

INFORMATION | VALKENBURG

Tourist office The VVV is located on the Theodoor Dorrenplein 5 (Mon–Sat 9am–5pm; July & Aug Mon–Sat 9am–5.30pm, Sun 10am–4pm; ☎0900 555 9798, ⓦvvvzuidlimburg.nl), has maps and information on all Valkenburg's attractions, as well as lists of the dozens of hotels and pensions.

ACCOMMODATION AND EATING

Den Driesch Heunsbergerweg 1 ☎043 601 2025, ⓦcampingdendriesch.nl. The nearest campsite to the centre of town is a short walk up Daalhemerweg from Grendelplein, and attracts a young crowd. Guests have free access to the nearby swimming pool. April–Dec. **€25**

Gaudi Grendelplein 14 ☎043 601 5333, ⓦhotelgaudi .nl. Inspired by the Spanish architect and centrally located, this hotel has fifteen basic but perfectly adequate and colourful rooms. The Spanish restaurant serves a great paella for only €14.50 or tapas platter for €17.50. **€65**

Hostellerie Valckenborgh Hovetstraat 3 ☎043 601 2484, ⓦvalckenborgh.nl. Family-run hotel where you can choose between classic budget rooms or larger, more modern rooms with rain shower and flat-screen TV. The downstairs restaurant with a cosy fireplace mainly serves regional dishes. **€80**

La Casa Grotestraat 25–27 ☎043 601 2180, ⓦla-casa .nl. This centrally located hotel has eight modern, comfortable rooms with warm wooden floors and kitschy knick-knacks. The Spanish/Italian restaurant downstairs dishes up everything from pizzas and pastas to a Spanish tapas platter. **€80**

Roermond and around

ROERMOND, the focal point of central Limburg, is something of an oddity. While not especially exciting, it does have a rich Catholic heritage, as numerous shrines to the Virgin attest – a legacy of several hundred years of Hapsburg hegemony. It was also the home town of that most prolific of architects, P.J.H. Cuypers, who dotted the whole country with his fancy neo-Gothic structures. Today, the town's greatest asset is its position: Roermond lies on the banks of the **River Maas**, at the point where it meanders into the small, artificial lakes of the **Maasplassen**. Come summertime, these lakes fill with small boats, windsurfers and waterskiers as holidaymakers take to the water or fish under the town's skyline. The town also claims to have Europe's largest designer outlet centre, attracting busloads of German and even Russian tourists shopping for bargains.

Roermond also makes a useful base for visiting **De Meinweg** national park and the nearby village of **Thorn**, as well as being a handy stopover on the way to Maastricht and the south, or Aachen, Düsseldorf and Cologne in Germany.

Munsterkerk

Munsterplein • April–Oct daily 2–5pm, Sat closes 4pm • Free

Built in Romanesque style in the thirteenth century, the **Munsterkerk** was much altered and Gothicized by P.J.H. Cuypers, who lived and worked in Roermond for much of his life. Inside, the main thing to see is the polychrome thirteenth-century tomb of Gerhard III and his wife Margaret of Brabant.

Around the Markt

The large sloping square of the **Markt** is the town's main plaza. On its eastern side is the early eighteenth-century **Stadhuis**, a dull building that's easily overlooked, while the larger streets leading south from the Markt – Marktstraat, Neerstraat and Minderbroeders Singel – are home to some later and much more attractive architecture. Neerstraat 38 and 10 are good examples of Roermond's alluring twentieth-century **facades**, the majority of which are Art Nouveau, often strongly coloured with heavily moulded vegetal patterns and designs, sometimes with stylized animal heads and grotesque characters.

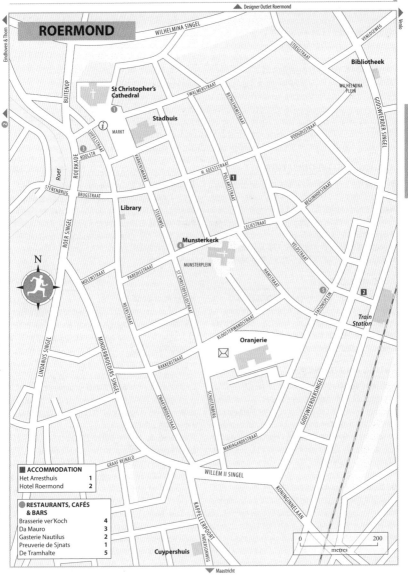

ROERMOND

Designer Outlet Roermond

Eindhoven & Thorn

Venlo

WILHELMINA SINGEL

STEEGSTRAAT

VENLOSEWEG

Bibliotheek

BUITENOP

St Christopher's
Cathedral

SWALMERSTRAAT

BETHLEHEMSTRAAT

WILHELMINA
PLEIN

GODSWEERDER SINGEL

Stadhuis

MARKT

VOOGDIJSTRAAT

UILESTRAAT

KOOLSTR

ROERKADE

H. GEESTSTRAAT

POLLAERTSTRAAT

BEGIJNHOFSTRAAT

Roer

VARENSTRAAT

STENENBRUG

BRUGSTRAAT

STEENWEG

LELIESTRAAT

Library

ROER SINGEL

VELDSTRAAT

Munsterkerk

MOLENSTRAAT

PAREDISSTRAAT

MUNSTERPLEIN

ST.CHRISTOFFELSTRAAT

HAMSTRAAT

N

NEERSTRAAT

KLOOSTERWANDSTRAAT

STATIONSPLEIN

**Train
Station**

LINDANUS SINGEL

MINDERBROEDERS SINGEL

KLOOSTERWANDSTRAAT

Oranjerie

GODSWEERDERSINGEL

BAKKERSTRAAT

ZWARTBROEKSTRAAT

SCHUITENBERG

MARIAGARDESTRAAT

GRAAF REINALD

WILLEM II SINGEL

KONINGINNELAAN

KAPPELLERPOORT

ANDERSONWEG

Cuypershuis

Maastricht

■ **ACCOMMODATION**
Het Arresthuis — 1
Hotel Roermond — 2

● **RESTAURANTS, CAFÉS
& BARS**
Brasserie ver'Koch — 4
Da Mauro — 3
Gasterie Nautilus — 2
Preuverie de Sjnats — 1
De Tramhalte — 5

0   metres   200

The Cuypershuis

Pieter Cuyperstraat 1 • Tues–Sun 11am–4.30pm • €6 • ⓦ cuypershuisroermond.nl

Roermond's principal claim to architectural fame is celebrated at the **Cuypershuis**, the
building in which P.J.H. Cuypers (1827–1921) lived and worked for many years.
Cuypers was the Netherlands' foremost ecclesiastical architect in the nineteenth
century, his work paralleling that of the British Gothic Revivalist, Augustus Pugin.
Almost every large city in the country has a Catholic church by him – those in
Eindhoven, Leeuwarden and Hilversum are notable – though his two most famous
buildings are secular: the Rijksmuseum and Centraal Station in Amsterdam. Inside the

Cuypershuis, you can see exhibits on the architect and examples of his work, as well as a small private chapel, and a large extension in which masses of decorative panels, mouldings and fixtures were produced.

Designer Outlet Roermond

Stadsweide 2 • Fri–Wed 10am–7pm, Thurs 10am–8pm • ⓦ designer-outlet-roermond.nl

Roermond's main tourist attraction is its most commercial, an immense designer outlet with over a hundred and fifty stores selling everything from Armani to Burberry and Gucci at sharp prices. The centre is one of Europe's largest designer outlets, attracting almost four million visitors a year and boosting Roermond's economy enormously. Be prepared for hordes of bargain shoppers and traffic jams at weekends.

ARRIVAL AND INFORMATION

ROERMOND

By train The train station is at Stationsplein 8, a straight ten- to fifteen-minute walk into the centre of town. Regular trains connect Roermond to Venlo (every 30min; 23min), Maastricht (every 30min; 30min) and Amsterdam (every 30min; 1h 55min).

Tourist office The VVV is on Markt 17 (April–Oct Mon–Fri 9.30am–5.30pm, Sat 9.30am–4pm; Nov–March Mon

1–5pm, Tues–Sat 9.30am–5pm, Sun noon–4pm; ☏ 0475 335 847, ⓦ vvvmiddenlimburg.nl). It can provide details of fishing and boat trips along the River Maas (April–Sept).

Boat rental Watersportschool Frissen, Hatenboer 75 (☏ 0475 327 873, ⓦ watersportschool.nl), rents out five-person boats for €60 a day.

ACCOMMODATION

Het Arresthuis Pollartstraat 7 ☏ 0475 870 870, ⓦ hetarresthuis.nl. This former prison has been converted into a stylish, modern and funky hotel. The 105 old prison cells have become 36 luxurious rooms equipped with all mod cons behind the original cell doors. **€160**

Hotel Roermond Stationsplein 9 & 13 ☏ 0475 332 325, ⓦ hotelroermond.nl. Right next to the train station, this hotel has rather basic but spacious rooms with modern bathrooms. Downstairs, there's a large restaurant with an inviting terrace. **€92**

EATING AND DRINKING

Brasserie ver'Koch Munsterplein 22 ☏ 0475 795 361, ⓦ verkoch.nl. Amenable place located in the former residence of local art photographer Victor Mathieu Koch, with kitschy chandeliers and large black and white pictures on the wall. It serves a wide array of coffees, scrumptious club sandwiches and pastas for around €12. Sun & Mon 11am–6pm, Tues, Wed & Fri 10am–6pm, Thurs 10am–9pm, Sat 9am–6pm.

Da Mauro Koolstraat 8 ☏ 0475 317 759, ⓦ damauro.nl. Original Italian specialties such as truffle pasta, *misto di mare* or *scallopine romana* for around €24 per main dish. If you're feeling flush, splash out on the four-course seasonal menu for €39.50. Daily except Wed 5–10.30pm.

Gasterie Nautilus Maasboulevard 2 ☏ 0475 335 174, ⓦ gasterienautilus.nl. Overlooking the yachts moored in

the marina, this is a popular café in summertime with a great terrace. The menu is seasonal, so expect stews in winter and lots of fish specialties in summer for around €20 a main dish. Daily noon–9pm.

Preuverie de Sjnats Markt 24 ☏ 0475 331 413. A locals' hangout with a great terrace right on the bustling Markt square. It serves a good range of beers and simple lunch fair such as hamburgers, toasties and *kroketten* or regional fruit tart. Mon–Fri 10.30am–1am, Sat 10am–2/3am, Sun 11am–7pm.

De Tramhalte Stationsplein 17 ☏ 0475 333 453. This typical brown café is as good as any on the lively if unpretentious Stationsplein. It's a great spot for coffee and fruit tart, or choose from its wide array of speciality beers. Daily from noon–2am, later at weekends.

Nationaal Park De Meinweg

Just 9km from Roermond, Netherlands largest national park, **Nationaal Park de Meinweg** is an excellent region for walking and cycling, with forests and fens that extend to the German border. It comprises 16 square kilometres of oak, birch and pine trees, dotted with small lakes and heathland, and is home to adders and (shy) wild boar. A network of **cycle paths** crosses the park, all connected and well signposted. The Bezoekerscentrum (visitors' centre) hands out cycle path maps, as well as a detailed map of the 36km **Meinweg** route, for those who feel particularly fit. The route takes you through the national park and along the Roer valley, as well as crossing the "Iron

Rhine", a disused railroad which was used to transport freight from Antwerp to the German Ruhr from 1877 but was closed down in 1991. There are also several **walking routes**, ranging between two and seven kilometres, all departing from the Bezoekerscentrum and with different themes.

ARRIVAL AND INFORMATION NATIONAAL PARK DE MEINWEG

By bus Take the bus from Roermond train station in the direction of Herkenbosch (Mon–Fri bus #78 twice hourly; Sat & Sun bus #178 or #179 hourly). Get off at the Meinweg stop and follow the Bezoekerscentrum signs.

By bike Cycling from Roermond is an option; it's a 9km ride following signs to the village of Herkenbosch. From Herkenbosch, follow signs to Keulsebaan, then turn left down the Meinweg to reach the Bezoekerscentrum and the entrance to the park. You can rent a bike from the

Rijwielshop at Roermond station (€10/day for a three-geared bike).

Information The park is open daily from dawn to dusk ⓦ np-demeinweg.nl. Its visitor centre, just before the entrance (April–Oct Tues–Sun 10am–5pm; Nov–March Wed 12.30 –4.30pm, Sat & Sun 10am –4pm) sells maps with routes and starting points for walkers and cyclists, and has a small nature museum.

Thorn

It's easy to see why the village of **THORN** is a favourite of travel agents' posters, and something of a tourist honeypot. Its houses and farms are all painted **white**, a tradition for which no one seems to have a credible explanation, but one which has a striking photogenic effect. The farms intrude right into the village itself, giving Thorn a barnyard friendliness that's enhanced by its cobblestone streets, the closed-shuttered propriety of its houses and, at the centre, the Abdijkerk.

The Abdijkerk

Kerkberg • April–Oct Mon noon–5pm, Tues–Sun 10am–5pm; Nov–March Sat & Sun noon–4pm • €3, joint ticket with the museum €5

The **Abdijkerk** was founded at the end of the tenth century by a powerful count, Ansfried, and his wife Hilsondis, as a sort of religious retirement home after Ansfried had finished his tenure as bishop of Utrecht. Under his control the abbey and the land around it was granted the status of an independent principality under the auspices of the Holy Roman Empire, and it was in the environs of the abbey that the village developed.

The abbey was unusual in having a **double cloister** that housed both men and women (usually from local noble families), a situation that carried on right up until the French invasion of 1797, after which the monks and nuns were dispersed and all the abbey buildings, save the church, destroyed. Most of what can be seen of the church today dates from the fifteenth century, with some later tidying up by P.J.H. Cuypers. The interior decoration, though, is congenially Baroque, with some good memorials and side chapels. If you're into the macabre, head for the **crypt** beneath the chancel, which has a couple of glass coffins containing conclusively dead members of the abbey from the eighteenth century: this and other highlights are described in the notes that you can pick up on entry (in English) for a self-guided walking tour.

Museum Land of Thorn

Wijngaard 14 • April–Oct Mon noon–5pm, Tues–Sun 10am–5pm; Nov–March Tues–Sun 11am–4pm • €3, joint ticket with the abbey €5 • ⓦ museumhetlandvanthorn.nl

Thorn has one small museum, the **Museum Land of Thorn**, in the historic heart of the village. It details the history of Thorn, hosts temporary exhibitions of art and houses a three-dimensional painting of the village. The permanent collection consists of Gallic coins, Roman ceramics, fossils and objects made of flint among others.

ARRIVAL AND INFORMATION THORN

By bus Regular buses run from Roermond bus station to Thorn (buses #72 & #73; every 30min; 35min).

By bike The round trip from Roermond train station to Thorn is roughly 30km, along the River Maas, following LF

Route 5b (Roermond to Thorn). Take a map (available at the Roermond VVV; see p.288), as the signposting is patchy. To return, follow the 5a signs.

Tourist office The VVV near the entrance to the museum at Wijngaard 8 (April–Oct Mon 1–5pm, Tues–Fri 10am–5pm, Sat & Sun 10am–4pm; Nov–March Tues–Fri 11am–4pm, Sat & Sun 11am–3pm; ☎0475 561 085) can help with regional information.

ACCOMMODATION

Crasborn Hoogstraat 6 ☎0475 561 281, ⓦwww .hotelcrasborn.nl. Located right in front of the Abdijkerk, with an intimate garden terrace, free wi-fi and flat-screen TVs. The restaurant dishes up specialties such as red mullet fillet or traditional meat stew at affordable prices. **€69**

Hostellerie La Ville Blanche Hoogstraat 2 ☎0475 562 341, ⓦvilleblanche.nl. This atmospheric hotel offers surprisingly affordable luxury, with a lush garden and many authentic touches, such as wooden beams in some guest rooms. It also has a fine restaurant serving mainly regional specialties and an intimate cellar bar. **€79**

Venlo

Just a few kilometres from the German border, **VENLO** has been repeatedly destroyed and recaptured throughout its history, particularly during World War II, when most of its ancient buildings were knocked down during the Allied invasion of Europe. As a result the town is short of specific sights, but it's pleasant enough to stroll around the cramped streets of Venlo's centre, which wind around the town's architectural highlight, the fancily turreted and onion-domed **Stadhuis**, a much-modified building dating from the sixteenth century.

Limburgs Museum

Keulsepoort 5 • Tues–Sun 11am–5pm • €8 • ⓦ limburgsmuseum.nl

The **Limburgs Museum**, near the train station, houses the city's historical artefacts. Its highlight is the largest collection of nineteenth-century kitchenware in western Europe. They also have an extensive film collection, the oldest of which dates from 1911. The museum is especially suitable for children, with child-friendly but educational exhibits about life in former eras.

Van Bommel van Dam

Deken van Oppensingel 8 • Tues–Sun 11am–5pm • €6 • ⓦ vanbommelvandam.nl

Founded in 1971, **Van Bommel van Dam** is Limburg's first museum of contemporary art. It's permanent collection focuses principally on Dutch artists, with work by the CoBrA movement, informal art and the Zero movement. The gallery also hosts regular temporary exhibitions of the contemporary work by mostly local artists. To get here from the train station, take the third right off the roundabout.

ARRIVAL AND INFORMATION   VENLO

By train Venlo's train station is south of the centre, a 10-minute walk from the Markt. Regular train services connect Venlo to Roermond (every 30min; 23min), Amsterdam (every 30min; 2h) and Den Haag/The Hague (every 30min; 2hr 25min).

Tourist office The VVV is at Nieuwstraat 40–42 (Mon noon–5pm, Tues–Sat 10am–5pm; ☎077 354 3800, ⓦvvvvenlo.nl), about 600m west from the train station, towards the pedestrianized part of town. They have details of boat trips and can help find accommodation.

ACCOMMODATION AND EATING

D'n Dorstigen Haen Markt 26 ☎077 354 7397, ⓦdehaen.nl. Your best bet for a simple meal or drinks in an atmospheric setting, located right in front of the Stadhuis. Don't expect haute cuisine but their steaks and spare ribs for around €15 are good value for money. It also claims to have one of the largest whisky collections in Europe. Daily 11.30am–9.30pm.

★ **Puur** Parade 7 ☎077 351 5790, ⓦhotelpuur.nl. The trendiest hotel in town is a hospitable place with basic but stylish rooms and a breakfast area with an industrial feel. All the rooms are decorated with a different theme – varying from nautical to cosy – and have colour in abundance. **€90**

Wilhelmina Kaldenkerkerweg 1 ☎077 351 6251,

ⓦ hotel-wilhelmina.nl. A well-established hotel, which has been here for 125 years, has 43 basic but spacious rooms and a decent restaurant serving mainly regional dishes. Wi-fi is included and there's free parking. Centrally located near the train station. **€90**

Noord-Brabant

Noord-Brabant, the Netherlands' largest province, stretches from the North Sea to the German border. Woodland and heath make up most of the scenery, the gently undulating arable land in striking contrast to the watery polders of the west. While it's unlikely to form the focus of an itinerary, the instantly likeable provincial capital of **Den Bosch** is well worth an overnight visit, as is **Breda**, whose cobbled and car-free centre enjoys a lively market that pulls in the crowds from far and wide. In contrast, **Eindhoven** lacks the historic interest of these towns, as hardly anything here was spared during World War II. It is, however, renowned for its modern architecture and design and has a fairly vibrant nightlife. North of **Tilburg** is the province's other highlight, for kids at least – the **Efteling** theme park, set deep in the woods.

Originally part of the independent Duchy of Brabant, Noord-Brabant was occupied by the Spanish, and eventually split in two when its northern towns joined the revolt against Spain. This northern part was ceded to the United Provinces in 1648; the southern half formed what today are the Belgian provinces of Brabant and Antwerp. The Catholic influence is still strong here: the region takes its religious festivals seriously and if you're here in February and March, the boozy **carnivals** (especially in **Bergen-op-Zoom** and Den Bosch) are must-sees. Towns even change their names for the occasion: Den Bosch becomes Oeteldonk, Tilburg is Kruikenstad and people in Bergen-op-Zoom live in Krabbegat during the festivities. The tradition derives from the Burgundy version of carnival, and the names refer to what the main industry of the cities used to be: Eindhoven, for example, becomes Lampegat, referring to Philips producing light bulbs.

Overloon

The affluent little town of **OVERLOON** in Noord-Brabant was rebuilt following its destruction in World War II during a fierce battle in October 1944 in which 2400 men died. The final stages of the battle took place in the woods to the east of the town, where hand-to-hand fighting was needed to secure the area, and it's on this site that a moving museum to commemorate the battle has been built.

Nationaal Oorlogs-en Verzetsmuseum

Museumpark 1 · Mon–Fri 10am–5pm, Sat & Sun 11am–5pm · €14 · ⓦ oorlogsmuseum-overloon.nl

Founded with the military hardware that was left behind after the battle, the purpose of the **Nationaal Oorlogs-en Verzetsmuseum** (National War and Resistance Museum) is openly didactic: "Not merely a monument for remembrance, it is intended as an admonition and warning, a denouncement of war and violence". In showing the machinery of war, including tanks, rocket launchers, armoured cars, a Bailey bridge and a V1 flying bomb, the museum powerfully achieves this, making it a moving experience and a poignant prelude to its excellent collection of documents and posters. Touring the museum takes around a couple of hours.

Eindhoven

EINDHOVEN is not your typical Dutch city and has few historical sights of interest. This is mainly because the town – which was granted city rights in 1232 – only grew to any size in the twentieth century: in 1900 Eindhoven's population was approximately 4700, but a century later it had passed 200,000, making it the country's fifth largest city.

6

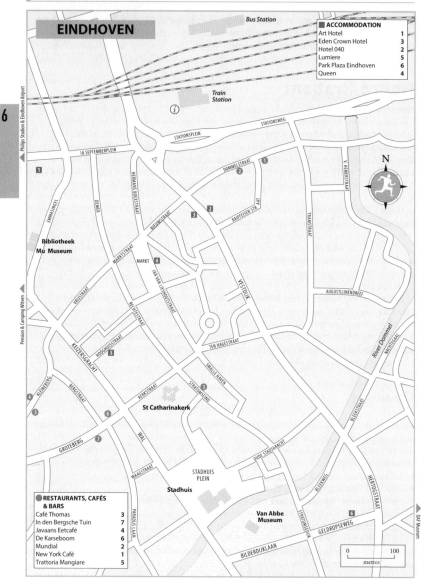

EINDHOVEN

Bus Station

Train Station

Philips Station & Eindhoven Airport

Pension & Camping Wirven

STATIONSWEG

STATIONSPLEIN

18 SEPTEMBERPLEIN

DOMMELSTRAAT

HERMANS BOEXSTRAAT

EMMASINGEL

DEMER

NIEUWSTRAAT

RAIFFEISEN STR

AAT

V. HEMESTRAAT

TRAMSTRAAT

N

Bibliotheek
Mu Museum

MARKTSTRAAT

MARKT

VRIJSTRAAT

JAN VAN LIESHOUTSTRAAT

VESTDIJK

AUGUSTIJNENDREEF

BECHTELSTRAAT

River Dommel

NACHTEGAAL

KEIZERSGRACHT

HOOGHUISSTRAAT

TEN HAGESTRAAT

SMALLE HAVEN

KLEINBERG

BERGSTRAAT

KERKSTRAAT

STRATUMSEIND

BLEEKSTRAAT

GROTEBERG

WAL

St Catharinakerk

WAAGSTRAAT

OUDE STADSGRACHT

BLEEKWEG

HERTOGSTRAAT

PARADIJSLAAN

STADHUIS
PLEIN

Stadhuis

STRATUMSEDIJK

Van Abbe
Museum

GELDROPSEWEG

DAF Museum

BILDERDIJKLAAN

ACCOMMODATION

Art Hotel	1
Eden Crown Hotel	3
Hotel 040	2
Lumiere	5
Park Plaza Eindhoven	6
Queen	4

RESTAURANTS, CAFÉS & BARS

Café Thomas	3
In den Bergsche Tuin	7
Javaans Eetcafé	4
De Karseboom	6
Mundial	2
New York Café	1
Trattoria Mangiare	5

0   100
metres

What happened in between was **Philips**, the multinational electrical firm: the town is home to Philips' research centre (the manufacturing plant had such trouble recruiting here, it relocated to Amsterdam), and the name of Eindhoven's benevolent dictator is everywhere – on bus stops, parks, even the stadium of the famous local football team, PSV Eindhoven. The town even moved the main train station (in the shape of a Philips transistor radio) to make sure all the company's employees could get to work faster.

What little there was of old Eindhoven was bombed to smithereens during World War II, but being a very modern city does have its advantages, with a leading modern design academy and many hi-tech multinationals based here. The annual internationally renowned **Dutch Design Week** draws almost 80,000 visitors, and all sorts of design projects can be found around town. The technical university draws in many international students making nightlife vibrant, with plenty of bars and clubs to choose from.

Van Abbe Museum

Bilderdijklaan 10 • Tues–Sun 11am–5pm • €10 • ⓦ vanabbemuseum.nl

Eindhoven's prime attraction is the first-rate **Van Abbe Museum**, with its superb collection of modern paintings that includes works by Picasso, Klein, Chagall, Kandinsky and Bacon. The museum, built in 1936 by architect Kropholler and expanded with a new wing designed by Cahen, is an attraction itself with a very pleasant café overlooking the Dommel River.

MU

Emmasingel 20 • Mon–Fri 10am–6pm, Sat 11am–5pm, Sun 1–5pm • €3 • ⓦ mu.nl

Inside the Witte Dame building, the **MU** is devoted solely to contemporary art and design. Its exhibitions frequently rotate, but it usually presents an innovative blend of design, fashion, music, architecture and new media. The work on display is mainly by young and upcoming artists, with some imaginative interpretations on show.

DAF Museum

Tongelresetraat 27 • Tues–Sun 10am–5pm • €7 • ⓦ dafmuseum.nl

The least taxing of Eindhoven's museums is the **DAF Museum**, devoted to the history of the Netherlands' only truck manufacturer. There are around forty trucks on display, as well as some fine examples of unique rally cars, though the museum's pride and joy is its 1968 DAF Siluro: built by Italian car designer, Giovanni Michelotti, it is named after and resembles a torpedo.

ARRIVAL AND INFORMATION   EINDHOVEN

By plane Eindhoven airport is at Luchthavenweg 25, about 9km northwest of town (ⓦ eindhovenairport.nl) with direct flights to London, Bristol and Dublin. As airport taxes are low, flying directly to Eindhoven is often cheaper than going to Schiphol airport. From the airport, bus #401 runs into the centre of town.

By train Eindhoven station is at Stationsplein 22, a five-minute walk to the Markt and the main shopping precinct. Regular trains connect Eindhoven to Roermond (every

30min; 30min); Venlo (every 30min; 35min); and Den Haag/The Hague (every 30min; 1hr 35min).

Tourist Office The VVV (Mon 10am–5.30pm, Tues–Fri 9am–5.30pm, Sat 10am–5pm; ☏ 0900 112 2363, ⓦ vvveindhoven.nl), right outside the train station at Stationsplein 17, is a great source of information, maps and walking routes. They can also book accommodation for a small fee, or provide a handy brochure on the city and a list of pensions.

ACCOMMODATION

For a city which is not a key tourist attraction, Eindhoven has a wide range of hotels, many of them in the heart of the town. As its hotels mainly cater for a corporate clientele during the week, you can often get a great bargain at the weekends, when prices drop enormously.

Art Hotel Lichttoren 22 ☏ 040 751 3500, ⓦ arthoteleindhoven.nl. The former Philips factory has been transformed into Eindhoven's newest hotel – a funky art hotel with 72 rooms divided over two buildings. Old Philips relics give the nod to its former function, and many industrial elements have been carefully saved. Prices can drop to a bargain €80 at the weekend. €173

Eden Crown Hotel Vestdijk 14–16 ☏ 040 844 4000, ⓦ wedencrownhotel.com. Right in the centre of town,

this 135-roomed hotel is in a rather plain building and caters to a mainly a corporate clientele. That said, it has all the trendy luxury and mod cons you would expect – if in a somewhat impersonal setting. Special deals are abundant for early bookers. €120

Hotel 040 Vestdijk 17 ☏ 040 244 9131, ⓦ hotel040eindhoven.com. One of the cheaper options in town, with 16 simple, clean and recently modernized rooms. It also has a shared dorm sleeping up to 10 people and is within crawling distance from Eindhoven's nightlife. **€82**, dorm bed **€32.50**

Lumiere Hooghuisstraat 31a ☏ 040 239 4950, ⓦ hotellumiere.nl. Right in the heart of town, this boutique hotel with 25 rooms has all the luxury you would expect with free wi-fi, large, comfortable beds and DVD-players in all the rooms. Breakfast is served in the next-door bakery. Weekend rates can go as low as €80. **€139**

Park Plaza Eindhoven Geldropseweg 17 ☏ 040 214 6500, ⓦ parkplaza.com. This modern hotel offers a high level of comfort, with recently refurbished contemporary rooms, an indoor pool and three Asian fine-dining restaurants. **€159**

Queen Markt 7 ☏ 040 245 2480, ⓦ queeneindhoven .nl. Recently revamped and enlarged, this hotel is in a great location above the Markt. Its forty rooms are basic but modern, decorated in natural colours with wooden elements. **€80**

EATING AND DRINKING

Eindhoven comes alive at night with the Kleine and Grote Berg being the best places for eating: the restaurants here offer a diverse range of international food. The main strip for drinking is the Stratumseind, which starts just south of Cuypers' gloomy neo-Gothic St Catherinakerk. This street, with its loud music and cheap beer, has the honour of being the longest bar street in the Netherlands. A little less crowded is the Dommelstraat, with a good range of restaurants and trendy bars.

Café Thomas Stratumseind 23, ⓦ cafethomas.nl. A decent café on the busy Stratumseind, in a monumental building with high ceilings, chandeliers and classy ornaments. The ear-splitting music mainly attracts a young student crowd. Thurs 8pm–2am, Fri & Sat 8pm–4am.

In den Bergsche Tuin Grote Berg 17 ☏ 040 243 7727, ⓦ indenbergschetuin.nl. Cosy eetcafé-cum-restaurant that's very popular with both students and large groups. It specializes in meat dishes (for around €18), or from Tuesday to Thursday you can eat a three-course meal for a bargain price of €24. Tues–Sun 5–10.30pm.

Javaans Eetcafe Kleine Berg 34 ⓦ javaanseetcafe .com. Not your typical Indonesian restaurant, as the owner has a passion for Elvis and motor cycles which shows in the interior and choice of music. The menu is authentic though, with a *rijsttafel* of Indonesian delicacies such as *soto ayam*, *babi kecap* and satay from €22.50. Daily 4.30–10pm.

De Karseboom Grote Berg ☏ 040 243 9597, ⓦ dekarseboomeindhoven.nl. An old-time favourite, this restaurant has been here for over thirty years and still pulls in the crowds. Daily specials for €14.50 and a great chateaubriand for two for €46. There's a great courtyard for warm evenings. Daily 5–10pm.

Mundial Dommelstraat 13 ☏ 040 237 7900, ⓦ cocktailbarmundial.nl. A relaxing spot with comfy lounge seats, and a wicked drinks menu where you can choose from over 40 cocktails in every imaginable flavour. The food menu features dishes from all over the globe, with mains around €17. Tues, Wed & Sun 5pm–midnight, Thurs 4pm–2am, Fri & Sat 4pm–3am.

New York Café Dommelstraat 9 ☏ 040 293 9227, ⓦ newyorkcafeeindhoven.nl. Located in a converted bank, this is one of the trendier spots on the Dommelstraat with a classy black and purple interior, brass chandeliers and a decent menu: mains such as duck breast, tilapia or lamb cost around €23. DJs at the weekend. Daily noon till after midnight.

Trattoria Mangiare Kleine Berg 67 ☏ 040 236 7088, ⓦ trattoriamangiare.nl. The best place for authentic Italian specialties, such as truffle spaghetti or ravioli with figs and Parma ham for around €15. The pizza (starting from €11.50) is made in a traditional wood oven. The decor is industrial-style and there's a beautiful inner courtyard for summer. Daily 11.30am–midnight.

's-Hertogenbosch (Den Bosch) and around

Capital of Noord-Brabant, **'s-HERTOGENBOSCH** is a lively town, particularly on Wednesdays and Saturdays, when its Markt fills with traders from all over the province. Better known as **Den Bosch** (pronounced "bos"), it merits a day or two's exploration. The town's full name – "the Count's Woods" – dates from the time when Henry I, Duke of Brabant, established a hunting lodge here in the twelfth century. Beneath the graceful townhouses of the old city flows the Binnendieze, its gloomy depths spanned by small wooden bridges. Staggered crossroads, winding streets and the twelfth-century town walls are vestiges of interminable warfare between the Protestants to the north and the Catholics to the south. The town's history is written into its street and house names – "Corn Bridge", "The Gun Barrel", "Painters' Street" and more – while its most famous son is the fifteenth-century artist **Hieronymous Bosch**. Den Bosch also makes a good base from which to visit the chilling **Camp Vught**, nearby.

6

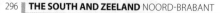

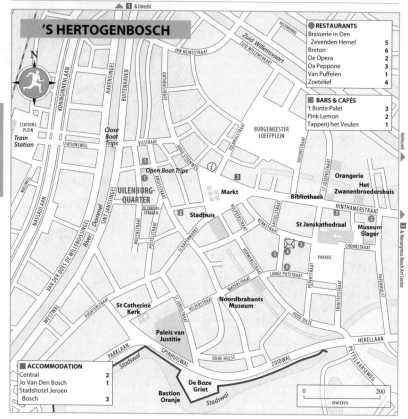

'S HERTOGENBOSCH

& Utrecht

RESTAURANTS
Brasserie in Den
  Zevenden Hemel   5
Breton   6
De Opera   2
Da Peppone   3
Van Puffelen   1
Zoetelief   4

BARS & CAFÉS
't Bonte Palet   3
Pink Lemon   2
Tapperij het Veulen   1

ACCOMMODATION
Central   2
Jo Van Den Bosch   1
Stadshotel Jeroen
Bosch   3

The Markt

If you were to draw a picture of the archetypal Dutch marketplace, it would almost certainly look like the **Markt** in Den Bosch. It's broad and cobbled, home to the province's largest market (Wed & Sat) and lined with typical seventeenth-century houses. In the middle is a **statue of Hieronymous Bosch**, palette in hand, while the sixteenth-century **Stadhuis** (guided tours Wed 3pm & Sat 1pm; €4) has a carillon that's played every Wednesday between 10 and 11am: it also chimes the half-hour to the accompaniment of a group of mechanical horsemen.

Uilenburg

The backstreets of Den Bosch are a mass of intriguing buildings and facades, with the **Uilenburg** quarter being particularly pleasant. Here, pint-sized houses squash up against each other; look out for the restored farmhouse opposite Molenstraat 29, and the picturesque Uilenburgstraatje bridge.

St Janskathedraal

Torenstraat 16 • Daily: April–Oct 10am–5pm; Nov–March 10am–4.30pm; restricted entrance during services • **Western Tower** guided tours April, May & Oct Wed, Sat & Sun at 1.30pm & 3pm; June–Sept Tues–Sun at 1.30pm & 3pm • €4 • ⓦ sint-jan.nl

From just about anywhere in the centre of town it's impossible to miss **St Janskathedraal**. Generally regarded as the finest Gothic church in the country, it was built between 1330 and 1530 and has recently undergone a massive restoration. But if Breda's Grote Kerk is

Gothic at its most intimate and exhilarating, then St Jan's is Gothic at its most gloomy, the garish stained glass – nineteenth-century or modern – only adding to the sense of dreariness that hangs over the nave. You enter beneath the oldest part of the cathedral, the western **tower**, blunt and brick-clad, it's oddly prominent amid the wild decoration of the rest of the exterior, which includes some nasty-looking creatures scaling the roof – symbols of the forces of evil that attack the church.

Inside, there's much of interest. The **Lady Chapel** near the entrance contains a thirteenth-century figure of the Madonna known as *Zoete Lieve Vrouw* ("Sweet Dear Lady"), famed for its miraculous powers in the Middle Ages and still much venerated today. The brass **font** in the southwest corner was the work of Alard Duhamel, who worked on the cathedral in the late fifteenth century. It's thought that the stone pinnacle, a weird twisted piece of Gothicism at the eastern end of the nave, was the sample piece that earned him the title of master mason.

Almost filling the west wall of the cathedral is an extravagant **organ case**, assembled in 1602. It was described by a Victorian visitor as "certainly the finest in Holland and probably the finest in Europe…it would be difficult to conceive a more stately or magnificent design". Equally elaborate, though on a much smaller scale, the south transept holds the **Altar of the Passion**, a retable made in Antwerp in around 1500. In the centre is a carved Crucifixion scene, flanked by Christ bearing the Cross on one side and a Lamentation on the other. Though rather difficult to make out, a series of carved scenes of the life of Christ run across the retable, made all the more charming by their attention to period (medieval) costume detail.

Zwanenbroedershuis

Hinthamerstraat 94 • Tues, Thurs & Sun 1.30–4.30pm • €5 • ⓦ zwanenbroedershuis.nl

Opposite the cathedral, the **Zwanenbroedershuis** has an intriguing collection of artefacts, liturgical songbooks and music scores that belonged to the Brotherhood of which Hieronymus Bosch was a member. Founded in 1318, there's nothing sinister about the Brotherhood: membership is open to all and its aim is to promote and popularize religious art and music.

Museum Slager

Choorstraat 16 • Tues–Sun 2–5pm • €4.50 • ⓦ museum-slager.nl

The **Museum Slager** contains the works of three generations of the Slager family who lived in Den Bosch. The paintings of the family's doyen, P.M. Slager (1841–1912), such as *Veterans of Waterloo*, have the most authority, but some of the other works are competent, encompassing the major trends in European art as they came and went.

Noordbrabants Museum

Verwersstraat 41 • Currently closed for major renovation and due to reopen, along with a new contemporary art and design museum at the end of 2012 • ⓦ noordbrabantsmuseum.nl

A few minutes' walk southwest of the cathedral, the **Noordbrabants Museum** is housed in an eighteenth-century building that was once the seat of the provincial commissioner and has been enlarged with two wings and complemented by a sculpture garden. The good-looking collection of local art and artefacts from prehistory to the present is excellent and interesting, while the downstairs galleries often hold superb temporary exhibitions of modern art. The permanent collection includes drawings and prints by Hieronymus Bosch, works by other medieval painters and assorted early torture equipment.

Hieronymus Bosch Art Centre

Jeroen Boschplein 2 • April–Oct Tues–Fri 11am–5.30pm, Sat & Sun noon–5.30pm; Nov–March Tues–Fri 11am–5pm, Sat & Sun noon–5pm • €6 • ⓦ jheronimusbosch-artcenter.nl

The **Hieronymus Bosch Art Centre**, in the St Jacobskerk, pays tribute to the life and work of Den Bosch's most prominent native son, the late-Gothic painter

Hieronymus Bosch (1450–1516), who lived in the town all his life. Bosch's fantastically vivid and tormented religious paintings won him the epithet "The master of the monstrous…the discoverer of the unconscious" from no less than Carl Jung. All the paintings on display in the centre are replicas of the original work, but the mayor of Den Bosch is currently trying to raise funds to get more original paintings here for a big exhibition in 2016, to commemorate 500 years of Hieronymus Bosch's death.

The City Walls

The southern limit of Den Bosch is marked by the old city walls. The **Bastion Oranje** once defended the southern section of the city walls but, like the walls themselves, it has long gone. Still remaining is a large cannon, **De Boze Griet** ("The Devil's Woman"), cast in 1511 in Cologne and bearing in German the inscription "Brute force I am called, Den Bosch I watch over". The only action she sees now is from the cows, chewing away in the watermeadows below.

Camp Vught

Lunettenlaan 600, 9km from Den Bosch • Tues–Fri 10am–5pm, Sat & Sun noon–5pm; April–Sept also Mon 10am–5pm • Free • ⑩ nmkampvught.nl • All information is in Dutch, but an English-speaking guide is available for €3.50 • Take bus #213 (hourly) from Den Bosch and get off at the Lunettenlaan stop: it's a 20min journey

Opened in January 1943, **Camp Vught** was the only official SS concentration camp in the Netherlands, modelled on camps in Germany. It was divided into two sections, one for political prisoners brought here from Belgium and the Netherlands, the other for Jews, who were, for the most part, subsequently moved to Westerbork (see p.230) before being transported on to the death camps in the east. Predictably, many people died here in the cruellest of circumstances or were executed in the woods nearby. Although it's a reconstruction, and only a fraction of the size it used to be, Camp Vught still makes a vivid impression. Next to the old camp are the walls of a high security prison, giving the location a rather eerie feel.

ARRIVAL AND DEPARTURE

DEN BOSCH

By train Den Bosch's train station is to the east of the centre, about a fifteen-minute walk away. Trains regularly run to Eindhoven (every 10min; 25min); Utrecht (every 15min; 30min); Amsterdam (every 30 min; 1hr); and Tilburg (every 20 min; 15min).

INFORMATION AND TOURS

Tourist office The VVV is at Markt 77 (April–Oct Mon 1–6pm, Tues–Fri 10am–6pm, Sat 10am–5pm; Nov–March Mon 1–5pm, Tues–Sat 10am–5pm; ☎0900 112 2334, ⑩vvvdenbosch.nl). The office, housed in De Moriaan, the oldest brick building in town, stocks the useful *Tourist Information Guide* (free) and *Walking tour 's-Hertogenbosch* (€2), which unearths all kinds of historical and architectural nuggets.

Boat trips A good way to see the town is on a boat trip. Traditional open boats depart from Molenstraat 15a, next to *Café van Puffelen* (April–Oct Mon 2–5.20pm, Tues–Sun 10am–5.20pm; every 20min; €7; reserve on ☎0900 202 0178, ⑩kringvriendenvanshertogenbosch.nl). Closed boats depart from St Janssingel near the Wilhelmina bridge, and tours take in the River Aa, Dommel and the Oude Dieze (May, Sept & Oct Wed, Sat & Sun; June–Aug Tues–Sat always at noon, 1.30pm, 3pm & 4.30pm; €8). Rederij Wolthuis, Leunweg 17 (☎073 631 2048, ⑩rederijwolthuis.nl), has information and takes reservations for closed-boat tours.

ACCOMMODATION

Den Bosch does not have a lot of hotels to choose from in the city centre, so you would be wise to book in advance. If the central hotels are filled up, there are a couple of large chain hotels just out of the city centre. The VVV has a list of the town's B&Bs.

Central Burgemeester Loeffplein 98 ☎073 692 6926, ⑩hotel-central.nl. Located smack on the Markt with 125 spacious, recently renovated rooms in warm red and brown shades. Breakfast is served in a fourteenth-century vault and they host occasional live jazz in one of their bars. **€178**

Jo van den Bosch Boschdijkstraat 39a ☎073 613 8205, ⊛www.jovandenbosch.nl. Small but intimate family-run hotel, with comfortable rooms all equipped with flat-screens, free wi-fi and modern bathrooms. There's also a well-known fish restaurant downstairs. **€111**

Stadshotel Jeroen Jeroen Boschplein 6 ☎073 610 3556, ⊛stadshoteljeroen.nl. The most appealing option in town, located right next to the Hieronymus Bosch Art Centre and with only four rooms, kitted out in basic but elegant style. The two suites offer more luxury with a kitchen and private sauna. **€120**

EATING AND DRINKING

You can find anything from inexpensive eetcafés to pricey restaurants in Den Bosch. Make sure you try the "Bossche Bol", a local speciality with chocolate and whipped cream – an absolute calorie bomb. Nightlife isn't particularly exciting but it's easy enough to wander up and down Hinthamerstraat or the streets that radiate from the Markt and find somewhere convivial to drink.

BARS AND CAFÉS

't Bonte Palet Hinthamerstaat 97 ☎073 613 2532. A tiny, popular bar with a cornucopia of kitsch hanging from the ceiling, and occasional live music. Seven beers on draft, an amenable owner and, unlike most Dutch bars, smoking is still allowed inside. Wed–Sun 3pm–2am.

Pink Lemon Minderbroederstraat 28 ☎073 614 4724, ⊛pinklemon.nl. The decor is very girly, with pink walls covered in rickety racks and old-fashioned plates. It's great if you have a sweet tooth, with muffins, chocolate fondue as well as all sorts of healthy fruit juices. The high tea is a joy. Mon & Sun noon–5pm, Tues–Sat 10am–5.30pm.

★ **Tapperij het Veulen** Korenbrugstraat 9 ☎073 612 3038. Typical brown café with oodles of atmosphere and at least forty beers by the bottle, mainly attracting an older clientele. The peanut shells on the floor add to the atmosphere, and there's an intimate terrace in summer. Mon–Thurs 3pm–1am, Fri 2pm–1.30am, Sat 11am–1.30am, Sun 2pm–1am.

RESTAURANTS

Brasserie in den Zevenden Hemel Korte Putstraat 13–17 ☎073 690 1451, ⊛indenzevendenhemel.nl. Located in a cosy street, and ideal for a romantic dinner, this restaurant uses seasonal ingredients to produce dishes with an international twist. Main courses such as codfish, black tiger prawn or lamb rack will set you back around €25/dish, or go for the three-course meal for €35.50. Sun–Thurs 5–10pm, Fri 5–10.30pm, Sat 4.30–10.30pm.

Breton Korte Putstraat 26 ☎073 513 4705, ⊛restaurantbreton.nl. Soberly decorated restaurant with an intimate terrace. The menu consists of numerous starter-sized dishes inspired by French, Italian and Japanese cuisine, such as fresh tuna salad with wasabi mayonnaise, escargots with garlic and crostini, which cost between €4 and €14. Lunch Tues–Sat noon–3pm; dinner Mon–Fri 5.30–10pm, Sat & Sun 5–10pm.

De Opera Hinthamerstraat 115–117 ☎073 613 7457, ⊛de-opera.nl. This small restaurant offers a range of wonderful Dutch/French cooking prepared with fresh organic ingredients and served in a relaxed setting: it's not cheap with a three-course meal for €40, but well worth a splurge. Tues–Sat 5–10pm.

Da Peppone Kerkstraat 77 ☎073 614 7894, ⊛dapeppone.nl. A little more chic than your standard pizzeria, *Da Peppone* serves tasty pizzas from €10 but also classic dishes such as osso bu co or *merluzzo* for around €20. Try the *pollo diavolo* (spicy chicken), their speciality. Tues–Sat 5–10pm.

Van Puffelen Molenstraat 4 ☎073 689 0414, ⊛lunchdinervanpuffelen.nl. Recently revamped and attractive eetcafé, right above the canal, with affordable *dagschotels* (daily specialities) and a three-course meal for €24.50. Mains such as codfish, spare ribs or Surf & Turf will set you back around €15. Tues–Sun 11am–10pm.

Zoetelief Korte Putstraat 10 ☎073 691 1430, ⊛zoetelief.nu. Large and stylish restaurant with a very decent menu featuring delicacies such as sashimi of scallops, and saltimbocca of monkfish: prices start at €20 for a main dish. Also serves a wide variety of tasty fingerfood and charcuterie which go down well with a glass of wine. Daily noon–3pm & 5–10pm.

Tilburg

Tilburg is a humdrum industrial town, its streets a maze of nineteenth-century houses and anonymous modern shopping precincts. It developed as a textile town, though today most of its mills have closed in the face of cheap competition from India and Southeast Asia. The main reason you might find yourself passing through is on your way to the action-packed **De Efteling** theme park. However, two decent museums within easy walking distance of the train station provide a worthwhile detour. There's no need to explore further – if that's as far as you get, you haven't missed much. That said, thrill seekers shouldn't miss the largest **funfair** in Benelux (⊕kermistilburg.nl), a ten-day event held annually at the end of July. Surprisingly, Monday is the busiest day of the fair as it was declared Pink Monday about a decade ago, attracting thousands of gays and lesbians from all over the country.

Nederlands Textielmuseum

Goirkestraat 96 • Tues–Fri 10am–5pm, Sat & Sun noon–5pm • €7 • ⊕ textielmuseum.nl

The **Nederlands Textielmuseum** is housed in an old mill with an adjacent modern glass building and displays aspects of the industry relating to design and textile arts. It houses a collection of textile designs by Dutch artists, a range of looms and weaving machines from around the world, and puts on demonstrations of weaving and spinning. Step out of the train station, walk west along Spoorlaan, turn right along Gasthuisring, and Goirkestraat is the fourth turn on the right.

De Pont modern art museum

Wilheminapark 1 • Tues–Sun 11am–5pm • €8 • ⊕ www.depont.nl

The **De Pont** modern art museum is located in a converted wool-spinning mill, a fifteen-minute walk from the station. Its permanent collection features renowned international artists such as James Turrell, Marlene Dumas and Thierry de Cordier, and it also hosts annual temporary exhibitions. Its main gallery space is complemented by more intimate side rooms, previously used for wool storage.

Koningshoeven

Eindhovenseweg 3, Berkel-Enschot • **Tasting room** April–Oct daily 11am–7pm; Nov–March daily 11am–6pm; free • **Guided tours of the brewery** April–Oct Mon–Fri 2pm, Sat & Sun 1.30pm & 3.30pm; Nov–March Fri 2pm, Sat & Sun 1.30pm & 3.30pm; €10, beer included • ⊕ koningshoeven.nl • Take bus #141 in the direction of Eindhoven and ask to be dropped at the Trappistenklooster

Five kilometres from the centre of town, **Koningshoeven monastery** is home to the brewery of **La Trappe**, the only Dutch Trappist beer. Trappist does not refer to the type of beer, but to the fact that it has been brewed by a particular order of monks, and the Koningshoeven monastery is one of only seven monasteries in the world that brew this beer.

De Efteling

Europalaan 1, Kaatsheuvel • Early Feb to early July & late Aug to early Nov daily 10am–6pm; early July to late Aug Sun–Fri 10am–8pm, Sat 10am–midnight; mid-Nov to early Feb daily 11am–6pm • €32 • ⊕ efteling.com • Bus #137 runs to De Efteling every half-hour from Tilburg (15min) and from Den Bosch (40min); in summer, the direct services #169 from Tilburg and #168 from Den Bosch are slightly faster • The park is well signposted just off the A261 between Tilburg and Waalwijk; parking costs €10

Hidden in the woods fifteen minutes' drive north of Tilburg, the prize-winning **De Efteling theme park** is one of the country's principal attractions. It's an excellent day out, and not just for children. The setting is superbly landscaped, especially in spring when the tulips are out. And while it's not Disney, it's certainly vast enough to swallow up the crowds.

Of the rides, Python is the most hair-raising, a roller-coaster twister with great views of the park before plunging down the track; De Bob, a bobsleigh run, is almost as exhilarating although over far too quickly, especially if you've queued for ages. Piranha takes you through some gentle whitewater rapids (expect to get wet). Of the quieter rides, Villa Volta is a slightly unsettling room that revolves around you, after a rather lengthy introduction in Dutch. For children, the Fairy-Tale Wood, where the park began – a hop from Gingerbread House to Troll King to Cinderella Castle – is popular. Vogel Rok and Droomvlucht are the best of the rides, and there are afternoon shows in the Efteling Theatre. In addition, there are a number of fairground attractions, canoes and paddleboats, and a great view over the whole shebang and the surrounding woods from the Pagoda. A sedate way to check whether you've missed anything is to take the steam train around the park. Prepare yourself for long queues on summer weekends; if you're not up to doing it all, skip the disappointing Haunted Castle and the Carnaval Festival.

ARRIVAL AND INFORMATION TILBURG

By train From the train station it's a ten-minute walk down Stationstraat to the main shopping area. Tilburg is well connected by train to Eindhoven (every 20min; 35min); 's Hertogenbosch (every 30min; 15min); and Den Haag/The Hague (every 30min; 1hr 15min).

Tourist office The VVV is at Nieuwlandstraat 34 (Mon 1–6pm, Tues–Fri 9.30am–6pm, Sat 10am–4pm; ☎ 0900 202 0815, ⓦ vvvtilburg.nl), a five-minute walk from the train station down Stationstraat.

ACCOMMODATION AND EATING

Studio Korte Heuvel 7 ☎ 013 543 6016, ⓦ studio -tilburg.nl. Your best bet for some night-time entertainment in a hip and industrial setting with DJs and live jam sessions. Also has a decent restaurant serving daily specialities for a mere €9.50 and a wicked cocktails list. Mon & Sun noon–1am, Tues & Wed 10am–2am, Thurs–Sat 10am–4am.

Het Wapen van Tilburg Spoorlaan 362 ☎ 013 542 2692, ⓦ hetwapenvantilburg.nl. The least expensive hotel in town with five rather bland but perfectly adequate doubles and two backpackers dorms. There's a lively bar-cum-restaurant downstairs serving dishes such as pasta, schnitzel and steaks for around €17. **€60**, dorm beds **€22.50**

Breda

BREDA, 20km west of Tilburg, is one of the prettier towns of Noord-Brabant, a pleasant, easy-going place to while away a night or two. A magnificent Gothic **cathedral** looms above the three-storey buildings that front its stone-paved main square, which is crammed with stallholders and shoppers on market days. There's a range of well-priced accommodation here too, plus inexpensive restaurants and lively bars, though ultimately it's less appealing than Den Bosch (see p.294) as a base for exploring central Noord-Brabant.

Breda also has an excellent **carnival**, which is celebrated with vim and gusto, and a top-notch, four-day annual **jazz festival** (ⓦ bredajazzfestival.nl), when some twenty stages are scattered around the centre; it usually starts on Ascension Day.

Brief history

While there's little evidence of it today, Breda developed as a strategic fortress town and was badly damaged following its capture by the Spanish in 1581. The local counts were scions of the House of Nassau, which married into the House of Orange in the early sixteenth century. The first prince of the Orange-Nassau line was **William the Silent**, who spent much of his life in the town and would probably have been buried here, had Breda not been in the hands of the Spanish at the time of his assassination in Delft (see p.166). In 1566 William was among the group of Dutch nobles who issued the **Compromise of Breda** – an early declaration against Spanish domination of the Low Countries. The town later fell to the Spanish, was retaken by Maurice, William's son, then captured once more by the Spanish, but finally ceded to the United Provinces in 1648. Curiously, King Charles II of England lived in Breda during part of his long exile and it was here, in 1660, that he issued his **Declaration of Breda**, an offer of amnesty to his former foes which greased the wheels of his return to the English throne.

Around the Grote Markt

The **Grote Markt** is the focus of life, site of a general **market** every Tuesday and Friday morning and a secondhand market every Wednesday morning, when stalls loaded with books, bric-a-brac, clothes and small furniture pieces push up against the **Grote Kerk**. From here, head southbound for Breda's main **shopping street** – the Karrestraat, which

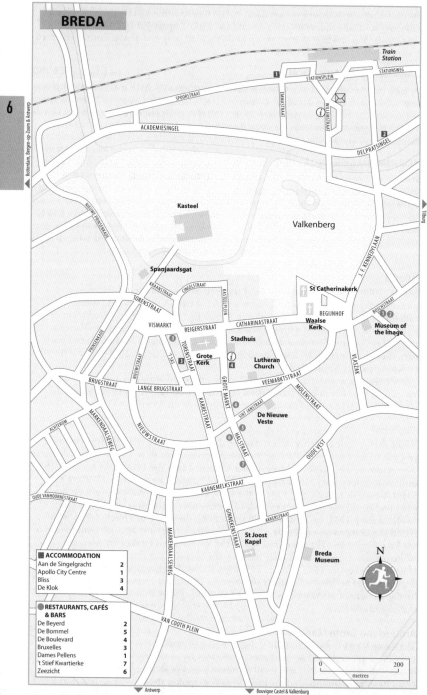

BREDA

Rotterdam, Bergen-op-Zoom & Antwerp

6

Train Station

STATIONSPLEIN

STATIONSWEG

SPOORSTRAAT

EMMASTRAAT

WILLEMSTRAAT

ACADEMIESINGEL

DELPRATSINGEL

Tilburg

NIEUWE PRINSENKADE

Kasteel

Valkenberg

J. F. KENNEDYLAAN

Spanjaardsgat

KRAANSTRAAT

CINGELSTRAAT

KASTEELPLEIN

St Catherinakerk

BOSCHSTRAAT

TORENSTRAAT

REIGERSTRAAT

CATHARINASTRAAT

BEGIJNHOF

Waalse Kerk

Museum of the Image

VISMARKT

PRINSENKADE

NIEUWSTRAAT

T-STS

TORENSTRAAT

Stadhuis

Grote Kerk

Lutheran Church

GROTE MARKT

VLASZAK

BRUGSTRAAT

LANGE BRUGSTRAAT

VEEMARKTSTRAAT

MOLENSTRAAT

MARKENDAALSEWEG

ACHTEROM

NIEUWSTRAAT

KARRESTRAAT

SINT JANSTRAAT

De Nieuwe Veste

HALSTRAAT

OUDE VEST

OUDE VANHOORNESTRAAT

KARNEMELKSTRAAT

MARKENDAALSEWEG

GINNEKENSTRAAT

AKKERSTRAAT

St Joost Kapel

Breda Museum

N

VAN COOTH PLEIN

ACCOMMODATION
Aan de Singelgracht	2
Apollo City Centre	1
Bliss	3
De Klok	4

RESTAURANTS, CAFÉS & BARS
De Beyerd	2
De Bommel	5
De Boulevard	4
Bruxelles	3
Dames Pellens	1
't Stief Kwartierke	7
Zeezicht	6

0	200
	metres

Antwerp

Bouvigne Castel & Valkenburg

turns into the Ginnekenstraat – where you'll primarily find large chain stores and the chic covered mall De Barones. There's more upmarket shopping nearby on Hallstraat, lined with boutique stores.

The Grote Kerk

Kerkplein 2 • Mon–Sat 10am–5pm, Sun 1–5pm • Mid-April to Dec free; Jan to mid-April €4; tower €5 • Ⓦ grotekerkbreda.nl

The main attraction on the Grote Markt is the Gothic **Grote Kerk**, whose stunningly beautiful bell tower reaches high into the sky. Inside, the main nave, with its richly carved capitals, leads to a high and mighty central crossing. Like the majority of Dutch churches, the Grote Kerk had its decorations either removed or obscured after the Reformation, but a few murals have been uncovered and they reveal just how colourful the church once was. The Grote Kerk's most remarkable feature is the **Mausoleum of Count Engelbrecht II**, a one-time Stadholder and captain-general of the Netherlands who died in 1504 of tuberculosis – vividly apparent in the drawn features of his intensely realistic face. Four kneeling figures (Caesar, Regulus, Hannibal and Philip of Macedonia) support a canopy that carries his armour, so skilfully sculpted that their shoulders seem to sag slightly under the weight. It's believed that the mausoleum was the work of Tomaso Vincidor of Bologna, but whoever created it imbued the mausoleum with grandeur without resorting to flamboyance; the result is both eerily realistic and oddly moving. During the French occupation the choir was used as a stable, but fortunately the sixteenth-century misericords, showing rustic scenes of everyday life, survived. A couple of the carvings are modern replacements – as you'll see from their subject matter.

The Kasteel

At the top of Kasteelplein sits the **Kasteel** – too formal to be forbidding and considerably rebuilt since the Compromise of Breda was signed here in 1566. Twenty-five years later the Spanish captured Breda, but it was regained in 1590 thanks to a neat trick by Maurice of Nassau's troops using the Trojan Horse strategy. The **Spanjaardsgat**, an early sixteenth-century water gate with twin defensive bastions just west of the Kasteel, is usually (but inaccurately) identified as the spot where this happened. Today the Kasteel is a military academy and there's no admission to its grounds, unless you join one of the VVV tours.

Begijnhof

Catherinastraat 45 • Daily 9am–6pm • Free • Ⓦ begijnhofbreda.nl

To the east of Kasteelplein, the **Begijnhof**, built in 1531, was until quite recently the only *hofje* in the Netherlands still occupied by Beguines. Today it has been given over to elderly women, some of whom look after the dainty nineteenth-century chapel at the rear, the St Catherinakerk, and tend the herb garden that was laid out several hundred years ago. To the right of the Begijnhof entrance is the **Waalse Kerk** (Walloon Church), where Peter Stuyvesant (1612–72), governor of New York when it was a Dutch colony, was married.

Museum of the Image

Boschstraat 22 • Tues–Sun 10am–5pm • €7.50 • Ⓦ motimuseum.nl

The city's newest museum, the **MOTI**, Museum of the Image, is well worth a visit – and not just for its location in one of Breda's oldest buildings, The Beyerd. Founded as a hospice in 1246 to provide shelter for pilgrims, it later became an old men's home. Inside, the basement of the museum hosts a permanent exhibition on a hundred years of Dutch graphic design, from magazine covers to old propaganda posters. On the ground floor imaginative temporary exhibitions are held: the displays change regularly, but the theme is always the same – how images affect us and can be interpreted.

ARRIVAL AND INFORMATION

By train The train station is at Stationsplein 16: from here, head down Willemstraat and cross the park for the town centre. Breda is well connected to Dordrecht (every 20min; 20min), 's Hertogenbosch (every 30min; 30min), Maastricht (every 30min; 1hr 50min) and Middelburg (every 30min; 1hr 15min).

Tourist office Breda has two VVV offices, one just outside

the train station, at Willemstraat 17–19 (Mon 1–5.30pm, Tues–Fri 9.30am–5.30pm, Sat 10am–4pm; ☎ 0900 522 2444, ⓦ vvvbreda.nl), about ten minutes' walk from the Grote Markt, where the second office is located at no. 38 (Wed–Fri 10.30am–5.30pm, Sat 10.30am–5pm; July & Aug also Tues 10.30am–5.30pm).

ACCOMMODATION

★ **B&B Aan de Singelgracht** Delpratsingel 14 ☎ 076 521 6271, ⓦ desingelgracht.nl. Within walking distance of the train station, this small B&B has been elegantly decorated, with an amazing eye for detail. Two of the rooms have original *bedstedes*, a bed built in a closet which was used until well into the nineteenth century. The suite is equipped with a sauna. **€105**

Apollo City Centre Stationsplein 14 ☎ 076 522 0200, ⓦ apollohotelsresorts.com. Recently revamped and conveniently located right next to the train station, this smart hotel has 88 well-equipped rooms in bright colours with funky wall-art. It's located in a converted post office, with many relics on the walls reminiscent of its former

function. The rooms are well insulated, so you won't hear the freight trains passing at night. Special deals are abundant. **€200**

Bliss Torenstraat 9 ☎ 076 533 5980, ⓦ www.blisshotel .nl. The place to pick if you want to splash out, with nine themed suites, located in the main shopping street in the centre of town. It has a good restaurant and a champagne bar to relax after a day of shopping. **€210**

De Klok Grote Markt 26–28 ☎ 076 521 4082, ⓦ hotel -de-klok.nl. Right in the centre of town, with basic but adequate rooms, some with views over the bustling market square. It's surprisingly inexpensive for the location, but fills up quickly in summer. **€98**

EATING, DRINKING AND NIGHTLIFE

Breda has a decent range of places to eat, many of them located around the Grote Markt and the streets running off it. Kebab joints and Turkish pizzas are plentiful at Havermarkt, a square packed with hole-in-the-wall eateries for late-night snacks. This is also the best place for drinking with plenty of bars that stay open late into the night.

De Beyerd Boschstraat 26 ☎ 076 521 4265, ⓦ beyerd .nl. The place to be for connoisseurs of Low Countries' beer, with its own on-tap brewery. There's also a good restaurant attached, serving main courses such as codfish or deer steak for €18.50. Mon, Tues, Thurs & Sun 10am–1am, Fri 10am–2am, Sat noon–2am.

De Bommel Halstraat 3 ☎ 076 521 2429, ⓦ debommel .nl. A large and lively café-bar frequented by a mix of customers – with occasional live music and DJs at weekends. It's extremely popular and often jam-packed, so not suited for the claustrophobic. Mon 11am–1am, Tues & Wed 10.30am–1am, Thurs & Fri 10.30–2am, Sat 11am–2am, Sun 3pm–2am.

De Boulevard St Janstraat 3 ☎ 076 514 6399, ⓦ boulevardbreda.nl. Located in an old theatre, this eetcafé mainly attracts families and people on a tight budget with its extremely cheap three-course meals for only €13.50. The café and theatre attract the crowds at weekends with DJs playing everything from disco to drum 'n' bass. Tues–Sun 10am–5pm.

Bruxelles Havermarkt 5 ☎ 076 521 5211, ⓦ bruxelles .nl. A lively café specializing in Belgian beers which go down well with the cheap daily specials such as spare ribs, steak or satay for only €8.50. They also have an impressive

whisky collection, specializing in Scottish malts. Mon 10am–1am, Tues–Thurs 10am–2am, Fri & Sat 10am–4am, Sun noon–1am.

Dames Pellens Boschstraat 24 ☎ 076 887 6929, ⓦ damespellens.nl. Modern and classy wine bar, serving French wines and champagne, to accompany the tasty cheese platters or fish pâté. At lunch they also serve salads and sandwiches for around €9. Tues–Sun noon–midnight.

't Stief Kwartierke Halstraat 32 ☎ 076 522 8493, ⓦ stiefkwartierke.nl. Intimate little lunchroom with warm red walls covered with black and white pictures. It mainly serves home-made specialities such as apple pie, chocolate tart, pancakes and salads. Also great for high tea with mouth-watering sweets and a wide variety of teas. Tues, Wed & Fri 9.30am–6pm, Thurs 9.30am–9pm, Sat 9.30am–5.30pm.

Zeezicht Ridderstraat 1 ☎ 076 514 8248, ⓦ cafezeezicht.nl. This upmarket café is good for its large choice of beers, lively terrace and inviting menu consisting of delicacies such as barramundi, lamb stew and stuffed turkey for around €18. Live music on Fridays. Daily 5–10pm.

Bergen-op-Zoom

BERGEN-OP-ZOOM, just 30km north of Antwerp, is an untidy town, a jumble of old and new buildings that are the consequence of being shunted between various European powers from the sixteenth century onwards. In 1576 Bergen-op-Zoom sided with the United Provinces against the Spanish and as a result was under near-continuous siege until 1622. This war-ravaged theme continued thereafter: the French bombarded the city in 1747 and took it again in 1795, though it managed to withstand a British attack in 1814. Bergen-op-Zoom's saving grace is its famous **February carnival** when almost every inhabitant – as well as revellers from all over Europe – joins in the Tuesday procession. It's a great time to be in the town, although you won't find any accommodation – the whole place gets packed out – so just do as the locals do and party all night.

6

Grote Markt

Walk straight out of the train station and you'll soon find yourself on the **Grote Markt**, most cheerful during summer when it's decked out with open-air cafés and the like. The **Stadhuis** (May–Oct Tues–Sun 1–4.30pm; €1.50) on the north side of the square, is Bergen's most attractive building, spruced up in recent years and comprising three separate houses: to the left of the gateway an alderman's house of 1397, to the right a merchant's house of 1480 and on the far right a building known as "De Olifant", whose facade dates from 1611. All of this is a lot more appealing than the blunt ugliness of the **Grote Kerk**, also on the Grote Markt, an unlucky building that's been destroyed by siege and fire innumerable times over the past four hundred years.

Markiezenhof Museum

Steenbergsestraat 8 • Tues–Sun 11am–5pm • €7.50 • ⓦ markiezenhof.nl

Walking northwest of Grote Markt, Fortuinstraat leads to the **Markiezenhof Museum**, a first-rate presentation of a collection that has a little of everything: domestic utensils and samplers from the sixteenth century onwards, sumptuous period rooms and architectural drawings as well as a permanent exhibition on fairground attractions on the top floor. All this is housed in a palace built by Anthonis Keldermans between 1485 and 1522 to a late-Gothic style that gives it the feel of an Oxford college.

Gevangenpoort

Lievevrouwestraat • May–Oct Tues–Sun 1–4.30pm • €1.50

Little was spared of old Bergen-op-Zoom: near the entrance to the Markiezenhof, the **Gevangenpoort** is practically all that remains of the old city defences, a solid-looking fourteenth-century gatehouse that was later converted into a prison which it remained until the 1930s. Today, the gatehouse is used for archeological exhibitions.

ARRIVAL AND INFORMATION
BERGEN-OP-ZOOM

By train The train station is an easy five-minute stroll south of the Grote Markt. Regular trains connect Bergen-op-Zoom with Rotterdam (hourly; 50min); Den Haag/The Hague (hourly; 1hr 15min); and Middelburg (every 30min; 35min).

Tourist office The VVV just off the Grote Markt at Kortemeestraat 19 (Mon 1–5pm; Tues–Sat 10am–5pm; May–Oct also Sun noon–4pm; ☎0164 277 482, ⓦvvvbrabantsewal.nl), has details of private rooms and issues free maps of the town centre.

ACCOMMODATION AND EATING

Beursplein 5 Beursplein 5 ☎0164 266 377, ⓦwww .hotelrestaurantbeursplein5.nl. Located on the handsomely restored Beursplein square near the Markiezenhof museum, this hotel offers simple but perfectly adequate rooms. The downstairs restaurant has

been revamped in bright blue colours: a three-course meal will set you back a mere €24. **€95**
De Bourgondiër Grote Markt 2 ☎0164 254 000, ⓦgrandcafehoteldebourgondier.nl. The most centrally located hotel with thirteen classy, up-to-the-minute rooms

decorated in warm shades. The pleasant café downstairs has a terrace overlooking the market square, and serves great waffles and pancakes as well as a wide variety of beers on draft. €92

HI hostel Boslustweg 1 ☎ 0164 233 261, ⓦ stayokay .com. Four kilometres out of town, amid the greenery, this HI hostel is perfectly suited for families with young children with its large playground and comfortable facilities. Take bus #22 from the station and it's a fifteen-minute walk from the Ziekenhuis (hospital) stop. Dorms €29

My Place Steenbergsestraat 1 ☎ 0164 233 844, ⓦ espressobar-myplace.com. Cosy little espresso bar

with colourful Baroque chairs and kitschy chandeliers serving every imaginable variety of coffee. Great iced cappuccinos, mochas and smoothies go down well with tasty muffins or cheesecake. Mon noon–3pm, Tues–Sat 10am–5.30pm, Sun noon–5pm.

De Teerkamer Grote Markt 13 ☎ 0164 239 345, ⓦ teerkamer.nl. Smack on the market square this is the place to be for a quick lunch or lingering dinner in an industrial setting combined with plush purple elements. The menu features everything from a simple chicken satay to a lip-smacking fish platter. Mon–Fri 11.30am–10pm, Sat 10.30am–10pm, Sun 12.30–10pm.

Zeeland

Luctor et Emergo, reads **Zeeland**'s slogan: "I struggle and I emerge", a reference to the interminable battle the province has waged with the sea. As its name suggests, the southwestern corner of the Netherlands is bound as much by water as land. Comprising three main peninsulas within the delta of the Rijn (Rhine), the Schelde and the Maas, this cluster of islands and semi-islands is linked by a complex network of dykes. This concrete web not only gives protection from flooding but also forms the main lines of communication between each sliver of land. The northernmost landmass, **Goeree-Overflakkee**, a little south of Rotterdam, is connected by two dams to **Schouwen-Duiveland**, while further south are **Noord and Zuid Beveland**, the western tip of which adjoins **Walcheren**. Furthest south of all is **Zeeuws Vlaanderen**, lying across the blustery waters of the Westerschelde on the Belgian mainland.

Before the Delta Project (see p.317) secured the area, fear of the sea's encroachment had prevented any large towns developing and consequently Zeeland remains a condensed area of low dunes and nature reserves, popular with holidaymakers escaping the cramped conurbations nearby. The province also has more sun than anywhere else in the Netherlands: the winds blow the clouds away, with spectacular sunsets guaranteed. Getting around is easy, with bus services making up for the lack of north–south train connections, though undoubtedly the best way to see these islands is to **cycle**, using **Middelburg** as a base and venturing out into its environs.

Middelburg

Sitting pretty on Walcheren island, compact **MIDDELBURG**, the largest town in Zeeland, is also its most likeable. The town's streets preserve some snapshots of medieval Holland, its cobbled alleyways echo the sea-trading days of the sixteenth century, and a scattering of museums and churches provide targets for your wanderings. Middelburg's centre holds a large Thursday **market** and if you can only make it for a day, this is the best time to visit. Set against the imposing backdrop of the Stadhuis and packed with local produce, it's an atmospheric event that's guaranteed to draw a crowd – including, if you're lucky, elderly couples in traditional costume. With a reasonable range of accommodation, Middelburg also makes an ideal base for exploring the surrounding area, including Veere, Domburg and the Delta Project, with good bus connections and excellent cycling along Walcheren's windswept coast.

Middelburg is an appealing town to explore, small enough to cover on foot and dotted with architectural clues that bear witness to its rich maritime past. The town owes its early growth to its position on a bend in the River Arne, making it easy to defend. The slight elevation on which it was built gave the settlement protection from

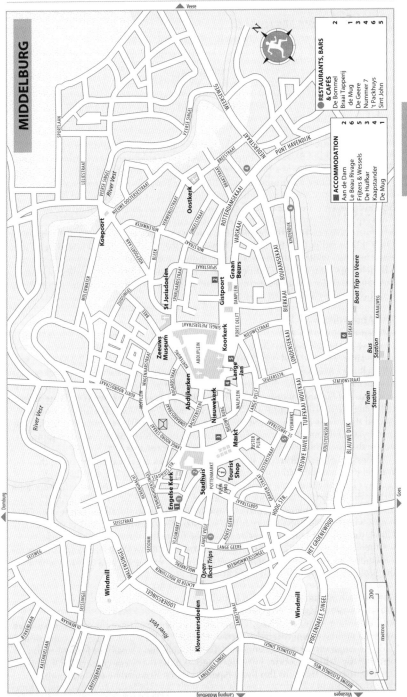

MIDDELBURG

Veere

N

■ **ACCOMMODATION**
Aan de Dam 2
Le Beau Rivage 6
Frijters & Wessels 5
De Huifkar 3
Kaapstander 4
De Mug 1

● **RESTAURANTS, BARS & CAFÉS**
De Bommel 2
Braai Tapperij de Mug 1
De Geere 3
Nummer 7 4
't Packhuys 5
Sint John 5

Koepoort

Oostkerk

St Jorisdoelen

Gistpoort

Graan Beurs

Zeeuws Museum

Koorkerk

Abdijkerken

Lange Jan

Nieuwekerk

Engelse Kerk

Stadhuis

Markt

Tourist Shop

Windmill

Open Boat Trips

Windmill

Klovenlersdoelen

Boat Trip to Veere

Bus Station

Train Station

0   200
metres

Domburg

Goes

Vlissingen

Camping Middelburg

Vlissingen

6

> ## MIDDELBURG'S FESTIVALS
>
> One of the town's most colourful **festivals** is **Ringrijderij**, a horseback competition where riders try to pick off rings with lances. It takes place in August at the Koepoort city gate near Molenwater, and in the central Abdijplein on one day in July; check with the tourist office for dates. Another major draw is the annual **Mosselfeesten** (ⓦ mosselfeesten.nl), a weekend in the second half of July devoted to celebrating the arrival of the fresh black mussels, of which Zeeland is particularly proud. The festival takes place around the Vlasmarkt, with live music and restaurants offering their own version of this regional speciality.

the sea and its streets slope down to the harbour. Look out for the surviving stone blocks at the end of **Brakstraat**, into which wooden planks were slotted, then bolstered with sandbanks, acting as a temporary dyke when floods threatened.

Though its **abbey** was founded in 1120, Middelburg's isolation restricted its development until the late Middle Ages when, being at the western end of the Scheldt estuary, it became rich off the back of the wool and cloth trade with Antwerp, Bruges and Ghent. Thereafter, it became both the market and administrative centre of the region. The town's **street names** – Houtkaai ("Timber Dock"), Korendijk ("Grain Dyke"), Bierkaai ("Beer Dock") – reveal how diverse its trade became, while house names like "London" and "Samarkand" tell of the routes Middelburg's traders plied. Kuiperspoort ("Barrelmaker's Port") is an alleyway off **Rouaansekaai** along which a string of warehouses have been restored, many of them now occupied by artists and musicians.

The Abdijkerken

Onderdentoren • April–Oct Mon–Fri 10.30am–5pm; May–Aug also Sat & Sun 1.30–5pm; free • **Tower** April–June, Sept & Oct Mon 1–5pm, Tues–Sun 11am–5pm; July & Aug daily 11am–5pm; €4

Badly damaged on several occasions, most recently by the Germans in 1940, Middelburg's **Abdijkerken** ("Abbey Churches") complex comprises three churches, parts of which date back to the thirteenth century. Little remains from the abbey's salad days as a centre of Catholic worship, since Middelburg was an early convert to Protestantism following the uprising against the Spanish, and in 1574 William the Silent's troops ejected the monks and converted the abbey to secular use. Thereafter, the complex was used by all and sundry, becoming at one time a gun factory and at another a mint, before the three churches were turned over to the Protestants.

Among the ecclesiastical trio, the **Nieuwe Kerk** has an organ case from 1692; the **Wandel Kerk** holds the triumphalist tomb of admirals Jan and Cornelis Evertsen, brothers killed fighting in a naval battle against the English in 1666; and the **Koor Kerk** retains the oldest decoration, including a fine Nicolai organ of 1478. Best of all, however, is the complex's landmark 91-metre **tower**, known locally as **Lange Jan** (Long John), whose **carillon** plays every fifteen minutes, with additional concerts year-round. Climb the 207 steps of the **tower** and you'll be treated to some fine views: in clear weather, the view from the top of the tower stretches across Walcheren and as far as the Zeelandbrug and the eastern Scheldt, all of which gives a good idea of how vulnerable the province is to the ebbs and flows of the sea.

The Zeeuws Museum

Abdij 3–4 • Tues–Sun 11am–5pm • €8.50 • ⓦ zeeuwsmuseum.nl

At the northern tip of the Abbey Churches in the centre of town, housed in what were once the monks' dormitories, the **Zeeuws Museum** holds a mixed bag of a collection with the emphasis on the Zeeland area. The museum has a small but fine collection of paintings by Adriaan Coorte, Joris Hoefnagel and the twentieth-century Realist painter Charley Toorop. There are also lively tapestries, commissioned by the local authorities

FROM TOP BERGEN-OP-ZOOM (P.305); THORN (P.289) >

between 1591 and 1604 to celebrate the naval battles against the Spanish, and a comprehensive display of local costumes. Take note, however, that regular temporary exhibitions often take over large parts of the museum, so the permanent collection is not always on display.

The Damplein

East of the centre and right next to the Abbey Churches, **Damplein** was restored to its original width by the demolition of a couple of rows of houses. It forms a quieter focus for bars than the Markt and is the site of the **Graanbeurs**, a grain exchange rebuilt in the nineteenth century, which today contains some intriguing and humorous stone plaques by international artists – a project known as "Podio del Mondo per l'Arte".

The Stadhuis

Markt 1 • Forty-minute guided tour of the mayor's office, council chambers, the Vleeshal and various reception rooms; April–Oct daily except Fri at 11.30am & 3.15pm • €4.25

Middelburg's **Stadhuis** is generally agreed to be Zeeland's finest building, a wonderfully eclectic mix of architectural styles. The towering Gothic facade is especially magnificent, dating from the mid-fifteenth century and built to a design by the Keldermans family from Mechelen in modern-day Belgium. Inside is the **Vleeshal**, a former meat hall that now houses temporary exhibitions of contemporary art, which can be visited on the guided tour.

The Stadhuis's impressive pinnacled **tower** was added in 1520, though the current tower, along with the Stadhuis itself and much of Middelburg's city centre, is only a reconstruction of the original. On May 17, 1940, the city was all but flattened by German bombing in the same series of raids that destroyed Rotterdam. Restoration was a long and difficult process, but so successful that you can only occasionally tell that the city's buildings have been patched up.

Kloveniersdoelen

On the western edge of town, at the end of Langeviele, is the landmark building, the **Kloveniersdoelen**. Built in 1607 in exuberant Flemish Renaissance style, this was the home of the city's civic guard, the arquebusiers, until the end of the eighteenth century, later becoming the local headquarters of the East India Company, and later still a military hospital. Restored in 1969 (as you might guess if you spot the weather vane), it's now a recital hall and is renowned for presenting new and experimental music.

ARRIVAL AND DEPARTURE   MIDDELBURG

By train From the train station at Kanaalweg 22, it's a short walk to the town centre: cross the bridge on Loskade, head up Segeersstraat and Lange Delft and you find yourself on the Markt. Trains connect Middelburg to Bergen-op-Zoom (every 30min; 40min); Goes (every 30min; 13min); and Roosendaal (every 30min; 50min).

By bus The main bus station is also at Kanaalweg 22, right in front of the train station. Regular buses connect Middelburg to Delta Expo (Mon–Fri 2 hourly, Sat hourly, Sun every 2hr; 30min); Renesse (hourly; 1hr); and Veere (Mon–Sat hourly; 12min).

INFORMATION AND TOURS

Tourist office Middelburg does not have an official VVV office, but you should be able to find whatever you need at the privately run Tourist Shop at Markt 51 (Mon 11am–6pm, Tues–Sat 9.30am–6pm, Sun 1–5pm; ☎0118 674 300, ⓦtouristshop.nl), which has details of summer events in the city, a list of private rooms and is well stocked with cycling maps for touring Zeeland's coast.

Boat trips Open-top boats offer trips on the canals,

leaving from the Lange Viele bridge on Achter de Houttuinen (April–Oct daily 11am–5pm; €6.50; ⓦrondvaartmiddelburg.nl). The return boat trip to Veere (May–Sept daily 10.15am & 2pm; €14; ⓦrederij -dijkhuizen.nl) leaves from near the train station.

Tours The Tourist Shop at Markt 51 (☎0118 674 300, ⓦtouristshop.nl) runs a guided walking tour (April–Oct daily except Fri 1.30pm; €4.75), which leaves from their office and lasts an hour and a half, taking in the city's main landmarks. Horse-drawn carriage rides operate from

Nieuwe Burg 38–40 (July & Aug Mon–Sat 11.30am–4.30pm; €3.50; 20min).

ACCOMMODATION

Aan de Dam Dam 31 ☏0118 643 773, ⓦhotelaandedam.nl. A well-kept treasure with eleven suites, all in different styles and varying sizes, but equally elegant. The garden is a real oasis in summer, a great spot to enjoy a high tea after a day of shopping. **€110**

Frijters & Wessels Reigerstraat 1 ☏0118 853 891, ⓦfrijtersenwessels.nl. The perfect combination of a homeware shop and an incredibly stylish B&B. This romantic hideaway with amenable owners has just two rooms and a small studio across the street. Breakfast is served in the shop downstairs. **€95**

De Huifkar Markt 19 ☏0118 612 998, ⓦhoteldehuifkar.nl. One of Middelburg's cheapest options, with basic but bright rooms. It's located right on the town's main square so can be noisy, especially on market days. Book ahead as they only have five rooms. **€59**

Kaepstander Koorkerkhof 10 ☏0118 640 767, ⓦkaepstander.nl. Small and basic rooms in a seventeenth-century former warehouse, but with great views of the Abbey Churches and a relaxing café downstairs. Some rooms have shared facilities and the breakfast is very simple. **€63**

Le Beau Rivage Loskade 19 ☏0118 638 060, ⓦlebeaurivage.nl. This small hotel has only nine rooms, all elegantly furnished with old Chesterfields and the like. Some rooms have balconies and there's free wi-fi. It's just a short walk from the main shopping area. **€79**

★ **De Mug** Vlasmarkt 54–56 ☏0118 614 851, ⓦdemug.nl. By far the most appealing and authentic option in town, these four spacious rooms are located in a renovated building, with a restaurant, popular bar and shop downstairs. The friendly owners will make you feel at home immediately. **€119**

EATING AND DRINKING

Most of Middelburg's bars, cafés and restaurants are on or near the Markt with a particular concentration along Vlasmarkt. Many are tourist-oriented and pricey for what you get, but there is a sprinkling of top-notch places too. On Thursdays, market stalls supply limitless cheap and tasty snacks, especially fresh fish and seafood. Look out for *bolus*, a circular sweetbread first brought to Middelburg by Portuguese Jews and best served hot with butter and a cup of coffee.

De Bommel Markt 85 ☏0118 636 093, ⓦcafebommel.nl. This is the pick of the bars along here; it's convenient for a quick bite with mains such as boeuf bourguignon and salmon fillet for around €16. Sun–Thurs 10am–1am, Fri & Sat 10am–2am.

Braai Tapperij de Mug Vlasmarkt 56 ☏0118 614 851, ⓦdemug.nl. Good Dutch-French cooking (mussels in season) at moderate prices, an excellent array of beers, and

occasional live jazz, all in an old-fashioned setting decorated with aged cognac barrels. Very popular, so book ahead. Tues–Sat 5.30–10pm.

De Geere Lange Viele 55 ☏0118 613 083, ⓦcafedegeere.nl. Daily specials for €8.50 and cheap beer are on offer at this centrally located café with red-brick walls and smart chandeliers. Regular main courses, such as deer steak or rib-eye, are pricier at around €20. For

CYCLING AROUND MIDDELBURG: ALONG THE WALCHEREN COAST

The **coast** north and west of Middelburg offers some of the Netherlands' finest beaches and excellent walking and cycling, although on midsummer weekends parts of it are mobbed with crowds of Dutch and German holidaymakers. Countless **cycling options** make the most of Walcheren's handsome coastline, with plenty of refreshments en route. With limited public transport available to transport bikes, most routes are best completed as loops. As a rule of thumb, red cycleway signs indicate utility paths, often parallel to a main road, while the green signs denote more scenic alternatives.

Possible **day-trips** include cycling west to Domburg, picking up signs to the Domburg HI hostel and continuing through the woods to Breezand. A cycleway follows the polder to Veere, from where you can ride alongside the Walcheren canal, cutting back to Middelburg. Alternatively, pick up the same canal out of town to Vlissingen, joining the cycleway that runs between dune and woodland to Zoutelande and Westkapelle: there's a fabulous stretch of dyke to cycle along in the direction of Domburg with spectacular sunsets out to sea and a photogenic lighthouse. A red-signposted cycle path leads directly back to Middelburg.

pudding, try their home-baked apple pie or brownies. Lunch Tues–Sat noon–2.30pm; dinner Tues–Thurs 5.30–9pm, Fri & Sat 5.30–9.30pm.

Nummer 7 Rotterdamsekaai ☎0118 627 077, ⓦrestaurantje.nl. This cosy restaurant with only a few tables serves a three-course meal for €35, using mainly regional ingredients combined with fresh seasonal products. Main courses such as scallops or beef go for around €25. Tues–Sat 5.30–9.30pm, Sun 1–8pm.

't Packhuys Kinderdijk 82 ☎0118 647 064, ⓦhetpackhuys.nl. Located in an old warehouse with a great waterfront terrace, this maritime-themed restaurant serves fabulous food, such as lobster soup, salads and lambs racks. Main courses are around €20 and a three-course meal costs €32.50. Wed–Sun 5–10pm.

Sint John Sint Janstraat 40 ☎0118 625 993, ⓦwww.sintjohn.nl. A tasteful mix of a brown café-cum-tearoom, serving many different artisan beers and a wide variety of coffee and tea blends. Try their home-made sweets and yoghurt ice cream. Mon–Sat 8.30am–6pm.

DIRECTORY

Bookshop De Drukkerij, Markt 51, has a wide selection of books, internet access and a popular café centred around a communal table.

Markets General market on the Markt is on Thurs (8am–4pm); there's also a book and curio market on Mon (May–Oct, 11am–5pm). Vismarkt has a flea market on the first Sat of the month (except Jan; 8am–4pm), and an art and antique market in summer (June–Aug ,Thurs 9am–4pm).

Police Achter de Houttuinen 10 ☎0900 8844.

Taxi Taxicentrale ☎0118 612 600.

Domburg

Sixteen kilometres from Middelburg, **DOMBURG** is the area's principal resort. It's been a favourite haunt for artists since early last century when Jan Toorop gathered together a group of like-minded painters (including, for a while, Piet Mondrian), who were inspired by the coastal scenery and the fine quality of the light. Aside from a museum which holds a small collection of Toorop's work, the main reason to come to Domburg is to walk over the dunes and through the woods or to cycle the coastal path. It's an easy ride 7km bike ride southwest of Domburg to the quieter beach resort of **Westkapelle**, with a picturesque lighthouse and a critical spot where the dyke was breached during the 1953 flood (see box, p.317).

Marie Tak van Poortvliet Museum

Ooststraat 10a • April–Oct Tues–Sun 1–5pm • €3.50 • ⓦ marietakvanpoortvlietmuseumdomburg.nl

The **Marie Tak van Poortvliet Museum** is housed inside a pavilion built by artist Jan Toorop (1858–1928) to exhibit his paintings. Today, the musuem displays works by members of the Domburg group such as Jacoba van Heemskerck, Ferdinand Hart Nibbrig and Charley Toorop, Jan Toorops' daughter, as well as hosting temporary exhibitions by local, less-known artists.

ARRIVAL AND INFORMATION   DOMBURG

By bus Bus #53 departs hourly from Middelburg to Domburg, following the longer, more scenic route along the Walcheren coast through Zoutlande and Westkapelle (50min). Bus #52 goes direct from Middleburg though Walcheren to Domburg in approximately 30 minutes.

Tourist office The VVV is at Schuitvlotstraat 32 (April–June, Sept & Oct Mon–Sat 9.30am–5.30pm, Sun 11am–3pm; July & Aug Mon–Sat 9am–6pm, Sun 11am–3pm; Nov–March Mon–Fri 10am–5pm, Sat 10am–2pm; ☎0118 583 484, ⓦvvvzeeland.nl). They can help with accommodation and provide a map of the village.

ACCOMMODATION

Beach house Domburg Beach ☎0118 570 055, ⓦslaapzand.nl. Modern, well equipped and right on the beach, these unique beach houses have great sea views: they sleep up to five people. Advance reservations advised. €485 for a weekend, €725 for a week.

Duinlust Badhuisweg 28 ☎0118 582 943, ⓦhotel duinlust.nl. Simple but pleasant hotel within easy walking distance of the beach. The rooms are basic but perfectly adequate, all with free wi-fi and most with balconies. €85

HI hostel Duinvlietweg 8 ☎0118 581 254, ⓦstayokay.com. A particularly scenic HI hostel, located in the thirteenth-century Kasteel Westhove which comes complete with a moat and is surrounded by a nature reserve. It's only a short stroll to the beach and less than

two kilometres from Domburg on bus route #53: ask to be dropped off at the castle. Dorm beds **€34**
Strandhotel Duinheuvel Badhuisweg 2 ☎0118 581 100, ⓦwilduin.nl. Upmarket establishment – within easy

walking distance of the beach – with 35 tastefully decorated rooms in minimalist style, and an art gallery downstairs. Most rooms have balconies, some with a sea view, and all have flat-screens and free wi-fi. **€135**

EATING AND DRINKING

Pizzeria Milano 't Groentje 11 ☎0118 581 251, ⓦmilanodomburg.nl. Tasty pizzas served in a modern setting, plus home-made Italian ice cream in summer. Pizzas start at €7.50 for a simple Margerita moving up to €14.50 for a Frutti di Mare. Mon–Fri 5–10pm, Sat & Sun 1–10pm; Oct–Feb closed on Tues & Wed.

Markt Zes Markt 6 ☎0118 582 373, ⓦmarktzes.nl. Right in the centre of town with a pleasant terrace. Wraps, toasties and *uitsmijters* make up the lunch menu, while excellent seafood such as a traditional fish stew for €19 is served at dinner. Occasional live music. Daily 11am–midnight.

Vlissingen

VLISSINGEN (Flushing), just 5km south of Middelburg, was previously an important ferry terminus, but its role as a transport hub for Belgium has dwindled due to the completion of the tunnel between Ellewoutsdijk and Terneuzen, a little way to the east. There's not a lot to see in the town, although the maritime museum warrants a couple of hours, and the assorted shipping that plies the choppy Westerschelde estuary has an appeal of its own.

Vlissingen's workaday centre won't detain you long, though you might drop by the improbably named **Cornelia Quackhofje**, an eighteenth-century almshouse for sailors, just north of the Lange Zelke shopping precinct. For more atmosphere, head for the **harbour**, whose bundle of pavement cafés and fresh fish-and-chip stalls is popular with Dutch and German tourists.

Zeeuws Maritiem Muzeeum

Nieuwendijk 11 • Mon–Fri 10am–5pm, Sat & Sun 1–5pm; Oct–March closed Mon • €8 • ⓦmuzeeum.nl

The **Zeeuws Maritiem Muzeeum** is the place to gen up on Zeeland's strong maritime traditions. The museum is divided into four themes – the sea, trade, glory and adventure. Multimedia presentations (in Dutch) explain the sea's crucial role in shaping Zeeland's livelihood, while excellent audiovisual displays reconstruct scenes of naval battles to dramatic effect. Exhibits include wares shipped along the trading routes of the Dutch East Indies such as nutmeg, ginger, salt, tea, silver, porcelain and even bricks.

Het Arsenaal

Arsenaalplein • July & Aug daily 10am–8pm; hours vary outside season but generally daily 10am–7pm; last admission 2hr before closing • €13 • ⓦarsenaal.com

Families will enjoy **Het Arsenaal**, a theme park where you can go on a simulated sea voyage, climb an observation tower and walk on a mocked-up sea bed among tanks of sharks. Kids can learn what skills they need to become a real pirate and find out what it was like to live on a pirate's ship. The petting pool where you can touch small sharks and rays is a real attraction.

The Westerschelde

The blustery walk along the Nieuwendijk offers views of the enormous vessels that sail the **WESTERSCHELDE**. Keeping to a narrow, often tortuous route, these container ships must negotiate the shallow waters and shifting sandbanks that sometimes reveal centuries-old wrecks. Further round the harbour, the promenade has a pleasant seaside feel, with a **beach** at the end. Alternatively, you can continue beyond the promenade on the green-signposted cycle path to Dishoek and Zouteland; along the way there are plenty of opportunities to lock your bike and hike up and over the dunes, emerging onto a beach that runs for miles.

6

ARRIVAL AND INFORMATION   VLISSINGEN

By train The train station is located in the harbour, next to the ferry terminal to Breskens, and an inconvenient ten-minute bus ride from the town centre. From Vlissingen regular trains serve Middelburg (every 30min; 8min).

By bus From Middelburg train station, catch bus #56 or #57 to the centre of Vlissingen; the journey takes about 25 minutes.

By ferry The ferry across the Westerschelde between Vlissingen and Breskens (every 30min; 20min) is located next to Vlissingen train station: buses #56 and #57 from Vlissingen town centre run to the port (10min). The ferry carries foot passengers and bicycles only and takes 20min. Ferries leave Vlissingen daily (5.45am–9.55pm), and there are buses on the other side from Breskens to the Belgian town of Bruges. In the opposite direction, the ferry departs Breskens daily (6.15am–10.25pm). Tickets are €2.80 per person each way, plus €1 for bicycles: check ⓦbba.nl for up-to-date information.

By tunnel The 6.6-kilometre tunnel beneath the Westerschelde, linking Ellewoutsdijk and Terneuzen, is open 24 hours a day; the toll for cars is €5.

Bike rental You can rent a bike from the train station next to the ferry terminal, which has a wide selection, including recumbents.

Tourist office The VVV is at Spuistraat 30 (April–Oct Mon 11am–5.30pm, Tues–Thurs 9.30am–5.30pm, Fri 9.30am–9pm, Sat 9.30am–5pm; Nov–March Mon 1–5.30pm, Tues–Thurs 9.30am–5.30pm, Fri 9.30am–9pm, Sat 9.30am–5pm; ☎0118 715 320, ⓦvvvzeeland.nl). It can provide a list of pensions as well as information on local cycling routes.

ACCOMMODATION

Belgische Loodsen Sociëteit Boulevard de Ruyter 4 ☎0118 413 608, ⓦbsoos.nl. This seafront hotel near the end of Nieuwendijk offers 11 basic rooms – the ones at the front have fabulous views of the passing ships. The downstairs restaurant serves reasonably priced fish dishes. **€100**

City Hostel Vlissingen Kerkstraat 10 ☎0118 415 200, ⓦcityhostel-vlissingen.nl. Located in two monumental buildings, this recently opened backpackers hostel has rooms sleeping up to 6 people. A three-course buffet dinner is served in the cosy downstairs café for only €15. Bicycle rent for €10. Dorm beds **€25**

EATING AND DRINKING

De Gecroonde Liefde Nieuwendijk 13 ☎0118 441 194, ⓦdegecroondeliefde.nl. Next to the maritime museum, this is your best bet for lunch with tasty sandwiches and salads followed by home-baked apple pie and lemon cheesecake. The interior is modern and minimalistic with a nice terrace in summer. Mon–Thurs 10am–6pm, Fri 10am–9pm, Sat & Sun noon–9pm; July & Aug also open till 9pm on Thurs.

Soif Bellamypark 14 ☎0118 410 516, ⓦso-if.nl. Located close to the harbour, *Soif* is a cheerful little place with lime-green walls and wooden floors. Like many restaurants in Vlissingen, seafood is their speciality; from fresh oysters and salmon to lobster and shrimps at reasonable prices. Daily noon–10pm.

De Beurs Beursplein 11 ☎0118 410 295, ⓦrestaurantdebeurs.nl. In Dutch Renaissance style and dating from 1635, one of Vlissingen's prettiest buildings now houses an agreeable restaurant with a terrace overlooking the harbour. It specializes in seafood and has a good-value three-course meal for €29.50. Daily 10am–10pm.

Veere

VEERE, some 8km northeast of Middelburg, is an attractive little town by the banks of the Veerse Meer that makes for a pleasant half-day visit. Today, it's a centre for all things maritime, its small harbour jammed with yachts and its cafés packed with weekend admirals, but a handful of buildings and a large church point to a time when Veere was wealthy and quite independent of other, comparable towns in Zeeland.

The town originally made its fortune through a fortuitous Scottish connection: in 1444 a certain Wolfert VI van Borssele, the lord of Veere, married Mary, daughter of James I of Scotland. As part of the dowry, van Borssele was granted a monopoly on trade with Scottish wool merchants and, in return, Scottish merchants living in Veere were granted special privileges. Veere declined economically once the wool trade started to deteriorate. The opening of the Walcheren canal linking the town to Middelburg and Vlissingen, in the nineteenth century gave it a stay of execution, but the

ZIERIKZEE (P.318) >

construction of the Veersegatdam and Zandkreekdam in the 1950s finally sealed off the port to seagoing vessels, and simultaneously created a freshwater lake ideal for watersports.

The town centre holds many fine old buildings dating from its heyday: their ornate workmanship leaves you in no doubt that the Scottish wool trade earned a bundle for the sixteenth- and seventeenth-century burghers of Veere. Many of the buildings (which are usually step-gabled with distinctive green and white shutters) are embellished with whimsical details that play on the owners' names or their particular line of business.

Museum Schotse Huizen
Kaai 25–27 • April–Oct daily 1–5pm • €4 • ⓦ schotsehuizen.nl

The **Museum Schotse Huizen** is housed in two former merchants' buildings, **Het Lammetje** (The Lamb) and **De Struys** (The Ostrich), dating from the mid-sixteenth century. Originally combined offices, homes and warehouses for the merchants, they now hold a rather lifeless collection of local costumes, old books, atlases and furniture, along with an exhibit devoted to fishing.

Stadhuis
Markt 5 • May–Oct daily 1–5pm • €1.50 • ⓦ schotsehuizen.nl

The town's **Stadhuis** is a typically opulent building, dating from the 1470s, with an out-of-scale Renaissance tower added a century later. Its facade is decorated with statues of the lords of Veere and their wives (Wolfert VI is third from the left) and, inside, a small museum occupies what was formerly the courtroom.

Grote Kerk
Oudestraat 26 • May–Sept Tues–Sun 11am–5pm • €3

Finished in 1560, Veere's **Grote Kerk** was badly damaged by fire a century later and subsequent restorations removed much of its decoration. In 1808 invading British troops used the church as a hospital and three years later Napoleon's army converted it into barracks and stables, destroying the stained glass, bricking up the windows and inserting five floors in the nave. Despite all this damage, the church's blunt 42-metre **tower** adds a glowering presence to the landscape, especially when seen from the town's watery surroundings. According to the original design, the tower was to have been three times higher, but even as it stands there's a great view from the top, back towards the pinnacled skyline of Middelburg and out across the Veerse Meer.

ARRIVAL AND INFORMATION   VEERE

By bus Bus #54 runs hourly from Middelburg to Veere.
By bike You can rent a bike from Middelburg train station (€7.50 a day) and take either the cycle path beside the main road or the circuitous but more picturesque route from the north side of town.

Tourist office Veere VVV is at Oudestraat 28 (April to mid-May & Oct Fri–Sun noon–4pm; mid-May to June & Sept Tues–Sun noon–4pm; July & Aug daily 10am–5pm; ☏ 0118 506 110, ⓦ vvvzeeland.nl): it can advise on boat rental and has details of private rooms.

ACCOMMODATION AND EATING

Bed & Brood Kerkstraat 7 ☏ 0118 502 081, ⓦ bed-en -brood.nl. A fourteenth- century house of worship which has been converted into a stylish B&B with very spacious rooms. Classical elements have been given a modern twist and the huge garden is perfect for escaping the tourist crowds. €90
De Campveerse Toren Kade 2 ☏ 0118 501 291, ⓦ campveersetoren.nl. This hotel has rooms in four separate buildings, all beautifully located overlooking the

water. All the rooms have a different feel but are equally stylish with an eye for detail. The restaurant is great for fresh seafood. €150
't Waepen van Veere Markt 23–27 ☏ 0118 501 231, ⓦ waepenvanveere.nl. Recently renovated in minimalist style with warm wooden floors, stylish chairs and flat-screen TVs. The classy restaurant serves regional oysters and has an extensive wine list of fine wines. €120

THE DELTA PROJECT AND THE DELTA EXPO

On February 1, 1953, a combination of an exceptionally high spring tide and powerful northwesterly winds drove the North Sea over the dykes to **flood** much of Zeeland. The results were catastrophic: 1855 people drowned, 47,000 homes and 500km of dykes were destroyed and some of the country's most fertile agricultural land was ruined by salt water. Towns as far inland as Bergen-op-Zoom and Dordrecht were flooded and Zeeland's road and rail network was wrecked. The government's response was immediate and massive. After patching up the breached dykes, work was begun on the **Delta Project**, one of the largest engineering schemes the world has ever seen and one of phenomenal complexity and expense.

The aim was to ensure the safety of Zeeland by radically shortening and strengthening its coastline. The major estuaries and inlets would be dammed, thus preventing unusually high tides surging inland to breach the thousands of kilometres of small **dykes**. Where it was impractical to build a dam – such as across the Westerschelde or Nieuwe Waterweg, which would have closed the seaports of Antwerp and Rotterdam respectively – secondary dykes were to be reinforced. New roads across the top of the dams would improve communications to Zeeland and Zuid-Holland and the freshwater lakes that formed behind the dams would enable precise control of the water table of the Zeeland islands.

It took thirty years for the Delta Project to be completed. The smaller, secondary dams – the **Veersegat**, **Haringvliet** and **Brouwershaven** – were built first to provide protection from high tides as quickly as possible, a process that also enabled engineers to learn as they went along. In 1968, work began on the largest dam, intended to close the Oosterschelde estuary that forms the outlet of the Maas, Waal and Rijn rivers. It soon ran into intense opposition from **environmental groups**, who pointed out that the mud flats were an important breeding ground for birds, while the estuary itself was a nursery for plaice, sole and other North Sea fish. The inshore fishermen saw their livelihoods in danger too: if the Oosterschelde were closed the oyster, mussel and lobster beds would be destroyed, representing a huge loss to the region's economy.

The environmental and fishing lobbies argued that strengthening the estuary dykes would provide adequate protection; the water board and agricultural groups raised the emotive spectre of the 1953 flood. In the end a compromise was reached, and in 1976 work began on the **Stormvloedkering** ("Storm Surge Barrier"), a gate that would stay open under normal tidal conditions, allowing water to flow in and out of the estuary, but close ahead of potentially destructive high tides.

DELTA EXPO

Faelweg 5, Vrouwenpolder • April–Oct daily 10am–5.30pm; check website for opening hours out of season • €22 • ⓦ neeltjejans.nl • From Middelburg, take bus #133 (2 hourly) from Langevieleweg, or cycle (1hr 30min) along national cycleway LF16 (noord)

Completed in 1986, the fascinating **Delta Expo**, signposted as Waterland Neeltje Jans, is on the Stormvloedkering. It's only once you're inside the Expo, though, that you get an idea of the scale of the project. It's best to start with the half-hour video presentation before taking in the exhibition, which is divided into three areas: the historical background of the Netherlands' water management problems; the technological developments that enabled the country to protect itself; the environmental consequences of applying the technologies and the solutions that followed. The Surge Barrier (and the Delta Project as a whole) has been a triumphant success: computer simulations predict most high tides, but if an unpredicted rise does occur, the sluice gates close automatically in a matter of minutes. If you cycle to the Expo on cycle route LF16, you'll run alongside open beaches and dunes, past wind turbines and onto the storm barrier itself, with ample opportunities to peer into the sluice gates: allow for blustery winds on the way back.

Suster Anna Markt 8 ⓣ 0118 501 557, ⓦ susteranna .nl. A warm and welcoming eatery serving pancakes, sandwiches and cakes in a homely atmosphere. It serves many different blends of tea and has an intimate garden terrace. Summer daily 10am–10pm; hours vary out of season.

Schouwen-Duiveland

The Storm Surge Barrier spans the mouth of the Oosterschelde estuary providing easy access over to the island of **Schouwen-Duiveland**. Most of the Dutch and German tourists who come here head directly to the western corner of the island for the acres of beach, pine forest and dune that stretches out between Burgh-Haamstede and **Renesse**, two villages situated 6km apart. In the summer, this western flank of the island is packed with families and predominantly young holidaymakers, making the most of its waterborne activities. **Zierikzee** further east is a more traditional affair, a miniature Middelburg that makes an appealing base for exploring the area, with some fine trips through the countryside out over one of Europe's longest (and perhaps windiest) bridges nearby.

If you're coming for peace and quiet, you should steer clear of the school holidays. Travel over the season's bookends in June and September and you'll have much of the long, pristine beaches to yourself, though the weather can be unpredictable, facilities dwindle with the approach of autumn, and storms can blot the sky.

Renesse

RENESSE, about 8km north of the Barrier, is a modern sprawl of bungalows just a kilometre from the beach, making an appealing base. Popular with the surfing and windsurfing crowd, its sixteen-kilometre beach is divided in summer into sectors, catering for families, surfers, kite-flyers and naturists. A free, open-top electric **bus** (9am–7pm) plies the length of the beach, linking hotels, campsites and the "Transferium" – the modern bus station on the edge of town that offers changing rooms, showers and bike rental, in an attempt to encourage holidaymakers to abandon their cars at the free car park alongside. Parking at the beach is limited to two hours.

INFORMATION
RENESSE

Tourist office The VVV is at Roelandsweg 1 (April to mid-May & mid-Sept to late Oct Mon–Sat 9am-5pm; mid-May to late June & early Sept to mid-Sept Mon–Sat 9am–5pm, Sun 10am–4pm; July & Aug daily 9am–7pm; Nov–March Mon 1–5pm, Fri & Sat 9am–5pm; 0900 2020 233, vvvzeeland.nl), and sells an excellent map of the beach, as well as walking and cycling trails on the island (€3).

ACTIVITIES

Surfing Windsurfing Renesse, De Zoom 15 (windsurfingrenesse.nl), rents out surfboards for €37.50 a day and provides lessons, as well as renting windsurfing equipment.
Windsurfing The best spot for windsurfing is at the Brouwersdam, 8km from Renesse, which links Schouwen-Duiveland to Goeree-Overflakkee and offers excellent windsurfing on one side, and one of Europe's cleanest beaches on the other. Halfway along the Brouwersdam, the Surfcentrum, at Ossenhoek 1, Kabbellaarsbank (0111 671 480, brouwersdam.nl), will rent a board and wetsuit for €35 a day. Tuition, small sailboats and four-bed dorms (€62.50/room) are also available. Take bus #104 from Renesse, and ask the driver for the Port Zélande stop.

ACCOMMODATION

The area is teeming with hotels, campsites and holiday homes and B&Bs. The VVV has a list of available accommodation, or try the English-language website renesse.nl, for accommodation and other holiday services. Book accommodation well in advance over the summer.

Hotel de Logerij Laône 15 0111 462 570, delogerij.nl. Within walking distance of both the town and beach, with 22 simple but perfectly adequate and clean rooms. You can rent bicycles at the reception. **€86.50**

Zierikzee and around

Schouwen-Duiveland's most interesting town, **ZIERIKZEE**, is situated about 14km east of the Barrier. The town's position at the intersection of shipping routes between England, Flanders and Holland made it an important port in the late Middle Ages and it was famed for its salt and madder – a root that, when dried and ground, produces a

6

CYCLING AROUND ZIERIKZEE

There's plenty of scope for exploring the countryside and coastline around Zierikzee by bike. To put colour in your cheeks, you could follow the bike lane over the wind-tunnel-like **Zeelandbrug**, a graceful bridge that spans the Oosterschelde south of Zierikzee, and is one of the longest bridges in Europe, at 5022m. Refreshments are available in Colijnsplaat on the other side: prevailing winds will be against you on the way out, so you can expect the journey back to take half the time. Alternatively, **Dreischor**, 8km northeast, makes for a pleasant half-day bike ride from Zierikzee. Here, the fourteenth-century St Adriaanskirche is surrounded by a moat and lush green lawns, encircled by a ring of attractive houses. Complete with waddling geese and a restored *travalje* (livery stable), it's an idyllic setting – although busy at weekends.

brilliant red dye. Today, it's a picturesque town of narrow cobbled streets and traditional gabled facades: encircled by a defensive canal – and best entered by one of two sixteenth-century water gates – Zierikzee's centre is small and easily explored. Although very popular with Dutch, German and Belgian tourists, the town makes a good base for a bike ride in the surrounding area, or a visit to the atmospheric **Watersnoodmuseum**.

Stadhuismuseum

Meelstraat 6 • Tues–Sat 11am–5pm, Sun 1–5pm • €7.50

Zierikzee's **Stadhuis** is easy enough to find – just head for the tall spire. Inside, the **Stadhuismuseum** has collections of silver, costumes and a regional history exhibition. It has been recently renovated and now incorporates part of the collection from the former Maritime Museum.

The Watersnoodmuseum

Weg van de Buitenlandse Pers 5, Ouwerkeric • Tues–Sun: April–Oct 11am–5pm; Nov–March 1–5pm • €8 • ⓦ www.watersnoodmuseum.nl

Six kilometres out of Zierikzee at Ouwerkeric, the recently enlarged **Watersnoodmuseum** commemorates the great floods of 1953 (see box, p.317), the catalyst for the massive Delta Project. Atmospherically set in four desolate caissons – the original concrete bunkers manoeuvred into place to plug a break in the dyke – the museum tells the story chronologically from the disaster to the current day and also covers future plans to keep the waters at bay. The first caisson holds construction machinery used in the 1950s, scale models showing the extent of the damage, old photographs and original newsreel footage beamed onto the wall. The second caisson focuses more on the human aspect, with interactive stories about the many victims of the flood. The third and fourth caissons give an insight into the reconstruction phase and future plans to keep Zeeland safe.

ARRIVAL AND INFORMATION
ZIERIKZEE

By bus Bus #132 shuttles between Goes and Zierikzee in half an hour.

Tourist office The VVV is at Nieuwe Haven 7 (Mon–Sat 10am–5pm; ⓣ 0900 202 0233, ⓦ vvvzeeland.nl) and can provide you a map of the town as well as details of where to stay.

Bike rental Bike Totaal, Weststraat 5 (ⓣ 0111 412 115; ⓦ jandejongefietsen.nl) rents out bikes for €7.50 a day.

ACCOMMODATION AND EATING

Pension Klaas Vaak Nieuwe Bogerdstraat ⓣ 0111 414 204, ⓦ pensionklaasvaak.nl. A simple pension located in a sixteenth-century building with seven plain but adequate rooms, all with free wi-fi. The big plus is a huge and lovely garden with a trampoline for kids. **€65**

Hotel Van Oppen China Garden Verrenieuwstraat 11 ⓣ 0111 412 288, ⓦ hotel-van-oppen.nl. Pretty average rooms, but with the big advantage of a large Chinese restaurant downstairs that specializes in fondue and Ti-pan dishes. **€70**

WAR GRAVES AT OOSTERBEEK, NEAR ARNHEM

Contexts

History

The country now known as the Netherlands didn't reach its present delimitations until 1830. Until then the borders of the entire region, formerly known as the Low Countries and including present-day Belgium and Luxembourg, were continually being redrawn following battles, treaties and alliances. Inevitably, then, what follows is, in its early parts at least, an outline of the history of the whole region, rather than a straightforward history of the Netherlands as such. Please note, incidentally, that the term "Holland" refers to the province – not the country – throughout.

Beginnings

Little is known of the **prehistoric** settlers of the Low Countries, their visible remains largely confined to the far north of the Netherlands, where mounds known as *terpen* were built to keep the sea at bay in Friesland and Groningen. There are also megalithic tombs (*hunebeds*) among the hills near Emmen in the northeast corner of the Netherlands, but quite how these tie in with the Iron Age culture that had established itself across the region by the fifth century BC is impossible to say.

Clearer details of the region begin to emerge at the time of **Julius Caesar**'s conquest of Gaul (broadly France) in 57 to 50 BC. He found three tribal groupings living in the region: the mainly Celtic **Belgae** (hence the nineteenth-century term "Belgium") settled by the Rhine, Maas and Waal to the south; the Germanic **Frisians** living on the marshy coastal strip north of the Scheldt; and the **Batavi**, another Germanic people, inhabiting the swampy riverbanks of what is now the southern Netherlands. The Belgae were conquered and their lands incorporated into the imperial province of **Gallia Belgica**, but the territory of the Batavi and Frisians was not considered worthy of colonization. These tribes were granted the status of allies, a source of recruitment for the Roman legions and curiosity for imperial travellers.

Romans and Merovingians

The Roman occupation of Gallia Belgica continued for 500 years until the legions were pulled back to protect the heartlands of the crumbling empire. As the empire collapsed in chaos and confusion, the Germanic **Franks**, who had been settling within Gallia Belgica from the third century, filled the power vacuum, establishing a **Merovingian** kingdom around their capital Tournai (in modern Belgium) with their allies the Belgae. A great swathe of forest extending from the Scheldt to the Ardennes separated this Frankish kingdom from the more confused situation to the north and east, where other tribes of Franks settled along the Scheldt and Leie, Saxons occupied parts of Overijssel and Gelderland, and the Frisians clung to the seashore.

57 BC	406 AD	695
The Romans reach the edge of what is now the Netherlands, but are not impressed by its marshes and bogs.	Barbarians cross the River Rhine in numbers; the Roman Empire recedes.	Christianity spreads across the Netherlands; St Willibrord becomes the first bishop of Utrecht.

Towards the end of the fifth century, the Merovingian king Clovis was converted to **Christianity** and the faith slowly filtered north, spread by energetic missionaries like St Willibrord, first bishop of Utrecht, from about 695, and St Boniface, who was killed by the Frisians in 754 in a final act of pagan resistance before they too were converted. Meanwhile, after the death of the last distinguished Merovingian king, Dagobert, in 638, power passed increasingly to the so-called "mayors of the palace", a hereditary position whose most outstanding occupant was **Charles Martel** (c.690–741). Martel inherited a large shambolic kingdom, whose military weakness he determined to remedy. Martel replaced the existing body of infantry led by a small group of cavalry with a mounted force of highly trained knights who bore their own military expenses in return for land – the beginnings of the **feudal system**. These reforms came just in time to save Christendom: in 711 the extraordinary Arab advance, which had begun early in the seventh century in modern-day Saudi Arabia, reached the Pyrenees and a massive Muslim army occupied southern France in preparation for further conquests. In the event, Martel defeated the invaders outside Tours in 732, one of Europe's most crucial engagements and one that saved France from Arab conquest for good.

The Carolingians

Ten years after Martel's death, his son, **Pepin the Short**, formally usurped the Merovingian throne with the blessing of the pope, becoming the first of the **Carolingian** dynasty, whose most famous member was **Charlemagne**, king of the west Franks from 768. In a dazzling series of campaigns, Charlemagne extended his empire south into Italy, west to the Pyrenees, north to Denmark and east to the Oder. His secular authority was bolstered by his coronation as the first **Holy Roman Emperor** in 800, a title bestowed on him by the pope in order to legitimize his claim as the successor to the emperors of imperial Rome.

The strength and stability of Charlemagne's court at Aachen spread to the Low Countries, bringing a building boom that created a string of superb Romanesque churches like Maastricht's St Servaas, and a trading bonanza along the region's principal rivers. However, unlike his Roman predecessors, Charlemagne was subject to the divisive inheritance laws of the Salian tribe of Franks, and after his death in 814, his kingdom was divided between his grandsons into three roughly parallel strips of territory, the precursors of France, the Low Countries and Germany.

The growth of the towns

The tripartite division of Charlemagne's empire placed the **Low Countries** between the emergent French- and German-speaking nations, a dangerous location, which was

814	900s	1083
The Emperor Charlemagne brings law and economic order to the Netherlands; it's short-lived.	Vikings raid the Netherlands by the boatload.	First historical record of the use of the term "Holland" to describe part of the Low Countries.

subsequently to influence much of its history. Amid the cobweb of local alliances that made up **early feudal western Europe** in the ninth and tenth centuries, however, this was not apparent. During this period, French kings and German emperors exercised a general authority over the region, but power was effectively in the hands of local lords who, remote from central control, brought a degree of local stability. From the twelfth century, feudalism slipped into a gradual decline, the intricate pattern of localized allegiances undermined by the increasing strength of certain lords, whose power and wealth often exceeded that of their nominal sovereign. Preoccupied by territorial squabbles, this streamlined nobility was usually willing to assist the **growth of towns** by granting charters that permitted a certain amount of **autonomy** in exchange for tax revenues and military and labour services. The first major cities were the cloth towns of Flanders – Bruges, Ieper (Ypres) and Ghent. Meanwhile, their smaller northern neighbours concentrated on trade, exploiting their strategic position at the junction of the region's main waterways – Amsterdam being a case in point.

Burgundian rule

By the late fourteenth century the political situation in the Low Countries was fairly clear: five lords controlled most of the region, paying only nominal homage to their French or German overlords. In 1419 **Philip the Good** of Burgundy succeeded to the countship of Flanders and by a series of adroit political moves gained control over Holland, Zeeland, Brabant and Limburg to the north, and Antwerp, Namur and Luxembourg to the south. He consolidated his power by establishing a strong central administration in Bruges and by restricting the privileges granted in the towns' charters. During his reign Bruges became a showcase for the **Hanseatic League**, a mainly German association of towns which acted as a trading group and protected their interests by an exclusive system of trading tariffs. Philip died in 1467 to be succeeded by his son, **Charles the Bold**, who was killed in battle ten years later, plunging his father's carefully crafted domain into turmoil. The French seized the opportunity to take back Arras and Burgundy and before the people of Flanders would agree to fight the French, they kidnapped Charles's daughter, Mary, and forced her to sign a charter that restored the civic privileges removed by her grandfather Philip.

The Habsburgs

After her release, Mary married the **Habsburg** Maximilian of Austria, who assumed sole authority when Mary was killed in a riding accident in 1482. **Maximilian** continued to implement the centralizing policies of Philip the Good, but in 1494, when he became Holy Roman Emperor, he transferred control of the Low Countries to his son, Philip the Handsome. The latter died in 1506 and his territories were passed on to Maximilian's grandson **Charles V**, who also became King of Spain and Holy Roman Emperor in 1516 and 1519, respectively. Charles was suspicious of the turbulent burghers of Flanders and, following in Maximilian's footsteps, favoured Antwerp at their expense; it soon became the greatest port in the empire, part of a general movement of trade and prosperity away from Flanders to the cities to the north.

1432	1482	1517
Philip the Good, the Duke of Burgundy, incorporates the Netherlands within his territories.	Mary of Burgundy killed in a riding accident; Netherlands absorbed into the Habsburg Empire.	Luther nails up his 95 theses against the sale of indulgences by the Catholic church; Protestants anxious.

Through sheer force of will and military might, Charles bent the merchant cities of the Low Countries to his will, but regardless of this display of force, a spiritual trend was emerging that would soon question not only the rights of the emperor but also rock the power of the Catholic Church itself.

The Reformation

An alliance of Church and State had dominated the medieval world: pope and bishops, kings and counts were supposedly the representatives of God on earth, and they combined to crush any religious dissent. Much of their authority relied on the ignorance of the population, who were dependent on priests for the interpretation of the scriptures, their view of the world carefully controlled. The **development of typography**, therefore, was a key factor in the **Reformation**, the stirring of religious revolt that stood sixteenth-century Europe on its head. For the first time, printers were able to produce relatively cheap bibles in quantity, and religious texts were no longer the exclusive property of the Church.

Consequently, as the populace snaffled up the bibles, so a welter of debate spread across much of western Europe under the auspices of theologians like **Erasmus of Rotterdam** (1465–1536), who wished to cleanse the Catholic Church of its corruptions, superstitions and extravagant ceremony; only later did many of these same thinkers – principally **Martin Luther** (1483–1546) – decide to support a breakaway church. In 1517, Luther produced his 95 theses against indulgences, rejecting – among other things – Christ's presence in the Eucharist and denying the Church's monopoly on the interpretation of the Bible. There was no way back, and when Luther's works were disseminated his ideas gained a European following among reforming groups that were soon branded **Lutheran** by the Catholic Church. Luther asserted that the Church's political power was subservient to that of the state, whereas the supporters of another great reforming thinker, **John Calvin** (1509–64), emphasized the importance of individual conscience and the need for redemption through the grace of Christ rather than the confessional.

The Revolt of the Netherlands

These seeds of **Protestantism** fell on fertile ground among the Low Countries' merchants, whose wealth and independence could not easily be accommodated within a rigid caste society. Similarly, their employees, the guildsmen and their apprentices, had a long history of opposing arbitrary authority, and were soon convinced of the need to reform an autocratic, venal church. In 1555, **Charles V abdicated**, transferring his German lands to his brother Ferdinand, and his Italian, Spanish and Low Countries territories to his son, the fanatically Catholic **Philip II**. In the short term, the scene was set for a bitter religious confrontation, while the dynastic ramifications of the division of the Habsburg Empire were to complicate European affairs for centuries.

After his father's abdication, **Philip II** decided to teach his heretical subjects a lesson they would not forget. He garrisoned the towns of the Low Countries with Spanish mercenaries, imported the Inquisition and passed a series of anti-Protestant edicts. However, other pressures on the Habsburg Empire forced him into a tactical withdrawal

1555	**1566**	**1579**
The resolutely Catholic Philip II of Spain prepares to weed out Protestant subjects in the Low Countries; Protestants very anxious.	Rebellious Protestants smash up hundreds of Catholic churches in the Iconoclastic Fury – Beeldenstorm in Dutch ("statue storm").	The seven provinces of the Netherlands break with Habsburg Spain, establishing the United Provinces; Protestants relieved.

and he transferred control to his sister, **Margaret of Parma**, in 1559. Based in Brussels, the equally resolute Margaret implemented the policies of her brother with gusto. In 1561 she reorganized the Church and created fourteen new bishoprics, a move that was construed as a wresting of power from civil authority, and an attempt to destroy the local aristocracy's powers of religious patronage. Protestantism – and Protestant sympathies – now spread to the nobility, who formed the "**League of the Nobility**" to counter Habsburg policy. The League petitioned Philip for moderation, but was dismissed out of hand by one of Margaret's Walloon advisers, who called them *ces geux* ("those beggars"), an epithet that was to be enthusiastically adopted by the rebels.

The Iconoclastic Fury
In 1565 a harvest failure caused a winter famine among the workers, and, after years of repression, they struck back: a Protestant sermon in the tiny Flemish textile town of Steenvoorde incited the congregation to purge the local church of its "papist idolatry"; the crowd attacked the church's reliquaries and shrines, smashed the stained-glass windows and terrorized the priests, thereby launching the **Iconoclastic Fury**, which spread like wildfire: within ten days churches had been ransacked from one end of the Low Countries to the other, nowhere more so than in Antwerp.

The ferocity of this outbreak shocked the upper classes into renewed support for Spain, and Margaret regained the allegiance of most nobles – with the principal exception of the country's greatest landowner, Prince William of Orange-Nassau, known as **William the Silent** (though William the Taciturn is perhaps a better translation). Of Germanic descent, William was raised a Catholic but the excesses and rigidity of Philip had caused him to side with the Protestant movement. A firm believer in individual freedom and religious tolerance, William became a symbol of liberty, but after the Fury had revitalized the pro-Spanish party, he prudently slipped away to his estates in Germany.

The Duke of Alva dispatched
Philip II was encouraged by the increase in support for Margaret and so, in 1567, he sent the **Duke of Alva**, with an army of 10,000 men, to the Low Countries to suppress his religious opponents absolutely. Margaret was, however, not at all pleased by Philip's decision and, when Alva arrived in Brussels, she resigned in a huff, thereby abandoning the Low Countries to military rule. One of Alva's first acts was to set up the Commission of Civil Unrest, which was soon nicknamed the "**Council of Blood**", after its habit of executing those it examined: no fewer than 12,000 citizens were killed by the commission, mostly for participating in the Fury. Initially the repression worked: in 1568, when William attempted an invasion from Germany, the towns, garrisoned by the Spanish, offered no support. William waited and considered other means of defeating Alva. In April 1572, a band of privateers entered Brielle on the Maas and captured it from the Spanish. This was one of several commando-style attacks by the so-called **Waterguezen**, or sea-beggars, who were at first obliged to operate from England, although it was soon possible for them to secure bases in the Netherlands, whose citizens had grown to loathe Alva and his Spaniards.

After the success at Brielle, the revolt spread rapidly: by June the rebels controlled most of the province of Holland and William was able to take command of his troops

1606	1625	1632	1648
Rembrandt born in Leiden, the ninth child of a miller.	Dutch found "New Amsterdam" – the forerunner of New York.	Johannes Vermeer born in Delft.	The Peace of Westphalia heralds Amsterdam's Golden Age.

in Delft. Alva and his son Frederick fought back, taking Gelderland, Overijssel and the towns of Zutphen and Naarden, and then Haarlem, where they massacred the Calvinist ministers and most of the defenders. But the Protestants retaliated: utilizing their superior naval power, the dykes were cut and the Spanish forces, unpaid and threatened with watery destruction, were forced to withdraw. Frustrated, Philip replaced Alva with **Luis de Resquesens**, who initially had some success in the south, where the Catholic majority was more willing to compromise with Spanish rule than their northern neighbours.

The Spanish Fury

William's triumphant relief of Leiden in 1574 increased the confidence of the rebel forces, and when de Resquesens died in 1576, his unpaid garrison in Antwerp mutinied and attacked the town, slaughtering some eight thousand of its people in what was known as the **Spanish Fury**. Though Spain still held several towns, the massacre alienated the south and pushed its inhabitants into the arms of William, whose troops now swept into Brussels, the heart of imperial power. Momentarily, it seemed possible for the whole region to unite behind William, and all signed the **Union of Brussels**, which demanded the departure of foreign troops as a condition for accepting a diluted Habsburg sovereignty. This was followed, in 1576, by the **Pacification of Ghent**, a regional agreement that guaranteed freedom of religious belief, a necessary precondition for any union between the largely Protestant north (the Netherlands) and Catholic south (Belgium and Luxembourg).

The end of the Revolt

Philip II was, however, not inclined to compromise, especially when he realized that William's Calvinist sympathies were upsetting his newly found Walloon and Flemish allies. The king bided his time until 1578, when, with his enemies still arguing among themselves, he sent another army from Spain to the Low Countries under the command of Alessandro Farnese, the **Duke of Parma**. Events played into Parma's hands. In 1579, tired of all the wrangling, seven northern provinces (Holland, Zeeland, Utrecht, Groningen, Friesland, Overijssel and Gelderland) broke with their southerly neighbours to sign the **Union of Utrecht**, an alliance against Spain that was to be the first unification of the Netherlands as an identifiable country – the so-called **United Provinces**. The agreement stipulated freedom of belief within the provinces, an important step since the struggle against Spain wasn't simply a religious one: many Catholics disliked the Spanish occupation and William did not wish to alienate this possible source of support. This liberalism did not, however, extend to freedom of worship, although to all intents and purposes a blind eye was turned to the celebration of Mass if it was done privately and inconspicuously – giving rise to the "hidden churches" (Schuilkerken) found throughout the Netherlands today. Meanwhile, in the south – and also in 1579 – representatives of the southern provinces signed the **Union of Arras**, a Catholic-led agreement that declared loyalty to Philip II in counterbalance to the Union of Utrecht in the north. Parma used this area as a base to recapture all of Flanders and Antwerp, which fell after a long and cruel siege in 1585. But Parma was unable to advance any further north and the Low Countries were, de facto, divided into two – the Spanish Netherlands and the United Provinces – beginning a separation

1652–1654	**1654**	**1665–1667**
First Anglo-Dutch War.	Carel Fabritius, potentially an artist of the first order, is killed in a gunpowder explosion in Delft aged just 32.	Second Anglo-Dutch War: the Dutch fleet sails up the Thames; England humiliated.

that would lead, after many changes, to the creation of three modern countries – Belgium, Luxembourg and the Netherlands.

The United Provinces (1579–1648)

Throughout the late sixteenth and seventeenth centuries, **Holland**, today comprising Noord- and Zuid-Holland, was by far the most dominant of the **United Provinces**, both economically and politically. While the individual provinces maintained a degree of decentralized independence, as far as the United Provinces as a whole were concerned, what Holland said pretty much went. The assembly of these United Provinces was known as the **States General** and it met at Den Haag (The Hague); it had no domestic legislative authority, and could only carry out foreign policy by unanimous decision, a formula designed to make potential waverers feel more secure. The role of **Stadholder** was the most important in each province, roughly equivalent to that of governor, though the same person could occupy this position in any number of provinces – and mostly did, with the Orange-Nassaus characteristically picking up five or six provinces at any one time. The **Council Pensionary** was another major post. The man who held either title in Holland was a centre of political power. Pieter Geyl, in his seminal *Revolt of the Netherlands*, defined the end result as the establishment of a republic which was "oligarchic, erastian [and] decentralized".

In 1584, a Catholic fanatic assassinated William the Silent at his residence in Delft. It was a grievous blow to the provinces and, as William's son **Maurice** was only 17, power passed to **Johan van Oldenbarneveldt**, the country's leading statesman and Council Pensionary of Rotterdam and ultimately Holland. Things were going badly in the war against the Spanish, but Oldenbarneveldt, somewhat to his own surprise, drove the Spanish back. International events then played into their hands: in 1588, the English defeated the Spanish Armada and the following year the powerful king Henry III of France died. Most important of all, Philip II of Spain, the scourge of the Low Countries, died in 1598, a necessary preamble to the **Twelve Year Truce** (1609–21) signed between the Habsburgs and the United Provinces, which grudgingly accepted the independence of the new republic.

The early seventeenth century

In the breathing space created by the Twelve Year Truce, the **rivalry** between Maurice and Oldenbarneveldt intensified and an obscure argument within the Calvinist church on predestination proved the catalyst for Oldenbarneveldt's downfall. This quarrel, between two Leiden theologians, began in 1612: one of them, **Armenius**, argued that God gave man the choice of accepting or rejecting faith; **Gomarus**, his opponent, believed that predestination was absolute – to the degree that God chooses who will be saved and who damned, with man powerless in the decision. This row between the two groups (known respectively as Remonstrants and Counter-Remonstrants) soon became attached to the political divisions within the republic. When a synod was arranged at Dordrecht to resolve the doctrinal matter, the province of Holland, led by Oldenbarneveldt, refused to attend, insisting on Holland's right to decide its own religious orthodoxies. At heart, he and his fellow deputies supported the provincial

1672	1688	1672–1674
Johan de Witt fails as a politician and the Dutch mob rip him to pieces – literally.	William III of Orange successfully invades England – and adds King of England to his several titles.	Third Anglo-Dutch War.

independence favoured by Remonstrant sympathizers, whereas Maurice sided with the Counter-Remonstrants, who favoured a strong central authority. The Counter-Remonstrants won at Dordrecht and Maurice, with his troops behind him, quickly overcame his opponents and had Oldenbarneveldt arrested. In May 1619 Oldenbarneveldt was **executed** in Den Haag "for having conspired to dismember the states of the Netherlands and greatly troubled God's church".

The Thirty Years' War (1618–1648)

With the end of the Twelve Year Truce in 1621, fighting with Spain broke out once again, this time as part of the more general **Thirty Years' War** (1618–48), a largely religious-based conflict between Catholic and Protestant countries that involved most of western Europe. In the Low Countries, the Spanish were initially successful, but they were weakened by war with France and by the fresh attacks of Maurice's successor, his brother **Frederick Henry**. From 1625, the Spaniards suffered a series of defeats on land and sea that forced them out of what is today the southern part of the Netherlands, and in 1648 they were compelled to accept the humiliating **Peace of Westphalia**, the general treaty that ended the Thirty Years' War. Under its terms, the independence of the United Provinces was formally recognized and the Dutch were even able to insist that the Scheldt estuary be closed to shipping, an action designed to destroy the trade and prosperity of Antwerp, which – along with the rest of modern-day Belgium – remained part of the Habsburg Empire. By this act, the commercial expansion and pre-eminence of Amsterdam was assured, and the Golden Age began.

The Golden Age

The brilliance of **Amsterdam**'s explosion onto the European scene is as difficult to underestimate as it is to detail. The size of the city's merchant fleet carrying Baltic grain into Europe had long been considerable and even during the long war with Spain it had continued to expand. Indeed, not only were the Spaniards unable to undermine it, but they were, on occasion, even obliged to use Dutch ships to supply their own troops – part of a burgeoning cargo trade that was another key ingredient of Amsterdam's economic success.

It was, however, the emasculation of Antwerp by the Treaty of Westphalia that launched a period of extraordinarily dynamic growth – the so-called **Golden Age** – and Amsterdam quickly became the emporium for the products of north and south Europe and the new colonies in the East and West Indies. Dutch banking and investment brought further prosperity, and by the mid-seventeenth century Amsterdam's wealth was spectacular. Taking their new-found riches as a sign of God's pleasure, the city's Calvinist bourgeoisie indulged in fine canal houses and commissioned images of themselves in group portraits. Civic pride knew no bounds: great monuments to self-aggrandizement, such as Amsterdam's new town hall, were hastily erected, and, if some went hungry, few starved, as the poor were cared for in municipal almshouses. The arts flourished and religious tolerance extended even to the traditional scapegoats, the **Jews**, and in particular the Sephardic Jews, who had been hounded from Spain by the Inquisition, but were guaranteed freedom from religious persecution under the

1700s	**1713**	**1720s**
Nautical folklore acclaims the legend of The Flying Dutchman, who captains a ghost ship that can never make port.	Treaty of Utrecht: Spain abandons the Spanish Netherlands (Belgium), which is passed to the Austrians.	The Netherlands starts to ossify – politically and economically.

terms of the Union of Utrecht of 1579. By the end of the eighteenth century, Jews accounted for ten percent of the city's inhabitants. Guilds and craft associations thrived, and in the first half of the seventeenth century the city's population quadrupled. Furthermore, although Amsterdam was the centre of this boom, economic ripples spread across much of the United Provinces. Dutch farmers were, for instance, able to sell all they could produce to the expanding city and a string of Zuider Zee ports cashed in on the flourishing Baltic trade.

The East and West India companies

Throughout the Golden Age, one organization that kept the country's coffers brimming was the **Dutch East India Company** (Vereenigde Oost-Indische Compagnie; VOC). Formed in 1602, this Amsterdam-controlled enterprise sent ships to Asia, Indonesia, and China to bring back spices, woods and other assorted valuables. The States General granted the company a trading monopoly in all lands east of the Cape of Good Hope and, for good measure, threw in unlimited military powers over the lands it controlled. As a consequence, the company became a colonial power in its own right, governing, at one time or another, parts of Malaya, Sri Lanka and parts of modern-day Indonesia. In 1621, the **West India Company** (Geoctroyeerde Westindische Compagnie or GWIC) was inaugurated to protect Dutch interests in the Americas and Africa. However, this second company never achieved the success of its sister, expending most of its energies in waging war on Spanish and Portuguese colonies from its base in Surinam. The company was dismantled in 1674, ten years after its nascent colony of New Amsterdam had been captured by the British and renamed **New York**. Elsewhere, the Netherlands held on to its colonies for as long as possible: Java and Sumatra remained under Dutch control until 1949.

Johan de Witt versus William III of Orange

Although the economics of the Golden Age were dazzling, the **politics** were dismal. Interminable wrangling dogged the United Provinces with one faction wanting a central, unified government under the pre-eminent **House of Orange-Nassau**, the other championing provincial autonomy. Frederick Henry died in 1647 and his successor, William II, lasted just three years before his death from smallpox. A week after William's death, his wife bore the son who would become William III of England, but in the meantime the leaders of the province of Holland seized their opportunity. They forced measures through the States General that abolished the position of Stadholder, thereby reducing the powers of the Orangists and increasing those of the provinces, chiefly Holland itself. Holland's foremost figure in these years was **Johan de Witt**, Council Pensionary to the States General. He guided the country through wars with England and Sweden, concluding a triple alliance between the two countries and the United Provinces in 1678. This didn't last, however, and when both France and England marched on the Provinces two years later, the republic was in deep trouble – previous victories had been at sea – and the army, weak and disorganized, could not withstand an attack. In panic, the country turned to **William III of Orange** for leadership and Johan de Witt was brutally murdered by a mob of Orangist sympathizers in Den

1750	1795	1815	1830
Handel visits the Netherlands to gee-up its musical scene.	Napoleon's Revolutionary army occupies the United Provinces.	Belgium and the Netherlands (forcibly) united as the "United Kingdom of the Netherlands".	Belgium revolts – and the Netherlands goes it alone.

WILLIAM THE SILENT COMES TO A STICKY END

Champion of the Protestants, **William the Silent**, Prince of Orange (1533–1584), did much to break the Habsburg hold on "The Netherlands". Recognizing his value to their Protestant enemies, the Habsburgs had placed a huge prize on his head, quite sufficient to attract a motley crew of adventurers and mercenaries. Despite tight security, an ardent Catholic and Habsburg agent **Balthasar Gérard** managed to secrete himself into William's household in Delft, shooting the prince as he was about to climb the stairs to his private chambers. Two of the three bullets went straight through William into the wall behind – and are still clearly visible in the Prinsenhof in Delft (see p.166). True or not, William's last words were said to have been "Lord have mercy upon me, and remember thy little flock", while Gérard came to a grisly end, dying after four days of torture.

Haag. By 1678, William had defeated the French and made peace with the English – and was rewarded (along with his wife Mary) with the English crown ten years later.

The United Provinces in the eighteenth century

Though William III had defeated the French, Louis XIV retained designs on the United Provinces and the pot was kept boiling in a long series of dynastic wars that ranged across northern Europe. In 1700, **Charles II of Spain**, the last of the Spanish Habsburgs, died childless, bequeathing the Spanish throne and control of the Spanish Netherlands to Philip of Anjou, Louis' grandson. Louis promptly forced Philip to cede the latter to France, which was, with every justification, construed as a threat to the balance of power by France's neighbours. The **War of the Spanish Succession** ensued, with the United Provinces, England and Austria forming the Triple Alliance to thwart the French king. The war itself was a haphazard, long-winded affair distinguished by the spectacular victories of the Duke of Marlborough at Blenheim, Ramillies and Malplaquet. It dragged on until the **Treaty of Utrecht** of 1713 in which France finally abandoned its claim to the Spanish Netherlands.

All this fighting had, however, drained the United Provinces' reserves and its slow economic and political decline began, accelerated by the ossification of its ruling class. This reflected the emergence of an increasingly **socially static society**, with power and wealth concentrated within a small, immovable elite. Furthermore, with the threat of foreign conquest effectively removed, the Dutch ruling class divided into two main camps – the **Orangists** and the pro-French "**Patriots**" – whose constant squabbling soon brought political life to a virtual standstill. The situation deteriorated even further in the latter half of the century and the last few years of the United Provinces present a sorry state of affairs.

French occupation

In 1795 the French invaded and swiftly swept their opponents aside. They were welcomed by the Patriots, who helped them dismantle the entrenched privileges of the merchant oligarchy, dissolving the United Provinces and establishing the **Batavian Republic** – named after the warlike Germanic Batavia tribe who inhabited the area around Nijmegen in classical times. As a result, the Dutch became, to all intents and purposes, part of the Napoleonic Empire and as such were obliged to wage

1853	1872	1890	1914
Vincent van Gogh born in a village near Breda.	Piet Mondrian born in Amersfoort; his father is a teacher.	Vincent van Gogh shoots himself – and dies 29 hours later.	The Netherlands stays neutral in World War I.

unenthusiastic war with England. In 1806, Napoleon appointed his brother **Louis** as king, but in the event Louis was not willing to allow the Netherlands to become a simple satellite of France; he ignored Napoleon's directives and after just four years of rule his brother forced Louis to abdicate. The country was then formally incorporated into the French Empire, and for three gloomy years suffered occupation and heavy taxation to finance French military adventures.

The United Kingdom of the Netherlands

Following Napoleon's disastrous retreat from Moscow, the Orangist faction surfaced to exploit weakening French control. In 1813, Frederick William, son of the exiled William V, returned to the country and eight months later, under the terms of the **Congress of Vienna** which concluded the Napoleonic Wars, was crowned King William I of the **United Kingdom of the Netherlands**, incorporating both the old United Provinces and the Spanish (Austrian) Netherlands. A strong-willed man, he spent much of the latter part of his life trying to control his disparate kingdom, but failed primarily because the Catholic south did not trust him. The southern provinces revolted against his rule and in 1830 the independent Kingdom of Belgium was proclaimed.

From 1830 to the early twentieth century

In 1839, a final fling of the military dice gave William most of Limburg, and all but ended centuries of territorial change within the Low Countries. The Netherlands benefited from this new stability both economically and politically, emerging as a unitary state with a burgeoning industrial and entrepôt economy. The outstanding political figure of the times, **Jan Rudolph Thorbecke**, formed three ruling cabinets (1849–53, 1862–66 and 1872, in the year of his death) and steered the Netherlands through these changes. The political parties of the late eighteenth century had wished to resurrect the power and prestige of the seventeenth-century Netherlands; Thorbecke and his allies resigned themselves to the country's reduced status and eulogized the advantages of being a small power. For the first time, from about 1850, liberty was seen as a luxury made possible by the country's very lack of power, and the malaise that had long disturbed public life gave way to a positive appreciation of the very narrowness of its national existence. One of the results of Thorbecke's liberalism was a gradual extension of the franchise, culminating in the **Act of Universal Suffrage** of 1917.

RANDOM THOUGHTS FROM THE NETHERLANDS

"I can't understand it. I can't even understand the people who can understand it" (Queen Juliana).

"I dream of painting and then I paint my dream" (Vincent van Gogh).

"This player heard the clock tick, but doesn't know what time it is…" (Johan Cruyff, who is famous for his gnomic statements).

"The Dutch are always right but seldom relevant" (EU diplomat at an EU summit meeting).

"To play Holland, you have to play the Dutch" (Another Dutch football manager reaches for the truth – this one is Ruud Gullit).

1917	1932	1940	1944/5
Dutch Parliament passes the Act of Universal Suffrage.	Afsluitdijk completed separating the old Zuider Zee (now the IJsselmeer) from the North Sea.	The Germans occupy the Netherlands in World War II.	Allied forces liberate the Netherlands, but the Dutch starve in the Winter of Hunger (Hongerwinter).

The war years

The Netherlands remained neutral in **World War I** and although it suffered privations from the Allied blockade of German war materials, this was offset by the profits accrued by continuing to trade with both sides. Similar attempts to remain neutral in **World War II** failed: the Germans invaded on May 10, 1940, destroying Rotterdam four days later, a salutary lesson that made prolonged resistance inconceivable. The Dutch army was quickly overwhelmed, Queen Wilhelmina fled to London to set up a government-in-exile, and members of the **NSB**, the Dutch fascist party, which had welcomed the invaders, were rewarded with positions of authority. Nevertheless, in the early stages of the occupation, life for the average Netherlander went on pretty much as usual, which is just what the Germans wanted – they were determined to transform the country by degrees. Even when the first roundups of the **Jews** began in late 1940, many managed to turn a blind eye, though the newly outlawed Dutch Communist Party did organize a widely supported strike to protest, a gesture perhaps, but an important one all the same.

As the war progressed, so the German grip got tighter and the Dutch **Resistance** stronger, its activities focused on destroying German supplies and munitions as well as the forgery of identity papers, a real Dutch speciality. The Resistance also trumpeted its efforts in a battery of underground newspapers, most notably *Het Parool* (The Password), which survives today. Inevitably, the Resistance paid a heavy price with some 23,000 of its fighters and sympathizers losing their lives, but Amsterdam's Jews took the worst punishment: in 1940, Amsterdam's Jewish population, swollen by refugees from Hitler's Germany, was around 140,000, but by the end of the war there were only a few thousand left, rendering the old Jewish quarter – the Jodenhoek – deserted and derelict.

Operation Market Garden

Liberation began from the south in the autumn of 1944. To speed the process, the Allies determined on **Operation Market Garden**, an ambitious plan to finish the war quickly by creating an Allied corridor stretching from Eindhoven to Arnhem. If it had been successful, the Allies would have secured control of the country's three main rivers and been able to drive on into Germany, thereby isolating the occupying forces in the western Netherlands. On September 17, 1944, the 1st Airborne Division parachuted into the countryside around Oosterbeek, a small village near the most northerly target of the operation, the **bridge at Arnhem**. However, German opposition was much stronger than expected and after heavy fighting the paratroopers could only take the northern end of the bridge. The advancing British army was unable to break through fast enough, and after four days the decimated battalion defending the bridge was forced to withdraw.

With the failure of Operation Market Garden, the Allies were obliged to resort to more orthodox military tactics. In their push towards Germany, they slowly cleared the east and south of the country in the winter and spring of 1944–45, leaving the coastal provinces pretty much untouched, though here lack of food and fuel created desperate conditions, with hundreds starving to death. Finally, on **May 5, 1945**, the remains of the German army in the Netherlands surrendered to the Canadians at Wageningen.

1944	1947	1953	1963
Betrayal and capture of Anne Frank in Amsterdam.	Johan Cruyff, arguably the greatest European footballer of all time, born in Amsterdam.	Hundreds die when the country's sea defences are breached; the Dutch pause for thought – and plan the Delta Project.	Jasper Grootveld kick-starts the playful/anarchist movement that sweeps the country's youth.

Postwar development

The **postwar years** were spent patching up the damage of occupation and liberation: Rotterdam was rebuilt in double-quick time, the dykes blown during the war were speedily repaired, and the canals and waterways were soon cleared of their accumulated debris. At the same time, the country began a vast construction programme, with modern suburbs mushrooming around every major city, especially Amsterdam, where almost all the land projected for use by the year 2000 was in fact used by 1970. The late 1940s and early 1950s saw an ill-advised colonial adventure, which could not prevent the Dutch from losing control of their principal Asian colonies, which were incorporated as **Indonesia**, in 1950.

Back home, **tragedy** struck on February 1, 1953, when an unusually high tide was pushed over Zeeland's sea defences by a westerly wind, flooding around 150 square kilometres of land and drowning over 1800 people. The response was to secure the area's future with the **Delta Project**, closing off the western part of the Scheldt and Maas estuaries with massive sea dykes. A brilliant and graceful piece of engineering, the main storm surge barrier on the Oosterschelde was finally completed in 1986. Amsterdam itself had already been secured by the completion of the **Afsluitdijk** between Noord-Holland and Friesland in 1932. This dyke separated the North Sea from the former Zuider Zee, which now became the freshwater **IJsselmeer**, and in 1976 a second dyke was added, carving the Markermeer from the IJsselmeer.

Counter-culture

The radical and youthful mass movements that swept across the West in the 1960s transformed Amsterdam from a middling, rather conservative city into a turbo-charged hotbed of hippy action – and where Amsterdam led, all the big cities of the Randstad followed. Initially, it was the Provos (see box, p.334) who led the counter-cultural charge, but in 1967 they dissolved themselves and many of their supporters moved on to the **squatter movement**, which opposed the wholesale destruction of low-cost (often old) urban housing as envisaged by many municipal councils. For many squatters, it seemed as if local councils were neglecting the needs of their poorer citizens in favour of business interests, and in Amsterdam, the epicentre of the movement, there were regular confrontations between the police and protestors at a handful of symbolic squats. The first major incident came in Amsterdam in March 1980 when several hundred police evicted squatters from premises on **Vondelstraat**. Afterwards there was widespread rioting, but this was small beer in comparison with the protests of April 30, 1980 – the **coronation day of Queen Beatrix** – when a mixed bag of squatters and leftists vigorously protested both the lavishness of the proceedings and the expense of refurbishing Beatrix's palace in Den Haag. Once again there was widespread rioting and this time it spread to other Dutch cities, though the unrest was short-lived.

At its peak, Amsterdam's squatter movement boasted around ten thousand activists, many of whom were involved in two more major confrontations with the police – the first at the Lucky Luyk squat, on Jan Luykenstraat, the second at the Wyers building in February 1984, when the squatters were forcibly cleared to make way for a hotel. Thereafter, the movement faded away, partly because of its failure to stop the developers, who could now claim, with limited justification, to be sensitive to community needs.

1975

Soft drugs (partly) decriminalized and the Netherlands wins the Eurovision contest with the timeless *Ding-a-dong* (or in Dutch *Ding dinge dong*), sung by Teach-In.

1976

Another decade, another dyke: the Houtribdijk dyke carves the Markemeer from the IJsselmeer.

THE PROVOS

In 1963, one-time window cleaner and magician extraordinaire **Jasper Grootveld** won celebrity status by painting "K" – for *kanker* ("cancer") – on cigarette billboards throughout Amsterdam. His actions inspired others, most notably **Roel van Duyn**, a philosophy student at Amsterdam University, who set up a left-wing-cum-anarchist movement known as the **Provos** – short for *provocatie* ("provocation") – and organized street "**happenings**" that proved fantastically popular among young Amsterdammers. The number of Provos never exceeded about thirty and the group had no coherent structure, but they did have one clear aim – to bring points of political or social conflict to public attention. More than anything they were masters of publicity, and pursued their "games" with a spirit of fun, promoting policies such as the popular **white bicycle plan**, which proposed that the council ban all cars in the city centre and supply 20,000 white bicycles for public use.

There were regular police–Provo confrontations, but it was the **wedding of Princess Beatrix** to Claus von Amsberg on March 10, 1966, that provoked the most serious unrest. Amsberg had served in the German army during World War II and many Netherlanders were offended by the marriage. Consequently, when hundreds took to the streets to protest, pelting the wedding procession with smoke bombs, a huge swathe of Dutch opinion supported them. Amsberg himself was jeered with the refrain "Give us back the bicycles", a reference to the commandeering of hundreds of bikes by the retreating German army in 1945. In June 1966, the students, workers and Provos looked likely to combine forces in protest at the government. In panic, the Hague politicians ordered the dismissal of Amsterdam's police chief, but in the event the Provos support had peaked and the workers proved far from revolutionary, settling for arbitration on their various complaints instead.

Into the twenty-first century

Throughout the 1990s, the country's street protests and major squats became a distant memory, though some of the old ideals were carried forward by the **Greens**, who attracted – and continue to attract – a small but significant following in every national election. One of the recurring political problems was the country's finely balanced system of **proportional representation**: time and again major issues became mired in long inter-party wheeling and dealing and politics often appeared little more than a bland business conducted by a disconnected political class.

In April 2002, this political class was deeply embarrassed by the publication of a damning report on the failure of the Dutch army to protect the **Bosnian Muslims** ensconced in the UN safe haven of **Srebrenica** in 1995. The report told a tale of extraordinary incompetence: the UN's Dutch soldiers were inadequately armed but refused American assistance, and watched as Serb troops separated Muslim men and women in preparation for the mass executions, which the Dutch soldiers did nothing to stop (though they were never involved). In a country that prides itself on its internationalism, the report was an especially hard blow and the whole of the Socialist PvdA-led government, under **Wim Kok**, resigned almost immediately – coincidentally in the same year as the Netherlands dropped the guilder in favour of the **euro**.

The rise and fall of Pim Fortuyn

In the national elections of May 2002, the three main parties suffered a shock when a new Rightist grouping – **Lijst Pim Fortuyn (LPF)** – swept to second place, securing

1980	**1984**	**1986**
The coronation of Queen Beatrix is marked by mass protests against the lavishness of the proceedings.	The last mass squat in Amsterdam meets a troublesome end.	The major part of the Delta Project is completed; the Dutch hope their western coast is secure from the perils of the sea.

seventeen percent of the national vote. The LPF was named after its founder and leader, Rotterdam's **Pim Fortuyn**, who was murdered a few days before the election by Volkert van der Graaf, an animal rights activist who claimed to have killed Fortuyn to stop him exploiting Muslims as scapegoats. Stylish and witty, openly gay, a pipe smoker and a former Marxist, Fortuyn was an important figure, who managed to cover several popular bases, from the need for law and order through to tighter immigration controls. Most crucially, he also attacked the liberal establishment's espousal of **multiculturalism** on the grounds that some representatives of minority ethnic groups were deeply reactionary, anti-gay and sexist. Politically, it worked a treat, but in the event Fortuyn's assassination holed the LPF, which rapidly unravelled, breaking up the governing coalition and then losing most of its seats in the general election of January 2003.

The murder of Theo van Gogh

The general election of 2003 saw a **Rightist alliance** – led by the right-of-centre VVD and the Catholic–Protestant CDA coalition – cobble together an administration under the leadership of **Jan Peter Balkenende**, a plain-speaking Harry Potter lookalike, described by a leading newspaper as "dull but 200 percent reliable". Superficially, therefore, it seemed that normal political service had been resumed, but there was an uneasy undertow, with Fortuyn's popularity pushing certain issues, particularly **immigration**, to the right. The situation got much worse – and race relations more tense – when, in late 2004, the film-maker **Theo van Gogh** was shot dead on an Amsterdam street by a Moroccan who objected to a film he had made "*Submission*" about Islamic violence against women. Sensing the danger, Amsterdam city council in general – and the mayor, **Job Cohen**, in particular – handled the situation with great aplomb, coining the slogan "keeping things together" (*de boel bij elkaar houden*) and organizing several, candlelit vigils.

AYAAN HIRSI ALI

Shown on Dutch TV in 2004, Theo van Gogh's film *Submission* was scripted by **Ayaan Hirsi Ali**, a one-time Somali refugee, who had successfully sought asylum in the Netherlands in 1992. Hirsi Ali progressed through Dutch society, obtaining a degree at Leiden University, working as a translator and becoming an MP for the VVD in 2003. She renounced Islam in 2002 and thereafter received death threats, obliging her to seek police protection and even forcing her into hiding. Hirsi Ali refused to be cowed and her pronouncements on Islam were hard-hitting and headline-grabbing. In an interview with the UK's *Daily Telegraph* in December 2004, she said: "But tell me why any Muslim man would want Islamic women to be educated and emancipated? Would a Roman voluntarily have given up his slaves?". Unfortunately for Hirsi Ali, she was engulfed by controversy of a different kind in 2006, when it turned out that her **application for asylum** had not been entirely truthful. Some supported Hirsi Ali, others argued that she should be stripped of her parliamentary seat, and the furore brought the governing coalition down amid an avalanche of mud-slinging. In the meantime, Hirsi Ali decided to parachute out of the whole mess, taking up a position in a conservative think-tank in Washington DC. Her autobiography, *Infidel*, was published in September 2006.

1990	2001
The World Cup: Frank Rijkaard, one of the Netherlands finest footballers, does a long-range spit at the German Rudi Völler that is famed for its accuracy; commentators suitably appalled.	The Netherlands is the first country in the world to recognize same-sex marriages.

To the present day

After the Ayaan Hirsi Ali crisis brought the government down (see box, p.335), the **national election of November 2006** saw modest gains for the far right and left, but not enough to unseat Balkenende, who proceeded to weld together yet another coalition. This unwieldy alliance did its best to cope with the banking crisis of 2008, when the government nationalized failing parts of the banking industry at huge cost to the taxpayer: there is now wide agreement that Dutch banks should be kept under much tighter legislative control with savings ultimately separated from speculation.

The coalition held together until February 2010, when the PvdA refused to prolong the Dutch army's engagement in Afghanistan and, in the ensuing elections, Mark Rutte, the leader of the VVD, became the Prime Minister in a minority administration in coalition with the CDA and with the tacit support of a newly emergent right-wing party the **Partij voor de Vrijheid** (Party For Freedom; PVV), which took fifteen percent of the popular vote under the leadership of Geert Wilders. The coalition didn't last long, however: in April 2012, Wilders stormed out of a meeting, refusing to support the government's plan to slice €16bn off the national budget. At time of writing, new elections are scheduled for September 2012.

Into the future

The PVV's leader **Geert Wilders** is a controversial and outspoken Eurosceptic whose views on Islam are regarded by many as being inflammatory: his combustible provocations – such as "I don't hate Muslims, I hate Islam" – seem to promise a bumpy ride ahead. However, he is obviously tapping a populist vein, and the general sense of angst that comes from the gap between how the Dutch conceive themselves and how things seem to be turning out. The vast majority want their country to be liberal and tolerant, and yet there are undoubtedly racial tensions; nearly everyone wants the Netherlands to be prosperous, and yet they have been stung by the worldwide recession; and while most of the Dutch are still proud of the progressive social policies they introduced in the 1960s and 1970s, these very policies are not wearing too well. The best illustration is in Amsterdam, where the country's liberal attitude to **soft drugs and prostitution** may once have seemed sane and pragmatic, but the result has been to turn the city into a target for thousands of tourists hell-bent on pursuing the city's twin indulgences. To a solid bloc of Amsterdammers, the Red Light District now seems unpleasant, if not downright offensive, and beginning in 2007 the city council began to reduce its size and curb its excesses. Neither have the country's coffeeshops avoided attention: Maastricht has banned most foreigners from using the city's coffeeshops and the rest of the country may follow suit – or may not: there has been endless discussion on the subject, both in the courts and among politicians. Other Netherlanders have simply given up and are voting with their feet: in 2011, 133,000 mostly middle-class Dutch citizens emigrated, one of the largest numbers ever.

2002	2004	2007	2012
Controversial politician Pim Fortuyn is assassinated.	Film-maker Theo van Gogh is murdered on an Amsterdam street.	Amsterdam city council moves to restrict and reduce its Red Light District.	The upstanding Job Cohen resigns as leader of the Labour Party (the PvdA).

Art

The following is the very briefest of introductions to a subject that has rightly filled volumes. Inevitably, it covers artists that lived and worked in both the Netherlands and Belgium, as these two countries have – along with Luxembourg – been bound together as the "**Low Countries**" for most of their history.

Beginnings: the Flemish Primitives

Throughout the medieval period, **Flanders**, in modern-day Belgium, was one of the most artistically productive parts of Europe, and it was here that the realist base of later Dutch painting developed. Today, the works of these early Flemish painters, the **Flemish Primitives**, are highly prized, and although examples are fairly sparse in the Netherlands, all the leading museums – especially Amsterdam's Rijksmuseum and Den Haag's Mauritshuis – have a healthy sample.

  Jan van Eyck (1385–1441) is generally regarded as the first of the Flemish Primitives, and has even been credited with the invention of oil painting – though it seems more likely that he simply perfected a new technique by thinning his paint with turpentine (at the time a new discovery), thus making it more flexible. The most famous of his works still in the Low Countries is the altarpiece in Belgium's Ghent Cathedral, which was revolutionary in its realism, for the first time using elements of native landscape in depicting biblical themes. Van Eyck's style and technique were to influence several generations of the region's artists.

Bouts and Goes

One of the most talented painters of his generation, **Dieric Bouts** (1415–75) was born in Haarlem but active in (Belgium's) Leuven. Bouts is recognizable by his stiff, rather elongated figures and penchant for horrific subject matter – the tortures of damnation for example – all set against carefully drawn landscapes. **Hugo van der Goes** (d.1482) was the next Ghent master after van Eyck, most famous for the Portinari altarpiece in Florence's Uffizi gallery. Van der Goes died insane and his later works have strong hints of his impending madness in their subversive use of space and implicit acceptance of the viewer's presence.

Memling, David and Bosch

Active in Bruges throughout his life, **Hans Memling** (1440–94) is best remembered for the pastoral charm of his landscapes and the quality of his portraiture, much of which survives on the rescued side panels of triptychs. **Gerard David** (1460–1523) was a native of Oudewater, near Gouda, but he moved to Bruges in 1484, becoming the last of the great painters to work in that city, producing formal religious works of traditional bent. Strikingly different, but broadly contemporaneous, was **Hieronymus Bosch** (1450–1516), who lived for most of his life in the Netherlands, though his style is linked to that of his Flemish contemporaries. His frequently reprinted religious allegories are filled with macabre visions of tortured people and grotesque beasts, and appear faintly unhinged at first, though it's now thought that these are visual representations of contemporary sayings, idioms and parables. While their interpretation is far from resolved, Bosch's paintings draw strongly on subconscious fears and archetypes, giving them a lasting, haunting fascination.

The sixteenth century

At the end of the fifteenth century, Flanders was in economic and political decline and the leading artists of the day were drawn instead to the booming port of **Antwerp**, also in present-day Belgium. The artists who worked here soon began to integrate the finely observed detail that characterized the Flemish tradition with the style of the Italian painters of the Renaissance. **Quentin Matsys** (1464–1530) introduced florid classical architectural details and intricate landscapes to his works, influenced perhaps by the work of Leonardo da Vinci. As well as religious works, he painted portraits and genre scenes, all of which have recognizably Italian facets – and in the process he paved the way for the Dutch genre painters of later years. **Jan Gossaert** (1478–1532) made the pilgrimage to Italy too, and his dynamic works are packed with detail, especially finely drawn classical architectural backdrops. He was the first Low Countries artist to introduce the subjects of classical mythology into his paintings, part of a steady trend towards secular subject matter.

The Bruegels

The middle of the sixteenth century was dominated by the work of **Pieter Bruegel the Elder** (c.1525–69), whose gruesome allegories and innovative interpretations of religious subjects are firmly placed in Low Countries settings. Pieter also painted exquisitely observed peasant scenes, though he himself was well connected in court circles in Antwerp and, later, Brussels. **Pieter Aertsen** (1508–75) also worked in the peasant genre, adding aspects of still life; his paintings often show a detailed kitchen scene in the foreground, with a religious episode going on behind. Bruegel's two sons, **Pieter Bruegel the Younger** (1564–1638) and **Jan Bruegel** (1568–1625), were lesser painters; the former produced fairly insipid copies of his father's work, while Jan developed a style of his own – delicately rendered flower paintings and genre pieces that earned him the nickname "Velvet". Towards the latter half of the sixteenth century highly stylized Italianate portraits became the dominant fashion, with **Frans Pourbus the Younger** (1569–1622) the leading practitioner. Frans hobnobbed across Europe, working for the likes of the Habsburgs and the Medicis.

The Dutch emerge

Meanwhile, there were artistic rumblings in the province of Holland. Leading the painterly charge was **Geertgen tot Sint Jans** (Little Gerard of the Brotherhood of St John; d.1490), who worked in Haarlem, initiating – in a strangely naive style – an artistic vision that would come to dominate Dutch painting in the seventeenth century. There was a tender melancholy in his work, which was very different from the stylized paintings produced in Flanders, and, most importantly, a new sensitivity to light. **Jan Mostaert** (1475–1555) took over after Geertgen's death, developing similar themes, but the first painter to effect real changes in northern painting was Leiden's **Lucas van Leyden** (1489–1533). Leyden's bright colours and narrative technique were refreshingly novel, and he introduced a new dynamism into what had become a rigidly formal treatment of devotional subjects. There was rivalry, of course. Eager to publicize Haarlem as the artistic capital of the northern Netherlands, **Karel van Mander** claimed **Jan van Scorel** (1495–1562) as the better painter, complaining, too, of van Leyden's dandyish ways. Certainly van Scorel's influence should not be underestimated. Like many of his contemporaries, van Scorel hotfooted it to Italy to view the works of the Renaissance, but in Rome his career went into overdrive when he found favour with Pope Hadrian VI, one-time bishop of Utrecht, who installed him as court painter in 1520. Van Scorel stayed in Rome for four years and when he returned to Utrecht, armed with all that papal prestige, he combined the ideas he had picked up in Italy with those underpinning Haarlem realism, thereby modifying what had previously been an independent artistic tradition once and for all. Among his several students, probably the most talented was **Maerten van Heemskerck** (1498–1574), who duly went off to Italy himself in 1532, staying there for five years before doubling back to Haarlem.

The Golden Age

The seventeenth century begins with **Karel van Mander** (1548–1606), Haarlem painter, art impresario and one of the few contemporary chroniclers of the art of the Low Countries. His *Schilderboek* of 1604 put Flemish and Dutch traditions into context for the first time, and in addition specified the rules of fine painting. Examples of his own work are rare – though Haarlem's Frans Hals Museum (see p.107) weighs in with a couple – but his followers were many. Among them was **Cornelius Cornelisz van Haarlem** (1562–1638), who produced elegant renditions of biblical and mythical themes; and **Hendrik Goltzius** (1558–1616), who was a skilled engraver and an integral member of van Mander's Haarlem academy. The enthusiasm these painters had for Italian art, combined with the influence of a late revival of Gothicism, resulted in works that combined **Mannerist** and **Classical** elements. An interest in realism was also felt, but, for them, the subject became less important than the way in which it was depicted: biblical stories became merely a vehicle whereby artists could apply their skills in painting the human body, landscapes, or copious displays of food. All of this served to break the religious stranglehold on art, and make legitimate a whole range of everyday subjects for the painter.

In what is now the Netherlands (and this was where the north and the south finally diverged) this break with tradition was compounded by the **Reformation**: the austere Calvinism that had replaced the Catholic faith in the United Provinces had no use for images or symbols of devotion in its churches. Instead, painters catered to the burgeoning middle class, and no longer visited (Catholic) Italy to learn their craft. Indeed, the real giants of the seventeenth century – Hals, Rembrandt, Vermeer – stayed in the Netherlands all their lives. Another innovation was that painting split into more distinct categories – genre, portrait, landscape – and artists tended (with notable exceptions) to confine themselves to one field throughout their careers.

Historical and religious painting

The artistic influence of Renaissance Italy may have been in decline, but Italian painters still had clout with the Dutch, most notably **Caravaggio** (1571–1610), who was much admired for his new realism. Taking Caravaggio's cue, many artists – Rembrandt for one – continued to portray classical subjects, but in a way that was totally at odds with the Mannerists' stylish flights of imagination. The Utrecht artist **Abraham Bloemaert** (1564–1651), though a solid Mannerist throughout his career, encouraged these new ideas, and his students – **Gerard van Honthorst** (1590–1656), **Hendrik Terbrugghen** (1588–1629) and **Dirck van Baburen** (1590–1624) – formed the nucleus of the influential **Utrecht School**, which followed Caravaggio almost to the point of slavishness. Honthorst was perhaps the leading figure, learning his craft from Bloemaert and travelling to Rome, where he was nicknamed "Gerardo delle Notti" for his ingenious handling of light and shade. In his later paintings, however, this was to become more routine technique than inspired invention, and though a supremely competent artist, Honthorst is somewhat discredited among critics today. Terbrugghen's reputation seems to have aged rather better; he soon developed a more individual style, with his later, lighter work having a great influence on the young Vermeer. After a jaunt to Rome, Baburen shared a studio with Terbrugghen and produced some fairly original work – work which also had some influence on Vermeer – but today he is the least studied member of the group and few of his paintings survive.

Without doubt, however, **Rembrandt** (see box, p.340) was the most original historical artist of the seventeenth century, also chipping in with religious paintings throughout his career. In the 1630s, Huygens procured for him his greatest commission – a series of five paintings of the Passion, beautifully composed and uncompromisingly realistic. Later, however, Rembrandt drifted away from the mainstream, ignoring the smooth brushwork of his contemporaries and choosing instead a rougher, darker and more disjointed style for his biblical and historical subjects. Throughout his career

REMBRANDT VAN RIJN

The gilded reputation of **Rembrandt van Rijn** (1606–69) is still relatively recent, but he is now justly regarded as one of the greatest and most versatile painters of all time. Born in Leiden, the son of a miller, he was a boy apprentice to local artist Jacob van Swanenburgh, before heading to Amsterdam to study under the fashionable Pieter Lastman. Soon he was painting commissions for the city elite and became an accepted member of their circle, with the poet and statesman **Constantijn Huygens** acting as his agent. In 1634, Rembrandt married **Saskia van Uylenburgh**, daughter of the burgomaster of Leeuwarden and quite a catch for a relatively humble artist. Five years later, the couple moved into a smart house on Jodenbreestraat, now the Rembrandthuis museum (see p.69), though these years were marred by the death of all but one of his children in infancy, the sole survivor being his much-loved **Titus** (1641–68).

In 1642 Rembrandt produced his most celebrated painting, **The Night Watch**, on display in the Amsterdam Rijksmuseum (see p.75), but thereafter his career went into decline, essentially because he forsook portraiture to focus on increasingly sombre and introspective **religious and historical works**. Traditionally, Rembrandt's change of direction has been linked to the death of Saskia in 1642, but he was also facing increased competition from a new batch of portrait artists, primarily Bartholomeus van der Helst, Ferdinand Bol and Govert Flinck. Whatever the reason, there were few takers for Rembrandt's later works, and in 1656 he was formally declared insolvent: four years later he was obliged to sell his house and goods, moving to much humbler premises in the Jordaan. By this time, he had a new cohabitee, **Hendrickje Stoffels** (a clause in Saskia's will prevented them from ever marrying), and in the early 1660s, she and Titus took Rembrandt in hand, sorting out his finances and his work schedule. With his money problems solved, a relieved Rembrandt then produced some of his finest paintings, emotionally deep and contemplative works with a rough finish, the paint often daubed with an almost trowel-like heaviness. One of his very last and most exquisite pictures, finished in 1668, is *The Jewish Bride*, now exhibited in Amsterdam's Rijksmuseum. Hendrickje died in 1663 and Titus in 1668, a year before his father.

Rembrandt maintained a large studio, and his influence extended to the next generation of Dutch painters. Some – Dou and Maes (see p.341) – were famous for their genre work, others turned to portraiture (see p.342).

Genre painting

The term **genre painting** initially applied to everything from animal paintings and still lifes through to historical works and landscapes, but later – from around the middle of the seventeenth century – referred only to **scenes of everyday life**. Its target market was the region's burgeoning middle class, who had a penchant for non-idealized portrayals of common scenes, both with and without symbols – or subtly disguised details – making one moral point or another. One of its early practitioners was Antwerp's **Frans Snijders** (1579–1657), who took up still-life painting where Aertsen (see p.338) left off, amplifying his subject – food and drink – to even larger, more sumptuous canvases. Snijders also doubled up as a member of the Rubens art machine (see p.334), painting animals and still-life sections for the master's works. In Utrecht, Hendrik Terbrugghen and Gerard van Honthorst adapted the realism and strong chiaroscuro learned from Caravaggio to a number of tableaux of everyday life, though they were more concerned with religious works (see p.339), while Haarlem's Frans Hals dabbled in genre too, but is better known as a portraitist. The opposite is true of one of Hal's pupils, **Adriaen Brouwer** (1605–38), whose riotous tavern scenes were well received in their day and collected by, among others, Rubens and Rembrandt. Brouwer spent only a couple of years in Haarlem under Hals before returning to his native Flanders, where he influenced the inventive **David Teniers the Younger** (1610–90), who worked in Antwerp and later in Brussels. Teniers' early paintings are Brouwer-like peasant scenes, although his later work is more delicate and diverse, including *kortegaardje*

– guardroom scenes that show soldiers carousing. **Adriaen van Ostade** (1610–85), on the other hand, stayed in Haarlem most of his life, skilfully painting groups of peasants and tavern brawls – though his later acceptance by the establishment led him to water down the realism he had learnt from Brouwer. He was teacher to his brother **Isaak** (1621–49), who produced a large number of open-air peasant scenes, subtle combinations of genre and landscape work.

Jan Steen

The English critic E.V. Lucas dubbed Teniers, Brouwer and Ostade "coarse and boorish" compared with **Jan Steen** (1625–79) who, along with Vermeer, is probably the most admired Dutch genre painter. Steen's paintings offer the same Rabelaisian peasantry in full fling, but they go their debauched ways in broad daylight, and nowhere do you see the filthy rogues favoured by Brouwer and Ostade. Steen offers more humour, too, as well as more moralizing, identifying with the hedonistic mob and reproaching them at the same time. Indeed, many of his pictures are illustrations of well-known contemporary proverbs – popular epithets on the evils of drink or the transience of human existence that were supposed to teach as well as entertain.

Gerrit Dou, his students and Nicholas Maes

Leiden's **Gerrit Dou** (1613–75) was one of Rembrandt's first pupils. It's difficult to detect any trace of the master's influence in his work, however, as Dou initiated a (genre) style of his own: tiny, minutely realized and beautifully finished views of a kind of ordinary life that was decidedly more genteel than Brouwer's – or even Steen's for that matter. He was admired, above all, for his painstaking attention to detail and he would, it's said, sit in his studio for hours waiting for the dust to settle before starting work. Among Dou's students, **Frans van Mieris** (1635–81) continued the highly finished portrayals of the Dutch bourgeoisie, as did **Gabriel Metsu** (1629–67) – perhaps Dou's most talented pupil – whose pictures often convey an overtly moral message. Another pupil of Rembrandt's, though a much later one, was **Nicholas Maes** (1629–93), whose early works were almost entirely genre paintings, sensitively executed and with an obvious didacticism. His later paintings show the influence of a more refined style of portraiture, which he had picked up in France.

Gerard ter Borch and Pieter de Hooch

As a native of Zwolle, **Gerard ter Borch** (1619–81) remained very much a provincial painter, despite trips to most of Europe's artistic capitals. He depicted the country's merchant class at play and became renowned for his curious doll-like figures and his ability to capture the textures of different cloths. His domestic scenes were not unlike those of **Pieter de Hooch** (1629–84), whose simple depictions of everyday life are deliberately unsentimental and have little or no moral commentary. De Hooch's favourite trick was to paint darkened rooms with an open door leading through to a sunlit courtyard, a practice that, along with his trademark rusty-red colour, makes his work easy to identify and, at its best, exquisite. That said, his later pictures lose their spartan quality, reflecting the increasing opulence of the Dutch Republic; the rooms are more richly decorated, the arrangements more contrived and the subjects less homely.

Johannes Vermeer

It was **Johannes Vermeer** (1632–75) who brought the most sophisticated methods to painting interiors, depicting the play of natural light on indoor surfaces with superlative skill – and the tranquil intimacy for which he is now famous the world over. Another observer of the well-heeled Dutch household and, like de Hooch, without a moral tone, he is regarded (with Hals and Rembrandt) as one of the big three Dutch painters – though he was, it seems, a slow worker. As a result, only about forty paintings can be attributed to him with any certainty. Living all his life in Delft,

Vermeer is perhaps the epitome of the seventeenth-century Dutch painter – rejecting the pomp and ostentation of the High Renaissance to record quietly his contemporaries at home, painting for a public that demanded no more than that: bourgeois art at its most complete.

Portraiture

Predictably enough, the ruling bourgeoisie of the United Provinces was keen to record and celebrate its success, and consequently portraiture was a reliable way for a young painter to make a living. **Michiel Jansz Miereveld** (1567–1641), court painter to Frederick Henry of Orange-Nassau in Den Haag, was the first real portraitist of the Dutch Republic, but it wasn't long before his stiff and rather conservative figures were superseded by the more spontaneous renderings of **Frans Hals** (1585–1666). Hals is perhaps best known for his "corporation pictures" – group portraits of the Dutch civil guard regiments that had been formed in most of the larger towns during the war with Spain, but subsequently became social clubs. These large group pieces demanded superlative technique, since the painter had to create a collection of individual portraits, and accord prominence based on the relative importance of the sitters and the size of the payment each had made. Hals also painted many individual portraits, making fleeting and telling expressions his trademark; his pictures of children are particularly sensitive. Later in life, however, his work became darker and more akin to Rembrandt's, spurred – it's conjectured – by his penury. **Rembrandt's early portraits** and self-portraits show the confident face of security, when he was on top of things and sure of his direction. While he would not always be the darling of the Amsterdam burghers, his fall from grace was still some way off when he completed *The Night Watch* (see p.75), a group portrait whose fluent arrangement of his subjects was almost entirely original.

Rembrandt's pupils

The early work of **Ferdinand Bol** (1616–80) was heavily influenced by Rembrandt, so much so that for centuries art historians couldn't tell the two apart, though Bol's later paintings are readily distinguishable, blandly elegant portraits which proved very popular with the wealthy. At the age of 53, Bol married a rich widow and promptly hung up his easel. A one-time apprentice silk mercer, **Govert Flinck** (1615–60) was perhaps Rembrandt's most faithful follower and he was certainly held in high esteem by the city council, which commissioned him to produce eight paintings for Amsterdam's new town hall, though in the event Flinck died before he could start work. Like Bol, Flinck married into money and his best paintings date from the 1630s. Most of the pitifully scarce extant work of **Carel Fabritius** (1622–54) is portraiture, but he died young, before he could properly realize his promise as probably the most gifted of all Rembrandt's students. Generally regarded as the teacher of Vermeer, he forms a link between the two masters, combining Rembrandt's technique with his own practice of painting figures against a dark background, prefiguring the lighting and colouring of Vermeer.

Landscapes

Aside from Pieter Bruegel the Elder (see p.338), whose depictions of his native surroundings make him the first true Low Countries landscape painter, **Gillis van Coninxloo** (1544–1607) stands out as the earliest Dutch landscapist. He imbued his native scenery with elements of fantasy, painting the richly wooded views he had seen on his travels around Europe as backdrops to biblical scenes. In the early seventeenth century, **Hercules Seghers** (1590–1638), apprenticed to van Coninxloo, carried on his mentor's style of depicting forested and mountainous landscapes, some real, others not; his work is scarce but is believed to have had considerable influence on the landscape work of Rembrandt himself. **Esaias van der Velde**'s (1591–1632) quaint and unpretentious scenes show the first real affinity with the Dutch countryside, but while his influence was likewise considerable, he was soon overshadowed by his pupil **Jan van**

THE GOLDEN AGE: THE DUTCH ARTIST AS SPECIALIST

Most of the leading Dutch painters of the seventeenth century could, if push came to shove, try their brush at pretty much anything, but some preferred to specialize. Among them, **Paulus Potter** (1625–54) came up trumps with his animals, producing a string of lovingly executed paintings of cows and horses. **Pieter Saenredam** (1597–1665), on the other hand, zoned in on architecture, becoming famous for his finely realized paintings of Dutch church interiors, as did **Emanuel de Witte** (1616–92), though his churches lack the austere crispness of the former. Haarlem's **Gerrit Berckheyde**'s (1638–98) interest was architecture too, but he limited his views to the outside of buildings, painting glossy townscapes with a precise eye and cool detachment. Nautical scenes in praise of the Dutch navy were the speciality of **Willem van der Velde II** (1633–1707), whose melodramatic canvases, complete with churning seas and chasing skies, are a delight. Two Haarlem painters dominated the field of still life – **Pieter Claesz** (1598–1660) and **Willem Heda** (1594–1680) – in which objects were gathered together to remind the viewer of the transience of human life and the meaninglessness of worldly pursuits. Thus, a skull would often be shown alongside a book, pipe or goblet, and some half-eaten food.

Goyen (1596–1656), a remarkable painter who belongs to the so-called "**tonal phase**" of Dutch landscape painting. Van Goyen's early pictures were highly coloured and close to those of his teacher, but it didn't take him long to develop a marked touch of his own, using tones of green, brown and grey to lend everything a characteristic translucent haze. A long-neglected artist, van Goyen only received recognition with the arrival of the Impressionists, when his fluid and rapid brushwork was at last fully appreciated.

Another "tonal" painter, Haarlem's **Salomon van Ruysdael** (1600–70) was also directly affected by Esaias van der Velde, and his simple and atmospheric, though not terribly adventurous, landscapes were for a long time consistently confused with those of van Goyen. More esteemed is his nephew, **Jacob van Ruysdael** (1628–82), generally considered the greatest of all Dutch landscapists, whose fastidiously observed views of quiet flatlands dominated by stormy skies were to influence European landscapists right up to the nineteenth century; John Constable certainly acknowledged a debt to him.

Rubens and his followers

Down in the south, in Antwerp, **Pieter Paul Rubens** (1577–1640) was easily the most important exponent of the Baroque in northern Europe. Born in Siegen, Westphalia, he was raised in Antwerp, where he entered the painters' guild in 1598. Two years later, he became court painter to the Duke of Mantua and thereafter he travelled extensively in Italy, absorbing the art of the High Renaissance and classical architecture. By the time of his return to Antwerp in 1608 he had acquired an enormous artistic vocabulary and, as with his Dutch contemporaries, the paintings of Caravaggio were to greatly influence his work. His first major success was *The Raising of the Cross*, painted in 1610 and displayed today in Antwerp cathedral. A large, dynamic work, it caused a sensation at the time, establishing Rubens' reputation and leading to a string of commissions that enabled him to set up his own studio.

The division of labour in **Rubens' studio** – and the talent of the artists working there (who included Anthony van Dyck and Jacob Jordaens) – ensured an extraordinary output of excellent work. The degree to which Rubens personally worked on a canvas would vary – and would determine its price. From the early 1620s onwards he turned his hand to a plethora of themes and subjects – religious works, portraits, tapestry designs, landscapes, mythological scenes, ceiling paintings – each exhibiting an acute **sense of light**, in association with colour and form. The drama in his works comes from the vigorous animation of his characters. His large-scale allegorical works, especially, are packed with heaving, writhing figures that appear to tumble out from the canvas.

In addition to his career as an artist, Rubens undertook diplomatic missions to Spain and England, and used these opportunities to study the works of other artists and – as in the case of Velázquez – to meet them personally. In the 1630s, **gout** began to hamper his activities, and his painting became more domestic and meditative. **Hélène Fourment**, his second wife, was the subject of many of these later portraits and she also served as a model for characters in his allegorical paintings, her figure epitomizing the buxom, well-rounded women found throughout his work.

Anthony van Dyck and Jacob Jordaens

Rubens' influence on the artists of the period was enormous. The huge output of his studio meant that his works were universally seen and also widely disseminated by the engravers he employed to copy his work. Chief among his followers was the portraitist **Anthony van Dyck** (1599–1641), who worked in Rubens' studio from 1618, often taking on the depiction of religious figures in his master's works, or at least those that required particular sensitivity and pathos. Eventually, van Dyck developed his own distinct style and technique, establishing himself as court painter to Charles I of England, and creating portraits of a nervous elegance that would influence the genre there for the next 150 years. **Jacob Jordaens** (1593–1678) was also an Antwerp native who studied under Rubens. Although he was commissioned to complete several works left unfinished by Rubens at the time of his death, his robustly naturalistic works have an earthy – and sensuous – realism that is quite different and distinct in style and technique.

The eighteenth century

In the eighteenth century, the Netherlands' economic decline was mirrored by a gradual deterioration in the quality and originality of Dutch painting. The subtle delicacies of the great paintings of the Golden Age were replaced by finicky still lifes and minute studies of flowers, or overly finessed portraiture and religious scenes: the work of **Adrian van der Werff** (1659–1722) is typical. Of the era's other big names, **Jacob de Wit** (1695–1754) painted burgher ceiling after ceiling in flashy style. He also benefited from a relaxation in the laws against Catholics, decorating several of their (newly legal) churches. The eighteenth century's only painter of any real talent was **Cornelis Troost** (1697–1750) who, although he didn't produce anything stunningly original, painted competent portraits and some neat, faintly satirical pieces that have since earned him the title of "The Dutch Hogarth". Cosy interiors also continued to prove popular, and the Haarlem painter **Wybrand Hendriks** (1744–1831) satisfied demand with numerous proficient examples.

The nineteenth century

Born in Overijssel, **Johann Barthold Jongkind** (1819–91) was the first important Dutch artist to emerge in the nineteenth century, painting landscapes and seascapes that were to influence Monet and the early Impressionists. He spent most of his life in France and his work was exhibited in Paris with the Barbizon painters, though he owed less to them than to van Goyen and the seventeenth-century "tonal" artists of the United Provinces. Jongkind's work was a logical precursor to the art of the **Hague School**. Based in and around Den Haag between 1870 and 1900, this prolific group of painters tried to re-establish a characteristically Dutch school of painting. They produced atmospheric studies of the dunes and polders around Den Haag, nature pictures that are characterized by grey, rain-filled skies, windswept seas, and silvery, flat beaches. **J.H. Weissenbruch** (1824–1903) was a founding member, a specialist in low, flat beach scenes dotted with stranded boats. The banker-turned-artist **H.W. Mesdag** (1831–1915) did the same but with more skill than imagination, while **Jacob Maris** (1837–99), one of three artist brothers, was perhaps the most typical, with his rural and sea scenes heavily covered by grey, chasing skies.

Anton Mauve (1838–88) is better known, an exponent of soft, pastel landscapes and an early teacher of van Gogh. Profoundly influenced by the French Barbizon painters – Corot, Millet et al – he went to Hilversum near Amsterdam in 1885 to set up his own group, which became known as the "**Dutch Barbizon**". **Jozef Israëls** (1826–1911) has often been likened to Millet, though it's generally agreed that he had more in common with the Impressionists, and his best pictures are his melancholy portraits and interiors. Lastly, **Johan Bosboom**'s (1817–91) church interiors may be said to sum up the romanticized nostalgia of the Hague School; shadowy and populated by figures in seventeenth-century dress, they seem to yearn for the country's Golden Age.

Very different, and slightly later, **Jan Toorop** (1858–1928) went through multiple artistic changes, radically adapting his technique from a fairly conventional pointillism through a tired Expressionism to Symbolism with an Art Nouveau feel. Roughly contemporary, **George Hendrik Breitner** (1857–1923) was a better painter, and one who refined his style rather than changed it. His snapshot-like impressions of his beloved Amsterdam figure among his best work.

Vincent van Gogh
Vincent van Gogh (1853–90) was one of the least "Dutch" of Dutch artists, and he spent most of his relatively short painting career in France. After countless studies of Dutch peasant life – studies which culminated in his sombre *Potato Eaters* – he went to live in Paris with his art-dealer brother Theo. There, under the influence of the Impressionists, he lightened his palette, following the pointillist work of Seurat and "trying to render intense colour and not a grey harmony". Two years later he went south to Arles, the "land of blue tones and gay colours", and, struck by the brilliance of the Mediterranean light, began to develop his characteristic style. A disastrous attempt to live with Gauguin, and the much-publicized episode in which he cut off part of his ear and presented it to a local prostitute, led to his committal in an asylum at St-Rémy. Here he produced some of his most famous, and most Expressionistic, canvases – strongly coloured and with the paint thickly, almost frantically, applied. Van Gogh is now one of the world's most popular – and popularized – painters, and Amsterdam's **Van Gogh Museum** has the world's finest collection of his work (see p.76).

Twentieth-century and contemporary art
The Netherlands today boasts a vibrant art scene with all the major cities possessing at least a couple of art galleries that showcase regular exhibitions of contemporary art. Among modern Dutch artists, look out for the abstract work of **Edgar Fernhout** (1912–74) and **Ad Dekkers** (1938–74); the reliefs of **Jan Schoonhoven** (1914–94); the multimedia productions of **Jan Dibbets** (b.1941); the imprecisely coloured geometric designs of **Rob van Koningsbruggen** (b.1948); the smeary Expressionism of **Toon Verhoef** (b.1946); the exuberant figures of **Rene Daniels** (b.1950); the exquisite realism of **Karel Buskes** (b.1962) and **Joke Frima** (b.1952); and the witty, hip furniture designs of **Piet Hein Eek** (b.1967) – to name just ten of the more important figures.

De Stijl and Piet Mondrian
Probably the Netherlands's most influential twentieth-century art movement – and the only specifically Dutch one – is **De Stijl** (The Style), whose leading proponent was **Piet Mondrian** (1872–1944). Mondrian developed the realism he had learned from the Hague School painters, via Cubism, into a complete abstraction of form which he called **Neo-Plasticism**. Mondrian was something of a mystic, and this was to some extent responsible for the direction that De Stijl – and his paintings – took: canvases painted with grids of lines and blocks made up of the three primary colours plus white, black and grey. Mondrian believed this freed his art from the vagaries of personal perception, making it possible to obtain what he called "a true vision of reality".

De Stijl took other forms too: there was a magazine of the same name, and the movement introduced new concepts into every aspect of design, from painting to interior design and architecture. But in all these media, lines were kept simple, colours bold and clear. **Theo van Doesburg** (1883–1931) was a De Stijl co-founder and major theorist. His work is similar to Mondrian's except for the noticeable absence of thick, black borders and for the diagonals that he introduced into his work, calling his paintings "contra-compositions" – which, he said, were both more dynamic and more in touch with the twentieth century. **Bart van der Leck** (1876–1958) was the third member of the circle, identifiable by white canvases covered by randomly placed interlocking coloured triangles. Mondrian split with De Stijl in 1925, going on to attain new artistic extremes of clarity and soberness before moving to New York in the 1940s and producing atypically exuberant works such as *Victory Boogie Woogie* – named for the artist's love of jazz and now owned by Den Haag's Gemeentemuseum (see p.158).

The Bergen School, De Ploeg and Magic Realism
During and after De Stijl, a number of other movements flourished in the Netherlands, though their impact was not so great and their influence was largely local. The Expressionist **Bergen School** was probably the most localized, its best-known exponent, **Charley Toorop** (1891–1955), daughter of Jan, developing a distinctively glaring but strangely sensitive realism. **De Ploeg** (The Plough), centred in Groningen, was headed by **Jan Wiegers** (1893–1959) and influenced by Ernst Ludwig Kirchner and the German Expressionists; the group's artists set out to capture the uninviting landscapes around their native town, and produced violently coloured canvases that hark back to van Gogh. Another group, known as the **Magic Realists**, surfaced in the 1930s, painting quasi-surrealistic scenes that, according to their leading light, **Carel Willink** (1900–83), revealed "a world stranger and more dreadful in its haughty impenetrability than the most terrifying nightmare".

CoBrA and Karel Appel
Postwar Dutch art began with **CoBrA** – a loose grouping of like-minded painters from Denmark, Belgium and the Netherlands, whose name derives from the initial letters of their respective capital cities. Their first exhibition at Amsterdam's Stedelijk Museum in 1949 provoked a furore, at the centre of which was **Karel Appel** (1921–2006), whose brutal abstract Expressionist pieces, plastered with paint inches thick, were, he maintained, necessary for the era – indeed, inevitable reflections of it. "I paint like a barbarian in a barbarous age," he claimed. In the graphic arts, the most famous twentieth-century Dutch figure was **Maurits Cornelis Escher** (1898–1972), whose Surrealistic illusions and allusions were underpinned by his fascination with mathematics. Many remain unconvinced by Escher, but the Dutch took a liking to his work and he now has his own museum in Den Haag (see p.155).

Books

Most of the books listed below are in print and in paperback, and those that are **out of print** (o/p) should be easy to track down either in secondhand bookshops or through Amazon's used and secondhand book service (ⓦamazon.co.uk or ⓦamazon.com). While we recommend all the books listed below, we have marked our particular favourites with ★.

AMSTERDAM

★ **Geert Mak** *Amsterdam: A Brief Life of the City.* First published in 1995, this infinitely readable trawl through the city's past is a simply wonderful book – amusing and perceptive, alternately tart and indulgent. It's more a social history than anything else, so – for example – it's here you'll find out quite why Rembrandt lived in the Jewish Quarter and why the city's merchant elite ossified in the eighteenth century. It's light and accessible enough to read from cover to cover, but its index of places makes it easy to dip into as well.

Heather Reyes (ed.) *City-Pick Amsterdam.* Enjoyable anthology of writing about Amsterdam, including big

names – Alain de Botton, Cees Nooteboom – and small. Divided into themes – "Water, water everywhere", "Amsterdam the tolerant" and so forth.

★ **Manfred Wolf (ed.)** *Amsterdam: A Traveler's Literary Companion* (o/p). One of a series published by Whereabouts Press (ⓦwhereaboutspress.com), this anthology tries to get to the heart of Amsterdam. Contains a well-chosen mix of travel pieces, fiction and reportage, uncovering a low-life aspect to the city that exists beyond the tourist spots. A high-quality and evocative selection, and often the only chance to read some of this material in translation. Published in 2001.

ART

Anthony Bailey *A View of Delft.* Concise, startlingly well-researched book on Vermeer, with an accurate and well-considered exploration of his milieu.

Wayne Franits *Dutch Seventeenth-century Genre Painting: Its Stylistic and Thematic Evolution.* Well-argued, immaculately researched and attractively illustrated book – the best on its subject. Hardly deckchair reading, perhaps, but fascinating all the same.

★ **R.H. Fuchs** *Dutch Painting* (o/p). As complete an introduction to the subject – from Flemish origins to the postwar period – as you could wish for, in just a couple of hundred pages. Published in the 1970s and sadly out of print, there's still nothing better.

Melissa McQuillan *Van Gogh.* Extensive, in-depth look at Vincent's paintings, as well as his life and times. Superbly researched and illustrated.

Steven Naifeh & Gregory White Smith *Van Gogh: The Life.* This new book on van Gogh has received mixed reviews, but it is a thunderous volume, whose 955 pages explore the man's life, times and art in exhaustive detail.

Simon Schama *Rembrandt's Eyes.* Published in 1999, this

erudite work received good reviews, but it's very, very long – and often very long-winded.

★ **Mariet Westerman** *The Art of the Dutch Republic 1585–1718.* This excellently written, immaculately illustrated and enthralling book tackles its subject thematically, from the marketing of works of art to an exploration of Dutch ideologies. Highly recommended. Also by Westerman is an all-you-could-ever-want-to-know book about *Rembrandt.*

★ **Christopher White** *Rembrandt.* White is something of a Rembrandt specialist, writing a series of books on the man and his times. Most of these books are expensive and aimed at the specialist art market, but this particular title is perfect for the general reader. Well illustrated with a wonderfully incisive and extremely detailed commentary. Published in 1984, but still very much on song.

Frank Wynne *I was Vermeer: The Forger who Swindled the Nazis.* The art forger Han van Meegeren fooled everyone, including Hermann Goering, with his "lost" Vermeers, when in fact he painted them himself. This story of bluff, bluster and fine art is an intriguing tale no doubt, but Wynne's book of 2007, though extremely well informed, is overly written.

BIOGRAPHY

Ayaan Hirsi Ali *Infidel: My Life.* This powerful and moving autobiography by one of the Netherlands' most controversial figures, begins with Ali's harsh, sometimes brutal, childhood in Somalia and then Saudi Arabia, where her grandmother insisted she have her clitoris cut off when she was 5. Later, in 1992, Ali came to the Netherlands partly to evade an arranged marriage. Thereafter, she

made a remarkable transition from factory cleaner to MP, becoming a leading light of the rightist VVD political party and remaining outspoken in her denunciations of militant Islam (see box, p.335). She now lives in the US.

A.C. Grayling *Descartes: The Life and Times of a Genius.* One of the greatest philosophers of all time, René Descartes (1596–1650) was a key figure in the transition from medieval to early modern Europe. He also made major contributions to optics and geometry and, among his miscellaneous travels, spent time living in Amsterdam. This crisply written, erudite biography deals skilfully with the philosophy – Grayling himself a philosophy professor – and argues that Descartes was almost certainly a Jesuit spy acting on behalf of the Habsburg interest during his time in the Netherlands.

Carol Ann Lee *Roses from the Earth: the Biography of Anne Frank*. Among an army of publications trawling through the life of the young Jewish diarist, this is probably the best, written in a straightforward and insightful manner without sentimentality. Lee's *The Hidden Life of Otto Frank* is equally clear, lucid and interesting. The first was first published in 1999, the second four years later.

HISTORY

Paul Arblaster *A History of the Low Countries*. Welcome addition to the limited range of English-language books on this wide-ranging subject. Arblaster covers the ground methodically, with impeccable research, and has added lots of fascinating detail – and all in just 322 pages. An excellent survey.

J.C.H. Blom (ed.) *History of the Low Countries*. Books on the totality of Dutch history are thin on the ground, so this heavyweight volume fills a few gaps, though it's hardly sun-lounger reading. A series of historians weigh in with their specialities, from Roman times onwards, and its forte is in picking out those cultural, political and economic themes that give the region its distinctive character. Blom has also edited a second, top-notch anthology, *The History of the Jews in the Netherlands*.

Mike Dash *Tulipomania*. An examination of the introduction of the tulip into the Low Countries at the height of the Golden Age – and the extraordinarily inflated and speculative market that ensued. There's a lot of padding and scene-setting, but it's an engaging read, with nice detail on seventeenth-century Amsterdam, Leiden and Haarlem. Also by Dash is *Batavia's Graveyard*, a tale of mutiny and cannibalism among the shipwrecked crew of the East India Company's *Batavia*.

Pieter Geyl *The Revolt of The Netherlands 1555–1609* and *The Netherlands in the Seventeenth Century 1609–1648*. These detailed accounts of the Netherlands during its formative years chronicle the uprising against the Spanish and the formation of the United Provinces. First published in 1932, they have long been regarded as classic texts on the subject, if rather a hard and ponderous read.

Lisa Jardine *The Awful End of Prince William the Silent*. Great title for an intriguing book on the premature demise of one of the country's most acclaimed heroes, who was assassinated in Delft in 1584. At just 160 pages, the tale is told succinctly, but – unless you have a particular interest

in early firearms – there is a bit too much information on guns.

John Nichol & Tony Rennell *Arnhem: The Battle for Survival* Operation Market Garden (see p.262) has attracted a good deal of attention over the years, both as history and memoir. This latest historical addition leaves no parachute unfurled.

Henk van Nierop *Treason in the Northern Quarter* Thoughtful, studious account of the reasons for – and ideologies behind – the Revolt of the Netherlands. The chapter on "Treason" – who to did what to whom and why – is illuminating.

★ **Geoffrey Parker** *The Dutch Revolt* and *The Army of Flanders and the Spanish Road 1567–1659*. The first of these two titles provides a compelling account of the struggle between the Netherlands and Spain and is quite the best thing you can read on the period. The second may sound academic, but it gives a fascinating insight into the Habsburg army that occupied the Low Countries for well over a hundred years – how it functioned, was fed and moved from Spain to the Low Countries along the so-called Spanish Road.

Simon Schama *The Embarrassment of Riches: An Interpretation of Dutch Culture in the Golden Age*. Long before his reinvention on British TV, Schama specialized in Dutch history, and this chunky volume draws on a huge variety of archive sources. Also by Schama, *Patriots and Liberators: Revolution in the Netherlands 1780–1813* focuses on a less familiar period of Dutch history and is particularly good on the Batavian Republic set up in the Netherlands under French auspices. Both are heavyweight tomes, and leftists might well find Schama a little too reactionary. See also Schama's *Rembrandt's Eyes* (p.347).

Andrew Wheatcroft *The Habsburgs; Embodying Empire*. Excellent and well-researched trawl through the family's history, from eleventh-century beginnings to its eclipse at the end of World War I. Enjoyable background reading.

LITERATURE

A.C. Baantjer *De Kok and the Dead Harlequin*. An ex-Amsterdam policeman, who racked up nearly forty years service, Baantjer is currently one of the most widely read authors in the Netherlands. This rattling good yarn, in the Inspector de Kok series, has all the typical ingredients – crisp plotting, some gruesomeness and a batch of nice characterizations on the way. For more, try *De Kok and the*

Somber Nude, though there will not be any new ones: Baantjer died in 2010.

Tracy Chevalier *Girl with a Pearl Earring*. Chevalier's novel is a fanciful piece of fiction, building a story around one of Vermeer's most enigmatic paintings. It's been a popular read and one that paints a detailed picture of seventeenth-century Delft, exploring its social structures and mores.

★ **Anne Frank** *The Diary of a Young Girl*. Lucid and moving, the most revealing book you can read on the plight of Amsterdam's Jews during the German occupation. An international bestseller since its publication in 1947.

★ **Willem Frederik Hermans** *The Dark Room of Damocles*. Along with Wolkers (see below), Mulisch (see below) and Gerard Reve, Hermans is considered one of the four major literary figures of the Dutch postwar generation. This title, first published in 1958, is about the German occupation and its concomitants – betrayal, paranoia and treason. Indeed, the reader is rarely certain what is truth and what is false. If this whets your appetite for Hermans, try the recently translated *Beyond Sleep*. Hermans died in 1995.

Etty Hillesum *An Interrupted Life: the Diaries and Letters of Etty Hillesum, 1941–43*. The Germans transported Hillesum, a young Jewish woman, from her home in Amsterdam to Auschwitz, where she died. As with Anne Frank's more famous journal, penetratingly written – though on the whole a tad less readable.

Arthur Japin *The Two Hearts of Kwasi Boachi*. Inventive re-creation of a true story in which the eponymous Ashanti prince was dispatched to the court of King William of the Netherlands in 1837. Kwasi and his companion Kwame were ostensibly sent to Den Haag to further their education, but there was a strong colonial subtext. Superb descriptions of Ashanti-land in its pre-colonial pomp. Also try Japin's *Lucia's Eyes*, an imaginative extrapolation of a casual anecdote found in Casanova's memoirs set mostly in eighteenth-century Amsterdam.

Otto de Kat *Julia*. From one of the country's most praised contemporary novelists, this is de Kat's latest work, an engaging exploration of love and regret in which a suicide leads back to the events of World War II. Also the comparable *Man on the Move*, set in the Dutch East Indies as the Dutch face the Japanese.

Sylvie Matton *Rembrandt's Whore*. Taking its cue from Chevalier's *Girl with a Pearl Earring*, this slim novel tries hard to conjure Rembrandt's life and times, with some success. Matton certainly knows her Rembrandt – she worked for two years on a film of his life. Published in 2001.

Sarah Emily Miano *Van Rijn*. Carefully composed re-creation of Rembrandt's milieu, based on the (documented) visit of Cosimo de Medici to the artist's house. As an attempt to venture into Rembrandt's soul it does well – but not brilliantly.

Deborah Moggach *Tulip Fever*. At first Moggach's novel seems no more than an attempt to build a story out of her favourite domestic Dutch interiors, genre scenes and still-life paintings. But ultimately the story is a basic one – of lust, greed, mistaken identity and tragedy. The Golden Age Amsterdam backdrop is well realized, but almost incidental.

Marcel Moring *In Babylon*. Popular Dutch author with an intense style and thought-provoking, philosophical content. *In Babylon* has an older Jewish man and his niece

trapped in a cabin in the eastern Netherlands where they ruminate on their family's history. Moring's *Dream Room* is also gracefully nostalgic in its concentration on the family of Boris and his son, David, while his latest novel, *In a Dark Wood*, is set in the town of Assen during the annual TT motorbike races.

Harry Mulisch *The Assault*. Set partly in Haarlem, partly in Amsterdam, this powerful novel (made into an excellent film) traces the story of a young boy who loses his family in a reprisal raid by the Nazis. Mulisch also wrote *The Discovery of Heaven*, a gripping adventure yarn; *The Procedure*, featuring a modern-day Dutch scientist investigating strange goings-on in sixteenth-century Prague; and *Siegfried: a Black Idyll*, whose central question is whether a work of imagination can help us understand the nature of evil in general and Hitler in particular. A well-respected literary figure for several decades, Mulisch died in Amsterdam in 2010, prompting a fulsome tribute from the Dutch prime minister.

Multatuli *Max Havelaar: Or, The Coffee Auctions of the Dutch Trading Company*. Classic, nineteenth-century Dutch satire of colonial life in the East Indies. Eloquent and intermittently amusing. If you have Dutch friends, they will be impressed (dumbstruck) if you have actually read it, not least since it's 352 pages long.

Saskia Noort *Back to the Coast*. One of the most popular/ populist contemporary novelists in the Netherlands, Noort sets this thriller on the Dutch coast where all sorts of fear and loathing ensue.

Cees Nooteboom *Rituals* (o/p). Nooteboom published his first novel in 1955, but only hit the literary headlines with this, his third novel, in 1980. The central theme of all his work is time; *Rituals* in particular is about the passing of time and ways of controlling the process. It is almost entirely set in Amsterdam, and paints a strong picture of the city while describing the inner life of Inni Wintrop.

Esther Verhoef *Rendezvous*. Verhoef is one of the Netherlands's most popular thriller writers and this tale of unfaithfulness and abandon has a French setting.

Janwillem van de Wetering *Tumbleweed*; *Hard Rain*; *Corpse on the Dyke*; *Outsider in Amsterdam*. Offbeat detective tales set in Amsterdam and the Dutch provinces. Humane, quirky and humorous, Wetering's novels have inventive plots and unusual characters in interesting locations, though the prose can be indigestible.

Tommy Wieringa *Caesarion*. Self-sacrifice and family tumult in the depths of East Anglia –written by one of the Netherlands most promising contemporary writers.

Jan Wolkers *Turkish Delight* (o/p). Wolkers, who died in 2007, was one of the Netherlands' best-known artists and writers, and this is an early novel, a close examination of the relationship between a bitter, working-class sculptor and his young, middle-class wife. If you like it, try Wolkers' *Horrible Tango* (o/p).

Dutch

It's unlikely that you'll need to speak anything other than English while you are in the Netherlands: the Dutch have a seemingly innate talent for languages, and your attempts at speaking theirs may be met with some bewilderment – though this can have as much to do with your pronunciation (Dutch is very difficult to get right) as their surprise that you're making an effort. That said, the Dutch words and phrases below are useful, especially in the more rural parts of the country, and we have also included a basic food and drink glossary, though menus are nearly always multilingual – where they aren't, ask and one will almost invariably appear. As for phrasebooks, the *Rough Guide to Dutch* is pocket-sized, with a good dictionary section (English–Dutch and Dutch–English) as well as a menu reader; it also provides a useful introduction to grammar and pronunciation.

Pronunciation

Dutch is **pronounced** much the same as English. However, there are a few Dutch sounds that don't exist in English, which can be difficult to get right without practice.

Consonants

Double-consonant combinations generally keep their separate sounds in Dutch: kn, for example, is never like the English "knight". Note also the following consonants and consonant combinations:

j is an English y

ch and **g** indicate a throaty sound, as at the end of the Scottish word loch.

ng as in bring

nj as in onion

y is not a consonant, but another way of writing ij

Vowels and diphthongs

A good rule of thumb is that doubling the letter lengthens the vowel sound.

a is like the English apple

aa like cart

e like let

ee like late

o as in pop

oo in pope

u is like the French tu if preceded by a consonant; it's like wood if followed by a consonant

uu is the French tu

au and **ou** like how

DOUBLE DUTCH???

Dutch is a Germanic language – the word itself is a corruption of "Deutsche", a label inaccurately given by English sailors in the seventeenth century – and indeed, although the Dutch are at pains to stress the differences between the two languages, if you know any German you'll spot many similarities. Spoken Dutch, however, is – far from consistent, with a hatful of regional dialects: the inhabitants of Amsterdam have a very different accent and slang to someone, say, from The Hague, while in Limburg the dialect is closer to German and Flemish than to Dutch. The Netherlands has a second official language too, **Fries**, the pride and joy of the people of Friesland – and incomprehensible to everyone else.

ei and **ij** as in fine, though this varies strongly from region to region; sometimes it can sound more like lane

oe as in soon

eu is like the diphthong in the French leur

ui is the hardest Dutch diphthong of all, pronounced like how but much further forward in the mouth, with lips pursed (as if to say "oo").

WORDS AND PHRASES

BASICS

yes	ja
no	nee
please	alstublieft
thank you	dank u or bedankt
hello	hallo or dag
good morning	goedemorgen
good afternoon	goedemiddag
good evening	goedenavond
goodbye	tot ziens
see you later	tot straks
Do you speak English?	Spreekt u Engels?
I don't understand	Ik begrijp het niet
women/men	vrouwen/mannen
children	kinderen
men's/women's toilets	heren/dames
I want…	Ik wil…
I don't want to	Ik wil niet…(+verb)
I don't want any…	Ik wil geen… (+noun)
How much is…?	Wat kost…?

TRAVEL, DIRECTIONS AND SHOPPING

How do I get to…?	Hoe kom ik in…?
Where is…?	Waar is…?
How far is it to…?	Hoe ver is het naar…?
When?	Wanneer?
far/near	ver/dichtbij
left/right	links/rechts
straight ahead	rechtdoor
airport	luchthaven
post office	postkantoor
Post box	postbus
stamp(s)	postzegel(s)
money exchange	geldwisselkantoor
cash desk	kassa
railway platform	spoor or perron

ticket office	loket
here/there	hier/daar
good/bad	goed/slecht
big/small	groot/klein
open/closed	open/gesloten
push/pull	duwen/trekken
new/old	nieuw/oud
cheap/expensive	goedkoop/duur
hot/cold	heet or warm/koud
with/without	met/zonder
North	noord
South	zuid
East	oost
West	west

USEFUL CYCLING TERMS

brake	rem
broken	kapot
chain	ketting
cycle path	fietspad
handlebars	stuur
pedal	trapper
pump	pomp
puncture	lek
tyre	band
wheel	wiel

MONTHS OF THE YEAR

January	januari
February	februari
March	maart
April	april
May	mei
June	juni
July	juli

SIGNS AND ABBREVIATIONS

AUB Alstublieft: please (also shown as SVP, from French)
BG Begane grond: ground floor
BTW Belasting Toegevoegde Waarde: VAT
geen toegang no entry
gesloten closed
ingang entrance
K kelder: basement
let op! attention!

heren/dames men's/women's toilets
open open
T/M Tot en met: up to and including
toegang entrance
uitgang exit
VA vanaf: from
VS Verenigde Staten: United States
VVV Tourist office
ZOZ please turn over (page, leaflet, etc)

August	augustus	**1am**	een uur 's nachts
September	september		
October	oktober	**NUMBERS**	
November	november	**0**	nul
December	december	**1**	een
		2	twee
DAYS AND TIMES		**3**	drie
Monday	maandag	**4**	vier
Tuesday	dinsdag	**5**	vijf
Wednesday	woensdag	**6**	zes
Thursday	donderdag	**7**	zeven
Friday	vrijdag	**8**	acht
Saturday	zaterdag	**9**	negen
Sunday	zondag	**10**	tien
yesterday	gisteren	**11**	elf
today	vandaag	**12**	twaalf
tomorrow	morgen	**13**	dertien
tomorrow morning	morgenochtend	**14**	veertien
year	jaar	**15**	vijftien
month	maand	**16**	zestien
week	week	**17**	zeventien
day	dag	**18**	achttien
hour	uur	**19**	negentien
minute	minuut	**20**	twintig
What time is it?	Hoe laat is het?	**21**	een en twintig
It's…	Het is…	**22**	twee en twintig
3.00	drie uur	**30**	dertig
3.05	vijf over drie	**40**	veertig
3.10	tien over drie	**50**	vijftig
3.15	kwart over drie	**60**	zestig
3.20	tien voor half vier	**70**	zeventig
3.25	vijf voor half vier	**80**	tachtig
3.30	half vier	**90**	negentig
3.35	vijf over half vier	**100**	honderd
3.40	tien over half vier	**101**	honderd een
3.45	kwart voor vier	**200**	twee honderd
3.50	tien voor vier	**201**	twee honderd een
3.55	vijf voor vier	**500**	vijf honderd
8am	acht uur 's ochtends	**525**	vijf honderd vijf en twintig
1pm	een uur 's middags		
8pm	acht uur 's avonds	**1000**	duizend

MENU READER

BASIC TERMS

boter	butter	**koud**	cold
boterham/broodje	sandwich/roll	**nagerechten**	desserts
brood	bread	**patat/friet**	chips/french fries
dranken	drinks	**peper**	pepper
eieren	eggs	**pindakaas**	peanut butter
groenten	vegetables	**sla/salade**	salad
honing	honey	**slagroom**	whipped cream
hoofdgerechten	main courses	**soep**	soup
huzarensalade	potato salad with pickles	**stokbrood**	french bread
kaas	cheese	**suiker**	sugar

uitsmijter	ham or cheese with eggs on bread
vegetarisch	vegetarian
vis	fish
vlees	eat
voorgerechten	starters/hors d'oeuvres
vruchten	fruit
warm	hot
zout	salt

MEAT AND POULTRY

biefstuk (duitse)	hamburger
biefstuk (hollandse)	steak
eend	duck
fricandeau	roast pork
fricandel	frankfurter-like sausage
gehakt	minced meat
kalfsvlees	veal
kalkoen	turkey
karbonade	a chop
kip	chicken
kroket	spiced veal or beef hash, coated in breadcrumbs
lamsvlees	lamb
lever	liver
ossenhaas	tenderloin beef
rookvlees	smoked beef
spek	bacon
worst	sausages

FISH

forel	trout
garnalen	prawns
haring	herring
kabeljauw	cod
makreel	mackerel
mosselen	mussels
oesters	oysters
paling	eel
schelvis	haddock
schol	plaice
tong	sole
zalm	almon

VEGETABLES

aardappelen	potatoes
bloemkool	cauliflower
bonen	beans
champignons	mushrooms
erwten	peas
hutspot	mashed potatoes and carrots
knoflook	garlic
komkommer	cucumber

prei	leek
rijst	rice
sla	salad, lettuce
stampot andijvie	mashed potato and endive
stampot boerenkool	mashed potato and cabbage
uien	onions
wortelen	carrots
zuurkool	sauerkraut

COOKING TERMS

belegd	filled or topped
doorbakken	well-done
gebakken	fried or baked
gebraden	roast
gegrild	grilled
gekookt	boiled
geraspt	grated
gerookt	smoked
gestoofd	stewed
half doorbakken	medium-done
rood	rare

SWEETS AND DESSERTS

appelgebak	apple tart or cake
drop	Dutch liquorice, available in *zoet* (sweet) or *zout* (salted) varieties
gebak	pastry
ijs	ice cream
koekjes	biscuits
oliebollen	traditional sweet sold at New Year – something like a doughnut
pannenkoeken	pancakes
pepernoten	Dutch ginger nuts
poffertjes	small pancakes, fritters
(slag)room	(whipped) cream
speculaas	spice and cinnamon-flavoured biscuit
stroopwafels	waffles
taai-taai	spicy Dutch cake
vla	custard

FRUITS AND NUTS

aardbei	strawberry
amandel	almond
appel	apple
appelmoes	apple purée
citroen	lemon
druiven	grape
framboos	raspberry
hazelnoot	hazelnut

kers	cherry	karnemelk	buttermilk
kokosnoot	coconut	koffie	coffee
peer	pear	koffie verkeerd	coffee with warm milk
perzik	peach	kopstoot	beer with a jenever chaser
pinda	peanut	melk	milk
pruim	plum/prune	met ijs	with ice
		met slagroom	with whipped cream
DRINKS		pils	Dutch beer
anijsmelk	aniseed-flavoured	proost!	cheers!
	warm milk	sinaasappelsap	orange juice
appelsap	apple juice	thee	tea
bessenjenever	blackcurrant gin	tomatensap	tomato juice
chocomel	chocolate milk	vruchtensap	fruit juice
citroenjenever	lemon gin	wijn	wine
droog	dry	(wit/rood/rosé)	(white/red/rosé)
frisdranken	soft drinks	vieux	Dutch brandy
jenever	Dutch gin	zoet	sweet

DUTCH GLOSSARY

Abdij Abbey.

Amsterdammertje Phallic-shaped bollard placed in rows alongside many Amsterdam streets to keep drivers off pavements and out of the canals.

Begijnhof Similar to a *hofje* but occupied by Catholic women (*begijns*) who led semi-religious lives without taking full vows.

Belfort Belfry.

Beurs Stock exchange.

Botermarkt Butter market.

Brug Bridge.

Burgher Member of the upper or mercantile classes of a town, usually with certain civic powers.

Gasthuis Hospice for the sick or infirm.

Gemeente Municipal, as in Gemeentehuis (town hall).

Gerechtshof Law Courts.

Gezellig A hard term to translate – something like "cosy", "comfortable" and "inviting" all in one – which is said to lie at the heart of the Dutch psyche.

Gilde Guild.

Gracht Canal.

Groentenmarkt Vegetable market.

Grote Kerk Literally "big church" – the main church of a town or village.

Hal Hall.

Hijsbalk Pulley beam, often decorated, fixed to the top of a gable to lift goods and furniture. Essential in canal houses whose staircases were narrow and steep, *hijsbalken* are still very much in use today.

Hof Courtyard.

Hofje Almshouse, usually for elderly women who could look after themselves but needed small charities such as food and fuel; usually a number of buildings centred around a small, enclosed courtyard.

Huis House.

Ingang Entrance.

Jeugdherberg Youth hostel.

Kasteel Castle.

Kerk Church.

Koning King.

Koningin Queen.

Koninklijk Royal.

Kunst Art.

Lakenhal Cloth hall.

Markt Central town square and the heart of most Dutch communities, normally still the site of weekly markets.

Molen Windmill.

Nederland The Netherlands.

Nederlands Dutch.

OMGANG Procession.

Paleis Palace.

Plein A square or open space.

Polder An area of land reclaimed from the sea.

Poort Gate.

Raadhuis Town hall.

Randstad Literally "rim-town", this refers to the urban conurbation that makes up much of Noord- and Zuid-Holland, stretching from Amsterdam in the north to Rotterdam and Dordrecht in the south.

Rijk State.

Schouwburg Theatre.

Schepezaal Alderman's hall.

Schone Kunsten Fine arts.

Sierkunst Decorative arts.

Spionnetje Small mirror on a canal house enabling the occupant to see who is at the door without descending the stairs.

Spoor Train station platform.

Stadhuis The most common word for a town hall.

Stedelijk Civic, municipal.

Steeg Alley.
Steen Stone.
Stichting Institute or foundation.
Straat Street.
Toegang Entrance.
Toren Tower.
Tuin Garden.

Uitgang Exit.
Vleeshuis Meat market.
Volkskunde Folklore.
Waag Old public weigh house, a common feature of most towns.
Weg Way.
Wijk District (of a city).

ART AND ARCHITECTURAL GLOSSARY

Ambulatory Covered passage around the outer edge of the choir of a church.

Apse Semicircular protrusion (usually) at the east end of a church.

Art Deco Geometrical style of art and architecture popular in the 1930s.

Art Nouveau Style of art, architecture and design based on highly stylized vegetal forms. Especially popular in the early part of the twentieth century.

Baroque The art and architecture of the Counter-Reformation, dating from around 1600 onwards. Distinguished by extreme ornateness, exuberance and by the complex but harmonious spatial arrangement of interiors.

Carillon A set of tuned church bells, either operated by an automatic mechanism or played by a keyboard.

Carolingian Dynasty founded by Charlemagne; mid-eighth to early tenth century. Also refers to art of the period.

Caryatid A sculptured female figure used as a column.

Chancel The eastern part of a church, often separated from the nave by a screen (see "rood screen"). Contains the choir and ambulatory.

Classical Architectural style incorporating Greek and Roman elements – pillars, domes, colonnades etc – at its height in the seventeenth century and revived, as Neoclassical, in the nineteenth century.

Clerestory Upper story of a church with windows.

Diptych Carved or painted work on two panels. Often used as an altarpiece – both static and, more occasionally, portable.

Expressionism Artistic style popular at the beginning of the twentieth century, characterized by the exaggeration of shape or colour; often accompanied by the extensive use of symbolism.

Flamboyant Florid form of Gothic.

Fresco Wall painting – durable through application to wet plaster.

Gable The triangular upper portion of a wall – decorative or supporting a roof – which is a feature of many Dutch canal houses. Initially fairly simple, they became more ostentatious in the late seventeenth century, before turning to a more restrained Classicism in the eighteenth and nineteenth centuries.

Genre painting In the seventeenth century the term "genre painting" applied to everything from animal paintings and still lifes through to historical works and landscapes. In the eighteenth century, the term came only to be applied to scenes of everyday life.

Gothic Architectural style of the thirteenth to sixteenth centuries, characterized by pointed arches, rib vaulting, flying buttresses and a general emphasis on verticality.

Merovingian Dynasty ruling France and parts of the Low Countries from the sixth to the middle of the eighth century. Refers also to art, etc, of the period.

Misericord Ledge on choir stall on which the occupant can be supported while standing; often carved with secular subjects (bottoms were not thought worthy of religious subjects).

Neoclassical A style of Classical architecture revived in the nineteenth century, popular in the Low Countries in the early nineteenth century.

Neo-Gothic Revived Gothic style of architecture popular between the late eighteenth and nineteenth centuries.

Renaissance The period of European history marking the end of the medieval period and the rise of the modern world. Defined, among many criteria, by an increase in classical scholarship, geographical discovery, the rise of secular values and the growth of individualism. Began in Italy in the fourteenth century. Also refers to the art and architecture of the period.

Retable Altarpiece.

Rococo Highly florid, light and intricate eighteenth-century style of architecture, painting and interior design, forming the last phase of Baroque.

Romanesque Early medieval architecture distinguished by squat, heavy forms, rounded arches and naive sculpture.

Rood screen Decorative screen separating the nave from the chancel. A rood loft is the space above it.

Stucco Marble-based plaster used to embellish ceilings, etc.

Transept Arms of a cross-shaped church, placed at ninety degrees to nave and chancel.

Triptych Carved or painted work on three panels.

Tympanum Sculpted, usually recessed, panel above a door.

Vauban Seventeenth-century military architect, whose fortresses still stand all over Europe – including the Low Countries; hence the adjective Vaubanesque.

Small print and index

A ROUGH GUIDE TO ROUGH GUIDES

Published in 1982, the first Rough Guide – to Greece – was a student scheme that became a publishing phenomenon. Mark Ellingham, a recent graduate in English from Bristol University, had been travelling in Greece the previous summer and couldn't find the right guidebook. With a small group of friends he wrote his own guide, combining a highly contemporary, journalistic style with a thoroughly practical approach to travellers' needs.

The immediate success of the book spawned a series that rapidly covered dozens of destinations. And, in addition to impecunious backpackers, Rough Guides soon acquired a much broader readership that relished the guides' wit and inquisitiveness as much as their enthusiastic, critical approach and value-for-money ethos.

These days, Rough Guides include recommendations from budget to luxury and cover more than 200 destinations around the globe, as well as producing an ever-growing range of eBooks and apps.

Visit **roughguides.com** to see our latest publications.

Rough Guide credits

Editor: Mandy Tomlin
Layout: Anita Singh
Cartography: Swati Handoo
Picture editor: Rhiannon Furbear
Proofreader: Karen Parker
Managing editor: Keith Drew
Assistant editor: Dipika Dasgupta
Production: Rebecca Short
Cover design: Nicole Newman, Anita Singh
Editorial assistant: Olivia Rawes

Senior pre-press designer: Dan May
Design director: Scott Stickland
Travel publisher: Joanna Kirby
Digital travel publisher: Peter Buckley
Reference director: Andrew Lockett
Operations coordinator: Becky Doyle
Publishing director (Travel): Clare Currie
Commercial manager: Gino Magnotta
Managing director: John Duhigg

Publishing information

This sixth edition published January 2013 by
Rough Guides Ltd,
80 Strand, London WC2R 0RL
11, Community Centre, Panchsheel Park,
New Delhi 110017, India
Distributed by the Penguin Group
Penguin Books Ltd,
80 Strand, London WC2R 0RL
Penguin Group (USA)
375 Hudson Street, NY 10014, USA
Penguin Group (Australia)
250 Camberwell Road, Camberwell,
Victoria 3124, Australia
Penguin Group (NZ)
67 Apollo Drive, Mairangi Bay, Auckland 1310,
New Zealand
Penguin Group (South Africa)
Block D, Rosebank Office Park, 181 Jan Smuts Avenue,
Parktown North, Gauteng, South Africa 2193
Rough Guides is represented in Canada by Tourmaline
Editions Inc. 662 King Street West, Suite 304, Toronto,
Ontario M5V 1M7
Printed in Singapore by Toppan Security Printing Pte. Ltd.

© Martin Dunford, Phil Lee and Suzanne Morton-Taylor 2013
Maps © Rough Guides
No part of this book may be reproduced in any form
without permission from the publisher except for the
quotation of brief passages in reviews.
368pp includes index
A catalogue record for this book is available from the
British Library
ISBN: 978-1-40936-192-3

Help us update

We've gone to a lot of effort to ensure that the sixth
edition of **The Rough Guide to the Netherlands** is
accurate and up-to-date. However, things change – places
get "discovered", opening hours are notoriously fickle,
restaurants and rooms raise prices or lower standards. If
you feel we've got it wrong or left something out, we'd like
to know, and if you can remember the address, the price,
the hours, the phone number, so much the better.

Please send your comments with the subject line
"**Rough Guide the Netherlands Update**" to ✉ mail
@uk.roughguides.com. We'll credit all contributions and
send a copy of the next edition (or any other Rough Guide
if you prefer) for the very best emails.

Find more travel information, connect with fellow
travellers and book your trip on ⊕ roughguides.com

ABOUT THE AUTHORS

Martin Dunford is one of the founders and the former publisher of Rough Guides and has worked in travel publishing for over 25 years. He is the author of more than ten guidebooks and also works as a freelance writer and as a publishing and digital consultant to the travel industry. He travels to the Netherlands regularly, and when not on the road, he lives in Blackheath, London, with his wife and two daughters.

Phil Lee A one-time deckhand in the Danish merchant navy, Phil Lee has been writing for Rough Guides for well over twenty years. His other books in the series include Canada, Amsterdam, Norfolk & Suffolk, Mallorca & Menorca and Belgium & Luxembourg. He lives in Nottingham, where he was born and raised.

Suzanne Morton-Taylor has been working as a travel writer for Rough Guides since 2006 and has contributed to the Amsterdam, Australia, Norway and Belgium & Luxembourg guides, among others.

Acknowledgements

Martin Dunford I'd like to thank my co-authors, Phil and Suzanne; Rianne Ojeh from the Netherlands Board of Tourism for helping to smooth the way, and indeed all the hoteliers and restauranteurs who helped me on the ground; and of course Caroline, Daisy and Lucy for trips to Holland, past, present and future.
Phil Lee would like to thank his editor, Mandy Tomlin, for her careful implementation of the new Rough Guide design in the preparation of this new edition of *The Rough Guide to the Netherlands*. I would also like to express my appreciation to my ever-helpful co-authors, Suzanne Morton-Taylor and Martin Dunford.
Suzanne Morton-Taylor would like to thank Mandy Tomlin for her patience in explaining the redesign and the thorough job she did editing this new edition of *The Rough Guide to the Netherlands*. Special thanks – as always – to my co-authors Phil Lee and Martin Dunford for all their help and "gezelligheid".

Readers' letters

Thanks to all the readers who have taken the time to write in with comments and suggestions (and apologies if we've inadvertently omitted or misspelt anyone's name):

Annemarie Beers; J. G. Brekelmans; Johanneke Braam; Eveline Colijn; Sjoerd van Eeden; Lieke Heerschop; Lindy Heijmering; Eke van Heynegen; Dave Himelfield; Marten Hoeksma; Richard Jones; Klaas de Jong; Sabine Koch; Robert van Kuyk; Joost van der Kwaak; Rosa Lopez; Jeffrey Maisels; Jan Pieter; Frank de Ruijter; George Saba; Manon Schilder; Richard Shaffer; Marissa Verdonk; and Keeley Warren.

Photo credits

All photos © Rough Guides except the following:
(Key: t-top; c-centre; b-bottom; l-left; r-right)

p.1 SuperStock/van der Meer Rene
p.2 SuperStock/Ludovic Maisant
p.4 Corbis/Murat Taner
p.5 4Corners/Sandra Raccanello/SIME
p.9 Getty Images; Gallo Images/Neil Overy (tr);
SuperStock/Frans Lemmens (b)
p.10 Corbis/Olaf Kraak
p.11 Corbis/Frank Krahmer (c); Floris Leeuwenberg (t); Will Pryce (b)
p.12 Visit Holland/Jochen Tack
p.13 Alamy/Mediacolor's (b) Visit Holland/Den Haag Marketing (t,c)
p.14 Visit Holland/(t, c, b)
p.15 Corbis/Keren Su (b)
p.16 Corbis (bl); Visit Holland (tl)
p.17 Alamy/David Robertson (t)
p.18 Alamy/Frans Lemmens (t); Picture Contact BV (b)
p.19 Visit Holland (tl)
p.20 Corbis/Ethel Davies/Robert Harding (tc);
Visit Holland/(tl, tr)
p.22 Getty Images/Photolibrary
p.47 Corbis/Sylvain Sonnet
p.100 Corbis/Frank Krahmer

p.115 AWL Images/Travel Pix Collection (b); SuperStock/Travel Library Limited (tr)
p.131 Corbis/Manfred Mehlig (t); Getty Images/Bjorn Svensson (bl)
p.142 Corbis/Gary Cook
p.183 Visit Holland (b)
p.192 SuperStock/Richard Semik
p.195 Alamy/Erik Lam Boats
p.211 Visit Holland/(b)
p.232 SuperStock/Frans Lemmens
p.235 Corbis/Ronald Jansen/Foto Natura
p.272 SuperStock/van der Meer Rene
p.295 SuperStock/imagebroker.net (b); Malherbe Marcel (tl); Ton Koene (tr)
p.309 Alamy/Lourens Smak (t); Robert Harding Picture Library/van der Meer Rene (b)
p.315 Alamy/Scott Hortop Travel

Front cover Flowering bulb fields © Frans Lemmens/Getty Images
Back cover Amsterdam Canal © Corbis/Image Source (top); Beach cabins, Vlissingen © SuperStock/imagebroker .net (right); Cheese Market, Alkmaar © Visit Holland (left)

Index

Maps are marked in grey

Map symbols

The symbols below are used on maps throughout the book

✈	Airport	♦	Point of interest	)(	Bridge	▨	Building
★	Bus/taxi stop	@	Internet access	⊠	Gate	▨	Cemetery
P	Parking	🍺	Beer Brewery	⍭	Garden	▨	Park
✉	Post office	⊙	Statue	⚠	Campsite	▨	Beach/dune
✛	Hospital	♟	Museum	△	Hostel		
ⓘ	Information office	Ⓜ	Metro station	✡	Synagogue		
Ⓒ	Telephone office	Ⓣ	Tram stop		Church		

Listings key

- ■ Accommodation
- ● Eating
- ■ Drinking & Nightlife
- ● Shops